Sports or/and Special Populations: Training Physiology in Health and Sports Performance

Sports or/and Special Populations: Training Physiology in Health and Sports Performance

Editor

Felipe Aidar

MDPI

Basel • Beijing • Wuhan • Barcelona • Belgrade • Novi Sad • Cluj • Manchester

Editor
Felipe Aidar
Department of Physical Education
Federal University of Sergipe
Aracaju
Brazil

Editorial Office
MDPI
St. Alban-Anlage 66
4052 Basel, Switzerland

This is a reprint of articles from the Special Issue published online in the open access journal *Healthcare* (ISSN 2227-9032) (available at: www.mdpi.com/journal/healthcare/special_issues/Sports_Special_Populations).

For citation purposes, cite each article independently as indicated on the article page online and as indicated below:

Lastname, A.A.; Lastname, B.B. Article Title. *Journal Name* **Year**, *Volume Number*, Page Range.

ISBN 978-3-0365-9053-0 (Hbk)
ISBN 978-3-0365-9052-3 (PDF)
doi.org/10.3390/books978-3-0365-9052-3

Contents

About the Editor

Felipe Aidar

Adjunct Professor at the Department of Physical Education at the Federal University of Sergipe. Physical Education Professional, Third Dan Black Belt in Judo. Reserve Officer of the Minas Gerais Military Fire Department. In the academic area, he holds a PhD and Master's degree in Sports Sciences from the University of Trás os Montes and Alto Douro-UTAD-Portugal. Graduate and Bachelor in Physical Education from Centro Universitário do Triângulo–UNITRI, Graduate in Military Sciences with an emphasis on Social Defense from the Minas Gerais Military Police Academy, Bachelor of Law from Cruzeiro do Sul University, Degree in Pedagogy from the University of Uberaba - UNIUBE and a Degree in Biological Sciences from Centro Universitário Claretiano.

Preface

I thank everyone who believed and believes that a safe approach, through scientific knowledge, can positively impact people's lives. Physical activity every day has become an important tool in preventing diseases, improving quality of life and improving physiological indicators for people in general and for athletes. Thus, the production of knowledge in this area is fundamental for all people. In this sense, the content of this reprint tends to positively impact the area of human knowledge and, above all, the lives of those involved.

Felipe Aidar
Editor

healthcare MDPI

Editorial

Sports and Special Populations: Training Physiology in Health and Sports Performance

Felipe J. Aidar [1,2,3]

[1] Graduate Program of Physiological Science, Federal University of Sergipe (UFS), São Cristovão 49100-000, Brazil; fjaidar@gmail.com
[2] Group of Studies and Research of Performance, Sport, Health and Paralympic Sports (GEPEPS), Federal University of Sergipe (UFS), São Cristovão 49100-000, Brazil
[3] Graduate Program of Physical Education, Federal University of Sergipe (UFS), São Cristovão 49100-000, Brazil

Health is increasingly being studied, notably concerning preventive measures for health issues [1–3]. Problems related to modern lifestyles, particularly the effects of hypokinesia, have been a focal point in recent research [4,5]. Therefore, engaging in regular exercise along with ensuring a healthy diet, among other factors, are believed to play a decisive role in promoting health [1,4]. In this sense, engagement in sports would positively impact health indicators [3,5]. However, several factors influence athletes' success, rehabilitation, and physical preparation [6,7].

Furthermore, parasport and special populations have been extensively researched, and the performance and health of these populations have been affected by the relationship between stress, maturation, training load, and recovery [8,9]. Additionally, environmental approaches aiming to enhance efficiency and physiological adaptation in relation to training and intervention methods are being explored [10,11]. However, in various situations and conditions, the stimulus–performance–adaptation relationship may vary and can interfere with recovery, performance, and health [12,13].

Thus, topics such as training load monitoring; stress and physiological responses exhibited during exercise or sports; post-exercise recovery processes; alterations due to stress and/or training load; and the physiology of training in health and athletic performance could significantly impact health. In this context, 19 published studies related to the subject have been identified.

We begin with stress assessment, where the influence of slow breathing on acute stress among handball coaches was evaluated. It was indicated that implementing respiratory control could improve stress conditions during official games, with potential impacts on health [14].

Another study investigated the impact of sleep deficiency on oxidative stress, PCR-us, and cortisol levels associated with different intensities of aerobic exercise. Exercises of varying intensities were compared, and the results suggested that lower exercise intensity was more effective in mitigating the negative effects of sleep deficiency [15].

Furthermore, one study compared resistance training based on speed and percentages. Training based on percentages was found to be more effective in maintaining resistance to high-power speed, while speed-based training had a greater impact on explosive power adaptations [16].

Another focus of research was on individuals with disabilities, including people with Down's syndrome, and their relationship with training and swimming. The body composition and physical restriction profiles of competitive swimmers and moderately active (detrained) individuals with Down's syndrome were compared. The results indicated that competitive swimming had a positive effect on reducing the tendency toward obesity and improving the strength, efficiency, and balance of this population [17].

Citation: Aidar, F.J. Sports and Special Populations: Training Physiology in Health and Sports Performance. *Healthcare* **2023**, *11*, 2198. https://doi.org/10.3390/healthcare11152198

Received: 21 July 2023
Accepted: 28 July 2023
Published: 4 August 2023

Aquatic activities were also evaluated with respect to the health, psychological, and social indicators in people with disabilities. Significant improvements were observed in the mentioned conditions, as well as in social relationships and the inclusion of individuals with disabilities, with increased support for their parents [18].

Furthermore, concerning individuals with disabilities, a scale was developed to predict the pre-service intentions of physical activity instructors for people with disabilities. The scale addressed the constructs, followed by the behavioral beliefs, that were influenced by teaching experience regarding physical activity for people with disabilities. The influence of parents and close associates of individuals with disabilities, as well as the beliefs of those involved in teaching physical activity to this group, were also observed [19].

The relative importance and priority of factors to be considered in the administration of physical activities for people with disabilities were also evaluated. The type of facility and the provider of information were considered highly important, and it was observed that programs within sports facilities had a higher priority. The utilization of these locations by individuals with disabilities seems to be a crucial point outlined by this approach [20].

In the realm of parasports, studies were focused on various sports. Notably, the Paralympic Games (PG) are considered one of the world's largest events, with increasing media coverage and participation. One study aimed to investigate the variation in the number of gold, silver, bronze, and total medals in the Summer Paralympic Games from 1992 to 2016. It was observed that several external factors could influence performance indicators, including an increase in the number of participants and greater and better government investment. Additionally, it was noted that preparation should be based on a multidisciplinary team, meaning that improvement in performance relies on knowledge and investment from governments [21].

Within this paralympic perspective, the participation of the Portugal team in the Tokyo 2020 Paralympic Games was evaluated through sociodemographic and psychosocial variables (positive and negative effects, life satisfaction, resilience, and social support). The Paralympic athletes presented high levels of life satisfaction, high positive affect, low negative affect, and substantial levels of resilience and social support, which appeared to be essential variables for these athletes [22].

A South Korean study also assessed the physical and sports needs of people with disabilities and how these needs should be reflected in policies and practices to improve their quality of life. The results indicated that para-sport projects should be community-focused, and the environment should be stable for the professionals involved, especially in sports facilities. Additionally, continuous capacity development should be prioritized. Facilities should be utilized more effectively by people with disabilities, and effective communication should be encouraged to help them understand the importance of physical activity and sports for their health [23].

In Brazil, the effect of different warm-up types on the strength and skin temperature of para-powerlifting athletes was evaluated. The results showed that there were no significant differences between warm-ups with stretching and specific exercises or the lack of engagement in warm-ups. However, thermal images demonstrated that traditional warm-up methods better suited the objectives of para-powerlifting [24]. The relationship between individuals with disabilities and the immune system was also assessed, including with respect to chronic low-grade inflammatory states and immunodepression. The impact of disability on various variables, ranging from physical fitness to well-being, quality of life, sleep, and nutritional aspects, among others, was examined. The study also analyzed the variability of parameters related to exercise/physical activity and the intra- and inter-individual variability of the immune response to exercise. Overall, moderate-intensity training was associated with optimal immunity and resistance to infections, such as upper respiratory tract infections, among athletes. Intense training periods with insufficient recovery times could lead to a temporary state of immunosuppression, which should resolve with a few days of rest/recovery from exercise [25].

Furthermore, research from Italy focused on para-rowing, wherein a scoping review enhanced by bibliometric analyses provided a comprehensive synthesis of knowledge related to the sport. The academic community of para-rowing was found to consist of 78 researchers, 16 (20.51%) of whom were highly interconnected. The study identified gaps in areas such as sports nutrition, doping, and psychological aspects among para-rowers who are not visually impaired [26]. The same Italian group evaluated paralympic powerlifting (PP) through a scoping literature review enhanced by a bibliometric analysis using large databases. The results indicated that the community studying the sport was poorly interconnected, with most authors contributing to only one article. However, one author was a central node in the author network, with 59.5% of the reviewed scientific material attributed to a Brazilian research group. The study suggested the need for increased connectivity within the research community and highlighted the significant growth potential of the sport [27].

In addition to these studies, other modalities were also investigated. For instance, badminton was evaluated through a visual reaction training system for improving footwork (VRTS) among badminton players. The results indicated that badminton footwork agility training through VRTS could enhance players' skills and agility in this sport [28].

Environmental aspects were also studied, particularly training at different altitudes. Concentrations of erythropoietin (EPO), hemoglobin (Hb) levels, and VO2max values were assessed. Living and training at higher altitudes were associated with improvements in EPO, Hb, and VO2max compared to locations closer to sea level. Training at altitude was found to be favorable for enhancing sports performance [29].

In conventional swimming, the use of playful methods has been shown to have positive effects on sports learning. Two different swimming learning programs, one alternative and the other standardized, were evaluated. The alternative swimming learning program proved to be more efficient or equally effective compared to the standardized method regarding water skills, technique, swimming performance, and salivary cortisol concentration [30].

Basketball was also a subject of study, particularly the prevalence of back pain and musculoskeletal disorders and associated factors among basketball players. The corresponding study found a high prevalence of cervical pain, followed by lumbar and back pain, among basketball players. Preventive programs were recommended to improve the health and sports performance of these athletes [31].

Additionally, a study evaluated military personnel and their visceral adipose tissue (VAT) in relation to inflammatory processes. The study suggested that quantifying VAT could be used to estimate the risk of developing metabolic syndrome (MS). The results indicated that VAT $\geq$ 1025.0 cm^3 (1086.0 g) was associated with MS risk factors and served as a predictor of the disease presenting good indicators of sensitivity and specificity [32].

In this context, this Special Issue covers current and varied topics, with broad relevance for both sports and occupational health, thereby making significant contributions to overall health. Furthermore, it was observed that there was a considerable body knowledge focused on people with disabilities, resulting in significant advancements in paralympic sports and the control of loads and variables related to this sector and thus contributing to the improvement of their life conditions and health.

Conflicts of Interest: The authors declare no conflict of interest.

References

1. Aidar, F.J.; Jacó de Oliveira, R.; Gama de Matos, D.; Chilibeck, P.D.; de Souza, R.F.; Carneiro, A.L.; Machado Reis, V. A Randomized Trial of the Effects of an Aquatic Exercise Program on Depression, Anxiety Levels, and Functional Capacity of People Who Suffered an Ischemic Stroke. *J. Sports Med. Phys. Fit.* **2018**, *58*, 1171–1177. [CrossRef]
2. Aidar, F.J.; Silva, A.J.; Reis, V.M.; Carneiro, A.; Carneiro-Cotta, S. A study on the quality of life in ischaemic vascular accidents and its relation to physical activity. *Rev. Neurol.* **2007**, *45*, 518–522. [PubMed]

3. Aidar, F.J.; Gama de Matos, D.; de Souza, R.F.; Gomes, A.B.; Saavedra, F.; Garrido, N.; Carneiro, A.L.; Reis, V. Influence of Aquatic Exercises in Physical Condition in Patients with Multiple Sclerosis. *J. Sports Med. Phys. Fit.* **2018**, *58*, 684–689. [CrossRef] [PubMed]
4. Aidar, F.J.; de Matos, D.G.; de Oliveira, R.J.; Carneiro, A.L.; Cabral, B.G.D.A.T.; Dantas, P.M.S.; Reis, V.M. Relationship between Depression and Strength Training in Survivors of the Ischemic Stroke. *J. Hum. Kinet.* **2014**, *43*, 7–15. [CrossRef] [PubMed]
5. Aidar, F.J.; de Oliveira, R.J.; Silva, A.J.; de Matos, D.G.; Carneiro, A.L.; Garrido, N.; Hickner, R.C.; Reis, V.M. The Influence of the Level of Physical Activity and Human Development in the Quality of Life in Survivors of Stroke. Health Qual. *Life Outcomes* **2011**, *9*, 89. [CrossRef]
6. Aidar, F.J.; Dantas, E.F.; Almeida-Neto, P.F.; Neto, F.R.; Garrido, N.D.; Cabral, B.G.; Figueiredo, T.; Reis, V.M. Can Post-Exercise Hemodynamic Response Be Influenced by Different Recovery Methods in Paraplegic Sportsmen? *Int. J. Environ. Res. Public Health* **2022**, *19*, 1772. [CrossRef]
7. Aidar, F.J.; Cataldi, S.; Badicu, G.; Silva, A.F.; Clemente, F.M.; Bonavolontà, V.; Greco, G.; Getirana-Mota, M.; Fischetti, F. Does the Level of Training Interfere with the Sustainability of Static and Dynamic Strength in Paralympic Powerlifting Athletes? *Sustainability* **2022**, *14*, 5049. [CrossRef]
8. Aidar, F.J.; Fraga, G.S.; Getirana-Mota, M.; Marçal, A.C.; Santos, J.L.; de Souza, R.F.; Ferreira, A.R.P.; Neves, E.B.; Zanona, A.D.F.; Bulhões-Correia, A.; et al. Effects of Ibuprofen Use on Lymphocyte Count and Oxidative Stress in Elite Paralympic Powerlifting. *Biology* **2021**, *10*, 986. [CrossRef]
9. Aidar, F.J.; Fraga, G.S.; Getirana-Mota, M.; Marçal, A.C.; Santos, J.L.; de Souza, R.F.; Vieira-Souza, L.M.; Ferreira, A.R.P.; de Matos, D.G.; de Almeida-Neto, P.F.; et al. Evaluation of Ibuprofen Use on the Immune System Indicators and Force in Disabled Paralympic Powerlifters of Different Sport Levels. *Healthcare* **2022**, *10*, 1331. [CrossRef]
10. Bezerra, L.A.; de Melo, H.F.; Garay, A.P.; Reis, V.M.; Aidar, F.J.; Bodas, A.R.; Garrido, N.D.; de Oliveira, R.J. Do 12-Week Yoga Program Influence Respiratory Function of Elderly Women? *J. Hum. Kinet.* **2014**, *43*, 177–184. [CrossRef]
11. Barros, N.D.A.; Aidar, F.J.; Marçal, A.C.; Santos, J.L.; de Souza, R.F.; Menezes, J.L.; Gomes, M.Z.; de Matos, D.G.; Neves, E.B.; Carneiro, A.L.G.; et al. Effects of Resistance Training on Oxidative Stress Markers and Muscle Damage in Spinal Cord Injured Rats. *Biology* **2021**, *11*, 32. [CrossRef] [PubMed]
12. de Jesus, J.B.; Aidar, F.J.; de Souza Leite Junior, J.A.; Menezes, J.L.; Silva, A.F.; Carvutto, R.; Poli, L.; Cataldi, S.; Messina, G.; Banja Fernandes, T.L.; et al. Analysis of Post-Exercise Acute Hemodynamic Sustainability in Different Training Methods in Paralympic Powerlifting Athletes. *Sustainability* **2022**, *14*, 14817. [CrossRef]
13. de Souza, R.F.; de Matos, D.G.; Lopes Dos Santos, J.; Andrade Lima, C.; Reis Pires Ferreira, A.; Moreno, G.; Santos Oliveira, A.; Dutra Pereira, D.; Knechtle, B.; Aidar, F.J. Effects of Ibuprofen during 42-Km Trail Running on Oxidative Stress, Muscle Fatigue, Muscle Damage and Performance: A Randomized Controlled Trial. *Res. Sports Med. Print* **2022**, 1–11. [CrossRef] [PubMed]
14. Nikolovski, Z.; Vrdoljak, D.; Foretić, N.; Perić, M.; Marić, D.; Fountoulakis, C. Acute and Long-Lasting Effects of Slow-Paced Breathing on Handball Team Coach's Match Stress. *Healthcare* **2023**, *11*, 1242. [CrossRef] [PubMed]
15. Park, J.-S.; Murlasits, Z.; Kim, S. The Effect of Aerobic Exercise on Variation of Oxidative Stress, Hs-CRP and Cortisol Induced by Sleep Deficiency. *Healthcare* **2023**, *11*, 1201. [CrossRef]
16. Zhang, M.; Li, D.; He, J.; Liang, X.; Li, D.; Song, W.; Ding, S.; Shu, J.; Sun, X.; Sun, J. Effects of Velocity-Based versus Percentage-Based Resistance Training on Explosive Neuromuscular Adaptations and Anaerobic Power in Sport-College Female Basketball Players. *Healthcare* **2023**, *11*, 623. [CrossRef]
17. Querido, A.; Costa, M.J.; Araújo, D.; Sampaio, A.R.; Vilas-Boas, J.P.; Corredeira, R.; Daly, D.J.; Fernandes, R.J. Swimmers with Down Syndrome Are Healthier and Physically Fit than Their Untrained Peers. *Healthcare* **2023**, *11*, 482. [CrossRef]
18. Vernerova, A.; Marova, I.; Chmelik, F. The Role of Volunteers in a Swimming Organization for Persons with Disabilities. *Healthcare* **2022**, *10*, 2149. [CrossRef]
19. Kim, K.; Lee, Y. Development and Validation of a Scale Measuring Intention toward Participating in Pro Bono of Pre-Service Physical Activity Instructors for the Activation of Physical Activity for the Disabled: Based on the Theory of Planned Behavior. *Healthcare* **2022**, *10*, 2094. [CrossRef]
20. Oh, A.-R.; Kim, K. A Study on the Establishment of Physical Activity Environment for People with Disabilities in South Korea. *Healthcare* **2022**, *10*, 1638. [CrossRef]
21. Jacinto, M.; Monteiro, D.; Matos, R.; Antunes, R. Gold Medals, Silver Medals, Bronze Medals, and Total Medals: An Analysis of Summer Paralympic Games from 1992 to 2016. *Healthcare* **2022**, *10*, 1289. [CrossRef] [PubMed]
22. Mira, T.; Monteiro, D.; Costa, A.M.; Morouço, P.; Matos, R.; Antunes, R. Tokyo 2020: A Sociodemographic and Psychosocial Characterization of the Portuguese Paralympic Team. *Healthcare* **2022**, *10*, 1185. [CrossRef] [PubMed]
23. Oh, A.; So, W.-Y. Assessing the Needs of People with Disabilities for Physical Activities and Sports in South Korea. *Healthcare* **2022**, *10*, 265. [CrossRef]
24. de Aquino Resende, M.; Aidar, F.J.; Vasconcelos Resende, R.B.; Reis, G.C.; de Oliveira Barros, L.; de Matos, D.G.; Marçal, A.C.; de Almeida-Neto, P.F.; Díaz-de-Durana, A.L.; Merino-Fernández, M.; et al. Are Strength Indicators and Skin Temperature Affected by the Type of Warm-Up in Paralympic Powerlifting Athletes? *Healthcare* **2021**, *9*, 923. [CrossRef] [PubMed]
25. Sellami, M.; Puce, L.; Bragazzi, N.L. Immunological Response to Exercise in Athletes with Disabilities: A Narrative Review of the Literature. *Healthcare* **2023**, *11*, 1692. [CrossRef] [PubMed]

26. Puce, L.; Biz, C.; Trompetto, C.; Marinelli, L.; Currà, A.; Cavaggioni, L.; Formica, M.; Vecchi, V.; Cerchiaro, M.C.; Trabelsi, K.; et al. A Scoping Review with Bibliometric Analysis of Para-Rowing: State of the Art and Future Directions. *Healthcare* **2023**, *11*, 849. [CrossRef] [PubMed]
27. Puce, L.; Trabelsi, K.; Trompetto, C.; Mori, L.; Marinelli, L.; Currà, A.; Faelli, E.; Ferrando, V.; Okwen, P.; Kong, J.D.; et al. A Bibliometrics-Enhanced, PAGER-Compliant Scoping Review of the Literature on Paralympic Powerlifting: Insights for Practices and Future Research. *Healthcare* **2022**, *10*, 2319. [CrossRef] [PubMed]
28. Kuo, K.-P.; Liao, C.-C.; Kao, C.-C. Improving Special Ability Performance of Badminton Players through a Visual Reaction Training System. *Healthcare* **2022**, *10*, 1454. [CrossRef]
29. Dragos, O.; Alexe, D.I.; Ursu, E.V.; Alexe, C.I.; Voinea, N.L.; Haisan, P.L.; Panaet, A.E.; Albina, A.M.; Monea, D. Training in Hypoxia at Alternating High Altitudes Is a Factor Favoring the Increase in Sports Performance. *Healthcare* **2022**, *10*, 2296. [CrossRef]
30. Papadimitriou, K.; Loupos, D. The Effect of an Alternative Swimming Learning Program on Skills, Technique, Performance, and Salivary Cortisol Concentration at Primary School Ages Novice Swimmers. *Healthcare* **2021**, *9*, 1234. [CrossRef]
31. de Carvalho Borges, S.C.; Mendonça, C.R.; Ferreira Silva, R.M.; De Vitta, A.; Noll, M. Prevalence and Risk Factors of Musculoskeletal Disorders in Basketball Players: Systematic Review and Meta-Analysis. *Healthcare* **2023**, *11*, 1190. [CrossRef] [PubMed]
32. da Rosa, S.E.; Costa, A.C.; Fortes, M.S.R.; Marson, R.A.; Neves, E.B.; Rodrigues, L.C.; Ferreira, P.F.; Filho, J.F. Cut-Off Points of Visceral Adipose Tissue Associated with Metabolic Syndrome in Military Men. *Healthcare* **2021**, *9*, 886. [CrossRef] [PubMed]

healthcare MDPI

Review

Immunological Response to Exercise in Athletes with Disabilities: A Narrative Review of the Literature

Maha Sellami [1], Luca Puce [2] and Nicola Luigi Bragazzi [3,*]

[1] Physical Education Department, College of Education, Qatar University, Doha P.O. Box 2713, Qatar
[2] Department of Neuroscience, Rehabilitation, Ophthalmology, Genetics, Maternal and Child Health (DINOGMI), University of Genoa, 16132 Genoa, Italy
[3] Laboratory for Industrial and Applied Mathematics (LIAM), Department of Mathematics and Statistics, York University, Toronto, ON M3J 1P3, Canada
* Correspondence: bragazzi@yorku.ca

Abstract: For a person with a disability, participating in sports activities and/or competitions can be a challenge for the immune system. The relationship between exercise and immunity response in disabled athletes is, indeed, extremely complex for several reasons, including (1) the chronic low-grade inflammatory and immunodepression—"secondary immune deficiency"—state imposed by the disability/impairment; (2) the impact of the disability on an array of variables, spanning from physical fitness to well-being, quality of life, sleep, and nutritional aspects, among others, which are known to mediate/modulate the effects of exercise on human health; (3) the variability of the parameters related to the exercise/physical activity (modality, frequency, intensity, duration, training versus competition, etc.); and (4) the intra- and inter-individual variability of the immunological response to exercise. In able-bodied athletes, previously published data described several exercise-induced changes affecting various immunological subsets and subpopulations, ranging from neutrophils to lymphocytes, and monocytes. Broadly, moderate intensity workout is accompanied by optimal immunity and resistance to infections such as upper respiratory tract infections (URTI) in athletes. Periods of intense training with insufficient recovery can cause a temporary state of immunosuppression, which should end with a few days of rest/recovery from exercise. Disabled athletes are relatively overlooked and understudied with respect to their able-bodied counterparts. Findings from the few studies available on paralympic and disabled athletes are here summarized and analyzed utilizing a narrative approach to review and determine the major features of the immunological and inflammatory responses to exercise in this specific population. Moreover, a few studies have reported behavioral, dietary, and training strategies that can be adopted to limit exercise-induced immunosuppression and reduce the risk of infection in people with disabilities. However, given the paucity of data and contrasting findings, future high-quality investigations on paralympic and disabled athletes are urgently needed.

Keywords: immune system; disabled athletes; infection; lymphocytes; cytokines; narrative review

Citation: Sellami, M.; Puce, L.; Bragazzi, N.L. Immunological Response to Exercise in Athletes with Disabilities: A Narrative Review of the Literature. *Healthcare* **2023**, *11*, 1692. https://doi.org/10.3390/healthcare11121692

Academic Editor: Felipe Aidar

Received: 14 March 2023
Revised: 26 May 2023
Accepted: 1 June 2023
Published: 9 June 2023

1. Introduction

"People with disabilities" or "disabled people" are broad umbrella terms and expressions that refer to a group of individuals or a specific population that is particularly socially vulnerable and exhibits special needs. These subjects often experience societal stigma, discrimination, and marginalization, reporting as well multiple social disadvantages and either structural or perceived barriers [1,2], such as lack of accommodations and inequities/disparities in perceived quality of life and health-related outcomes, as well as in the use of/access to healthcare provisions [3,4].

According to the currently available body of scholarly research, adults living with disabilities are up to four times more likely to report their health to be fair or poor compared with their able-bodied counterparts [5]. These disparities can be due to both inherent/intrinsic and extrinsic factors, which include the type of impairment and underlying co-morbidities, and ableism, respectively [3]. The lack or scarcity of accessible information, specifically devised for people with disabilities, increases the barriers they may experience, which is dramatically impactful [3]. These factors are cascading and compound, requiring, as such, an intersectional lens to be properly addressed. Besides subjective health-related outcomes, including perceived quality of life, disabled individuals are at an increased risk of poor objective outcomes because of a "triple jeopardy", which includes disability itself, reduced access to healthcare and rehabilitation provisions, and inadequate or ineffective policies, which are not truly disability-inclusive. For example, the efforts in terms of public health measures and the non-pharmaceutical interventions (NPIs) implemented to mitigate against the burden posed by the still ongoing Coronavirus Disease 2019 (COVID-19) pandemic have had some adverse social impacts, especially on marginalized and stigmatized communities [6].

Exercise can exert beneficial effects by enhancing the quality of life [7–10] and protecting against disorders such as communicable [11,12] and chronic-degenerative ones [13,14]. On the other hand, if acute and particularly intense, strenuous, and vigorous, exercise practiced by elite athletes can result in the insurgence of infectious diseases, muscle injuries, inflammation, or cardiovascular disorders [15,16]. The management and treatment of these accidents are hindered by a delayed diagnosis because there are no proactive policies that would enable an early, rapid, and efficient diagnosis. Continuous monitoring of the athlete is, indeed, rarely carried out. This is extremely relevant for disabled athletes and para-athletes who are at higher risk for infections [17,18] as well as chronic, non-communicable conditions [17].

There are several stressors and challenges affecting disability sports participation. Some stressors that impact athletes, including elite athletes, in general, may disproportionately and more commonly affect (elite) athletes with disabilities. Other stressors may instead be unique to (elite) disabled athletes [18]. Stressors and challenges from either or both categories include post-exercise (acute or chronic) pain, overtraining, and injury in often rather complex medical situations (with the need to distinguish sports fatigue or discomfort from sports injuries and disability). Moreover, there can also be organizational issues, including the lack of sufficient adaptive sports infrastructures or facilities, malfunctioning sports equipment, the generally high costs associated with new technologies, and logistical challenges in travel to competition sites. Other stressors are represented by challenging sleep conditions and reduced sleep quantity and/or quality in Paralympic villages or during competitions of national/international interest [19,20]. Furthermore, the pinnacle of para-sports is characterized by rapidly escalating levels of competitiveness and consequently increased training loads and demands. This pressure can also reverberate in the coaching and training environment, with some negative behaviors, such as demeaning comments, non-inclusive language, and derogatory attitudes [19]. Finally, since assignment/allocation to a given disability sports class for the competition is not fully data-driven and evidence-based, there is a risk of being misclassified or assigned to the wrong category [19].

Understanding the impact of these stressors and challenges on the physical and mental health of disabled and Paralympic athletes would shed light on the etiology of health-related symptoms and disorders in this specific athletic population and help devise effective symptom management and preventative strategies, accordingly [19]. In particular, these stressors can impair the immune system [21,22].

However, there is a dearth of data concerning the immunological and inflammatory response to exercise in this specific population of athletes. Therefore, to fill in this gap of knowledge, we conducted the present review of the literature.

2. Material and Methods

2.1. Search Strategy

We mined the major scholarly electronic database MEDLINE via its publicly available interface PubMed. The search string included keywords related to the immune system, disability/impairment, and the sports arena (Table 1). Truncated words (wildcard option) and Medical Subject Headings (MeSH) terms were used where appropriate. Gray literature was consulted by surfing Google Scholar.

Table 1. Search strategy adopted in the present review.

Search Strategy	Selection Criteria
Keywords	(interleukin OR cytokine OR chemokine OR myokine OR inflammation OR inflammatory OR immunity OR "immune system" OR "immune response" OR immunological OR monocytes OR lymphocytes OR neutrophils OR phagocytosis OR granulocytes OR "natural killer" OR "NK cells") AND ("disabled athletes" OR "athletes with disabilities" OR "Paralympics" OR "para-athletes" OR "wheelchair basketball" OR "wheelchair fencing" OR "wheelchair rugby" OR "wheelchair tennis" OR "sitting volleyball" OR (("Down syndrome" OR "intellectual disability" OR "spinal cord injury" OR paraplegia OR paraplegic OR diplegia OR diplegic OR tetraplegia OR tetraplegic OR quadriplegia OR quadriplegic OR ataxia OR athetosis OR hypertonia OR "motor disability" OR wheelchair) AND (exercise OR "physical activity"))) NOT (rats OR rodents OR mice OR mouse OR "animal model")
Inclusion criteria	All ages, any sex/gender groups, any para-sports disciplines All paralympic categories, athletes with disabilities, sufficiently trained people with disabilities
Exclusion criteria	Able-bodied athletes Non-paralympic categories/athletes without disabilities People with disabilities undergoing rehabilitation protocols
Hand-searched target journals	Arch Phys Med Rehabil; Br J Sports Med; Endocr Metab Immune Disord Drug Targets; Int J Sport Nutr Exerc Metab; Int J Sports Physiol Perform; J Intellect Disabil Res; Spinal Cord

No time or language filters were applied. Extensive cross-referencing and hand-consultation of target journals were carried out.

2.2. Inclusion and Exclusion Criteria

The inclusion criteria devised according to the "Population (P)/Intervention (I)/ Comparisons or Comparators (O)/Outcomes (O)" (PICOS) components were the following: studies with sufficiently trained people with disabilities, disabled athletes, and para-athletes (P); subjected to any type of training/conditioning protocol and/or vitamin supplementation or dietary strategy (I); compared across different para-sports disciplines, or with their able-bodied counterparts or stratified according to weekly training duration and frequency, internal and external training load (C); and studies reporting immunological and inflammatory response to exercise (O). The following study designs (S) were considered: quantitative investigations, either prospective or retrospective, or randomized clinical trials (RCTs). The exclusion criteria were as follows: studies recruiting only able-bodied athletes (P); rehabilitation protocols for non-athlete individuals with disabilities (I); and reporting parameters other than immunological/inflammatory ones (O). Studies designed as qualitative or lacking quantitative details, commentaries, editorials, letters to the editor, or expert opinions (S) were not deemed eligible. Review articles were not included as well but were scanned to increase the chance of obtaining all the relevant studies on the designated topic.

2.3. Data Abstraction

Two independent authors (LP and NLB) designed and performed the search, screened the literature, and identified the relevant studies to be included in the present review. The agreement between the two authors was computed according to the kappa statistics and was found to be excellent.

3. Results

3.1. Immunity and Inflammation in Disabled Individuals and Athletes: General Observations in Athletes with Spinal Lesions

In some disabilities such as spinal lesions, autonomic innervation can be altered (the so-called "autonomic dysreflexia") with an impaired humoral and cellular immune response [23] and a systemic low-grade inflammatory state characterized by the levels of circulating inflammatory biomarkers up to 2–3 times higher than in able-bodied subjects [24]. For instance, in people with chronic spinal cord injury, the levels of certain immunoglobulins (such as IgA and IgG2) are elevated [25]. On the other hand, a case-controlled study could not find any differences in the pre- and post-vaccination ratio for IgG, IgA, and IgM response to Pneumovax 23 vaccine between injured and non-injured subjects [26]. In terms of cellular immunity, total and CD4+ T-cell frequencies were found to be increased in chronic spinal cord injury patients. CD4+ T-cells and B cells tended to shift towards memory phenotypes, in (sub-)acute and chronic spinal cord injury, respectively. Decreased immunoglobulin IgG+ and increased IgM+ B cell frequencies were found to reflect disability severity, correlating with the "American Spinal Injury Association" (ASIA) impairment scale (AIS) scores. Finally, B cell responses were comprised of an increased frequency of CD74+ cells and CD74 expression level within total B cells and B cell subsets, respectively [27]. Other studies found evidence of elevated or impaired immunological mediators [28,29].

The innate immune system is altered as well. For example, in several motor disabilities, there is a neuroinflammatory environment [30]. Interleukin 6 (IL-6), which is a single-chain glycoprotein produced and released by monocytes, endothelial cells, and adipose tissue is an activator of inflammation and a strong recruiter of immune cells after the insurgence of some injuries, including spinal cord injury [31]. This cytokine, together with other cytokines and chemokines produced by injured tissues, is released into circulation and acts as a chemoattractant for circulating monocytes which migrate to and infiltrate the injury site where they differentiate into macrophages, monocyte-derived macrophages, or MDMs [31]. It is a pro-inflammatory cytokine and, in addition, an anti-inflammatory myokine involved in an array of cellular and biochemical processes such as lipid oxidation and improvement/enhancement of insulin-stimulated glucose uptake [32].

C-reactive protein (CRP) is an annular, ring-shaped pentameric protein belonging to the family of pentraxins and pattern recognition receptors (PRRs). It is an acute-phase protein found in blood plasma, synthesized, and secreted by the liver, and whose circulating levels increase in response to inflammation, following IL-6 release by macrophages and T cells. It binds to lysophosphatidylcholine expressed on the surface of dead or dying cells (and some types of bacteria) to promote the activation of the complement system via C1q [33]. CRP concentrations have been found to be altered in subjects with spinal cord injuries [33,34]. Regardless of some contrasting findings reported [35], it is, however, a very common clinical observation that people with neurogenic bladder, such as those with multiple sclerosis, cerebral palsy, Parkinson's disease, spina bifida, and spinal cord injury, are at a higher risk for indwelling urinary catheters, thus developing genitourinary infections [36,37]. Besides genitourinary issues, they are also at a higher risk for respiratory/pulmonary impairment/infection and metabolic syndrome, including overweight and obesity, dyslipidemia, diabetes, malignancies, poor wound healing, and pressure ulcers [38,39].

Specifically concerning disabled athletes, the relationship between training-related parameters, such as weekly training volume, intensity, frequency and recovery, internal and external training load, immunity, and immune system, and infection rate in the population of athletes with disabilities appears to be rather complex. In several para-sports disciplines, athletes tend to produce large training loads because of movement inefficiency and to maximize beneficial adaptions which could exert a detrimental impact on an athlete's health by resulting in insufficient recovery [40,41], significantly impairing immunity, and thus leading to illnesses, such as infections as well as chronic-degenerative disorders.

Epidemiological surveys among disabled athletes with spinal lesions have found a higher incidence of upper respiratory tract infections (URTIs) among those with higher training loads and heavier training. For instance, Furusawa et al. [42] computed the number of URTI episodes in wheelchair marathoners during the 1 month before the race (the 18th Oita International Wheelchair Marathon) and the 2-week post-race period at 0.086 ± 0.036/week and 0.089 ± 0.040/week, respectively (versus 0.139 ± 0.046/week and 0.072 ± 0.047/week, among the controls). Even though overall, no significant differences could be detected between the before and after the race periods in marathoners, or between the two populations during each period, the number of URTIs in the 2 weeks after the race was higher in those who trained by running more than 65 km/week.

Disabled athletes and paralympic athletes with spinal lesions may have also high levels of hematological indexes of inflammation and platelet activation and high prevalence rates of cardiovascular disease (CVD) [17,43,44] because of autonomic dysreflexia and their poor autonomic cardiovascular control [43,44] (Figure 1).

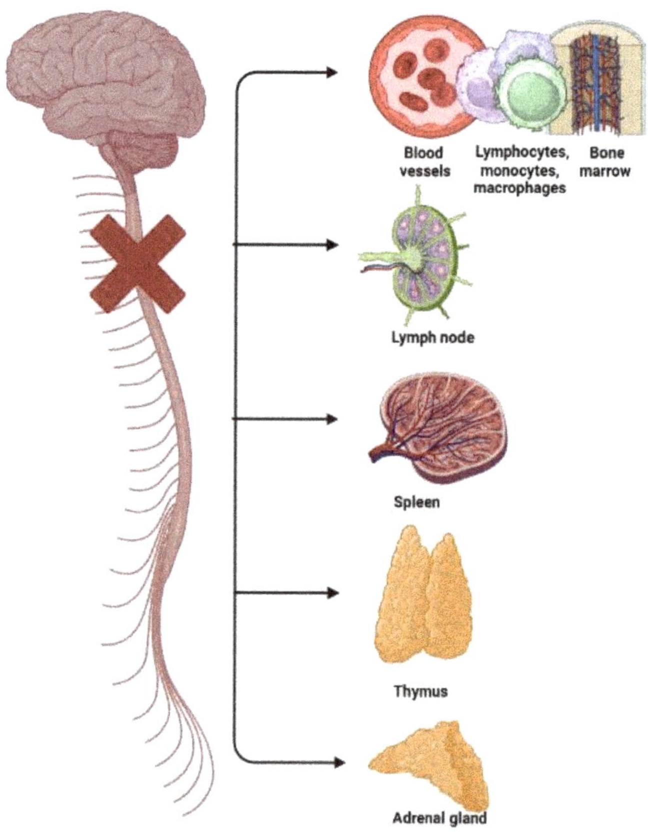

Figure 1. Disruption and breakdown of the outflow of signals (from the central nervous system to primary and secondary lymphoid tissues/organs—bone marrow, spleen, thymus, and lymph nodes—and to the adrenal gland, and their blood vessels; and vice versa from these tissues to the brain) causing immunological impairments in subjects with spinal cord injuries.

3.2. *Immunity and Inflammation in Disabled Individuals and Athletes: General Observations in Athletes with Intellectual Disabilities*

Developmental disorders associated with intellectual disabilities [45] can show a plethora of neuro-inflammatory and/or neuro-immunological features. Of note, individuals with Down syndrome can exhibit signs and symptoms of chronic immune impairment and dysregulation, such as higher prevalence rates of immune and autoimmune/autoinflammatory disorders, which can result in hospitalization during respiratory viral infections and impose a higher burden of mortality from severe infections and complications, including pneumonia and sepsis [46–48]. Immune defects affect both the innate and adaptive immune systems, potentially involving every actor of human immunity from T and B cells to monocytes and neutrophils. Subjects with Down syndrome can show impaired neutrophil chemotaxis, abnormal levels of circulating cytokines, and suboptimal antibody production. Other features of the immune system may also be dysregulated such as the gamma-delta T-cell function, the inflammasome, the Toll-like receptors (TLRs), and their cascades [48].

Moreover, individuals with Down syndrome are at a higher risk of infections also due to non-immunological defects, including abnormal anatomical structures such as tracheomalacia or small ear canal, and gastro-esophageal reflux [46].

Of note, subjects with Down syndrome can have abnormal articular anatomy at the level of the upper cervical joints C1–C2, which can be foot or rockered instead of being normally cup-shaped [49]. For instance, Tassone and Duey-Holtz [50] identified other abnormalities such as hypoplasia of C1, the abnormal body structure of C2, the hypoplastic posterior arch of C1, and fusions contributing to upper cervical instabilities and potentially leading to spinal cord injuries, adding further disability.

In the next sections, we overview the effects of exercise on the mucosal humoral immune system and the non-mucosal humoral and cellular immunity.

3.3. Mucosal Humoral Immunity in Disabled Athletes

Leukocytes include granulocytes, lymphocytes, and monocytes. Granulocytes (neutrophils, eosinophils, and basophils) represent 60–70% of the circulating leukocytes, while lymphocytes represent 20–25% of the pool. The main types of lymphocytes are CD4+ (helper T) lymphocytes, CD8+ (cytotoxic, suppressor) T lymphocytes, B lymphocytes, and natural killer (NK) cells. B cells secrete immunoglobulins (Ig): IgA, IgG, IgM, IgD, and IgE. IgG and IgM are found mainly in plasma, while IgA is more localized in extracellular fluids within the human body, including mucous secretions. The latter type of mucosal immunity is particularly important and studied in the context of physical activity and sports.

The adaptive humoral immune defense in mucosal secretions (saliva) and at mucosal surfaces (respiratory, gastrointestinal, and genitourinary tracts) is to a large extent mediated by secretory IgA (sIgA) antibodies, which represent the first line of defense against pathogens, especially cold-causing viruses [49]. Both saliva composition and sIgA secretion rate can be affected by parasympathetic and sympathetic nerve stimulation (the so-called "integrative autonomic-immune physiological processing" system) [51,52]. Exercise and training, by stimulating the autonomic system, can potentially lead to changes in the mucosal humoral immune compartment [52], but the impact of these alterations on health- and performance-related outcomes is still unclear.

We were able to find five studies [53–57] focusing on the effects of exercise on mucosal humoral immunity in disabled athletes: four [53–56] in athletes with spinal cord injuries and one [57] in subjects with Down syndrome.

Stephenson et al. [53] recruited a sample of seven elite para triathletes over 34 weeks. There was a significant negative correlation between athletes' weekly training duration and sIgA secretion rate ($p = 0.028$) with changes in training duration accounting for 12.7% of the variance. However, no significant relationships between external or internal training load or upper respiratory tract illness (URI) and sIgA parameters could be detected. These findings contrast with previous results by Leicht et al. [54], who presented a negative correlation between training load and sIgA ($p = 0.04$) at 12 predefined time points over five months of training in a sample of fourteen elite tetraplegic athletes. No statistically significant relationship could be found between sIgA levels and subsequent upper respiratory symptoms (URS) occurrence. Finally, sIgA responses did not differ between athletes with and without URS.

In terms of sIgA responses after acute bouts of exercise, Leicht et al. [55] recruited seven highly trained wheelchair rugby athletes with tetraplegia. They carried out two separate highly strenuous sessions, lasting 23 and 41.5 min, respectively, with an aerobic or an interval focus. sIgA secretion rate and α-amylase were found to be unaffected by exercise during both sessions. On the other hand, the increases in sIgA concentration (by 67 ± 29%) 30 min after exercise during the aerobic session were accompanied by parallel decreases in saliva flow rate (by 35 ± 22%). The authors hypothesized that the disruptive impact of the disability-induced sympathetic dysfunction on sIgA secretion rate in tetraplegic athletes may be compensated by mechanisms such as reflex activity by a predominant contribution of the parasympathetic nervous system, which is intact and unaffected in tetraplegics, or by hypersensitivity of receptors.

In another study, Leicht et al. [56] recruited a sample of twenty-three wheelchair athletes, eight tetraplegics, seven paraplegics, and eight non-spinal cord-injured individuals. The athletes carried out two randomized and counterbalanced 60 min sessions on a treadmill consisting of constant load (60% peak oxygen uptake) and intermittent (80% and 40% peak oxygen uptake) exercise blocks. sIgA secretion rate and α-amylase activity were found to be increased during exercise in all groups, especially greater in tetraplegics (by 60 ± 31% versus 30 ± 35% and 11 ± 25% in paraplegics and non-spinal cord-injured subjects, respectively).

In subjects with intellectual disabilities, Fornieles et al. [57] assessed the impact of resistance training on sIgA levels and hormone profile in 40 sedentary adults with Down syndrome, 24 of which were randomly assigned to the 12-week intervention (six stations, 3 days per week), and 16 acting as age-, gender-, and BMI-matched controls. Resistance training was found to significantly increase sIgA concentration ($p = 0.0120$; effect-size = 0.94).

The paucity of available data and partially conflicting results concerning mucosal immunity in the population of disabled athletes warrant further research, even though studies seem to suggest a positive role of acute exercise on mucosal immunologic function in disabled athletes, regardless of the precise type of disability.

3.4. Cytokines and Chemokines in Disabled Athletes

Twelve studies [58–69] investigating cytokines and chemokines in disabled athletes (ten [58–67] in persons with spinal cord injuries, and two [68,69] in those with Down syndrome) could be retrieved and synthesized in the current review.

Regarding neuromotor disabilities, Kouda et al. [58] explored the IL-6 responses to a 20 min arm crank ergometer exercise at 60% of maximum oxygen consumption in eight trained individuals with cervical spinal cord injuries (C6–C7) versus eight able-bodied trained healthy subjects. The plasma concentrations of IL-6, adrenaline, prostaglandin E_2 (PGE_2), and cortisol were measured before, immediately after the exercise, and one and two hours after exercise. At rest, the concentration of IL-6 was significantly higher in individuals with cervical spinal cord injuries (2.18 ± 0.44 pg/mL versus 1.02 ± 0.22 pg/mL, p-value < 0.05). In able-bodied subjects, the plasma IL-6 level increased significantly 1 h after exercise (1.91 ± 0.28 pg/mL, p-value < 0.05) and returned to the baseline level 2 h after exercise, whereas the IL-6 values were steady throughout the study in disabled individuals. The lack of exercise-related IL-6 response in individuals with cervical spinal cord injuries could be due to muscle atrophy and sympathetic nervous system dysfunction.

On the contrary, Umemoto et al. [59] investigated inflammatory response to exercise in a sample of six subjects with spinal cord injuries (T6-T10) versus seven able-bodied subjects. Both groups performed a 2 h arm crank ergometer exercise at 60%VO_{2max}. Several parameters, including plasma catecholamines, IL-6, tumor necrosis factor (TNF)-α, and high-sensitivity CRP (hsCRP) were collected and measured before exercise, 60 min exercise, immediately and 2 h after the completion of the exercise. The authors determined that the arm exercise resulted in a statistically significant increase (p-value < 0.01) in myoglobin and plasma IL-6 levels in both groups, without any difference between the two groups. The other parameters (plasma levels of creatine kinase, lactate dehydrogenase, TNF-α, and hsCRP) did not exhibit any change throughout the study in both groups.

Kinoshita et al. [60] analyzed a sample of five wheelchair basketball players with a spinal cord injury (T7–T12) taking part in the 2009 Mei-shin League of Wheelchair Basketball Games held at Wakayama, Japan. Approximately 1 h before the player's warm-up for the game and immediately after the game, blood samples were collected, measuring plasma IL-6, TNF-α, CRP levels, and blood cell count. Plasma IL-6 levels and the number of monocytes were found to be significantly increased after the game when compared with pre-game measurements (from 1.11 ± 0.66 pg/mL to 2.5 ± 1.29 pg/mL, and from 350 ± 246 per μL to 461 ± 266 per μL, respectively). No changes in other measurements (hematocrit, hemoglobin, red and white blood cell count) could be detected instead. Finally, the author determined a significant relationship between increased IL-6 levels and accumulated play duration ($r = 0.94$, p-value < 0.01), whereas no association between the monocyte count and play duration could be described. This seems to suggest that muscles, and not monocytes, can be the major source of increased IL-6 production and secretion into the blood, whilst monocytes could have been released from the vascular endothelium, as a consequence of the impact of exercise on hemodynamics. This study is limited by the absence of a control group, the low statistical power (59%), the low sample size (the recruitment of further wheelchair players would have enabled the achievement of a higher power), and the lack of serial blood measures.

Ogawa et al. [61] studied six athletes with cervical spinal cord injuries and eight athletes with thoracic and lumbar spinal cord injuries that took part in the 30th Oita International Wheelchair Marathon Race. The authors reported stable monocyte counts in the cervical spinal cord injury group and an increase in the thoracic–lumbar spinal cord injury group, 2 h after the wheelchair half marathon. The authors also described an increase in IL-6 concentrations in both groups (but lower in the cervical spinal cord injury group) and in adrenaline levels in the spinal cord injury group, which recovered to baseline values two hours after the race. Finally, a decrease in TNF-α levels two hours after the wheelchair half marathon was noted in the cervical spinal cord injury group but not in the spinal cord injury group. Adrenaline remained stable in the cervical spinal cord injury group and was lower compared with the spinal cord injury group.

Sasaki et al. [62] found that plasma IL-6 concentrations increased by 18.4-fold and by 9.4-fold in the full and half groups immediately after the race, respectively, recovering to baseline values after 2 h, whereas plasma TNF-α and hsCRP did not change. Plasma IL-6 and hsCRP pre- but not post-race values correlated negatively with the average wheelchair speed.

Hoekstra et al. [63] investigated the relationship between autonomic function and the inflammatory response to a wheelchair half-marathon in seventeen wheelchair athletes with ($n = 7$) and without cervical spinal cord injury ($n = 10$). Catecholamine post-race levels increased only in the non-cervical spinal cord injury group ($p = 0.036$), whilst the increase in IL-6 post-race concentrations was larger in wheelchair athletes without cervical spinal cord injury ($p = 0.040$).

Rosety-Rodriguez et al. [64] investigated a sample of 17 men with complete spinal cord injuries at or below T5, randomly allocated to the intervention ($n = 9$, a 12-week arm cranking exercise program of three sessions per week at a moderate work intensity of 50–65% of heart rate reserve) or control group ($n = 8$). Plasma levels of leptin, adiponectin, plasminogen activator inhibitor-1 (PAI-1), TNF-α, and IL-6 were gathered and measured. Plasma levels of leptin, tumor necrosis factor-alpha, and interleukin-6 were found to be significantly decreased after the completion of the training program. This study has several strengths, including its longitudinal design and random allocation (performed utilizing a concealed method).

Paulson et al. [65] analyzed a sample of twenty-six elite male wheelchair athletes (8 tetraplegics, with a level of injury at C6–C7, ten paraplegics, with a level of injury at T6-L1, and eight non-spinal-cord-injured controls). They carried out a submaximal exercise test followed by a graded exercise to exhaustion on a motorized treadmill. Blood samples were taken before, after, and 30 min after exercise and assessed for levels of IL-6, IL-10, IL-1 receptor antagonist (IL-1RA), TNF-α, epinephrine, and cortisol. Circulating IL-6 concentrations were elevated after and 30 min after exercise and increased by approximately fivefold in non-injured subjects and paraplegics ($p = 0.003$), whereas concentrations in tetraplegics did not change from baseline values. IL-10, IL-1ra, and TNF-α levels were unaffected by exercise in all groups; however, both spinal-cord-injured groups presented elevated concentrations of IL-10 compared with non-spinal-cord-injured groups ($p = 0.001$).

Cavalcante et al. [66] assessed the effects of a wheelchair basketball-based intervention (2 h, twice a week) involving physical and tactical conditioning techniques in a sample of 48 males aged 18–55 years, 21 of which were allocated to the experimental group and 27 were allocated to the control group. The authors were able to find a significant improvement in urinary tract infections and urine culture in pre- and post-intervention antibiograms, respectively. Moreover, the intergroup comparison presented a decrease in infection caused by *Klebsiella pneumoniae*, as well as an increase in the time variability of partially activated thromboplastin, average corpuscular hemoglobin, and hemoglobin and platelets. In the experimental group, there was an increase in hemoglobin and hematocrit and a decrease in glycated hemoglobin. Regarding the intragroup comparison, there was a reduction in the levels of IL-6 before intervention and CRP after intervention.

Manns et al. [67] analyzed twenty-two men with functionally complete paraplegia (aged 39 ± 9 years, with a mean duration of injury of 17 ± 9 years and a level of injury at T2-L2). The main outcome measures were peak aerobic capacity, physical activity, and functional ability as assessed using the Physical Activity and Disability Scale and the Self-Report Functional Measure, respectively. Circulating glucose, insulin, HDL-C, triglycerides, total cholesterol, IL-6, and CRP levels were also collected and measured. The results showed that lower peak aerobic capacities correlated with lower HDL-C and lower physical activity levels, which, in turn, were associated with higher fasting glucose, lower HDL-C levels, and larger abdominal sagittal diameters. These were found to be associated with higher fasting glucose, higher fasting, and post-load insulin, lower HDL-C, higher triglycerides, and higher CRP levels.

Finally, Raguzzini et al. [68] determined that after a simulated wheelchair basketball match, growing IL-6 levels correlated with basal energy expenditure ($r = 0.778$, p-value < 0.05) and inversely correlated with the percentage of fat mass ($r = -0.762$, p-value < 0.05).

To summarize, exercise has been consistently determined to improve low-grade systemic inflammation in disabled athletes with spinal cord injuries by decreasing and increasing plasma levels of pro-inflammatory and anti-inflammatory cytokines, respectively. Slightly contrasting findings reported may be due to some methodological differences, such as the muscle mass of the participating subjects in the studies, the period of training each subject had undergone before the study, or the timing of the collection of parameters.

Regarding subjects with intellectual disabilities, Ordonez et al. [69] recruited 20 premenopausal obese young women with Down syndrome, 11 of which were randomly assigned to the intervention group (a 10-week aerobic training program, three sessions per week, consisting of a 30–40-min treadmill exercise at a work intensity of 55–65% of peak heart rate). Plasmatic levels of TNF-α, IL-6, hsCRP, and fibrinogen were assessed. Plasmatic levels of TNF-α (11.7 ± 1.6 versus 9.2 ± 1.3 pg/mL, $p = 0.022$), IL-6 (8.2 ± 1.1 versus 6.1 ± 0.9 pg/mL, $p = 0.014$) and hsCRP (0.62 ± 0.11 versus 0.53 ± 0.09 mg/dl, $p = 0.009$) significantly decreased in the intervention group.

Rosety-Rodriguez et al. [70] recruited a sample of 40 young male adults with Down Syndrome, 24 of whom were randomly allocated to the intervention group (a 12-week program of resistance circuit training with six stations, 3 days per week). Plasma levels of leptin, adiponectin, CRP, and TNF-α were collected and assessed. They were found to be significantly decreased after the completion of the training program.

To summarize, a 10/12-week training program is effective in reducing pro-inflammatory cytokines and acute phase proteins in women and men with Down syndrome.

3.5. Neutrophils in Disabled Athletes

Neutrophil granulocytes play a major role in the immune system, representing the "first line of defense" against invading pathogens. Disabled people may have impaired neutrophil function in terms of altered phagocytosis and microorganism clearance. For instance, neutrophils play a key role in the pathogenesis of spinal cord injury, even if the precise cellular and molecular mechanisms underlying spinal lesions must be elucidated yet [71]. Neutrophil chemotaxis, as previously mentioned, is impaired in individuals with Down syndrome [72]. There are a few studies investigating neutrophils in disabled athletes. Most importantly, the measurement of neutrophils in response to exercise and recovery time was not yet elucidated in the existing few studies. In able-bodied athletes, moderate exercise has been shown to increase defense functions while extreme exercise decreases some without affecting others. The absolute number of neutrophils increases during and after an acute exercise [16].

For example, Levada-Pires et al. [73] recruited a sample of 10 male wheelchair basketballers aged 33.8 $\pm$ 2.7 years with a spinal cord injury (at T1-L3). Neutrophil levels and function were assessed on rest and 60 min after the basketball match. Phagocytosis capacity was found to be decreased by 75%, whereas the percentage of cells with integral plasma membrane was reduced by 17%. A fivefold increase in the proportion of cells with mitochondrial membrane polarization was reported. DNA fragmentation and phosphatidylserine externalization could not be observed. Finally, the authors described an increase in neutral lipid accumulation of 30% and a twofold increase in ROS production. The authors concluded that sport, in this specific case basketball play, can induce a significant decrease in neutrophil function (in terms of phagocytosis capacity and production of ROS) and an increase in neutrophil death (by necrosis) in wheelchair athletes. This study warrants the need for specific training and conditioning strategies for basketball players in wheelchairs and other disabled athletes to enhance athletic performance and improve disabled athletes' health.

Of note, no article could be found exploring the effect of exercise on neutrophil function in persons with Down syndrome.

3.6. Natural Killer Cells in Disabled Athletes

Natural killer (NK) cells are a major class of cytotoxic lymphocytes and, more generally speaking, innate lymphoid cells (ILCs). They represent from 5% to 20% of all circulating lymphocytes in humans.

NK cells are lymphocytes historically called "natural killer cells" because of their ability to spontaneously lyse tumors or infected cells in the absence of prior specific immunization. This property distinguishes them from CD8+ T cells (cytotoxic). NK cells are one of the components of so-called "innate" immunity. NK cytotoxicity is exerted by different mechanisms, generally such as those employed by CD8+ T cells, such as perforin-dependent cytotoxicity. Following recognition of the target cell, the NK cell degranulates: it releases at the synapse the contents of its cytoplasmic granules, especially perforin which forms pores in the membrane of the target cell [16]. Concerning NK in disabilities such as spinal cord injury, the amount of NK cells can be altered, and their cytotoxic activity (NKCA) can be found to be compromised [74].

A few studies [75–79] investigated NK cells in disabled athletes or persons with disabilities taking part in regular exercise programs. A study by Furusawa et al. [75] found that competitive wheelchair racers with a T5–L1 spinal cord injury exhibited decreased peripheral NK cells and NKCA immediately after a wheelchair full marathon. However, these parameters recovered to baseline values after just one night of rest. Different findings were reported by Furusawa et al. [76] who found a short-term increase in NKCA among disabled recreational athletes with a T7–L1 spinal cord injury after a wheelchair half marathon. The mechanism underlying such an increase was found to be adrenaline-independent [77].

Ueta et al. [78] assessed NKCA response to a 2 h arm crank ergometer exercise at 60% of maximum oxygen consumption (VO_{2max}) in seven subjects with a T11–L4 spinal cord injury and six able-bodied persons. Two different NKCA response patterns could be identified, with NKCA in able-bodied subjects increasing at 60 min of exercise and immediately after the exercise, staying elevated up to 2 h after exercise, decreasing in the spinal cord injury group immediately after exercise and recovering to baseline values 2 h after exercise. Plasma adrenaline in both groups increased significantly immediately after exercise and returned to baseline level 2 h after exercise. Plasma cortisol levels were stable. In the spinal cord injury group, PGE_2 levels significantly increased immediately 2 h after exercise and then normalized, while they were stable in able-bodied athletes.

However, Nowak et al. [79] reported an increase in NK counts in a sample of paralympic rowers who took part in the preparatory stages before the Paralympic Games in Rio, 2016. These conflicting results concerning NK immunity in the population of disabled athletes warrant further research.

3.7. *Lymphocytes in Disabled Athletes*

The amount of lymphocytes increases during exercise and decreases after long-term exercise. Studies of lymphocyte subpopulations all show a decrease in the different lymphocyte subpopulations, whether these are TCD4+, TCD8+, BCD19+, NK CD56+ (NCAM), or NK CD16+. During exercise, the CD4+/CD8+ ratio decreases due to the greater increase in TCD8+. The number of NK CD94+ or NK CD94− increases in absolute number despite a decrease in CD94. Memory T cells CD45 RO+ are preferentially recruited, and true naïve T CD45 RO-CD62L (L-selectine) increases during exercise. The study of T-cell telomeres suggests that exercise allows redistribution of activated T lymphocytes and not a repopulation from newly produced cells. While it was well described in the literature, the biphasic model of leukocytosis–lymphopenia during and after exercise and their activity during exercise is not yet explained nor described in all paralympic categories [16].

Ten studies [17,58,75–82] assessed lymphocyte counts in disabled athletes. Most studies could not find significant changes in lymphocyte counts before and after a sports event, except the studies by Ueta et al. [78], which reported a 1.9-fold increase (from $1.67 \pm 0.6 \times 10^9/L$ to $3.07 \pm 1.8 \times 10^9/L$) and by Klokker et al. [81], in which the extent of the change was not specified. Other changes in lymphocyte counts were reported by Nowak et al. [79] in a sample of paralympic rowers. The authors found a decrease in the counts of total T lymphocytes. Moreover, shifts in T lymphocyte subsets were described with higher percentages of suppressor/cytotoxic and lower percentages of helper/inducer T lymphocyte subsets. No changes in B lymphocytes could be reported. Noteworthily, Yamanaka et al. [82] could not find any changes in total lymphocyte counts for disabled athletes with a spinal cord injury (C6–C7), but, on the contrary, computed a 1.4-fold increase for their able-bodied counterparts. Similarly, Kouda et al. [58] observed no changes in disabled athletes and reported a 1.3-fold increase in able-bodied athletes.

Finally, Bernardi et al. [17] investigated hematological indexes of inflammation and platelet activation in paralympic athletes with spinal cord injury (n = 25, 13 with and 12 with low spinal lesions), lower (n = 15) or upper (n = 10) limb amputation competing in power, intermittent (mixed metabolism), and endurance sports during the London 2012 and Sochi 2014 Paralympics. Inflammation scores did not differ among the groups; however, subjects with a high spinal lesion exhibited lower lymphocyte counts compared with para-athletes with lower limb amputation and higher indexes of platelet activation (mean platelet volume, platelet distribution width, ratio between mean platelet volume and platelet, ratio between mean platelet volume and lymphocyte, and ratio between platelet distribution width and lymphocyte). These data seem to suggest that para-athletes with lower limb amputation may have a higher cardiometabolic risk, whilst those with high spinal injuries may have a higher platelet-derived cardiovascular risk.

3.8. The Impact of Particular Training Strategies on the Immune System in Disabled Athletes

Humans can adapt to a variety of environments. Exposure to hypoxic conditions can induce the expression of hypoxia-inducible factors (HIFs), which act as major regulators of several cellular and molecular pathways involved in processes such as cell proliferation, stem cell function, glycolysis, erythropoiesis, and angiogenesis, as well as immune regulation. More specifically, HIFs contain sequences at the level of promoter regions of genes important to immune regulation. From a clinical standpoint, hypobaric chambers can control chronic inflammation in several inflammatory conditions, including autoimmune/autoinflammatory diseases and systemic inflammation in HIV-infected subjects on antiretroviral treatment (ART). Induction of hypoxia is an effective immunotolerogenic inducer in subjects with HIV infection [83].

However, in the absence of adequate acclimatization protocols, exposure to high altitudes can result in potentially life-threatening issues, such as gastrointestinal problems including gastrointestinal tract bleeding and inflammation. In an animal model study by Khanna et al. [84], in which Sprague–Dawley rats were exposed to 7620 m of hypobaric hypoxia in an animal decompression chamber, intestinal mucosal damage could be described in terms of increased mucosal permeability and disruption of intestinal villi, as well as upregulation of sIgA and proinflammatory cytokines (IL-17) and markers including TLR type 4 (TLR-4) and inducible nitric oxide synthase (iNOS). NK cell and dendritic cell populations were found to be increased, whilst the number of naive T cells was significantly decreased in Peyer's patches. To summarize, hypobaric hypoxia may activate the gastrointestinal–immune axis and dysregulate Th_{17} cells and proinflammatory molecules. IL-17-producing CD4+ T helper cells (Th_{17}) require, indeed, to differentiate stimulation of the aryl hydrocarbon receptor (AhR) pathway, with a key role played by HIF-1-alpha (HIF-1α).

Specifically concerning disabled athletes, Park et al. [85] evaluated the effects of a 2-week exercise training program in hypobaric hypoxic conditions (week 1: simulated altitude 2000 m; 596 mmHg; week 2: simulated altitude 3000 m; 526 mmHg) created by the environmental control chambers on exercise performance (continuous aerobic exercise and anaerobic interval exercise) and immune function in six Korean national cycling athletes with disabilities. The exercise training frequency was 60 min (5 days per week). The authors determined that the number of leukocytes and NK cells significantly decreased, whilst the number of eosinophils, B, and T cells significantly increased.

3.9. The Impact of Particular Dietary Strategies on the Immune System in Disabled Athletes

We were able to find three studies [86–88] addressing the impact of particular dietary strategies on the immune system and the inflammatory state in disabled athletes.

Marques et al. [86] investigated the effects of docosahexaenoic acid (DHA)-rich fish oil (FO) supplementation (3 g/day for 30 days) on neutrophil function in a sample of eight male wheelchair basketball players before and after acute exercise. In the absence of DHA-rich FO supplementation, acute exercise was found to lead to the loss of membrane integrity, ROS production, and high mitochondrial membrane potential in neutrophils, and reduced the phagocytic capacity and IL-6 production by the neutrophils, confirming the results of the previous study by Levada-Pires et al. [73]. These effects could be counteracted by FO supplementation. An et al. [84] conducted a double-blind, randomized, crossover study and recruited ten wheelchair basketball players (aged 34.5 $\pm$ 8.9 years; lean body mass of 34.3 $\pm$ 10.0 kg) who had spinal cord injury and had undergone amputation leucine-enriched essential amino acid (LEAA) supplementation. Of these ten players, nine participated in the final test, receiving LEAA supplements (three times 4.0 g/day), or a placebo. Parameters related to muscular fatigue and inflammatory response were measured before the intense exercise and 4 days after recovery. LEAA supplementation significantly inhibited circulating IL-6 levels (p-value < 0.05), without affecting TNF-α and creatinine kinase concentrations. Finally, Al-Rubaye et al. [88] performed a cross-sectional study recruiting 100 disabled athletes with hemodialysis and hemophilia. The overall dietary inflammatory index (DII) score was −2.83, indicating anti-inflammatory dietary uptake. However, no statistically significant association could be found between the DII of the participants and the components of their body composition, such as body mass index (BMI), waist circumference, waist–hip ratio, fat mass percentage, and fat-free mass percentage.

3.10. The Impact of Particular Pharmacological Strategies on the Immune System in Disabled Athletes

We were able to identify three studies [89–91] covering the impact of specific pharmacological strategies on the immune system and inflammatory state in disabled athletes.

Aidar et al. [89] conducted a randomized, placebo-controlled trial and recruited 10 Paralympic Powerlifting athletes at the national level, aged 27.13 ± 5.57 years. They underwent a warm-up and a 5 × 5 at 80–90% of 1 RM, ingesting ibuprofen 15 min before and 5 h after training. Ibuprofen ingestion resulted in greater peak torque values (p = 0.04, at 24 h) and lower fatigue index (p = 0.01, at 24 h), whereas there was no impact on oxidative stress markers. Blood indicators, including leukocytes, with the use of ibuprofen were higher than with a placebo ($p < 0.001$). In another work, Aidar et al. [90] conducted a randomized, placebo-controlled trial and recruited a sample of 20 Paralympic powerlifting athletes (10 at the national level aged 32.50 ± 3 years, and 10 at the regional level aged 30.75 ± 5.32 years). Athletes underwent a warm-up and a 5 × 5 at 80% of 1 RM, with half of the subjects ingesting ibuprofen 15 min before the commencement of the training. Ibuprofen ingestion resulted in greater peak torque values (p = 0.007) and lower fatigue index (p = 0.002) in the national level group. Leukocytes, with the use of ibuprofen in the national-level group, were greater in concentration than in the regional-level group (p = 0.001). Similarly, neutrophils in the national-level group treated with ibuprofen were greater in concentration than in the regional-level group treated with ibuprofen and placebo (p = 0.025). Lymphocytes in the national-level group treated with ibuprofen were lower in concentration than in the regional-level group treated with ibuprofen and placebo (p = 0.001). Monocytes in the national-level group with ibuprofen and placebo were lower in concentration than in the regional-level group treated with ibuprofen (p = 0.049). Hemoglobin, hematocrit, and erythrocyte values were higher in concentration at the national level in athletes treated with ibuprofen and placebo than at the regional level in those treated with ibuprofen and placebo (p-value < 0.05). Ammonia levels were higher in concentration in the national-level group treated with ibuprofen (p = 0.007) and placebo (p = 0.038) compared to the regional-level group treated with ibuprofen and placebo, respectively. Fraga et al. [91] recruited eight Paralympic powerlifting athletes (aged 27.0 ± 5.3 years) competing at the national level who underwent a warm-up and a 5 × 5 at 85–90% of 1 RM. Ingestion of ibuprofen or placebo occurred 15 min before and 5 h after training. Maximal isometric force only decreased in the placebo condition, with a significant increase between 24 and 48 h in the ibuprofen condition, whilst the post-exercise rate of force development decreased significantly for both conditions. Muscle temperature decreased significantly at 48 h after exercise in the placebo condition, while deltoid muscle temperature 48 h after exercise was higher in the ibuprofen condition. Finally, creatine kinase was higher in concentration with the placebo than with ibuprofen 48 h after exercise, whilst alanine aminotransferase was lower in concentration 24 h after the training with ibuprofen. Immediately after training, aspartate aminotransferase increased with a placebo, while with ibuprofen it increased after 24 h.

4. Discussion

There is a limited number of studies on the immunological response to physical activity/exercise in people with disabilities on a range of selected immunological parameters (Table 2).

Table 2. Main features of selected studies included in the present systematic review.

Study	Athlete Population	Training/Exercise	Studied Parameters	Major Findings
		Mucosal Humoral Immunity		
Stephenson et al. [35]	Seven elite para triathletes	34-week training	Weekly training duration, sIgA, URI **Measurements**: Weekly saliva samples	- Negative correlation between weekly training duration and sIgA secretion rate ($p = 0.028$) - No relationships between external or internal training load or URI and sIgA parameters - No significant difference in SIgA when URI is present or not
Leicht et al. [36]	Fourteen elite tetraplegic athletes	Five months of training	Training load, sIgA, URS **Measurements**: Throughout the study's duration Before 11 am and before any physical activity Self-reported	- Negative correlation between training load and sIgA ($p = 0.04$) - No relationship between sIgA and URS - No difference in SIgA between athletes with and without URS
Leicht et al. [37]	Seven highly trained wheelchair rugby athletes with tetraplegia	Two separate highly strenuous sessions, lasting 23 and 41.5 min	sIgA secretion rate and concentration, and α-amylase **Measurements**: Saliva was collected before, after, and 30 min after exercise Blood lactate before and immediately after the training session	- sIgA secretion rate and α-amylase unaffected by exercise - Increased sIgA concentration post aerobic session accompanied by decreases in saliva flow rate - No difference for saliva in osmolality
Leicht et al. [38]	Twenty-three wheelchair athletes (eight tetraplegics, seven paraplegics, and eight non-spinal cord-injured participants)	Two randomized and counterbalanced 60 min sessions on a treadmill	sIgA secretion rate and α-amylase activity **Measurements**: Before, during, after, and 30 min after exercise	- Increased sIgA secretion rate and α-amylase activity
		Cytokines and Chemokines		
Kinoshita et al. [60]	Five wheelchair basketball players with spinal cord injuries	2009 Mei-shin League of Wheelchair Basketball Games	Plasma IL-6, TNF-α, CRP levels, blood cell count, and accumulated play duration **Measurements**: 1 h before warm-up and after the game	- Increased plasma IL-6 level and the number of monocytes - Significant relationship between increased IL-6 levels and accumulated play duration - No significant correlation between increased monocyte number and IL-6 level changes
Ogawa et al. [61]	Six athletes with cervical spinal cord injuries and eight athletes with thoracic and lumbar spinal cord injury	30th Oita International Wheelchair Marathon Race	- IL-6 - (TNF)-α - adrenaline and blood cell **Measurements**: Before, immediately after, and 2 h after the race 24 h recovery	- Stable increased monocyte counts (depending on the disability) - Increased IL-6 - Decreased TNF-α
Sasaki et al. [62]	Twenty-eight men with spinal cord injury (16 full-marathon racers, full-group and 12 half-marathon racers, half-group)	28th Oita International Wheelchair Marathon Race, Japan	- IL-6 - (TNF)-α - Sensitivity C-reactive protein **Measurements**: 24 h and immediately before and after the race	- Increased IL-6 - Correlation between plasma IL-6 and hsCRP and average wheelchair speed - TNF-α and hsCRP did not change - No correlation between IL-6 and wheelchair performance
Hoekstra et al. [63]	Seventeen men athletes with cervical spinal cord injury or without	Oita 2016 Wheelchair half-marathon	- Adrenaline and noradrenaline - IL-6 - eHsp72 **Measurements**: Before, after, and 1 h after race	- Large increase in IL-6 after race in NON-CSCI - No change in eHsp72 concentration - Increased plasma adrenaline and noradrenaline levels in NON-CSCI ($p < 0.036$)
An et al. [87]	Ten wheelchair basketball players with spinal cord injuries and amputation (nine in the final test)	Korean Paralympic wheelchair basketball league	Inflammatory response Muscular fatigue **Measurements**: Before the intense exercise and 4 days after recovery	- Significant inhibition of IL-6 levels in the ELAA-treated group - No changes in TNF-a and creatinine kinase levels - Significant improvement in the whole body and back muscle soreness values
		Neutrophils		
Levada-Pires et al. [73]	Ten male wheelchair basketballers with a spinal cord injury (T1-L3)	Basketball match	Neutrophil levels and function	- Decreased phagocytosis capacity - Increased percentage of cells with the integral plasma membrane - Increased proportion of cells with mitochondrial membrane polarization - Increased neutral lipid accumulation - Increased ROS production

Table 2. *Cont.*

Study	Athlete Population	Training/Exercise	Studied Parameters	Major Findings
Marques et al. [86]	Eight male wheelchair basketball players	DHA-rich FO supplementation	Neutrophil function	- Loss of membrane integrity - ROS production - High mitochondrial membrane potential - Decreased phagocytic capacity and IL-6 production
Natural Killer Cells				
Furusawa et al. [75]	Competitive wheelchair racers with T5-L1 spinal cord injury	Wheelchair full marathon	Peripheral NK cell counts and NKCA	Decreased peripheral NK cells and NKCA
Furusawa et al. [76]	Disabled recreational athletes with T7-L1 spinal cord	Wheelchair half marathon	NKCA	Short-term increase in NKCA
Ueta et al. [78]	Seven spinal-cord-injured individuals	2 h arm crank ergometer exercise at 60% of VO_{2max}	NKCA	Decreased NKCA, recovering after 2 h
Yamanaka et al. [82]	Eight spinal-cord-injured individuals (C6-C7)	20-min arm crank ergometer exercise at 60% of VO_{2max}	NKCA	No changes in NKCA
Nowak et al. [79]	Paralympic rowers	Paralympic Games in Rio, 2016	NK cell counts	Increased NK cell counts
Lymphocytes				
Banno et al. [77]	Six cervical spinal cord injury individuals and seven individuals with T4 and L1 spinal cord injuries in a wheelchair half-marathon race	The 29th Oita International Wheelchair Marathon Race	NKCA cell count **Measurements**: Before, after, and 2 h after recovery	No changes in the lymphocyte counts
Furusawa et al. [75]	Nine male wheelchair marathon athletes with spinal cord injuries between T5 and T12	15th Oita International Wheelchair Marathon Race	NK cell counts **Measurements**: The day before, immediately after, and 1 day after the race	No changes in the lymphocyte counts
Furusawa et al. [76]	Seven men wheelchair racers with spinal cord injuries between T7 and L1	International Wheelchair Marathon Race in Japan	NK cell counts **Measurements**: The day before, immediately after, and 1 day after the race	No changes in the lymphocyte counts
Nash [80]	Individuals with quadriplegia	Cycling exercise	Immune system NK cell counts Cytotoxicity **Measurements**: NA	- No production of an archetypical leukocytosis - Raising in NK cell number and cytotoxicity for 1.5 h after exercise - Immune system is responsive to exercise challenge
Ueta et al. [78]	Seven individuals with spinal cord injury between T11 and L4 Six able-bodied individuals	Arm crank ergometer exercise at 60% of VO_{2max}	NKCA **Measurements**: Before, during, and immediately after the exercise	Increased lymphocyte counts ($p < 0.05$) Decreased NKCA in SCI Significant increases in plasma adrenaline No changes in plasma cortisol
Klokker et al. [81]	Eleven subjects with spinal cord injury (five paraplegic individuals and six quadriplegic individuals)	30 min electrically stimulated cycling exercise	NK cells **Measurements**: Before, at the end of the exercise, and 2 h after the exercise	Increased lymphocyte counts
Nowak et al. [79]	Two Paralympic rowers	Rowing ergometer until exhaustion	Cardiorespiratory fitness Lymphocyte counts **Measurements**: Blood samples 3 times The day before testing, 5 min after exercise, and after the recovery period	Increased lymphocyte counts

4.1. Mucosal Humoral Immunity in Disabled Athletes

In able-bodied athletes, several important acquired (specific) immune functions including antigen presentation by monocytes/macrophages and derived cells, immunoglobulin production by B cells, T-cell cytokine production, and proliferation (e.g., interferon-gamma), are reduced after prolonged exercise. Mucosal immune protection may also be compromised. For example, sIgA response to intense and strenuous exercise is variable, even though it is generally accepted that very prolonged exercise sessions such as triathlon may result in lower sIgA. Trying to explain these variations, several scientists claim the role of stress biological amines and hormones (including catecholamines and cortisol) together with the disruption of pro-/anti-inflammatory cytokine balance, especially in cellular environments characterized by higher IL-6 secretion.

However, for athletes with disabilities, contradictory findings could be reported. One study [53] found no significant relationships between external or internal training load or URI and sIgA parameters. These results are in contrast with other studies [54,55], which presented a negative correlation between training load and sIgA in a sample of elite tetraplegic athletes. On the other hand, no statistically significant relationship could be found between sIgA levels and subsequent URS occurrence. Finally, sIgA responses did not differ between athletes with and without URS. In addition, it is important to mention here that all samples were taken before and after the acute exercise, and it resulted in increased sIgA during recovery in tetraplegic athletes, contrary to previous studies with able-bodied athletes.

The dearth of currently available data and the reporting of partially conflicting results concerning mucosal immunity in the population of disabled athletes (see also studies [56,57]) warrant further research. In this context, it is important to highlight the role of exercise duration and intensity on humoral immunity and consider these parameters as external factors playing a key role in the modulation and fine-tuning of the adaptation to training and exercise when it comes to exploring humoral immunity responses in disabled individuals. This should be investigated together with other relevant variables, such as the concentrations of cortisol and other molecules known to influence (or confound) the expression of sIgA. Moreover, a more diverse representation of disabilities would be appreciated in that virtually all available studies focus on spinal cord injury, as such overlooking other kinds of impairment and other disabilities.

4.2. Neutrophils in Disabled Athletes

Based on the currently available body of scholarly data on able-bodied athletes, it appears that exercises of low to moderate intensity (60% VO_{2max}) and of medium duration (approximately 60 min) exert less stress on the immune system than prolonged sessions (over 90 min) of intense effort (greater than 75% VO_{2max}). Moderate-intensity exercise results in a reduced response to stress hormones, which is associated with a more favorable immune response. The increase in the number of polymorphonuclear neutrophils (innate immune cells) and the improvement in their functionality, as well as the increase in the number of monocytes and certain lymphocytes (NK cells), following moderate exercise plead in favor of an improvement of the immune defenses in response to moderate activity. Neutrophils represent about 60% of leukocytes and participate in the immune response. Their function is to migrate to infected sites where they bind, ingest, and kill pathogens. Neutrophils play an important role as mediators of inflammation. On the one hand, neutrophils release various substances that contribute to the inflammatory reaction and the recruitment of other immune system cells to the site of infection. On the other hand, recent studies have shown that neutrophils are not only involved in promoting this response, but also take part in the resolution and repair of damaged tissues.

During an infection or in the event of tissue damage such as spinal cord injuries, neutrophils communicate and interact with various cells of the immune system (macrophages, NK cells, T lymphocytes, and B lymphocytes) by "orchestrating" the evolution of immune responses, both innate and adaptive. Neutrophils activate pro-inflammatory responses eliciting macrophages that phagocyte debris and clean the damaged tissue in spinal cord injury. In addition, neutrophils can play a key role in different conditions and biological/physiological events, such as the responses and adaptations to physical exercise in individuals with disabilities.

Of interest, in spinal cord injury, Levada-Pires et al. [73] reported decreased phagocytic activity in response to intense physical activity with increased ROS production. Similarly, Marques et al. [86] reported an increase in ROS but also lower phagocytic capacity and

IL-6 production. Regulation of neutrophil production and pro-anti-inflammatory status in spinal cord injury remains unclear and based on very few studies, while it is certain that neutrophils perform different important immune functions. Their inadequate response or dysregulation can also lead to the development of different disease states, including immunological impairments and chronic inflammation.

4.3. Lymphocytes in Disabled Athletes

In able-bodied athletes, the practice of exercises/physical activities of any intensity can produce pro-inflammatory cytokines, even though higher levels of inflammatory mediators are generally reported after intense and prolonged exercise. This stimulates a complementary anti-inflammatory response, the homeostasis of which can help clear infections and reduce inflammation, resulting in beneficial health effects. Studies found, indeed, that both moderate and intense intensity exercise may release pro-inflammatory cytokines with the subsequent promotion of anti-inflammatory molecule production. Anti-inflammatory mediators are then released to combat the pro-inflammatory response and restore immunological balance [92].

In able-bodied athletes, during exercise, increases in the number of lymphocytes have been reported in various lymphocyte subsets/subpopulations, including CD4+ or CD8+ T lymphocytes as well as CD19+ B lymphocytes and CD16+ or CD56+ NK lymphocytes. The most increased populations are NK cells and CD8+ lymphocytes, inducing a decrease in the CD4+/CD8+ ratio that can reach values in the range of 30–60% [93]. An increase in NK cells can lead to a decrease in T cells. Concerning disabled athletes, conflicting results were found in the studies conducted on the spinal-cord-injured (paraplegics or tetraplegics) in the modulation of the response and adaption to exercise and overviewed in the present review.

Most of these studies measured the lymphocyte count before, immediately after the exercise/competition, and during recovery. Only three studies [78,79,81] found no changes in lymphocyte count in response to marathon races in disabled participants. However, other investigations were able to find increased lymphocyte counts in response to low–to-moderate intensity exercises such as arm crank ergometer exercise at 60% of VO_{2max} or electrical stimulation lasting up to 30 min. Similarly, only one study [79] conducted in a sample of Paralympic rowers showed leukocytosis following maximal exercise. Disparities in results may be due to the sample size chosen and the methodology adopted (such as the study design) but, most importantly, to the exercise modality (in terms of duration and intensity). Leukocytosis and then post-exercise lymphopenia constitute the biphasic response to intense exercise [94], even though these "biphasic changes" are generally overlooked and understudied in the disabled athlete population.

As previously mentioned, further explanations of this and other immunological phenomena may be linked to the impact of cortisol and biological amines, such as catecholamines, which are known to be important mediators of immunological responses in a number of different disabilities/impairments, especially in spinal cord injury.

4.4. Natural Killer Cells in Disabled Athletes

NK cells are large granular lymphocytes that belong to the innate compartment of the human immune system. They participate in the immunosurveillance of tumors and in the early control of microbial infections. These cells are capable of killing tumor cells while sparing healthy ones according to the "immunological theory of the self". They also produce proinflammatory cytokines such as interferon-gamma (IFN-y) which participate in the orientation and modulation of the adaptive immune response. NK cells produce other pro-inflammatory cytokines, but also immunoregulatory ones, such as the immunosuppressive IL-10, growth factors, such as the granulocyte-macrophage colony-stimulating factor (GM-CSF) and the granulocyte colony-stimulating factor (G-CSF), as well as other various chemokines.

In disabled people with neurological impairments such as multiple sclerosis, immunopathological studies have largely focused on adaptive T and B lymphocytes. Regarding NK cells, their precise involvement remains unclear and even controversial [95,96]. On the one hand, it has been observed that blocking the infiltration of NK cells into the central nervous system can cause symptom exacerbation, such as in an experimental model of autoimmune encephalitis, but other observations have shown a pro-inflammatory role of the NK cells through their interaction with T and B lymphocytes and antigen-presenting cells. On the other hand, patients suffering from relapsing–remitting multiple sclerosis with significant NK cell activity are more prone to disease progression and more active and developing lesions [95,96].

In other conditions, such as exercise/sport and physical activity, it has been well determined that in able-bodied athletes, regardless of the exercise modality (in terms of duration and intensity), NK activity can increase due to the increase in the number of NK cells. However, according to some observations, NKCA can also stay unchanged or even be reduced depending on the intensity and duration of the exercise [97]. During the exercise, recruited NKs can have a high response to IL-2 stimulation [98]. After a long, intense exercise, the concentration of circulating NK cells and functional NK activity decrease below baseline values. This decrease is maximal 2 to 4 h after exercise [99].

In the present review focused on disabled athletes, disparities in results were noted in the studies overviewed. While some investigations reported decreased NK cells in wheelchair athletes and spinal-cord-injured ones, others reported an increased count or no changes. These discrepancies could be due to the different test/competition chosen for the assessment of exercise-induced changes in NK cells. For instance, elevated NK cell counts were detected in response to long-duration and intense competitions, while decreases or no changes in NK cell levels were detected in response to exercises conducted at lower intensities. Conflicting findings may also be due to compensatory mechanisms specific to the type of disability/impairment under study and involve, for example, other mediators, such as biological amines (catecholamines).

4.5. *Cytokines and Chemokines in Disabled Athletes*

A growing body of scholarly research has consistently shown that exercise may help reduce pro-inflammatory cytokines in a number of circumstances and clinical populations, including former cancer patients [100]. The previously published data suggest that combined aerobic and resistance training may help reduce pro-inflammatory markers in former prostate and breast cancer patients by increasing the counts of lymphocytes, including NK cells [101–104].

Under normal conditions, immune cells generally do not produce cytokines: they can produce them only after being activated, in general by pathogenic agents or in particular circumstances, including exercise/physical activity. In response to physical exercise, there is an increase in plasma levels of IL-1 and especially IL-6 [105]. After a marathon race, there is also an increase in TNF-α, IL-1β, and IL-6. This elevation is followed by an increase in IL-1RA, soluble TNF receptors, and IL-10 with anti-inflammatory properties [106,107]. Chemokines such as IL-8, MIP1α, and MIP1β can also rise in concentration after a marathon [108]. In the urine, the presence of proinflammatory cytokines was observed after exercise (including TNF-α, IL1β, IL-6, IL-2 receptor, and IFN-γ, among others) [109,110].

Studies overviewed in the present review suggested that cytokines play a major role in the etiopathogenesis of the damage in spinal-cord-injured people as well as during the recovery and rehabilitation periods. Studying the variation of immunological parameters at rest and in response to physical activity/exercise can help find potentially new strategies targeting a specific type of disability/impairment.

Increased IL-6 levels after exercise can be found in wheelchair athletes in some studies, while disparities could be noted in the reporting of TNF-α and hsCRP concentrations, which were the most measured immunological parameters. The discordant results in the studies overviewed in the present review can be explained by taking into account several factors such as the type of physical activity (intensity and duration) and the nature and sensitivity of the test, as well as the precise type of disability/impairment (for instance, level and completeness of spinal cord injury).

4.6. Behavioral, Dietary, and Training Strategies in Disabled Athletes

For a person with a disability, participating in sports activities and/or competitions can be a challenging condition for the immune system. The relationship between exercise and immunity response in disabled athletes is, indeed, extremely complex for several reasons, including (1) the chronic low-grade inflammatory and immunodepression—"secondary immune deficiency"—state imposed by the disability/impairment; (2) the impact of the disability on an array of variables, spanning from physical fitness to well-being, quality of life, sleep, and nutritional aspects, among others, which are known to mediate/modulate the effects of exercise on human health; (3) the variability of the parameters related to the exercise/physical activity (modality, frequency, intensity, duration, training versus competition, etc.); and (4) the intra- and inter-individual variability of the immunological response to exercise.

In able-bodied athletes, the previously published data describe several exercise-induced changes affecting various immunological subsets and subpopulations, ranging from neutrophils to lymphocytes, and monocytes. Broadly, moderate-intensity workout is accompanied by optimal immunity and resistance to infections such as URTI in athletes. Periods of intense training with insufficient recovery can cause a temporary state of immunosuppression, which should end with a few days of rest/recovery from exercise. Disabled athletes are relatively overlooked and understudied compared to their able-bodied counterparts. Findings from the few studies available on paralympic and disabled athletes have been here summarized and analyzed utilizing a narrative approach to review and determine the major features of the immunological and inflammatory responses to exercise in this specific population. Moreover, only a few studies have reported behavioral, dietary, and training strategies that can be adopted to limit exercise-induced immunosuppression and reduce the risk of infection in people with disabilities. However, given the paucity of data and contrasting findings, future high-quality investigations on paralympic and disabled athletes are urgently needed.

5. Conclusions

In general, a few studies have explored immunological responses in disabled athletes, especially from a comparative perspective (athletes with versus without disabilities/impairments), which would be paramount in dissecting the molecular and cellular basis of the adaptation to exercise in this specific, unique population. Disabled athletes are generally overlooked and understudied, whilst research could help unlock new viable approaches and strategies to counteract the poor health-related outcomes imposed by the disability/impairment.

There is a limited number of studies on the immunological response to physical activity/exercise in people with disabilities on selected immunological parameters. Findings from these few studies suggested no impact of acute and chronic exercise (in terms of training load, intensity, and duration) on salivary antibodies in spinal-cord-injured (tetraplegic and paraplegic) athletes, regardless of the precise type of impairment. However, when it comes to more intense exercises, there was an impaired sIgA secretion rate and α-amylase activity. Only very few studies reported no changes in lymphocyte counts in response to intense exercise (marathon competition), while others suggested an increased count in response to progressive maximal exercise. Similarly, studies reported an increase in lymphocytes when measured in low–moderate intensity exercise in spinal-cord-injured athletes (either in populations of paraplegics and/or tetraplegics). In other words, moderate physical activity seems, therefore, to have a protective effect on the human body in disabled subjects by promoting the detachment of leukocytes and their diffusion in the blood system and by the recruitment of neutrophil cells which can have a "booster effect" on the immune system. Conversely, if the activity is too intense, the natural defense functions will be upgraded to properly adjust the pro- and anti-inflammatory balance. Harnessing these anti-inflammatory abilities may hold the key to new strategies for the treatment of inflammatory diseases, especially in the disabled population, which exhibits a chronic low-grade inflammatory state combined with immunodepression ("secondary immune deficiency"). Furthermore, NK cell count was found unchanged or reduced in spinal cord injury and wheelchair athletes during low intense competition, while it increased in more intensive sporting events in disabled athletes, even though this could be due to the type of disability/impairment (level and completeness of the lesion). Concerning cytokines, increased IL-6 levels were generally reported in wheelchair athletes, while contradictory findings regarding interferons and other chemokines were reported.

Further high-quality investigations are needed to clarify the reasons underlying conflicting findings regarding immunological parameters in disabled athletes, also leveraging molecular big data [106], next-generation immunological assays (i.e., the so-called "immunomics") [111], and including the measurement of other molecules, such as biological amines (catecholamines) and hormones (cortisol) which are known to mediate/modulate the immunological responses to exercise within a more comprehensive, integrative, and systems-based approach.

Author Contributions: N.L.B. conceived and designed the study. M.S., L.P. and N.L.B. drafted and critically revised the manuscript. All authors have read and agreed to the published version of the manuscript.

Funding: This research received no external funding.

Institutional Review Board Statement: Not applicable.

Informed Consent Statement: Not applicable.

Data Availability Statement: Not applicable.

Conflicts of Interest: The authors declare no conflict of interest.

References

1. Mithen, J.; Aitken, Z.; Ziersch, A.; Kavanagh, A.M. Inequalities in social capital and health between people with and without disabilities. *Soc. Sci. Med.* **2015**, *126*, 26–35. [CrossRef] [PubMed]
2. Rowland, M.; Peterson-Besse, J.; Dobbertin, K.; Walsh, E.S.; Horner-Johnson, W. Expert Panel on Disability and Health Disparities. Health outcome disparities among subgroups of people with disabilities: A scoping review. *Disabil. Health J.* **2014**, *7*, 136–150. [CrossRef]
3. Kamalakannan, S.; Bhattacharjya, S.; Bogdanova, Y.; Papadimitriou, C.; Arango-Lasprilla, J.C.; Bentley, J.; Jesus, T.S.; Refugee Empowerment Task Force International Networking Group of The American Congress of Rehabilitation Medicine. Health Risks and Consequences of a COVID-19 Infection for People with Disabilities: Scoping Review and Descriptive Thematic Analysis. *Int. J. Environ. Res. Public Health* **2021**, *18*, 4348. [CrossRef] [PubMed]
4. Krahn, G.L.; Walker, D.K.; Correa-De-Araujo, R. Persons with disabilities as an unrecognized health disparity population. *Am. J. Public Health* **2015**, *105* (Suppl. S2), S198–S206. [CrossRef] [PubMed]
5. Altman, B.M.; Bernstein, A. *Disability and Health in the United States, 2001–2005*; National Center for Health Statistics: Hyattsville, MD, USA, 2008.
6. Shakespeare, T.; Ndagire, F.; Seketi, Q.E. Triple jeopardy: Disabled people and the COVID-19 pandemic. *Lancet* **2021**, *397*, 1331–1333. [CrossRef] [PubMed]
7. Gill, D.L.; Hammond, C.C.; Reifsteck, E.J.; Jehu, C.M.; Williams, R.A.; Adams, M.M.; Lange, E.H.; Becofsky, K.; Rodriguez, E.; Shang, Y.T. Physical activity and quality of life. *J. Prev. Med. Public Health* **2013**, *46* (Suppl. S1), S28–S34. [CrossRef]
8. Hacker, E. Exercise and quality of life: Strengthening the connections. *Clin. J. Oncol. Nurs.* **2009**, *13*, 31–39. [CrossRef]
9. Puce, L.; Marinelli, L.; Mori, L.; Pallecchi, I.; Trompetto, C. Protocol for the study of self-perceived psychological and emotional well-being of young Paralympic athletes. *Health Qual Life Outcomes* **2017**, *15*, 219. [CrossRef]
10. Puce, L.; Marinelli, L.; Girtler, N.G.; Pallecchi, I.; Mori, L.; Simonini, M.; Trompetto, C. Self-Perceived Psychophysical Well-Being of Young Competitive Swimmers with Physical or Intellectual Impairment. *Percept Mot. Ski.* **2019**, *126*, 862–885. [CrossRef]
11. da Silveira, M.P.; da Silva Fagundes, K.K.; Bizuti, M.R.; Starck, É.; Rossi, R.C.; de Resende ESilva, D.T. Physical exercise as a tool to help the immune system against COVID-19: An integrative review of the current literature. *Clin. Exp. Med.* **2021**, *21*, 15–28. [CrossRef]

12. Chastin, S.F.M.; Abaraogu, U.; Bourgois, J.G.; Dall, P.M.; Darnborough, J.; Duncan, E.; Dumortier, J.; Pavón, D.J.; McParland, J.; Roberts, N.J.; et al. Effects of Regular Physical Activity on the Immune System, Vaccination and Risk of Community-Acquired Infectious Disease in the General Population: Systematic Review and Meta-Analysis. *Sports Med.* **2021**, *51*, 1673–1686. [CrossRef] [PubMed]
13. Nilsson, M.I.; Bourgeois, J.M.; Nederveen, J.P.; Leite, M.R.; Hettinga, B.P.; Bujak, A.L.; May, L.; Lin, E.; Crozier, M.; Rusiecki, D.R.; et al. Lifelong aerobic exercise protects against inflammaging and cancer. *PLoS ONE* **2019**, *14*, e0210863. [CrossRef] [PubMed]
14. Peres, A.; Branchini, G.; Marmett, B.; Nunes, F.B.; Romão, P.R.T.; Olean-Oliveira, T.; Minuzzi, L.; Cavalcante, M.; Elsner, V.; Lira, F.S.; et al. Potential Anticarcinogenic Effects from Plasma of Older Adults After Exercise Training: An Exploratory Study. *Front. Physiol.* **2022**, *13*, 855133. [CrossRef] [PubMed]
15. Friman, G.; Wesslén, L. Special feature for the Olympics: Effects of exercise on the immune system: Infections and exercise in high-performance athletes. *Immunol. Cell Biol.* **2000**, *78*, 510–522. [CrossRef]
16. Sellami, M.; Gasmi, M.; Denham, J.; Hayes, L.D.; Stratton, D.; Padulo, J.; Bragazzi, N. Effects of Acute and Chronic Exercise on Immunological Parameters in the Elderly Aged: Can Physical Activity Counteract the Effects of Aging? *Front. Immunol.* **2018**, *9*, 2187. [CrossRef]
17. Bernardi, M.; Fedullo, A.L.; Di Giacinto, B.; Squeo, M.R.; Aiello, P.; Dante, D.; Romano, S.; Magaudda, L.; Peluso, I.; Palmery, M.; et al. Cardiovascular Risk Factors and Haematological Indexes of Inflammation in Paralympic Athletes with Different Motor Impairments. *Oxid Med. Cell Longev.* **2019**, *2019*, 6798140. [CrossRef]
18. Puce, L.; Trabelsi, K.; Ammar, A.; Jabbour, G.; Marinelli, L.; Mori, L.; Kong, J.D.; Tsigalou, C.; Cotellessa, F.; Schenone, C.; et al. A tale of two stories: COVID-19 and disability. A critical scoping review of the literature on the effects of the pandemic among athletes with disabilities and para-athletes. *Front. Physiol.* **2022**, *13*, 967661. [CrossRef]
19. Swartz, L.; Hunt, X.; Bantjes, J.; Hainline, B.; Reardon, C.L. Mental health symptoms and disorders in Paralympic athletes: A narrative review. *Br. J. Sport. Med.* **2019**, *53*, 737–740. [CrossRef]
20. Silva, A.; Pinto Pinheiro, L.S.; Silva, S.; Andrade, H.; Pereira, A.G.; Rodrigues da Silva, F.; Guerreiro, R.; Barreto, B.; Resende, R.; Túlio de Mello, M. Sleep in Paralympic athletes and its relationship with injuries and illnesses. *Phys. Ther. Sport.* **2022**, *56*, 24–31. [CrossRef]
21. Segerstrom, S.C.; Miller, G.E. Psychological stress and the human immune system: A meta-analytic study of 30 years of inquiry. *Psychol. Bull.* **2004**, *130*, 601–630. [CrossRef]
22. Puce, L.; Okwen, P.M.; Yuh, M.N.; Akah Ndum Okwen, G.; Pambe Miong, R.H.; Kong, J.D.; Bragazzi, N.L. Well-being and quality of life in people with disabilities practicing sports, athletes with disabilities, and para-athletes: Insights from a critical review of the literature. *Front. Psychol.* **2023**, *14*, 1071656. [CrossRef] [PubMed]
23. Kenney, M.J.; Ganta, C.K. Autonomic nervous system and immune system interactions. *Compr. Physiol.* **2014**, *4*, 1177–1200. [CrossRef] [PubMed]
24. Neefkes-Zonneveld, C.R.; Bakkum, A.J.; Bishop, N.C.; van Tulder, M.W.; Janssen, T.W. Effect of long-term physical activity and acute exercise on markers of systemic inflammation in persons with chronic spinal cord injury: A systematic review. *Arch. Phys. Med. Rehabil.* **2015**, *96*, 30–42. [CrossRef] [PubMed]
25. Shnawa, A.; Lee, S.; Papatheodorou, A.; Gibbs, K.; Stein, A.; Morrison, D.; Bloom, O. Elevated levels of IgA and IgG2 in individuals with chronic spinal cord injury. *J. Spinal Cord Med.* **2021**, *45*, 728–738. [CrossRef] [PubMed]
26. Lynch, A.C.; Palmer, C.; Lynch, A.C.; Anthony, A.; Roake, J.A.; Frye, J.; Frizelle, F.A. Nutritional and immune status following spinal cord injury: A case controlled study. *Spinal Cord* **2002**, *40*, 627–630. [CrossRef]
27. Fraussen, J.; Beckers, L.; van Laake-Geelen, C.C.M.; Depreitere, B.; Deckers, J.; Cornips, E.M.J.; Peuskens, D.; Somers, V. Altered Circulating Immune Cell Distribution in Traumatic Spinal Cord Injury Patients in Relation to Clinical Parameters. *Front. Immunol.* **2022**, *13*, 873315. [CrossRef]
28. Bank, M.; Stein, A.; Sison, C.; Glazer, A.; Jassal, N.; McCarthy, D.; Shatzer, M.; Hahn, B.; Chugh, R.; Davies, P.; et al. Elevated circulating levels of the pro-inflammatory cytokine macrophage migration inhibitory factor in individuals with acute spinal cord injury. *Arch. Phys. Med. Rehabil.* **2015**, *96*, 633–644. [CrossRef]
29. Stein, A.; Panjwani, A.; Sison, C.; Rosen, L.; Chugh, R.; Metz, C.; Bank, M.; Bloom, O. Pilot study: Elevated circulating levels of the proinflammatory cytokine macrophage migration inhibitory factor in patients with chronic spinal cord injury. *Arch. Phys. Med. Rehabil.* **2013**, *94*, 1498–1507. [CrossRef]
30. Longbrake, E.E.; Lai, W.; Ankeny, D.P.; Popovich, P.G. Characterization and modeling of monocyte-derived macrophages after spinal cord injury. *J. Neurochem.* **2007**, *102*, 1083–1094. [CrossRef]
31. Nakamura, M.; Okada, S.; Toyama, Y.; Okano, H. Role of IL-6 in spinal cord injury in a mouse model. *Clin. Rev. Allergy Immunol.* **2005**, *28*, 197–204. [CrossRef]
32. Muñoz-Cánoves, P.; Scheele, C.; Pedersen, B.K.; Serrano, A.L. Interleukin-6 myokine signaling in skeletal muscle: A double-edged sword? *FEBS J.* **2013**, *280*, 4131–4148. [CrossRef] [PubMed]
33. Gibson, A.E.; Buchholz, A.C.; Martin Ginis, K.A. C-Reactive protein in adults with chronic spinal cord injury: Increased chronic inflammation in tetraplegia vs paraplegia. *Spinal Cord.* **2008**, *46*, 616–621. [CrossRef] [PubMed]
34. Davies, A.L.; Hayes, K.C.; Dekaban, G.A. Clinical correlates of elevated serum concentrations of cytokines and autoantibodies in patients with spinal cord injury. *Arch. Phys. Med. Rehabil.* **2007**, *88*, 1384–1393. [CrossRef]

35. Hellenbrand, D.J.; Quinn, C.M.; Piper, Z.J.; Morehouse, C.N.; Fixel, J.A.; Hanna, A.S. Inflammation after spinal cord injury: A review of the critical timeline of signaling cues and cellular infiltration. *J. Neuroinflamm.* **2021**, *18*, 284. [CrossRef]
36. Leslie, S.W.; Tadi, P.; Tayyeb, M. Neurogenic Bladder and Neurogenic Lower Urinary Tract Dysfunction. In *StatPearls [Internet]*; StatPearls Publishing: Treasure Island, FL, USA, 2022.
37. Burns, S.P. Acute respiratory infections in persons with spinal cord injury. *Phys. Med. Rehabil. Clin. N. Am.* **2007**, *18*, 203–216, v–vi. [CrossRef] [PubMed]
38. DeVivo, M.J.; Rause, J.S.; Lammertse, D.P. Recent trends in mortality and causes of death among persons with spinal cord injury. *Arch. Phys. Med. Rehabil.* **1999**, *80*, 1411–1419. [CrossRef]
39. Tallqvist, S.; Kauppila, A.M.; Vainionpää, A.; Koskinen, E.; Bergman, P.; Anttila, H.; Hämäläinen, H.; Täckman, A.; Kallinen, M.; Arokoski, J.; et al. Prevalence of comorbidities and secondary health conditions among the Finnish population with spinal cord injury. *Spinal Cord.* **2022**, *60*, 618–627. [CrossRef]
40. Paulson, T.A.; Mason, B.; Rhodes, J.; Goosey-Tolfrey, V.L. Individualized Internal and External Training Load Relationships in Elite Wheelchair Rugby Players. *Front. Physiol.* **2015**, *6*, 388. [CrossRef]
41. Bishop, N.C.; Gleeson, M. Acute and chronic effects of exercise on markers of mucosal immunity. *Front. Biosci.* **2009**, *14*, 4444–4456. [CrossRef]
42. Furusawa, K.; Tajima, F.; Okawa, H.; Takahashi, M.; Ogata, H. The incidence of post-race symptoms of upper respiratory tract infection in wheelchair marathon racers. *Spinal Cord.* **2007**, *45*, 513–517. [CrossRef]
43. Filho, J.A.; Salvetti, X.M.; de Mello, M.T.; da Silva, A.C.; Filho, B.L. Coronary risk in a cohort of Paralympic athletes. *Br. J. Sports Med.* **2006**, *40*, 918–922. [CrossRef] [PubMed]
44. West, C.R.; Wong, S.C.; Krassioukov, A.V. Autonomic cardiovascular control in Paralympic athletes with spinal cord injury. *Med. Sci. Sports Exerc.* **2014**, *46*, 60–68. [CrossRef] [PubMed]
45. Di Marco, B.; Bonaccorso, C.M.; Aloisi, E.; D'Antoni, S.; Catania, M.V. Neuro-Inflammatory Mechanisms in Developmental Disorders Associated with Intellectual Disability and Autism Spectrum Disorder: A Neuro-Immune Perspective. *CNS Neurol. Disord. Drug Targets* **2016**, *15*, 448–463. [CrossRef]
46. Ram, G.; Chinen, J. Infections and immunodeficiency in Down syndrome. *Clin. Exp. Immunol.* **2011**, *164*, 9–16. [CrossRef] [PubMed]
47. Espinosa, J.M. Down Syndrome and COVID-19: A Perfect Storm? *Cell Rep. Med.* **2020**, *1*, 100019. [CrossRef]
48. Huggard, D.; Doherty, D.G.; Molloy, E.J. Immune Dysregulation in Children with Down Syndrome. *Front. Pediatr.* **2020**, *8*, 73. [CrossRef]
49. Machida, M.; Rocos, B.; Taira, K.; Nemoto, N.; Oikawa, N.; Kinoshita, T.; Kozu, T.; Nakanishi, K. The Association between Radiographic and MRI Cervical Spine Parameters in Patients with Down Syndrome. *Cureus* **2022**, *14*, e25046. [CrossRef]
50. Tassone, J.C.; Duey-Holtz, A. Spine concerns in the Special Olympian with Down syndrome. *Sport. Med. Arthrosc Rev.* **2008**, *16*, 55–60. [CrossRef]
51. MacDonald, T.T. The mucosal immune system. *Parasite Immunol.* **2003**, *25*, 235–246. [CrossRef]
52. Carpenter, G.H.; Garrett, J.R.; Hartley, R.H.; Proctor, G.B. The influence of nerves on the secretion of immunoglobulin A into submandibular saliva in rats. *J. Physiol.* **1998**, *512 Pt 2*, 567–573. [CrossRef]
53. Stephenson, B.T.; Hynes, E.; Leicht, C.A.; Tolfrey, K.; Goosey-Tolfrey, V.L. Brief Report: Training Load, Salivary Immunoglobulin A, and Illness Incidence in Elite Paratriathletes. *Int. J. Sport. Physiol. Perform.* **2019**, *14*, 536–539. [CrossRef] [PubMed]
54. Leicht, C.A.; Bishop, N.C.; Paulson, T.A.W.; Griggs, K.E.; Goosey-Tolfrey, V. Salivary immunoglobulin A and upper respiratory symptoms during 5 months of training in elite tetraplegic athletes. *Int. J. Sport. Physiol. Perform.* **2012**, *7*, 210–217. [CrossRef] [PubMed]
55. Leicht, C.A.; Bishop, N.C.; Goosey-Tolfrey, V.L. Mucosal immune responses during court training in elite tetraplegic athletes. *Spinal Cord.* **2012**, *50*, 760–765. [CrossRef] [PubMed]
56. Leicht, C.A.; Bishop, N.C.; Goosey-Tolfrey, V.L. Mucosal immune responses to treadmill exercise in elite wheelchair athletes. *Med. Sci. Sports Exerc.* **2011**, *43*, 1414–1421. [CrossRef] [PubMed]
57. Fornieles, G.; Rosety, M.A.; Elosegui, S.; Rosety, J.M.; Alvero-Cruz, J.R.; Garcia, N.; Rosety, M.; Rodriguez-Pareja, T.; Toro, R.; Rosety-Rodriguez, M.; et al. Salivary testosterone and immunoglobulin A were increased by resistance training in adults with Down syndrome. *Braz. J. Med. Biol. Res.* **2014**, *47*, 345–348. [CrossRef]
58. Kouda, K.; Furusawa, K.; Sugiyama, H.; Sumiya, T.; Ito, T.; Tajima, F.; Shimizu, K. Dose 20-min arm crank ergometer exercise increase plasma interleukin-6 in individuals with cervical spinal cord injury? *Eur. J. Appl. Physiol.* **2012**, *112*, 597–604. [CrossRef]
59. Umemoto, Y.; Furusawa, K.; Kouda, K.; Sasaki, Y.; Kanno, N.; Kojima, D.; Tajima, F. Plasma IL-6 levels during arm exercise in persons with spinal cord injury. *Spinal Cord.* **2011**, *49*, 1182–1187. [CrossRef]
60. Kinoshita, T.; Nakamura, T.; Umemoto, Y.; Kojima, D.; Moriki, T.; Mitsui, T.; Goto, M.; Ishida, Y.; Tajima, F. Increase in interleukin-6 immediately after wheelchair basketball games in persons with spinal cord injury: Preliminary report. *Spinal Cord.* **2013**, *51*, 508–510. [CrossRef]
61. Ogawa, T.; Nakamura, T.; Banno, M.; Sasaki, Y.; Umemoto, Y.; Kouda, K.; Kawasaki, T.; Tajima, F. Elevation of interleukin-6 and attenuation of tumor necrosis factor-α during wheelchair half marathon in athletes with cervical spinal cord injuries. *Spinal Cord.* **2014**, *52*, 601–605. [CrossRef]

62. Sasaki, Y.; Furusawa, K.; Tajima, F.; Nakamura, T.; Kouda, K.; Kanno, N.; Kawasaki, T.; Umemoto, Y.; Shimizu, K. Wheelchair marathon creates a systemic anti-inflammatory environment in persons with spinal cord injury. *Clin. J. Sport Med.* **2014**, *24*, 295–301. [CrossRef]
63. Hoekstra, S.P.; Leicht, C.A.; Kamijo, Y.I.; Kinoshita, T.; Stephenson, B.T.; Goosey-Tolfrey, V.L.; Bishop, N.C.; Tajima, F. The inflammatory response to a wheelchair half-marathon in people with a spinal cord injury—The role of autonomic function. *J. Sport. Sci.* **2019**, *37*, 1717–1724. [CrossRef] [PubMed]
64. Rosety-Rodriguez, M.; Camacho, A.; Rosety, I.; Fornieles, G.; Rosety, M.A.; Diaz, A.J.; Bernardi, M.; Rosety, M.; Ordonez, F.J. Low-grade systemic inflammation and leptin levels were improved by arm cranking exercise in adults with chronic spinal cord injury. *Arch. Phys. Med. Rehabil.* **2014**, *95*, 297–302. [CrossRef] [PubMed]
65. Paulson, T.A.; Goosey-Tolfrey, V.L.; Lenton, J.P.; Leicht, C.A.; Bishop, N.C. Spinal cord injury level and the circulating cytokine response to strenuous exercise. *Med. Sci. Sport. Exerc.* **2013**, *45*, 1649–1655. [CrossRef] [PubMed]
66. Cavalcante, R.N.; Santos, A.C.S.; Rodrigues, R.A.S.; Napoleão, A.C.B.; Balogun, S.O.; Andrade, B.R.M.; Fett, C.A.; Zavala, A.A.Z.; Arunachalam, K.; Oliveira, R.G. Wheelchair basketball improves the treatment of urinary tract infection in people with motor disabilities: A clinical trial. *Rev. Assoc. Med. Bras.* **2022**, *68*, 559–567. [CrossRef]
67. Manns, P.J.; McCubbin, J.A.; Williams, D.P. Fitness, inflammation, and the metabolic syndrome in men with paraplegia. *Arch. Phys. Med. Rehabil.* **2005**, *86*, 1176–1181. [CrossRef]
68. Raguzzini, A.; Toti, E.; Bernardi, M.; Castellucci, F.; Cavedon, V.; Fedullo, A.L.; Milanese, C.; Sciarra, T.; Peluso, I. Post-Exercise Ketosis, Salivary Uric Acid and Interleukin-6 after a Simulated Wheelchair Basketball Match. *Endocr Metab Immune Disord Drug Targets* **2021**, *21*, 2055–2062. [CrossRef]
69. Ordonez, F.J.; Rosety, M.A.; Camacho, A.; Rosety, I.; Diaz, A.J.; Fornieles, G.; Garcia, N.; Rosety-Rodriguez, M. Aerobic training improved low-grade inflammation in obese women with intellectual disability. *J. Intellect. Disabil. Res.* **2014**, *58*, 583–590. [CrossRef]
70. Rosety-Rodriguez, M.; Camacho, A.; Rosety, I.; Fornieles, G.; Rosety, M.A.; Diaz, A.J.; Rosety, M.; Ordonez, F.J. Resistance circuit training reduced inflammatory cytokines in a cohort of male adults with Down syndrome. *Med. Sci. Monit* **2013**, *19*, 949–953. [CrossRef]
71. McCreedy, D.A.; Abram, C.L.; Hu, Y.; Min, S.W.; Platt, M.E.; Kirchhoff, M.A.; Reid, S.K.; Jalufka, F.L.; Lowell, C.A. Spleen tyrosine kinase facilitates neutrophil activation and worsens long-term neurologic deficits after spinal cord injury. *J. Neuroinflamm.* **2021**, *18*, 302. [CrossRef]
72. Sreedevi, H.; Munshi, A.K. Neutrophil chemotaxis in Down syndrome and normal children to Actinobacillus actinomycetem-comitans. *J. Clin. Pediatr. Dent.* **1998**, *22*, 141–146.
73. Levada-Pires, A.C.; Santos, V.C.; Marques, C.G.; Alves, S.R.; Pithon-Curi, T.C.; Cury-Boaventura, M.F.; Curi, R. Neutrophil function in Wheelchair Basketball players with Paraplegia. *Med. Sci. Sport. Exerc.* **2010**, *42*, 368. [CrossRef]
74. Laginha, I.; Kopp, M.A.; Druschel, C.; Schaser, K.D.; Brommer, B.; Hellmann, R.C.; Watzlawick, R.; Ossami-Saidi, R.R.; Prüss, H.; Failli, V.; et al. Natural Killer (NK) Cell Functionality after human Spinal Cord Injury (SCI): Protocol of a prospective, longitudinal study. *BMC Neurol.* **2016**, *16*, 170. [CrossRef] [PubMed]
75. Furusawa, K.; Tajima, F.; Tanaka, Y.; Ide, M.; Ogata, H. Short-term attenuation of natural killer cell cytotoxic activity in paraplegic athletes during wheelchair marathon. *Arch. Phys. Med. Rehabil.* **1998**, *79*, 1116–1121. [CrossRef]
76. Furusawa, K.; Tajima, F.; Ueta, M.; Ogata, H. Activation of natural killer cell function in recreational athletes with paraplegia during wheelchair half marathon race. *Arch. Phys. Med. Rehabil.* **2003**, *84*, 706–711. [CrossRef] [PubMed]
77. Banno, M.; Nakamura, T.; Furusawa, K.; Ogawa, T.; Sasaki, Y.; Kouda, K.; Kawasaki, T.; Tajima, F. Wheelchair half-marathon race increases natural killer cell activity in persons with cervical spinal cord injury. *Spinal Cord.* **2012**, *50*, 533–537. [CrossRef] [PubMed]
78. Ueta, M.; Furusawa, K.; Takahashi, M.; Akatsu, Y.; Nakamura, T.; Tajima, F. Attenuation of natural killer cell activity during 2-h exercise in individuals with spinal cord injuries. *Spinal Cord.* **2008**, *46*, 26–32. [CrossRef] [PubMed]
79. Nowak, R.; Buryta, R.; Krupecki, K.; Zając, T.; Zawartka, M.; Proia, P.; Kostrzewa-Nowak, D. The Impact of the Progressive Efficiency Test on a Rowing Ergometer on White Blood Cells Distribution and Clinical Chemistry Changes in Paralympic Rowers During the Preparatory Stage before the Paralympic Games in Rio, 2016—A Case Report. *J. Hum. Kinet.* **2017**, *60*, 255–263. [CrossRef]
80. Nash, M.S. Immune responses to nervous system decentralization and exercise in quadriplegia. *Med. Sci. Sport. Exerc.* **1994**, *26*, 164–171. [CrossRef]
81. Klokker, M.; Mohr, T.; Kjaer, M.; Galbo, H.; Pedersen, B.K. The natural killer cell response to exercise in spinal cord injured individuals. *Eur. J. Appl. Physiol. Occup. Physiol.* **1998**, *79*, 106–109. [CrossRef]
82. Yamanaka, M.; Furusawa, K.; Sugiyama, H.; Goto, M.; Kinoshita, T.; Kanno, N.; Takaoka, K.; Tajima, F. Impaired immune response to voluntary arm-crank ergometer exercise in patients with cervical spinal cord injury. *Spinal Cord.* **2010**, *48*, 734–739. [CrossRef]
83. Ziliotto, M.; Rodrigues, R.M.; Chies, J.A.B. Controlled hypobaric hypoxia increases immunological tolerance by modifying HLA-G expression, a potential therapy to inflammatory diseases. *Med. Hypotheses* **2020**, *140*, 109664. [CrossRef]
84. Khanna, K.; Mishra, K.P.; Chanda, S.; Eslavath, M.R.; Ganju, L.; Kumar, B.; Singh, S.B. Effects of Acute Exposure to Hypobaric Hypoxia on Mucosal Barrier Injury and the Gastrointestinal Immune Axis in Rats. *High Alt. Med. Biol.* **2019**, *20*, 35–44. [CrossRef] [PubMed]

85. Park, H.Y.; Jung, W.S.; Kim, J.; Hwang, H.; Kim, S.W.; An, Y.; Lee, H.; Jeon, S.; Lim, K. Effects of 2-Week Exercise Training in Hypobaric Hypoxic Conditions on Exercise Performance and Immune Function in Korean National Cycling Athletes with Disabilities: A Case Report. *Int. J. Environ. Res. Public Health* **2020**, *17*, 861. [CrossRef] [PubMed]
86. Marques, C.G.; Santos, V.C.; Levada-Pires, A.C.; Jacintho, T.M.; Gorjão, R.; Pithon-Curi, T.C.; Cury-Boaventura, M.F. Effects of DHA-rich fish oil supplementation on the lipid profile, markers of muscle damage, and neutrophil function in wheelchair basketball athletes before and after acute exercise. *Appl. Physiol. Nutr. Metab.* **2015**, *40*, 596–604. [CrossRef] [PubMed]
87. An, Y.H.; Kim, J.; Kim, H.J.; Lim, K. Effects of leucine-enriched essential amino acid supplementation on muscular fatigue and inflammatory cytokines in wheelchair basketball players. *Phys. Act. Nutr.* **2020**, *24*, 38–46. [CrossRef] [PubMed]
88. Al-Rubaye, T.E.M.; Sobhani, V.; Shab-Bidar, S.; Djafarian, K. Association of the dietary inflammatory index and body composition among Paralympic athletes with hemodialysis and hemophilia. *Clin. Nutr. ESPEN.* **2022**, *49*, 504–509. [CrossRef]
89. Aidar, F.J.; Fraga, G.S.; Getirana-Mota, M.; Marçal, A.C.; Santos, J.L.; de Souza, R.F.; Ferreira, A.R.P.; Neves, E.B.; Zanona, A.F.; Bulhões-Correia, A.; et al. Effects of Ibuprofen Use on Lymphocyte Count and Oxidative Stress in Elite Paralympic Powerlifting. *Biology* **2021**, *10*, 986. [CrossRef]
90. Aidar, F.J.; Fraga, G.S.; Getirana-Mota, M.; Marçal, A.C.; Santos, J.L.; de Souza, R.F.; Vieira-Souza, L.M.; Ferreira, A.R.P.; de Matos, D.G.; de Almeida-Neto, P.F.; et al. Evaluation of Ibuprofen Use on the Immune System Indicators and Force in Disabled Paralympic Powerlifters of Different Sport Levels. *Healthcare* **2022**, *10*, 1331. [CrossRef]
91. Fraga, G.S.; Aidar, F.J.; Matos, D.G.; Marçal, A.C.; Santos, J.L.; Souza, R.F.; Carneiro, A.L.; Vasconcelos, A.B.; Da Silva-Grigoletto, M.E.; van den Tillaar, R.; et al. Effects of Ibuprofen Intake in Muscle Damage, Body Temperature and Muscle Power in Paralympic Powerlifting Athletes. *Int. J. Environ. Res Public Health* **2020**, *17*, 5157. [CrossRef]
92. Cerqueira, É.; Marinho, D.A.; Neiva, H.P.; Lourenço, O. Inflammatory Effects of High and Moderate Intensity Exercise-A Systematic Review. *Front. Physiol.* **2020**, *10*, 1550. [CrossRef]
93. Shek, P.N.; Sabiston, B.H.; Buguet, A.; Radomski, M.W. Strenuous exercise and immunological changes: A multiple-time-point analysis of leukocyte subsets, CD4/CD8 ratio, immunoglobulin production and NK cell response. *Int. J. Sport. Med.* **1995**, *16*, 466–474. [CrossRef] [PubMed]
94. Hansen, J.B.; Wilsgård, L.; Osterud, B. Biphasic changes in leukocytes induced by strenuous exercise. *Eur. J. Appl. Physiol. Occup. Physiol.* **1991**, *62*, 157–161. [CrossRef] [PubMed]
95. Beliën, J.; Goris, A.; Matthys, P. Natural Killer Cells in Multiple Sclerosis: Entering the Stage. *Front. Immunol.* **2022**, *13*, 869447. [CrossRef]
96. Liu, M.; Liang, S.; Zhang, C. NK Cells in Autoimmune Diseases: Protective or Pathogenic? *Front. Immunol.* **2021**, *12*, 624687. [CrossRef] [PubMed]
97. Millard, A.L.; Valli, P.V.; Stussi, G.; Mueller, N.J.; Yung, G.P.; Seebach, J.D. Brief Exercise Increases Peripheral Blood NK Cell Counts without Immediate Functional Changes, but Impairs their Responses to ex vivo Stimulation. *Front. Immunol.* **2013**, *4*, 125. [CrossRef] [PubMed]
98. Shephard, R.J.; Rhind, S.; Shek, P.N. Exercise and the immune system. Natural killer cells, interleukins and related responses. *Sport. Med.* **1994**, *18*, 340–369. [CrossRef]
99. Shephard, R.J.; Shek, P.N. Effects of exercise and training on natural killer cell counts and cytolytic activity: A meta-analysis. *Sport. Med.* **1999**, *28*, 177–195. [CrossRef]
100. Zimmer, P.; Baumann, F.T.; Bloch, W.; Schenk, A.; Koliamitra, C.; Jensen, P.; Mierau, A.; Hülsdünker, T.; Reinart, N.; Hallek, M.; et al. Impact of exercise on pro inflammatory cytokine levels and epigenetic modulations of tumor-competitive lymphocytes in Non-Hodgkin-Lymphoma patients-randomized controlled trial. *Eur. J. Haematol.* **2014**, *93*, 527–532. [CrossRef]
101. Parent-Roberge, H.; Fontvieille, A.; Maréchal, R.; Wagner, R.; Fülöp, T.; Pavic, M.; Riesco, E. Effects of combined exercise training on the inflammatory profile of older cancer patients treated with systemic therapy. *Brain Behav. Immun. Health* **2019**, *2*, 100016. [CrossRef]
102. Khosravi, N.; Hanson, E.D.; Farajivafa, V.; Evans, W.S.; Lee, J.T.; Danson, E.; Wagoner, C.W.; Harrell, E.P.; Sullivan, S.A.; Nyrop, K.A.; et al. Exercise-induced modulation of monocytes in breast cancer survivors. *Brain Behav. Immun. Health* **2021**, *14*, 100216. [CrossRef]
103. Hagstrom, A.D.; Marshall, P.W.; Lonsdale, C.; Papalia, S.; Cheema, B.S.; Toben, C.; Baune, B.T.; Fiatarone Singh, M.A.; Green, S. The effect of resistance training on markers of immune function and inflammation in previously sedentary women recovering from breast cancer: A randomized controlled trial. *Breast Cancer Res. Treat.* **2016**, *155*, 471–482. [CrossRef] [PubMed]
104. Hanson, E.D.; Sakkal, S.; Que, S.; Cho, E.; Spielmann, G.; Kadife, E.; Violet, J.A.; Battaglini, C.L.; Stoner, L.; Bartlett, D.B.; et al. Natural killer cell mobilization and egress following acute exercise in men with prostate cancer. *Exp. Physiol.* **2020**, *105*, 1524–1539. [CrossRef] [PubMed]
105. Fischer, C.P. Interleukin-6 in acute exercise and training: What is the biological relevance? *Exerc. Immunol. Rev.* **2006**, *12*, 6–33. [PubMed]
106. Nieman, D.C.; Henson, D.A.; Smith, L.L.; Utter, A.C.; Vinci, D.M.; Davis, J.M.; Kaminsky, D.E.; Shute, M. Cytokine changes after a marathon race. *J. Appl. Physiol* **2001**, *91*, 109–114. [CrossRef] [PubMed]
107. Docherty, S.; Harley, R.; McAuley, J.J.; Crowe, L.A.N.; Pedret, C.; Kirwan, P.D.; Siebert, S.; Millar, N.L. The effect of exercise on cytokines: Implications for musculoskeletal health: A narrative review. *BMC Sport. Sci. Med. Rehabil.* **2022**, *14*, 5. [CrossRef]

108. Shin, Y.O.; Lee, J.B. Leukocyte chemotactic cytokine and leukocyte subset responses during ultra-marathon running. *Cytokine* **2013**, *61*, 364–369. [CrossRef]
109. Ostrowski, K.; Rohde, T.; Asp, S.; Schjerling, P.; Pedersen, B.K. Pro- and anti-inflammatory cytokine balance in strenuous exercise in humans. *J. Physiol.* **1999**, *515 Pt 1*, 287–291. [CrossRef]
110. Sprenger, H.; Jacobs, C.; Nain, M.; Gressner, A.M.; Prinz, H.; Wesemann, W.; Gemsa, D. Enhanced release of cytokines, interleukin-2 receptors, and neopterin after long-distance running. *Clin. Immunol. Immunopathol.* **1992**, *63*, 188–195. [CrossRef]
111. Sellami, M.; Elrayess, M.A.; Puce, L.; Bragazzi, N.L. Molecular Big Data in Sports Sciences: State-of-Art and Future Prospects of OMICS-Based Sports Sciences. *Front. Mol. Biosci.* **2022**, *8*, 815410. [CrossRef]

healthcare

MDPI

Article

Acute and Long-Lasting Effects of Slow-Paced Breathing on Handball Team Coach's Match Stress

Zoran Nikolovski [1,2], Dario Vrdoljak [1,*], Nikola Foretić [1,2], Mia Perić [1], Dora Marić [1] and Charalampos Fountoulakis [3]

1 Faculty of Kinesiology, University of Split, 21000 Split, Croatia
2 High Performance Sport Center, Croatian Olympic Committee, 10000 Zagreb, Croatia
3 College for Humanistic Sciences, ICPS, 121 31 Athens, Greece
* Correspondence: darvrd@kifst.hr

Abstract: Stress was previously defined as a response to any demand for change. These demands are noticeable during sport events, not only in athletes but also in coaches. Therefore, this study aimed to determine the influence of slow-paced breathing (SPB) on acute stress to handball coaches during official matches. One professional handball coach, aged 37 (height, 180 cm; weight, 80 kg), took part in the study. His salivary cortisol (C) concentration and alpha-amylase (AA) activity were measured, and his heart rate (HR) was monitored during six official matches. In the first three matches the SPB training protocol was not followed. From match four to match six, the coach performed SPB training every day and directly before the match. The decrease observed in AA was statistically significant with a large effect size (1.80). The trend of change in HR is visible and similar for matches with and without SPB. However, for SPB matches, there is a lower starting point compared to matches without SPB (89.81 ± 6.26 and 96.62 ± 8.10, respectively). Moreover, values of AA on SPB matches were smaller before the match (93.92 ± 15.89) compared to the same time point in non-SPB matches (115.30 ± 26.00). For AA, there is a significant effect size in the half-time (2.00) and after the match (−2.14). SPB matches showed a lower increase in AA. SPB might be used as one of the possible tools that could help coaches in achieving a desirable mental state during the match.

Keywords: stress; hormones; salivary glands; endocrine; autonomic nervous system

check for updates

Citation: Nikolovski, Z.; Vrdoljak, D.; Foretić, N.; Perić, M.; Marić, D.; Fountoulakis, C. Acute and Long-Lasting Effects of Slow-Paced Breathing on Handball Team Coach's Match Stress. *Healthcare* **2023**, *11*, 1242. https://doi.org/10.3390/healthcare11091242

Academic Editor: Felipe Aidar

Received: 1 March 2023
Revised: 24 April 2023
Accepted: 25 April 2023
Published: 26 April 2023

1. Introduction

Stress was previously defined as a non-specific response to any demand for change, or as "the rate of wear and tear on the body" [1]. It is usually characterized as individual and personal, which differs among given types of tasks [2]. Stress is connected to negative emotions, and therefore, influenced by two major components. Specifically, cause (e.g., major events or daily hassles) and effect (e.g., subjective response, divided between stress appraisal and emotional response) of stress [3–5]. Furthermore, some of the most stressful environments are perceived by the sports participants. Both coaches and athletes are exposed to competitive stress, which is defined as an ongoing transaction between an individual and the environmental demands. Competitive stress is, primarily and directly, associated with competitive performance. It is influenced by the competitive stressors (environmental demands) and competitive strains (an individual's negative psychological, physical, and behavioral responses to competitive stressors). These factors are the main cause of competitive anxiety and may lead to a negative emotional response to competitive stressors [6]. According to previous studies, athletes have reported that their sensation of stress has been influenced by performance-related, intra- and interpersonal, self-presentational, and organizational issues [7,8]. On the other hand, sports coaches operate within complex, changing environments of matches and deal with athletes and their own stress reactions simultaneously. Specifically, coaches lead athletes to improve their physical, technical, mental, and tactical skills, as well as facilitate their personal and social development. They also contribute to wider societal agendas, such as improving health, youth engagement, social inclusion, lifelong learning, and community regeneration [9]. Furthermore, this complex stressful environment in which coaches exist could lead to burnout [10,11]. This state could lead athletes to perceive such coaches negatively [10,11]. Additionally, there are significant potential health costs of the psychological stress experienced by coaches [9].

The performance of a coach and its effectiveness is often connected with the efficiency and success of his athletes [12]. As previously stated, coaches must accomplish multiple roles and deal with technical, physical, organizational, and psychological challenges in their jobs. It is not surprising that because of high demands, coaches confront various levels of stress [13]. Therefore, coping with stress is an important factor leading to success for coaches [14,15]. According to previous studies, there are several ways of stress management leading to mitigating negative effects that might impact performance [16–18]. Strategies that are easy to practice and proven to be useful are breathing techniques [19]. Specifically, diaphragmatic breathing has been widely incorporated in routines for general stress reduction, due to its effect on the parasympathetic nervous system. Lowering blood pressure and HR, a simultaneous increase in peripheral skin temperature, and an overall sense of relaxation are some of its effects [20]. Moreover, studies have shown that slow-paced breathing (SPB) could also be a useful tool in managing stress [21,22]. SPB has positive effects on physiological indicators of arousal and vagal flow, including changes in cardiac rhythm, HR and HRV [21–23]. Thus, some authors believe that breathing strategies may be useful in managing stress effectively, for both athletes and coaches [24]. However, a vast majority of studies use different measurement methods, such as psychological measures (questionnaires) [25,26], heart rate (HR), breathing frequency [27,28], and biological markers (e.g., cortisol and alpha-amylase) [29].

The most commonly used methods for monitoring cognitive load and stress in athletes are questionnaires [30]. These questionnaires often refer to the anxiety levels of sports' participants and examine the influence of the match as the main stressor. The questionnaire used in a study by Arruda, Aoki, Paludo and Moreira [31] had a high correlation with the difficulty of the match. Apart from the subjective indicators, heart rate variability (HRV) showed to be a good objective measure of stress. HRV is defined as the ability of the heart to produce fluctuations in the beat-to-beat interval in response to different situations [32]. It was previously shown that HRV variables change depending on stress and can distinguish between different stressors [33]. In terms of biomarker monitoring, cortisol (C) reflects the activation of the hypothalamic–pituitary–adrenocortical axis, which is involved in the physiological stress response [34]. C is frequently used as a biomarker of the physical and mental (psychological) stress-related functioning of athletes [35]. Alpha-amylase (AA) is an enzyme that catalyzes the hydrolysis of starch into smaller carbohydrate molecules, such as maltose [36]. Additionally, AA reflects the activity of the sympathetic nervous system. It has been shown that physical activity consistently increases AA activity and concentration [37]. Moreover, levels of AA are highly related to an increase in noradrenalin, and consequently, reflect the state of arousal [38]. Biological markers have also been used as indicators of stress caused by sports activity [31,39]. For example, Moreira, McGuigan [35] showed an increase in C and AA regarding mental exertion during physical activity.

Hunt, Rushton, Shenberger and Murayama [40] compared diaphragmatic breathing (DB) and progressive muscle relaxation techniques. The results showed that DB is easy to apply and is an effective tool for athletes to cope with stressors. According to the authors, during DB a lower rate of respiration, higher tidal volume, lower HR, and higher HRV were observed. Additionally, there is evidence that SPB has a positive effect regarding adaptation to psychological stress before and after physical exertion [41]. According to Thelwell, Weston and Greenlees [42], world-class coaches reported relaxation breathing as a rarely used stress-coping strategy. However, the literature review showed good results of stress management in sports while practicing breathing exercises [40,41]. Therefore, the aim of this study was to determine the possible influence of SPB on acute stress in handball coaches during official matches. The authors hypothesize that SPB could have an effect on stress biomarkers and HR. Moreover, if proven to be effective, SPB can be used by handball coaches as a stress coping practice.

2. Materials and Methods

2.1. Participant

One professional EHF master handball coach (kinesiology professor), aged 37 (height, 180 cm; weight, 80 kg), with 19 years of coaching experience in handball, participated in the study. The participant's stress was measured in 6 official matches, during which a total of 33 saliva samples were collected. During the course of the study, the subject coached a club in the first Qatar Handball League, which was a cup finalist, and at the end of the season achieved 8th place. The participant was informed about the procedures and aims of the research. He signed an inform consent form and participated voluntarily. All experimental procedures were completed following the declaration of Helsinki (2008), and they were approved by the corresponding authors' institutional research ethics board (Ethics Board Approval No. 2181-205-02-05-18-002).

2.2. Procedures

Salivary C concentration and AA activity were measured, and the HR was monitored. Samples for stress markers (HR, C, and AA) were collected during one rest day to establish the baseline circadian rhythm. Additionally, samples from six official matches in the first Qatar Handball League were collected too. To establish the baseline circadian rhythm of biomarkers, the coach spent the day without physical activity, fasting in his apartment. During the course of the day, from 9:00 a.m. to 9:30 p.m., 10 saliva samples were collected, and his HR was monitored at the same time points [38]. Baseline values corresponded to the same time of sample collection during the matches. Due to the circadian variability of the measured markers, values varied during the day. Prior to collecting saliva samples, the subject stayed still (sitting) for 10 min, and during that period, his HR was continuously monitored (the average values were taken as a result).

In the second half of the study, stress markers were tracked before, during, and after the handball matches (Scheme 1). The coached team won three out of six matches (1st match, 34 to 29; 2nd match, 30 to 34; 3rd match, 32 to 28; 4th match, 27 to 30; 5th match, 23 to 30; and 6th match, 34 to 31). All six matches were held in the same hall (QHA sports hall), with 5000 seating places; the dimension of the court was 20 × 40 m, and the temperature ranged between 23 and 25 °C. The matches took place during a period of 35 days, and were scheduled between 4:30 p.m. and 8:30 p.m.

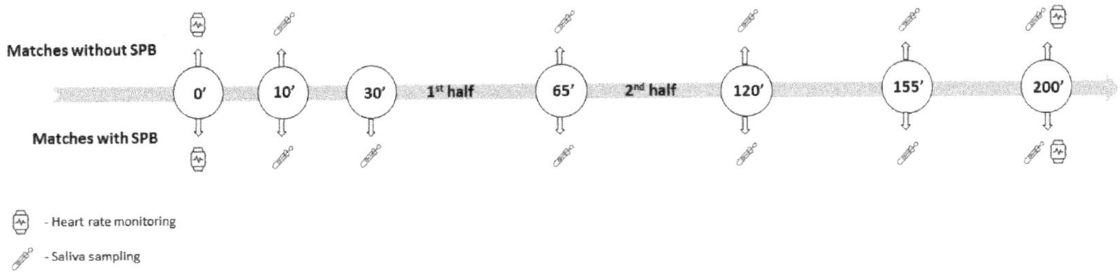

Scheme 1. Data collection timeline: 20 minutes before the match, at halftime, directly after the match, and 45 and 90 min after the match; for SPB matches: data collection before the match.

2.3. Design

In the course of the first three matches, SPB training or any other stress-relieving protocol was not performed. In the rest of the text, these matches are labeled as NOSPB matches. From match four to match six, the coach performed SPB training twice a day. To assess the SPB breathing frequency profile, the Biograph Infiniti version 6.0.4 was used. The subject entered the mindroom–special room for psychological testing, where the researcher gave him guidelines on how to practice diaphragmatic/abdominal breathing. To guarantee proper abdominal breathing, the participant practiced it for some time (i.e., using diaphragmatic breathing). Inhalation happened through the nose, whereas exhalation happened through pursed lips. A report of testing was generated when the test was complete, including the coach's performance across all four primary HRV measures (i.e., heart rate (Max–Min), pNN50, SDNN, LF percent of total power) and whether he was able to properly follow the breathing pacer. The participant was asked to complete a low-breathing test, following the pacer on the screens, and providing feedback to the researcher about whether he felt comfortable with the pace at the end of the test to ensure that the calculated breathing frequency was indeed his individualized (resonant) breathing frequency. Our subject took 4.5 complete breaths per minute, with inhalations lasting 4.5 seconds and exhalations lasting 9.1 seconds. The subject was told to download a free breathing app (paced breathing app, Trex LLC, Greenbelt, Maryland USA), which is only a breath pacer, and install it on his smartphone. The participant was instructed to undertake a 20 min exercise on his mobile app at home and 30 min before the match in the coach's room. Prior to the study of immediate influence of SPB on stress on the handball coach during matches, the participant practiced SPB training during a 25-day period, twice a day, with a total of 920 min of slow-paced breathing in 46 sessions.

2.4. Instruments

Saliva samples were taken at 5 collection points: 30 min before the match (BM), at halftime (HT), directly after the match (EM), and 45 (45) and 90 (90) min after the match; for the matches with SPB, one more point is included: 20 minutes before the match (SPBBM) (Scheme 1). The coach avoided eating a major meal an hour before sample collection and rinsed his mouth thoroughly with water 10 min before each sample collection. For this purpose, SalivaBio Oral Swabs-SOS (Salimetrics LLC, State College, PA, USA) were used; they were placed underneath the tongue on the floor of the mouth for 2 min. After collection, the swabs were placed into a storage tube and immediately refrigerated. Within 2 h of sampling, the samples were frozen at below −20 °C until centrifugation. On the day of the analysis, the samples were completely thawed and centrifuged at 1500× *g* for 15 min. After centrifugation, assays were performed. Saliva cortisol and alpha-amylase were analyzed with a commercially available enzyme-linked immunosorbent assay (ELISA) purchased from Salimetrics LLC (State College, PA, USA) on a microplate reader (Infinite 200PRO, Tecan, Mannendorf, Switzerland). All samples were analyzed in the same batch to avoid intra-assay variability.

HR was measured using a heart rate monitor (Polar M430, Polar Electro, Kempele, Finland) that the coach wore for a total of 4 h: 30 min before the match, throughout the match, and 90 min after it (Scheme 1).

2.5. Statistics

The non-parametric/parametric nature of the variables was tested using the Kolmogorov–Smirnov test procedure. The calculation of the descriptive statistic parameters included means, standard deviations, and percentages (for HR and biomarkers values). The differences among the measurements of salivary biomarkers were calculated by the magnitude-based Cohen's effect size (ES) statistic, with modified qualitative descriptors (trivial ES: <0.2; small ES: 0.21–0.60; moderate ES: 0.61–1.20; large ES: 1.21–1.99; and very large ES: >2.0) [41]. The percentage of change was calculated accordingly and presented as percentage values. Firstly, we deducted two measurements between biomarkers (e.g., C before the activity and in the middle of the activity). Secondly, the first measurement was divided with the difference obtained by the previous step (e.g., C before activity). For example,

$$\begin{gathered}\text{Difference} = \text{C(atthemiddleoftheactivity)} - \text{C(beforetheactivity)} \\ \text{Percentageofchange} = \frac{\text{Difference}}{\text{C(beforetheactivity)}}\text{x}100\end{gathered} \quad (1)$$

Statistica ver. 13.0 (Dell Inc., Austin, TX, USA) was used for the analyses, and a *p*-level of 95% ($p < 0.05$) was applied.

3. Results

3.1. Acute Effect of Slow-Paced Breathing on HR, C, and AA before the Matches When SPB Was Performed

Figure 1 shows the acute influence of SPB on biomarker values at BM and SPBBM time points. There was a clear decrease in HR (89.81 ± 6.26) and AA (61.47 ± 31.51) comparing the values before and after (86.00 ± 10.30; 21.90 ± 3.84, respectively) SPB. A statistically significant decrease was observed in AA with a large effect size (1.80), whereas the values of the HR did not achieve statistical significance. Further statistical analysis showed that C was not influenced by SPB. Regardless, we noticed an increase in C levels after the SPB period, although without statistical significance.

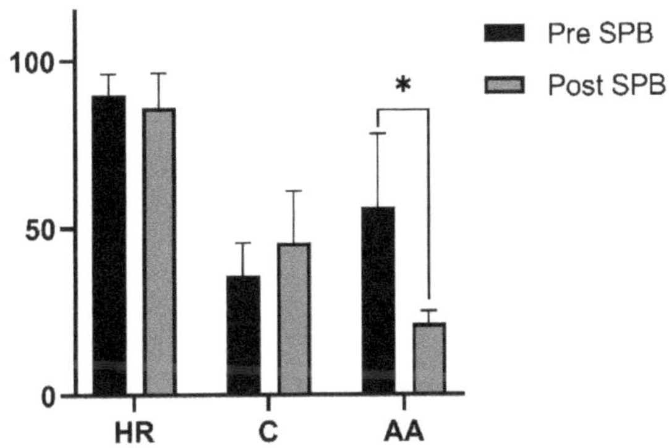

Figure 1. Acute effect of slow-paced breathing (SPB) on heart rate (HR), cortisol (C), and alpha-amylase (AA), with significant differences between SPB and NOSPB indicated with * for a large ES difference.

3.2. Effects of Slow-Paced Breathing on Heart Rate

The HR dynamics before, during, and after the matches are presented in Figure 2. The results show a trend of dynamics for matches with and without SPB. In both SPB and NOSPB similar trend in HR change was observed. However, there is a visible lower starting point at BM for SPB matches (89.81 ± 6.26) and a smaller increase at HT (93.92 ± 15.89) compared to the matches when SPB was not executed (96.62 ± 8.10 and 115.30 ± 26.00, respectively). Additionally, the differences of HR after the match are noticed in both the 45- and 90-minute measurement points.

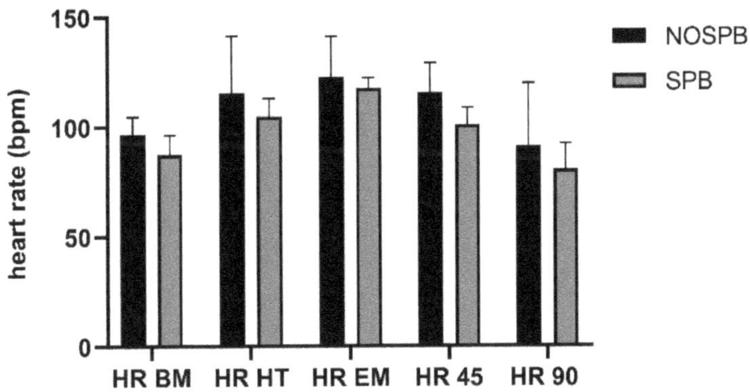

Figure 2. Acute effect of slow-paced breathing (SPB) on heart rate (HR).

3.3. Effects of Slow-Paced Breathing on C

Figure 3 shows the dynamics of C and its differences before, during, and after the match. C dynamics did not show a significant effect size in regard to SPB. However, it is visible that the change between the first two points of measurement (BM and HT) differ between NOSPB (BM, 0.40 ± 0.07; HT, 0.44 ± 0.18) and SPB (0.31 ± 0.11; 0.29 ± 0.05, respectively). In the NOSPB matches, the increase in C can be noticed, and in the SPB matches, C is almost constant. The rest of the timeline reveals the decrease in C for both conditions, respectively.

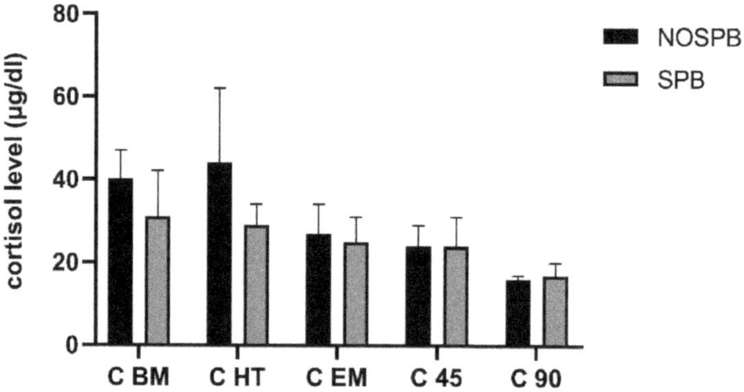

Figure 3. Acute effect of slow-paced breathing (SPB) on cortisol (C).

3.4. Effects of Slow-Paced Breathing on AA

Alpha-amylase dynamics and the differences of its levels relative to match time points are presented in Figure 4. AA dynamics exhibit a very large effect size in the HT (2.00)(NOSPB, 123.99 ± 10.17; SPB, 86.24 ± 24.66) and 90 (3.50)(31.81 ± 4.63; 46.75 ± 3.87, respectively) measuring point, whereas in the EM (128.67 ± 10.17; 86.24 ± 24.66, respectively), it presented large ES (1.51). Specifically, SPB matches showed a lower increase in AA throughout the whole match. After that, AA had a decreasing trend after the match. However, 90 minutes after the match, lower values in NOSPB matches (31.81 ± 4.63) in comparison to SPB (46.75 ± 3.87) are noticed.

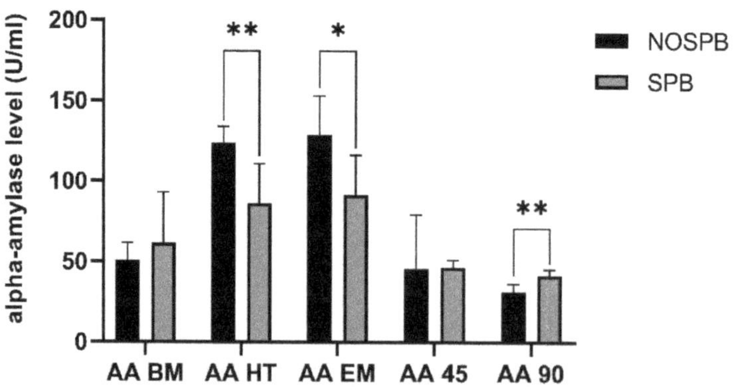

Figure 4. Acute effect of slow-paced breathing (SPB) on alpha-amylase (AA), with significant differences between SPB and NOSPB indicated with * for a large ES difference, and ** for very large ES. NOSPB—matches in the period when SPB was not applied.

The percentages of change in all measured parameters are presented in Figure 5. The results imply that SPB influenced all biomarkers before and/or throughout the match.

HR had the biggest increase in the first two points of measurement. The SPB matches demonstrated a smaller increase (40%) than NOSPB (144%) in AA. Similar results were noticed in C (SPB–8%; NOSP 11%) and HR (SPB 5%; NOSPB 19%). In the second half of the matches, AA exhibit a lesser increase (SPB 6%; NOSP 4%). Additionally, HR experienced a bigger increase in SPB (24%). C had a bigger decrease in NOSPB (−39%) than SPB (−12%).

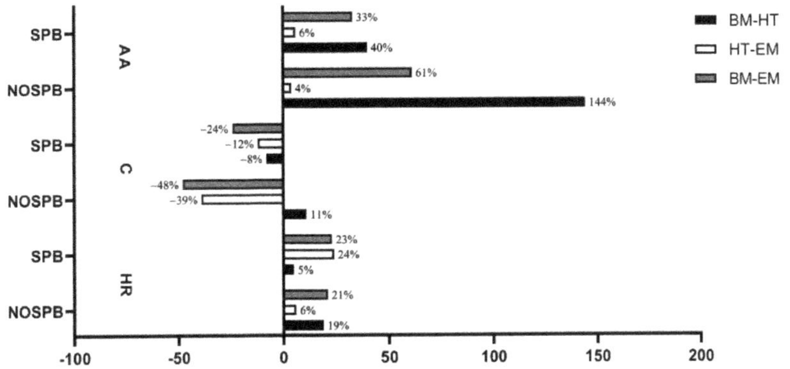

Figure 5. Percentage of change for HR, C, and AA between normal match environment and match with SPB, at different time points. SPB—matches in the period when SPB was applied; NOSPB—matches in the period when SPB was not applied; AA—alpha-amylase; C—cortisol; HR—heart rate.

4. Discussion

Precompetitive anxiety and arousal play an important role in coaching at a high level [22]. There is an evident lack of studies researching stress coping tools and stress handling strategies for coaches. This study was carried out in order to find a simple and effective strategy to deal with competitive stress for coaches. Accordingly, we report several important findings: (1) SPB influences all measured stress biomarkers; (2) A long lasting effect of SPB was detected; and (3) HR and AA have similar dynamics under the influence of SPB, acute and long-lasting, while there is no effect of SPB on C level. These findings corroborate the hypothesis that SPB could help coaches mitigate the influence of stressors during handball matches.

As reported previously, a competition setting elicits a higher stress response in coaches compared to trainings. It was speculated that the pre-competitive effect increases stress biomarkers levels (HR, C, and AA) [43]. This effect is an anticipated response to the stressful situations [44,45]. This leads to the triggering of the sympathetic nervous system (verified as an increase in HR and AA) and the hypothalamic–pituitary–adrenal axis (observed as an increase in C) [46]. Altogether, it may induce the development of negative emotional states and the disruption of decision making [47,48]. Therefore, it is of major importance to cope with stressful situations in order to gain the optimal state of arousal and a low level of anxiety before the competition.

According to Hunt, Rushton [40], diaphragmatic breathing (DB) has been shown to be a good technique to cope with stressful situations. Specifically, the authors examined the influence of DB on psychological stress in 76 varsity athletes. DB was compared to progressive relaxation and was shown to be a better tool for stress management. Another study showed how SPB has a positive effect on psychological stress after physical exertion. Hence, it can be noted that SPB has similar effects as DB [41]. The above-mentioned studies have similar findings to our study, where the effect of SPB is evident in all measured biomarkers. Specifically, SPB decreased HR and AA immediately after the breathing sessions (a higher effect size (1.80) is observed in AA), while C increased after the SPB. This finding could be explained by the circadian rhythm of C. While C during measuring drops, AA increases [38].

Blum, Rockstroh and Göritz [49] reported the influence of SPB on HRV. The participants of their study carried out the task after which the SPB was performed, followed by another task. The results showed a decrease in HR after SPB. Additionally, the chronic effects of SPB on HR and vagal tone were examined in other studies. In one study, a single session of SPB (preceded by a familiarization session) was capable of enhancing the vagal tone under cognitive stress [41]. Additionally, the duration of the breathing sessions had an influence on the spontaneous respiratory frequency in the resting measurement. Specifically, the respiratory frequency appears to decrease with the session duration, thus potentially contributing to additional relaxing effects [50]. However, these studies did not examine the long-lasting effects of SPB (completing a single session), and therefore, there is a need for future studies to address this effect in multiple sessions over a longer period of time. These long-lasting effects have been previously shown, but only few parameters were taken into consideration. Blum, Rockstroh and Göritz [49] concluded that regular breathing exercises could influence HRV in the long term. Furthermore, slow-paced breathing appears to be a promising cost-effective technique to improve subjective sleep quality and cardiovascular function during sleep in young healthy individuals [51].

In our study, the long-lasting effect of SPB was demonstrated. As the coach practiced SPB daily, this caused all the measured biomarkers to drop. Specifically, HR and C, at the BM point of measurement, showed lower values in the SPB matches (6.8 bpm, 0.16 μg/dL). This finding suggests that the coach started match preparations at a lower level of stress, which could possibly be a consequence of SPB practice. Hence, our findings might have implications in the sports competition scenario.

Lastly, the effects of SPB could also be noticed through the dynamics of AA and HR, throughout the match. The acute influence of SPB was mentioned previously, as studies reported similar findings to ours [41,49]. Moreover, Kant [45] examined the effects of a relaxation schedule on the arousal levels and performance of college handball players. The results of their study showed the effects of breathing techniques. However, those studies reported the chronic effect on vagal tone, HR, and HRV, whereas in our study, the stress markers C and AA are also included. The dynamics of C is similar for both SPB and NOSPB matches, and show a decrease before, during, and after the match. On the other hand, AA and HR dynamics differs from C. An AA and HR increase was noticed until HT, and then there was a decrease. Specifically, the AA and HR percentage of change for the SPB matches was smaller than in the NOSPB matches. In the BM point, there is even a larger effect size between SPB and NOSPB for AA (1.80).

5. Conclusions

In conclusion, the main goal of every sports coach should be the fast and clear understanding of game situations and good decision making. To fulfill such roles, the coach must remain calm, optimally aroused and with as little stressful interferences as possible. Our study introduced SPB as one of the possible tools that could help handball coaches in achieving a desirable mental state during a match. The results indicate that the application of SPB could decrease the level of stress in an acute and long-lasting manner.

The main limitation of this study is the small sample size of the matches used and the monitoring of a single coach. The study failed to assess some very important stress biomarkers that could better explain the handball coach's emotional and physical stress. The relationships of adrenalin, blood glucose, and breathing frequency with the biomarkers used in our study (HR, AA, and C) had been previously studied and could have given us a better insight into the stress state. The mentioned study limitations limit the generalization of results since the study was only focused on one subject and on an insufficient number of relevant stress biomarkers. Future studies should include more coaches and a higher number of matches. Additionally, monitoring a greater number of biomarkers (e.g., glucose and other hormones connected to stress) could give us more robust and clearer explanations of the gathered data.

Author Contributions: Conceptualization, Z.N., N.F. and C.F.; methodology, Z.N. and C.F.; software, D.V.; validation, D.V. and N.F.; formal analysis, Z.N.; investigation, Z.N. and C.F.; resources, Z.N.; data curation, M.P.; writing—original draft preparation, D.V., N.F. and Z.N.; writing—review and editing, M.P. and D.M; visualization, D.M.; supervision, N.F.; project administration, M.P. All authors have read and agreed to the published version of the manuscript.

Funding: This research received no external funding.

Institutional Review Board Statement: The study was conducted in accordance with the Declaration of Helsinki, and approved by the Institutional Ethics Committee of Faculty of Kinesiology, University of Split (Ethics Board Approval No. 2181-205-02-05-18-002).

Informed Consent Statement: Informed consent was obtained from all subjects involved in the study.

Data Availability Statement: Not available.

Conflicts of Interest: The authors declare no conflict of interest.

References

1. Selye, H. *The Stress of Life*; McGraw-Hill: New York, NY, USA, 1956.
2. Fink, G. Chapter 1—Stress, Definitions, Mechanisms, and Effects Outlined: Lessons from Anxiety. In *Stress: Concepts, Cognition, Emotion, and Behavior*; Fink, G., Ed.; Academic Press: San Diego, CA, USA, 2016; pp. 3–11.
3. Holmes, T.H.; Rahe, R.H. The social readjustment rating scale. *J. Psychosom. Res.* **1967**, *11*, 213–218. [CrossRef] [PubMed]
4. Lazarus, R.S.; Folkman, S. *Stress, Appraisal, and Coping*; Springer: Berlin/Heidelberg, Germany, 1984.
5. Kopp, M.S.; Thege, B.K.; Balog, P.; Stauder, A.; Salavecz, G.; Rózsa, S.; Purebl, G.; Ádám, S. Measures of stress in epidemiological research. *J. Psychosom. Res.* **2010**, *69*, 211–225. [CrossRef]
6. Mellalieu, S.D.; Hanton, S.; Fletcher, D. *A Competitive Anxiety Review: Recent Directions in Sport Psychology Research*; Nova Science Publishers: New York, NY, USA, 2009.
7. Noblet, A.J.; Gifford, S.M. The sources of stress experienced by professional Australian footballers. *J. Appl. Sport Psychol.* **2002**, *14*, 1–13. [CrossRef]
8. Holt, N.L.; Hogg, J.M. Perceptions of stress and coping during preparations for the 1999 women's soccer world cup finals. *Sport Psychol.* **2002**, *16*, 251–271. [CrossRef]
9. Fletcher, D.; Scott, M. Psychological stress in sports coaches: A review of concepts, research, and practice. *J. Sports Sci.* **2010**, *28*, 127–137. [CrossRef] [PubMed]
10. Baker, J.; Côté, J.; Hawes, R. The relationship between coaching behaviours and sport anxiety in athletes. *J. Sci. Med. Sport* **2000**, *3*, 110–119. [CrossRef]
11. Blanchard, C.M.; Amiot, C.E.; Perreault, S.; Vallerand, R.J.; Provencher, P. Cohesiveness, coach's interpersonal style and psychological needs: Their effects on self-determination and athletes' subjective well-being. *Psychol. Sport Exerc.* **2009**, *10*, 545–551. [CrossRef]
12. Gould, D.; Greenleaf, C.; Guinan, D.; Chung, Y. A survey of US Olympic coaches: Variables perceived to have influenced athlete performances and coach effectiveness. *Sport Psychol.* **2002**, *16*, 229–250. [CrossRef]
13. Olusoga, P.; Butt, J.; Hays, K.; Maynard, I. Stress in Elite Sports Coaching: Identifying Stressors. *J. Appl. Sport Psychol.* **2009**, *21*, 442–459. [CrossRef]
14. Balk, Y.A.; Englert, C. Recovery self-regulation in sport: Theory, research, and practice. *Int. J. Sport. Sci. Coach.* **2020**, *15*, 273–281. [CrossRef]
15. Olusoga, P.; Maynard, I.; Hays, K.; Butt, J. Coaching under pressure: A study of Olympic coaches. *J. Sports Sci.* **2012**, *30*, 229–239. [CrossRef]
16. Debanne, T.; Fontayne, P. A study of a successful experienced elite handball coach's cognitive processes in competition situations. *Int. J. Sport. Sci. Coach.* **2009**, *4*, 1–16. [CrossRef]
17. Lee, Y.; Kim, S.-H.; Joon-Ho, K. Coach leadership effect on elite handball players' psychological empowerment and organizational citizenship behavior. *Int. J. Sport. Sci. Coach.* **2013**, *8*, 327–342. [CrossRef]
18. Harinath, K.; Malhotra, A.S.; Pal, K.; Prasad, R.; Kumar, R.; Kain, T.C.; Rai, L.; Sawhney, R.C. Effects of Hatha yoga and Omkar meditation on cardiorespiratory performance, psychologic profile, and melatonin secretion. *J. Altern. Complement. Med.* **2004**, *10*, 261–268. [CrossRef] [PubMed]
19. Davis, M.; Eshelman, E.R.; McKay, M. *The Relaxation and Stress Reduction Workbook*; New Harbinger Publications: Oakland, CA, USA, 2008.
20. Harvey, J. Diaphragmatic breathing: A practical technique for breath control. *Behav. Ther.* **1978**, *1*, 13–14.
21. Kobayashi, H. Does paced breathing improve the reproducibility of heart rate variability measurements? *J. Physiol. Anthropol.* **2009**, *28*, 225–230. [CrossRef]
22. Stark, R.; Schienle, A.; Walter, B.; Vaitl, D. Effects of paced respiration on heart period and heart period variability. *Psychophysiology* **2000**, *37*, 302–309. [CrossRef]

23. Sandercock, G.; Gladwell, V.; Dawson, S.; Nunan, D.; Brodie, D.; Beneke, R. Association between RR interval and high-frequency heart rate variability acquired during short-term, resting recordings with free and paced breathing. *Physiol. Meas.* **2008**, *29*, 795. [CrossRef]
24. Kudlackova, K.; Eccles, D.W.; Dieffenbach, K. Use of relaxation skills in differentially skilled athletes. *Psychol. Sport Exerc.* **2013**, *14*, 468–475. [CrossRef]
25. Korre, M.; Farioli, A.; Varvarigou, V.; Sato, S.; Kales, S.N. A survey of stress levels and time spent across law enforcement duties: Police chief and officer agreement. *Polic. A J. Policy Pract.* **2014**, *8*, 109–122. [CrossRef]
26. Kop, N.; Euwema, M.C. Occupational stress and the use of force by Dutch police officers. *Crim. Justice Behav.* **2001**, *28*, 631–652. [CrossRef]
27. Sin, N.L.; Sloan, R.P.; McKinley, P.S.; Almeida, D.M. Linking daily stress processes and laboratory-based heart rate variability in a national sample of midlife and older adults. *Psychosom. Med.* **2016**, *78*, 573. [CrossRef]
28. Punita, P.; Saranya, K.; Kumar, S.S. Gender difference in heart rate variability in medical students and association with the level of stress. *Natl. J. Physiol. Pharm. Pharmacol.* **1970**, *6*, 431. [CrossRef]
29. Marques, A.H.; Silverman, M.N.; Sternberg, E.M. Evaluation of stress systems by applying noninvasive methodologies: Measurements of neuroimmune biomarkers in the sweat, heart rate variability and salivary cortisol. *Neuroimmunomodulation* **2010**, *17*, 205–208. [CrossRef]
30. Fuster, J.; Caparrós, T.; Capdevila, L. Evaluation of cognitive load in team sports: Literature review. *PeerJ* **2021**, *9*, e12045. [CrossRef]
31. Arruda, A.F.S.; Aoki, M.S.; Paludo, A.C.; Moreira, A. Salivary steroid response and competitive anxiety in elite basketball players: Effect of opponent level. *Physiol. Behav.* **2017**, *177*, 291–296. [CrossRef]
32. Camm, A.J.; Malik, M.; Bigger, J.T.; Breithardt, G.; Cerutti, S.; Cohen, R.J.; Coumel, P.; Fallen, E.L.; Kennedy, H.L.; Kleiger, R.E. Heart rate variability: Standards of measurement, physiological interpretation and clinical use. Task Force of the European Society of Cardiology and the North American Society of Pacing and Electrophysiology. *Circulation* **1996**, *93*, 1043–1065.
33. Morales, J.; Álamo, J.M.; García-Massó, X.; López, J.L.; Serra-Añó, P.; González, L.-M. Use of heart rate variability in monitoring stress and recovery in judo athletes. *J. Strength Cond. Res.* **2014**, *28*, 1896–1905. [CrossRef]
34. Stajer, V.; Vranes, M.; Ostojic, S.M. Correlation between biomarkers of creatine metabolism and serum indicators of peripheral muscle fatigue during exhaustive exercise in active men. *Res. Sports Med.* **2020**, *28*, 147–154. [CrossRef]
35. Moreira, A.; McGuigan, M.R.; Arruda, A.F.S.; Freitas, C.G.; Aoki, M.S. Monitoring internal load parameters during simulated and official basketball matches. *J. Strength Cond. Res.* **2012**, *26*, 861–866. [CrossRef]
36. Granger, D.A.; Kivlighan, K.T.; El-Sheikh, M.; Gordis, E.B.; Stroud, L.R. Salivary α-amylase in biobehavioral research: Recent developments and applications. *Ann. N. Y. Acad. Sci.* **2007**, *1098*, 122–144. [CrossRef]
37. Kivlighan, K.T.; Granger, D.A. Salivary α-amylase response to competition: Relation to gender, previous experience, and attitudes. *Psychoneuroendocrinology* **2006**, *31*, 703–714. [CrossRef] [PubMed]
38. Nater, U.M.; Rohleder, N.; Schlotz, W.; Ehlert, U.; Kirschbaum, C. Determinants of the diurnal course of salivary alpha-amylase. *Psychoneuroendocrinology* **2007**, *32*, 392–401. [CrossRef] [PubMed]
39. Moreira, A.; Aoki, M.S.; Franchini, E.; da Silva Machado, D.G.; Paludo, A.C.; Okano, A.H. Mental fatigue impairs technical performance and alters neuroendocrine and autonomic responses in elite young basketball players. *Physiol. Behav.* **2018**, *196*, 112–118. [CrossRef] [PubMed]
40. Hunt, M.G.; Rushton, J.; Shenberger, E.; Murayama, S. Positive effects of diaphragmatic breathing on physiological stress reactivity in varsity athletes. *J. Clin. Sport Psychol.* **2018**, *12*, 27–38. [CrossRef]
41. Laborde, S.; Lentes, T.; Hosang, T.J.; Borges, U.; Mosley, E.; Dosseville, F. Influence of slow-paced breathing on inhibition after physical exertion. *Front. Psychol.* **2019**, *10*, 1923. [CrossRef] [PubMed]
42. Thelwell, R.; Weston, N.J.V.; Greenlees, I. Coping with stressors in elite sport: A coach perspective. *Eur. J. Sport Sci.* **2010**, *10*, 243–253. [CrossRef]
43. Foretić, N.; Nikolovski, Z.; Marić, D.; Gabrilo, G.; Sekulić, D.; Jaksić, D.; Drid, P. Stress Levels in Handball Coaching–Case Study: Preliminary Analysis of the Differences between Training and Match. *Int. J. Environ. Res. Public Health* **2022**, *19*, 10251. [CrossRef]
44. Sewell, D.F.; Edmondson, A.M. Relationships between field position and pre-match competitive state anxiety in soccer and field hockey. *Int. J. Sport Psychol.* **1996**, *27*, 159–172.
45. Kant, S. Relaxation as Related to Arousal and Performance in Handball. *Int. J. Phys. Educ. Sports* **2017**, *2*, 71–73.
46. Boyce, W.T.; Ellis, B.J. Biological sensitivity to context: I. An evolutionary–developmental theory of the origins and functions of stress reactivity. *Dev. Psychopathol.* **2005**, *17*, 271–301. [CrossRef] [PubMed]
47. Preston, S.D.; Buchanan, T.W.; Stansfield, R.B.; Bechara, A. Effects of anticipatory stress on decision making in a gambling task. *Behav. Neurosci.* **2007**, *121*, 257. [CrossRef]
48. Eysenck, M.W.; Derakshan, N.; Santos, R.; Calvo, M.G. Anxiety and cognitive performance: Attentional control theory. *Emotion* **2007**, *7*, 336. [CrossRef] [PubMed]
49. Blum, J.; Rockstroh, C.; Göritz, A.S. Heart rate variability biofeedback based on slow-paced breathing with immersive virtual reality nature scenery. *Front. Psychol.* **2019**, *10*, 2172. [CrossRef] [PubMed]

50. You, M.; Laborde, S.; Zammit, N.; Iskra, M.; Borges, U.; Dosseville, F. Single Slow-Paced Breathing Session at Six Cycles per Minute: Investigation of Dose-Response Relationship on Cardiac Vagal Activity. *Int. J. Environ. Res. Public Health* **2021**, *18*, 12478. [CrossRef]
51. Laborde, S.; Hosang, T.; Mosley, E.; Dosseville, F. Influence of a 30-Day Slow-Paced Breathing Intervention Compared to Social Media Use on Subjective Sleep Quality and Cardiac Vagal Activity. *J. Clin. Med.* **2019**, *8*, 193. [CrossRef]

healthcare

Systematic Review

Prevalence and Risk Factors of Musculoskeletal Disorders in Basketball Players: Systematic Review and Meta-Analysis

Silvia Cristina de Carvalho Borges [1], Carolina Rodrigues Mendonça [1], Regina Márcia Ferreira Silva [2,*], Alberto De Vitta [3] and Matias Noll [1,2,*]

[1] Health Science, Universidade Federal de Goiás, Goiânia 74001-970, Brazil
[2] Departament of Education, Instituto Federal Goiano, Ceres 76300-000, Brazil
[3] Departament of Physical Therapy, Centro Universitário das Faculdades Integradas de Ourinhos, Ourinhos 19909-100, Brazil
* Correspondence: regina.silva@ifg.edu.br (R.M.F.S.); matias.noll@ifgoiano.edu.br (M.N.)

Abstract: Musculoskeletal disorders characteristically induce pain and limitations in mobility, ability, and overall functioning. In athletes, including basketball players, disorders such as back pain, postural changes, and spinal injuries are common. This systematic review aimed to evaluate the prevalence of back pain and musculoskeletal disorders in basketball players and ascertain the associated factors. Methods: The Embase, PubMed, and Scopus databases were searched for studies published in English without a time limit. Using STATA, meta-analyses were performed to estimate the prevalence of pain and musculoskeletal disorders of the back and spine. Results: Of the 4135 articles identified, 33 studies were included in this review, with 27 studies included in the meta-analysis. Of these, 21 were used for the meta-analysis of back pain, 6 articles were used for the meta-analysis of spinal injury, and 2 studies were used for the meta-analysis of postural changes. The overall prevalence of back pain was 43% [95% CI, −1% to 88%]; of these, the prevalence of neck pain was 36% [95% CI, 22–50%], the prevalence of back pain was 16% [95% CI, 4–28%], the prevalence of low back pain was 26% [95% CI, 16–37%], the prevalence of thoracic spine pain was 6% [95% CI, 3–9%]. The combined prevalence of spinal injury and spondylolysis was 10% [95% CI, 4–15%], with a prevalence of spondylolysis of 14% [95% CI, 0.1–27%]. The combined prevalence of hyperkyphosis and hyperlordosis was 30% [95% CI, 9–51%]. In conclusion, we found a high prevalence of neck pain, followed by low back pain and back pain, in basketball players. Thus, prevention programs are important to improve health and sports performance.

Keywords: back pain; athletes; sport

Citation: de Carvalho Borges, S.C.; Mendonça, C.R.; Ferreira Silva, R.M.; De Vitta, A.; Noll, M. Prevalence and Risk Factors of Musculoskeletal Disorders in Basketball Players: Systematic Review and Meta-Analysis. *Healthcare* **2023**, *11*, 1190. https://doi.org/10.3390/healthcare11081190

Academic Editor: Felipe Aidar

Received: 7 March 2023
Revised: 11 April 2023
Accepted: 17 April 2023
Published: 21 April 2023

1. Introduction

Approximately 1.71 billion people worldwide suffer from musculoskeletal disorders that affect multiple areas or body systems, such as joints, bones, muscles, and spine; they are characterized by pain and limitations in mobility, ability, and overall level of functioning [1–3]; and necessitate rehabilitation [1]. Unlike that in the general population, musculoskeletal disorders can be exacerbated in athletes. Athletes frequently experience musculoskeletal disorders, with back pain being one of the most common symptoms [4–6]. Several sports are characterized by the need for specific movements, which may result in excessive spinal stress [7].

A study of elite German athletes from different sports reported that 77% of the athletes reported low back pain, followed by neck pain (63%) and thoracic spine pain (46%) [8]. Another study of 1114 elite German athletes from various sports reported an 89% prevalence of low back pain [9]. In another study of athletes from Finland, 46% of the basketball players who participated in the study had low back pain [10].

Basketball players frequently suffer from low back and neck pain [7–11], which confers a high risk for spinal injuries [7], and lumbar spine injuries are common in basketball players [12,13]. A study that longitudinally evaluated all injuries in the National Basketball Association (NBA) players over a 17-year period found that 10.2% of all injuries involved the lumbar spine and 0.9% of all injuries were due to lumbar disk degeneration [4].

Moreover, postural changes are common in players of various sports due to the repetitive and unilateral overload of the body during sports practice [14,15]. Furthermore, the trend of spinal curvature changes in basketball players, when compared to that in non-athletes, suggests an effect of regular basketball training on the degree of curvature of thoracic kyphosis and lumbar lordosis [16].

Basketball is an asymmetric sport that involves repetitive unilateral movements [15]. Therefore, the practice of this sport may promote pain and/or injury to the spine due to the number of throws and dribbles during a practice session or game [15]. Therefore, it is necessary to determine the prevalence of postural changes and back pain, as they may affect players' mobility and ability. Despite the importance of this topic, no systematic reviews of back pain and postural changes in basketball players have been published.

Therefore, this systematic review aimed to evaluate the prevalence of back pain whose causes remain uncertain and probably multifactorial and musculoskeletal disorders in basketball players. This research is intended to identify factors that are associated with musculoskeletal disorders and pain in basketball players to contribute to the implementation of spinal pain and injury prevention and treatment interventions and programs to improve the health, quality of life, and sports performance of basketball players.

2. Materials and Methods

2.1. Protocol and Registration

The protocol (PROSPERO CRD42020201653) of this systematic review was registered in the International Prospective Register of Systematic Reviews and was published as an article [17]. The systematic review followed the Preferred Reporting Items for Systematic Reviews and Meta-Analyses methodology [18]. Ethical approval was not required because this review involved an analysis of previously published data.

2.2. Identification of Relevant Studies

Studies published in English were searched without any restriction on the publication period. The search was performed in three databases (Embase, PubMed, and Scopus) on 6 March 2022. The main search terms were "back pain", "postural changes", "players", and "basketball". The general search strategy is described in Table 1 and was adapted for the different databases (Supplementary Material).

Table 1. General search strategy for the identification of published articles.

1	("musculoskeletal disorder" OR "musculoskeletal disorders" OR "musculoskeletal disease" OR "musculoskeletal diseases" OR "musculoskeletal injuries" OR "musculoskeletal injury" OR posture OR "postural evaluation" OR "postural changes" OR scoliosis OR kyphosis OR lordosis OR spondylolysis OR "back pain" OR "low back pain" OR "back injuries" OR "lumbar pain" OR "neck pain" OR "spinal pain" OR "abnormalities in spine" OR "spine pain" OR "cervical pain" OR backache OR backaches OR "back ache" OR "back aches" OR "cumulative trauma disorders")
2	(players OR player OR sportsman OR athletes OR athlete OR sportsmen OR sportswoman OR sportswomen)
3	(basket OR basketball OR sports OR sport)
4	(1) AND (2) AND (3)

The review followed the PECO structure (population, exposure, comparators, and outcomes) [19]. In this article, "P" represents players, "E" represents basketball sport, "C" represents spine regions (lumbar spine, cervical spine, thoracic spine), and "O" represents the prevalence of back pain and musculoskeletal disorders (postural changes and spinal injuries) in basketball players and associated factors.

Musculoskeletal disorders include fractures, acute soft tissue injuries (i.e., bruises, sprains, or strains); non-articular and non-rheumatic soft tissue disorders, tissue disorders including local myofascial pain syndrome and systemic fibromyalgia, arthritis, neurological disorders, amputations, and problems of postoperative rehabilitation following interventional orthopedic procedures [20]. Functional disorders that were evaluated in this review included traumatic injuries of the spine and injuries of the spinal cord, nerve roots, bone structure, and disk ligaments of the spine [21]. Postural changes considered included scoliosis, kyphosis, and lordosis. Back pain was defined as pain in the cervical, thoracic, and/or lumbar spine [22–24].

Inclusion criteria were: (a) basketball players of both sexes; (b) age up to 50 years (articles with other age groups were included, provided the data were presented separately); (c) observational studies (longitudinal, cross-sectional, cohort, and case-control); (d) assessment of musculoskeletal disorders or back pain in basketball players (articles with other injuries were included, provided the data are presented separately); (e) publications in English; and (f) studies with players from communities of different nationalities. Both specific and non-specific back pain were included.

Articles based on the following criteria were excluded: (a) studies with basketball players that pertained to injuries in other body regions (knee, shoulder, hip, ankle) unless back and spine data were presented separately or could be calculated; (b) paralympic athletes and/or players with physical or mental disabilities; (c) mixed sports samples, unless basketball player data were presented separately or could be calculated; (d) experimental studies; and (e) studies with incomplete data.

This search included full articles published without the restriction of the search period, and excluded books, book chapters, case reports, commentaries, letters, editorials, and systematic reviews. Articles for which the full text could not be retrieved from online databases were requested by email from the authors of the papers.

2.3. Study Selection

Articles found in the databases were imported into Mendeley [25] software, where we excluded duplicate studies. Subsequently, the Rayyan software [26] was used to read the titles and abstracts of the studies, and articles that did not meet the previously established eligibility criteria were excluded. Next, the full texts of the selected studies were read to confirm their eligibility. All steps were performed by two reviewers (SCCB and MSVF), and disagreements, if any, were resolved by a third reviewer (MN). The flowchart of the study selection is shown in Figure 1.

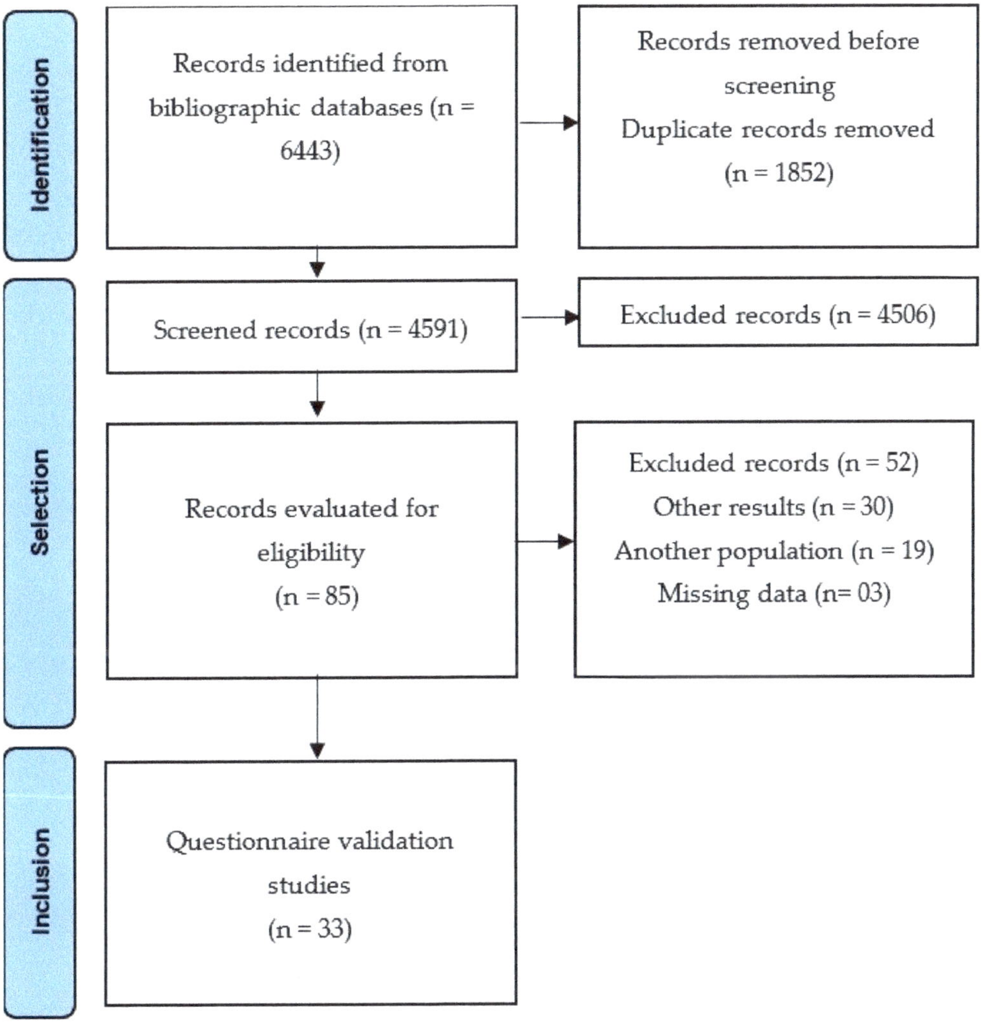

Figure 1. Preferred Reporting Items for Systematic Reviews and Meta-Analyses (PRISMA) flow diagram of articles included in this review.

2.4. Data Extraction

The following data were extracted from the selected studies: author and year of publication, type of study, country of origin, population, sex, age group, type of change, tool, prevalence of postural change and injuries, location, and prevalence of back pain. The full description of the extracted data is included in Tables 2–5.

We performed a meta-analysis with the data that were extracted to ascertain the prevalence of back pain, postural changes, and spinal injuries. However, these data were insufficient to perform a meta-analysis of the associated factors.

2.5. Examiner Training

Authors participating in the eligibility assessments were trained in the inclusion/exclusion criteria for studies and assessed the eligibility of 50 sample abstracts before they began reviewing the articles [27]. Besides performing standardized analyses using Mendeley and Rayyan software [25,26], the authors were trained to use risk-of-bias analysis tools through the examination of five non-included articles.

2.6. Methodological Quality and Risk of Bias

The included articles were assessed for methodological quality and risk of bias by using the Grading of Recommendations, Assessment, Development, and Evaluations-GRADE [28] or the Downs and Black checklist [29]. GRADE is a method that serves transparency and simplicity by enabling the classification of the quality of evidence into four categories: very low quality, low quality, moderate quality, and high quality. GRADE has been adopted worldwide because of its rigorous methodological classification and ease of use [28].

An adapted version of the Downs and Black checklist that was proposed by Noll was used [30], wherein each item indicates: (A) clearly stated objective; (B) clearly described main outcomes; (C) clearly defined sample characteristics; (D) clearly described distribution of main confounders; (E) clearly defined main findings; (F) random variability in estimates provided; (G) loss to follow-up described; (H) probability values provided; (I) representative target sample of the population; (J) representative sample recruitment of the population; (K) analyses adjusted for different follow-up times; (L) properly used statistical tests; (M) valid/reliable primary outcomes; (N) sample recruited from the same population; (O) adequate adjustment for confounders; and P) sample loss to follow-up considered (corresponding to items 1–3, 5–7, 9–12, 17, 18, 20, 21, 25, and 26). Items G and P were applied only to longitudinal studies, whereas items K and N were applied only to the case-control and longitudinal studies. Scores reach 100% at 12, 14, and 16 points for cross-sectional, case-control, and longitudinal studies, respectively. Scores above 70% were used to define a low risk of bias [29]. The Downs and Black checklist was identified as one of the two tools that were most frequently used in systematic reviews, which were registered in PROSPERO from 2011 to 2018 [31].

The scores were used to determine the methodological quality of the studies while considering five aspects: presentation, external validity, internal validity-bias, internal validity-confounders, and statistical power for inferences [29]. The risk of bias was assessed independently by two examiners. The prevalence of data identified in the studies was used for the data synthesis strategy.

2.7. Statistical Analysis

Meta-analyses were performed to estimate the prevalence of back pain, spinal injuries, and postural changes. Data were presented graphically in Forest plots to estimate the prevalence rates with 95% confidence intervals (CI). Statistical I^2 values were calculated to quantify the degree of heterogeneity between studies, with values of 25–50% representing moderate heterogeneity and values > 50% representing large heterogeneity among the studies [32]. Publication bias was assessed using Egger's test. All analyses were performed using STATA (version 16.0; StataCorp, College Station, TX, USA).

3. Results

The stages of study selection are presented in Figure 1. According to the eligibility criteria, 6443 studies were identified, of which 1852 duplicate records were excluded. After screening the title and abstract, 4591 articles were selected; among these, 4506 did not meet the eligibility criteria, and 85 articles were included for a full-text review.

In this stage, 52 studies were excluded because they assessed other sports (n = 19), had different outcomes (n = 30), or were missing data (n = 3). Finally, 33 studies were included in this systematic review [6–8,10,11,16,33–59] (Table 2). Moderate interrater agreement (98%) was found between the two examiners.

3.1. Risk of Bias and Evaluation of the Quality of Studies

Of the articles included, 69.7% of the studies obtained ethical approval (n = 23) [6,7,10,11,16,34–36,38–40,44–48,50,51,53–56,59] and 51.5% clearly reported that there were no conflicts of interest (n = 17) [6,7,10,11,16,33,34,36–38,45,46,50,51,53,56,58].

The quality of evidence was low quality in 57.6% (n = 19) [6,10,11,16,37–51] and very low quality in 42.4% (n = 14) [7,8,33–36,52–59] of studies, respectively (Table 3). A total of 78.8% of the articles had a low risk of bias (n = 26) [6–8,10,11,16,33,34,36–47,49–51,54,57,58].

3.2. Main Characteristics of the Studies

In total, 72.7% (n = 24) of the articles were published between 2011 and 2022 [6–8,10,11,16,33,34,36,38–42,45–47,49–52,56–58]; 45.4% of the studies were conducted on the European continent (n = 15) (Table 4) [7,8,10,16,33,34,37,39,42,46–50,57]. With regard to the type of pain, back pain was addressed in 60.6% of the articles (n = 20) [6–8,11,34,35,37,38,42,43,46,47,49,50,54–56,58,59]; 48.5% of the articles investigated spine injuries (n = 16) [35,36,39–41,43–46,48,51–55,57].

The majority of the studies, 69.7% (n = 23), included participants from both sexes [6,8,10, 33,34,37,38,40–50,52–55,58]. The average age of the participants ranged from 11.47 ± 2.10 [33] to 24.4 ± 4.7 years [36]. The sample size varied widely across studies, with a minimum of 10 [16] and a maximum of 5,566,124 players [41]. Furthermore, 63.6% (n = 21) of the articles were cross-sectional [6–8,11,34,37,38,40–42,44,45,47,48,52–55,57–59] (Table 4).

The vast majority of studies, a total of 14, did not present the period in which low back pain was assessed [6,38–41,43–46,48,52,55,57]. A total of 8 studies assessed low back pain in the last 3 to 6 months [33,35–37,42,51,56,59], 5 studies assessed it over a period of one year [10,16,34,47,50], 4 studies assessed it over a lifetime [7,8,11,54], and finally, 2 studies assessed it within the last 3 to 5 five years [49,53]. The detailed characteristics of the studies included in the systematic review are shown in Table 4.

Table 2. Characteristics of the studies included in the systematic review and their outcome variables.

Author/Year	Design Country	No. Participants (% Male)	Age (Years/Mean and Standard Deviation)	Training Level	Tool	Postural Changes/ Prevalence	Spine Injuries/ Prevalence	Definition of Back Pain	Pain Location/Prevalence
Abdollahi et al. [51]	Retrospective Iran	204 (100%)	26.37 ± 7.42	Professional Super League and First Division League	Retrospective Injury Questionnaire (RIQ)	*	Upper back injury: 6.38% Lumbar injury: 48.53%	*	*
Auvinen et al. [37]	Cross-sectional Finland	4314 (51.5%)	15 to 16 years	Moderate to vigorous Up to once a month, 2–4 times a month, and at least twice a week	Questionnaire	*	*	*	All: 88.5%, up to once a month 24.6%, 2–4 times a month; 9.4%, at least twice a week Neck pain: 44.5%, up to once a month (reference group) 12.2%, 2–4 times a month 4.7%, at least twice a week Backache: 44.3%, up to once a month (reference group) 12.4%, 2–4 times a month −4.7%, at least twice a week.
Farahbakhsh et al. [7]	Cross-sectional Iran	52 (100%)	16.1± 1.1 years	Hours/week 11.6± 8.2	Questionnaire	*	*	Point prevalence, Prevalence of chronic pain Yearly prevalence, Sports-lifePrevalence, Lifetime prevalence	Total: Point prevalence 61.6% (N = 32) Prevalence of chronic pain 28.8% Neck pain: 36.53% 13.46% 36.53% 46.15% 57.69%. Low back pain: 25% 15.38% 50% 65.38% 63.46%

Table 2. *Cont.*

Author/Year	Design Country	No. Participants (% Male)	Age (Years/Mean and Standard Deviation)	Training Level	Tool	Postural Changes/ Prevalence	Spine Injuries/ Prevalence	Definition of Back Pain	Pain Location/Prevalence
Grabara [52]	Cross-sectional Poland	52 (57.7%)	14 to 17 years	Training experience [years] 4.05 ± 0.58	Rippstein plurimeter	Hyperkyphosis: 21.2% Hypolordosis: 42.3% Hyperlordosis: 13.4%	*	*	*
Grabara [16]	Longitudinal Follow-up: 2 years Poland	10 (100%)	13–15 years	Training over a 2-year period	Plurimeter-V Gravity Inclinometer	Hyperkyphosis: 70% in almost 3 months after engagement in regular sports activity 70% after 1 year 60% after 2 years Hypokyphosis: 0% in almost 3 months after engaging in regular sports activity 20% after 1 year 10% after 2 years Hyperlordosis: 0% in almost 3 months after engaging in regular sports activity 10% after 1 year 0% after 2 years Hypolordosis: 70% in nearly 3 months after engaging in regular sports activity 30% after 1 year 50% after 2 years	*	*	*

Table 2. *Cont.*

Author/Year	Design Country	No. Participants (% Male)	Age (Years/Mean and Standard Deviation)	Training Level	Tool	Postural Changes/ Prevalence	Spine Injuries/ Prevalence	Definition of Back Pain	Pain Location/Prevalence
Greene et al. [53]	Cross-sectional Follow-up: 1 year United States	33 (57.6%)	19 ± 1 years	College athletes	16-item questionnaire	*	Low back injury: Injury during the 1999/2000 season 18.2% History of low back injury in the last 5 years 27.3%	*	*
Habelt et al. [39]	Longitudinal Follow-up: 10 years Switzerland	168 (100%)	10–19 years	*	Clinical examination, Radiographic assessment (anteroposterior and lateral view), ultrasound, or MRI scan.	*	Spine injury: 1.8%	*	*
Hagiwara et al. [38]	Cross-sectional Japan	590 (56.1%)	6–15 years	Training per day on weekends (hours) ≤3304 (51.5) and >3286 (48.5)	Self-reported questionnaires	*	*	*	Low back pain: 12.9%
Hangai et al. [54]	Cross-sectional Japan	63 (69.8%)	19.7 ± 0.9 years	Athletes' career time (years) 9.2 ± 1.8	MRI and clinical examination/Self-reported questionnaire	*	Disk Degeneration: 42.9%	*	Low back pain: during life: 81% During the previous 4 weeks: 17.7%
Hickey et al. [59]	Cross-sectional Australia	49(0%)	16–18 years	Young elite women's basketball players	Medical records	*	Disk-related pain, spondylolysis, and acute fracture of a lumbar transverse process: 14.9%	Mechanical/facet joint-related low back pain Acute-chronic	Low back pain: 6.3%
Ichikawa et al. [55]	Cross-sectional Japan	16 male and female athletes	*	*	Radiography	*	Spondylolysis: 12.5%	*	Low back pain: 25%

Table 2. *Cont.*

Author/Year	Design Country	No. Participants (% Male)	Age (Years/Mean and Standard Deviation)	Training Level	Tool	Postural Changes/ Prevalence	Spine Injuries/ Prevalence	Definition of Back Pain	Pain Location/Prevalence
Iwamoto et al. [43]	Retrospective 14-year period Japan	1229 (55.2%)	11–49 years	Class 2 = low recreational: sports activity once or twice a week; Class 3 = high recreational: sports activity; >3 times/week, and belonging to an elementary or high school team or other sports team; Class 4 = competitive: competitive sports activity and belonging to a professional, semi-professional, or university sports team	Radiographies or MRI/Database	*	Lumbar disc disease: 6.6.% Lumbar Spondylolysis: 2%	Non-traumatic pain	Low back pain: 2.9%
Keene et al. [44]	Cross-sectional United States	216 (male and female athletes)	*	College athletes	Review of training room medical records and hospital files	*	Total: 5.6% Strain: 5.1% Sprain: 0.5%	*	*
Kerr et al. [45]	Cross-sectional United States	19,991 (61.5%)		Athlete exposure was defined as the participation of 1 athlete in 1 school-sanctioned training or competition	Online Injury Surveillance System: Reporting Information Online	*	Trunk Displace-ments/Separations: 12.9% M = 7.7% F = 5.2%	*	*
Leppänen et al. [46]	Prospective Study Finland	201 (49.7%)	15.7 ± 1.7 years	College athletes	Questionnaire including information such as age, sex, injury history, playing experience, and family history of musculoskeletal disorders	*	Muscle/tendon: 26.9% Joint/ligament: 4.5% Bone injury: 5.5%	*	Low back pain: 9.95%

Table 2. *Cont.*

Author/Year	Design Country	No. Participants (% Male)	Age (Years/Mean and Standard Deviation)	Training Level	Tool	Postural Changes/ Prevalence	Spine Injuries/ Prevalence	Definition of Back Pain	Pain Location/Prevalence
Meron et al. [41]	Cross-sectional United States	5,566,124 (55.6%)	*	An athlete exposure was defined as an athlete (154) participating in one practice, competition, or performance	High School Reporting Information Online injury surveillance system	*	Cervical spine injury: 0.0006%	*	*
Nagano et al. [56]	Prospective study Japan	54 (0%)	19.0 ± 2.8 years	College athletes	Modified Japanese version of the OSTRC questionnaire	*	*	*	Backache: 14.4%
Noormohammadpour et al. [11]	Cross-sectional Iran	140 (0%)	22.7 ± 2.7 years	Female college athletes competing in the National College Student Sports Olympics	Self-reported questionnaire	*	*	Point prevalence Yearly prevalence Sports-life Prevalence Lifetime Prevalence	Low back pain: 22.9% 47.9% 48.6% 68.6%
Nowak et al. [57]	Cross-sectional Poland	58 (100%)	17 ± 1.4 years	Professional players (club players), amateur league (amateur players)	Original questionnaire consisting of 28 items	*	Neck injury and back injury: 12.1%	*	*
Owen et al. [58]	Cross-sectional Japan	63 male and female athletes	20 ± 1 years	Well-trained male and female athletes who have spent a minimum of 5 years playing the sport	Subjective questionnaire	*	*	*	Back pain: 1.6%
Pasanen et al. [47]	Cross-sectional Finland	207 (48.8%)	14.9 ± 1.6 years	Young players that were official members of participating teams and had played official games in the previous season.	Questionnaire based on the Nordic standardized musculoskeletal symptoms questionnaire and on its modified version for athletes.	*	*	*	Low Back Pain: 45.4%

Table 2. *Cont.*

Author/Year	Design Country	No. Participants (% Male)	Age (Years/Mean and Standard Deviation)	Training Level	Tool	Postural Changes/ Prevalence	Spine Injuries/ Prevalence	Definition of Back Pain	Pain Location/Prevalence
Rossi et al. [48]	Cross-sectional A retrospective analysis Italy	174 male and female athletes	15–27 years	Athletes referred to the Institute of Sport Sciences of the Italian Olympic Committee	Radiographic findings	*	Spondylolysis with low back pain: 9.77%	*	*
Rossi et al. [49]	Longitudinal 3-year follow-up Finland	203 (49.3%)	14.9 ± 1.6 years	Training hours (mean, standard deviation): 215.1 (102.9)	Nordic standardized questionnaire on musculoskeletal symp-toms/modified version for athletes	*	*	Non-traumatic Acute Traumatic / AcuteTraumatic	Total: 11.9% Low back pain: 8.4% 3% Back pain: 0.5%
Rossi et al. [10]	Longitudinal 3-year follow-up Finland	271 male and female athletes	16.2 ± 1.7 years	Hours of team practice during follow-up, average hours: 244.8	Nordic standardized questionnaire on musculoskeletal symp-toms/modified version for athletes	*	*	*	Low back pain: 46%
Rossi et al. [50]	Prospective cohort study Finland	128 male and female athletes	14.7 ± 1.5 years	Elite basketball players	Nordic standardized questionnaire of musculoskeletal symptoms	*	*	*	Low back pain: 25%
Sarcevic and Tepavcevic [33]	Case-control Serbia	38 male and female athletes Group of cases: 19 Control group: 19	11.5 ± 2.1 years 11.7 ± 1.9 years	Physical activity level, hours per week 3.03 ± 0.55, 3.04 ± 0.64	Checkup-Adams' forward Bend test and scoliometer measurement	Adolescent idiopathic scoliosis: 100%	*	*	*
Schneider et al. [42]	Cross-sectional Germany	182 (70.9%)	15.5 ± 1.3 years	Elite youth basketball players from Germany's three elite youth leagues	Sets of items from a previously validated and tested questionnaire	*	*	*	Back pain: 7 days: 34.3% 12-month prevalence rates: 70.9% More intense pain: 16.4% Neck pain: 7 days: 26.5% 12-month prevalence rates: 65.2% More intense pain: 6.1%

Table 2. *Cont.*

Author/Year	Design Country	No. Participants (% Male)	Age (Years/Mean and Standard Deviation)	Training Level	Tool	Postural Changes/ Prevalence	Spine Injuries/ Prevalence	Definition of Back Pain	Pain Location/Prevalence
Schulz et al. [34]	Cross-sectional Germany	11 (18.2%)	19 years old	Basketball played 20.6 h per week	Self-developed survey with 59 items	*	*	*	Back pain: 54.5%
Selhorst et al. [40]	Cross-sectional United States	194 (60.3%)	15.0 ± 1.8 years	*	Radiographies	*	Spondylolysis: 33%	*	*
Silva et al. [35]	Longitudinal Brazil	66 (0%)	23 years	Elite Women's Basketball Athletes. The teams played on average twice a week, and trained on average five times a week, which resulted in 76 matches and 375 training sessions.	Injury data were recorded by a physical therapist	*	Low back/back/neck injury: 33.3%	*	Low back pain: 12.1%
Trompeter et al. [8]	Cross-sectional Germany	518 (46.5%)	20.9 ± 4.8 years	Elite German athletes participating in the German Confederation of Olympic Sports	The questionnaire was based on the Nordic Questionnaire and a questionnaire developed by von Korff	*	*	Lifetime prevalence; 12-month prevalence; Point prevalence	Back pain: 91% 91% 67% Low back pain: 91% 86% 43%
Weiss et al. [36]	Prospective cohort study 24-week follow-up New Zealand	13 (100%)	24.4 ± 4.7 years	Competitive experience, 5.9 ± 3.6 years	Self-reported OSTRC injury questionnaire	*	Excessive use of lower back: 15.4%	*	*
Yabe et al. [6]	Cross-sectional Japan	592 (56.1%)	12–14 years	Training per day during the week: 2 h on average	Self-reported questionnaire	*	*	*	Low back pain: 12.8%

* Information missing in the article; ±, Standard deviation; BP, Back pain; F, Female; M, Male.

Table 3. Assessment of methodological quality and strength of evidence.

Study (Year)	Conflicts of Interest	Ethical Approval	Downs and Black Checklist																		GRADE
			A	B	C	D	E	F	G	H	I	J	K	L	M	N	O	P	Total	Score #	
Abdollahi et al. [51]	No	*	1	1	1	1	1	1	-	1	1	1	-	1	1	-	1	-	12/12	100%	●●○○
Auvinen et al. [37]	No	Yes	1	1	1	1	1	1	-	1	1	1	-	1	1	-	1	-	12/12	100%	●●○○
Farahbakhsh et al. [7]	No	Yes	1	1	1	0	1	1	-	1	0	0	-	1	1	-	1	-	9/12	75%	●○○○
Grabara [52]	*	Yes	1	1	1	0	1	1	-	0	0	0	-	1	1	-	0	-	7/12	58.3%	●○○○
Grabara [16]	No	Yes	1	1	1	0	1	1	1	1	0	0	1	1	1	1	0	1	12/16	75%	●●○○
Greene et al. [53]	*	Yes	1	1	1	0	1	0	-	1	0	0	-	1	1	-	0	-	7/12	58.3%	●○○○
Habelt et al. [39]	*	*	1	1	1	0	1	1	1	0	1	0	1	1	1	1	0	1	12/16	75%	●●○○
Hagiwara et al. [38]	No	Yes	1	1	1	1	1	1	-	1	1	1	-	1	1	-	1	-	12/12	100%	●●○○
Hangai et al. [54]	No	Yes	1	1	1	1	1	1	-	1	0	1	-	1	1	-	1	-	11/12	91.7%	●○○○
Hickey et al. [59]	*	Yes	1	1	1	0	1	0	-	0	1	1	-	1	1	-	0	-	8/12	66.7%	●○○○
Ichikawa et al. [55]	*	*	1	1	0	0	1	1	-	0	0	1	-	1	1	-	0	-	7/12	58.3%	●○○○
Iwamoto [43]	*	*	1	1	1	1	1	1	-	1	1	1	-	1	1	-	0	-	11/12	91.7%	●●○○
Keene et al. [44]	*	*	1	1	1	0	1	1	1	1	0	1	1	1	1	1	0	1	13/16	81.3%	●●○○
Kerr et al. [45]	No	Yes	1	1	1	0	1	1	-	1	1	1	-	1	1	-	0	-	10/12	83.3%	●●○○
Leppänen et al. [46]	No	Yes	1	1	1	0	1	0	-	1	1	1	-	1	1	-	1	-	10/12	83.3%	●●○○
Meron et al. [41]	*	Yes	1	1	1	0	1	1	-	1	1	1	-	1	1	-	0	-	10/12	83.3%	●●○○
Nagano et al. [56]	No	Yes	1	1	1	0	1	0	-	1	0	0	-	1	1	-	1	-	8/12	66.7%	●○○○
Noormohammadpour et al. [11]	No	Yes	1	1	1	1	1	1	-	1	1	1	-	1	1	-	1	-	12/12	100%	●●○○
Nowak et al. [57]	*	*	1	1	1	0	1	1	-	1	0	1	-	1	1	-	0	-	9/12	75%	●○○○
Owen et al. [58]	No	Yes	1	1	1	1	1	1	-	1	1	1	-	1	1	-	1	-	12/12	100%	●○○○
Pasanen et al. [47]	*	Yes	1	1	1	0	1	1	-	1	1	1	-	1	1	-	1	-	11/12	91.7%	●●○○
Rossi et al. [48]	*	*	1	1	1	0	1	0	-	0	1	1	-	1	1	-	0	-	8/12	66.7%	●●○○
Rossi et al. [49]	*	Yes	1	1	1	1	1	1	-	1	1	1	-	1	1	-	1	-	12/12	100%	●●○○
Rossi et al. [10]	No	Yes	1	1	1	1	1	1	1	1	1	1	1	1	1	1	1	0	15/16	93.8%	●●○○
Rossi et al. [50]	No	Yes	1	1	1	0	1	1	-	1	1	1	-	1	1	-	1	-	11/12	91.7%	●●○○
Sarcevic et al. [33]	No	Yes	1	1	1	1	1	1	-	1	0	1	1	1	1	1	0	-	12/14	85.7%	●○○○

Table 3. *Cont.*

Study (Year)	Conflicts of Interest	Ethical Approval	Downs and Black Checklist																		GRADE
			A	B	C	D	E	F	G	H	I	J	K	L	M	N	O	P	Total	Score #	
Schneider et al. [42]	*	Yes	1	1	1	0	1	1	-	1	1	1	-	1	1	-	0	-	10/12	83.3%	●●○○
Schulz et al. [34]	No	*	1	1	1	0	1	1	-	1	1	0	-	1	1	-	0	-	9/12	75%	●○○○
Selhorst et al. [40]	*	*	1	1	1	0	1	0	-	1	1	1	-	1	1	-	0	-	9/12	75%	●●○○
Silva et al. [35]	*	Yes	1	1	1	0	1	0	-	1	0	1	-	1	1	-	0	-	8/12	66.7%	●○○○
Trompeter et al. [8]	*	*	1	1	0	0	1	1	-	1	1	0	1	1	1	1	0	-	10/14	71.4%	●○○○
Weiss et al. [36]	No	Yes	1	1	1	0	1	1	-	1	0	1	1	1	1	1	0	-	11/14	78.6%	●○○○
Yabe et al. [6]	No	Yes	1	1	1	1	1	1	-	1	1	0	-	1	1	-	1	-	11/12	91.7%	●●○○

Downs and Black checklist: (A) clearly stated objective; (B) clearly described main outcomes; (C) clearly defined sample characteristics; (D) clearly described distribution of main confounders; (E) clearly defined main findings; (F) random variability in the estimates provided; (G) loss to follow-up described; (H) probability values provided; (I) representative target sample of the population; (J) representative sample recruitment of the population; (K) analyses adjusted for different follow-up times; (L) properly used statistical tests; (M) valid/reliable primary outcomes; (N) sample recruited from the same population; (O) adequate adjustment for confounders; and (P) sample loss to follow-up considered (corresponding to items 1–3, 5–7, 9–12, 17,18, 20, 21, 25, 26). *, not informed, -, not applied. Items G and P were applied to only longitudinal studies. Items K and N were applied to only case-control and longitudinal studies. # Scores reach 100% at 12, 14, and 16 points for cross-sectional, case-control, and longitudinal studies, respectively. GRADE, Grading of Recommendations, Assessment, Development, and Evaluations; were one filled circle, very low quality; two filled circles, low quality; three filled circles, moderate quality; and four filled circles, high quality.

Table 4. Characteristics of the studies included in the systematic review.

Characteristics	Categories	Number of Studies (%)
Year of Publication	1982–2000	3 (9.0%)
	2001–2010	6 (18.2%)
	2011–2022	24 (72.7%)
Region		
America	Brazil	1 (3.1%)
	USA	5 (15.2%)
Africa	-	-
Asia	Iran	3 (9%)
	Japan	7 (21.1%)
Europe	Germany	3 (9%)
	Poland	3 (9%)
	Finland	6 (18.1%)
	Switzerland	1 (3.1%)
	Italy	1 (3.1%)
	Serbia	1 (3.1%)
Oceania	Australia	1 (3.1%)
	New Zealand	1 (3.1%)
Study design	Case-control	1 (3.1%)
	Retrospective	2 (6%)
	Prospective	4 (12.1%)
	Longitudinal	5 (15.2%)
	Cross-sectional	21 (63.6%)
Sex	Male only	6 (18.2%)
	Female only	4 (12.1%)
	Both sexes	23 (69.7%)
Sample size	<100	15 (45.5%)
	100–500	12 (36.4%)
	501–1000	2 (6%)
	>1000	4 (12.1%)
Participants	Postural changes	3 (9.1%)
	Back pain and spine injuries	6 (18.2%)
	Spine injuries	10 (30.3%)
	Back pain	14 (42.4%)

Table 5. Associated Factors.

Author	Associated Factors
Auvinen et al. [37]	-
Farahbakhsh et al. [7]	The highest risk of neck pain at all times was observed among basketball players compared to other sports groups ($p < 0.05$; OR [95% CI 1.54–7.25]).
Grabara [52]	-
Grabara [16]	-
Greene et al. [53]	-
Habelt et al. [39]	-
Hagiwara et al. [38]	Upper limb pain was significantly associated with low back pain (OR: 7.86 [95% CI 3.93–15.72], $p < 0.001$). Shoulder pain was significantly associated with training per week (>4 days) (OR: 4.15; 95% CI: 1.29–13.40) and low back pain (OR: 13.77 [95% CI 5.70–33.24], $p < 0.001$).
Hangai et al. [54]	Logistic regression analysis of participants with disc degeneration, including a basketball group, adjusted for sex and obesity (OR: 1.61 [95% CI 0.78–3.35], $p = 0.1982$)

Table 5. *Cont.*

Author	Associated Factors
Hickey et al. [59]	-
Ichikawa et al. [55]	-
Iwamoto et al. [43]	-
Keene et al. [44]	-
Kerr et al. [45]	-
Leppãnen et al. [46]	Female players had a higher incidence of overuse injuries compared to male basketball players (IRR 1.61 [95% CI 1.07–2.46], $p < 0.05$. Previous injury was significantly associated with low-back overuse injuries in basketball and floorball players (OR 3.99 [CI 1.48–10.78], $p = 0.01$)
Meron et al. [41]	For sports that allow comparison between the sexes, females had higher basketball injury rates (RR, 2.02 [CI 1.01–4.03], $p < 0.05$)
Nagano et al. [56]	-
Noormohammadpour et al. [11]	-
Nowak et al. [57]	The differences in stretching before a workout or game between players training up to three times a week and players training four or more times a week were statistically significant ($\chi 2 = 8.926$, $p = 0.012$, V = 0.392)
Owen et al. [58]	After matching participants based on the status of back pain and height, basketball players showed signs of intervertebral disc hypertrophy ($p \leq 0.043$)
Pasanen et al. [47]	Family history of musculoskeletal disorders (OR 2.02 [95% CI 1.22–3.34]) and higher age (OR 1.22 [95% CI 1.05–1.41]) were associated with low back pain in basketball and floorball players.
Rossi and Dragoni [48]	-
Rossi et al. [49]	-
Rossi et al. [10]	There was a small increase in the risk of low back pain with a one-degree decrease in the right leg during the SLVDJ landing (HR 1.09 [95% CI 1.02–1.17] per one-degree decrease in the APF). Basketball and floorball players. All LBP Femur–pelvic angle, right side HR 1.09 (1.02–1.17) 0.014 Gradual onset non-traumatic LBP Femur–pelvic angle, right side HR 1.09 (1.01 to 1.18) 0.021
Rossi et al. [50]	None of the risk factors investigated were associated with low back pain in univariate Cox analyses.
Sarcevic and Tepavcevic [33]	-
Schneider et al. [42]	-
Schulz et al. [34]	-
Selhorst et al. [40]	Presence of spondylolysis in male basketball athletes RR (95% CI) = 1.05 (0.89–1.24) Presence of spondylolysis in female basketball athletes RR (95% CI) = 0.98 (0.86–1.12) Overall: Male athletes were 1.5 times more likely to have spondylolysis than female athletes ($p = 0.01$).

Table 5. *Cont.*

Author	Associated Factors
Silva et al. [35]	Older athletes were more likely to have consecutive injuries than younger athletes during the study period. This comparison was statistically significant (p = 0.010).
Trompeter et al. [8]	Among basketball players, these problems, along with a high frequency of jumping and landing, can lead to back pain. Compared with control subjects, significantly higher rates of back pain were found in those who participated in elite rowing, dancing, fencing, gymnastics, underwater rugby, water polo, shooting, basketball, field hockey, track and field, ice hockey, and figure skating.
Weiss et al. [36]	The mean weekly prevalence of all reported overuse conditions was 63% (95% CI 60–66), and that of severe overuse conditions was 7.3% (95% CI: 7.1–7.6).
Yabe et al. [6]	Participants with lower extremity pain had higher rates of low back pain, with an OR (95% CI) of 6.21 (3.57–10.80), than participants without lower extremity pain. Moreover, there was a significant association between knee/ankle pain and low back pain. Compared with participants without knee/ankle pain, the OR (95% CI) for low back pain was 4.25 (2.55–7.07) for participants with knee pain and 3.79 (2.26–6.36) for participants with ankle pain.

CI, confidence interval; OR, odds ratio; RR, Relative Risk; Cramér's V, V is a measure of association between two nominal variables; $\chi 2$, chi-square. SLVDJ: single leg drops vertical jump.

3.3. Assessment of the Prevalence of Spinal Injuries and Postural Changes

Of the tools used to assess spinal injuries, 31.3% were radiographs (n = 5) [39,40,43,48,55], 31.3% were questionnaires (n = 5) [36,46,51,53,57], and 18.8% comprised medical records (n = 3) [35,44,59]. The other studies used different tools to assess the prevalence of spine injuries, with 18.8% using magnetic resonance imaging (n = 3) (Table 3) [39,43,54]. Plurimeters (inclinometers) (n = 2) [16,52] were used in 66.7% of cases, and the Checkup-Adams' forward bend test and scoliometer measurement (n = 1) [33] were used in 33.3% of cases to assess postural changes.

The most common diagnoses were spondylolysis in 31.3% of the studies (n = 5) [40,43,48,55,59], lumbar spine injuries in 25% (n = 4) [35,36,51,53], and cervical spine injuries in 18.8% (n = 3) [35,41,57]. Of these studies, 43.8% (n = 7) examined more than one postural change [35,43,44,46,51,57,59]. Among the postural changes, the most common abnormalities were hyperlordosis, hypolordosis, and hyperkyphosis in 66.7% of the studies (n = 2) [16,52].

For spinal injuries, the prevalence of low back injuries was 48.5% (n = 204) [51], whereas that of disk degeneration, spondylolysis, back injuries (lumbar, dorsal, and cervical), overuse injuries, and trunk displacement/separation in players was 42.9% (n = 63) [54], 33% (n = 194) [40], 33.3% (n = 66) [35], 15.4% (n = 13) [36], and 12.9% (n = 19,991), respectively [45]. With regard to postural changes, the prevalence of hyperkyphosis was 70% (n = 10) [16], and hypolordosis was 42.3% (n = 52) [52].

3.4. Assessment of the Prevalence of Back Pain

To assess the prevalence of back pain, self-reported questionnaires were used in 80% of the studies (n = 16) [6–8,10,11,34,37,38,42,46,47,49,50,54,56,58] and medical records in 10% (n = 2) [35,59]. In 80% (n = 16) of the studies, low back pain was identified [6–8,10,11,37,38,43,46,47,49,50,54–56,59]; in 25% (n = 5) of the studies reported back pain [8,34,42,49,58]. In 25% (n = 5) of the studies, more than one outcome was reported for the location of back pain [7,8,37,42,49].

The prevalence of low back pain and back pain was 91% in 21 players [8], the prevalence of low back pain was 81% in 63 players [54], and of back pain was 70.9% in 182 participants [42]. The prevalence of neck pain ranged from 44.5% in a sample of 4314 players [37] to 26.5% in a sample of 182 players [42].

3.5. Associated Factors

Studies reported sex and age as factors that were associated with musculoskeletal disorders. Female basketball players had a higher injury rate than male players (IRR, 1.11 [CI: 0.44–2.71]; RR, 2.02 [CI: 1.01–4.03]) [46,51]. Furthermore, higher age was associated with low back pain (OR, 1.22 [CI: 1.05–1.41], $p < 0.008$) [7] and were more likely to suffer consecutive injuries ($p = 0.010$) [40]. Data on the associated factors found in the articles are presented in Table 5 but were insufficient to perform a meta-analysis.

4. Meta-Analysis

The overall prevalence of back pain was 43% [confidence interval (CI) of 95%: −1% to 88%] (Figure 2). Statistical heterogeneity between studies was high (I2 = 91.76%, $p < 0.001$). Thus, we performed a meta-regression analysis (tau2 = 0, I2 = 0.00). The analysis showed that heterogeneity had no influence on the result of the analysis. Using Egger's regression test, we found no evidence of publication bias in the meta-analysis of the overall prevalence of pain ($p = 0.081$).

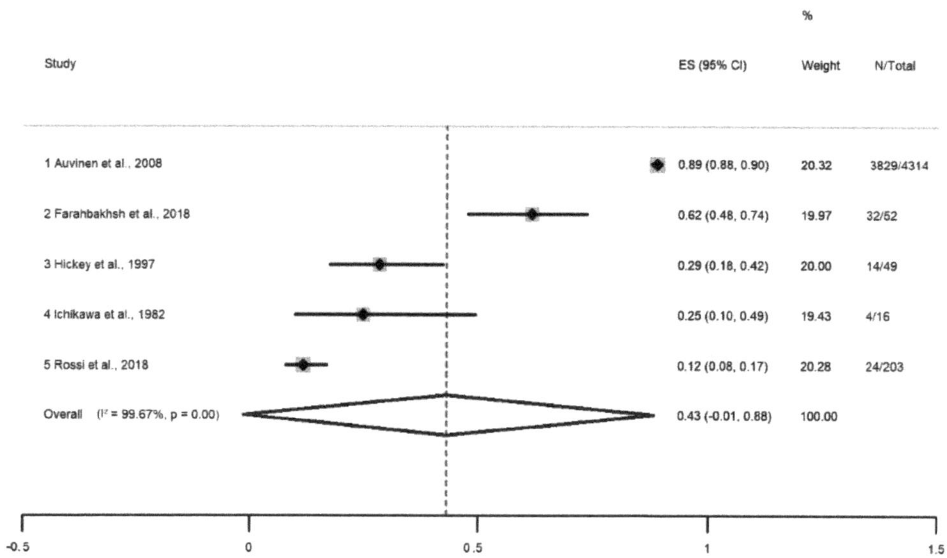

Figure 2. Meta-analysis of overall prevalence of back pain [7,10,37,55,59].

The prevalence of neck pain was 36% [95% CI, 22–50%], back pain was 16% [95% CI, 4–28%] (Figure 3), of low back pain was 26% [95% CI, 16–37%], and of thoracic spine pain was 6% [95% CI, 3–9%]. The combined prevalence of pain was 26% [95% CI, 17–34%]. There was high statistical heterogeneity for both back pain (I2 = 97.04%, $p = 0.001$) and low back pain (I2 = 99.37%, $p = 0.001$). Similarly, we performed a meta-regression analysis (Tau2 = 20.82, I2 = 0.001). The analysis showed that heterogeneity had no influence on the outcome of the analysis. Using the Egger regression test, we found evidence of publication bias in the meta-analysis of pooled prevalence ($p = 0.001$).

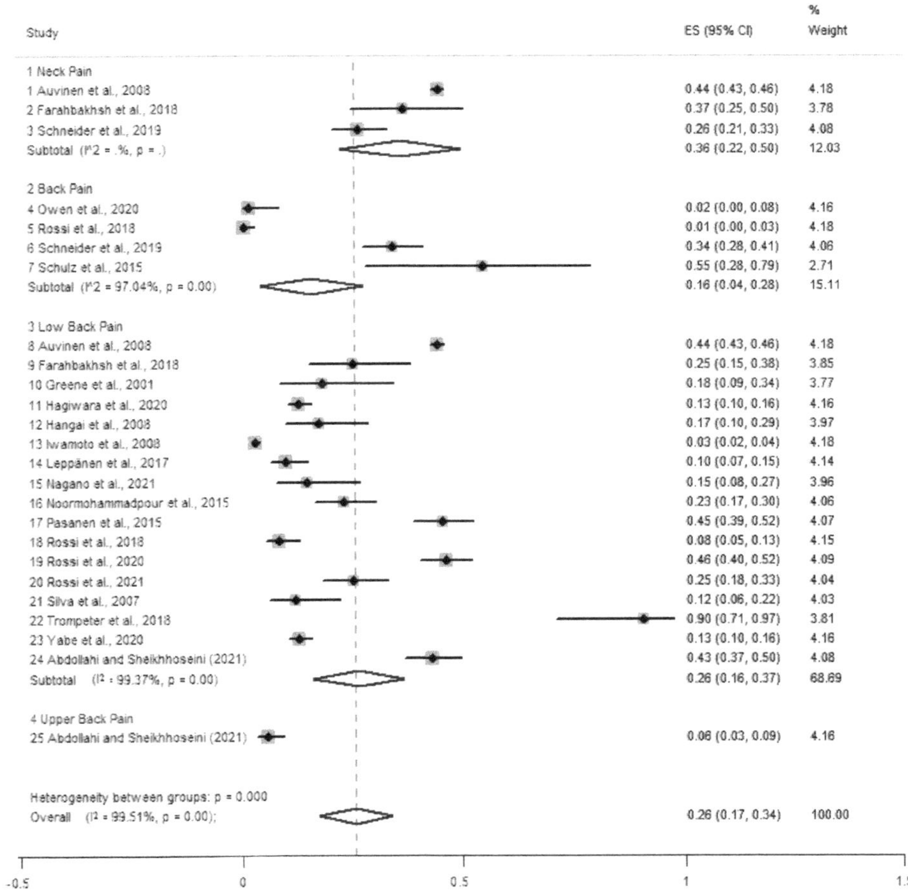

Figure 3. Meta-analysis of prevalence of neck pain, back pain, and low back pain [6–11,34,35,37,38,42,43,46,47,49–51,53,54,56,58].

The pooled prevalence of spine injury and spondylolysis was 10% [95% CI, 4–15%] (Figure 4). The prevalence of spine injury was 3% [95% CI, 1–5%], and spondylolysis was 14% [95% CI, 0.1–27%]. There was high statistical heterogeneity for spondylolysis (I2 = 96.85%, $p = 0.001$). Therefore, we performed a meta-regression (tau2 = 0, I2 = 0.001). The analysis showed that heterogeneity had no influence on the outcome of the analysis. Egger's regression test showed no evidence of publication bias ($p = 0.187$).

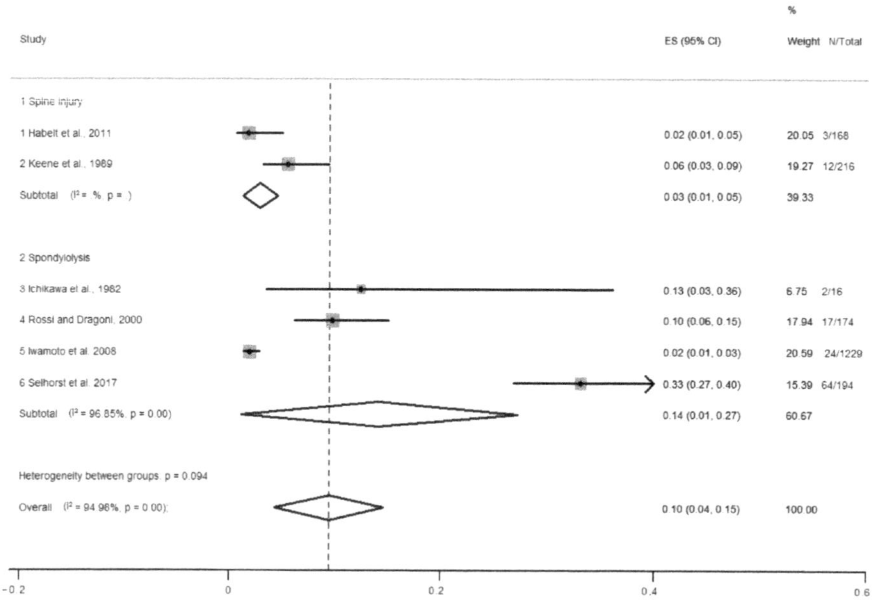

Figure 4. Meta-analysis of pooled prevalence of spinal injury and spondylolysis. [39,40,43,44,48,55].

The pooled prevalence of hyperkyphosis and hyperlordosis was 30% [95% CI, 9–51%] (Figure 5). The prevalence of hyperkyphosis was 28%, and of hyperlordosis was 13%. There was no evidence of statistical heterogeneity (I2 = 0.001).

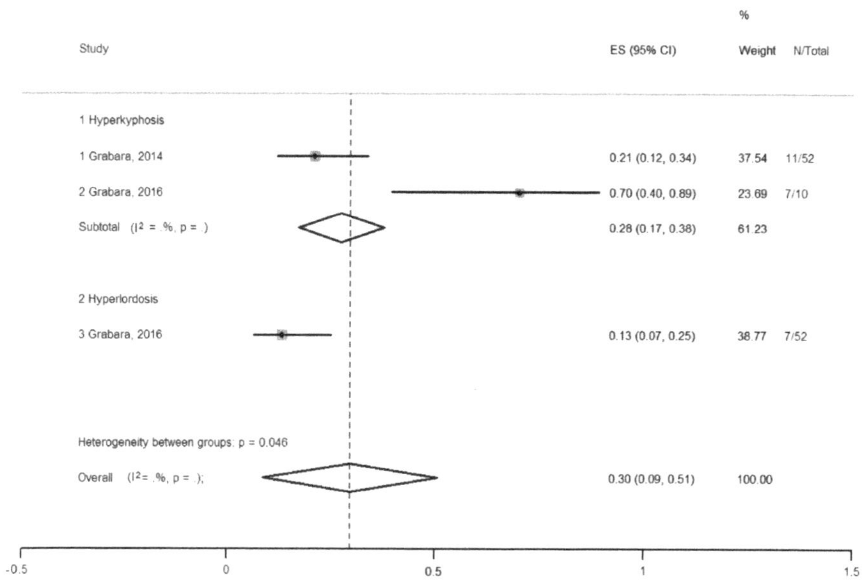

Figure 5. Meta-analysis of pooled prevalence of hyperkyphosis and hyperlordosis [16,52].

5. Discussion

This is the first systematic review to examine the prevalence of back pain and musculoskeletal disorders in basketball players and to ascertain the associated factors. Our findings suggest a high overall prevalence of back pain, with neck pain and low back pain being the most prevalent. Among musculoskeletal disorders, spondylolysis was most prevalent among spinal injuries. The prevalence of hyperkyphosis was highest among postural changes. Sex and age were associated with musculoskeletal disorders in this review, but the data were insufficient to perform a meta-analysis.

This review found an overall prevalence of back pain of 43% in basketball players. These results corroborate the findings of Pasanen et al. [47], who showed that one in six young elite basketball players reported back pain as the predominant pain [47]. Our data indicate a prevalence of neck pain of 36% in basketball, which is consistent with Safiri et al. [60], which showed that the number of cases of neck pain in women was 166.0 million (118.7–224.8), whereas in men it was 122.7 million (87.1–167.5) [59].

Similarly, there were 568.4 million (95% IU: 505.0–640.6 million) cases of low back pain worldwide in 2019 [60], and our study showed a prevalence of 25% of low back pain in basketball players. According to Kim et al. [61], who studied college basketball players, the prevalence of low back pain was 69.8% in the last year of training and 84.1% throughout life [61]. In 2022, low back pain remained the largest contributor to the total number of cases of musculoskeletal disorders. There are 570 million cases worldwide, which account for 7.4% of years lived with disability [62].

Our study found a prevalence of spinal injuries of 3%. In addition to the direct effects of back injury on general health, the indirect effects of this injury could lead to the irreversible loss of future young athletes [1–3]. Furthermore, our study found a pooled prevalence of spine injuries and spondylolysis of 10% and a prevalence of spondylolysis of 14%. Spondylolysis is an anatomic defect or fracture of the pars interarticularis (part of the neural arch located between the superior and inferior articular facets) of the vertebral arch, which occurs in the fifth lumbar vertebra (L5) in 85% to 95% of cases [63]. The higher percentage of spondylolysis can be explained by the risk factors for the development of this injury, which includes repetitive hyperextension and rotation of the lumbar spine that may occur in sports such as basketball [64].

Given the strong association between low back pain and sports activities that involve hyperextension with rotation of the lumbar spine, spondylolysis is a major concern in adolescent athletes [65]. This suggests that more frequent basketball training may have a negative effect on spinal positioning in basketball players [66]. Our study showed a pooled prevalence of hyperkyphosis and hyperlordosis of 30%, with a prevalence of hyperkyphosis of 28% and of hyperlordosis of 13%, in the sample.

In the study of basketball players conducted by Nam et al. [67], the sample had curvature values in the range of 37–42°, which represents a difference of approximately 10° as compared with the normal range [68]. In addition, Kaplan [69], when comparing basketball players and a control group to determine posture, found that the basketball group had a lateral spinal curvature, head positioned in the right sagittal plane, pelvic tilt, and thoracic kyphosis [70].

The first limitation of this study is the limitation may be different periods of back pain; example, we have studies that did not mention the period in which the prevalence was verified [6,38–41,43–46,48,52,55,57], and we also have studies that verified the prevalence in the last three months [33,42] up to the last five years [53]. Second, lack of definition of back pain in many studies, and the fact that different tools were used in the assessment of back pain [69], spinal injuries, and postural changes in the included studies, which makes it difficult to compare the results. Third, some studies could not be fully retrieved. Fourth, most studies had a cross-sectional design, which does not allow an inference of cause and effect. The strengths of this study include the performance of a meta-analysis that provided a general estimate of the prevalence of back pain, spinal injuries, and postural changes in basketball players. To our knowledge, this is the first systematic review to summarize the evidence of the association between these musculoskeletal disorders in basketball players, which allows us to clarify some gaps in the literature and make recommendations for future research.

In this sense, future studies should consider the severity and duration of back pain, spine injuries, and postural changes to prevent players from withdrawing from sports for a long time [71]. The relationship between back pain, spine injuries, and postural changes should be further investigated, and the associated factors need to be analyzed. The results of our study indicate that clarifying the relationship between back pain, injuries, and postural changes is important for developing actions and programs to prevent and treat musculoskeletal disorders, thus contributing to the health and sports performance of basketball players. It is important for health professionals to be aware of the origin of back pain, spinal injuries, and postural changes, as well as the protective mechanisms that can be adopted for more effective interventions.

6. Conclusions

We found a significant overall prevalence of back pain in basketball players. On comparing the prevalence of this pain in the general population, the value found was lower, suggesting that basketball players have a lower prevalence of back pain than the general population. The most prevalent types of back pain were neck pain and low back pain, the most prevalent musculoskeletal disorder was spondylolysis, and the most prevalent postural change was hyperkyphosis.

Supplementary Materials: The following supporting information can be downloaded at: https://www.mdpi.com/article/10.3390/healthcare11081190/s1, Table S1: Database search strategy.

Author Contributions: Conceptualization, S.C.d.C.B., C.R.M., R.M.F.S. and M.N.; methodology, S.C.d.C.B., C.R.M., R.M.F.S. and M.N.; software, S.C.d.C.B., C.R.M., R.M.F.S. and M.N.; validation, S.C.d.C.B., C.R.M., R.M.F.S. and M.N.; formal analysis, S.C.d.C.B., C.R.M., R.M.F.S. and M.N.; investigation, S.C.d.C.B., C.R.M., R.M.F.S. and M.N.; resources, S.C.d.C.B., C.R.M., R.M.F.S. and M.N.; data curation, S.C.d.C.B., C.R.M., R.M.F.S. and M.N.; writing—original draft preparation, S.C.d.C.B., C.R.M., R.M.F.S. and M.N.; writing—review and editing, S.C.d.C.B., C.R.M., R.M.F.S., A.D.V. and M.N.; visualization, S.C.d.C.B., C.R.M., R.M.F.S., A.D.V. and M.N.; supervision, A.D.V. and M.N.; project administration, A.D.V. and M.N. All authors have read and agreed to the published version of the manuscript.

Funding: This research received no external funding.

Institutional Review Board Statement: Not applicable.

Informed Consent Statement: Not applicable.

Data Availability Statement: Additional data can be obtained from the authors.

Acknowledgments: The authors would like to show their gratitude to Instituto Federal Goiano, Universidade Federal de Goiás and the Research Group on Child and Adolescent Health (www.gpsaca.com.br (accessed on 4 April 2023)) for the support.

Conflicts of Interest: The authors declare no conflict of interest.

References

1. Cieza, A.; Causey, K.; Kamenov, K.; Hanson, S.W.; Chatterji, S.; Vos, T. Global estimates of the need for rehabilitation based on the Global Burden of Disease study 2019: A systematic analysis for the Global Burden of Disease Study 2019. *Lancet* **2020**, *396*, 2006–2017. [CrossRef] [PubMed]
2. Williams, A.; Kamper, S.J.; Wiggers, J.H.; O'Brien, K.M.; Lee, H.; Wolfenden, L.; Yoong, S.L.; Robson, E.; McAuley, J.H.; Hartvigsen, J.; et al. Musculoskeletal conditions may increase the risk of chronic disease: A systematic review and meta-analysis of cohort studies. *BMC Med.* **2018**, *16*, 167. [CrossRef]
3. Hartvigsen, J.; Hancock, M.J.; Kongsted, A.; Louw, Q.; Ferreira, M.L.; Genevay, S.; Hoy, D.; Karppinen, J.; Pransky, G.; Sieper, J.; et al. What low back pain is and why we need to pay attention. *Lancet* **2018**, *391*, 2356–2367. [CrossRef]

4. Sheikhhoseini, R.; Kavianifard, M.; Nejad, S.E.H.; Piri, H. Comparison of the Mechanical Energy Transfer of Gait in Female Athletes with and without Non-Specific Chronic Low Back Pain. *Women's Health Bull.* **2020**, *7*, 12–17. Available online: https://womenshealthbulletin.sums.ac.ir/article_46712_f86e34cc6613495d4c04affd80e1cc91.pdf (accessed on 13 January 2021).
5. Ball, J.R.; Harris, C.B.; Lee, J.; Vives, M.J. Lumbar Spine Injuries in Sports: Review of the Literature and Current Treatment Recommendations. *Sports Med.-Open* **2019**, *5*, 26. [CrossRef] [PubMed]
6. Yabe, Y.; Hagiwara, Y.; Sekiguchi, T.; Momma, H.; Tsuchiya, M.; Kanazawa, K.; Itaya, N.; Yoshida, S.; Sogi, Y.; Yano, T.; et al. High prevalence of low back pain among young basketball players with lower extremity pain: A cross-sectional study. *BMC Sports Sci. Med. Rehabil.* **2020**, *12*, 40. [CrossRef]
7. Farahbakhsh, F.; Akbari-Fakhrabadi, M.; Shariat, A.; Cleland, J.A.; Farahbakhsh, F.; Seif-Barghi, T.; Mansournia, M.A.; Rostami, M.; Kordi, R. Neck pain and low back pain in relation to functional disability in different sport activities. *J. Exerc. Rehabil.* **2018**, *14*, 509–515. [CrossRef]
8. Fett, D.; Trompeter, K.; Platen, P. Back pain in elite sports: A cross-sectional study on 1114 athletes. *PLoS ONE* **2017**, *12*, e0180130. [CrossRef]
9. Trompeter, K.; Fett, D.; Brüggemann, G.-P.; Platen, P. Prevalence of Back Pain in Elite Athletes. *Ger. J. Sport. Med. Zeitschrift. Fur. Sport.* **2018**, *69*, 240–246. Available online: https://www.germanjournalsportsmedicine.com/archive/archive-2018/issue-7-8/prevalence-of-back-pain-in-elite-athletes/ (accessed on 31 January 2021). [CrossRef]
10. Rossi, M.K.; Pasanen, K.; Heinonen, A.; Äyrämö, S.; Räisänen, A.M.; Leppänen, M.; Myklebust, G.; Vasankari, T.; Kannus, P.; Parkkari, J. Performance in dynamic movement tasks and occurrence of low back pain in youth floorball and basketball players. *BMC Musculoskelet. Disord.* **2020**, *21*, 350. [CrossRef]
11. Noormohammadpour, P.; Rostami, M.; Mansournia, M.A.; Farahbakhsh, F.; Shahi, M.H.P.; Kordi, R. Low back pain status of female university students in relation to different sport activities. *Eur. Spine J.* **2015**, *25*, 1196–1203. [CrossRef]
12. Zuckerman, S.L.; Wegner, A.M.; Roos, K.G.; Djoko, A.; Dompier, T.P.; Kerr, Z.Y. Injuries sustained in National Collegiate Athletic Association men's and women's basketball, 2009/2010–2014/2015. *Br. J. Sports Med.* **2018**, *52*, 261–268. [CrossRef]
13. Makovicka, J.L.; Deckey, D.G.; Patel, K.A.; Hassebrock, J.D.; Chung, A.; Tummala, S.V.; Hydrick, T.C.; Pena, A.; Chhabra, A. Epidemiology of Lumbar Spine Injuries in Men's and Women's National Collegiate Athletic Association Basketball Athletes. *Orthop. J. Sports Med.* **2019**, *7*, 2325967119879104. [CrossRef]
14. Grabara, M.; Hadzik, A. Postural variables in girls practicing volleyball. *Biomed. Hum. Kinet.* **2009**, *1*, 67–71. [CrossRef]
15. Wojtys, E.M.; Ashton-Miller, J.A.; Huston, L.J.; Moga, P.J. The Association between Athletic Training Time and the Sagittal Curvature of the Immature Spine. *Am. J. Sport. Med.* **2000**, *28*, 490–498. [CrossRef] [PubMed]
16. Grabara, M. Sagittal spinal curvatures in adolescent male basketball players and non-training individuals—A two-year study. *Sci. Sport.* **2016**, *31*, e147–e153. [CrossRef]
17. Borges, S.C.D.C.; Fernandes, M.D.S.V.; Noll, P.R.E.S.; Azevedo, V.D.; Silva, R.M.F.; Mendonça, C.R.; Noll, M. Musculoskeletal disorders in basketball players and associated factors: A systematic review protocol with meta-analysis. *F1000Research* **2021**, *10*, 557. [CrossRef]
18. Page, M.J.; McKenzie, J.E.; Bossuyt, P.M.; Boutron, I.; Hoffmann, T.C.; Mulrow, C.D.; Shamseer, L.; Tetzlaff, J.M.; Akl, E.A.; Brennan, S.E.; et al. The PRISMA 2020 Statement: An Updated Guideline for Reporting Systematic Reviews. *BMJ* **2021**, *372*, n71. [CrossRef] [PubMed]
19. Morgan, R.L.; Whaley, P.; Thayer, K.A.; Schünemann, H.J. Identifying the PECO: A framework for formulating good questions to explore the association of environmental and other exposures with health outcomes. *Environ. Int.* **2018**, *121*, 1027–1031. [CrossRef]
20. Brahme, A. *Comprehensive Biomedical Physics*; Newnes: Oxford, UK, 2014.
21. Zhang, S.; Wadhwa, R.; Haydel, J.; Toms, J.; Johnson, K.; Guthikonda, B. Spine and Spinal Cord Trauma: Diagnosis and Management. *Neurol. Clin.* **2013**, *31*, 183–206. [CrossRef]
22. Beynon, A.M.; Hebert, J.J.; Lebouef-Yde, C.; Walker, B.F. Potential risk factors and triggers for back pain in children and young adults. A scoping review, part II: Unclear or mixed types of back pain. *Chiropr. Man. Ther.* **2019**, *27*, 61. Available online: https://chiromt.biomedcentral.com/articles/10.1186/s12998-019-0281-8 (accessed on 11 January 2021). [CrossRef]
23. Beynon, A.M.; Hebert, J.J.; Hodgetts, C.J.; Boulos, L.M.; Walker, B.F. Chronic physical illnesses, mental health disorders, and psychological features as potential risk factors for back pain from childhood to young adulthood: A systematic review with meta-analysis. *Eur. Spine J.* **2020**, *29*, 480–496. [CrossRef] [PubMed]
24. Noll, M.; Kjaer, P.; Mendonça, C.R.; Wedderkopp, N. Motor performance and back pain in children and adolescents: A systematic review and meta-analysis protocol. *Syst. Rev.* **2020**, *9*, 212. [CrossRef] [PubMed]
25. Reiswig, J. Mendeley. *J. Med. Libr. Assoc.* **2010**, *98*, 193–194. [CrossRef]
26. Ouzzani, M.; Hammady, H.; Fedorowicz, Z.; Elmagarmid, A. Rayyan—A web and mobile app for systematic reviews. *Syst. Rev.* **2016**, *5*, 210. [CrossRef] [PubMed]
27. Noll, M.; Kjaer, P.; Mendonça, C.R.; Wedderkopp, N. Motor performance and back pain in children and adolescents: A systematic review. *Eur. J. Pain* **2022**, *26*, 77–102. [CrossRef] [PubMed]
28. Guyatt, G.H.; Oxman, A.D.; Vist, G.E.; Kunz, R.; Falck-Ytter, Y.; Alonso-Coello, P.; Schünemann, H.J. GRADE: An emerging consensus on rating quality of evidence and strength of recommendations. *BMJ* **2008**, *336*, 924–926. [CrossRef] [PubMed]
29. Downs, S.H.; Black, N. The feasibility of creating a checklist for the assessment of the methodological quality both of randomised and non-randomised studies of health care interventions. *J. Epidemiol. Community Health* **1998**, *52*, 377–384. [CrossRef] [PubMed]

30. Noll, M.; De Mendonça, C.R.; De Souza Rosa, L.P.; Silveira, E.A. Determinants of eating patterns and nutrient intake among adolescent athletes: A systematic review. *Nutr. J.* **2017**, *16*, 46. Available online: https://nutritionj.biomedcentral.com/articles/10.1186/s12937-017-0267-0 (accessed on 12 January 2021). [CrossRef] [PubMed]
31. Farrah, K.; Young, K.; Tunis, M.C.; Zhao, L. Risk of bias tools in systematic reviews of health interventions: An analysis of PROSPERO-registered protocols. *Syst. Rev.* **2019**, *8*, 280. Available online: https://systematicreviewsjournal.biomedcentral.com/articles/10.1186/s13643-019-1172-8 (accessed on 20 April 2021). [CrossRef]
32. Higgins, J.P.T.; Thompson, S.G.; Deeks, J.J.; Altman, D.G. Measuring inconsistency in meta-analyses. *BMJ* **2003**, *327*, 557–560. [CrossRef] [PubMed]
33. Šarčević, Z.; Tepavčević, A. Association between adolescent idiopathic scoliosis and sacroiliac joint dysfunction in young athletes: A case control study. *Medicine* **2019**, *98*, e15161. [CrossRef] [PubMed]
34. Schulz, S.S.; Lenz, K.; Büttner-Janz, K. Severe back pain in elite athletes: A cross-sectional study on 929 top athletes of Germany. *Eur. Spine J.* **2015**, *25*, 1204–1210. [CrossRef]
35. Da Silva, A.S.; Abdalla, R.J.; Fisberg, M. Incidence of musculoskeletal injuries in elite female basketball athletes. *Acta Ortopédica Bras.* **2007**, *15*, 43–46. [CrossRef]
36. Weiss, K.J.; McGuigan, M.R.; Besier, T.F.; Whatman, C.S. Application of a Simple Surveillance Method for Detecting the Prevalence and Impact of Overuse Injuries in Professional Men's Basketball. *J. Strength Cond. Res.* **2017**, *31*, 2734–2739. [CrossRef] [PubMed]
37. Auvinen, J.P.; Tammelin, T.H.; Taimela, S.P.; Zitting, P.J.; Mutanen, P.O.A.; Karppinen, J.I. Musculoskeletal Pains in Relation to Different Sport and Exercise Activities in Youth. *Med. Sci. Sports Exerc.* **2008**, *40*, 1890–1900. [CrossRef]
38. Hagiwara, Y.; Yabe, Y.; Sekiguchi, T.; Momma, H.; Tsuchiya, M.; Kanazawa, K.; Yoshida, S.; Sogi, Y.; Yano, T.; Onoki, T.; et al. Upper Extremity Pain Is Associated with Lower Back Pain among Young Basketball Players: A Cross-Sectional Study. *Tohoku J. Exp. Med.* **2020**, *250*, 79–85. [CrossRef]
39. Habelt, S.; Hasler, C.C.; Steinbrück, K.; Majewski, M. Sport injuries in adolescents. *Orthop. Rev.* **2011**, *3*, e18. [CrossRef]
40. Selhorst, M.; Fischer, A.; MacDonald, J. Prevalence of Spondylolysis in Symptomatic Adolescent Athletes: An Assessment of Sport Risk in Nonelite Athletes. *Clin. J. Sport Med.* **2019**, *29*, 421–425. Available online: https://journals.lww.com/cjsportsmed/Fulltext/2019/09000/Prevalence_of_Spondylolysis_in_Symptomatic.12.aspx (accessed on 13 January 2021). [CrossRef]
41. Meron, A.; McMullen, C.; Laker, S.R.; Currie, D.; Comstock, R.D. Epidemiology of Cervical Spine Injuries in High School Athletes Over a Ten-Year Period. *PM&R* **2018**, *10*, 365–372. [CrossRef]
42. Schneider, S.; Sauer, J.; Berrsche, G.; Schmitt, H. No Pain, No Gain? Prevalence, Location, Context, and Coping Strategies with Regard to Pain Among Young German Elite Basketball Players. *J. Hum. Kinet.* **2019**, *69*, 179–189. [CrossRef] [PubMed]
43. Iwamoto, J.; Takeda, T.; Sato, Y.; Matsumoto, H. Retrospective case evaluation of gender differences in sports injuries in a Japanese sports medicine clinic. *Gend. Med.* **2008**, *5*, 405–414. [CrossRef]
44. Keene, J.S.; Albert, M.J.; Springer, S.L.; Drummond, D.S.; Clancy, W.G.J. Back Injuries in College Athletes. *Clin. Spine Surg.* **1989**, *2*, 190–195. Available online: https://journals.lww.com/jspinaldisorders/Fulltext/1989/09000/Back_Injuries_in_College_Athletes.7.aspx (accessed on 14 January 2021). [CrossRef]
45. Kerr, Z.Y.; Collins, C.L.; Pommering, T.L.; Fields, S.K.; Comstock, R.D. Dislocation/Separation Injuries Among US High School Athletes in 9 Selected Sports: 2005–2009. *Clin. J. Sport Med.* **2011**, *21*, 101–108. Available online: https://journals.lww.com/cjsportsmed/Fulltext/2011/03000/Dislocation_Separation_Injuries_Among_US_High.5.aspx (accessed on 13 January 2021). [CrossRef] [PubMed]
46. Leppänen, M.; Pasanen, K.; Kannus, P.; Vasankari, T.; Kujala, U.M.; Heinonen, A.; Parkkari, J. Epidemiology of Overuse Injuries in Youth Team Sports: A 3-year Prospective Study. *Int. J. Sport. Med.* **2017**, *38*, 847–856. [CrossRef]
47. Pasanen, K.; Rossi, M.; Parkkari, J.; Kannus, P.; Heinonen, A.; Tokola, K.; Myklebust, G. Low Back Pain in Young Basketball and Floorball Players. *Clin. J. Sport Med.* **2016**, *26*, 376–380. Available online: https://journals.lww.com/cjsportsmed/Fulltext/2016/09000/Low_Back_Pain_in_Young_Basketball_and_Floorball.4.aspx (accessed on 14 January 2021). [CrossRef]
48. Rossi, F.; Dragoni, S. The prevalence of spondylolysis and spondylolisthesis in symptomatic elite athletes: Radiographic findings. *Radiography* **2001**, *7*, 37–42. [CrossRef]
49. Rossi, M.K.; Pasanen, K.; Heinonen, A.; Myklebust, G.; Kannus, P.; Kujala, U.M.; Tokola, K.; Parkkari, J. Incidence and risk factors for back pain in young floorball and basketball players: A Prospective study. *Scand. J. Med. Sci. Sport.* **2018**, *28*, 2407–2415. [CrossRef]
50. Rossi, M.K.; Pasanen, K.; Heinonen, A.; Äyrämö, S.; Leppänen, M.; Myklebust, G.; Vasankari, T.; Kannus, P.; Parkkari, J. The standing knee lift test is not a useful screening tool for time loss from low back pain in youth basketball and floorball players. *Phys. Ther. Sport* **2021**, *49*, 141–148. [CrossRef]
51. Abdollahi, S.; Sheikhhoseini, R. Sport-related injuries in Iranian basketball players: Evidence from a retrospective epidemiologic study (2019–20). *Phys. Sportsmed.* **2022**, *50*, 406–413. [CrossRef]
52. Grabara, M. Anteroposterior curvatures of the spine in adolescent athletes. *J. Back Musculoskelet. Rehabil.* **2014**, *27*, 513–519. [CrossRef]
53. Greene, H.S.; Cholewicki, J.; Galloway, M.T.; Nguyen, C.V.; Radebold, A. A History of Low Back Injury is a Risk Factor for Recurrent Back Injuries in Varsity Athletes. *Am. J. Sport. Med.* **2001**, *29*, 795–800. [CrossRef]
54. Hangai, M.; Kaneoka, K.; Hinotsu, S.; Shimizu, K.; Okubo, Y.; Miyakawa, S.; Mukai, N.; Sakane, M.; Ochiai, N. Lumbar Intervertebral Disk Degeneration in Athletes. *Am. J. Sport. Med.* **2008**, *37*, 149–155. [CrossRef]

55. Ichikawa, N.; Ohara, Y.; Morishita, T.; Taniguichi, Y.; Koshikawa, A.; Matsukura, N. An aetiological study on spondylolysis from a biomechanical aspect. *Br. J. Sports Med.* **1982**, *16*, 135–141. [CrossRef] [PubMed]
56. Nagano, Y.; Shimada, Y.; Sasaki, N.; Shibata, M. Prevalence and Burden of Physical Problems in Female College Basketball Athletes: A 135-Day Prospective Cohort Study. *Open Access J. Sports Med.* **2021**, *12*, 55–60. [CrossRef] [PubMed]
57. Nowak, A.; Pytel, A.; Molik, B.; Marszalek, J. Characteristics of injuries of young adult male basketball players. *Adv. Rehabil.* **2019**, *2019*, 35–46. [CrossRef]
58. Owen, P.J.; Hangai, M.; Kaneoka, K.; Rantalainen, T.; Belavy, D.L. Mechanical loading influences the lumbar intervertebral disc. A cross-sectional study in 308 athletes and 71 controls. *J. Orthop. Res.* **2021**, *39*, 989–997. [CrossRef]
59. Hickey, G.J.; Fricker, P.A.; McDonald, W.A. Injuries to Young Elite Female Basketball Players Over a Six-Year Period. *Clin. J. Sport Med.* **1997**, *7*, 252–256. [CrossRef]
60. Safiri, S.; Kolahi, A.-A.; Hoy, D.; Buchbinder, R.; Mansournia, M.A.; Bettampadi, D.; Ashrafi-Asgarabad, A.; Almasi-Hashiani, A.; Smith, E.; Sepidarkish, M.; et al. Global, regional, and national burden of neck pain in the general population, 1990–2017: Systematic analysis of the Global Burden of Disease Study 2017. *BMJ* **2020**, *368*, m791. [CrossRef]
61. Chen, S.; Chen, M.; Wu, X.; Lin, S.; Tao, C.; Cao, H.; Shao, Z.; Xiao, G. Global, regional and national burden of low back pain 1990–2019: A systematic analysis of the Global Burden of Disease study 2019. *J. Orthop. Transl.* **2022**, *32*, 49–58. [CrossRef]
62. Kim, J.H.; Lee, G.H.; Cho, S.T. Prevalence of and risk factors for lower back pain in university basketball players. *Arthrosc. Orthop. Sport. Med.* **2021**, *8*, 54–60. [CrossRef]
63. Ackery, A.D.; Detsky, A.S. Reducing lifelong disability from sports injuries in children. *Can. Med. Assoc. J.* **2011**, *183*, 1235. [CrossRef] [PubMed]
64. Hu, S.S.; Tribus, C.B.; Diab, M.; Ghanayem, A.J. Spondylolisthesis and Spondylolysis. *JBJS* **2008**, *90*, 656–671. Available online: https://journals.lww.com/jbjsjournal/Fulltext/2008/03000/Spondylolisthesis_and_Spondylolysis.25.aspx (accessed on 13 April 2021).
65. Cavalier, R.; Herman, M.J.; Cheung, E.V.; Pizzutillo, P.D. Spondylolysis and Spondylolisthesis in Children and Adolescents: I. Diagnosis, Natural History, and Nonsurgical Management. *JAAOS-J. Am. Acad. Orthop. Surg.* **2006**, *14*, 417–424. Available online: https://journals.lww.com/jaaos/Fulltext/2006/07000/Spondylolysis_and_Spondylolisthesis_in_Children.4.aspx (accessed on 13 April 2021). [CrossRef] [PubMed]
66. Zusman, N.L.; Somogyi, R.D.; Barney, N.A.; Yang, S.; Halsey, M.F. Adolescents with spondylolysis have lower SRS-22 scores than controls and peers with pre-operative idiopathic scoliosis. *Spine Deform.* **2021**, *9*, 135–140. [CrossRef]
67. Nam, H.J.; Lee, J.-H.; Hong, D.-S.; Jung, H.C. The Effect of Wearing a Customized Mouthguard on Body Alignment and Balance Performance in Professional Basketball Players. *Int. J. Environ. Res. Public Health* **2020**, *17*, 6431. [CrossRef]
68. Chen, X.; Biro, I. Lumber Lordosis Motions Monitor Using Formetric Imaging Analysis. *J. Med. Imaging Health Inform.* **2020**, *10*, 1190–1194. [CrossRef]
69. Azevedo, V.D.; Silva, R.M.F.; Borges, S.C.D.C.; Fernandes, M.D.S.V.; Miñana-Signes, V.; Monfort-Pañego, M.; Noll, P.R.E.S.; Noll, M. Evaluation Instruments for Assessing Back Pain in Athletes: A Systematic Review Protocol. *Healthcare* **2020**, *8*, 574. [CrossRef]
70. Kaplan, D. Evaluating the Effect of 12 Weeks Football Training on the Posture of Young Male Basketball Players. *J. Educ. Train. Stud.* **2018**, *6*, 47–53. [CrossRef]
71. Silveira, E.A.; Romeiro, A.M.D.S.; Noll, M. Guide for scientific writing: How to avoid common mistakes in a scientific article. *J. Hum. Growth Dev.* **2022**, *32*, 341–352. [CrossRef]

healthcare

Article

The Effect of Aerobic Exercise on Variation of Oxidative Stress, hs-CRP and Cortisol Induced by Sleep Deficiency

Jong-Suk Park [1], Zsolt Murlasits [2] and Sangho Kim [1,*]

[1] School of Global Sport Studies, Korea University, Sejong-si 30019, Republic of Korea; model200@korea.ac.kr
[2] Institute of Sport Sciences and Physical Education, Faculty of Sciences, University of Pécs, 7624 Pécs, Hungary; drmurla@gamma.ttk.pte.hu
* Correspondence: ksh1905@korea.ac.kr; Tel.: +82-44-860-1371

Abstract: The aim of this study was to investigate the impact of sleep deficiency (SD) on oxidative stress, hs-CRP and cortisol levels and to examine the effects of different intensities of aerobic exercise on these parameters under SD conditions. Thirty-two healthy male university students participated in the study and underwent both normal sleep (NS, 8 h of sleep per night for 3 consecutive days) and SD (4 h of sleep per night for 3 consecutive days). After the SD period, the participants performed treatment for 30 min according to their assigned group [sleep supplement after SD (SSD), low-intensity aerobic exercise after SD (LES), moderate-intensity aerobic exercise after SD (MES), high-intensity aerobic exercise after SD (HES)]. Sleep-related factors were measured at NS and SD, while oxidative stress, hs-CRP and cortisol levels were measured at NS, SD and immediately after treatment by group (AT). The results showed that actual total sleep time (ATST) was significantly reduced during SD compared to NS ($p < 0.001$), while the visual analogue scale (VAS) and Epworth sleepiness scale (ESS) were significantly increased during SD compared to NS ($p < 0.001$). The difference in reactive oxygen metabolites (d-ROMs) and cortisol levels showed a significant interaction effect ($p < 0.01$, $p < 0.001$, respectively), with LES showing a decrease in d-ROMs and cortisol levels compared to SD ($p < 0.05$). Similarly, SSD showed a decrease in cortisol levels compared to SD ($p < 0.05$), while HES led to a significant increase in d-ROMs and cortisol levels compared to SD ($p < 0.05$). Biological antioxidant potential (BAP) and hs-CRP did not show any significant effect ($p > 0.05$). These results suggest that LES is the most effective exercise intensity for mitigating the negative effects of SD.

Keywords: sleep deficiency; aerobic exercise; oxidative stress; hs-CRP; cortisol

Citation: Park, J.-S.; Murlasits, Z.; Kim, S. The Effect of Aerobic Exercise on Variation of Oxidative Stress, hs-CRP and Cortisol Induced by Sleep Deficiency. *Healthcare* **2023**, *11*, 1201. https://doi.org/10.3390/healthcare11081201

Academic Editors: Felipe Aidar and Axel Steiger

Received: 23 February 2023
Revised: 10 April 2023
Accepted: 19 April 2023
Published: 21 April 2023

1. Introduction

Sleep is a biological activity that is necessary for survival and well-being. It plays a vital role in brain function and systemic physiology, such as metabolism, a function of immunological, hormonal and cardiovascular systems [1]. The quantity and quality of sleep are critical factors in physical performance and well-being [2,3]. Although sleep is a critical aspect of human health, sleep deficiency (SD) has become a prevalent problem in modern society. The proportion of people who experience SD has been rapidly increasing in both the United States and South Korea [4,5].

In humans, SD has been associated with various detrimental health effects. SD has been linked to increased activity of the hypothalamic–pituitary–adrenal (HPA) axis, resulting in elevated levels of cortisol and catecholamines, as well as increased oxidative stress, high sensitivity C-reactive protein (hs-CRP) and immune cytokines [6–8]. SD can also impact metabolism and the immune system, leading to a higher risk of diseases such as obesity, type 2 diabetes, hypertension, cardiovascular disease and higher mortality rates [9–11]. Therefore, it is important to find effective interventions to prevent and mitigate the negative effects of SD on health and well-being.

Regular exercise has been widely recommended as an intervention method for chronic diseases, such as obesity, metabolic syndrome, type 2 diabetes and cardiovascular disease [12,13]. Previous studies have shown that regular aerobic exercise can decrease blood pressure, reduce the risk of cardiovascular diseases and improve blood lipid levels [14,15]. Additionally, moderate endurance exercise can enhance immune function [16]. People with SD engage in exercise for leisure and to maintain their health because of its health benefits. However, the effects of aerobic exercise on people with SD have not been extensively studied.

Previous studies have reported that exercise may alleviate health problems associated with SD [17–19]. For instance, one study found that moderate exercise can prevent memory impairment resulting from SD [17]. Another study reported that aerobic exercise performed under SD conditions can reduce metabolites that cause insulin resistance and increase those that alleviate depressive symptoms caused by SD [18]. Moreover, physical activity can have beneficial effects on factors associated with obesity in people with SD [19]. However, people with sleep problems should be cautions when exercising because epidemiologic studies suggest that they have a higher risk of developing coronary heart disease, sudden cardiac death, myocardial infarction, stroke and angina [20,21]. Therefore, people with SD should be careful when applying the same exercise intensity as healthy people due to their higher risk of health complications. Despite this, the efficiency and safety of aerobic exercise as an intervention for health problems caused by SD have not been thoroughly investigated, and the most effective exercise intensity for optimal health benefits under SD conditions remains unclear.

Most sleep-related studies have focused on complete sleep deprivation lasting 24 h. However, in reality, partial sleep restriction, such as SD, is more common and may have different effects on health and performance. Therefore, future studies should investigate the effects of partial sleep restriction on various aspects of health and functioning, as well as the potential benefits of interventions, such as exercise, in mitigating the negative effects of SD.

Therefore, this study aims to examine the negative effects of SD on oxidative stress, hs-CRP and cortisol levels and to investigate the potential effects of aerobic exercise in reducing these the negative impacts. Through this study, we aim to evaluate the efficacy and safety of aerobic exercise under SD conditions.

2. Materials and Methods

2.1. Participants

The study's sample size was determined using G*Power software (version 3.1.9.2), with a power (1-β) of 0.95, a significance level (α) of 0.05 and an effect size of 0.4. This resulted in a calculated sample size of 28 participants. However, to account for a potential dropout rate of 10%, 32 healthy male university students with a normal body mass index (BMI) who did not exercise regularly were recruited. Participants were excluded from the study if they (1) reported a habitual sleep duration of less than 7 h, (2) had an irregular sleep–wake schedule, (3) were diagnosed with a circadian or sleep disorder, (4) were smokers, (5) exercised regularly, (6) had musculoskeletal or neurological disease or (7) had metabolic, cardiovascular or chronic inflammatory disease. All participants were informed about the purpose and procedures of the study and provided written consent. Participants were randomly assigned to one of four groups: the sleep supplement after SD (SSD, $n = 8$), the low-intensity aerobic exercise after SD (LES, $n = 8$), the moderate-intensity aerobic exercise after SD (MES, $n = 8$) and the high-intensity aerobic exercise after SD (HES, $n = 8$) (Figure 1).

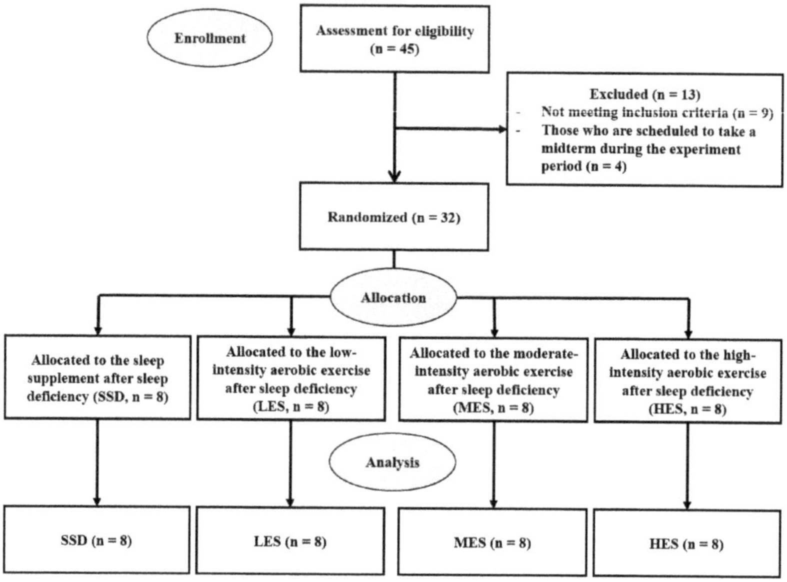

Figure 1. Flow chart.

The study was approved by the Institutional Review Board of Korea University (1040548-KU-IRB-16-286-A-1) before the experiment and was conducted by their guidelines and the Declaration of Helsinki (1964). Additionally, the study was registered with the Clinical Research Information Service (CRIS), a public trial registry of the Republic of Korea (CRIS-KCT0006684).

2.2. Experimental Procedure

The experimental procedure of this study is illustrated in Figure 2. Initially, to determine the exercise intensity of the participants, maximal oxygen uptake (VO_2 max) was measured using a graded treadmill exercise test one week before the normal sleep (NS) period. Subsequently, all participants underwent two different sleep conditions. Referring to previous studies [22,23], the first sleep condition was NS, with 8 h of sleep per night for 3 consecutive nights (from 11 p.m. to 7 a.m.). The second sleep condition was SD, with only 4 h of sleep per night for 3 consecutive nights (from 3 a.m. to 7 a.m.). To maintain consistency, the researchers provided the participants with the same daily diet consisting of 3 meals of 900 kcal each and prohibited any consumption except water after dinner, as well as prohibiting exercise during the experimental periods. The participants' sleep was conducted in their own homes to avoid any disturbances due to an unfamiliar environment. The sleep environment was kept dark and quiet by turning off the lights during sleeping hours, and the researchers supervised the participants using mobile messages to ensure adherence to the experimental protocols. Following the SD periods, participants underwent a 30-min treatment according to their assigned group. Blood samples were collected from participants three times for blood analysis: after normal sleep, after sleep deficiency and immediately after the group treatment (AT).

2.3. Treadmill Test

In the study, the VO_2 max of each participant was measured before the NS period to determine the exercise intensity for the exercise groups. To minimize variability, the measurement was performed at the same time (9:00~11:00), and participants were required to fast overnight and abstain from alcohol consumption the day before the experiment. Participants performed a maximal exercise test using a treadmill (Cosmed T150, h/p

Cosmos, Nussdorf-Traunstein, Germany) and an autonomous respiratory gas analyzer (TrueOne 2400, ParvoMedics, Inc., Salt Lake City, UT, USA). The Bruce protocol was used as the loading method, which involved increasing both speed and grade at 3-min intervals. The Bruce protocol used in this study is considered an appropriate exercise protocol for healthy adults.

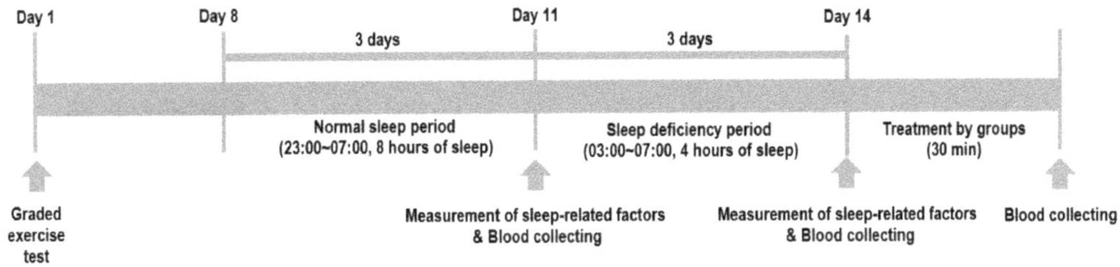

Figure 2. Experimental procedure.

During the exercise, the researcher encouraged the participants to reach their maximum exercise capacity. The researchers monitored the participants' heart rate (HR) and the results of the gas analysis, including ventilation, oxygen consumption, respiration exchange ratio (RER) and respiratory rate. This study determined VO_2 max using objective criteria, including an HR greater than 90% of HRmax (calculated as 220 minus the participant's age), a plateau in the oxygen uptake curve, an RER greater than 1.15 during the test and the participant's report of fatigue. All tests were performed in a room maintained at constant temperature (23~24 °C) and relative humidity (50~55%).

2.4. Measurement of Sleep-Related Factors

The participants in the study were provided with a wearable activity tracker (Fitbit Charge 2, Fitbit Inc., USA) to measure their sleep and daily activity levels during the experiment period. The tracker was worn on the participant's non-dominant wrist and equipped with a built-in triaxial accelerometer, altimeter, heart rate monitor and vibration motor. Fitbit devices are known to have a high accuracy rate of 98% when identifying sleep stages compared to polysomnography and have an inter-device reliability greater than 96% [24]. The actual total sleep time (ATST), sleep time of rapid eye movement (REM), sleep time of light sleep, sleep time of deep sleep, daily activity levels and calorie expenditure during each sleep period were recorded. The mean values of these variables over three days for each sleep period were used for analysis. In addition, we calculated the proportion of REM sleep, light sleep and deep sleep relative to the ATST.

The sleep quality, daytime sleepiness and fatigue of the participants during the experiment period were assessed using the Pittsburgh Sleep Quality Index (PSQI), the Epworth Sleepiness Scale (ESS) and the Visual Analogue Scale (VAS). The PSQI is a 19-item self-rated questionnaire that measures subjective sleep quality. The questions are divided into seven components, with each component scored on a scale of 0 to 3, where higher scores indicate poorer sleep quality. The PSQI score is the sum of the component scores, with a range of 0–21. The ESS is a widely used scale that measures sleepiness and consists of 8 self-rated items, each scored from 0 to 3, that assess a participant's likelihood of dozing off in various everyday situations. The ESS score is calculated as the sum of the individual item scores, with a range of 0–24. The VAS is used to measure subjective fatigue levels and consists of a 10-cm line with endpoints labeled "I do not feel tired." and "I feel extremely tired, exhausted." Participants marked a point on the line that corresponded to their level of fatigue, and the VAS score was calculated as the distance in centimeters from the marked point to the left end of the line. The score ranged from 0 to 10, where higher scores indicate higher levels of fatigue. The PSQI was measured during the recruitment, while the ESS and

VAS were measured at three different time points: during recruitment, after three days of NS and after three days of SD.

2.5. Treatment of Groups

Based on the participants' VO_2 max, they performed aerobic exercise on a treadmill for 30 min according to their assigned groups [LES (40% of VO_2 max), MES (60% of VO_2 max) or HES (80% of VO_2 max)] in the morning after the SD period. The exercise was performed on a treadmill using the Bruce protocol, and the target exercise intensity was maintained by adjusting the speed while maintaining a constant treadmill incline. The tests were performed in a controlled environment at room temperature (23~24 °C) and relative humidity (50~55%). Meanwhile, the SSD group was given a sleep supplement for 30 min after the SD period. They slept on a bed in the laboratory. To create a conducive sleeping environment, the laboratory lights were turned off, and a black curtain was used to block out outdoor lights. Additionally, the temperature and humidity in the laboratory were maintained at 24~25 °C and 40~50%.

2.6. Analysis of Oxidative Stress, hs-CRP and Cortisol

To analyze oxidative stress, hs-CRP and cortisol levels, 10 mL of blood was collected from the median cubital vein of participants at three different time points: at rest after NS, at rest after SD and immediately after treatment by group (AT). After allowing the blood samples to clot for 20 min at room temperature, the serum was separated by centrifugation at 3000 rpm for 15 min at room temperature using a centrifuge (Union 32R, Hanil Co., Inchun, Korea). The collected serum was then stored immediately at −80 °C until analysis.

Serum was used to measure markers of oxidative stress [reactive oxygen metabolites (d-ROMs) and biological antioxidant potential (BAP)] using the free radical analytical system (FRAS4 evolvo; H&D srl, Parma, Italy). The measurement of d-ROMs was performed using the d-ROMs kits (IKIT100 d-ROMs, H&D srl, Parma, Italy). Measurement of BAP was performed with BAP kits (IKIT100 BAP, H&D srl, Parma, Italy). In addition, hs-CRP and cortisol were measured using an immunoassay analysis system (i-CHROMATM reader, Boditech Med Inc., Chuncheon, Korea). Measurement of hs-CRP was performed using hs-CRP assay kits (CFPC-6, Boditech Med Inc., Chuncheon, Korea), and cortisol was measured using cortisol assay kits (CFPC-24, Boditech Med Inc., Chuncheon, Korea).

2.7. Statistical Analysis

The statistical analysis of this study was performed using SPSS software (version 25.0, IBM Corp, Armonk, NY, USA). Normal distribution of all data was confirmed through the Shapiro-Wilk test, and data are presented as mean ± standard deviation.

To evaluate significant differences in participants' baseline characteristics and exercise-related factors among treatment groups, a one-way analysis of variance (ANOVA) was performed, followed by Tukey's post-hoc test. For the analysis of sleep-related factors, oxidative stress, hs-CRP and cortisol levels, two-way repeated measures ANOVA was used to investigate significant differences between the treatment groups and time points. If a significant interaction between the treatment group and time points was identified, a one-way repeated measures ANOVA with Bonferroni post-hoc test was used to compare differences among time points within each group separately. Additionally, a one-way ANOVA with Bonferroni post-hoc test was used to identify differences among treatment groups at each time point. The statistical significance level (α) was set at 0.05 for all analyses.

3. Results

3.1. Participant Characteristics

Table 1 shows the baseline characteristics of the variables for each experimental group. No significant differences were found among groups for any of the factors ($p > 0.05$). Therefore, it identified that the baseline characteristics of groups were homogeneous.

Table 1. The difference in participant baseline characteristics among treatment groups.

Variables	SSD (n = 8)	LES (n = 8)	MES (n = 8)	HES (n = 8)	F	p
Age (years)	20.38 ± 0.52	21.88 ± 2.10	21.38 ± 2.00	21.50 ± 1.77	1.172	0.361
Height (cm)	176.88 ± 4.36	176.88 ± 3.27	174.63 ± 4.47	174.13 ± 5.19	0.887	0.460
Weight (kg)	75.23 ± 8.82	78.68 ± 11.78	70.38 ± 7.13	70.78 ± 5.74	1.657	0.199
BMI (kg/m^2)	24.03 ± 2.14	25.06 ± 2.95	23.05 ± 1.63	23.36 ± 2.21	1.216	0.322
VO_2 max (mL/kg/min)	53.33 ± 4.57	52.12 ± 6.77	51.79 ± 5.37	53.29 ± 7.40	0.134	0.939
PSQI (point)	4.13 ± 0.64	3.25 ± 1.28	3.25 ± 0.71	3.25 ± 1.48	1.285	0.299
ESS (point)	4.00 ± 0.93	3.13 ± 1.46	4.25 ± 1.03	3.63 ± 0.92	1.567	0.219
VAS (point)	1.69 ± 0.39	1.75 ± 0.45	1.60 ± 0.61	1.64 ± 0.28	0.167	0.918

Data are expressed as the mean ± standard deviation. Statistical analysis was performed using one-way ANOVA to analyze the differences among treatment groups. Abbreviations: SSD, sleep supplement after sleep deficiency; LES, low-intensity aerobic exercise after sleep deficiency; MES, moderate-intensity aerobic exercise after sleep deficiency; HES, high-intensity aerobic exercise after sleep deficiency; BMI, body mass index; PSQI, Pittsburgh Sleep Quality Index; ESS, Epworth Sleepiness Scale; VAS, Visual Analogue Scale.

3.2. The Differences in Sleep-Related Factors and Exercise-Related Factors among Groups

Data are expressed as the mean ± standard deviation. The results of the statistical analysis on the differences in sleep-related factors between the treatment group and time are presented in Table 2. The analysis showed significant differences only at the main effect time point for ATST, ESS and VAS ($p < 0.001$). The post-hoc analysis revealed that ATST significantly decreased in the SD compared to the NS ($p < 0.001$), while ESS and VAS significantly increased in the SD compared to the NS ($p < 0.001$). However, there were no significant differences in proportion of REM sleep, proportion of light sleep, proportion of deep sleep and calorie consumption per day.

Table 2. The differences in sleep-related factors among groups.

Variables		NS	SD	F	p
ATST (min)	SSD	397.46 ± 7.97	212.88 ± 19.09 ***	G: 2.218	0.108
	LES	417.25 ± 10.32	220.42 ± 8.68 ***	T: 2556.327	<0.001
	MES	410.13 ± 17.67	227.38 ± 21.37 ***	G*T: 2.438	0.085
	HES	416.54 ± 25.93	208.17 ± 9.96 ***		
REM (%ATST)	SSD	19.73 ± 2.90	20.91 ± 2.60	G: 0.368	0.776
	LES	19.38 ± 6.24	18.39 ± 1.90	T: 3.425	0.075
	MES	20.92 ± 4.51	18.47 ± 2.42	G*T: 1.699	0.190
	HES	20.66 ± 2.86	17.43 ± 4.22		
Light sleep (%ATST)	SSD	62.17 ± 6.06	61.83 ± 6.19	G: 1.059	0.382
	LES	63.58 ± 9.80	66.28 ± 10.90	T: 2.522	0.123
	MES	60.82 ± 5.68	59.78 ± 6.46	G*T: 1.948	0.145
	HES	61.15 ± 3.41	68.02 ± 4.91		
Deep sleep (%ATST)	SSD	18.10 ± 4.92	18.51 ± 3.95	G: 0.661	0.583
	LES	17.03 ± 6.34	19.08 ± 6.41	T: 1.296	0.265
	MES	18.26 ± 3.82	21.75 ± 4.87	G*T: 1.685	0.193
	HES	18.20 ± 3.23	16.30 ± 3.28		
Calorie consumption per day (kcal)	SSD	2889.56 ± 581.33	2819.92 ± 316.27	G: 2.307	0.098
	LES	3149.38 ± 494.18	3183.29 ± 427.43	T: 0.136	0.715
	MES	2802.00 ± 431.44	2745.17 ± 123.59	G*T: 0.866	0.471
	HES	2697.50 ± 156.25	2883.25 ± 314.22		
ESS (points)	SSD	5.00 ± 3.21	11.25 ± 4.83 ***	G: 0.808	0.500
	LES	3.38 ± 1.92	9.38 ± 3.11 ***	T: 90.868	<0.001
	MES	5.25 ± 1.91	10.00 ± 4.28 **	G*T: 2.229	0.107
	HES	3.75 ± 1.75	13.38 ± 5.48 ***		

Table 2. *Cont.*

Variables		NS	SD	*F*	*p*
VAS (points)	SSD	4.29 ± 1.76	7.44 ± 1.58 ***	G: 0.741	0.536
	LES	3.65 ± 1.60	6.99 ± 0.84 ***	T: 176.454	<0.001
	MES	3.26 ± 1.42	6.96 ± 1.26 ***	G*T: 1.262	0.306
	HES	3.36 ± 1.25	7.91 ± 0.76 ***		

Data are expressed as mean ± standard deviation. Statistical analysis was performed using a two-way repeated measures ANOVA. Abbreviations: NS, normal sleep; SD, sleep deficiency; SSD, sleep supplement after sleep deficiency; LES, low-intensity aerobic exercise after sleep deficiency; MES, moderate-intensity aerobic exercise after sleep deficiency; HES, high-intensity aerobic exercise after sleep deficiency; ATST, actual total sleep time; REM, rapid eye movement; ESS, Epworth sleepiness scale; VAS, visual analogue scale; G, group; T, time; G*T, interaction of group and time. *** denotes a significant difference compared to NS within each group ($p < 0.001$). ** denotes a significant difference compared to NS within each group ($p < 0.01$).

Table 3 shows the differences in exercise-related factors among the exercise groups. The results of the analysis indicate that all exercise-related factors among groups were significantly different ($p < 0.001$). Additionally, it was found that all factors were significantly higher in the order of LES, MES and HES. These findings suggest that the sleep intervention was applied equally across all groups, and the exercise intensity assigned to each group was carried out well.

Table 3. The differences in exercise-related factors among groups.

Variables	LES (a)	MES (b)	HES (c)	*F*	*p*	Post-hoc
VO_2 (mL/kg/min)	21.25 ± 2.74	33.71 ± 2.96	43.31 ± 4.93	72.320	<0.001	a < b < c
HR (beats)	120.60 ± 9.36	145.41 ± 9.28	172.15 ± 2.83	87.783	<0.001	a < b < c
Speed (mph)	2.32 ± 0.32	3.08 ± 0.22	4.16 ± 0.65	35.651	<0.001	a < b < c
Calorie consumption (kcal)	250.25 ± 25.52	352.75 ± 56.53	455.88 ± 48.32	41.033	<0.001	a < b < c
Running distance (m)	2297.25 ± 250.89	2912.25 ± 142.36	3651.38 ± 457.08	37.766	<0.001	a < b < c

Data are expressed as the mean ± standard deviation. Statistical analysis was performed using one-way ANOVA. Abbreviations: LES, low-intensity aerobic exercise after sleep deficiency; MES, moderate-intensity aerobic exercise after sleep deficiency; HES, high-intensity aerobic exercise after sleep deficiency; HR, heart rate.

3.3. *The Differences in Oxidative Stress, hs-CRP and Cortisol among Groups*

The differences in oxidative stress, hs-CRP and cortisol levels between groups and time are presented in Table 4. The d-ROMs showed a significant interaction effect ($p < 0.01$) and a main effect of time ($p < 0.001$). The post-hoc analysis indicated a significant increase in d-ROMs levels in all groups after SD compared to NS ($p < 0.001$). However, the LES group showed a significant decrease in d-ROMs levels at AT compared to SD ($p < 0.001$), while the HES group showed a significant increase compared to SD ($p < 0.01$). Additionally, the LES and MES groups had significantly lower d-ROMs levels in AT than the HES group ($p < 0.05$).

Similarly, cortisol levels showed a significant interaction effect ($p < 0.001$) and the main effect of time ($p < 0.001$). Post-hoc analysis revealed a significant increase in cortisol levels after SD compared to NS in all groups ($p < 0.05$). However, in the AT, both the SSD and LES groups showed a significant decrease compared to SD ($p < 0.05$), while the HES group showed a significant increase compared to SD ($p < 0.05$). Moreover, the levels of cortisol in AT were significantly lower in the SSD and LES groups than in the MES and HES groups ($p < 0.05$).

On the other hand, hs-CRP showed a significant difference in the main effect of time ($p < 0.01$), and the post-hoc analysis indicated a significant increase in all groups after SD compared to NS ($p < 0.05$). In contrast, BAP did not exhibit any significant difference in either the main or interaction effect ($p > 0.05$).

Table 4. The differences in oxidative stress, hs-CRP and cortisol between groups and times.

Variables		NS	SD	AT	F	p
d-ROMs (U.Carr)	SSD	279.25 ± 24.01	342.75 ± 15.59 ***	341.00 ± 16.54 ***	G: 1.476	0.242
	LES	262.88 ± 11.19	344.25 ± 11.47 ***	313.88 ± 26.46 ***###a	T: 215.466	<0.001
	MES	262.63 ± 20.15	342.13 ± 28.92 ***	332.00 ± 17.14 ***a	G*T: 3.735	0.003
	HES	274.00 ± 24.28	338.00 ± 24.05 ***	356.00 ± 26.55 ***#		
BAP (μmol/L)	SSD	2414.50 ± 178.93	2426.13 ± 174.40	2431.88 ± 119.59	G: 1.609	0.210
	LES	2473.25 ± 121.38	2584.50 ± 77.97	2562.63 ± 59.85	T: 1.301	0.217
	MES	2497.00 ± 169.42	2491.63 ± 181.33	2481.25 ± 130.23	G*T: 0.580	0.580
	HES	2408.88 ± 159.52	2471.38 ± 181.33	2484.50 ± 100.26		
hs-CRP (mg/L)	SSD	0.36 ± 0.31	0.52 ± 0.47 *	0.42 ± 0.39	G: 0.923	0.442
	LES	0.30 ± 0.13	0.46 ± 0.25 *	0.45 ± 0.24	T: 8.458	0.003
	MES	0.43 ± 0.24	0.75 ± 0.69 *	0.71 ± 0.66	G*T: 0.433	0.780
	HES	0.53 ± 0.43	0.76 ± 0.47 *	0.69 ± 0.51		
cortisol (nmol/L)	SSD	418.26 ± 78.94	478.20 ± 92.46 *	330.05 ± 86.32 *#ab	G: 1.471	0.244
	LES	371.57 ± 81.70	441.61 ± 99.08 *	364.77 ± 47.76 #ab	T: 10.826	<0.001
	MES	364.02 ± 62.19	446.65 ± 103.21 *	448.20 ± 97.23 *	G*T: 6.605	<0.001
	HES	393.50 ± 75.85	455.54 ± 45.63 *	516.90 ± 37.71 *#		

Data are expressed as the mean ± standard deviation. Statistical analysis was performed using a two-way repeated measures ANOVA. Abbreviations: NS, normal sleep; SD, sleep deficiency; AT, immediately after treatment by group; SSD, sleep supplement after sleep deficiency; LES, low-intensity aerobic exercise after sleep deficiency; MES, moderate-intensity aerobic exercise after sleep deficiency; HES, high-intensity aerobic exercise after sleep deficiency; d-ROMS, reactive oxygen metabolites; BAP, biological antioxidant potential; hs-CRP, high sensitive C-reactive protein; G, group; T, Time; G*T, interaction of group and time. * denotes a significant difference compared to NS within each group ($p < 0.05$). *** denotes a significant difference compared to NS within each group ($p < 0.001$). # denotes a significant difference compared to SD within each group ($p < 0.05$). ### denotes a significant difference compared to SD within each group ($p < 0.001$). a denotes a significant difference compared to HES at the AT ($p < 0.05$). b denotes a significant difference compared to MES at the AT ($p < 0.05$).

4. Discussion

This study aimed to investigate the effects of aerobic exercise on oxidative stress, hs-CRP and cortisol levels induced by SD. Through this investigation, the study aimed to confirm the safety and effectiveness of aerobic exercise under SD conditions.

Sleep duration and quality are crucial factors for maintaining good health in humans. To assess participants' sleep status, this study used a wearable activity tracker and a self-reported questionnaire to measure sleep duration and quality. The PSQI is typically used as a tool to evaluate sleep quality [25], while the ESS measures daytime sleepiness [26] and the VAS assesses the current level of fatigue [27]. The study found a significant decrease in ATST after SD compared to NS, while the ESS and VAS scores significantly increased after SD compared to NS. These findings are consistent with previous studies that have shown significant impacts of SD on sleep quantity and quality [28–30]. Regarding the ESS, a score of less than 8 indicates no daytime sleepiness, while a score of 9 or more indicates presence of daytime sleepiness [31]. Daytime sleepiness is directly related to nighttime sleep duration, and it increases when there is complete or partial sleep deprivation [32]. In this study, all groups had an ESS score of 9 or higher after three days of SD, indicating the presence of daytime sleepiness due to lack of sleep. A higher VAS score indicates greater fatigue [33]. In this study, the VAS score also increased more in SD than in NS, indicating that fatigue felt by individuals increased due to lack of sleep. Therefore, three days of SD in this study caused daytime sleepiness and fatigue during the day, indicating that three days of SD was well induced.

In this study, we found no significant difference in the daily calorie consumption between the NS period and SD period, indicating that the participants' physical activity levels remained consistent across both periods. Furthermore, to control for the possible impact of diet on the dependent variables, we provided the same number of calories in the lunch boxes provided to the participants during the experiment period. These measures were taken to ensure that any confounding factors that could affect the dependent variables were minimized and controlled for in this study.

Oxidative stress occurs when the production of reactive oxygen species (ROS) outweighs the endogenous antioxidant capacity. The intrinsic mechanism of inflammation is the generation of ROS, which can lead to a reduction of antioxidants and increased oxidative stress. Oxidative stress can increase inflammation by inducing pro-inflammatory cytokines. Therefore, oxidative stress and inflammation are strongly connected [34]. Oxidative stress plays a crucial role in various human diseases, such as dyslipidemia, diabetes, hypertension, atherosclerosis, metabolic disorders, cardiovascular diseases, cancer and neurodegenerative diseases [35]. In the relationship between sleep and oxidative stress, it is known that sleep reduces oxidative stress by removing oxidants produced during the daytime [36]. In previous studies, it has been shown that SD increases oxidative stress in the brain [37,38] and causes oxidative damage [39,40]. This study found a significant interaction effect between the treatment group and time on the concentration of d-ROMs, which indicates oxidative stress. Specifically, d-ROMs concentrations were significantly higher after SD than NS in all groups. Furthermore, the concentration of d-ROMs after LES was significantly decreased compared to SD, whereas the concentration of d-ROMs after HES was significantly increased compared to SD. In contrast, the concentration of BAP, which represents antioxidant capacity, did not significantly differ between NS and SD. Therefore, this study found that SD for 3 days caused oxidative stress without affecting the concentration of BAP, which represents antioxidant capacity. These findings are consistent with previous studies [37–39]. The increase in oxidative stress observed after SD in this study is likely due to an imbalance between oxidative stress and antioxidant defense mechanisms, as the antioxidant defense mechanisms were not upregulated despite the persistent state of stress. Additionally, exposure to light during nighttime wakefulness can suppress the release of melatonin, which has antioxidant capabilities [41]. Prolonged wakefulness and increased metabolic activity can lead to abnormal ROS production, which can alter cell membrane structure and composition and inhibit antioxidant enzyme activity. Chronic exposure to oxidative stress can impair antioxidant defense mechanisms. Therefore, this study suggests that SD for 3 days acts as a chronic stressor that induces oxidative stress and dysfunction of the antioxidant system. Thus, adequate sleep is crucial for alleviating oxidative stress and maintaining overall health.

Regarding exercise performance under SD, this study found that low- and high-intensity exercise have different effects on oxidative stress induced by SD. These findings are in agreement with previous studies [38,40,42]. A previous study showed that acute sleep deprivation increased oxidative stress in the hippocampus, cortex and amygdala, while treadmill exercise prevented the sleep deprivation-induced increase in oxidative stress [38]. However, exhaustive exercise following SD increased oxidative stress [40,42]. The effect of exercise on the redox balance is complex, depending on the intensity, duration and training level of the exercise [43]. Since exercise increases oxygen consumption, more ROS is produced during exercise than during rest. Excessive exercise induces an increase in oxidative stress, causing lipid peroxidation, DNA damage and protein oxidation in the human body [44,45]. Additionally, excessive exercise causes tissue damage, which induces inflammatory reactions and secondary reactive oxygen compounds produced by neutrophil activity [46]. However, low- and moderate-intensity exercises have been shown to decrease oxidative stress [47,48]. It has also been reported that the exercise intensity, which can protect free radicals and ROS caused by aerobic exercise through self-mechanism, such as antioxidant enzymes without the supplement of external antioxidants, is less than 70% of VO_2 max [49].

On the other hand, few studies have investigated the effect of napping as an intervention method to reduce oxidative stress induced by SD. The present study investigated the effect of SSD on oxidative stress and found no significant effect. This result suggests that a 30-min nap may not provide sufficient time for the activity of antioxidant enzymes to increase and reduce oxidative stress. Therefore, LES is an effective intervention for reducing oxidative stress caused by SD, while HES has a negative effect that may even exacerbate oxidative stress. However, MES and SSD have no impact on changes in oxidative stress.

Exposure to stress from various factors can activate both the nervous and endocrine systems, which may impact immune function [50]. Cortisol, a hormone that reflects stress levels, is a type of glucocorticoid that plays a critical role in maintaining body homeostasis [51]. Continuous exposure to high levels of cortisol due to stress can lead to various pathological conditions, such as weight loss, hyperglycemia, hypertension and the inhibition of immune function [52]. SD and sleep disorders are known to induce stress in the body. In this study, the concentration of cortisol showed an interaction effect between the group and time. Specifically, cortisol concentrations were significantly higher after SD than NS in all groups. Furthermore, the concentrations of cortisol after both LES and SSD were significantly decreased compared to SD, while the concentration of cortisol after HES was significantly increased compared to SD. In contrast, the concentration of cortisol after MES did not significantly differ from that after SD.

This finding is consistent with previous studies that have reported an increase in cortisol levels following SD [33,53–55]. SD activates the HPA axis, resulting in the release of cortisol. Prolonged SD has been shown to cause adrenal hypertrophy, heightened activity in the sympathetic nervous system (SNS) and release of adrenaline [56]. Sleep restriction can also lead to an increase in the ghrelin hormone, which stimulates the HPA axis and cortisol production [41,57]. Moreover, SD activates the SNS, leading to HPA axis activation, which causes stress and a subsequent increase in cortisol levels. Thus, through these mechanisms, the present study suggests that SD for 3 days triggered stress in the body and resulted in an increase in cortisol levels.

The relationship between exercise and cortisol has been well-established in previous studies, which have shown that high-intensity exercise leads to an increase in cortisol levels, while low-intensity exercise results in a decrease in cortisol levels [58,59]. The greater the intensity of exercise, the greater the increase in the circulating levels of epinephrine and norepinephrine [60]. In this study, cortisol concentrations decreased with LES and increased with HES, which is consistent with these findings. The intensity of exercise influences the cortisol response of the HPA axis. During high-intensity exercise, the plasma cortisol concentration is high because the secretion rate is faster than the removal rate. Conversely, the decrease in plasma cortisol levels during low-intensity exercise is due to the removal rate being faster than the secretion rate in the adrenal cortex. These changes seem to be due to a combination of hemoconcentration and HPA axis stimulus [58]. The present study also found a reduction in cortisol levels in the SSD, which is consistent with previous studies [61,62]. The reduction in cortisol levels with napping could be attributed to slow-wave sleep inhibiting the HPA axis and cortisol release, as well as the elevated release of catecholamines by the sympathoadrenal system observed following SD [61,62]. Thus, these findings suggest that SSD and LES are effective interventions for reducing stress by removing cortisol caused by SD. However, HES acts as another stressor, which is negative in the body.

On the other hand, inflammation is a vital immune response that helps maintain tissue homeostasis and combat infection in various harmful conditions [63]. In humans, sleep is known to be closely linked to the immune system, which is a critical defense mechanism in our body. Sleep regulates the function of the immune system and impacts the activation and regulation of inflammatory cytokines [64]. SD or sleep deprivation can have significant adverse effects on the ability to fight infections and alter the intensity and nature of inflammatory responses [65]. Additionally, sleep deprivation can lead to an increase in sympathetic activity, resulting in increased production of pro-inflammatory cytokines, such as IL-1β, IL-6 and TNF-α [66].

CRP is a widely used biomarker of inflammation, and it is considered an indicator of the likelihood of cardiovascular disease. Elevated levels of CRP have been independently associated with the progression of atherosclerosis in humans [67,68]. The hs-CRP provides a more sensitive and accurate measurement of CRP at lower concentration levels. In this study, No significant interaction effect between group and time was observed on hs-CRP concentration. However, the concentration of hs-CRP was significantly increased in the SD compared to NS. This finding is consistent with previous studies that have reported an association between SD and increased hs-CRP levels [69,70]. The mechanism through which SD leads to an increase in CRP is related to the activation of a pro-inflammatory signaling pathway that is regulated by toll-like receptors (TLRs) and nuclear factor kappa-beta (NF-κB) [64]. TLRs, one of the innate immune components, are stimulated by SD and induce the production of inflammatory cytokines [71]. Additionally, SD stimulates the activation of NF-kB in the brain, which is related to sleep regulation [72].

In the present study, the change in hs-CRP according to the treatment groups after SD was also measured. While all treatment groups showed a tendency to decrease compared to after SD, there was no significant difference. This result is consistent with earlier studies [61,73]. It is known that hs-CRP increases during an inflammatory response and is a non-specific response to cell and tissue metabolism, serving as an increased risk factor for cardiovascular disease prognostic factors [74]. In the present study, although there was no positive effect, such as a reduction in hs-CRP, the absence of an increase in hs-CRP after treatment suggests that the treatment groups are not risk factors for cardiovascular disease. However, further research is necessary to clarify the theory behind these results as the amount of nap and exercise duration may not have been sufficient stimuli to induce hs-CRP changes.

One of the main limitations of our study is that the induced state of SD was only for three consecutive days, which may not fully reflect the long-term effects of chronic SD. Although our study demonstrated the positive effects of a single session of aerobic exercise on individuals with SD, caution should be exercised in extrapolating these findings to individuals with chronic SD or shift workers. Additionally, the short duration of our SD protocol may not fully reflect the long-term effects of chronic SD. Furthermore, in this study, the presence or absence of snoring, bruxism and sleep abnormalities, such as chronic obstructive sleep apnea, were determined based on the participants' self-report, which may have limitations. Therefore, future studies should consider using polysomnography to accurately assess the participants' sleep state during participant selection and experiment. Moreover, the single session of aerobic exercise performed in our study may not accurately reflect the effects of regular exercise on SD over an extended period. Further studies are needed to confirm the beneficial effects of exercise in patients with chronic SD or shift workers, as well as to assess the effectiveness of long-term exercise in reducing the adverse effects of SD.

5. Conclusions

This study found that SD increased cortisol and hs-CRP levels, as well as induced oxidative stress. During the SD condition, LES was observed to have a positive effect on reducing oxidative stress and stress hormone levels, whereas HES had negative effects by increasing oxidative stress and stress hormone levels. Therefore, the study suggests that LES is a more suitable exercise intensity for individuals experiencing SD, as it can help reduce oxidative stress and hormone levels that may lead to various health problems. These findings could have significant implications for developing exercise programs for individuals with sleep problems, as well as for the prevention and treatment of related health conditions.

Author Contributions: Conceptualization, J.-S.P. and S.K.; methodology: J.-S.P., Z.M. and S.K.; validation of data: J.-S.P. and S.K.; formal analysis: J.-S.P.; investigation: S.K.; writing original draft: J.-S.P.; visualization: J.-S.P., Z.M. and S.K.; writing—review and editing, Z.M. and S.K.; supervision: S.K.; funding acquisition, S.K. All authors have read and agreed to the published version of the manuscript.

Funding: This work was supported by the National Research Foundation of Korea (NRF) grant funded by the Korea government (MSIT) (No. 2017R1A2B1011886).

Institutional Review Board Statement: The study was approved by the Institutional Review Board of Korea University (1040548-KU-IRB-16-286-A-1) before the experiment and was conducted by their guidelines and the Declaration of Helsinki (1964). Additionally, the study was registered with the Clinical Research Information Service (CRIS), a public trial registry of the Republic of Korea (CRIS-KCT0006684).

Informed Consent Statement: All participants were informed about the purpose and procedures of the study and provided written consent.

Data Availability Statement: The data presented in the study can be available from the corresponding author upon reasonable request.

Acknowledgments: The authors would like to thank all participants who consented and participated in this study.

Conflicts of Interest: The authors declare no conflict of interest.

References

1. Panel, C.C.; Watson, N.F.; Badr, M.S.; Belenky, G.; Bliwise, D.L.; Buxton, O.M.; Buysse, D.; Dinges, D.F.; Gangwisch, J.; Grandner, M.A. Joint Consensus Statement of the American Academy of Sleep Medicine and Sleep Research Society on the Recommended Amount of Sleep for a Healthy Adult: Methodology and Discussion. *J. Clin. Sleep Med.* **2015**, *11*, 931–952.
2. Malhotra, R.K. Sleep, Recovery, and Performance in Sports. *Neurol. Clin.* **2017**, *35*, 547–557. [CrossRef] [PubMed]
3. Castelli, L.; Walzik, D.; Joisten, N.; Watson, M.; Montaruli, A.; Oberste, M.; Roveda, E.; Zimmer, P. Effect of Sleep and Fatigue on Cardiovascular Performance in Young, Healthy Subjects. *Physiol. Behav.* **2022**, *256*, 113963. [CrossRef]
4. Ford, E.S.; Cunningham, T.J.; Croft, J.B. Trends in Self-Reported Sleep Duration among US Adults from 1985 to 2012. *Sleep* **2015**, *38*, 829–832. [CrossRef] [PubMed]
5. Shin, D.; Hur, J.; Cho, K.-H.; Cho, E.-H. Trends of Self-Reported Sleep Duration in Korean Adults: Results from the Korea National Health and Nutrition Examination Survey 2007–2015. *Sleep Med.* **2018**, *52*, 103–106. [CrossRef]
6. Faraut, B.; Boudjeltia, K.Z.; Kerkhofs, M. Neutrophil Counts: An Immune Sensor of Sleep Debt? *J. Sleep Res.* **2012**, *21*, 325–326.
7. McEwen, B.S. Sleep Deprivation as a Neurobiologic and Physiologic Stressor: Allostasis and Allostatic Load. *Metabolism* **2006**, *55*, S20–S23. [CrossRef]
8. Vgontzas, A.N.; Mastorakos, G.; Bixler, E.O.; Kales, A.; Gold, P.W.; Chrousos, G.P. Sleep Deprivation Effects on the Activity of the Hypothalamic–Pituitary–Adrenal and Growth Axes: Potential Clinical Implications. *Clin. Endocrinol.* **1999**, *51*, 205–215. [CrossRef] [PubMed]
9. Covassin, N.; Singh, P. Sleep Duration and Cardiovascular Disease Risk: Epidemiologic and Experimental Evidence. *Sleep Med. Clin.* **2016**, *11*, 81–89. [CrossRef]
10. Shan, Z.; Ma, H.; Xie, M.; Yan, P.; Guo, Y.; Bao, W.; Rong, Y.; Jackson, C.L.; Hu, F.B.; Liu, L. Sleep Duration and Risk of Type 2 Diabetes: A Meta-Analysis of Prospective Studies. *Diabetes Care* **2015**, *38*, 529–537. [CrossRef]
11. Vgontzas, A.N.; Liao, D.; Pejovic, S.; Calhoun, S.; Karataraki, M.; Basta, M.; Fernández-Mendoza, J.; Bixler, E.O. Insomnia with Short Sleep Duration and Mortality: The Penn State Cohort. *Sleep* **2010**, *33*, 1159–1164. [CrossRef]
12. Galasso, L.; Montaruli, A.; Jankowski, K.S.; Bruno, E.; Castelli, L.; Mulè, A.; Chiorazzo, M.; Ricceri, A.; Erzegovesi, S.; Caumo, A.; et al. Binge Eating Disorder: What Is the Role of Physical Activity Associated with Dietary and Psychological Treatment? *Nutrients* **2020**, *12*, 3622. [CrossRef]
13. Janiszewski, P.M.; Ross, R. Physical Activity in the Treatment of Obesity: Beyond Body Weight Reduction. *Appl. Physiol. Nutr. Metab.* **2007**, *32*, 512–522. [CrossRef]
14. Cornelissen, V.A.; Smart, N.A. Exercise Training for Blood Pressure: A Systematic Review and Meta-analysis. *J. Am. Heart Assoc.* **2013**, *2*, e004473. [CrossRef]
15. Farrell, S.W.; Finley, C.E.; Grundy, S.M. Cardiorespiratory Fitness, LDL Cholesterol, and CHD Mortality in Men. *Med. Sci. Sports Exerc.* **2012**, *44*, 2132–2137. [CrossRef]
16. Liu, D.; Wang, R.; Grant, A.R.; Zhang, J.; Gordon, P.M.; Wei, Y.; Chen, P. Immune Adaptation to Chronic Intense Exercise Training: New Microarray Evidence. *BMC Genom.* **2017**, *18*, 29. [CrossRef]
17. Zagaar, M.; Dao, A.; Levine, A.; Alhaider, I.; Alkadhi, K. Regular Exercise Prevents Sleep Deprivation Associated Impairment of Long-Term Memory and Synaptic Plasticity in the CA1 Area of the Hippocampus. *Sleep* **2013**, *36*, 751–761. [CrossRef]
18. Park, J.-S.; Kim, Y.-J.; Heo, W.; Kim, S. The Study of Variation of Metabolites by Sleep Deficiency, and Intervention Possibility of Aerobic Exercise. *Int. J. Environ. Res. Public. Health* **2022**, *19*, 2774. [CrossRef] [PubMed]
19. Park, J.S.; Heo, N.B.; Byun, Y.H.; Hwang, M.H.; Kim, S.H. The Relation Analysis of Obesity and Blood Lipid on Total Physical Activity Level in Short Sleeping Adults. *J. Sport Leis. Stud.* **2014**, *57*, 879–892. [CrossRef]

20. Gami, A.S.; Olson, E.J.; Shen, W.K.; Wright, R.S.; Ballman, K.V.; Hodge, D.O.; Herges, R.M.; Howard, D.E.; Somers, V.K. Obstructive Sleep Apnea and the Risk of Sudden Cardiac Death: A Longitudinal Study of 10,701 Adults. *J. Am. Coll. Cardiol.* **2013**, *62*, 610–616. [CrossRef] [PubMed]
21. Sabanayagam, C.; Shankar, A. Sleep Duration and Cardiovascular Disease: Results from the National Health Interview Survey. *Sleep* **2010**, *33*, 1037–1042. [CrossRef]
22. Dinges, D.F.; Pack, F.; Williams, K.; Gillen, K.A.; Powell, J.W.; Ott, G.E.; Aptowicz, C.; Pack, A.I. Cumulative Sleepiness, Mood Disturbance, and Psychomotor Vigilance Performance Decrements during a Week of Sleep Restricted to 4–5 Hours per Night. *Sleep* **1997**, *20*, 267–277.
23. van Leeuwen, W.M.; Lehto, M.; Karisola, P.; Lindholm, H.; Luukkonen, R.; Sallinen, M.; Härmä, M.; Porkka-Heiskanen, T.; Alenius, H. Sleep Restriction Increases the Risk of Developing Cardiovascular Diseases by Augmenting Proinflammatory Responses through IL-17 and CRP. *PLoS ONE* **2009**, *4*, e4589. [CrossRef] [PubMed]
24. Montgomery-Downs, H.E.; Insana, S.P.; Bond, J.A. Movement toward a Novel Activity Monitoring Device. *Sleep Breath.* **2012**, *16*, 913–917. [CrossRef] [PubMed]
25. Buysse, D.J.; Reynolds III, C.F.; Monk, T.H.; Berman, S.R.; Kupfer, D.J. The Pittsburgh Sleep Quality Index: A New Instrument for Psychiatric Practice and Research. *Psychiatry Res.* **1989**, *28*, 193–213. [CrossRef] [PubMed]
26. Johns, M.W. A New Method for Measuring Daytime Sleepiness: The Epworth Sleepiness Scale. *Sleep* **1991**, *14*, 540–545. [CrossRef] [PubMed]
27. Ofer Levy, M.D.; Amit-Vazina, M.; Segal, R.; Tishler, M. Visual Analogue Scales of Pain, Fatigue and Function in Patients with Various Rheumatic Disorders Receiving Standard Care. *Sat* **2015**, *29*, 22.
28. Lund, H.G.; Reider, B.D.; Whiting, A.B.; Prichard, J.R. Sleep Patterns and Predictors of Disturbed Sleep in a Large Population of College Students. *J. Adolesc. Health* **2010**, *46*, 124–132. [CrossRef]
29. Pikovsky, O.; Oron, M.; Shiyovich, A.; Perry, Z.H.; Nesher, L. The Impact of Sleep Deprivation on Sleepiness, Risk Factors and Professional Performance in Medical Residents. *Sat* **2013**, *30*, 22.
30. Purim, K.S.; Guimarães, A.T.B.; Titski, A.C.K.; Leite, N. Sleep Deprivation and Drowsiness of Medical Residents and Medical Students. *Rev. Colégio Bras. Cir.* **2016**, *43*, 438–444. [CrossRef]
31. Kaliyaperumal, D.; Elango, Y.; Alagesan, M.; Santhanakrishanan, I. Effects of Sleep Deprivation on the Cognitive Performance of Nurses Working in Shift. *J. Clin. Diagn. Res.* **2017**, *11*, CC01–CC03. [CrossRef] [PubMed]
32. Carskadon, M.A.; Dement, W.C. Nocturnal Determinants of Daytime Sleepiness. *Sleep* **1982**, *5*, S73–S81. [CrossRef] [PubMed]
33. Joo, E.Y.; Yoon, C.W.; Koo, D.L.; Kim, D.; Hong, S.B. Adverse Effects of 24 Hours of Sleep Deprivation on Cognition and Stress Hormones. *J. Clin. Neurol.* **2012**, *8*, 146–150. [CrossRef]
34. Kim, C.H.; Vaziri, N.D. Hypertension Promotes Integrin Expression and Reactive Oxygen Species Generation by Circulating Leukocytes. *Kidney Int.* **2005**, *67*, 1462–1470. [CrossRef] [PubMed]
35. Taniyama, Y.; Griendling, K.K. Reactive Oxygen Species in the Vasculature: Molecular and Cellular Mechanisms. *Hypertension* **2003**, *42*, 1075–1081. [CrossRef]
36. Ikeda, M.; Ikeda-Sagara, M.; Okada, T.; Clement, P.; Urade, Y.; Nagai, T.; Sugiyama, T.; Yoshioka, T.; Honda, K.; Inoué, S. Brain Oxidation Is an Initial Process in Sleep Induction. *Neuroscience* **2005**, *130*, 1029–1040. [CrossRef]
37. Alzoubi, K.H.; Khabour, O.F.; Salah, H.A.; Abu Rashid, B.E. The Combined Effect of Sleep Deprivation and Western Diet on Spatial Learning and Memory: Role of BDNF and Oxidative Stress. *J. Mol. Neurosci.* **2013**, *50*, 124–133. [CrossRef] [PubMed]
38. Vollert, C.; Zagaar, M.; Hovatta, I.; Taneja, M.; Vu, A.; Dao, A.; Levine, A.; Alkadhi, K.; Salim, S. Exercise Prevents Sleep Deprivation-Associated Anxiety-like Behavior in Rats: Potential Role of Oxidative Stress Mechanisms. *Behav. Brain Res.* **2011**, *224*, 233–240. [CrossRef]
39. Silva, R.H.; Abílio, V.C.; Takatsu, A.L.; Kameda, S.R.; Grassl, C.; Chehin, A.B.; Medrano, W.A.; Calzavara, M.B.; Registro, S.; Andersen, M.L. Role of Hippocampal Oxidative Stress in Memory Deficits Induced by Sleep Deprivation in Mice. *Neuropharmacology* **2004**, *46*, 895–903. [CrossRef]
40. Kholghi, G.; Alipour, V.; Rezaie, M.; Zarrindast, M.-R.; Vaseghi, S. The Interaction Effect of Sleep Deprivation and Treadmill Exercise in Various Durations on Spatial Memory with Respect to the Oxidative Status of Rats. *Neurochem. Res.* **2023**. [CrossRef]
41. Schüssler, P.; Uhr, M.; Ising, M.; Weikel, J.C.; Schmid, D.A.; Held, K.; Mathias, S.; Steiger, A. Nocturnal Ghrelin, ACTH, GH and Cortisol Secretion after Sleep Deprivation in Humans. *Psychoneuroendocrinology* **2006**, *31*, 915–923. [CrossRef]
42. Liu, W.; Luo, R.; Tang, C.; Zhao, X.; Zeng, S. Serumal oxidative stress status of acute exhaustive exercise rats following sleep deprivation. *Chin. J. Tissue Eng. Res.* **2007**, *53*, 7710–7713.
43. Pingitore, A.; Lima, G.P.P.; Mastorci, F.; Quinones, A.; Iervasi, G.; Vassalle, C. Exercise and Oxidative Stress: Potential Effects of Antioxidant Dietary Strategies in Sports. *Nutrition* **2015**, *31*, 916–922. [CrossRef]
44. Malaguti, M.; Angeloni, C.; Garatachea, N.; Baldini, M.; Leoncini, E.; Collado, P.S.; Teti, G.; Falconi, M.; Gonzalez-Gallego, J.; Hrelia, S. Sulforaphane Treatment Protects Skeletal Muscle against Damage Induced by Exhaustive Exercise in Rats. *J. Appl. Physiol.* **2009**, *107*, 1028–1036. [CrossRef] [PubMed]
45. Michailidis, Y.; Jamurtas, A.Z.; Nikolaidis, M.G.; Fatouros, I.G.; Koutedakis, Y.; Papassotiriou, I.; Kouretas, D. Sampling Time Is Crucial for Measurement of Aerobic Exercise-Induced Oxidative Stress. *Med. Sci. Sports Exerc.* **2007**, *39*, 1107–1113. [CrossRef]

46. Leeuwenburgh, C.; Heinecke, J.W. Oxidative Stress and Antioxidants in Exercise. *Curr. Med. Chem.* **2001**, *8*, 829–838. [CrossRef]
47. Finaud, J.; Lac, G.; Filaire, E. Oxidative Stress: Relationship with Exercise and Training. *Sports Med.* **2006**, *36*, 327–358. [CrossRef] [PubMed]
48. Gimenes, C.; Gimenes, R.; Rosa, C.M.; Xavier, N.P.; Campos, D.H.S.; Fernandes, A.A.H.; Cezar, M.D.M.; Guirado, G.N.; Cicogna, A.C.; Takamoto, A.H.R. Low Intensity Physical Exercise Attenuates Cardiac Remodeling and Myocardial Oxidative Stress and Dysfunction in Diabetic Rats. *J. Diabetes Res.* **2015**, *2015*, 457848. [CrossRef]
49. Eom, W.S. The Effect of 12 Weeks Aerobic Exercise with Different Exercise Intensity on Lipid Peroxidation (MDA) and Antioxidant Enzyme (SOD). *Exer. Sci.* **2004**, *13*, 335–350.
50. Woo, J.M.; Kim, G.M.; Kim, S.A. A Case of Mental Ill Health Caused by Job Stress after Job Reallocation. *Korean J. Occup. Environ. Med.* **2003**, *15*, 205–212. [CrossRef]
51. Miller, D.B.; O'Callaghan, J.P. Neuroendocrine Aspects of the Response to Stress. *Metab. Clin. Exp.* **2002**, *51*, 5–10. [CrossRef]
52. Boscaro, M.; Barzon, L.; Fallo, F.; Sonino, N. Cushing's Syndrome. *Lancet* **2001**, *357*, 783–791. [CrossRef]
53. Guyon, A.; Balbo, M.; Morselli, L.L.; Tasali, E.; Leproult, R.; L'Hermite-Balériaux, M.; Van Cauter, E.; Spiegel, K. Adverse Effects of Two Nights of Sleep Restriction on the Hypothalamic-Pituitary-Adrenal Axis in Healthy Men. *J. Clin. Endocrinol. Metab.* **2014**, *99*, 2861–2868. [CrossRef] [PubMed]
54. Song, H.; Sun, X.; Yang, T.; Zhang, L.; Yang, J.; Bai, J. Effects of Sleep Deprivation on Serum Cortisol Level and Mental Health in Servicemen. *Int. J. Psychophysiol.* **2015**, *96*, 169–175. [CrossRef]
55. Thorsley, D.; Leproult, R.; Spiegel, K.; Reifman, J. A Phenomenological Model for Circadian and Sleep Allostatic Modulation of Plasma Cortisol Concentration. *Am. J. Physiol. Endocrinol. Metab.* **2012**, *303*, E1190–E1201. [CrossRef] [PubMed]
56. Rechtschaffen, A.; Gilliland, M.A.; Bergmann, B.M.; Winter, J.B. Physiological Correlates of Prolonged Sleep Deprivation in Rats. *Science* **1983**, *221*, 182–184. [CrossRef]
57. Spiegel, K.; Tasali, E.; Penev, P.; Cauter, E.V. Brief Communication: Sleep Curtailment in Healthy Young Men Is Associated with Decreased Leptin Levels, Elevated Ghrelin Levels, and Increased Hunger and Appetite. *Ann. Intern. Med.* **2004**, *141*, 846–850. [CrossRef] [PubMed]
58. Hill, E.E.; Zack, E.; Battaglini, C.; Viru, M.; Viru, A.; Hackney, A.C. Exercise and Circulating Cortisol Levels: The Intensity Threshold Effect. *J. Endocrinol. Investig.* **2008**, *31*, 587–591. [CrossRef]
59. Hayes, L.D.; Bickerstaff, G.F.; Baker, J.S. Interactions of Cortisol, Testosterone, and Resistance Training: Influence of Circadian Rhythms. *Chronobiol. Int.* **2010**, *27*, 675–705. [CrossRef]
60. Natale, V.M.; Brenner, I.K.; Moldoveanu, A.I.; Vasiliou, P.; Shek, P.; Shephard, R.J. Effects of Three Different Types of Exercise on Blood Leukocyte Count during and Following Exercise. *Sao Paulo Med. J.* **2003**, *121*, 9–14. [CrossRef]
61. Faraut, B.; Boudjeltia, K.Z.; Dyzma, M.; Rousseau, A.; David, E.; Stenuit, P.; Franck, T.; Van Antwerpen, P.; Vanhaeverbeek, M.; Kerkhofs, M. Benefits of Napping and an Extended Duration of Recovery Sleep on Alertness and Immune Cells after Acute Sleep Restriction. *Brain. Behav. Immun.* **2011**, *25*, 16–24. [CrossRef]
62. Vgontzas, A.N.; Pejovic, S.; Zoumakis, E.; Lin, H.-M.; Bixler, E.O.; Basta, M.; Fang, J.; Sarrigiannidis, A.; Chrousos, G.P. Daytime Napping after a Night of Sleep Loss Decreases Sleepiness, Improves Performance, and Causes Beneficial Changes in Cortisol and Interleukin-6 Secretion. *Am. J. Physiol. Endocrinol. Metab.* **2007**, *292*, E253–E261. [CrossRef] [PubMed]
63. Medzhitov, R. Inflammation 2010: New Adventures of an Old Flame. *Cell* **2010**, *140*, 771–776. [CrossRef]
64. Lee, S.J.; Kim, J. Inflammation and Insufficient or Disordered Sleep. *Korean J. Clin. Lab. Sci.* **2015**, *47*, 97–104. [CrossRef]
65. Chennaoui, M.; Sauvet, F.; Drogou, C.; Van Beers, P.; Langrume, C.; Guillard, M.; Gourby, B.; Bourrilhon, C.; Florence, G.; Gomez-Merino, D. Effect of One Night of Sleep Loss on Changes in Tumor Necrosis Factor Alpha (TNF-α) Levels in Healthy Men. *Cytokine* **2011**, *56*, 318–324. [CrossRef]
66. Palagini, L.; Maria Bruno, R.; Gemignani, A.; Baglioni, C.; Ghiadoni, L.; Riemann, D. Sleep Loss and Hypertension: A Systematic Review. *Curr. Pharm. Des.* **2013**, *19*, 2409–2419. [CrossRef] [PubMed]
67. Chen, J.; Huang, L.; Song, M.; Yu, S.; Gao, P.; Jing, J. C-Reactive Protein Upregulates Receptor for Advanced Glycation End Products Expression and Alters Antioxidant Defenses in Rat Endothelial Progenitor Cells. *J. Cardiovasc. Pharmacol.* **2009**, *53*, 359–367. [CrossRef]
68. Zhou, Y.; Han, W.; Gong, D.; Man, C.; Fan, Y. Hs-CRP in Stroke: A Meta-Analysis. *Clin. Chim. Acta* **2016**, *453*, 21–27. [CrossRef]
69. Irwin, M.R.; Olmstead, R.; Carroll, J.E. Sleep Disturbance, Sleep Duration, and Inflammation: A Systematic Review and Meta-Analysis of Cohort Studies and Experimental Sleep Deprivation. *Biol. Psychiatry* **2016**, *80*, 40–52. [CrossRef]
70. Chiang, J.-K. Short Duration of Sleep Is Associated with Elevated High-Sensitivity C-Reactive Protein Level in Taiwanese Adults: A Cross-Sectional Study. *J. Clin. Sleep Med.* **2014**, *10*, 743–749. [CrossRef]
71. Irwin, M.R.; Wang, M.; Campomayor, C.O.; Collado-Hidalgo, A.; Cole, S. Sleep Deprivation and Activation of Morning Levels of Cellular and Genomic Markers of Inflammation. *Arch. Intern. Med.* **2006**, *166*, 1756–1762. [CrossRef] [PubMed]
72. Kuo, T.-H.; Pike, D.H.; Beizaeipour, Z.; Williams, J.A. Sleep Triggered by an Immune Response in Drosophila Is Regulated by the Circadian Clock and Requires the NFκB Relish. *BMC Neurosci.* **2010**, *11*, 17. [CrossRef] [PubMed]

73. Sauvet, F.; Arnal, P.J.; Tardo-Dino, P.E.; Drogou, C.; Van Beers, P.; Bougard, C.; Rabat, A.; Dispersyn, G.; Malgoyre, A.; Leger, D. Protective Effects of Exercise Training on Endothelial Dysfunction Induced by Total Sleep Deprivation in Healthy Subjects. *Int. J. Cardiol.* **2017**, *232*, 76–85. [CrossRef] [PubMed]
74. Ridker, P.M.; Bassuk, S.S.; Toth, P.P. C-Reactive Protein and Risk of Cardiovascular Disease: Evidence and Clinical Application. *Curr. Atheroscler. Rep.* **2003**, *5*, 341–349. [CrossRef] [PubMed]

healthcare

MDPI

Review

A Scoping Review with Bibliometric Analysis of Para-Rowing: State of the Art and Future Directions

Luca Puce [1], Carlo Biz [2,*], Carlo Trompetto [1,3], Lucio Marinelli [1,3], Antonio Currà [4], Luca Cavaggioni [5,6], Matteo Formica [3,7], Vittorio Vecchi [2], Maria Chiara Cerchiaro [2], Khaled Trabelsi [8,9], Nicola Luigi Bragazzi [10,*] and Pietro Ruggieri [2]

1 Department of Neuroscience, Rehabilitation, Ophthalmology, Genetics, Maternal and Child Health (DINOGMI), University of Genoa, 16132 Genoa, Italy
2 Orthopedics and Orthopedic Oncology, Department of Surgery, Oncology and Gastroenterology (DiSCOG), University of Padova, 35128 Padova, Italy
3 IRCCS Ospedale Policlinico San Martino, 16132 Genoa, Italy
4 Academic Neurology Unit, A. Fiorini Hospital, 04019 Terracina, Italy
5 Department of Biomedical Sciences for Health, Università Degli Studi di Milano, 20129 Milan, Italy
6 Obesity Unit and Laboratory of Nutrition and Obesity Research, Department of Endocrine and Metabolic Diseases, Istituto Auxologico Italiano IRCCS, 20145 Milan, Italy
7 Orthopedic Clinic, Department of Integrated Surgical and Diagnostic Sciences (DISC), University of Genoa, 16132 Genoa, Italy
8 Research Laboratory: Education, Motricity, Sport and Health, EM2S, LR19JS01, University of Sfax, Sfax 3000, Tunisia
9 High Institute of Sport and Physical Education, University of Sfax, Sfax 3000, Tunisia
10 Laboratory for Industrial and Applied Mathematics (LIAM), Department of Mathematics and Statistics, York University, Toronto, ON M3J 1P3, Canada
* Correspondence: carlo.biz@unipd.it (C.B.); robertobragazzi@gmail.com (N.L.B.)

Abstract: Para-rowing is a format of rowing practiced by people with different types of disabilities, thanks to adapted equipment set-ups and regulations. Para-rowing made its debut recently at the 2008 Paralympic Games. According to the mandate of the "International Paralympic Committee", para-rowers should be enabled to pursue sporting excellence. Therefore, rigorous research is needed in terms of well-designed, high-quality studies. To the best of our knowledge, there are no systematic appraisals of the body of scholarly evidence in the field of para-rowing. As such, a scoping review enhanced by bibliometric analyses was carried out to provide a comprehensive synthesis of knowledge related to para-rowing for the perusal of practitioners and athletes. By mining eighteen major databases, 17 studies were retained in the present review. The included studies were found to focus on a range of aspects involving health, the etiology of injuries (n = 5), psychological and physiological responses (n = 5), performance, biomechanical analysis (n = 4), and new analytical approaches for kinematic assessments and predictions of mechanical outputs in para-rowers (n = 3). The scholarly community on para-rowing consists of 78 researchers, 16 (20.51%) of whom are highly interconnected. The most prolific author was Smoljanović T., from Croatia, with three items/documents. In total, 93.6% of scholars have authored one single document. Topological features indicated a highly fragmented and dispersed, poorly connected community characterized by a high number of clusters and a low strength of connections. In terms of publication years, the first scholarly article dates back to 2008, with four articles (23.5%) published in the current year, showing an increasing interest in this para-sports discipline. Finally, gaps in current research on para-rowing were identified in terms of overlooked topics, including sports nutrition, doping, and psychological aspects in para-rowers other than those with visual impairment.

Keywords: paralympic sport; para-rowing; scoping review; bibliometric analysis

check for updates

Citation: Puce, L.; Biz, C.; Trompetto, C.; Marinelli, L.; Currà, A.; Cavaggioni, L.; Formica, M.; Vecchi, V.; Cerchiaro, M.C.; Trabelsi, K.; et al. A Scoping Review with Bibliometric Analysis of Para-Rowing: State of the Art and Future Directions. *Healthcare* **2023**, *11*, 849. https://doi.org/10.3390/healthcare11060849

Academic Editors: Felipe Aidar and Herbert Löllgen

Received: 11 January 2023
Revised: 28 February 2023
Accepted: 9 March 2023
Published: 13 March 2023

1. Introduction

Para-rowing or adaptive rowing or adaptive sculling is a format of rowing practiced by people with different types of disabilities, especially thanks to adapted equipment set-ups and regulations [1]. These adaptations and/or technical modifications are needed to facilitate its practice in the presence of impairments in muscle and joint functions (i.e., strength, or range of motion, ROM), movement deficiencies (athetosis/hypertonia/ataxia), differences in physical structure (lower limb deficiency/amputation), and/or a range of sensory and physical disabilities (visual impairment, orthopedic impairments, and upper/lower motor neuron syndrome) [2]. Para-rowing made its debut for the first time, at the 2008 Paralympic regattas in Beijing, in 1000 m races. This distance was adopted at the 2012 and 2016 Paralympic games, when, in 2017, a new rule change doubled the distance. At the Tokyo 2020 Paralympic games, para-rowing used the same distance as its Olympic counterpart—2000 m. According to the para-rowing classification regulations of the World Rowing Association [3], para-rowers are assigned to three different sport classes based on sex/gender and level of physical function: PR1 (with minimal or no trunk function, with preserved arm and shoulder function to propel the boat, and with poor sitting balance, for which they require to be strapped to the boat/seat), PR2 (with functional use of arms and trunk, but weak/absent leg function to slide the seat), or PR3 (with residual function in the legs which allows para-rowers to slide the seat). PR3 functional class also includes rowers with intellectual and vision impairment. Para-rowing can be practiced either individually or as a team discipline, composed of two or four para-rowers. Specifically, there are four events: two singles (PR1 Men's Single Sculls—PR1M1x and PR1 Women's Single Sculls—PR1W1x), one of a man and woman couple (PR2 Mixed Double Sculls—PR2Mix2x) and one with a double couple of two men and two women (PR2 Mixed Double Sculls—PR2Mix2x). The hulls of para-rowing boats are generally larger and heavier than able-bodied single and double sculls and are equipped with special seats that vary according to the athlete's disability. For example, in the PR1 and PR2 sports classes, the boats have fixed seats with backrests. Sometimes, in the case of athletes belonging to the PR1 sports class, the boats can have further modifications and be equipped with flotation systems that act as stabilizers (known as pontoons) and are fixed to the oarlocks of the boat to ensure further lateral balancing (optional for PR2 rowers). Further adaptions can be represented by strapping: chest straps are needed for PR1 rowers for increased stability, whereas knee straps are used for PR2 rowers to prevent any flexion or extension of the knee during rowing. Able-bodied rowers apply techniques that maximize the drive of the legs, followed by the back and arms in a synchronized manner [4]. When parts of this kinetic chain are lost due to physical impairments, these techniques cannot be implemented. This results in decreased performance and impaired rowing technique by the para-rowers especially in sports classes PR1 and PR2 [5]. For example, the PR1 rowers' current world records are approximately 3 min slower (about 7 vs. 10 min) than their counterparts without physical disabilities [6]. Furthermore, the former has a higher stroke rate at the expense of a shorter stroke length [7]. However, competition times and time discrepancies between sports classes have improved a lot in recent years probably due to the growing technical and scientific support for these athletes [8]. Finally, despite the disability-induced fatigue, para-athletes undergo training frequencies, volumes, and intensities very similar to able-bodied athletes of the same level [9].

According to the mandate of the "International Paralympic Committee" (IPC), para-rowers should be enabled to pursue sporting excellence [10]. Therefore, rigorous research is needed in terms of well-designed studies. To the best of our knowledge, there are no systematic appraisals of the body of scholarly evidence in the field of para-rowing. The existing body of literature includes anecdotal stories and personal experiences, as well as single case reports and manuals/handbooks. There exist reviews on rowing, but, in para-rowing, the areas of the athlete's body that are subjected to higher force transmission are altered [5].

As such, given the unique challenges of para-rowing, this investigation was carried out to provide a comprehensive synthesis of knowledge related to this para-sports discipline for the perusal of both practitioners and athletes, to better inform training protocols and conditioning strategies, as well as for the para-rowing scholarly community, to offer guidance for future studies and research.

2. Materials and Methods

2.1. Study Protocol, Study Conceptual Design, and Development

An a priori study protocol was drafted before formally commencing the study research, but it could not be submitted and registered within the "International prospective register of systematic reviews" (PROSPERO,) in that PROSPERO does not accept anymore scoping reviews or literature scans. Given our research aims, the present literature review was performed and designed as a scoping review enhanced by bibliometric analyses [11]. Arksey and O'Malley's five-step methodology [12] was followed as well as the "Patterns-Advances-Gaps-Evidence for Practice-Recommendations" (PAGER) framework developed by Bradbury-Jones et al. [13]. More in detail, the aim was to synthesize the body of currently available research on para-rowing in terms of evidence, knowledge and practice gaps, recommendations and policies, prospects, and directions in the field, for the benefit of both the sports and scholarly communities.

Arksey and O'Malley's five-step methodology [12] consists of (i) identifying and developing the research question(s), (ii) identifying the body of relevant scholarly studies, (iii) selecting the studies to retain in the review, based on well-defined inclusion/exclusion criteria, (iv) extracting and charting the data (either quantitative or qualitative), and (v) collating, summarizing, and reporting the major findings of the studies included in the present review.

Building on the previous steps, the PAGER framework [12] consists of (i) synthesizing the key findings in terms of unique key themes/thematic areas (P), (ii) discovering and dissecting the dynamic underlying these themes (A), (iii) identifying underdeveloped/overlooked themes that warrant future research (G), (iv) advising relevant stakeholders from the sports and scholarly communities and informing/shaping practices (E), and (v) guiding future research (R).

2.2. Identification of Relevant Studies

The following keywords were used: "adaptive rowing", "adaptive sculling", "para rowing", "para rower", "para rowers", "paralympic rower", and "paralympic rowers". These keywords were combined in a search string using the "OR" Boolean connector. Eighteen major electronic, scholarly databases (namely, Scopus, Gale Academic OneFile, IngentaConnect Journals, ProQuest Central, Science Citation Index Expanded (Web of Science), PubMed Central, Factiva, ROAD or Directory of Open Access Scholarly Resources, Journals@Ovid Complete, Taylor and Francis Journals Complete, Taylor and Francis CRKN Social Science and Humanities, Web of Science, Taylor & Francis CRKN Science and Technology, Nursing and Allied Health Database, Web of Science—Science Citation Index Expanded—2022, Scholars Portal Journals: Open Access, Web of Science—Social Sciences Citation Index—2022, and Scholars Portal Journals) were mined from inception using the Omni academic search tool, without language filters/restrictions. The search was conducted up to 17 February 2022. Citation information was exported using the "Research Information Systems" (RIS) file format, which is a standardized tag format developed to enable citation programs to exchange and share data related to citation information.

2.3. Study Selection and Inclusion/Exclusion Criteria

As recommended by the Joanna Briggs Institute (JBI), the Population (or Participants), Concept, and Context (PCC) mnemonic was employed as a guide to constructing a clear and meaningful title and framing and developing the subsequent research question(s).

Inclusion and exclusion criteria [14] were the following: studies focusing on para-rowing and with athletes, exposed to any kind of interventional strategy (if any, either a warm-up or training/conditioning program, nutritional supplementation, pharmacological intervention, recovery strategy, etc.), compared against other disabled or able-bodied athletes, assessed in terms of age, sex/gender, functional sport class, years of experience and training, competing level—regional, national, international-, type of disability/impairment and if congenital/acquired). Studies were retained if they focused on any outcome relevant to para-rowing (kinematic, biomechanical, physiological, psychological or psycho-physiological, epidemiological, methodological, etc.). Any study design was deemed eligible: any original study with sufficient (quantitative/qualitative) details was scrutinized. Reviews were not included but were scanned to increase the chance of finding any relevant study, whereas commentaries, letters to the editor, editorials, expert opinions, or technical notes without sufficient details were discarded. Articles were also excluded if focusing on other Paralympic disciplines or reporting data in such a way that it was not possible to disaggregate them, and extract data related to para-rowing only. Finally, non-peer-reviewed items (including conference proceedings and abstracts, theses/dissertations, (e)books/(e)book chapters, newsletter articles, and reports, among others) were not deemed eligible.

2.4. Bibliometrics Analysis

Using ad hoc extraction, processing, visualization, and bibliometric software, including VOSviewer version 1.6.18, Gephi, and Cytoscape [15], data extracted from MEDLINE via PubMed and RIS reference manager files were mapped and visualized as graphs/networks and investigated from a quantitative standpoint, by computing a range of several graph theory/network-related indicators. Finally, the number of papers per year was also visualized as a time series. Further details are described in our previous publication, to which the reader is referred [15].

3. Results

3.1. Literature Search

The initial literature search yielded a pool of 157 items (n = 18 from Scopus, n = 17 from Gale Academic OneFile, n = 15 from IngentaConnect Journals, n = 14 from ProQuest Central, n = 12 from Science Citation Index Expanded (Web of Science), n = 11 from PubMed Central, n = 8 from Factiva, n = 8 from ROAD, n = 7 from Journals@Ovid Complete, n = 7 from Taylor & Francis Journals Complete, n = 6 from Taylor & Francis CRKN Social Science and Humanities, n = 6 from Web of Science, n = 6 from Taylor & Francis CRKN Science and Technology, n = 5 from the Nursing and Allied Health Database, n = 5 from Web of Science—Science Citation Index Expanded—2022, n = 4 from Scholars Portal Journals: Open Access, n = 4 Web of Science—Social Sciences Citation Index—2022, and n = 4 from Scholars Portal Journals).

A total of 111 items were duplicated and were, as such, removed, and 46 items were inspected, by looking at the title and/or abstract. Based on the inclusion/exclusion criteria, eleven items were discarded based on their study design/format (newsletter articles (n = 4), books and ebooks (n = 3), theses and dissertations (n = 2), reports (n = 1), book chapters (n = 1)). Out of 35 studies, further ten studies were excluded not being related to the research topic/research aims or questions. Twenty-five studies were scrutinized in the full text. Out of these 25 items, 8 studies [16–23] were excluded with reason (n = 2, not reporting sufficient quantitative/qualitative details; n = 4, not disaggregating data according to para-sports discipline; n = 2 reporting details of another study (letter and response to the editor). Finally, 17 studies [5–7,24–37] were retained in the present scoping review. The included studies were found to focus on a range of aspects involving health, the etiology of injuries (n = 5), psychological and physiological responses (n = 5), performance, biomechanical analysis (n = 4), and new analytical approaches for kinematic assessments and predictions of mechanical outputs in para-rowers (n = 3). The flow-chart adopted in the present scoping review is pictorially depicted in Figure 1.

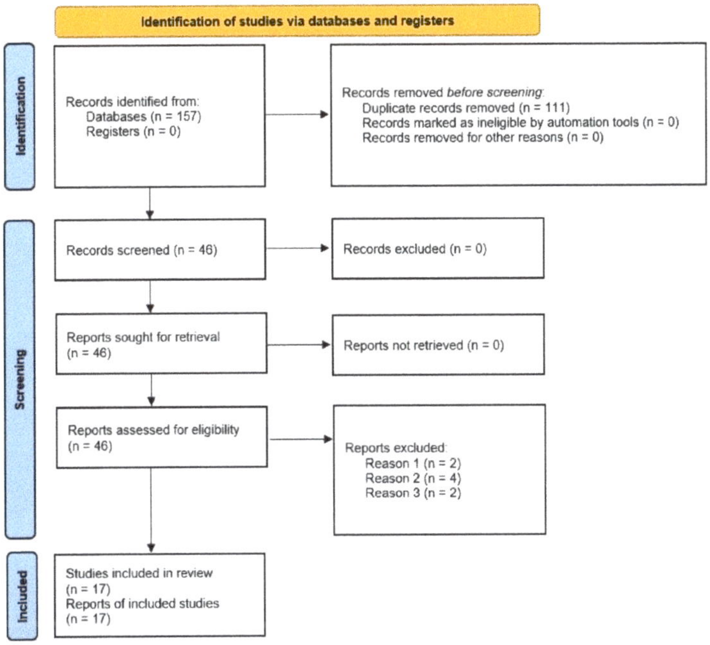

Figure 1. Flowchart adopted in the present scoping review.

3.2. Psychological and Physiological Responses in Para-Rowing

This section included five studies [24–28], which are overviewed in Table 1. Of these, four studies [24–27] investigated physiological responses to para-rowing. Only one study [28], on the other hand, investigated the psychological aspects.

Zoppi et al. [24] examined changes in anthropometric (body mass and skinfold), physiological (muscle strength, power at 4 mM blood lactate, and fatigue index), and performance (1000 m trial) parameters throughout 32 weeks of training in a sample of eight Afro-Brazilian para-rowers (aged 25 ± 5.3 years). Four participants had a unilateral traumatic above-the-knee amputation, one subject had a unilateral hip disarticulation, one individual had Class 5 cerebral palsy, one subject had Class 4 cerebral palsy, and one subject had a neurological impairment (a complete lesion at the L3 level). The training protocol was designed in 4 phases (phase 1 or incorporation phase: 6 weeks, phase 2 or basic phase: 6 weeks, phase 3 or specific phase: 12 weeks, and phase 4 or competitive phase: 8 weeks), which were different in terms of volume and intensity, intending to achieve peak form in the last phase. The studied anthropometric characteristics remained stable during the initial phases of training with a significant drop in body mass in the penultimate ($p \leq 0.05$) and last phase ($p \leq 0.1$) and in body fat in the last phase ($p \leq 0.05$). Regarding physiological parameters, muscle strength significantly improved in all three trials performed (lying T-bar row, barbell bench press, and 45° leg press with one repetition max) after phase 3, with a peak in phase 4 ($p < 0.01$) In addition, during maximal intensity exercise (1000 m trials), power at 4 mM blood lactate and fatigue index improved in all phases and in the penultimate and last phase, respectively ($p < 0.01$). However, no significant variation in power output was found. Finally, performance improved immediately after phases 1 and 2 ($p < 0.01$ compared to the start of training) with a peak after phase 3, which was maintained until the end of phase 4 ($p < 0.01$ compared to the start of training and to phases 1 and 2).

Table 1. Main characteristics of the study included in the present scoping review concerning psychological and physiological responses in para-rowing. Abbreviations: BF (body fat); BM (body mass); EMG (electromyography); FI (fatigue index); IF (Impact Factor); NA (not available); SCI (spinal cord injury); w (weeks); y (years).

Study, Study Design	Journal, IF (2022), Scimago Ranking, Subject Areas and Categories	Sample Size, Sex, Age, Experience, Type of Disability	Sports Class	Aim(s)	Outcome Measures	Findings
Zoppi et al., 2014 [24]; Longitudinal study	Journal of Exercise Physiology Online, NA, Q4; Medical Phsyiology	8; Male; 25 ± 5.3 y; International level; Physical disability	3 LTAMix4+, 3 TAMix2x, 2 ASM1x	Evaluation of physiological and performance changes during a training season (32 w)	BM, muscular strength, power at 4 mM blood lactate, FI, and a 1000 m time-trial	Outcomes improved
Porto et al., 2008; [25]; Comparative (case–control) study	Research in Sports Medicine; 3.661; Q1–Q2; Medicine (miscellaneous); orthopedics and sports medicine; physical trherapy, sports therapy and rehabilitation; sports science	8; Male; 30 ± 9.25 y; International level; Physical disability	NA	Evaluation of anthropometric and physical characteristics of motor disabled para-rowers	Upper body anaerobic threshold, peak, mean, and lower anaerobic power, peak anaerobic power to weight ratio, FI, BF, handgrip strength	Similar strength levels and fatigue, but a higher anaerobic threshold and peak anaerobic weight/power ratio, similar BM, but lower BF with respect to disabled controls; higher FI and lower anaerobic threshold with lower anaerobic performance capacity and higher weight/peak anaerobic power ratio with respect to able-bodied controls
Nowak et al., 2017 [26]; Case series	Journal of Human Kinetics; 2.923; Q1–Q2, Physical therapy, sports therapy and rehabilitation; medical physiology; sports science	2; 1 male, 1 female; 26 and 38 y; from 6 to 10 y of training experience; Physical disability	TAMix2x	Evalution of the impact of the Progressive Efficiency Test on a rowing ergometer on clinical chemistry parameters	Cardiorespiratory fitness, blood count, white blood cell distribution, and 30 clinical chemistry variables	Changes in study variables, with a few exceptions (no changes in B lymphocyte distribution)
Tiller et al., 2018 [27]; Case report	Journal of Applied Physiology; 3.880; Q1–Q2; Medicine (miscellaneous); Physiology and medical physiology; Sports science	1; Male; 28 y; Elite; SCI	ASM1x	Evaluation of diaphragm fatigue on a rowing ergometer (1000 m)	Pulmonary ventilation and gas exchange, diaphragm EMG-derived indexes of neural respiratory drive, and intrathoracic pressure-derived indexes of respiratory mechanics	Decrease in diaphragm neuromuscular efficiency during exercise
Rich et al., 2022 [28]; Interpretative Phenomeno-logical Analysis	International Journal of Environmental Research and Public Health; 4.614; Q2; Public health, environmental and occupational health	8; 7 female and 1 male; 40.5 ± 16.3 y (22–66); Elite; Visual impairment (4 B3, 2 B2, 2 B1)	NA	To capture elite para-rowers' embodied experiences with their engagement in sport	Benefits and challenges, barriers, and facilitators	Empowerment through para-rowing, rowing through feel, changing perceptions, and establishing influential, supportive, inclusive, and meaningful relationships.

To understand whether high training loads lead to higher levels of fitness, Porto et al. [25] compared the physiological (aerobic, anaerobic, strength levels, and fatigue index) and anthropometric (body mass and body fat) parameters of eight top para-rowers (aged 30 $\pm$ 9.25 years) matched with a control group of eight wheelchair basketball players (aged 45.4 $\pm$ 9.6 years) who did not practice regularly. Furthermore, to better understand how motor disabilities compromise performance in the para-rower group, a comparison with literature data concerning high-level able-bodied rowers was conducted on the studied parameters. The authors showed that para-rowers tended to have similar strength levels and fatigue, but a higher anaerobic threshold ($p < 0.01$) than the control disabled group. However, among all the anaerobic performance outcomes studied, only the peak anaerobic weight/power ratio was significantly higher (6.5 $\pm$ 1.1 W/Kg vs. 7.5 $\pm$ 0.9 W/Kg, $p = 0.0387$). Regarding the anthropometric parameters, the two groups of people with disabilities had similar body mass, but the para-rowers had significantly lower body fat. Compared with high-level able-bodied rowers, the para-rowers showed ten times greater fatigue levels and a 37% lower anaerobic threshold with lower anaerobic performance capacity. Specifically, mean, and lower anaerobic power were 26% and 54% lower, respectively. Contrary to all the trends, the weight/peak anaerobic power ratio was 25% higher in para-rowers.

While the physiological response and adaption to exercise have been highly studied in able-bodied athletes, there is a significant dearth of data concerning post-exercise changes in athletes with disabilities.

In this regard, Nowak et al. [26] recruited two para-rowers from a Polish adaptive rowing settle TAMix2x qualified for the Paralympic Games in Rio, 2016. The authors conducted a progressive test on a rowing ergometer until exhaustion, assessing a range of parameters including cardiorespiratory fitness, complete blood count, white blood cell distribution, and thirty clinical chemistry variables. Exercise-induced changes could be detected for all metabolites under study (glucose, creatinine, urea, uric acid, and both total and direct bilirubin), as well as for albumin, total protein levels, aspartate transaminase activity, and white blood cell count. Concerning the latter two variables, a post-exercise increase was found for both parameters, but with a different post-recovery response, characterized by a two-fold decrease and increase, respectively. The percentages of natural killer cells and total T lymphocytes were found to be higher and lower after the exercise, respectively. Of interest, although changes in T lymphocyte subset distribution could be noted (with higher and lower percentages of suppressor/cytotoxic and helper/inducer cells), no changes in B lymphocyte distribution could be observed.

Tiller et al. [27] conducted a case study to evaluate diaphragm fatigue (measuring pre- and post-exercise changes in the transdiaphragmatic pressure response of contraction to anterolateral magnetic stimulation of the phrenic nerves) in a spinal cord injured para-rower (aged 28 years old) during a test on a rowing ergometer (1000 m). In addition, pulmonary ventilation and gas exchange, diaphragm electromyography (EMG)-derived indices of neural respiratory drive, and respiratory mechanics indices derived from intrathoracic pressure were evaluated. The para-rower completed the test in 3.89 min at an average power of 248 W, with peak oxygen uptake and pulmonary ventilation of 3.46 L/min and 150 L/min, respectively. The blood lactate concentration reached 15.8 mmol/L (8 min after exercise). The breath/stroke ratio was 1:1 in the initial part of the test (0–400 m). Subsequently (after 400 m), a reduction in respiratory time and an increase in ventilatory drive resulted in a breath/stroke ratio of 2:1. From baseline, the reduction in transdiaphragmatic pressure at 15–20 min after exercise was 33% (61 vs. 41 cm H_2O) with a partial recovery of 12% at 30–35 min (41 vs. 50 cm H_2O) (10–15% reduction is already considered muscle fatigue). The muscle fatigue that occurred was associated with a reduction in the neuromuscular efficiency of the diaphragm. Specifically, the inspiratory transdiaphragmatic pressure decreased throughout the test, whereas the EMG value tended to increase (16.0 vs. 3.0 as the ratio of the two outcome measures studied). Finally, after the test, due to an increase in tidal volume (from 2.7 to 3.1 L), an increase in absolute ventilation was found (from 13.6 to

18.7 L), whereas the transdiaphragmatic pressure and the EMG of the diaphragm decreased (133 to 53 cmH_2O; 91 to 58% of the maximal value of the Root Mean Square, RMS_{max}).

In addition, Rich et al. [28] aimed to capture elite para-rowers' embodied experiences with their engagement in sport, in terms of benefits and challenges, barriers, and facilitators, by conducting an interpretative phenomenological analysis. The authors recruited eight participants with a visual impairment aged 40.5 ± 16.3 years old (22–66), representing three countries: seven of them were female, and one was male. Five of the participants' visual impairments were congenital. According to the USABA Visual Impairment Classification System, four participants reported having B3 vision (low vision), two reported having B2 vision (travel vision), and two reported having B1 vision (blind). The authors were able to extract four major themes: namely, (i) empowerment through para-rowing, (ii) rowing through feel, (iii) changing perceptions, and (iv) establishing influential, supportive, inclusive, and meaningful relationships. Para-rowing allowed them to overcome fears related to their impairment and cope with their acuity/vision loss, abate apprehensions, gain independence and psychological benefits, including resilience, self-esteem, confidence, and self-advocacy, and generate opportunities as well as social connections, relationships, and networking, in terms of shared commonalities and mutual support. Para-rowers were also able to better manage their time and build self-discipline, set, and achieve new goals. Finally, para-rowing was considered more accessible for people with visual impairments than other Paralympic sports disciplines, being "based on feel, regardless of sight" and given that no additional equipment and special accommodations/modifications were necessary for rowing and racing with a visual impairment. On the other hand, participants also experienced negative feelings and emotions, due to ableism derived from ignorance and the stigma of visual impairment: para-rowers had to make an effort to either formally or informally educate their coaches and peers toward acceptance of their disability. Para-rowing was perceived as a second-class and less legitimate sport in comparison with rowing, and para-rowers' athleticism, and achievements were underscored with respect to their able-bodied counterparts.

3.3. *Health, Injuries, and Risk Factors in Para-Rowing*

Five studies [5,7,29–31] explored the determinants of health and injuries, including their risk factors, in para-rowing. Studies included are briefly overviewed in Table 2.

Smolyanović et al. [7] conducted a case study on the management of a rib stress fracture in a PR1 rower (23 years old) caused by pressure occurring in the chest strap area during hyperflexion of the torso in the catch position. Two different strategies were followed by the coaching staff: (1) pause from activity until the athlete no longer felt tenderness on palpation and deep inspiration (5 weeks) (2) the use of a protective orthosis to relieve the pressure of the chest strap on the chest has been studied and applied. However, the para-rower during the forced stop was unable to maintain the specific physical form of rowing, compromising his athletic preparation and giving up participating in a world championship.

Soo Hoo et al. [29] conducted a retrospective survey of non-elite athletes with disabilities to assess their demographics, training regimen, and injuries. Of the total of 61 athletes approached, 43 athletes participated in the study and five of whom practiced rowing (4 females and 1 male). The main and extremely interesting finding was that none of the rowers were injured in the last 12 months, whereas around half of participants in sled hockey (50%), wheelchair basketball (44%) and wheelchair rugby (43%) suffered an injury. Data on training regimens, on the other hand, are in line with those of rowers. Specifically, most athletes trained in their sport almost all year round with an average of about 8 h per week. Regarding the diagnosis, spinal cord injury was the most frequent (51%) and was predominant in rowers (100%). Finally, athletes with disabilities involved in rowing and basketball had a higher incidence of spasticity (80% and 100%, respectively) than the overall average (42%).

Table 2. Main characteristics of the study included in the present scoping review concerning health, injuries, and risk factors in para-rowing. Abbreviations: IF (Impact Factor); NA (not available); SCI (spinal cord injury); y (years).

Study, Study Design	Journal, IF (2022), Scimago Ranking, Subject Areas and Categories	Sample Size, Sex, Age, Experience, Type of Disability	Sports Class	Aim(s)	Outcome Measures	Findings
Smoljanović et al., 2013 [5]; Review study	British Journal of Sports Medicine; 18.473; Q1; Medicine (miscellaneous); orthopedics and sports medicine; physical therapy, sports therapy and rehabilitation; sports science	NA	NA	To evaluate the potential injuries and health risks associated with regulation changes in para-rowing	NA	No potential health risks
Smolyanović et al., 2011 [7]; Case study	Croatian Medical Journal; 2.415; Q3; Medicine (miscellaneous)	1; male; 23 y; <1 y of experience training; physical disability (SCI, T9 complete paraplegia)	PR1	To evaluate the management of a rib stress fracture	NA	The athletic preparation was compromised and the athlete had to give up participating in a world championship
Soo Hoo et al., 2019 [29]; Retrospective survey	Journal of Injury, Function and Rehabilitation; 2.218; Q1–Q2–Q3; Medicine (miscellaneous); neurology and clinical neurology; physical therapy, sports therapy and rehabilitation; rehabilitation; sports science	5; 4 females, 1 male; 3 30–40 y; Non-elite; Physical disability	NA	To evaluate and assess the demographics, training regimen, and injury rate in para-rowing	Self-report data	No injuries reported in para-rowers. Half of the participants in other sports had been injured. Training regimen was 8 h per week. SCI was the most common disability
Thornton et al., 2017 [30]; Review study	Sports medicine; 11.928; Q1; Medicine (miscellaneous); orthopedics and sports medicine; physical therapy, sports therapy and rehabilitation; sports science	NA	NA	Analysis of the risk factors of disability-dependent injuries	NA	Volume and intensity of exercise, as well as the type of impairment, as the main risk factors of injury
Nowak et al., 2022 [31]; Comparative, survey-based study	International Journal of Environmental Research and Public Health; 4.614; Q2; Public health, environmental and occupational health	35; 27 males and 8 females; $14 \leq 29$ y; NA; Physical disability	NA	To evaluate the degree of adoption of healthy lifestyles	Self-report data	Experience, training volume and intensity, education, social, economic-financial, and employment status, and marital status were predictors of the uptake of health-related behaviors

As of 2017, the race distance for para-rowers has changed from 1000 m to 2000 m for all events. The review by Smoljanović et al. [5] analyzes the potential injuries and health risks associated with this regulation change in PR1 and PR2 rowers. The authors find no significant evidence that increasing distance and consequently race time leads to more problems. However, it is recommended to modify the training program in order to prepare the athletes for the doubled distance.

Thornton et al.'s review [30] analyzed the risk factors of disability-dependent injuries. For example, a para-rower with a leg strength deficit will compensate more with the other leading to imbalances in the entire kinetic chain and contributing to possible lower back injuries. Furthermore, the skin lesion of the stump caused by the prosthesis in the amputee athlete can compromise athletic preparation until the skin heals. Additionally, special attention should be paid to athletes with spinal cord injuries. Athletes with this condition may be at increased risk for bone fractures and/or joint dislocations and pressure sores. The latter problem can cause an increase in muscle spasticity and in case of severe infection even death. Finally, the chest straps create high pressure on the athlete's chest, placing them at risk for rib stress fractures.

Nowak et al. [31] performed a comparative study, assessing the degree of adoption of healthy lifestyles in people with disabilities, using wheelchairs in their daily lives, and practicing wheelchair basketball, wheelchair rugby, and para-rowing. The sample consisted of 176 participants, aged 19–49 years old (mean age 34.41 $\pm$ 8.56 years), mostly under 40, from all over Poland, men (83.5%), city-dwellers, in formal relationships, with higher education, working professionally, and assessing their financial situation as good. 35 were para-rowing athletes. Compared with the average participants, they were more often unmarried, lived off their pension, and rated their finance lower. 42.9% of them won the title of the Polish Champions. With respect to the others, they reported a lower intensity of health behaviors in general and in four categories of correct eating habits, preventive behaviors, positive mental attitude, and health practices. Compared with Polish Champions, amateur rowers with disabilities achieved the poorest results in terms of preventive behaviors but the highest results in positive mental attitudes. Training every day and having the longest weekly exercise, having received higher education, being in a better financial situation, being employed, married, and being rural residents correlated with a greater intensity of health-related behaviors.

3.4. Biomechanics of the Para-Rowing Strokes

Four studies [6,32–34] provided insight into the biomechanics of rowing in the Paralympic setup. These are briefly overviewed in Table 3.

In one case study, Schaffert and Mattes [32] used biomechanical measurements combined with questionnaires to examine the effects of acoustic feedback on mean boat speed in seven training sessions of the same rowing crew (coxed four) with visual impairment (aged 34.8 $\pm$ 10.6 years). The training consisted of five blocks of 500 m at two different intensities (20 and 22 rpm). In both intensities, in the first, third, and fifth blocks, acoustic feedback is provided, whereas in the second and fourth blocks it is not. Furthermore, a baseline was obtained once for each intensity. The authors found that the three blocks with acoustic feedback for both intensities were faster than the baseline (0.08 $\pm$ 0.01 $m{\cdot}s^{-1}$; $p < 0.01$). In the highest intensity test (22 rpm), a different speed was found between blocks with acoustic feedback. Specifically, the first block was slower than the third (0.08 $\pm$ 0.01 $m{\cdot}s^{-1}$; $p = 0.001$; effect size, ES = 1.11) and the fifth (0.07 $\pm$ 0.01 $m{\cdot}s^{-1}$; $p = 0.001$; ES = 0.93). Furthermore, the blocks without acoustic feedback of both intensities (second and fourth blocks) were faster than baseline but slower than with acoustic feedback. From the analysis of the time structure of the rowing cycle, the acoustic feedback would seem capable of optimizing the time course of boat acceleration, mainly during the recovery phase, reducing its fluctuations and thus increasing the speed. Finally, the positive effects of acoustic feedback are also confirmed by both athletes and coaches (by completing a questionnaire) who generally perceive a better smoothness of the movement performed during the recovery phase compared to without acoustic feedback.

Table 3. Main characteristics of the study included in the present scoping review concerning the biomechanics of para-rowing. Abbreviations: IF (Impact Factor); NA (not available); SCI (spinal cord injury); y (years).

Study, Study Design	Journal, IF (2022), Scimago Ranking, Subject Areas and Categories	Sample Size, Sex, Age, Experience, Type of Disability	Sports Class	Aim(s)	Outcome Measures	Findings
Severin et al., 2021 [6]; Case study	Frontiers in Sports and Active Living; NA; NA; NA	1; Female; 30 y; Elite; Physical disability (incomplete SCI)	PR1	To evaluate the effects of adjusting seat and backrest angle on performance, physiology, and biomechanics parameters	Rowing performance, physiology, and biomechanics	Outcomes improved
Schaffert and Mattes, 2015 [32]; Case series	Journal of Sports Sciences; 3.943; Q1; Orthopedics and sports medicine; physical therapy, sports therapy and rehabilitation; sports science	6; 3 males and 3 females; 34.8 ± 10.6 y; International level; Visual impairment	P3 mixed coxed four	To examine the effects of acoustic feedback on mean boat speed	Mean velocity, stroke rate, and power output	Outcomes improved
Held et al., 2022 [33]; Multiple single case in-field testing as a part of randomized crossover trial verified by a repeated measurement trial	Frontiers in Physiology; 4.755; Q1; Physiology and medical physiology	1; Male; 37 y; Elite; Physical disability	PR1	To examine the changing oar rotation axis position in indoor and in-field	Catch angle using a 3D motion capture system	Outcome increased
Cutler et al., 2017 [34]	Journal of Sports Sciences; 3.943; Q1; Orthopedics and sports medicine; physical therapy, sports therapy and rehabilitation; sports science	NA	NA	Comparison of kinematic movement patterns between able-bodied and adapted para-rowing set-ups	Handle pull force, kinematics stroke length, and posture (grip/landing angles on specific joints) plus data from literature	Greater trunk angle, higher stroke rate, and less vertical displacement in para rowers than able-bodied rowers

Held et al. [33] compared kinematic and physiological data and performance during tasks performed with two different boat configurations. Specifically, this was carried out with a standard setup (NORM: with the oar in front of the axis of rotation) vs. a modified setup (GATE: with the oar behind the axis of rotation) in a sample of 15 able-bodied rowers and a PR1 rower. The able-bodied and the para-rower performed, respectively 2 and 24 timed trials of 2 min each. The former was in an indoor rowing tank, whereas the latter was in the water. Both performed the time trials in both NORM and GATE setups in randomized order at maximum intensity with legs and trunk fixed with straps and with a fixed stroke rate (34 rpm). The result shared by all participants indicates that GATE (compared to NORM) enables larger catch angles. Specifically, for this output parameter, there was a mean increase of 97% ($p < 0.001$) and 12% ($p = 0.021$) for able-bodied athletes and for para-athletes, respectively. However, no changes in the shape of the force-angle curve (position of peak force and ratio of mean to maximum force) were found. Furthermore, with GATE, able-bodied athletes experience an increase in total stroke length ($p < 0.010$), rowing power (55.8 $\pm$ 57.3%, $p < 0.010$), and work per stroke (59.7 $\pm$ 67.2%, $p < 0.010$). In the Paralympic athlete, on the other hand, these performance parameters are unchanged. Concerning the specific parameters of the para-rower, the economy of the rowing (power or speed per oxygen uptake) and the speed of the boat did not show significant differences between the two setups used.

Cutler et al. [34] investigated how para-rowing configurations change physiological measures (handle pull force), kinematics (stroke length), and posture (grip/landing angles on specific joints) in ergometer rowing. In total, 17 able-bodied rowers (9 men and 8 women) completed three 10-stroke trials in each rowing configuration (PR1, PR2, and PR3). Physiological and kinematic parameters in the PR3 configurations were comparable to values for the able-bodied literature and decreased with configurations. Specifically, handle force decreased from PR3 to PR2 set-up by 22% and from PR2 to PR1 by 42%. Similarly, stroke length decreased with the PR3 to PR2 setting by 25% and PR3 to PR1 by 47%. For both parameters, men performed better than women. Regarding posture in the PR 2 setups, the rowers used a greater lumbar angle at the catch (37° vs. 29°) and at the finish (−42° vs. −39°) of the stroke compared to the PR3 setups. On the other hand, the flexion of the elbow joint at the finish of the stroke was 11° and 7° greater, respectively, in the PR1 setup compared to PR3 and PR2. Finally, shoulder abduction at the finish of the stroke increased from LTA to TA ($p = 0.014$), LTA to AS ($p = 0.001$), and TA to AS ($p = 0.006$) configurations.

In a case study, Severin et al. [6], compared the effects of a more inclined seat and backrest on rowing performance, physiology, and biomechanics parameters in a PR1 world champion woman athlete (aged 30 years old). The test protocol consisted of three 4 min phases performed with a target power of 100 W (SUBMAX test) and an all-out effort (MAX test) in three different seat configurations (conA: 25° from the vertical plane and 7.5° from the horizontal, conB: 25° from the vertical plane and 0o from that to the horizontal, conC: 5° from the vertical plane and 0° from the horizontal plane). During SUBMAX due to the nature of the task (target power 100 W) similar virtual distances were recorded (conA: 793, conB: 793, conC: 787 m). However, in the usual setups (conC), the peak force (conA: 509, conB: 458, conC: 312 N) and impulse (conA: 172, conB:158, conC: 97 N·s) were lower as well as the stroke length (conA: 81, conB: 78, conC: 67 cm) compared to the other two setups. To compensate for this result, there was an increase in stroke rate (conA: 27, conB: 31, conC: 49 strokes·min^{-1}) at the expense of increase in VO_2 (conA: 34.4, conB: 35.4, conC: 39.6 mL·kg^{-1}·min^{-1}). Similarly, in the MAX task, the conC configuration was less performing in terms of distance covered (conA: 934, conB: 918, (conC: 856 M), peak force (conA: 408 N, conB: 418 N, conC: 331 N), stroke length (conA: 79, conB: 77, conC: 68 cm), and stroke rate (conA: 51, conB: 54, conC: 56 rpm). However, these differences were smaller than in SUBMAX test. Regarding the kinematic parameters, the para-athlete was able to perform a greater extension of the trunk in setups conA and conB compared to conC. Finally, an increase in flexion in the elbow and shoulder joints in the SUBMAX task during the driving phase was found in conA and conB compared with conC.

3.5. Emerging Analytical Approaches for Kinematic Assessments and Predictions of Mechanical Outputs in Para-Rowers

Three studies [35–37] developed new analytical approaches for kinematics assessments and predictions of mechanical outputs in para-rowers. These studies are overviewed in Table 4.

In a multi-time assessment (longitudinal search), it is critical that the test chosen can consistently reproduce the same outcome between visits, provided all other variables remain the same. In this regard, Euiler and Finley [35] assessed the repeatability of the para-rowing stroke and analyzed EMG data (muscle activity of the upper, middle, and lower trapezius, anterior and posterior deltoid, latissimus dorsi, and infraspinatus) and kinematic of the rowing stroke (humero-thoracic plane of elevation, angle of elevation, and trunk flexion and extension, and trunk rotation) in a sample of 10 para-rowers (7 males and 3 females aged, 41.6 ± 13.4 years old) with low experience, to determine the trial-to-trial reliability of three submaximal rowing trials (20 strokes each). Muscle activity and kinematics data were reliable with moderate to excellent and excellent intraclass correlation coefficients, respectively.

Schwingel et al. [36] conducted a study with a dual objective: to analyze the safety and tolerability of performing the one-repetition maximum tests (1RM) and compare the 1RM–measured values with linear and exponential equation models (12 different equations) for predicting 1RM. Two upper body strength exercises (Flat barbell bench press and Lying T-bar row) and one lower body (45-degree leg press) were performed by 9 male para-rowers (mean age; 30 6 7.9 years, 7 one-legged amputees and 2 with cerebral palsy). From qualitative analysis, the 1RM test proved to be well-tolerated and safe also for athletes with a disability. However, for body strength exercises, the estimate of maximal strength can be replaced by prediction equations. In fact, although the predicted values were slightly underestimated, they were accurate and reliable. Furthermore, the authors did not find statistical differences between exercises ($p = 0.84$ and 0.23 for lying T-bar row and flat barbell bench press, respectively). For lower body exercise, on the other hand, a highly significant difference between measured and predicted values were found ($p < 0.01$).

People affected with upper motor neuron syndrome may benefit from functional electrical stimulation (FES) through the electrical elicitation of paralyzed muscles [22]. FES has been integrated with rowing (FES Rowing) also allowing people with paraplegia to row without adapting to boat configurations [20]. To maximize the benefits of FES Rowing, the intensity of a muscle's stimulation should be greatest when its force-producing potential is greatest. This is possible by monitoring the joint angles of the specific muscle during rowing. Concerning that point, Vieira et al. [37] compared a biomechanical model for knee joint angle estimation with actual knee angle changes (measured with inertial sensors) during three sets of 30 strokes (each at a different stroke rate of 18, 24, and 32 spm) in indoor rowing in a sample of 15 able-bodied (age range 20–35 years) and 11 PR3 rowers (23–47 years). This model was based on real-time measurements of handle and seat position for each stroke transmitted by an adapted rowing machine. The authors found that the mean squared error (RMSE) between calculated vs. estimated was generally low (3.8 to 5.1 degrees). Furthermore, the estimation error differed significantly within the rowing cycle ($p < 0.001$) and not for group and stroke rate ($p > 0.267$). Specifically, the highest RMSE values occurred during 20–50% and 80–100% of the rowing cycle ($p < 0.003$) with a peak during the mid-recovery (average 8 deg). Additionally, for the two groups and for the three-stroke rates, the onset of knee flexion was consistently underestimated (~5%, $p < 0.001$). Based on these results, the biomechanical model used proved to be reliable and capable of replacing the less economical inertial sensors for kinematic analysis.

Table 4. Main characteristics of the study included in the present scoping review concerning emerging analytical approaches for kinematic assessments and predictions of mechanical outputs in para-rowing. Abbreviations: EMG (electromyography); IF (Impact Factor); NA (not available); y (years).

Study, Study Design	Journal, IF (2022), Scimago Ranking, Subject Areas and Categories	Sample Size, Sex, Age, Experience, Type of Disability	Sports Class	Aim(s)	Outcome Measures	Findings
Euiler and Finley, 2022 [35]; Modeling study	Journal of Sport Rehabilitation; 2.203; Q2–Q3; Orthopedics and sports medicine; physical therapy, sports therapy and rehabilitation; rehabilitation; sports science	10; 7 males and 3 females; 41.6 ± 13.4 y; various levels of experience; Physical disability	NA	To assess the reliability of upper-extremity muscle activity and kinematics during adaptive rowing	Muscle EMG assessment (peak muscle activity, mean muscle activity), and kinematics of the rowing stroke	Good to excellent reliability
Schwingel et al., 2009 [36]; Modeling study	Journal of Strength and Conditioning Research; 4.415; Q1; Medicine (miscellaneous); orthopedics and sports medicine; physical therapy, sports therapy and rehabilitation; sports science	9; Male; 30 ± 7.9 y; International level; Physical disability	NA	To assess the accuracy of predicting one repetition maximum (1RM) equations	Linear and exponential equation models (12 different equations)	Good accuracy for upper and lower body strength
Vieira et al., 2018 [37]; Modeling study	IEEE Transactions on Neural Systems and Rehabilitation Engineering; 4.528; Q1–Q2; Medicine (miscellaneous), internal medicine, neuroscience (miscellaneous), rehabilitation, biomedical engineering, computer science applications	11; NA; 23–47 y; International level; Physical disability	LTA-PD	Design and testing of a biomechanical model for the estimation of knee joint angle during indoor rowing	Knee angle changes (measured with inertial sensors)	High accuracy of the model (average error less than 2° compared to the traditional method)

3.6. Bibliometrics-Based Analysis of Para-Rowing Scientific Output

The bibliometrics analysis enabled us to identify 78 researchers (nodes), 16 (20.51%) of whom were highly interconnected (Figure 2). The resulting graph (Figure 2) consisted of 202 links (edges), with a total link strength of 209, and 14 clusters. The most prolific author was Smoljanović, T., with 3 items/documents (representing 17.6% of the scientific output overviewed in the present scoping review). The list of the ten most productive scholars can be found in Table 1. In total, 93.6% of scholars have authored one single document. The main topological features of the scholarly community of authors on PR are shown in Tables 5 and 6: these features indicate a highly fragmented and dispersed, poorly connected community characterized by a relatively high number of clusters and a low strength of connections. In terms of publication years, the first scholarly article dates back to 2008, with four articles (23.5%) published in the current year, showing an increasing interest in this para-sports discipline.

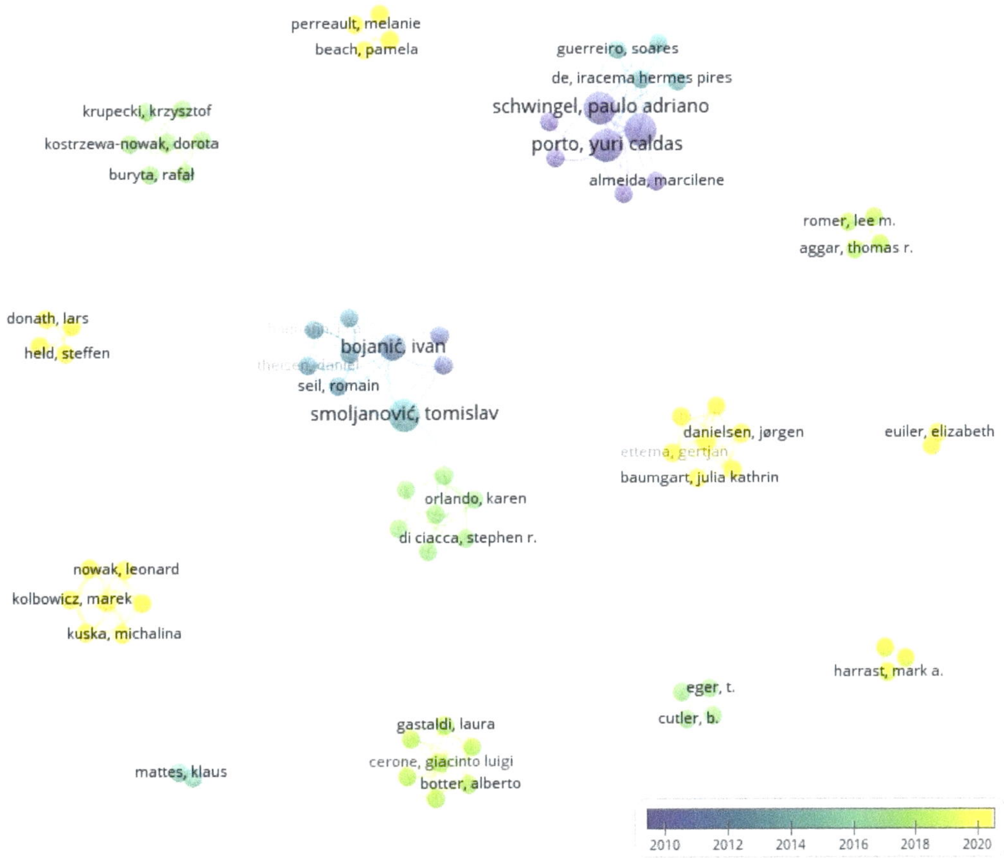

Figure 2. Bibliometric map showing connections of the authors in the field of para-rowing.

Table 5. The ten most productive authors on para-rowing.

Author	Country	Number of Documents (%)	Number of Links	Total Link Strength	Author Cluster	Publication Year Range
Smoljanović T.	Croatia	3 (17.6%)	15	16	2	2011–2017
Porto Y.C.	Brazil	3 (17.6%)	10	14	1	2008–2014
Schwingel P.A.	Brazil	3 (17.6%)	10	14	1	2008–2014
Zoppi C.C.	Brazil	3 (17.6%)	10	14	1	2008–2014
Bojanić I.	Croatia	2 (11.8%)	8	9	2	2011–2013
Di Ciacca S.R.	Canada	1 (5.9%)	7	7	5	2017
Lebrun C.M.	Canada	1 (5.9%)	7	7	5	2017
Orlando K.	Canada	1 (5.9%)	7	7	5	2017
Thornton J.S.	Canada	1 (5.9%)	7	7	5	2017
Vinther A.	Denmark	1 (5.9%)	7	7	5	2017

Table 6. The main topological features of the scholarly community of authors on para-rowing.

Topological Feature	Value
Avg. Number of neighbors	6.75
Network diameter	2
Network radius	1
Characteristic path length	1.55
Clustering coefficient	0.94
Network density	0.45
Network heterogeneity	0.37
Network centralization	0.63
Connected components	13

The top institution was the University of Zagreb, Zagreb (Croatia). In terms of journals, the studies included in our review were published in 15 scholarly journals, in the field of sports science, orthopedics and sports medicine, physical therapy, sports therapy, and rehabilitation, medicine (miscellaneous), physiology and medical physiology, rehabilitation, public health, environmental, and occupational health, biomedical engineering, computer science applications, internal medicine, neuroscience (miscellaneous), biophysics, and neurology/neurology (clinical). The two top journals were the International Journal of Environmental Research and Public Health (IJERPH) and the Journal of Sports Sciences. More than half of the journals (53.3%) were top journals in their fields. More in detail, four journals (namely, the British Journal of Sports Medicine, the Journal of Strength and Conditioning Research, Frontiers in Physiology, and the Journal of Sports Sciences) were first quartile (Q1) journals, whereas four other journals (IJERPH, the Journal of Applied Physiology, the Journal of Human Kinetics, Research in Sports Medicine, and IEEE Transactions on Neural Systems and Rehabilitation Engineering) were Q1-second quartile (Q2) scholarly journals. In terms of citations, the most cited article was the study by Thornton et al. [30], with 36 citations, according to Scopus. Finally, in terms of funding, this was reported by six articles: more specifically, several sponsors/funding sources could be identified, including universities and research centers, research councils and foundations, and Ministries/governmental agencies and institutions.

4. Discussion

4.1. Psychological and Physiological Responses in Para-Rowing

Due to the nature of their disabilities, para-rowers have exhibited lower fitness levels than their able-bodied counterparts [25]. Indeed, some disabilities limit the physiological functioning of these athletes. For example, spinal cord injuries, which are the most commonly reported type of impairment in para-rowers, can lead to impaired cardiovascular and respiratory function, characterized by decreased peak heart rate, inability to increase tidal volume, exercise-induced hypotension, and increased fatigue [27,38]. In addition, decreases in strength (impaired neural recruitment), and ROM, as well as increased muscle stiffness, spasticity, spastic dystonia, and impaired coordination, have been found in athletes with cerebral palsy [39,40]. However, from the studies retained in the present scoping review, two important and highly interconnected aspects emerged, stating the beneficial effect of training. The first aspect is that para-rowers tolerate the training load of able-bodied rowers relatively well, allowing for increases in performance-outcomes aspects such as muscle strength, anaerobic power, and aerobic power [24]. The second is that with the right training program, para-rowers did not show any inflammatory symptoms, indicating high levels of immunological adaption [26]. Regarding the psychological aspects, para-rowing is an empowering, engaging, and accessible sports discipline that can provide athletes with meaningful connections and social networking, enabling them to overcome stigma and disability-related fears and apprehensions [28].

4.2. Health, Injuries, and Risk Factors in Para-Rowing Injuries

The rowing of an able-bodied rower represents a sequence of movements that are part of a single kinetic chain in which the trunk acts as a link generating and transferring forces from the legs and arms to the oar [4,41]. In para-rowers, this is not the case due to the limited joints and body segments used. This results in isolated repetitive force generation of joints and functional segments and an increased risk of injury [7,30]. In addition, increasing stroke rate, boat weight and racing time add further stress to the musculoskeletal system [5]. The initial-to-mid drive phase is particularly critical in the PR1 and PR2 sports classes. In fact, to reach the maximal stroke length, in these phases they perform larger amplitudes of forward flexion of the trunk (in the PR2 class) and shoulder flexion (in PR1 and PR2 classes) in comparison to PR3 class and/or able-bodied rowers, which can be potentially harmful [34]. Additionally, PR1 rowers with minimal trunk control bend as much as possible at the chest strap, creating stress on the upper thoracic region with a high risk of rib fractures [7]. However, para-rowing compared to other Paralympic sports such as sled hockey, wheelchair basketball, and wheelchair rugby would seem the safest [29]. Finally, most rowers in class PR1 and PR2 have a spinal cord injury. The former generally have lesions in the thoracic spine while the latter have lesions in the lower thoracic or lumbosacral spine [22]. It is, therefore, conceivable that the greater risk of injury within these sports classes is closely connected to the underlying pathology. For example, lesions attributable to autonomic dysreflexia, spastic hypertonia and osteoporosis (such as bone fractures resulting from small traumas) [30].

4.3. Biomechanics of the Para-Rowing Strokes

The biomechanics of the para-rower is significantly altered mainly due to the pathology. Equipment adjustments made to minimize intra-class differences can make this situation worse. In fact, it has been observed that rowing with a PR2 setup or even more with a PR1 setup alters the range of motion and measures of handle strength and stroke length even for able-bodied athletes [34]. In this regard, various strategies have been studied to implement the para-rowing set-ups, some of which have proved to be useful, while others have proved to be difficult to transfer to the para-rowers. For example, because of the importance of allowing trunk extension in para-rowers with minimal residual trunk function, a more inclined seat and backrest were used [6]. This modification allowed a more trunk motion and a longer stroke length combined with a lower stroke rate. In fact, moving the oar from in front of the axis of rotation to behind the axis of rotation instead made biomechanical improvements primarily for able-bodied athletes [33]. This confirms that applying the discoveries made in the world of able-bodied to the para-athlete populations could be a mistake. The latter is a widely heterogeneous world with intra- and interdependent implications of the specific type of impairment. Finally, an acoustic feedback strategy was studied for athletes with visual impairment during training sessions [32]. Acoustic feedback has proved to be useful for optimizing the time course of boat acceleration during the rowing phase (mainly during the recovery phase). Specifically, the para-rowers performed a more regular sliding movement in the recovery phase compared to the situation without feedback, increasing the force output in the drive phase and consequentially the speed of the boat [16,21].

4.4. Emerging Analytical Approaches for Kinematic Assessments and Predictions of Mechanical Outputs in Para-Rowers

Having reliable, validated measures is of paramount importance in the field of research. Para-rowing stroke-related metrics have shown excellent repeatability [35]. The 1RM test is relatively safe and easy to evaluate and correlates well with sports performance [42]. However, pulling to the maximum implies maximum stress for the involved structures, such as muscles, tendons, joints, and even neural networks. For this reason, in para-athletes, the 1RM test is often replaced by alternative tests to prevent injuries, technical failures, and fatigue [43–45]. While in the upper limb both methods (i.e., 1RM and alternative tests) can be used to assess the intensity of resistance training, in the lower limb 1RM is more accurate than alternative tests, especially for athletes with one leg amputated [36]. Besides strength assessment, biomechanical evaluation is also fundamental. The latter is usually carried out by using inertial sensors, which are generally expensive and require calibration efforts, which is rather a time- and resource-consuming procedure [46]. A study developed a significantly less expensive and similarly reliable methodology, that can be easily implemented in the setting of para-rowing. More specifically, the adaptation of the rowing machine enabled the provision of real-time data on handle and seat position, that a subject-specific biomechanical model was able to relate to the knee joint angle [37].

4.5. Bibliometrics-Based Analysis of Para-Rowing Scientific Output

A few bibliometrics studies have investigated scholarly interest in Paralympic disciplines. Of interest, the most over-represented countries such as Croatia, Brazil, and Canada, did not qualify as top counties in terms of medals awarded. Recently, our group assessed publishing trends related to Paralympic powerlifting [15]. Compared with the Paralympic powerlifting community, the para-rowing community appears to be less connected, more fragmented, and dispersed. Of note, no hub authors could be identified, and the number of documents/items are more homogeneously distributed among authors, with the most prolific scholar having coauthored three studies. For para-rowing, Canada was over-represented as a country, while Brazil was over-represented for Paralympic powerlifting. Finally, also in terms of temporal trends, publication years were more homogeneously represented and distributed from 2008 to 2022. In the sports arena, scientific collaboration is of paramount importance in that it can enhance the quality of research, by improving performance-related outcomes, establishing networks, and achieving more sustainable development. This is even more true in the Paralympic world, where the complexity of the issues makes collaborations vital for the advancement of knowledge. Therefore, further efforts are warranted to improve the scientific collaboration among authors interested in para-rowing.

4.6. Gaps in Knowledge and Future Directions

Overall, a relative paucity of evidence-based studies was identified, particularly in the domain of physiology, probably due, at least partially, to the recent debut of para-rowing at the Paralympic Games. The presence of mostly case studies, anecdotal reports, articles based on personal experiences, and/or investigations mainly focusing on a single type of impairment makes it difficult to have a comprehensive understanding of how various impairments could affect the physiological response to exercise and adapted rowing. Accurate, rigorous knowledge of these aspects could serve a two-fold role: (i) to preserve, and, potentially, enhance, the health and well-being of the para-athlete, and (ii) to plan individualized interventions, and devise specific protocols, conditioning, and training methods, which are appropriate based on the specific type of disability. For example, it can be anticipated that athletes with visual and intellectual disabilities show very different physiological responses to exercise than athletes with spinal cord injuries. Additionally, there could be a significant degree of variability among athletes with the same impairment. For instance, in subjects paralyzed with spinal cord injuries, disability depends on the level at which spinal cord is injured and varies whether the impairment is congenital or acquired [47,48].

To ensure fair competition, athletes with similar levels of activity limitation due to their impairments should be in the same sports class and compete against each other. However, one of the major limitations of para-rowing is a lack of evidence-based classification to assess the true impact of impairment on performance. Furthermore, a broad range of disabilities and just three sports classes (PR1, 2 and 3) might give some athletes an advantage over others. Therefore, it is necessary to develop tests that describe impairment and define the relationship between impairment and rowing performance outcomes. In other words, a correct classification method should be based on scientific evidence and not on expert opinions.

The use of technology to measure motor disability has proven useful in several Paralympic sports [49] and could also be used in para-rowing. For example, para-swimming technology has enabled more objective and reliable tests to be designed which are likely to be included in the next revision of the World Para Swimming classification [50–52]. Moreover, also as far as injury is concerned, data is still lacking in this athlete population [30]. In most rowing injury cases there is a history of inaccurate management of load parameters with increased intensity/length of training associated with poor recovery [7]. However, training methodology and periodization theory of peak performance represent relatively under-explored and overlooked research areas in the existing academic literature. Additionally, to our knowledge, training methods for maintaining conditioning during periods of inactivity have never been explored.

The limited body of evidence can lead the less expert coach to manage the para-athlete as an able-bodied athlete, compromising their preparation and, in the worst case, their health. While kinematic evaluations have been extensively studied, topics such as sports nutrition, doping, and psychology have been relatively underdeveloped and overlooked. Psychological aspects have been investigated only in athletes with loss of visual acuity, who do not represent the most commonly described para-rower, usually affected by spinal cord injury.

Therefore, in para-rowing, further studies are warranted involving a broad range of impairments and disabilities, with particular attention paid to spinal cord injury. Finally, although in recent years COVID-19 has dramatically impacted the Paralympic sport arena [53], there are no published studies investigating this topic, which deserves to be explored.

5. Conclusions

The current literature review covered several domains and aspects of para-rowing, namely (i) psychological and physiological aspects and responses in para-rowing, (ii) epidemiology and risk factors of para-rowing injuries, (iii) biomechanics of the para-rowing strokes, and (iv) emerging analytical approaches for kinematic assessments and prediction of mechanical outputs in para-rowers. This literature review was complemented by a bibliometrics-based analysis of para-rowing scientific output. This information can be used by both practitioners and athletes, to enhance their expertise and knowledge of training protocols and conditioning strategies. However, several gaps were identified in terms of underdeveloped or overlooked topics (namely, sports nutrition, doping, and psychological aspects in para-rowers other than those with visual impairment), warranting further research in the field.

Author Contributions: Conceptualization, L.P. and N.L.B.; methodology, N.L.B.; software, N.L.B. and L.M.; validation, L.P., L.M. and N.L.B.; formal analysis, N.L.B. and L.M.; investigation, L.P. and N.L.B.; resources, L.P. and N.L.B.; data curation, N.L.B.; writing—original draft preparation, L.P. and N.L.B.; writing—review and editing, L.P., C.B., C.T., L.M., A.C., L.C., M.F., V.V., M.C.C., P.R., K.T. and N.L.B.; visualization, N.L.B.; supervision, L.P. and N.L.B.; project administration, L.P. and N.L.B.; funding acquisition, C.B. and P.R. All authors have read and agreed to the published version of the manuscript.

Funding: This research received no external funding.

Institutional Review Board Statement: Not applicable.

Informed Consent Statement: Not applicable.

Data Availability Statement: Not applicable.

Conflicts of Interest: The authors declare no conflict of interest.

References

1. The Official Website of FISA, The International Rowing Federation. Adaptive. Available online: http://www.worldrowing.com/rowing/adaptive (accessed on 1 December 2022).
2. The Official Website of International Paralympic Committee. Available online: http://www.paralympic.org/rowing/classification (accessed on 2 December 2022).
3. The Official Website of FISA, The International Rowing Federation. Available online: https://worldrowing.com/technical/para-rowing-classification/ (accessed on 1 December 2022).
4. Warmenhoven, J.; Cobley, S.; Draper, C.; Smith, R. Over 50 Years of Researching Force Profiles in Rowing: What Do We Know? *Sport. Med.* **2018**, *48*, 2703–2714. [CrossRef]
5. Smoljanović, T.; Bojanić, I.; Hannafin, J.A.; Urhausen, A.; Theisen, D.; Seil, R.; Lacoste, A. Complete Inclusion of Adaptive Rowing Only 1000 m Ahead. *Br. J. Sport. Med.* **2013**, *47*, 819–825. [CrossRef] [PubMed]
6. Severin, A.C.; Danielsen, J.; Falck Erichsen, J.; Wold Eikevåg, S.; Steinert, M.; Ettema, G.; Baumgart, J.K. Case Report: Adjusting Seat and Backrest Angle Improves Performance in an Elite Paralympic Rower. *Front. Sport. Act. Living* **2021**, *3*, 625656. [CrossRef]
7. Smoljanović, T.; Bojanić, I.; Pollock, C.L.; Radonić, R. Rib Stress Fracture in a Male Adaptive Rower from the Arms and Shoulders Sport Class: Case Report. *Croat. Med. J.* **2011**, *52*, 644–647. [CrossRef] [PubMed]
8. The Official Website of International Paralympic Committee. Available online: https://www.paralympic.org/tokyo-2020/results/rowing (accessed on 5 December 2022).
9. Puce, L.; Marinelli, L.; Pierantozzi, E.; Mori, L.; Pallecchi, I.; Bonifazi, M.; Bove, M.; Franchini, E.; Trompetto, C. Training Methods and Analysis of Races of a Top Level Paralympic Swimming Athlete. *J. Exerc. Rehabil.* **2018**, *14*, 612–620. [CrossRef] [PubMed]
10. Tweedy, S.M.; Connick, M.J.; Beckman, E.M. Applying Scientific Principles to Enhance Paralympic Classification Now and in the Future. *Phys. Med. Rehabil. Clin. N. Am.* **2018**, *29*, 313–332. [CrossRef]
11. Munn, Z.; Pollock, D.; Price, C.; Aromataris, E.; Stern, C.; Stone, J.; Barker, T.H.; Godfrey, C.M.; Clyne, B.; Booth, A.; et al. Investigating Different Typologies for the Synthesis of Evidence: A Scoping Review Protocol. *JBI Evid. Synth.* **2022**, *Publish Ahead of Print*. [CrossRef]
12. Arksey, H.; O'Malley, L. Scoping Studies: Towards a Methodological Framework. *Int. J. Soc. Res. Methodol.* **2005**, *8*, 19–32. [CrossRef]
13. Bradbury-Jones, C.; Aveyard, H.; Herber, O.R.; Isham, L.; Taylor, J.; O'Malley, L. Scoping Reviews: The PAGER Framework for Improving the Quality of Reporting. *Int. J. Soc. Res. Methodol.* **2022**, *25*, 457–470. [CrossRef]
14. Saaiq, M.; Ashraf, B. Modifying "Pico" Question into "Picos" Model for More Robust and Reproducible Presentation of the Methodology Employed in A Scientific Study. *World J. Plast. Surg.* **2017**, *6*, 390–392.
15. Puce, L.; Trabelsi, K.; Trompetto, C.; Mori, L.; Marinelli, L.; Currà, A.; Faelli, E.; Ferrando, V.; Okwen, P.; Kong, J.D.; et al. A Bibliometrics-Enhanced, PAGER-Compliant Scoping Review of the Literature on Paralympic Powerlifting: Insights for Practices and Future Research. *Healthcare* **2022**, *10*, 2319. [CrossRef] [PubMed]
16. Schaffert, N.; Mattes, K. Authors' Response to the Letter to the Editor: "Effects of Acoustic Feedback Training in Elite-Standard Para-Rowing" by Schaffert and Mattes. *J. Sport. Sci.* **2015**, *33*, 1632–1636. [CrossRef] [PubMed]
17. da Silva, L.F.; de Almeida-Neto, P.F.; de Matos, D.G.; Riechman, S.E.; de Queiros, V.; de Jesus, J.B.; Reis, V.M.; Clemente, F.M.; Miarka, B.; Aidar, F.J.; et al. Performance Prediction Equation for 2000 m Youth Indoor Rowing Using a 100 m Maximal Test. *Biology* **2021**, *10*, 1082. [CrossRef]
18. Daud, A.; Safir, O.A.; Gross, A.; Kuzyk, P.R.T. Return to Paralympic Rowing After Partial Joint Transplantation: A Case Report. *JBJS Case Connect.* **2021**, *11*, e20.00808. [CrossRef] [PubMed]
19. Wong, R.N.; Stewart, A.L.; Sawatzky, B.; Laskin, J.J.; Borisoff, J.; Mattie, J.; Sparrey, C.J.; Mortenson, W.B. Exploring Exercise Participation and the Usability of the Adaptive Rower and Arm Crank Ergometer through Wheelchair Users' Perspectives. *Disabil. Rehabil.* **2022**, *44*, 3915–3924. [CrossRef] [PubMed]

20. Andrews, B.; Gibbons, R.; Wheeler, G. Development of Functional Electrical Stimulation Rowing: The Rowstim Series. *Artif. Organs* **2017**, *41*, E203–E212. [CrossRef]
21. Hill, H. Letter to the Editor Concerning the Article "Effects of Acoustic Feedback Training in Elite-Standard Para-Rowing" by Schaffert and Mattes. *J. Sport. Sci.* **2015**, *33*, 1637–1638. [CrossRef]
22. Hettinga, D.M. Adaptive Rowing. In *Rowing*; Secher, N.H., Volianitis, S., Eds.; Blackwell Publishing Ltd.: Oxford, UK, 2007; pp. 141–144, ISBN 978-1-4443-1261-4.
23. Cardoso, R.; Rios, M.; Carvalho, D.D.; Monteiro, A.S.; Soares, S.; Abraldes, J.A.; Gomes, B.B.; Vilas Boas, J.P.; Fernandes, R.J. Mechanics and energetic analysis of rowing with Big blades with Randall foils. *Int. J. Sport. Med.* **2022**. [CrossRef]
24. Zoppi, C.C.; Guerreiro, S.; Porto, Y.C.; de Mélo Montenegro, I.H.P.; Montenegro, M.; Fulgêncio Alves da Silva, T.; Schwingel, P.A. Physiological and Performance Improvements during a Training Season in Paralympic Rowers. *J. Exerc. Physiol. Online* **2014**, *17*, 88–101.
25. Porto, Y.C.; Almeida, M.; de Sá, C.C.; Schwingel, P.A.; Zoppi, C.C. Anthropometric and Physical Characteristics of Motor Disabilited Paralympic Rowers. *Res. Sport. Med.* **2008**, *16*, 203–212. [CrossRef]
26. Nowak, R.; Buryta, R.; Krupecki, K.; Zając, T.; Zawartka, M.; Proia, P.; Kostrzewa-Nowak, D. The Impact of the Progressive Efficiency Test on a Rowing Ergometer on White Blood Cells Distribution and Clinical Chemistry Changes in Paralympic Rowers During the Preparatory Stage Before the Paralympic Games in Rio, 2016—A Case Report. *J. Hum. Kinet.* **2017**, *60*, 255–263. [CrossRef] [PubMed]
27. Tiller, N.B.; Aggar, T.R.; West, C.R.; Romer, L.M. Exercise-Induced Diaphragm Fatigue in a Paralympic Champion Rower with Spinal Cord Injury. *J. Appl. Physiol.* **2018**, *124*, 805–811. [CrossRef] [PubMed]
28. Rich, J.; Lieberman, L.J.; Beach, P.; Perreault, M. "Moving Freely in Space with Power and Not Be Afraid": An Interpretative Phenomenological Analysis of the Experiences of Elite Rowers with Visual Impairment. *IJERPH* **2022**, *19*, 14059. [CrossRef]
29. Soo Hoo, J.A.; Latzka, E.; Harrast, M.A. A Descriptive Study of Self-Reported Injury in Non-Elite Adaptive Athletes. *J. Inj. Funct. Rehabil.* **2019**, *11*, 25–32. [CrossRef] [PubMed]
30. Thornton, J.S.; Vinther, A.; Wilson, F.; Lebrun, C.M.; Wilkinson, M.; Di Ciacca, S.R.; Orlando, K.; Smoljanović, T. Rowing Injuries: An Updated Review. *Sport. Med.* **2017**, *47*, 641–661. [CrossRef] [PubMed]
31. Nowak, M.A.; Kolbowicz, M.; Kuska, M.; Sygit, K.; Sygit, M.; Nowak, L.; Kotarska, K. The Intensity of the Health Behaviors of People Who Practice Wheelchair Basketball, Wheelchair Rugby and Para-Rowing. *IJERPH* **2022**, *19*, 7879. [CrossRef]
32. Schaffert, N.; Mattes, K. Effects of Acoustic Feedback Training in Elite-Standard Para-Rowing. *J. Sport. Sci.* **2015**, *33*, 411–418. [CrossRef]
33. Held, S.; Rappelt, L.; Wicker, P.; Donath, L. Changing Oar Rotation Axis Position Increases Catch Angle During Indoor and In-Field Para-Rowing: A Randomized Crossover Trial Verified by a Repeated Measurement Trial. *Front. Physiol.* **2022**, *13*, 833646. [CrossRef]
34. Cutler, B.; Eger, T.; Merritt, T.; Godwin, A. Comparing Para-Rowing Set-Ups on an Ergometer Using Kinematic Movement Patterns of Able-Bodied Rowers. *J. Sport. Sci.* **2017**, *35*, 777–783. [CrossRef]
35. Euiler, E.; Finley, M. Reliability of Upper-Extremity Muscle Activity and Kinematics During Adaptive Rowing. *J. Sport Rehabil.* **2022**, *31*, 926–932. [CrossRef]
36. Schwingel, P.A.; Porto, Y.C.; Dias, M.C.M.; Moreira, M.M.; Zoppi, C.C. Predicting One Repetition Maximum Equations Accuracy in Paralympic Rowers with Motor Disabilities. *J. Strength Cond. Res.* **2009**, *23*, 1045–1050. [CrossRef] [PubMed]
37. Vieira, T.; Cerone, G.L.; Gastaldi, L.; Pastorelli, S.; Oliveira, L.F.; Gazzoni, M.; Botter, A. Design and Test of a Biomechanical Model for the Estimation of Knee Joint Angle During Indoor Rowing: Implications for FES-Rowing Protocols in Paraplegia. *IEEE Trans. Neural. Syst. Rehabil. Eng.* **2018**, *26*, 2145–2152. [CrossRef] [PubMed]
38. Gee, C.M.; Lacroix, M.A.; Stellingwerff, T.; Gavel, E.H.; Logan-Sprenger, H.M.; West, C.R. Physiological Considerations to Support Podium Performance in Para-Athletes. *Front. Rehabilit. Sci.* **2021**, *2*, 732342. [CrossRef]
39. Puce, L.; Bragazzi, N.L.; Currà, A.; Marinelli, L.; Mori, L.; Cotellessa, F.; Chamari, K.; Ponzano, M.; Samanipour, M.H.; Nikolaidis, P.T.; et al. Not All Forms of Muscle Hypertonia Worsen With Fatigue: A Pilot Study in Para Swimmers. *Front. Physiol.* **2022**, *13*, 902663. [CrossRef]
40. Puce, L.; Pallecchi, I.; Chamari, K.; Marinelli, L.; Innocenti, T.; Pedrini, R.; Mori, L.; Trompetto, C. Systematic Review of Fatigue in Individuals With Cerebral Palsy. *Front. Hum. Neurosci.* **2021**, *15*, 598800. [CrossRef] [PubMed]
41. Buckeridge, E.M.; Bull, A.M.J.; McGregor, A.H. Biomechanical Determinants of Elite Rowing Technique and Performance: Rowing Technique and Performance. *Scand. J. Med. Sci. Sport.* **2015**, *25*, e176–e183. [CrossRef] [PubMed]
42. Grgic, J.; Lazinica, B.; Schoenfeld, B.J.; Pedisic, Z. Test–Retest Reliability of the One-Repetition Maximum (1RM) Strength Assessment: A Systematic Review. *Sport. Med. Open* **2020**, *6*, 31. [CrossRef] [PubMed]
43. Loturco, I.; Pereira, L.A.; Winckler, C.; Santos, W.L.; Kobal, R.; McGuigan, M. Load–Velocity Relationship in National Paralympic Powerlifters: A Case Study. *Int. J. Sport. Physiol. Perform.* **2019**, *14*, 531–535. [CrossRef]
44. Neto, F.R.; Dorneles, J.R.; Aidar, F.J.; Gonçalves, C.W.; Veloso, J.; Costa, R.R.G. Validation of the Repetitions in Reserve Rating Scale in Paralympic Powerlifting Athletes. *Int. J. Sport. Med.* **2022**, *43*, 366–372. [CrossRef]
45. Aidar, F.J.; Brito, C.J.; de Matos, D.G.; de Oliveira, L.A.S.; de Souza, R.F.; de Almeida-Neto, P.F.; de Araújo Tinoco Cabral, B.G.; Neiva, H.P.; Neto, F.R.; Reis, V.M.; et al. Force–Velocity Relationship in Paralympic Powerlifting: Two or Multiple-Point Methods to Determine a Maximum Repetition. *BMC Sport. Sci. Med. Rehabil.* **2022**, *14*, 159. [CrossRef]

46. Worsey, M.T.; Espinosa, H.G.; Shepherd, J.B.; Thiel, D.V. A Systematic Review of Performance Analysis in Rowing Using Inertial Sensors. *Electronics* **2019**, *8*, 1304. [CrossRef]
47. Mills, P.B.; Krassioukov, A. Autonomic function as a missing piece of the classification of paralympic athletes with spinal cord injury. *Spinal Cord* **2011**, *49*, 768–776. [CrossRef] [PubMed]
48. Le Toquin, B.; Schipman, J.; De Larochelambert, Q.; Saulière, G.; Duncombe, S.; Toussaint, J.F. Is the visual impairment origin a performance factor? Analysis of international-level para swimmers and para athletes. *J. Sport. Sci.* **2022**, *40*, 489–497. [CrossRef]
49. Beckman, E.M.; Connick, M.J.; Tweedy, S.M. Assessing muscle strength for the purpose of classification in Paralympic sport: A review and recommendations. *J. Sci. Med. Sport* **2017**, *20*, 391–396. [CrossRef]
50. Nicholson, V.P.; Spathis, J.G.; Hogarth, L.W.; Connick, M.J.; Beckman, E.M.; Tweedy, S.M.; Payton, C.J.; Burkett, B.J. Establishing the Reliability of a Novel Battery of Range of Motion Tests to Enable Evidence-Based Classification in Para Swimming. *Phys. Ther. Sport* **2018**, *32*, 34–41. [CrossRef] [PubMed]
51. Payton, C.; Hogarth, L.; Burkett, B.; Van De Vliet, P.; Lewis, S.; Oh, Y.-T. Active Drag as a Criterion for Evidence-Based Classification in Para Swimming. *Med. Sci. Sport. Exerc.* **2020**, *52*, 1576–1584. [CrossRef] [PubMed]
52. Hogarth, L.; Oh, Y.; Osborough, C.; Osborough, C.; Formosa, D.; Hunter, A.; Alcock, A.; Burkett, B.; Payton, C. Passive Drag in Para Swimmers with Physical Impairments: Implications for Evidence-based Classification in Para Swimming. *Scand. J. Med. Sci. Sport.* **2021**, *31*, 1932–1940. [CrossRef]
53. Puce, L.; Trabelsi, K.; Ammar, A.; Jabbour, G.; Marinelli, L.; Mori, L.; Kong, J.D.; Tsigalou, C.; Cotellessa, F.; Schenone, C.; et al. A Tale of Two Stories: COVID-19 and Disability. A Critical Scoping Review of the Literature on the Effects of the Pandemic among Athletes with Disabilities and Para-Athletes. *Front. Physiol.* **2022**, *13*, 967661. [CrossRef]

healthcare

MDPI

Article

Effects of Velocity-Based versus Percentage-Based Resistance Training on Explosive Neuromuscular Adaptations and Anaerobic Power in Sport-College Female Basketball Players

Mingyang Zhang [1,†], Duanying Li [2,†], Jiaxin He [1], Xingyue Liang [1], Dongyu Li [3], Wenfeng Song [2], Shicong Ding [2], Jie Shu [1], Xiaoning Sun [2,*] and Jian Sun [2,*]

1 Digital Physical Training Laboratory, Guangzhou Sport University, Guangzhou 510500, China
2 Department of Physical Education, Guangzhou Sport University, Guangzhou 510500, China
3 School of Athletic Training, Guangzhou Sport University, Guangzhou 510500, China
* Correspondence: sunxn@gzsport.edu.cn (X.S.); sunjian@gzsport.edu.cn (J.S.)
† These authors contributed equally to this work and share first authorship.

Abstract: The purpose of this study was to compare the impact of velocity-based resistance training (VBRT) and percentage-based resistance training (PBRT) on anaerobic ability, sprint performance, and jumping ability. Eighteen female basketball players from a Sport College were randomly divided into two groups: VBRT (n = 10) and PBRT (n = 8). The six-week intervention consisted of two sessions per week of free-weight back squats with linear periodization from 65% to 95%1RM. In PBRT, the weights lifted were fixed based on 1RM percentage, while in VBRT, the weights were adjusted based on individualized velocity profiles. The T-30m sprint time, relative power of countermovement jump (RP-CMJ), and Wingate test were evaluated. The Wingate test assessed peak power (PP), mean power (MP), fatigue index (FI), maximal velocity (Vmax), and total work (TW). Results showed that VBRT produced a very likely improvement in RP-CMJ, Vmax, PP, and FI (Hedges' g = 0.55, 0.93, 0.68, 0.53, respectively, $p < 0.01$). On the other hand, PBRT produced a very likely improvement in MP (Hedges' g = 0.38) and TW (Hedges' g = 0.45). Although VBRT showed likely favorable effects in RP-CMJ, PP, and Vmax compared to PBRT ($p < 0.05$ for interaction effect), PBRT produced greater improvements in MP and TW ($p < 0.05$ for interaction effect). In conclusion, PBRT may be more effective in maintaining high-power velocity endurance, while VBRT has a greater impact on explosive power adaptations.

Keywords: load-velocity relationship; autoregulation; load monitoring; fixed-loading; resistance training; Wingate anaerobic performance

Citation: Zhang, M.; Li, D.; He, J.; Liang, X.; Li, D.; Song, W.; Ding, S.; Shu, J.; Sun, X.; Sun, J. Effects of Velocity-Based versus Percentage-Based Resistance Training on Explosive Neuromuscular Adaptations and Anaerobic Power in Sport-College Female Basketball Players. *Healthcare* **2023**, *11*, 623. https://doi.org/10.3390/healthcare11040623

Academic Editor: Felipe Aidar

Received: 2 February 2023
Revised: 14 February 2023
Accepted: 16 February 2023
Published: 20 February 2023

1. Introduction

"Traditionally, resistance training (RT) has been prescribed based on a percentage of an individual's one-repetition maximum (1RM), referred to as percentage-based resistance training (PBRT) [1]. This involves setting a fixed load based on a baseline %1RM before training, meaning the intensity is determined by the individual's %1RM. However, PBRT is unable to account for changes in muscle performance caused by life stressors and fatigue [2]. With the rise of linear position transducers (LPTs), strength training coaches can now gather real-time and kinetic data, leading to the widespread use of velocity-based resistance training (VBRT) [2,3]. VBRT is a novel form of autoregulated RT that adjusts intensity and volume based on an individualized load-velocity profile (LVP) regression equation [2,4,5]. This involves using the mean concentric velocity (MCV) of the first repetition as a measure of performance to adjust the training load. Trainers perform the exercise with maximal effort and the velocity of the concentric phase is recorded across different loads. Thresholds are established at each relative load or velocity loss, which are then used to adjust the subsequent training load and control the training volume [6]. By monitoring MCV data based on LVP, VBRT allows for training loads to be adjusted based on the athlete's physiological state and strength performance [7]. Notably, in contrast to PBRT, VBRT offers a more personalized approach to load prescription [2].

Recently, there have been several controlled trials that have compared the effects of VBRT and PBRT on physical performance measures such as strength, linear sprint, change of direction, jump, and aerobic endurance [8–10]. This comparison has become a focus in the field of strength and conditioning, and while these studies provide useful insights for coaches, the results in terms of muscle strength remain controversial and the mechanisms behind the adaptations are not fully understood [1,3,9,11]. To further shed light on this topic, this study aims to compare the two training protocols on lower limb muscular function and power performance in greater depth. The originality of this study lies in its exploration of the effects of VBRT and PBRT on anaerobic performance adaptations, an area that has not been studied in depth before.

Basketball is a sport that requires high levels of intensity and is largely based on anaerobic metabolism. Anaerobic power and capacity play a crucial role in determining the physical fitness and overall game performance of basketball players, particularly in defensive and offensive transitions [12]. To assess anaerobic performance in professional basketball players, the Wingate anaerobic power test (WAnT) has been widely used due to its reliability. The results of a study by Apostolidis et al. [13] showed a strong correlation between the mean power in the WAnT and the performance of basketball players, including control dribbling and high-intensity shuttle running.

This study aimed to compare the effects of VBRT and PBRT on lower-limb power and anaerobic performance in off-season female basketball players from a Sport College over a six-week linear mesocycle. The hypothesis was that VBRT, based on recent studies [1,9,10], would result in greater improvements in anaerobic performance compared to PBRT.

2. Materials and Methods

2.1. Participants

The study recruited 18 female basketball players from the Sport College Basketball Association (SCBA) Championship winning team. The players, who had an average age of 22.3 $\pm$ 1.8 years, height of 169.7 $\pm$ 7 cm, and body mass of 60.4 $\pm$ 5.8 kg, were randomly assigned to either the VBRT group (n = 10) or the PBRT group (n = 8) using card markers drawn by an uninformed researcher. The distribution of playing positions was equal among the groups to reduce the impact of position on anaerobic capacity [14]. The inclusion criteria were age over 18 years, at least 2 years of RT experience, no musculoskeletal injuries in the past 6 months, completion of a 10-week basketball training prior to the study, and a negative result from the Functional Movement Screen (FMS) test.

Participants were required to provide written informed consent prior to participating in the study. The study was approved by the local Ethics Committee and was in accordance with the Declaration of Helsinki. This ensured that the study was conducted in a fair and ethical manner, with the participants' wellbeing and rights being of utmost importance.

2.2. Experimental Design

All participants took part in a 6-week training program, which was conducted twice a week on Monday and Wednesday and followed a progressive mesocycle design. The program consisted of three load phases, each with specific training objectives (as shown in Figure 1). Participants performed two RT programs that only varied in amount of weight lifted and number of repetitions (velocity-based vs. percentage-based). The training volume in both programs corresponded to the number of repetitions. Additionally, both groups were verbally encouraged to perform a maximal voluntary contraction at the concentric phase with a standardized body posture during RT. The RT sessions were completed in the afternoon (3:30–4:00 p.m.), were separated by 48 h, and avoided holidays. Both RT programs consisted of free-weight back squats and bench presses and were supervised and monitored by two conditioning training coaches.

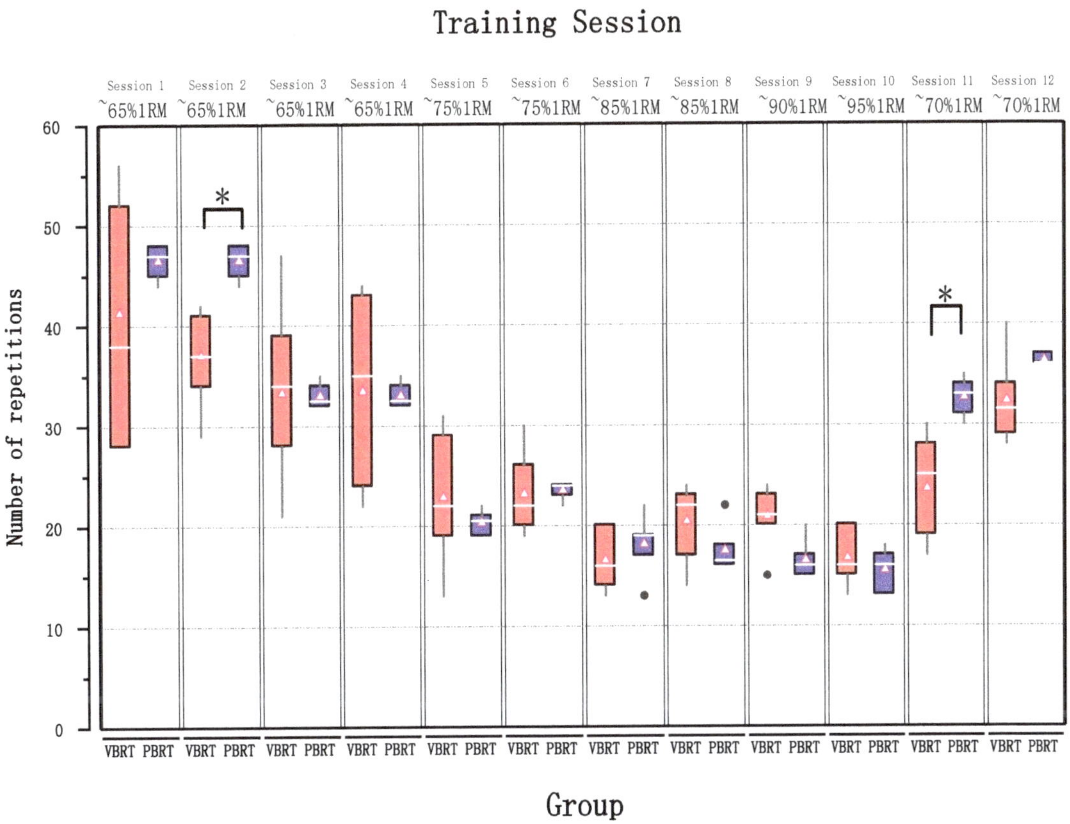

Figure 1. Number of repetitions in the squat exercise performed between VBRT and PBRT. Data are mean ± SD. VBRT: velocity-based resistance training. PBRT: percentage-based (%1RM) resistance training. Statistically significant differences between groups: * $p < 0.05$.

All tests were conducted in a laboratory setting, with a minimum of 48 h of rest and under similar time (±0.5 h) and environmental conditions (~27 °C and ~68% humidity). The outcomes of anaerobic performance, sprint, jump performance, and body composition were evaluated at the baseline (before randomization) and at the end of the intervention. The training loads (weights and repetitions) and kinematic data were continuously recorded during each session.

2.3. Testing Procedure

Before the baseline assessment, participants were asked to come to the laboratory and complete an informed consent form and questionnaire. Their personal information such as age, height, and weight was recorded, and a standardized warm-up was conducted. The warm-up included fascial relaxation, self-prescribed dynamic stretching, activation exercises, and barbell mobility work, which lasted approximately 20 min. After the warm-up, participants underwent a familiarization session with all laboratory tests to ensure they fully understood the testing procedures and to guarantee that they adhered to the strict technical requirements during the tests. This was followed by a barbell back squat repetition session to familiarize the participants with the equipment and technique.

All participants who met the inclusion criteria were permitted to participate in the study after the familiarization. Outcomes were evaluated at week 1 and week 7, where participants came to the laboratory to complete three sessions of assessments. These included body composition and 1 repetition maximum (1RM) assessment in session 1, jump, sprint test, and LVP assessment in session 2, and Wingate anaerobic test in session 3. Both baseline and post-test followed the same standardized warm-up protocol. The 1RM and LVP assessments were used to determine the training loads, but only performed at baseline. To minimize experimental error, the basketball coaches instructed all players to maintain a consistent diet and sleep pattern and monitored their additional resistance training during the intervention.

2.4. Measurements

2.4.1. Anaerobic Power Performance

All participants performed the Wingate Anaerobic Test (WAnT) on a mechanically braked cycle ergometer (Monark© 894E, Varberg, Sweden). Participants were instructed to remain seated and complete a standardized warm-up, which involved riding at 60 revolutions per minute for 3–4 min at 60W, followed by two 5-s no-load sprints at 90 rpm. After a brief interval, participants began a 30-s all-out effort to maintain maximum speed with a resistance of 7.5% body mass. Verbal encouragement was provided throughout the test.

The peak power (PP), mean power (MP), and fatigue index (FI) were recorded and analyzed. The data was collected in the laboratory and processed using the Monark software.

2.4.2. Jump and Sprint Testing

Relative peak power during a countermovement jump (RP-CMJ) and sprint ability were used as markers of explosive lower-limb power and athletic performance in basketball players. The RP-CMJ was conducted in three trials, with a 30-s rest in between, using the Smartjump wireless test mat (SmartJump; FusionSport, Coopers Plains, Queensland, Australia). Participants placed their hands on their hips, lowered themselves to the optimal level, and then jumped as high as possible. Following the CMJ, the participants completed three 30-m sprint trials with a 3-min rest in between. Sprint time was measured using the Smartspeed fusion sport (2 smart scans and pro, Australia), and a 1.5-m light gate was set up for the 30-m distance. The highest RP-CMJ and the fastest sprints were selected for further analysis. The test-retest reliability was high, with a coefficient variation of 0.99% and 1.4% for the T-30m and RP-CMJ, respectively. The intraclass correlation coefficients (ICC) with 95% confidence intervals (CI) were 0.968 (95% CI: 0.933–0.987) for T-30m, and 0.991 (95% CI: 0.981–0.996) for RP-CMJ.

2.4.3. Body Composition

Body composition was evaluated using a bioelectrical impedance analysis (InBody 770 Body Composition Analyzer, Biospace, Seoul, South Korea) [15]. Relevant parameters, including muscle mass (MM), free-fat mass (FFM), and body mass index (BMI) were measured. Body composition assessments were performed at least 3 days after the last training session. The assessment was performed before warm-up and there were no cases of menstrual period. The laboratory had an internal temperature range of 24–26 °C. All participants were required to participate in body composition assessments in a fasted and dehydrated state (no prior water or food for 4 h).

2.4.4. 1-RM Assessment

Body composition was evaluated using a bioelectrical impedance analysis device (InBody 770 Body Composition Analyzer, Biospace, Seoul, South Korea). The parameters measured included muscle mass (MM), free-fat mass (FFM), and body mass index (BMI). The assessments were performed at least 3 days after the participants' last training sessions, before their warm-ups. To minimize any impact of menstrual cycle, all participants were assessed when not in their menstrual period. The laboratory was maintained at a temperature range of 24–26 °C, and participants were required to be in a fasted and dehydrated state (no food or water consumed for 4 h prior) during the assessments.

2.4.5. LVP Assessment

The LPT was used to measure MCV during the free-weight back squat. Participants performed a protocol that included sets of 3 reps at 40%, 60%, 80%, and 90% of their baseline 1RM, with three minutes of rest between sets. The fastest MCV was used to calculate the LVP regression equation [9]. The individualized LVPs were determined by plotting MCV against load and applying a line of best fit, using the Gymaware cloud's reporter. The MCV corresponding to 65–95% of 1RM was used to adjust daily lifted weights during the VBRT.

2.5. Resistance Training Program

The PBRT was based on a fixed load calculated from the baseline 1RM [11]. In contrast, the VBRT group performed auto-regulation training, adjusting the weight and reps according to the achieved Mean Concentric Velocity (MCV) and the target velocity from the Load-Velocity Profile (LVP). The VBRT group's session target velocity was equivalent to the relative load in the PBRT group [9], albeit with different lifted weights. The specific velocity zones for each repetition and relative load were calculated for the VBRT group. If the MCV was 0.06 or 0.12 m/s above or below the target velocity, the next set weight was adjusted by 5% or 10% of the 1-RM [9]. The training information was provided to the strength coaches through visual and audio feedback.

During each training session, the average velocity was continuously monitored, and the appropriate load adjustments were made for each participant in the VBRT group. To ensure consistency, all participants utilized 20 kg barbells. The VBRT group also used LPTs (Gymaware Power Tool; Kinetic Performance Technologies, Australia), attached 60 cm to the right of the barbell center, to collect real-time concentric velocity data during the back squat exercise in every session.

2.6. Statistical Analysis

The descriptive statistics were presented as mean (standard deviation) or median (range). Test-retest reliability was evaluated through coefficient of variation (CV) and ICC with 95% CI. The one-way random effects model was used for this evaluation. To check for normality, the Shapiro-Wilk test was used, and Levene's test was used to determine homogeneity of variance. In case of abnormal distribution or heterogeneity, the Mann-Whitney U test and Wilcoxon test were used to examine within-group and between-group differences, respectively. However, if the data was normally distributed and had homogeneous variance, the *T*-test was used. A two-way analysis of variance (ANOVA) with repeated measures was performed to analyze the time effects and time x group interactions to identify the best performing group. If there were significant group interactions, between-group comparisons were performed with the Bonferroni post-hoc test.

Statistical significance was determined at a two-tailed $p < 0.05$. In addition, the clinical significance of the effect size (ES) of the within-group and between-group differences was evaluated using magnitude-based inference [16]. The standard mean difference (SMD), calculated as the mean change divided by the baseline standard deviation, and its associated measures, including the smallest worthwhile change (0.2 times the baseline standard deviation) and Hedges' g, were computed and used to determine the magnitude of the difference [16]. The effect size was calculated based on the Cohen scale, with positive SMD values indicating effects that favored the VBRT group, while negative SMD values indicated effects favoring the PBRT group. The magnitude of the effect was considered trivial (SMD < 0.2), small (0.2 to 0.59), moderate (0.6 to 1.19), or large (1.2 to 2.0) [16]. The likelihood of harmful or beneficial effects was estimated as almost certainly not likely (less than 0.5%), very unlikely (0.5% to 5%), unlikely (5% to 25%), possible (25% to 75%), likely (75% to 95%), very likely (95% to 99%), or almost certain (greater than 99.5%) [16]. In cases where both the harmful and beneficial changes were greater than 5%, the difference was considered unclear. The magnitude-based inferential statistics and intraclass correlation coefficients were calculated using a custom spreadsheet [17], with data analysis performed using jamovi 2.2.2 and R.

3. Results

No significant differences between VBRT and PBRT were found at baseline for all descriptive variables (Table 1).

Table 1. Participants characteristics.

Characteristic	VBRT	PBRT	*p*-Value	SMD
Age (y) *	22.6 ± 1.6	22.0 ± 2.0	0.49	0.32
Training years (y) *	7.8 ± 3.4	8.2 ± 2.6	0.85	0.1
Height (cm) *	169.8 ± 6.0	169.4 ± 8.1	0.9	0.06
Body mass (kg) *	60.0 ± 4.8	61.0 ± 7.7	0.92	0.04
Fat mass (kg) *	21.8 ± 6.1	21.5 ± 4.6	0.92	0.05
Muscle mass (kg) *	43.1 ± 3.1	45.1 ± 4.6	0.3	0.49
BMI *	21.7 ± 1.9	21.4 ± 2.1	0.78	0.13
Fat Free Mass (FFM) *	45.9 ± 3.3	46.6 ± 4.1	0.7	0.04
FMS test ~	16 (13–16)	15 (13–16)	0.39	0.39
The deep squat ~	2 (2–3)	2 (2–3)	1	0
Back squat 1-RM (kg) *	81.0 ± 12.4	85.9 ± 6.9	0.33	−0.45
R-SQ 1RM *	1.3 ± 0.2	1.4 ± 0.2	0.34	−0.45
Total work (J) *	12,492.2 ± 1294.4	12,262.3 ± 1709.1	0.75	0.15

Data are median (range) or mean ± SD. *p*-values for * *t*-test and ~ Mann–Whitney U-test are applied to test for differences between VBRT and PBRT groups.

3.1. Training Loads

The training data is depicted in Figure 1. After a six-week intervention, the VBRT group performed fewer repetitions compared to the PBRT group (31.1 ± 8.7 vs. 33.9 ± 12.17, respectively; $p < 0.05$). However, no significant difference was observed in the average weight lifted between the two groups (60.7 ± 11.9 vs. 63 ± 11.9, $p > 0.05$). The VBRT group experienced a higher intensity in weightlifting, as evidenced by a higher %1RM (80.2 ± 5.9% vs. 72 ± 6.5%, respectively) compared to the PBRT group.

3.2. Body Composition

No significant within-group differences were observed from baseline to post-intervention, and no time or group by time interaction effect was found for any of the lower limb muscle mass related parameters (Table 2).

Table 2. Results of lower limb muscle mass and morphological development.

Outcome	VBRT (n = 10)		SMD (95%CI)	PBRT (n = 8)		SMD(95%CI)	RM-ANOVA	
	Baseline	Post-Intervention		Baseline	Post-Intervention		Time	Group × Time
BM (kg)	60.0 ± 4.2	59.6 ± 5.0	−0.08 (−0.22, 0.03)	61.0 ± 7.7	61.2 ± 7.8	−0.02 (−0.07, 0.11)	0.636	0.305
FFM (kg)	45.9 ± 3.3	46.5 ± 4.0	0.15 (−0.22, 0.56)	46.6 ± 4.1	46.5 ± 4.2	−0.03 (−0.17, 0.11)	0.557	0.391
BMI (kg/m²)	21.7 ± 1.9	21.5 ± 1.9	−0.1 (−0.24, 0.02)	21.4 ± 2.1	21.4 ± 2.0	−0.01 (−0.12, 0.09)	0.189	0.308
MM (kg)	43.1 ± 3.1	43.1 ± 3.6	0 (−0.20, 0.20)	45.1 ± 4.6	44.8 ± 4.7	−0.05 (−0.14, 0.04)	0.609	0.609
HC (cm)	93.3 ± 2.5	93.1 ± 3.0	−0.08 (−0.24, 0.06)	92.8 ± 4.1	92.6 ± 4.1	−0.04 (−0.14, 0.03)	0.174	0.887
LLC (cm)	50.2 ± 1.3	50.0 ± 1.5	−0.17 (−0.48, 0.1)	50.4 ± 3.2	50.4 ± 3.1	−0.02 (−0.11, 0.07)	0.256	0.443
RLC (cm)	50.3 ± 1.4	50 ± 1.5	−0.2(−0.55, 0.09)	50.7 ± 3.3	50.5 ± 3.2	−0.04 (−0.14, 0.04)	0.116	0.571

Abbreviations: BM = body mass; FFM = Fat Free Mass; BMI = body mass index, BMI = mass (kg)/height^2 (m); MM = muscle mass; HC: hip circumference; LLC, RLC: left leg circumference, right leg circumference.

3.3. WAnT Performance

T Significant time effects were observed for maximal velocity (Vmax), total work (TW), and the related outcomes of PP, MP, and PD ($p < 0.05$). Results from separate analyses indicated that only within-group differences from baseline to post-intervention were significant in Vmax for the VBRT group ($p < 0.001$, effect size [ES] = 0.93) and in the related outcomes of PP ($p < 0.01$, ES = 0.5 to 0.68; see Figure 2A,B) and PD ($p < 0.01$,

ES = 0.51 to 0.58; see Figure 2E) for the VBRT group. However, only the PBRT group showed significant improvements in MP ($p < 0.01$, ES = 0.38; see Figure 2C,D) and TW ($p < 0.01$, ES = 0.45; see Figure 2F). A significant "group × time" interaction effect was observed for MP and TW ($p < 0.05$; see Figure 2C,F). No significant group by time interaction effect was noted for the remaining anaerobic-related outcomes (see Table 3).

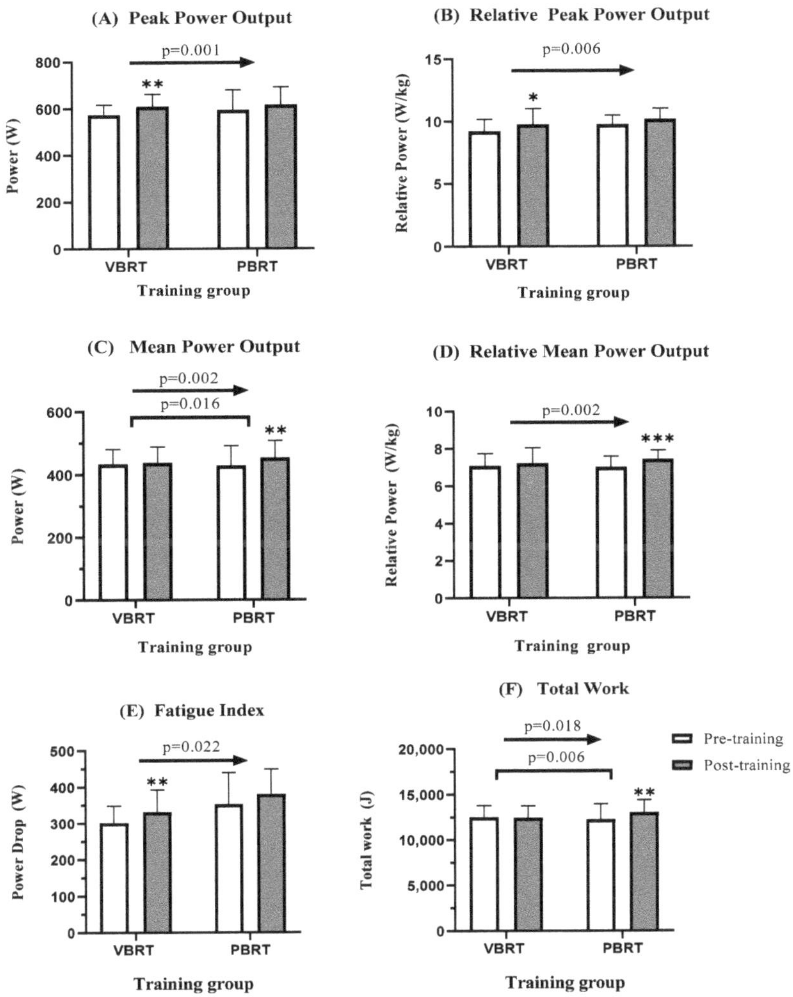

Figure 2. Mean changes in absolute (**A**) and relative peak power output (**B**), absolute (**C**) and relative mean power output (**D**), fatigue index (**E**) and total work (**F**) for the Wingate anaerobic power test after 6 weeks of training. * indicates significant difference baseline vs post-intervention: * $p < 0.05$, ** $p < 0.01$, *** $p < 0.001$; → indicates significant time effect; p-value show significant group by time effect.

Table 3. Results of mechanisms of lower limb muscle anaerobic performance adaptation between VBRT and PBRT.

Outcome	VBRT				PBRT				RM-ANOVA	
	Baseline	Post-Intervention	SMD (95%CI)	Inference	Baseline	Post-Intervention	SMD (95%CI)	Inference	Time	Group × Time
30-m sprint (s)	4.78 ± 0.2	4.71 ± 0.2	−0.46 (−0.87, −0.16)	71/28/1 Unclear	4.8 ± 0.1	4.71 ± 0.2	−0.2 (−1.35, 0.87)	55/20/25 Unclear	0.053	0.197
RP-CMJ (W/kg)	45.7 ± 5.2	48.7 ± 5.3 **	0.55 (0.25, 0.99)	98/2/0 Very Likely	47.3 ± 3.5	47.4 ± 2.8	0.03 (−0.43, 0.51)	22/62/16 Unclear	0.012	0.018
T-PP (ms)	2976.5 ± 853.7	2932.5 ± 2817.7	−0.03 (−0.77, 0.7)	54/35/11 Unclear	2416.3 ± 995.4	2478.8.2 ± 1367	0.05 (−0.67, 0.55)	62/25/14 Unclear	0.639	0.568
V-max (m/s)	147.8 ± 13.1	160.5 ± 13.0 ***	0.94 (0.54, 1.37)	99.9/0.1/0 Almost	145 ± 17.8	154.2 ± 14.4	0.54 (−0.06, 1.31)	87/11/2 Possibly	0.001	0.501
TW (J)	12,492 ± 1294	12,420 ± 1318	0.05 (−0.34, 0.22)	4/81/15 Unclear	12,262 ± 1709	12,998 ± 1388 **	0.45 (0.25, 0.80)	96.5/3.4/0.0 Very Likely	0.018	0.006
PP [W]	572.7 ± 43.9	607.4 ± 54.0 **	0.68 (0.31, 1.21)	99/1/0 Very Likely	592.1 ± 87.4	615.3 ± 76.5	0.27 (−0.11, 0.74)	63.3/34.7/2.0 Unclear	0.001	0.524
RPP [W/kg]	9.2 ± 1.0	9.8 ± 1.3 *	0.5 (0.13, 1.31)	96/4/0 Very Likely	9.7 ± 0.8	10.2 ± 0.8	0.65 (−0.03, 1.58)	83.7/13.2/3.1 Possibly	0.006	0.672
MP [W]	432.8 ± 48.3	436.3 ± 51.4	0.07 (−0.16, 0.31)	15/83/2 Unclear	427.8 ± 63.1	451.8 ± 55.5 **	0.38 (0.23, 0.66)	97.4/2.6/0.0 Very Likely	0.002	0.016
RMP [W/kg]	7.1 ± 0.7	7.2 ± 0.9	0.16 (−0.09, 0.46)	49/49/2 Unclear	7.0 ± 0.6	7.4 ± 0.5 ***	0.7 (0.41, 1.22)	99.7/0.3/0.0 Almost	0.002	0.079
PD [W]	300.8 ± 47.0	331.0 ± 62.0 **	0.53 (0.26, 0.93)	98/2/0 Very Likely	351.6 ± 87.9	379.4 ± 69.6	0.33 (−0.28, 1.07)	65.1/29.4/5.5 Unclear	0.022	0.916
PD [W/kg]	4.9 ± 0.9	5.5 ± 1.1 **	0.5 (0.26, 0.88)	99/1/0 Very Likely	5.6 ± 0.9	6.1 ± 1.0	0.59 (−0.26, 1.49)	80.5/14.1/5.4 Possibly	0.008	0.981
PD [W/s]	10 ± 1.6	11 ± 2.1 **	0.53 (0.26, 0.93)	98/2/0 Very Likely	11.7 ± 2.9	12.6 ± 2.3	0.33 (−0.28, 1.07)	73.9/17.7/8.5 Possibly	0.022	0.916
PD [%]	53.3 ± 5.3	55.7 ± 5.6	0.41 (−0.11, 1.05)	80/18/2 Possibly	56.8 ± 7.2	60.5 ± 6.4	0.51 (−0.47, 1.7)	73.9/17.7/8.5 Possibly	0.083	0.679

Data are mean ± SD. * indicates significances difference = * $p < 0.05$, ** $p < 0.01$, *** $p < 0.001$. Inferences = magnitude-based inference; RM-ANOVA = repeated-measures analysis of variance; RP-CMJ = the relative power of countermovement jump, peak power (W)/body mass (kg); T-PP = time to peak power; TW = Total work; PP, RPP = absolute peak power and relative peak power output; MP = absolute mean power and relative mean power output; PD = power drop for the Wingate anaerobic power test; VBRT = velocity-based resistance training; PBRT= (%1RM) percentage-based resistance training. CI = confidence interval; SMD = standardized mean difference; Inference = magnitude based.

3.4. *Jump and Sprint Performance*

A significant time effect ($p = 0.012$) and group-by-time interaction effect ($p = 0.018$) were observed for RP-CMJ. The VBRT group showed a very likely improvement in RP-CMJ (7.0%; ES = 0.55) compared to baseline (Figure 3a). A comparison of between-group effects revealed that VBRT was more likely to be beneficial for RP-CMJ (Figure 3b). However, no group-by-time interaction and no significant improvement were found for T-30m (Table 3, Figure 3a).

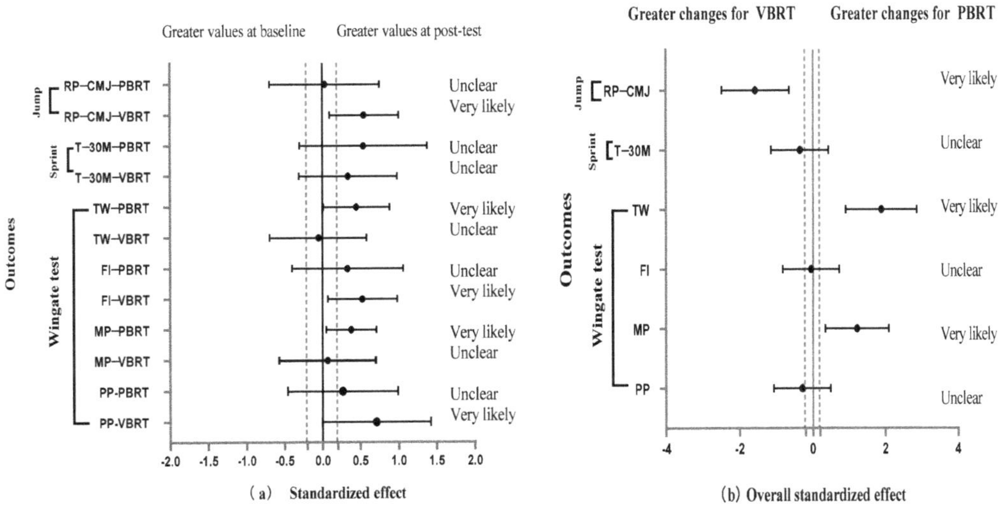

Figure 3. Standardized effect (90%CI) in all outcomes (**a**) between baseline and post−test and (**b**) between VBRT and PBRT groups. RP−CMJ = the relative power of countermovement jump, peak power(W)/body mass(kg); T−30 m = 30 m sprint running time; TW = total work; PP = peak power output; MP = mean power output; FI = fatigue index for the Wingate anaerobic test.

3.5. Training Effect

When comparing the power adaptation between the VBRT and PBRT (Figure 3), VBRT was very likely preferable for RP-CMJ (SMD = 0.55), whereas PBRT was very likely more beneficial for TW (SMD = 0.45) and MP (SMD = 0.38).

4. Discussion

The purpose of this study was to compare the effects of two load prescription methods, VBRT and PBRT, during a six-week progressive resistance training program on lower-limb power adaptation in female basketball players. The results showed that VBRT elicited greater improvements in RP-CMJ, Vmax, and PP compared to PBRT, which had more favorable effects on MP and TW. The findings support the notion that VBRT is effective in improving vertical jump performance, as evidenced by previous studies in various populations. The mechanisms behind these improvements may be attributed to the higher load and fewer repetitions implemented in the VBRT program, which reduced mechanical stress and fatigue while improving power output.

The study evaluated the impact of two resistance training methods, individualized MCV-based and %1RM-based on CMJ height and T-30M. After a six-week intervention, the results showed that only the VBRT elicited improvements in RP-CMJ. This finding is supported by previous studies, including Orange et al. [11] which compared the effects of strength and jumping performance of rugby league players with seven-week VBRT and PBT, and found a likely improvement in CMJ height for both groups, although there were no significant differences between groups. Another study by Banyard et al. [9] found likely improvements in the fastest velocity of loaded CMJ (PV-CMJ) in 24 trained men with VBRT. The systematic review [18] also supports the use of velocity loss metrics as a monitoring tool in strength training, as it can improve CMJ height to varying degrees.

The present study aimed to assess the effects of resistance training on lower-limb explosive power output using the relative power output of the CMJ as a direct variable. The findings suggest that VBRT is more effective than PBRT or different velocity loss interventions in improving vertical jump performance, including peak velocity and CMJ height.

This has been observed in various populations, including players, fitness enthusiasts, and female athletes. The results provide valuable insights for sports that require high jumping ability, such as basketball and volleyball. The higher load and fewer repetitions mechanism of VBRT may explain its superior efficacy [19]. Additionally, routine strength training can lead to a decrease in velocity and power output with an increase in repetitions. High velocity-loss and high repetition resistance training can result in a significant reduction in type IIX fibers, which may negatively impact strength development and prolong recovery [20]. Velocity-based prescription and monitoring velocity loss can mitigate these issues by ensuring higher quality completion of each repetition and reducing unnecessary mechanical stress and fatigue [18]. The present study highlights the importance of heavy intensity and slightly fewer repetitions in enhancing explosive power.

The results regarding the effects on sprint ability in both groups are inconclusive due to the lack of plyometrics and linear sprint training in the six-week intervention. Previous studies have shown mixed results. Banyard et al. study on adult trained males (n = 24) reported that VBRT improved 10 m and 20 m sprint performance (10 m: ES = 1.24; 20 m: ES = 1.27). However, a larger study on youth football players over 12 weeks of maximum velocity (VG) and maximal strength (RMG) training found that only VG improved 30m sprint performance ($p < 0.001$; ES = −1.26) [21]. Further research is required to determine whether VBRT can improve sprint performance.

Currently, most studies on WAnT have focused on the acute effects of non-strength training interventions. The limited and complex nature of laboratory-based studies has resulted in a scarcity of research examining the impact of resistance training on anaerobic performance. In a study by Rønnestad et al. [22], 16 elite cyclists were subjected to 25 weeks of combined endurance and percentage-based half-squat training (E + S) or endurance training only (E). Results showed a moderate effect of E + S on relative peak power (PP) in the WAnT (ES = 0.76). Pallares et al. [23] also demonstrated the effectiveness of VBRT through improved parallel-squat PP and MP) (ES = 0.15–0.56). While these studies suggest that VBRT or PBRT may have a positive effect on anaerobic performance, the underlying mechanism remains unclear. Moreover, there is a lack of direct comparative research in this field.

The anaerobic metabolic capacity is influenced by several factors including age, gender, and muscle mass. PP during the WAnT reflects the energy-generating capacity of the ATP-CP system and is dependent on muscle mass and maximum leg strength [24], particularly the amount of FFM. MP during the test reflects the energy generated from glycolysis and represents muscle endurance [25]. Previous research has shown that high velocity-loss RT can increase muscle cross-sectional area (CSA) and muscle volume, particularly in the vastus lateralis and intermedius muscles, with the use of higher loads and fewer repetitions [26]. However, the current study did not observe significant changes in FFM and muscle mass, which may be due to differences in the number of repetitions and overall training volume compared to previous studies. Thus, it is inappropriate to draw conclusions on the relationship between neuromuscular adaptations and muscle mass or hypertrophy based on the results of this study.

The present study aimed to investigate the relationship between muscle fiber type and anaerobic capacity, as manifested in the percentage of fast-muscle fibers. Our findings showed a positive correlation between the high percentage of fast-muscle fibers and high anaerobic power output during contraction, as well as maximum knee extension force, contraction force, and velocity. The dominance of fast muscle fibers in maximum instantaneous power output and short-duration anaerobic power was also observed. In exercises that heavily rely on anaerobic metabolic energy, faster muscle fibers or larger cross-sectional area can sustain maximal power output for a relatively longer period. Lahti et al. [27] demonstrated that high-intensity training, such as the VBRT employed in this study, can induce a shift in fiber type towards type IIa fast muscle fibers and enhance explosive power in athletes. Therefore, athletes can increase the proportion of fast fibers through training and thereby shift the force-velocity curve toward the right and upward. In the overview of the literature and theory, the higher intensity and lower volume prescription observed in this study during VBRT group may explain the observed increase in PP and V-max, as well as RP and peak velocity of the CMJ were also considered. It seemed possible that these results were also due to the feedback during RT that inspired the athletes to accomplish concentric velocity in VBRT [28], which contributed to heavier lifting weights, as well as faster and fewer repetitions, thus possibly inducing a shift in type IIa fast muscle fibers or a positive shift in the force-velocity curve. Myofibrillar subclasses can be converted rather quickly into a more active type II subclass through RT programs, and high-intensity exercises appear to facilitate the conversion of myofibrillar subclasses from type IIx to type IIa. Higher VL allowed for greater volume, thus maximizing muscle hypertrophy, while the lower VL triggered positive neuromuscular-specific adaptations [26]. Our results also showed that VBRT induced greater adaptation of faster and less fatigue-resistant muscle fibers, whereas the PBRT resulted in higher muscle endurance and time to exhaustion but had less impact on power output. Further studies are needed to examine the differences in changes in force-velocity relationship between these two strength methods. This research has practical implications for athletic performance and neuromuscular adaptations, as it provides novel insights into the differences between VBRT and PBRT from an anaerobic power capacity perspective.

The finding suggests that the two strength training methods, VBRT and PBRT, induce distinct neuromuscular adaptations. Both high power anaerobic endurance and instantaneous explosive power are key physical fitness factors crucial for basketball performance. By monitoring real-time muscle contraction velocity during strength training, a method can be prescribed that utilizes higher intensity loading weights, promotes specific adaptations, and reduces fatigue. This study sheds light on the underlying mechanisms of action of both VBRT and PBRT, reducing the potential for subjective bias from physical fitness experts and athletes. As a result, it provides a basis for choosing the appropriate strength training method for specific training goals, rather than dismissing previous training approaches.

This study found that VBRT was effective in improving PP, V-max, and RP-CMJ in basketball players. These results provide new insights into the differential impact of VBRT and PBRT and could aid in the selection of strength training programs for sports that require high jumping ability. The use of velocity-based prescription and monitoring in resistance training programs was emphasized by these findings, highlighting their practical significance in improving athletic performance in sports such as basketball and volleyball.

The limitations of this study include the inability to determine changes in muscle fiber type or percentage distributions and a small sample size. These limitations highlight the need for future research with a larger sample size to confirm the transformation of fiber types. Despite these limitations, the study should be acknowledged for its contribution to the field of sports science by exploring the influence of VBRT on female basketball players, which is an understudied area [29]. Further research is needed to expand upon the results and address the limitations of the study.

5. Conclusions

The results of this study demonstrate that after six weeks of back squat training with different load prescription protocols, VBRT and PBRT are different as regards improving physical parameters related to basketball performance. Specifically, VBRT was effective in improving PP, V-max, and RP-CMJ, while PBRT was more beneficial in improving MP and TW. These findings suggest that PBRT might target high power velocity endurance, whereas VBRT might primarily induce greater instantaneous mechanical power for explosive adaptations.

Author Contributions: M.Z., D.L. (Duanying Li), J.H., X.S. and J.S. (Jian Sun) designed the study. M.Z., X.L., J.H., J.S. (Jie Shu) and D.L. (Dongyu Li) involved in baseline test, experimental preparation, and data collection. M.Z., W.S., S.D., J.S. (Jie Shu) and D.L. (Duanying Li) contributed to the statistical analyses and interpretation. M.Z., X.S. and J.S. (Jian Sun) wrote the original draft and revised it. All authors provided comments, approved the final version of the manuscript and agreed to be accountable for all aspects of the work in ensuring that questions related to the accuracy or integrity of any part of the work are appropriately investigated and resolved. All persons designated as authors qualify for authorship, and all those who qualify for authorship are listed. All authors have read and agreed to the published version of the manuscript.

Funding: This work was supported by the National Social Science Foundation of China and Excellent Doctoral dissertation Project. Project name: Research on systematic biological principles of performance training in competitive sports (Grant No. 20FTYB008).

Institutional Review Board Statement: The studies involving human participants were reviewed and approved by the Ethics Committee of Guangzhou Sport University (2022LCLL-02). The trial was registered at www.chictr.org.cn (accessed on 21 December 2022). The participants provided their written informed consent to participate in this study.

Informed Consent Statement: Informed consent was obtained from all subjects involved in the study.

Data Availability Statement: The original contributions presented in the study can be directed to the corresponding authors. Written informed consent has been obtained from the patients to publish this paper.

Acknowledgments: The authors would like to thank all of the participants for providing their valuable time in volunteering for this study, and Guangzhou Sport University, which provided all testing equipment. We confirm that the experiments comply with the current laws of the country in which they were performed and there is no conflict of interest to declare.

Conflicts of Interest: The authors declare no conflict of interest.

References

1. Dorrell, H.F.; Smith, M.F.; Gee, T.I. Comparison of Velocity-Based and Traditional Percentage-Based Loading Methods on Maximal Strength and Power Adaptations. *J. Strength Cond. Res.* **2020**, *34*, 46–53. [CrossRef] [PubMed]
2. Weakley, J.; Mann, B.; Banyard, H.; Mclaren, S.; Garcia-Ramos, A. Velocity-Based Training: From Theory to Application. *Strength Cond. J.* **2020**, *43*, 31–49. [CrossRef]
3. Zhang, M.; Tan, Q.; Sun, J.; Ding, S.; Yang, Q.; Zhang, Z.; Lu, J.; Liang, X.; Li, D. Comparison of Velocity and Percentage-based Training on Maximal Strength: Meta-analysis. *Int. J. Sport. Med.* **2022**, *43*, 981–995. [CrossRef] [PubMed]
4. Nevin, J. Autoregulated Resistance Training: Does Velocity-Based Training Represent the Future? *Strength Cond. J.* **2019**, *41*, 34–39. [CrossRef]
5. Hickmott, L.M.; Chilibeck, P.D.; Shaw, K.A.; Butcher, S.J. The Effect of Load and Volume Autoregulation on Muscular Strength and Hypertrophy: A Systematic Review and Meta-Analysis. *Sport. Med.-Open* **2022**, *8*, 1–35. [CrossRef]
6. González-Badillo, J.J.; Marques, M.C.; Sánchez-Medina, L. The importance of movement velocity as a measure to control resistance training intensity. *J. Hum. Kinet.* **2011**, *29*, 15–19. [CrossRef]
7. González-Badillo, J.J.; Sánchez-Medina, L. Movement velocity as a measure of loading intensity in resistance training. *Int. J. Sports Med.* **2010**, *31*, 347–352. [CrossRef]
8. Montalvo-Perez, A.; Alejo, L.B.; Valenzuela, P.L.; Gil-Cabrera, J.; Talavera, E.; Luia, A.; Barranco-Gil, D. Traditional Versus Velocity-Based Resistance Training in Competitive Female Cyclists: A Randomized Controlled Trial. *Front. Physiol.* **2021**, *12*, 586113. [CrossRef]
9. Banyard, H.G.; Tufano, J.J.; Weakley, J.J.S.; Wu, S.; Jukic, I.; Nosaka, K. Superior Changes in Jump, Sprint, and Change-of-Direction Performance but Not Maximal Strength Following 6 Weeks of Velocity-Based Training Compared With 1-Repetition-Maximum Percentage-Based Training. *Int. J. Sports Physiol. Perform.* **2020**, *16*, 232–242. [CrossRef]
10. Zhang, M.; Liang, X.; Huang, W.; Ding, S.; Li, G.; Cui, X.; Li, C.; Zhou, Y.; Sun, J.; Li, D. The Effects of Velocity-based Versus Percentage-based Resistance Training on Athletic Performances in Sport-Collegiate Female Basketball Players. *Front. Physiol.* **2023**, *13*, 2739. [CrossRef]
11. Orange, S.T.; Metcalfe, J.W.; Robinson, A.; Applegarth, M.J.; Liefeith, A. Effects of In-Season Velocity- Versus Percentage-Based Training in Academy Rugby League Players. *Int. J. Sports Physiol. Perform.* **2020**, *15*, 554–561. [CrossRef]
12. Ziv, G.; Lidor, R. Physical attributes, physiological characteristics, on-court performances and nutritional strategies of female and male basketball players. *Sports Med.* **2009**, *39*, 547–568. [CrossRef] [PubMed]
13. Apostolidis, N.; Nassis, G.; Bolatoglou, T.; Geladas, N. Physiological and technical characteristics of elite young basketball players. *J. Sports Med. Phys. Fit.* **2004**, *44*, 157–163.
14. Hoare, D.G. Predicting success in junior elite basketball players–the contribution of anthropometic and physiological attributes. *J. Sci. Med. Sport* **2000**, *3*, 391–405. [CrossRef] [PubMed]

15. Campa, F.; Toselli, S.; Mazzilli, M.; Gobbo, L.A.; Coratella, G. Assessment of body composition in athletes: A narrative review of available methods with special reference to quantitative and qualitative bioimpedance analysis. *Nutrients* **2021**, *13*, 1620. [CrossRef] [PubMed]
16. Hopkins, W.G.; Marshall, S.W.; Batterham, A.M.; Hanin, J. Progressive statistics for studies in sports medicine and exercise science. *Med. Sci. Sports Exerc.* **2009**, *41*, 3–13. [CrossRef]
17. Hopkins, W.G. Spreadsheets for analysis of controlled trials, with adjustment for a subject characteristic. *Sport Sci.* **2006**, *10*, 46–50.
18. Pareja-Blanco, F.; Rodriguez-Rosell, D.; Sanchez-Medina, L.; Sanchis-Moysi, J.; Dorado, C.; Mora-Custodio, R.; Yanez-Garcia, J.M.; Morales-Alamo, D.; Perez-Suarez, I.; Calbet, J.A.L.; et al. Effects of velocity loss during resistance training on athletic performance, strength gains and muscle adaptations. *Scand. J. Med. Sci. Sports* **2017**, *27*, 724–735. [CrossRef]
19. Sanchez-Medina, L.; González-Badillo, J.J. Velocity loss as an indicator of neuromuscular fatigue during resistance training. *Med. Sci. Sports Exerc.* **2011**, *43*, 1725–1734.
20. Enoka, R.M.; Duchateau, J. Muscle fatigue: What, why and how it influences muscle function. *J. Physiol.* **2008**, *586*, 11–23.
21. Ortega, J.A.F.; Reyes, Y.G.D.l.; Peña, F.R.G. Effects of strength training based on velocity versus traditional training on muscle mass, neuromuscular activation, and indicators of maximal power and strength in girls soccer players. *Apunt. Sports Med.* **2020**, *55*, 53–61. [CrossRef]
22. Rønnestad, B.R.; Hansen, J.; Hollan, I.; Ellefsen, S. Strength training improves performance and pedaling characteristics in elite cyclists. *Scand. J. Med. Sci. Sports* **2015**, *25*, e89–e98. [CrossRef] [PubMed]
23. Pallares, J.G.; Cava, A.M.; Courel-Ibanez, J.; Gonzalez-Badillo, J.J.; Moran-Navarro, R. Full squat produces greater neuromuscular and functional adaptations and lower pain than partial squats after prolonged resistance training. *Eur. J. Sport Sci.* **2020**, *20*, 115–124. [CrossRef] [PubMed]
24. Izquierdo, M.; Ibanez, J.; Hakkinen, K.; Kraemer, W.J.; Ruesta, M.; Gorostiaga, E.M. Maximal strength and power, muscle mass, endurance and serum hormones in weightlifters and road cyclists. *J. Sports Sci.* **2004**, *22*, 465–478. [CrossRef]
25. Wilmore, J.H.; Costill, D.L.; Gleim, G.W. Physiology of sport and exercise. *Med. Sci. Sports Exerc.* **1995**, *27*, 792. [CrossRef]
26. Pareja-Blanco, F.; Alcazar, J.; Cornejo-Daza, P.J.; Sanchez-Valdepenas, J.; Rodriguez-Lopez, C.; Hidalgo-de Mora, J.; Sanchez-Moreno, M.; Bachero-Mena, B.; Alegre, L.M.; Ortega-Becerra, M. Effects of velocity loss in the bench press exercise on strength gains, neuromuscular adaptations, and muscle hypertrophy. *Scand. J. Med. Sci. Sports* **2020**, *30*, 2154–2166. [CrossRef]
27. Lahti, J.; Jimenez-Reyes, P.; Cross, M.R.; Samozino, P.; Chassaing, P.; Simond-Cote, B.; Ahtiainen, J.; Morin, J.B. Individual Sprint Force-Velocity Profile Adaptations to In-Season Assisted and Resisted Velocity-Based Training in Professional Rugby. *Sports* **2020**, *8*, 74. [CrossRef]
28. Randell, A.D.; Cronin, J.B.; Keogh, J.W.; Gill, N.D.; Pedersen, M.C. Effect of instantaneous performance feedback during 6 weeks of velocity-based resistance training on sport-specific performance tests. *J. Strength Cond. Res.* **2011**, *25*, 87–93. [CrossRef]
29. Gantois, P.; Nakamura, F.; Alcazar, J.; Fortes, L.; Pareja-Blanco, F.; Fonseca, F. The effects of different intra-set velocity loss thresholds on lower-limb adaptations to resistance training in young adults: A systematic review and meta-analysis. *SportRXiv* **2021**. [CrossRef]

healthcare

MDPI

Article

Swimmers with Down Syndrome Are Healthier and Physically Fit than Their Untrained Peers

Ana Querido [1,2,3,*], Mário J. Costa [2,3], Dália Araújo [2,3], António R. Sampaio [1,2,3], João P. Vilas-Boas [2,3], Rui Corredeira [4], Daniel J. Daly [5] and Ricardo J. Fernandes [2,3]

1 N2i, Polytechnic Institute of Maia, 4475-690 Maia, Portugal
2 Centre of Research, Education, Innovation and Intervention in Sport, CIFI2D, Faculty of Sport, University of Porto, 4200-450 Porto, Portugal
3 Porto Biomechanics Laboratory, LABIOMEP-UP, Faculty of Sport, University of Porto, 4200-450 Porto, Portugal
4 Research Centre in Physical Activity, Health and Leisure, CIAFEL, Faculty of Sport, University of Porto, 4200-450 Porto, Portugal
5 Faculty of Movement and Rehabilitation Sciences, Katholiek Universiteit Leuven, 3001 Leuven, Belgium
* Correspondence: d012072@umaia.pt

Abstract: While there are positive benefits from physical activity participation for individuals with Down syndrome, little is known about the effects of swimming training. The aim of this study was to compare the body composition and physical fitness profile of competitive swimmers and moderately active (untrained) individuals with Down syndrome. The Eurofit Special test was applied to a group of competitive swimmers (n = 18) and a group of untrained individuals (n = 19), all with Down syndrome. In addition, measurements were taken to determine body composition characteristics. The results showed differences between swimmers and untrained subjects in height, sum of the four skinfolds, body fat %, fat mass index and all items of the Eurofit Special test. Swimmers with Down syndrome exhibited physical fitness levels near to the Eurofit standards, although lower fitness levels were attained by these persons when compared to athletes with intellectual disability. It can be concluded that the practice of competitive swimming seems to counteract the tendency for obesity in persons with Down syndrome and also helps to increase strength, speed and balance.

Keywords: physical fitness; body composition; health; measurement; Down syndrome

Citation: Querido, A.; Costa, M.J.; Araújo, D.; Sampaio, A.R.; Vilas-Boas, J.P.; Corredeira, R.; Daly, D.J.; Fernandes, R.J. Swimmers with Down Syndrome Are Healthier and Physically Fit than Their Untrained Peers. *Healthcare* **2023**, *11*, 482. https://doi.org/10.3390/healthcare11040482

Academic Editors: Herbert Löllgen and João Paulo Brito

Received: 27 December 2022
Revised: 3 February 2023
Accepted: 4 February 2023
Published: 7 February 2023

1. Introduction

Down syndrome, a form of intellectual disability, is a genetic disorder caused by the presence of the whole (or part) of an extra copy of chromosome 21, with a global incidence estimation of 1 in 1000 to 1 in 1200 live births [1]. These individuals, present distinctive physical features, are predisposed to a higher incidence of cardiovascular disease [2], diabetes [3], osteoporosis and obesity, and more susceptible to a premature and significant decline in function with age [4]. Despite this, the infant Down syndrome survival rate, as well as life expectancy in general, continues to increase [5,6].

Lack of regular physical activity has been identified as one of the most significant health risks and people living with chronic conditions or disability are now being given recommendations for the first time [7]. This inactivity results in an increased threat of chronic conditions (e.g., cardiovascular disease and type 2 diabetes) [8] and is considered as a predictor of mortality in the Down syndrome population [9]. Literature indicates low fitness levels in these individuals [10–12], which may be related to sedentary lifestyles [13], limited social and recreational opportunities [14] and/or low motivation to be physically active [15]. Nevertheless, several studies have indicated positive benefits from physical activity participation for these individuals [16–18] and evidence suggests that physical activity can increase their physical fitness [19]. Specifically, aquatic exercise has been shown to offer benefits for people with intellectual disabilities in terms of cardiorespiratory endurance, muscular endurance, speed, static balance and agility [20,21].

There has been an increasing interest from people with Down syndrome in competitive swimming, with the participation of ~200 swimmers at the 2022 World Championships held in Portugal. Even if physical activity and sport are meaningful to many people, including those with intellectual disabilities, research in this topic has focused mainly on inactive participants [22], while trained individuals are scarcely studied [23]. In the specific case of competitive swimming, one study showed that an 18 week training intervention did not promote clear changes in jumping performance or body composition in swimmers with Down syndrome [24]. In a contrasting study, 33 weeks of swimming training lead to improved health status and swimming skills [25]. So, some mixed findings exist on how swimmers with Down syndrome may react to swimming training and exhibit improved physical form in comparison to their non-swimmer peers. This lack of evidence makes us question if swimmers with Down syndrome, even those at the top level, still remain healthier, or show better physical condition than their peers who are not involved in any intensive sport participation.

Thus, the aim of this study was to assess the body composition and the physical fitness profile of competitive swimmers with Down syndrome and to compare them to untrained peers. It was hypothesized that: (i) swimmers would present lower values than untrained individuals for Body Mass Index (BMI), percentage of total body fat (fat%) and Fat Mass Index (FMI), and higher values for Lean Body Mass (LBM); and (ii) swimmers would also present higher physical fitness values than untrained counterparts.

2. Materials and Methods

2.1. Participants

To be elegible for this study, trained participants had to be, as minimum, national competitive swimmers, being involved in a minimum of 6 h of swimming training per week, for at least 3 years. To be a part of the control group, participants could not be involved in any kind of competitive sport practice for the last 3 years.

Thirty-three individuals with Down syndrome participated in this study: 18 were national or international level trained swimmers and 19 were untrained persons with Down syndrome. Trained swimmers were 22.2 ± 5.4 years, practiced 7.4 ± 0.8 h per week over the entire year and had been involved in swimming training for several years. More than half of the participants were part of the National Federation Swimming Team and participated in DSISO International Championships. Untrained individuals were 26.6 ± 8.2 years and were involved in two 45 min sessions a week of general physical activity. All individuals, or their parents, gave written informed consent to participate in this study, which was approved by the local ethics committee (under the code: CEFAD 19.2020) and carried out according to the Declaration of Helsinki.

2.2. Procedures and Measures

The body measurements included height, weight and four skinfolds (triceps, biceps, subscapular and supra-iliac, using a Harpender skinfold caliper). BMI (in kg/m^2) was defined as body mass (in kg, measured using an electronic weighing scale) divided by height squared (in m). The fat% and LBM were derived from the measured skinfolds, using the equation proposed by Durnin & Wommersley [26] and the FMI was calculated as fat mass/height^2. All measurements were made on the right side of the body by the same evaluator and were repeated three times, with the mean values being used [27]. The classification of obesity was made according to the World Health Organization technical report as follows [28]: underweight if BMI $\leq$ 18.4, normal weight if BMI 18.5–24.9, overweight if BMI 25–29.9, obesity if BMI 30–39.9 and morbid obesity if BMI $\geq$ 40.

To evaluate physical fitness, the Eurofit Special test was used, as follows [29]: (i) explosive lower limb strength was determined with a standing broad jump; (ii) upper limb strength was determined using a 2 kg medicine ball push performed with the preferred arm—from a standing position, the ball was placed in the palm, supported by the second hand and pushed forward in a shot put like action; (iii) local muscle endurance was determined by the number of correctly completed sit-ups in 30 s; (iv) speed was measured for a 25 m run from a standing start measured to 0.1 s using a manual stopwatch; (v) flexibility was measured with the sit-and-reach test; and (vi) balance was determined by walking on a bench. Two test trials (Test A and Test B) were performed without shoes. In test A, the participant approached the bench, stepped onto it and walked forward. If Test A was successful, Test B is attempted. For test B the same process applies, with the bench in the upside-down position. Each test had to be completed in 30 s, with points recorded on the following scale: 1 point if the participant responds to the instructions; 2 points if the participant approaches the bench; 3 points if the participant walks 2 m without support or the entire bench with support (Test A); 4 points if the participant walks along the entire bench without support (Test A); 5 points if the participant walks 2 m without support or the entire bench with support (Test B); 6 points if the participant walks along the entire bench without support (Test B). A familiarization for all tests was allowed two weeks before the data collection to guarantee that the physical fitness tests were fully understood by the subjects and could therefore be carried out properly.

The results from the body mass, height and all the Eurofit items were then converted to percentile scores. This facilitated merging of gender groups for this study (14 males and four females swimmers and nine males and 10 females untrained). The norm scales for severe intellectual disabled individuals of 20 years old (top off age for the scale) were used [30]. This table was chosen for two main reasons: (i) most raw scores measured fit this table, particularly the control group, and (ii) 20 years was the closest age to the sample studied. Scores outside the scale were given the maximum or minimum points, as appropriate.

2.3. *Statistical Analysis*

Descriptive statistics were calculated for all the variables (raw values as well as percentile scores) and all data were checked for normality and homogeneity of variance using Shapiro-wilk and Levene tests, respectively. Mean and SD for all variables are presented. An independent sample t-test was used to verify if there were differences between groups on performance and body composition (independently of the sex). Cohen's d was calculated for effect size and interpreted as: small if $d \leq 0.2$, moderate if d between 0.2 and 0.5, and large if $d \geq 0.5$). The statistical significance was set at $p \leq 0.05$. Procedures were performed with SPSS Statistics (v. 27, IBM, SPSS Inc., Chicago, IL, USA).

3. Results

Table 1 presents the comparison of body composition and all variables of the Eurofit Special Test between trained swimmers and untrained subjects. The swimmers presented higher values for height and lower values for the sum of the skinfolds, BMI, fat% and FMI, all with large effect sizes. Concerning sex differences, male swimmers and untrained individuals were taller and had higher values for LBM and lower values for fat% than female counterparts. In the swimmers group, 10 persons were of normal weight, six were overweight, and two were obese whereas in the untrained group, seven were of normal weight, four were overweight, six were obese, and two were morbid obese. Thus, 44.4 and 52.6% of the participants were overweight or obese in swimmers and untrained individuals, respectively and 10.5% of the untrained group showed morbid obesity.

Table 1. Mean (± SD) and effect size values for the body composition and all variables of the Eurofit Special Test for trained swimmers and untrained subjects.

Variables	Swimmers			Untrained Subjects			Effect Size
	Males (n = 14)	Females (n = 4)	Total (n = 18)	Males (n = 9)	Females (n = 10)	Total (n = 19)	Cohen's d
BM (kg)	63.8 ± 11.3	53.8 ± 10.4	61.6 ± 11.6	67.5 ± 11.4	62.1 ± 12.8	64.7 ± 12.1	−0.26
Height (cm)	158.4 ± 5.7 a	145.8 ± 6.4	155.6 ± 7.8 c	155.1 ± 5.1 b	141.3 ± 6.7	147.9 ± 9.2	0.91
SS (mm)	47.9 ± 13.4	64.1 ± 22.1	51.5 ± 16.5 c	70.9 ± 23.4	91.8 ± 28.9	81.9 ± 27.9	−1.32
BMI	25.3 ± 3.1	25.9 ± 6.2	25.4 ± 3.8 c	28.3 ± 4.6	32.9 ± 13.3	30.7 ± 10.2	−0.76
Fat%	18.8 ± 3.7 a	29.7 ± 4.7	21.2 ± 6.0 c	24.2 ± 4.2 b	34.7 ± 5.3	29.8 ± 7.1	−1.30
LBM	23.5 ± 3.5 a	17.1 ± 2.6	22.1 ± 4.2	23.1 ± 2.8 b	18.1 ± 2.8	20.5 ± 3.7	0.40
FMI			9.3 ± 3.5 c			13.6 ± 6.1	−0.86
LJ (cm)	123.3 ± 40.7	91.0 ± 10.6	116.1 ± 9.1 c	89.6 ± 45.2 b	56.5 ± 32.6	72.1 ± 41.6	1.10
MB (cm)	384.8 ± 142.3 a	252.0 ± 102.9	355.3 ± 143.4 c	289.5 ± 139.1 b	200.8 ± 74.7	242.8 ± 116.0	0.86
Sit-ups	17.4 ± 3.8	16.0 ± 2.8	17.1 ± 3.6 c	8.7 ± 8.4	7.5 ± 6.7	8.1 ± 7.4	1.56
Speed (s)	5.2 ± 0.5 a	6.4 ± 0.7	5.5 ± 0.7 c	6.7 ± 1.7 b	8.6 ± 1.7	7.7 ± 1.9	−1.53
Flex (cm)	39.0 ± 8.3	42.9 ± 4.4	39.8 ± 7.7 c	29.8 ± 11.7	32.8 ± 10.1	31.4 ± 10.7	0.57
Bal (pts)	5.5 ± 0.7		5.4 ± 0.6 c	4.4 ± 1.1	3.6 ± 1.0	4.0 ± 1.1	1.55

BM = body mass, SS = skinfolds sum, BMI = body mass index, Fat % = percentage of total body fat, LBM = lean body mass, FMI = fat mass index, LJ = long jump, MB = medicine ball, Flex = flexibility, Bal = balance. Differences between genders in swimmers are identified by a, differences between genders in untrained individuals are identified by b and differences between swimmers and untrained individuals are identified by c ($p \leq 0.05$).

Swimmers with Down syndrome also scored better with large effect for long jump, medicine ball, sit-ups, speed and balance, while for flexibility there was a moderate effect.

Table 2 presents the percentile scores that are based on norms for severe intellectual disability without Down syndrome. Swimmers presented higher scores for all variables (groups were not different in body mass), with large effect sizes, except for the medicine ball throw with a moderate effect. Despite those differences, both swimmers and untrained subjects showed low percentile scores for height (28.8 ± 14.5 for swimmers), and medicine ball (36.7 ± 25.3 for swimmers) on the scale used.

Table 2. Mean (± SD) and effect size percentile values for all variables of the Eurofit Special Test, body mass and height for trained swimmers and untrained subjects.

Variables (Points)	Swimmers (n = 18)	Untrained Subjects (n = 19)	Mean Difference	Effect Size (d)
Body mass	51.2 ± 21.0	59.8 ± 22.3	−8.7	
Height	28.8 ± 14.5 a	16.0 ± 12.5	12.8	0.95
Long jump	55.9 ± 22.6 a	27.3 ± 27.3	28.6	1.14
Medicine ball	36.7 ± 25.3 a	20.5 ± 22.0	16.2	0.68
Sit-up	83.8 ± 18.8 a	39.6 ± 41.7	44.2	1.37
Speed	83.4 ± 9.0 a	50.2 ± 29.0	33.2	1.81
Flexibility	53.7 ± 13.8 a	33.0 ± 20.2	20.7	1.20
Balance	91.1 ± 9.9 a	53.9 ± 34.1	37.1	1.48

Differences between groups are identified by a ($p \leq 0.05$).

4. Discussion

The purpose of this study was to assess the body composition and the physical fitness profile of competitive swimmers with Down syndrome and to compare them with untrained individuals with the same condition. It was found that swimmers with Down syndrome present a healthier body composition and a higher physical fitness score than untrained individuals with Down syndrome.

4.1. Body Composition

Epidemiological studies often use BMI as a measure of weight status [31] since it is a good indicator of body fatness and easily calculated [32]. Nevertheless, several authors reported that BMI is not sufficient to describe the body composition of individuals [33–35]. Taking this into consideration, the fat mass index was also calculated here, due to the fact that fat mass is in part related to height [36]. Pitetti et al. [37] pointed out that ambiguous evidence exists regarding body composition in persons with Down syndrome and that the lack of consistency may involve methodological issues in measuring body composition or in the comparison of the weight status using different methods. Therefore, caution is urged when interpreting global statements on body composition in Down syndrome.

Numerous studies have reported that the prevalence of overweight and obesity are substantially higher in individuals with Down syndrome compared to their age-matched peers without disability, as well as those with intellectual disability but not related to Down syndrome [37]. Prasher [38] reported that ~48% of adults with Down syndrome were obese with ~27% being overweight and Rubin et al. [39] found ~48% of men and ~56% of women to be overweight or obese. In the present study, according to the BMI criteria, 55.6% of the swimmers and 36.8% of the untrained were normal weight, 33.3% of the swimmers and 21.1% of the untrained were overweight, 11.1% of the swimmers and 31.6% of the untrained were obese and 10.5% of the untrained were on the morbid obesity range. According to the fat% criteria, a much larger percentage of swimmers (83.3%) and a smaller percentage of untrained (31.6%) were considered normal. A much smaller percentage of swimmers were considered overweight (11.1%), while for the untrained the percentage rose to 63.2%, while 5.6% of the swimmers and 5.2% of the untrained were on the borderline range.

Although the equation described by Durnin & Womersley [26] to estimate body fat is not specific for Down syndrome, it was nevertheless previously used with this population [40]. These authors calculated the fat% in male adolescents with Down syndrome before and after a 12-week moderate aerobic training program. These adolescents decreased their fat mass percentage after the program (31.8 ± 3.7% pretest and 26.0 ± 2.3% posttest). We should note that male swimmers from our study presented much lower fat% than these adolescents (18.8 ± 3.7%).

In the current study, swimmers presented higher values for height and lower values for the sum of skinfolds, BMI, fat% and fat mass index than untrained peers. There was a large effect for all of the variables above, indicating that, not only swimmers are different from untrained, but that those differences are great. Gonzalez-Aguero et al. [19] stated that body composition in this specific population is, in general, poorer than what is observed in their peers without Down syndrome, as proven by higher BMI, lower levels of lean mass and reduced bone mass-related parameters. Bertapelli et al. [41] reported several causes for the augmented obesity in persons with Down syndrome, such as genetic, physiological, and environmental factors. However, as mentioned previously, the common term "obesity" used to describe physical characteristics in individuals with this condition might not always be valid [42]. For instance, a review by Gonzalez-Aguero et al. [19] reported mixed results and, if some studies indicate higher fatness values for people with Down syndrome [41,43–46], others present similar levels for persons with Down syndrome relative to persons without [42,43,47]. Despite these uncertainties, people with Down syndrome seem capable of improving their body composition values with training [40,44].

In athletes with Down syndrome or intellectual disability, systematic training seems to lead to healthier body composition, and, consequently, a better quality of life [19]. In a study from Aleixo et al. [48], with a small number of individuals with Down syndrome, differences in BMI between swimmers (24.3 ± 4.1) and untrained (36.8 ± 5.3) were observed, with swimmers being placed on the normal weight range and the untrained individuals at the obesity level. On the other hand, Balic et al. [16] analyzed 13 trained individuals who participated at the Special Olympics Games and seven sedentary adults, all with Down syndrome, and found no differences between both groups in BMI, height, weight and fat%. We may argue that, at the time of the study of Balic et al. [16] (approximately 20 years ago), the training for the Special Olympics started to be more demanding and not such an oriented and occupational practice. This training effect may also be the deciding factor for the differences between swimmers from our study and Climstein et al. [49]. These authors evaluated one group of 15 individuals with Down syndrome and one group of 17 non-Down syndrome and most of the subjects were actively involved in the Special Olympics program. When compared to the present study, Down syndrome individuals from Climstein et al. [49] presented higher values for fat% (26.1 ± 5.3%).

4.2. Physical Fitness

Swimmers presented better results for all the test items, indicating their better physical fitness profile. This higher score was confirmed when examining the percentile scores (Table 2) as swimmers with Down syndrome are more fit than untrained counterparts, presenting higher levels of strength, balance and flexibility.

Despite the fact that physical fitness is an important contributor to health in adults and youth, less is known in persons with disabilities, such as Down syndrome [42]. In a review on physical fitness and physical activity in children and adolescents with Down syndrome, Pitetti et al. [37] point out that peak aerobic capacity (VO_{2peak}) in both youth and adults with Down syndrome is reduced in comparison to their peers without disability and with other intellectual disabilities. The same authors highlight the fact that these persons can be responsive to aerobic endurance training, particularly with improvements in work capacity. Muscular strength is also lower in persons with Down syndrome when compared to their peers with normal development or with other intellectual disabilities [11,17,37,50–53]. According to Shields et al. [54], an improved strength in persons with Down syndrome has been associated with higher levels of physical activity. Muscular strength is a fundamental ability needed by persons with disabilities (with Down syndrome included) especially because: (i) their workplace activities typically emphasize physical rather than cognitive skills [54]; (ii) muscle weakness can impact their ability to perform everyday activities, including walking, eating, dressing and rising from a chair [17,51]; (iii) life expectancy is increasing for persons with Down syndrome [55] and maintenance of muscle strength is important to lead productive lives [56]; (iv) improving muscle strength may be important in controlling the high tendency for osteoporosis that persons with Down syndrome often demonstrate [50].

Hypotonia and hyper-flexibility, two characteristics of Down syndrome [57,58], have an impact on bone mass, muscular strength and power, gait and motor development [59]. All of these factors lead to the lower strength levels of persons with Down syndrome, but at the same time accent the importance of physical activity. For instance, Daly et al. [60] found that the strength differences between athletes with and without intellectual disabilities are in the range of 4–14% for male and 11–27% for female, being inferior for the athletes with intellectual disabilities. Despite this, much more specific data is needed on high-performance athletes with intellectual disability [23].

Swimming can be one of the activities that can make such a difference. According to Ylmaz et al. [21], aquatic exercises can be a good way of developing physical fitness and motor skill development for children with intellectual disabilities, as aquatics provide a very unique environment for these children. Perán et al. [61] stated that participating in competition is fundamental for individuals with Down syndrome. Although there is research on the effects of aquatic exercises on persons without disabilities, little has been done on persons with intellectual disabilities [62] and more specifically concerning competitive swimming for persons with Down syndrome, so the present study adds new evidence on what physical aspects may distinguish the Down syndrome subjects who are engaged in swimming programs from those who are not.

Comparing the results from the present study with those of Daly et al. [60] with high-performance athletes with intellectual disability, male swimmers with Down syndrome only scored better in the sit-and-reach test (cm) (39.0 ± 8.3 versus 34.0 ± 15.8 finalists and 35.7 ± 7.4 non-finalists) while low scores for the long jump (cm) and sit-ups were obtained

(123.3 ± 40.7 for long jump and 17.4 ± 3.8 for sit-ups versus 197.3 ± 26.3 and 23.0 ± 6.8 finalists and 181.9 ± 39.5 and 20.7 ± 4.7 non-finalists). Flexibility was slightly higher for female swimmers with Down syndrome (42.9 ± 4.4 versus 41.0 ± 8.9 finalists and 38.5 ± 8.0 non-finalists) but for the long jump and the sit-ups low scores can be observed (91.0 ± 10.6 and 16.0 ± 2.8 versus 154.6 ± 20.2 and 21.5 ± 6.1 finalists and 157.1 ± 24.9 and 18.2 ± 4.3 non-finalists).

As swimmers with Down syndrome from our study present higher levels of strength than untrained individuals with Down syndrome, we are led to conclude that swimmers have increased muscular hypertrophy, which in turn can reduce hypotonicity and balance dysfunctions and increase bone-mass related parameters [19]. Little is known about the effect of specific strength training in this population. Until recently, swimmers with Down syndrome rarely participated in specific dryland strength training. Van de Vliet et al. [23] studied elite athletes with intellectual disability and pointed out that good levels of fitness seem to be possible for these athletes, and it is likely that the training effect influenced the data. Likewise with athletes, Balic et al. [16] found that the active group of Special Olympians with Down syndrome exhibited significantly higher isometric strength than the sedentary group, also with Down syndrome. They suggested that long term exercise training may enhance physical fitness in individuals with Down syndrome.

Balance in people with Down syndrome is also a component of physical fitness that is usually inferior to the general population or individuals with intellectual disability without Down syndrome [18,63]. Muscle hypotonia may be responsible for balance problems that individuals with Down syndrome usually demonstrate [64]. The delay of maturation of the cerebellum and the relatively small size of cerebellum and brain stem in persons with Down syndrome may also be responsible for the disturbance of balance [65]. Despite these characteristics, individuals with Down syndrome seem capable of improving their balance through physical activity participation, and with this improve their well-being and the quality of life [18]. The swimmers from the current study presented good balance scores and were exceedingly better than the non-swimmers group.

As this was not a training study it is hard to conclude that differences in physical fitness are an outcome of the swimming training. Nevertheless, a study from Querido et al. [66] with six swimmers with Down syndrome evaluated for body composition and physical fitness in 2011 and 2014, found that in 3 years of training, swimmers with Down syndrome improved their physical fitness profile (especially strength) and their body composition characteristics.

In summary, it can be said that: (i) swimmers with Down syndrome present a healthier body composition than untrained individuals with Down syndrome, confirming the first hypothesis; (ii) swimmers with Down syndrome present higher physical fitness values than untrained individuals with Down syndrome, confirming the second hypothesis. This means that swimming educators, parents and/or institutions should see swimming as a sport that can take body composition and physical fitness of Down syndrome subjects to acceptable standards.

4.3. Limitations and Suggestions for the Future

We may point out several limitations to the present study. Larger sample sizes are needed (multi-center), if possible. Information about training characteristics should be more specific (volume, intensity, dry land training), and food intake characterized. Due to the lack of specific equations to estimate fat% and LBM for persons with Down syndrome, general equations were used. Although the participants had previous familiarizations with the tests, future studies should be carried with a test–retest procedure, to ensure that the physical fitness tests are completely understood. In the future it would also be important to perform an intervention program so it would be possible to conclude the effectiveness of swimming training on physical fitness, body composition and other complementary tests.

Author Contributions: Conceptualization, A.Q., D.J.D. and R.J.F.; methodology, D.A., J.P.V.-B. and R.J.F.; formal analysis, R.C. and D.J.D.; investigation, A.Q., M.J.C., D.A. and A.R.S.; writing—original draft preparation, A.Q. and M.J.C.; writing—review and editing, D.J.D. and R.J.F.; funding acquisition, A.R.S., J.P.V.-B. and R.J.F. All authors have read and agreed to the published version of the manuscript.

Funding: This research was founded by the Portuguese Foundation for Science and Technology (FCT), under the grant SFRH/BD/78513/2011.

Institutional Review Board Statement: The study was conducted in accordance with the Declaration of Helsinki, and approved by the local ethics committee (under the code: CEFAD 19.2020).

Informed Consent Statement: Informed consent was obtained from all subjects involved in the study.

Data Availability Statement: Not applicable.

Conflicts of Interest: The authors declare no conflict of interest.

References

1. Irving, C.; Basu, A.; Richmond, S.; Burn, J.; Wren, C. Twenty-year trends in prevalence and survival of Down syndrome. *Eur. J. Hum. Genet.* **2008**, *16*, 1336–1340. [CrossRef] [PubMed]
2. Hill, D.A.; Gridley, G.; Cnattingius, S.; Mellemkjaer, L.; Linet, M.; Adami, H.-O.; Olsen, J.H.; Nyren, O.; Fraumeni, J.F. Mortality and cancer incidence among individuals with Down syndrome. *Arch. Int. Med.* **2003**, *163*, 705–711. [CrossRef] [PubMed]
3. Hermon, C.; Alberman, E.; Beral, V.; Swerdlow, A. Mortality and cancer incidence in persons with Down's syndrome, their parents and siblings. *Ann. Hum. Genet.* **2001**, *65*, 167–176. [CrossRef] [PubMed]
4. Rimmer, J.H.; Heller, T.; Wang, E.; Valerio, I. Improvements in physical fitness in adults with Down syndrome. *Am. J. Ment. Retard.* **2004**, *109*, 165–174. [CrossRef] [PubMed]
5. Weijerman, M.E.; van Furth, A.M.; Noordegraaf, A.V.; van Wouwe, J.P.; Broers, C.J.M.; Gemke, R.J.B.J. Prevalence, neonatal characteristics, and first-year mortality of Down syndrome: A national study. *J. Pediatr.* **2008**, *152*, 15–19. [CrossRef] [PubMed]
6. Wu, J.; Morris, J.K. The population prevalence in Down's syndrome in England and Wales in 2011. *Eur. J. Hum. Genet.* **2013**, *21*, 1033–1034. [CrossRef]
7. World Health Organization. *WHO Guidelines on Physical Activity and Sedentary Behaviour*; World Health Organization: Geneva, Switzerland, 2020.
8. Chakravarthy, M.V.; Joyner, M.J.; Booth, F.W. An obligation for primary care physicians to prescribe physical activity to sedentary patients to reduce the risk of chronic health condition. *Mayo Clin. Proc.* **2002**, *77*, 165–173. [CrossRef]
9. Eyman, R.K.; Call, T.L. Life expectancy of persons with Down syndrome. *Am. J. Ment. Retard.* **1991**, *95*, 603–612. [PubMed]
10. Fernhall, B.; Tymeson, G.; Millar, A.L.; Burkett, L.N. Cardiovascular fitness testing and fitness levels of adolescents and adults with mental retardation including Down syndrome. *Educ. Train. Ment. Retard.* **1989**, *24*, 133–138.
11. Pitetti, K.H.; Climstein, M.; Mays, M.J.; Barrett, P.J. Isokinetic arm and leg strength of adults with Down syndrome: A comparative study. *Arch. Phys. Med. Rehab.* **1992**, *73*, 847–850.
12. Varela, A.M.; Sardinha, L.B.; Pitetti, K.H. Effects of an aerobic rowing training regímen in young adults with Down syndrome. *Am. J. Ment. Retard.* **2001**, *106*, 135–144. [CrossRef] [PubMed]
13. Draheim, C.C.; Williams, D.P.; McCubbin, J.A. Prevalence of physical inactivity and recommended physical activity in community-based adults with mental retardation. *Ment. Retard.* **2002**, *40*, 436–444. [CrossRef] [PubMed]
14. Fujiura, G.T.; Fitzsimons, N.; Marks, B. Predictors of BMI among adults with Down syndrome: The social context of health promotion. *Res. Dev. Disabil.* **1997**, *18*, 261–274. [CrossRef] [PubMed]
15. Kosma, M.; Cardinal, B.J.; Rintala, P. Motivating individuals with disabilities to be physically active. *Quest* **2002**, *54*, 116–132. [CrossRef]
16. Balic, M.; Mateos, E.; Blasco, C.; Fernhall, B. Physical fitness levels of physically active and sedentary adults with Down syndrome. *Adapt. Phys. Act. Q.* **2000**, *17*, 310–321. [CrossRef]
17. Carmeli, E.; Kessel, S.; Coleman, R.; Avalon, M. Effects of a treadmill walking programme on muscle strength and balance in elderly people with Down syndrome. *Geront* **2002**, *57*, 106–110. [CrossRef]
18. Tsimaras, V.; Fotiadou, E.G. Effect of training on the muscle strength and dynamic balance ability of adults with Down syndrome. *J. Strength Cond. Res.* **2004**, *18*, 343–347. [CrossRef]
19. González-Agüero, A.; Vicente-Rodríguez, G.; Moreno, L.A.; Balic-Guerra, M.; Ara, I.; Casajús, J.A. Health related physical fitness in children and adolescents with Down syndrome and response to training. *Scand. J. Med. Sci. Sport.* **2010**, *20*, 716–724. [CrossRef]
20. Fragala-Pinkham, M.A.; Haley, S.M.; O'Neil, M.E. Group aquatic aerobic exercise for children with disabilities. *Dev. Med. Child Neurol.* **2008**, *50*, 822–827. [CrossRef]
21. Yilmaz, I.; Ergu, N.; Konukman, F.; Agbuga, B.; Zorba, E.; Cimen, Z. The effects of water exercises and swimming on physical fitness of children with mental retardation. *J. Hum. Kinet.* **2009**, *21*, 105–111. [CrossRef]
22. Fernhall, B.; Pitetti, K.H. Limitations to physical work capacity in individuals with mental retardation. *J. Clin. Exerc. Physiol.* **2001**, *3*, 176–185.

23. Van De Vliet, P.; Rintala, P.; Fröjd, K.; Verellen, J.; Van Houtte, S.; Daly, D.J.; Vanlandewijck, Y.C. Physical fitness profile of elite athletes with intellectual disability. *Scand. J. Med. Sci. Sport.* **2006**, *16*, 417–425. [CrossRef] [PubMed]
24. González-Ravé, J.M.; Turner, A.; Phillips, S.M. Adaptations to swimming training in athletes with Down's syndrome. *Int. J. Environ. Res. Public Health* **2020**, *17*, 9175. [CrossRef] [PubMed]
25. Naczk, A.; Gajewska, E.; Naczk, M. Effectiveness of swimming program in adolescents with Down syndrome. *Int. J. Environ. Res. Public Health* **2021**, *18*, 7441. [CrossRef] [PubMed]
26. Durnin, J.V.G.A.; Wommersley, J. Body fat assessed from total body density and its estimation from skinfold thickness: Measurements on 481 men and woman aged from 16 to 72 years. *Br. J. Nutr.* **1974**, *32*, 77–92. [CrossRef]
27. Guidetti, L.; Franciosi, E.; Gallotta, M.C.; Emerenziani, G.P.; Baldari, C. Could sport specialization influence fitness and health of adults with mental retardation? *Res. Dev. Disabil.* **2010**, *31*, 1070–1075. [CrossRef]
28. World Health Organization. *Physical Status: The Use and Interpretation of Anthropometry*; WHO Technical Report Series Number 854; World Health Organization: Geneva, Switzerland, 1995.
29. Skowrónski, W.; Horvat, M.; Nocera, J.; Roswal, G.; Croce, R. Eurofit Special: European fitness battery score variation among individuals with intellectual disabilities. *Adapt. Phys. Act. Q.* **2009**, *26*, 54–67. [CrossRef]
30. Skowroński, W. Eurofit Specjalny. Test Sprawności Motorycznej Dla Osób z Upośledzeniem Umuslowym. Akademia Wychowania Fizycznego: Warsaw, Poland, 2007.
31. Melville, C.A.; Cooper, S.A.; McGrother, C.W.; Thorp, C.F.; Collacott, R. Obesity in adults with Down syndrome: A case-control study. *J. Intellect. Disabil. Res.* **2005**, *49*, 125–133. [CrossRef]
32. Husain, M. Body mass index for Saudi children with Down's syndrome. *Acta Pædiatr.* **2003**, *92*, 1482–1485. [CrossRef]
33. Hall, D.M.B.; Cole, T.J. What use is the BMI. *Arch. Dis. Child* **2000**, *91*, 283–286. [CrossRef]
34. Wells, J.C.K. A critique of the expression of paediatric body composition data. *Arch. Dis. Child* **2001**, *85*, 67–72. [CrossRef] [PubMed]
35. Wells, J.C.K.; Fewtrell, M.S. Measuring body composition. *Arch. Dis. Child* **2006**, *91*, 612–617. [CrossRef] [PubMed]
36. Magge, S.N.; O'Neill, K.L.; Shults, J.; Stallings, V.A.; Stettler, N. Leptin levels among prepubertal children with Down syndrome compared with their siblings. *J. Pediatr.* **2008**, *152*, 321–326. [CrossRef] [PubMed]
37. Pitetti, K.; Baynard, T.; Agiovlasitis, S. Children and adolescents with Down syndrome, physical fitness and physical activity. *J. Sport Health Sci.* **2013**, *2*, 47–57. [CrossRef]
38. Prasher, V.P. Overweight and obesity amongst Down's syndrome adults. *J. Intellect. Disabil. Res.* **1995**, *39*, 437–441. [CrossRef]
39. Rubin, S.S.; Rimmer, J.H.; Chicoine, B.; Bradock, D.; McGuire, D.E. Overweight prevalence in persons with Down syndrome. *Mental. Retard.* **1998**, *36*, 175–181. [CrossRef]
40. Ordoñez, F.; Rosety, M.; Rosety-Rodriguez, M. Influence of 12-week exercise training on fat mass percentage in adolescents with Down syndrome. *Med. Sci. Monit.* **2006**, *12*, CR416–CR419.
41. Bertapelli, F.; Gorla, J.I.; da Silva, F.F.; Costa, L.T. Prevalence of obesity and the body fat topography in children and teenagers with Down syndrome. *J. Hum. Growth Develop.* **2013**, *23*, 65–70. [CrossRef]
42. Izquierdo-Gomez, R.; Martínez-Gómez, D.; Tejero-Gonzalez, C.M.; Cabanas-Sánchez, V.; Ruiz Ruiz, J.; Veiga, Ó.L. Are poor physical fitness and obesity two features of the adolescent with Down syndrome? *Nutr. Hospital* **2013**, *28*, 1348–1351. [CrossRef]
43. Baptista, F.; Varela, A.; Sardinha, L.B. Bone mineral mass in males and females with and without Down syndrome. *Osteoporos. Int.* **2005**, *16*, 380–388. [CrossRef]
44. González-Agüero, A.; Ara, I.; Moreno, L.A.; Vicente-Rodríguez, G.; Casajús, J.A. Fat and lean masses in youths with Down syndrome: Gender differences. *Res. Develop. Disabil.* **2011**, *32*, 1685–1693. [CrossRef] [PubMed]
45. Mercer, V.S.; Lewis, C.L. Hip abductor and knee extensor muscle strength of children with and without Down syndrome. *Pediat. Phys. Ther.* **2001**, *13*, 18–26. [CrossRef]
46. Pitetti, K.H.; Fernhall, B. Comparing run performance of adolescents with mental retardation, with and without Down syndrome. *Adapt. Phys. Act. Q.* **2004**, *21*, 219–228.
47. Luke, A.; Sutton, M.; Schoeller, D.A.; Roizen, N.J. Nutrient intake and obesity in prepubescent children with Down syndrome. *J. Am. Diet. Assoc.* **1996**, *96*, 1262–1267. [CrossRef]
48. Aleixo, I.; Vale, S.; Figueiredo, P.; Corredeira, R.; Silva, A.; Fernandes, R.J. Comparison of body mass index between swimmers and non-trained individuals with Down syndrome. *J. Sport. Sci. Med.* **2009**, *8*, 194–195.
49. Climstein, M.; Pitetti, K.H.; Barrett, P.J.; Campbell, K.D. The accuracy of predicting treadmill VO_{2max} for adults with mental retardation, with and without Downs's syndrome, using ACSM gender- and activity-specific regression equations. *J. Intell. Disabil. Res.* **1993**, *37 Pt 6*, 521–531. [CrossRef]
50. Angelopoulou, N.; Tsimaras, V.; Christoulas, K.; Kokaridas, D.; Mandroukas, K. Isokinetic knee strength of individuals with mental retardation, a comparative study. *Percept. Motor. Ski.* **1999**, *88*, 849–855. [CrossRef]
51. Cowley, P.M.; Ploutz-Snyder, L.L.; Baynard, T.; Heffernan, K.; Jae, S.Y.; Hsu, S.; Lee, M.; Pitetti, K.H.; Reiman, M.P.; Fernhall, B. Physical fitness predicts functional tasks in individuals with Down syndrome. *Med. Sci. Sport. Exerc.* **2010**, *42*, 388–393. [CrossRef]
52. Horvat, M.; Pitetti, K.H.; Croce, R. Isokinetic torque, average power, and flexion/extension ratios in nondisabled adults and adults with mental retardation. *J. Orthop. Sport. Phys. Ther.* **1997**, *25*, 395–399. [CrossRef]
53. Shields, N.; Taylor, N. A student-led progressive resistance training program increases lower limb muscle strength in adolescents with Down syndrome: A randomized controlled trial. *J. Physiother.* **2010**, *56*, 187–193. [CrossRef]

54. Shields, N.; Taylor, N.; Fernhall, B. A study protocol of a randomized controlled trial to investigate if a community based strength training programme improves work task performance in young adults with Down syndrome. *BMC Pediatr.* **2010**, *10*, 17. [CrossRef] [PubMed]
55. Glasson, E.J.; Sullivan, S.G.; Hussain, R.; Petterson, B.A.; Montgomery, P.D.; Bittles, A.H. The changing survival profile of people with Down's syndrome: Implications for genetic counseling. *Clinic. Genet.* **2002**, *62*, 390–393. [CrossRef] [PubMed]
56. Croce, R.; Pitetti, K.H.; Horvat, M.; Miller, J. Peak-torque at average power, and hamstrings/quadriceps ratios in nondisabled adults and adults with mental retardation. *Arch. Phys. Med. Rehab.* **1996**, *77*, 369–372. [CrossRef] [PubMed]
57. Hawly, Y.; Nasrallah, M.; Fulelhan, G.E.H. Endocrine and musculoskeletal abnormalities in patients with Down syndrome. *Nat. Rev. Endocrinol.* **2009**, *5*, 327–334. [CrossRef]
58. Shields, N.; Dodd, K.J.; Abblitt, C. Do children with Down syndrome perform sufficient physical activity to maintain a good health? A pilot study. *Adapt. Phys. Act. Q.* **2009**, *26*, 307–320. [CrossRef]
59. Cissik, J.M. Down syndrome: An introduction for the strength and conditioning professional. *Strength Cond. J.* **2012**, *34*, 76–81. [CrossRef]
60. Daly, D.; Einarssson, I.; Vanlandewijck, Y. Race success in swimmers with intellectual disability. In Proceedings of the AETN 2014 XXXIV Congreso Interncional de la Associación Española de Técnicos de Natación: Swimming Science Seminar II, Facultad de Ciencias del Deporte, Universidad de Granada, Granada, Spain, 10–12 October 2014; pp. 55–60.
61. Peran, S.; Gil, J.; Ruiz, F.; Fernandez-Paster, V. Development of physical response after athletics training in adolescents with Down's syndrome. *Adapt. Phys. Activ. Q.* **1997**, *7*, 283–288. [CrossRef]
62. Einarsson, I.; Ólafsson, Á.; Hinriksdóttir, G.; Jóhannsson, E.; Daly, D.; Arngrímsson, S.Á. Differences in Physical activity among youth with and without intellectual disability. *Med. Sci. Sport. Exerc.* **2015**, *47*, 411–418. [CrossRef]
63. Connoly, B.; Michael, B. Performance of retarded children, with and without Down syndrome, on the Bruikinks-Oseretsky Test of Motor Proficiency. *Phys. Ther.* **1986**, *66*, 344–348. [CrossRef]
64. Connoly, B.; Morgan, S.; Russel, F. Evaluation of children with Down syndrome who participated in an early intervention program: Second follow-up study. *Phys. Ther.* **1984**, *64*, 1515–1519. [CrossRef]
65. Cowie, V. *A Study of the Early Development of Mongols*; Pergamon Press: Oxford, UK, 1970.
66. Querido, A.; Cardoso, C.; Vilas-Boas, J.P.; Corredeira, R.; Daly, D.; Fernandes, R.J. The added value of water for swimmers with Down syndrome. In *Book of Abstracts of the Aqua-Leuven*; Daly, D., Ed.; Faculty of Kinesiology and Rehabilitation Sciences, KU Leuven: Leuven, Belgium, 2015; p. 55.

healthcare

MDPI

Review

A Bibliometrics-Enhanced, PAGER-Compliant Scoping Review of the Literature on Paralympic Powerlifting: Insights for Practices and Future Research

Luca Puce [1], Khaled Trabelsi [2,3], Carlo Trompetto [1,4], Laura Mori [1,4], Lucio Marinelli [1,4], Antonio Currà [5], Emanuela Faelli [6,7], Vittoria Ferrando [6,7], Patrick Okwen [8], Jude Dzevela Kong [9], Achraf Ammar [10] and Nicola Luigi Bragazzi [9,*]

[1] Department of Neuroscience, Rehabilitation, Ophthalmology, Genetics, Maternal and Child Health (DINOGMI), University of Genoa, 16132 Genoa, Italy
[2] Research Laboratory: Education, Motricity, Sport and Health, EM2S, LR19JS01, University of Sfax, Sfax 3000, Tunisia
[3] High Institute of Sport and Physical Education of Sfax, University of Sfax, Sfax 3000, Tunisia
[4] Istituto di Ricovero e Cura a Carattere Scientifico (IRCCS) Ospedale Policlinico San Martino, 16132 Genova, Italy
[5] Academic Neurology Unit, A. Fiorini Hospital, 04019 Terracina, Italy
[6] Department of Experimental Medicine (DIMES), Section of Human Physiology, University of Genoa, 16132 Genoa, Italy
[7] Centro Polifunzionale di Scienze Motorie, University of Genoa, 16132 Genoa, Italy
[8] Effective Basic Services (eBASE), Bamenda 5175, Cameroon
[9] Laboratory for Industrial and Applied Mathematics (LIAM), Department of Mathematics and Statistics, York University, Toronto, ON M3J 1P3, Canada
[10] Academic Institute of Sport Sciences, Otto-von-Guericke University, 39104 Magdeburg, Germany
* Correspondence: bragazzi@yorku.ca

check for updates

Citation: Puce, L.; Trabelsi, K.; Trompetto, C.; Mori, L.; Marinelli, L.; Currà, A.; Faelli, E.; Ferrando, V.; Okwen, P.; Kong, J.D.; et al. A Bibliometrics-Enhanced, PAGER-Compliant Scoping Review of the Literature on Paralympic Powerlifting: Insights for Practices and Future Research. *Healthcare* **2022**, *10*, 2319. https://doi.org/10.3390/healthcare10112319

Academic Editor: Felipe Aidar

Received: 24 October 2022
Accepted: 17 November 2022
Published: 19 November 2022

Abstract: Paralympic powerlifting (PP), formerly known as "International Paralympic Committee" (IPC) powerlifting, is the format of powerlifting adapted for athletes with disabilities, and it differs from the version for able-bodied athletes in that it consists of bench press only. According to the mandate of the IPC, PP athletes should be enabled to achieve sporting excellence. As such, rigorous evidence is needed. However, to the best of our knowledge, there exists no systematic assessment of the body of scholarly evidence in the field of PP. Therefore, the present study was conducted to fill in this gap of knowledge, by conducting a scoping review of the literature enhanced by a bibliometrics analysis and by mining two major scholarly databases (MEDLINE via PubMed and Scopus). The aim was to provide a review/summary of the findings to date to help practitioners and athletes. Thirty-seven studies were retained in the present study. These covered the following thematic areas: (i) warm-up strategies ($n = 2$); (ii) aspects of training ($n = 2$); (iii) physiological aspects and responses ($n = 2$); (iv) psychological aspects and responses ($n = 2$); (v) biomechanics of bench press ($n = 8$); (vi) recovery strategy ($n = 5$); (vii) impact of the disability and type of disability ($n = 4$); (viii) epidemiology of PP ($n = 6$); and (ix) new analytical/statistical approaches for kinematics assessments, internal load monitoring, and predictions of mechanical outputs in strength exercises and in PP ($n = 6$). Bibliometrics analysis of the PP-related scientific output revealed that, despite having already become a paralympic sports discipline in 1984, only in the last few years, PP has been attracting a lot of interest from the community of researchers, with the first scholarly contribution dating back to 2012, and with more than one-third of the scientific output being published this year (2022). As such, this scholarly discipline is quite recent and young. Moreover, the community dealing with this topic is poorly interconnected, with most authors contributing to just one article, and with one single author being a hub node of the author network. Distributions of the number of articles and the authors/co-authors were found to be highly asymmetrical, indicating that this research is still in its infancy and has great room as well as great potential to grow. Reflecting this, many research topics are also overlooked and underdeveloped, with the currently available evidence being based on a few studies.

Keywords: para powerlifting; athletes with disabilities; scoping review; PAGER framework; bibliometrics

1. Introduction

Powerlifting, formerly known as "International Powerlifting Federation" (IPF) powerlifting, is a strength sport in which the maximum possible performance is sought in terms of kilos lifted on a single repetition over three barbell disciplines: namely, back squat (BS), bench press (BP), and deadlift. Each athlete has three attempts for each discipline and must perform at least one successful lift in each of them, otherwise, the athlete does not get a "total" and is disqualified from the competition. The sum or total of the best lift in each discipline determines the winner [1–3].

Paralympic powerlifting (PP), formerly known as "International Paralympic Committee" (IPC) powerlifting, is the format adapted for athletes with disabilities, and it differs from the version for able-bodied athletes in that it consists of BP only [4]. Another difference is disability-specific: whilst athletes competing in IPF powerlifting are required to place their feet on the floor, IPC para-athletes execute the lift with their torso, legs, and heels extended over a bench. To make this accessible and safe, the lower center section of the bench is wider than its IPF counterpart and is equipped with straps to stabilize the athlete. Additionally, IPC powerlifting requires an IPC license and appropriate classification status for all athletes. This system does not apply to IPF powerlifting [4].

According to the rules of the IPC, the PP discipline is open to male and female athletes aged at least 14 years, characterized by impairments in muscle and joint functions (i.e., strength, or range of motion, ROM), movement deficiencies (athetosis/hypertonia/ataxia), differences in physical structure (lower limb deficiency/amputation, leg length discrepancy, and short stature/dwarfism), and/or a range of physical disabilities (cerebral palsy, spinal cord injury, or poliomyelitis). Moreover, to be eligible, an athlete should be able to fully grip the bar without aids or prostheses, extending the arms with no more than a 20-degree loss of full extension on each elbow joint during the lift. All athletes compete in a single sports class, stratified into ten different weight categories per gender [4], specifically ranging from "49 kg" to "+107 kg" for men, and from "41 kg" to "+86 kg" for women [4]. In this para sport, the athletes can achieve world and Paralympic records equal to or, often, exceeding equivalent able-bodied BP records. Top PP athletes can lift more than three times their body weight. For example, during the Tokyo 2020 Games, a Malaysian male lifter weighing in at the "under 72 kg class" successfully lifted 228 kg. Para-athletes can generally reach these performance-related outcomes between their early- and mid-thirties, after many years of high-intensity daily training (5–6 times per week), and are very similar in terms of load parameters (volume, intensity, and recovery) as their able-bodied counterparts. Besides, para powerlifters dedicate all of their training time to the BP only, differently from able-bodied athletes who also have to dedicate their time to the other two powerlifting disciplines (BS and deadlift).

According to the mandate of the IPC, PP athletes should be enabled to achieve sporting excellence. As such, rigorous evidence is needed to effectively protect and promote PP athletes. This implies the design and implementation of studies aimed at the development and validation of an array of measures and indicators that can monitor and predict performance-related outcomes, the reliability of which has to be tested on large, representative samples [5].

However, to the best of our knowledge, there exists no systematic assessment of the body of scholarly evidence in the field of PP. Therefore, the present study was conducted to fill in this gap of knowledge and to provide a review/summary of the findings to date to help practitioners and athletes.

2. Materials and Methods

2.1. Study Design and Theoretical Framework

A literature review is aimed at collecting and appraising the body of evidence from the available scholarly literature, describing the state-of-the-art in terms of the latest advancements, consolidated current knowledge, and gaps in knowledge to address, and guiding future research in the field. Utilizing the "Search, AppraisaL, Synthesis and Analysis" (SALSA) framework, Grant and Booth have identified [6] 14 types of literature reviews based on the research needs, the depth and breadth of the research question(s), and the aims. According to the authors, a scoping review can be defined as a "preliminary assessment of potential size and scope of available research literature" with the "aims to identify nature and extent of research evidence (usually including ongoing research)" [6]. The research question is generally broad, and the researcher's aims include (i) providing the scholarly community with a (quick and rapid) scoping of the research area(s), (ii) understanding whether the research area(s) is/are worthy of carrying out a more systematic/systematized synthesis approach (i.e., a systematic/systematized review and/or a meta-analysis), (iii) summarizing/synthesizing the literature in terms of major findings, and (iv) identifying critical aspects and gaps in knowledge [6,7].

A scoping review is generally conducted when there exists a significantly heterogeneous body of literature and when no previous systematic review can be detected [8,9]. Here, we leveraged Arksey and O'Malley's five-step methodology (and subsequent theoretical refinements) [10,11], which consists of (i) identifying the research question(s), (ii) identifying the body of relevant studies, (iii) selecting the studies to include, (iv) charting the data, and (v) collating, summarizing, and reporting the results.

Moreover, the "Patterns-Advances-Gaps-Evidence for Practice-Recommendations" (PAGER) framework developed by Bradbury-Jones et al. [12] was here exploited. P enables the synthesis of the major findings in terms of unique key themes/thematic areas. A allows scholars to discover the dynamic unfolding of these themes. G enables the identification of under-developed/overlooked themes that should be explored and investigated in future research. E can provide relevant actors and stakeholders (athletes, coaches, instructors) with practical information that can be translated into relevant practices (i.e., training methodologies, conditioning strategies, etc.). Based on G, R can guide future research.

2.2. Research Question(s)

We aimed to summarize the body of existing research on PP by (i) appraising the available evidence, (ii) identifying the existing knowledge and practice shortcomings and gaps, (iii) translating evidence into training recommendations and policies, if possible, and (iv) outlining future prospects and directions in the field.

2.3. Identification of Relevant Studies

The following keywords were used: "paralympic powerlifting", "para powerlifting", "paralympic powerlifter", and "para powerlifter". These keywords were properly combined in a search string using the "OR" Boolean connector. Two major electronic, scholarly databases were searched from inception: namely, MEDLINE (via its freely available interface PubMed) and Scopus, without language filters/restrictions. The search was conducted from inception up to 1 October 2022.

2.4. Study Selection and Inclusion/Exclusion Criteria

Inclusion and exclusion criteria were devised according to the PICOS mnemonic: P (population), paralympic powerlifters; I (intervention), any kind of interventional strategy (warm-up or training/condition program, nutritional supplementation, pharmacological intervention, recovery strategy, etc.); C (comparison/comparator), any kind of comparison (between disabled and able-bodied athletes, the impact of age, sex/gender, weight category, years of experience and training, competing level—regional, national, international—the type of disability/impairment, and if congenital/acquired); O (outcome/outcomes), any outcome relevant to PP (kinematic, biomechanical, physiological, psychological or psychophysiological, epidemiological, methodological, etc.); S (study design), any original study with sufficient details. Reviews were not included but were scanned to increase the chance of getting any relevant study, whilst commentaries, letters to the editor, editorials, expert opinions, or technical notes without sufficient details were discarded. Articles were also excluded if focusing on other paralympic disciplines or reporting data in such a way that it was not possible to disaggregate them and extract data related to PP only.

2.5. Charting the Data

Data were abstracted utilizing an ad hoc designed and customized Excel spreadsheet.

2.6. Collating, Summarizing, and Reporting the Results

Abstracted data were presented in a narrative fashion, using tables and figures. Finally, findings were also visualized by means of bibliometrics/scientometrics, which is an emerging, highly specialized branch of information science that allows the rigorous, quantitative assessment of emerging research, in terms of topics, patterns, trends, and hot spots in the scientific literature [13].

2.7. Bibliometrics Analysis

Using VOSviewer version 1.6.18 [14], Gephi [15], and Cytoscape [16], data extracted from MEDLINE via PubMed and RIS reference manager files were mapped and visualized as graphs/networks of scholars (authors/co-authors, known as bibliographic—authorship/co-authorship—graphs/networks) and organizations/institutions. Moreover, the topology of these graphs/networks was investigated in-depth from a quantitative standpoint, by computing a range of several graph theory/network-related indicators, including (i) the number of scholars (authors/co-authors, in the case of a bibliographic graph/network), (ii) the number of countries, (iii) the number of items per author/research organization (both as absolute and relative (%) figures), (iv) the number of connected components (as a proxy for the connectivity of a network), (v) the average number of neighbors, (vi) the number of links, (vii) the total link strength (known also as total edge weight), (viii) the length of paths, such as the shortest paths (known as distance), the average shortest path length (known as the characteristic path length), and other related parameters, (ix) the network diameter and the network radius, (x) the network density, (xi) the network heterogeneity, (xii) the network centralization, (xiii) the number of scholar (author/co-author) clusters (also known as communities), (xiv) the number of research organization/institution clusters/communities, and finally, (xv) the clustering coefficient.

More specifically, graphs/networks were treated, modeled, and analyzed as "undirected networks". In graph/network theory, undirected networks can be defined as sets of objects (called nodes or vertices) that are connected/linked together, in which all the edges (known also as links) are bidirectional. In undirected networks, two nodes (scholars –authors/–coauthors, organizations, or institutions) are defined as connected if there is a path of edges between them. In addition, between any pair of nodes, there can be no more than one coupling link, even though each link has its own strength, represented by a positive figure, that is assigned in such a way that the higher (lower) this value, the stronger (weaker) the link. The strength of the link may vary, indicating, for instance, the number of quotations shared by two publications, the number of publications two researchers have co-authored, or the number of publications in which two terms/keywords occur together.

Within an undirected graph/network, all nodes that are pairwise connected form a connected component. The number of connected components is an indicator of paramount importance, in that it indicates the connectivity of a network—a lower (higher) number of connected components suggests stronger (weaker) connectivity. The length of a path is computed as the number of edges forming it. There may be multiple paths connecting two given nodes. The shortest path length, also called the distance between two nodes (node n and node m), is denoted by $L(n,m)$. The network diameter is the maximum distance between two nodes. If a network is disconnected, its diameter is the maximum of all diameters of its connected components, whilst the network radius can be defined as the minimum distance between two nodes.

Concerning graph/network paths and path lengths, the average shortest path length, also known as the characteristic path length, gives the expected distance between two connected nodes. Parameters related to the neighborhood include the neighborhood of a given node n, which is defined as the set of its neighbors. The connectivity of n, denoted by k_n, is the size of its neighborhood. The average number of neighbors indicates the average connectivity of a node in the network. A normalized version of this parameter is known as the network density. The density is a value between 0 and 1. It shows how densely the network is populated with edges (self-loops and duplicated edges are removed and ignored from the computation). A graph/network that contains no edges and solely isolated nodes has a density of 0. In contrast, the density of a clique is 1. The number of isolated nodes may provide insight into how the network density is distributed.

Another conceptually/theoretically related parameter is known as network centralization [17]. Graphs/networks, the topologies of which resemble a star, have a centralization close to 1, whereas decentralized networks are characterized by having a centralization close to 0. The network heterogeneity as a topological parameter reflects the tendency of a network to contain hub nodes [18]. In addition, the number of multi-edge node pairs indicates how often neighboring nodes are linked by more than one edge.

Finally, in undirected networks, items can be grouped into non-overlapping clusters, with a cluster being a unique set of items sharing common features included in a map [14]. The clustering coefficient C_n of a node n is defined as:

$$C_n = \frac{2e_n}{k_n(k_n - 1)}$$

where k_n is the number of neighbors of the node n, and e_n is the number of connected pairs between all the neighbors of the node n. The clustering coefficient is a ratio (namely, N/M), where N is the number of edges between the neighbors of the given node n, and M is the maximum number of edges that could possibly exist between the neighbors of the given node n. The clustering coefficient of a node is always a number between 0 and 1. The network clustering coefficient is defined as the average of the clustering coefficients for all nodes in the network. Nodes with less than two neighbors are assumed to have a clustering coefficient of 0.

Finally, the number of papers per year was also visualized as a time series.

3. Results

3.1. Literature Search

The initial literature search yielded a pool of 65 items (n = 37 from MEDLINE via PubMed and n = 28 from Scopus). A total of 21 items were duplicated and were, as such, removed, and 44 items were inspected. Seven studies [19–25] were excluded with reason (n = 2, not reporting sufficient details; n = 5, not disaggregating data according to para-sports discipline). Finally, 37 studies [26–62] were retained in the present scoping review. We found that the included studies focused on a range of aspects involving health, classification, the etiology of injuries, and performance.

3.2. Warm-Up Strategies in Paralympic Powerlifting

Two randomized, cross-over studies [26,27] in a sample of 12 elite Brazilian male PP athletes (aged 24.14 ± 6.21 years, body weight 81.67 ± 17.36 kg, experience 4.45 ± 0.31 years) [26] and in a sample of 15 elite Brazilian male PP athletes (aged 28.47 ± 5.79 years, body weight 81.75 ± 17.33 kg, experience 2.43 ± 1.03 years) [27] investigated the impact of three different warm-up conditions (no warm-up, traditional warm-up consisting of dynamic resistance exercises, and stretching warm-up) on a set of PP performance-related outcomes and variables. These included dynamic (1-RM and mean propulsive velocity) and isometric strength (rate of force development, maximum isometric force, time to maximum isometric force, fatigue index, impulse, variability, peak torque) and skin temperature. The authors found no differences among the experimental conditions with the exception of skin temperature over pectoral muscles (overall $p = 0.038$), in particular during the traditional warm-up vs. without a warm-up ($p = 0.049$), whereas the difference between stretching warm-up and without warm-up was borderline significant ($p = 0.064$). Finally, no differences could be detected between traditional and stretching warm-ups ($p = 0.934$). In addition, differences could be computed between the "after" condition without warm-up and stretch warm-up. Without warm-up demonstrated a difference in relation to a traditional warm-up in the "10 min later" condition. Another difference could be described for the maximum isometric force ($p = 0.005$), which was the highest in the without-warm-up condition. Overall, despite these differences, different types of warm-up methods do not seem to influence performance-related outcomes in elite PP athletes.

3.3. *Aspects of Training in Paralympic Powerlifting*

Aidar et al. [28] compared the effect of two different three-week training sessions (elastic bands vs. fixed resistance) conducted in randomized order, through static (maximum isometric force, peak torque, rate of force development, and time to maximum isometric force), dynamic indicators of force (1 repetition maximum, 1RM), and fatigue in a sample of 12 PP athletes (aged 28.60 ± 7.60 years). The authors found an increase in force between pre- and post-training for 1RM ($p = 0.018$, effect size (ES) = 0.412), maximum isometric force ($p = 0.011$, ES = 0.415), peak torque ($p = 0.012$, ES = 0.413), and the rate of force development ($p = 0.0002$, ES = 0.761), suggesting that training with the use of elastic bands has more detrimental effects compared to the method with fixed resistance, promoting overload, increasing fatigue, and decreasing strength.

Lopes Silva et al. [29] considered 4676 results (1683 achieved by female PP athletes, and 2993 achieved by male PP athletes) in the World Para Powerlifting events (Regional Games/Championships, World Cup, World Championships, and Paralympic Games) between 2014 and 2020, to determine the optimal preparation interval for success. The authors found that there were no significant sex-/gender-specific differences ($p = 0.37$). In addition, no differences could be computed in terms of weight categories ($p = 0.95$). Furthermore, the authors found that the longer intervals corresponded to the most important events. Specifically, the odds of winning a medal at the Paralympic Games were 2.17 ($p = 0.011$) times greater when preparation was ≥40 weeks than when preparation was less than 23 weeks. Considering the World Championships, the odds of winning a medal were 2.34 times greater ($p = 0.002$) when the interval varied from 23 to 31 weeks compared to a preparation interval of <23 weeks. World cup races, on the other hand, are generally career stages that are useful for the athlete to achieve physical fitness or qualification for higher-level competitions. In fact, athletes competing in these events were 1.69 times more likely to win a medal with preparation ranging from 22 to 30 weeks compared with preparation lasting < 11 weeks ($p = 0.004$). Finally, there were no significant differences between the interval of preparation for the Regional Games/Championships.

3.4. *Physiological Aspects and Responses in Paralympic Powerlifting*

Two studies [30,31] investigated the physiological responses in PP. Paz et al. [30] conducted a randomized cross-over trial to explore post-exercise hypotension after two high-intensity resistance-training sessions in a sample of ten national-level PP athletes (aged 26.1 ± 6.9 years; body weight 76.8 ± 17.4 kg). The authors found a decrease in systolic blood pressure by 5–9% after 90% and 95% of 1RM at 20–50 min post-exercise. Moreover, an increase in myocardial oxygen volume and the double product could be described immediately after and 5 min post-exercise, with the heart rate elevating post-exercise but returning to baseline values by 50 min after training sessions for both training conditions.

Aidar et al. [31] compared hemodynamic responses (systolic, diastolic, and mean blood pressure, heart rate, heart pressure product, and myocardial oxygen volume) in

PP vs. powerlifting before and after training and up to 60 min after training in a sample of 20 athletes. The systolic blood pressure increased after training ($p < 0.001$), and there were differences in the post-training and 30, 40, and 60 min later ($p = 0.021$), between 10 and 40 min after training ($p = 0.031$), and between the two samples ($p = 0.028$), with PP having a stronger and more persistent hypotensive effect, which remained present even after 50 min. Mean blood pressure showed a similar trend, with statistically significant differences between before and after ($p = 0.016$) and 40 min later ($p = 0.040$), and with lower values in PP athletes. Diastolic blood pressure, on the contrary, did not show any difference between powerlifters and PP athletes. Heart rate exhibited differences between before and after, and 5 and 10 min later ($p = 0.002$), and between after and 10, 20, 30, 40, 50, and 60 min later ($p < 0.001$). Heart pressure product and myocardial oxygen volume showed differences between before and after ($p = 0.006$) and between after and 5, 10, 20, 30, 40, 50, and 60 min later ($p < 0.001$). Overall, no risk of hemodynamic overload could be found in PP athletes as well as in their able-bodied counterparts, who exhibited clinically comparable responses to high-intensity resistance training [30,31].

3.5. Psychological Aspects and Responses in Paralympic Powerlifting

Only two studies [32,33] explored the psychophysiological responses in PP. Da Silva et al. [32] found that, in a sample of seven male athletes (aged 41.0 ± 10.1 years; body weight 84.7 ± 21.1 kg) undergoing a 4-week program of strength training, the increase in maximum dynamic strength ($p < 0.001$; ES = 0.50) was paralleled by an increase in stress as measured by means of the "Recovery Stress Questionnaire for Athletes" (RESTQ-Sport) scales, with significant increases in the lack of energy ($p < 0.022$; ES = 1.30), success ($p < 0.035$; ES = 0.33), and sleep quality ($p < 0.007$; ES = 0.62). Conversely, there was a post-training decrease in the scores of general well-being ($p < 0.012$; ES = 2.18), interval disturbances ($p < 0.021$; ES = 3.14), personal acceptance, and self-regulation ($p < 0.006$; ES = 2.21). The domains of tension ($p < 0.003$; ES = 1.32), fatigue ($p < 0.002$; ES = 0.72), mental confusion ($p < 0.002$; ES = 2.09), depression ($p < 0.001$; ES = 5.00), and anger ($p < 0.001$; ES = 4.75) reported significantly increased scores. Besides, the vigor domain score was found to be significantly reduced ($p < 0.001$; ES = 0.87). These negative changes in a set of psychophysiological indicators were potentially induced by overload. They can be utilized by coaches to monitor and control the internal training load, ideally customizing the prescription of training loads for PP athletes based on their individual responses.

The other study [33] is a qualitative case study highlighting the experiences and coping functions of a 35-year-old PP female athlete named Niza, from the socio-cultural context of an Islamic state in Malaysia. The author coupled Foucauldian theory with feminist post-structuralism, narrative inquiry, and a Gestalt phenomenological approach to identify the main discourses embedded within the narrative of the athlete, in an attempt to disentangle the complex dynamics of disability, athleticism, culture, ethnicity, and gender. Several themes emerged, including the initial negative reactions from her family members at the communication of the decision to pursue a career as an athlete, the barriers of society's conservative and exclusive attitudes toward women, and the lack of encouragement and support. Gradually, Niza was able to challenge this misconception through anticipatory and proactive coping functions, self-consciousness, and strong positive beliefs and became a confident, successful, and inspirational figure for other Muslim female athletes with disabilities.

3.6. Biomechanics of Bench Press in Paralympic Powerlifting

Eight studies [34–41] investigated the biomechanics of BP in PP, including the performance of PP under two different BP conditions (namely, with the legs tied and untied [34,35]), the impact of the choice of a specific grip width [36,37], the effects of arched and flat techniques [38], the impact of a partial vs. full range of movement (ROM) training [39], the evaluation of strength and muscle activation indicators in sticking point region [40], and the force output during different phases of the PP BP movement [41].

Guerra et al. [34] analyzed the variations in sEMG (muscle activity of *triceps brachii*—long head, anterior deltoid, and *pectoralis major*—sternal and clavicular portions), the velocity of the barbell displacement (maximum velocity and mean propulsive velocity), and power in the BP at various relative loads (40%, 60%, 80%, and 100% of 1RM) in a sample of 15 PP male athletes (aged 22.27 ± 10.30 years). The authors found no statistical differences in muscle activity in both BP conditions but indicated some intra-individual variability. Specifically, higher muscle activation values were found in the pectoral (sternal portion) than in the anterior deltoid ($p = 0.035$), with a 40% 1RM load in the tied condition. In the untied condition with a load of 60% of 1RM, on the other hand, muscle activation showed higher values in the pectoral (clavicular portion) than in the anterior deltoid ($p = 0.018$) and *triceps brachii* ($p = 0.046$). In the same condition but with a maximum load (100% 1RM), the brachial *triceps* had higher values than the anterior deltoid ($p = 0.047$). Comparing the velocity variables, significant differences were found ($p < 0.001$) between all loads (% 1RM) in both BP conditions, indicating a reduction in velocity due to the increase in the relative load. As for power, similar results were found. However, for the relative load of 40% of 1RM in the untied condition, power was lower than in the 60% and 80% of 1RM. Furthermore, power with a load of 100% of 1 RM differed from all other relative loads ($p < 0.001$) in both BP conditions. In conclusion, the findings showed the predominance of activation of the *pectoralis major* clavicular portion in the tied condition and *pectoralis major* sternal portion in the untied condition in loads of 40% to 60% 1RM, with greater muscle activation of the *triceps* in loads of 100% 1RM. Furthermore, a strong load–velocity relationship and, to a lesser extent, a strong load–power relationship were found. Mota et al. [35] recruited a sample of 16 male PPs, 8 of whom were trained (aged 26.25 ± 6.96 years) and 8 of whom were beginners (aged 30.29 ± 7.34 years), who conducted 40%, 45%, and 50% of 1RM in tied and untied conditions. No differences between those trained and beginners, as well as between the tied and untied conditions, in terms of average propulsive speed and average speed could be found. However, power at 40% of 1RM resulted in significantly higher values for the aforementioned variables in trained PP athletes across both conditions, tied ($p = 0.033$) and untied ($p = 0.024$), since it can be hypothesized that those trained develop more power than beginners. On the other hand, being tied does not create a performance advantage.

Dos Santos et al. [36,37] conducted two randomized controlled studies consisting of a sample of 15 elite Brazilian male PP athletes (aged 25.40 ± 3.30 years), which aimed at exploring the effects of using different grip widths on BP performance. In the first study, Dos Santos et al. [36] evaluated isometric (time and force spent to reach 30%, 50%, and 100% of the maximal isometric strength) and dynamic (mean propulsive velocity, and force production using 25%, 50%, and 100% of 1RM load) strength. In addition, an electromyographic evaluation was performed during the evaluation of the maximal isometric strength. All evaluations have been carried out with different grip widths in random order (bi-acromial distance: BAD, 1.3 BAD, 1.5 BAD, and 81 cm). Moderate and small effects were described for force production, with 25% ($p = 0.08$), 50% ($p = 0.41$), and 100% ($p = 0.66$) of 1RM load between the grip widths used, respectively. Large and moderate differences were computed between the mean propulsive velocity when performed with different grip widths using 25% ($p = 0.02$), 50% ($p = 0.15$), and 100% ($p = 0.18$) of the maximal dynamic strength load. The highest values for both force generation and mean propulsive velocity were obtained with the 1.5 BAD grip width. Greater lift distances were carried out during BP with 25% ($p = 0.05$) and 50% ($p = 0.02$) of 1RM in BAD conditions. No statistical difference was described in the force values at 30% ($p = 0.96$), 50% ($p = 0.91$), and 100% ($p = 0.91$) of maximal isometric strength between the different grip widths, with the 1.5 BAD grip width condition exhibiting the greatest force generation. Furthermore, statistically significant differences could be computed in time to achieve 30% ($p = 0.03$), 50% ($p = 0.03$), and 100% ($p = 0.03$) of the maximal isometric strength. Finally, sEMG showed moderate, although not statistically significant, effects in terms of muscle activation and the different amplitudes of the grip.

In the second study, Dos Santos et al. [37] analyzed variables related to the velocity of the barbell displacement (average velocity, average velocity propulsive, and velocity peak) carried out with loads of 30% and 50% of 1 RM with different grip widths in random order (BAD 1.3 × BAD, 1.5 × BAD). The authors found only a significant variable in this study. Specifically, the average velocity was higher with 1 × BAD at 30% of 1RM compared to the 1.3 × BAD. There was also an inverse relationship between load and velocity as the average velocity generated for 50% of the 1RM load was less than that applied for 30% of 1RM. Overall, the findings of these two studies [36,37] indicated the importance of choosing the proper grip width and its impact on muscle activation and performance-related outcomes.

The arched technique (or the arch bridge technique) is when the athlete performs a marked hyperlordosis in the spine, along with scapular retraction. Neto et al. [38] compared the arched and flat techniques in 23 experienced PP athletes vs. 20 beginners. The total load, the trajectory of the barbell in the sagittal plane, and the mean velocity of the barbell in eccentric and concentric phases were computed. No statistically significant differences between the arched and flat techniques for the total load could be found in terms of all analyzed outcomes, with trivial and moderate ESs for experienced and beginner PP athletes, respectively, and with higher values reported for the arched technique in experienced individuals and greater improvements reported for the arched technique in beginner subjects. During the eccentric phase of the BP, all outcome differences presented trivial-to-moderate ESs. The vertical displacement was lower in the arched technique compared with the flat technique for both experienced and beginner athletes, in eccentric and concentric phases. Finally, the root mean square error (RMSE) and the horizontal displacement exhibited nonsignificantly lower values in the arched technique in experienced athletes compared with beginner individuals during the eccentric and concentric phases of the BP. As such, according to this study [38], instead of imposing the arched technique, the most effective technique for experienced and beginner PP athletes should be identified by sports trainers and coaches, based on variables such as the injury level and its characteristics (i.e., structured severe scoliosis or high levels of spinal cord injury).

In training, partial movements are considered a variation of the BP and are generally used to improve control in particular areas of the trajectory or to stimulate the central nervous system without putting stress on it. Mendonça et al. [39] compared the fatigue index, the force production (maximum isometric force, time to maximum isometric force, and rate of strength development), the muscle thickness (clavicular and sternal portions of *pectoralis major*), and the variations in sEMG (muscle activity of the anterior portion of the deltoid muscle, the clavicular portion of the *pectoralis major*, and the sternal portion of the *pectoralis major*) involved in partial vs. full ROM before and after training in a sample of 12 athletes (aged 28.60 ± 7.60 years). In both exercise conditions, time in the rate of force development ($p < 0.001$, ES = 0.720) and time in the rate of strength development ($p = 0.014$, ES = 0.437) exhibited decreased values post-training. Moreover, the maximal isometric force decreased in post-training as well to a greater extent in full ROM ($p < 0.001$, ES = 3.53) than in partial ROM ($p < 0.001$; ES = 1.85), while the fatigue index increased solely in the partial ROM ($p < 0.001$; ES = 1.65). Regarding the other variables, the clavicular portion of the *pectoralis major* muscle thickness from pre- to post-training increased more in full ROM ($p < 0.001$; ES = 3.33) than in partial ROM ($p < 0.001$; ES = 2.34). Further, similar increases were found in the sternal portion of the *pectoralis major* muscle thickness between full ROM ($p < 0.001$; ES = 1.71) and partial ROM ($p < 0.001$; ES = 2.36). Finally, both portions of the *pectoralis major* were more active in full ROM ($p < 0.05$), while the *triceps* muscle was more active with partial ROM ($p < 0.05$). In conclusion, compared to a full lift, partial ROM training allows the management of higher workloads with fewer losses in muscle functions.

The concentric phase in the BP exercise is conventionally divided into three different regions: (i) pre-sticking: time from the lowest point of the bar to the maximum velocity of the bar, (ii) sticking: from the maximum velocity of the bar to the first minimum velocity of the bar, and (iii) post-sticking: from the moment the acceleration of the bar has returned positive up to the second peak of maximal velocity.

Aidar et al. [40], in a sample of 12 PP athletes (aged 26.56 ± 5.55 years), evaluated changes in strength indicators (maximum isometric force, rate of force development, and time to maximum isometric force), kinematic parameters (velocity and dynamics time), and sEMG muscle activity (pectoral, sternal and clavicular parts, deltoid and *triceps*) at different distances from the bar to the chest (5.0; 10.0; 15.0 and 25 cm). Furthermore, the velocity and dynamic time in the eccentric and concentric phases (pre-sticking, sticking, and post-sticking) were assessed. The authors found changes in velocity at the various points in the sticking region. Specifically, at 5.0 cm, velocity reaches its highest value (0.699 m/s), whilst at 10.0 cm, it tends to fall (0.198 m/s) ($p < 0.001$), and then increases at 15 cm (0.423 m/s) ($p < 0.04$) and at 25.0 cm (1.137 m/s) ($p < 0.001$). There were also differences in velocity between the pre-sticking region and the sticking region (1.98 ± 0.32 vs. 1.30 ± 0.43, $p = 0.039$) and in the dynamic time between the pre-sticking and the sticking region (0.40 ± 0.16 vs. 0.97 ± 0.37, $p = 0.021$). Regarding the strength indicators, the maximum isometric force showed an increase after the sticking point (10 cm) with significant differences between 5.0 and 15.0 cm ($p = 0.001$), 5.0 and 25.0 cm ($p < 0.001$), and 10.0 and 15.0 cm ($p = 0.012$). The rate of force development was higher at 25.0 cm than at 5 cm ($p = 0.004$) and 10.0 cm ($p < 0.001$). Finally, in the time to maximum isometric force, there were differences between 5.0 cm and 15.0 cm ($p < 0.001$), 5.0 cm and 25.0 cm ($p = 0.001$), 10.0 cm and 15.0 cm ($p < 0.05$), and 15.0 cm and 25.0 cm ($p < 0.05$). The electromyographic results did not indicate significant differences between the muscles and between the different distances studied. However, greater activation of the brachial *triceps* was found compared to the other muscles, mainly at 10.0 cm and 15.0 cm. In conclusion, in the sticking region, the strength and kinematic parameters tend to be altered despite the greater contribution of the *triceps* muscle. These findings have practical implications in that coaches should determine the sticking point and focus on it, devising proper and effective training and conditioning strategies for the point at which the failure occurs. This is anticipated to significantly improve PP outcomes.

Da Silva et al. [41] recruited six male (aged 26.5 ± 8.0 years) and four female (aged 39.8 ± 11.2 years) PP athletes who underwent 1 repetition at 95% intensity of 1RM three times with 5 min of rest between attempts. Electromyographic variables (root mean square (RMS), mean frequency, and median frequency) and kinematics (velocity of movement of the barbell) were evaluated in different sub-phases of the BP movement (sub-phases I and II for the eccentric phase and pre-sticking, sticking, and post-sticking for the concentric phase). There was no significant difference between the total velocity values of the eccentric and concentric phases. However, the eccentric phase was shorter than the concentric one. In the eccentric phase, differences in velocity were found between sub-phases I and II (149.36 ± 53.39 vs. 181.97 ± 47.01). In the concentric phase, on the other hand, the barbell velocity decreased during the sticking sub-phase compared to the pre-sticking phase (122.95 ± 35.92 vs. 179.39 ± 54.68), and the velocity increased again in the post-sticking phase (160.36 ± 65.09). Finally, the barbell velocity in sub-phase II and pre-sticking was significantly higher than in the sticking phase ($p < 0.05$). Regarding the electromyographic results, the RMS values obtained for the *triceps* were significantly lower than those of the pectoral and deltoid muscles for all the sub-phases studied ($p < 0.05$). Except for sub-phase I, where there were no differences in muscle activation, the deltoid had the maximum RMS values for all sub-phases ($p < 0.05$). The behavior common to all the muscles studied was that they had their maximum activation in the pre-sticking phase. In the mean and median frequency, on the other hand, the *triceps brachii* showed the highest values, followed by the deltoid and pectoral muscles. Furthermore, in the *triceps brachii*, statistically different values were found in all the movement sub-phases ($p < 0.05$). In both frequency parameters, all muscles showed significant differences in the post-sticking phase ($p < 0.05$). These results have practical implications in that sports trainers and coaches should develop resistance-training programs in such a way as to include variations in the BP execution and optimize PP performance-related outcomes.

3.7. Recovery Strategy in Paralympic Powerlifting

Five studies [42–46] explored the impact of post-exercise recovery in PP through physiological and biochemical assessments using different strategies. Aidar et al. [42] conducted a randomized, placebo-controlled trial and recruited 10 PP athletes at the national level, aged 27.13 ± 5.57 years. They underwent a warm-up and 5 × 5 at 80–90% of 1RM, ingesting ibuprofen 15 min before and 5 h after training. Ibuprofen ingestion resulted in positive effects, with greater peak torque values ($p = 0.04$, at 24 h) and a lower fatigue index ($p = 0.01$, at 24 h), even though there was no impact on oxidative stress markers. Blood indicators, including leukocytes, with the use of ibuprofen were higher than with the placebo ($p < 0.001$).

In another work, Aidar et al. [43] conducted a randomized, placebo-controlled trial and recruited a sample of 20 PP athletes (10 at the national level, aged 32.50 ± 3 years, and 10 at the regional level, aged 30.75 ± 5.32 years). Athletes underwent a warm-up and 5 × 5 at 80% of 1RM, with half of the sample ingesting ibuprofen 15 min before the commencement of the training. Ibuprofen ingestion resulted in greater peak torque values ($p = 0.007$) and a lower fatigue index ($p = 0.002$) in the national level group. Leukocytes, with the use of ibuprofen in the national level group, were greater than in the regional level group ($p = 0.001$). Similarly, neutrophils levels in the national-level group treated with ibuprofen were greater than those in the regional-level group treated with ibuprofen and a placebo ($p = 0.025$). Lymphocytes levels in the national-level group treated with ibuprofen were lower than those in the regional-level group treated with ibuprofen and a placebo ($p = 0.001$). Monocytes levels in the national level group with ibuprofen and a placebo were lower than those in the regional level with ibuprofen ($p = 0.049$). Hemoglobin, hematocrit, and erythrocyte values were higher at the national level with ibuprofen and the placebo than those at the regional level with ibuprofen and a placebo (p-value < 0.05). Ammonia levels were higher in the national level group with ibuprofen ($p = 0.007$) and a placebo ($p = 0.038$), with respect to the regional-level group with ibuprofen and a placebo, respectively.

Fraga et al. [44] recruited eight PP athletes (aged 27.0 ± 5.3 years) competing at the national level, who underwent a warm-up and 5 × 5 at 85–90% of 1RM. Ingestion of ibuprofen or a placebo occurred 15 min before and 5 h after training. The maximal isometric force only decreased in the placebo condition, with a significant increase between 24 and 48 h in the ibuprofen condition, whilst the post-exercise rate of force development decreased significantly for both conditions. Muscle temperature decreased significantly at 48 h post-exercise in the placebo condition, while deltoid muscle temperature at 48 h post-exercise was higher in the ibuprofen condition. Finally, creatine kinase levels were higher with the placebo than with ibuprofen 48 h after exercise, whilst alanine aminotransferase levels were lower 24 h after the training, with ibuprofen. Immediately after training, aspartate aminotransferase levels increase with the placebo, while with ibuprofen, they increase after 24 h. These findings, taken together, seem to indicate that the ingestion of ibuprofen exerts positive effects, in that it appears able to counteract, reduce, or at least partially delay the increases in the levels of creatine kinase and alanine/aspartate aminotransferases—an increase partly induced by the exercise and partly by the underlying disability in this population.

Sampaio et al. [45] investigated the impact of creatine supplementation on the recovery in a sample of 8 PP athletes aged 25.40 ± 3.30 years, undergoing training consisting of 5 × 5 at 85–90% of 1RM. There was no significant variation in the peak torque, rate of force development, time to maximum isometric force, and force with creatine supplementation, whilst the fatigue index after 7 days decreased ($p = 0.02$), making this supplementation a viable nutritional strategy for PP athletes.

dos Santos et al. [46] investigated how different post-workout recovery strategies (passive recovery, dry needling, and cold-water immersion) can impact homeostasis in a sample of twelve male PP athletes (aged 25.4 ± 3.3 years) undergoing strength training consisting of 5 × 5 at 120% of 1RM in the eccentric phase and 80% of 1RM in the concentric phase + 3 × 5 at 40% of 1RM. The maximal isometric force differed significantly among the three post-workout recovery strategies ($p = 0.046$). In particular, with passive recovery and dry needling, the maximal isometric force was found to decrease compared with the pretest value at 15 min and 2 h. Similarly, in cold-water immersion, it increased from 2 to 24 h and reached 20% more force after 24 h than at the baseline level. Biochemical blood indicators differed as well among the three post-workout recovery methods ($p = 0.006$). In more detail, cold-water immersion and dry needling led to increased levels of interleukin-2 (IL-2) from 24 to 48 h compared to that from 2 h to 24 h. On the other hand, interleukin-4 (IL-4) and interferon-gamma (IFN-γ) levels did not change significantly over time. These molecules, with the exception of IL-4, have a pro-inflammatory activity, which may be detrimental, but if finely regulated and controlled, they can play a key role in muscle repair and regeneration. Muscle thickness was another variable that differed according to the type of recovery strategy ($p = 0.002$). More specifically, with passive recovery, it increased and remained elevated, whilst with cryotherapy, it increased after 15 min and 2 h, whilst after dry needling, muscle thickness did not increase in any of the muscles analyzed, and after 2 h, muscle thickness was found to significantly decrease again in the *major pectoralis* muscle. Finally, pain pressure differed based on the post-workout recovery strategy in a muscle-specific way: differences could be described for acromial *pectoralis* ($p = 0.003$), but not for the deltoid muscle ($p = 0.085$). The pain pressure threshold was found to increase significantly immediately after all recovery methods (15 min). Then, it decreased for all muscles, with the lowest measurement computed 24 h after passive recovery, after which it started increasing again. A similar trend could be found for dry needling, even though the decrease was lower. Finally, after cold-water immersion, pain pressure stabilized after 15 min and increased after 2 h for acromial *pectoralis*. In conclusion, the various recovery strategies had differential effects in terms of the return to homeostasis in PP athletes, impacting edema, pain, and local and systemic recovery to varying degrees and with different, precise timing, with the dry needling method being effective in shorter-term recoveries, and with cold-water immersion being effective in shorter and longer recoveries.

3.8. Impact of the Disability and Type of Disability in Paralympic Powerlifting

Four studies [47–50] explored the impact of the disability and the type of disability in PP. Gołaś et al. [47] compared two elite flat BP athletes—an elite able-bodied athlete (aged 34 years, body weight 103 kg) and an athlete with a lower limb disability (aged 31 years, body weight 92 kg)—in terms of the activity of four muscles (*pectoralis major*, anterior deltoid, lateral and long heads of the *triceps brachii*). The peak activity of all the considered muscles significantly differed between the two athletes ($p = 0.001$, $p = 0.001$, $p = 0.0021$, and $p = 0.002$, respectively). Differences depended on the load: 60% to 100% 1RM ($p = 0.007$), 70% to 100% 1RM ($p = 0.016$), and 80% to 100% 1RM ($p = 0.032$). These findings can be explained by considering that keeping the feet on the bench leads to an increased engagement of upper body muscles and to their greater activation.

Szafraniec et al. [48] quantitatively assessed the impacts of a 6-week high-velocity strength training program on movement velocity and strength endurance measured one week before and one week after in eleven experienced powerlifting athletes with cerebral palsy vs. seven control subjects. While movement velocity increased in the cerebral palsy group only ($p = 0.016$), strength endurance increased in both groups ($p < 0.001$ and $p = 0.049$, respectively).

Teles et al. [49] compared PP athletes with (aged 30.57 ± 4.20 years) and without (aged 25.67 ± 4.52 years) spinal cord injuries in terms of the impact of dynamic (mean propulsive velocity, maximum velocity, and power) and static (maximum isometric force, time to maximum isometric force, rate of force development, impulse, variability and fatigue index) force and associated parameters at different intensities on performance-related outcomes. The two groups differed in terms of dynamic ($p < 0.05$) but not static force indicators. Concerning EMG, individuals with injured spinal cords exhibited differences between the *triceps* in relation to the previous deltoid ($p = 0.012$).

Aidar et al. [50] compared 10 PP athletes with spinal cord injuries (aged 30.00 ± 4.27 years) and 10 with other disabilities (aged 28.30 ± 4.92 years) in terms of the impact of a dynamic force (mean propulsive velocity, maximum velocity, and power), with loads of 40%, 60%, and 80% of 1RM in tied and untied conditions Athletes were also assessed in terms of static force (maximum isometric force, time to maximum isometric force, rate of force development, impulse, variability, and fatigue index). The authors found no differences between spinal cord injuries vs. other disabilities in dynamic and isometric strength indicators. However, spinal cord injuries at 80% of 1RM showed a higher mean propulsive velocity in the untied than in the tied condition ($p = 0.041$). Similarly, at 40% ($p = 0.004$) and 80% ($p = 0.023$) of 1RM, spinal cord injuries had a higher maximum velocity in the untied than in the tied condition. These studies [47–50], taken together, show that PP is a viable strategy in people living with disabilities, in that persons with injuries, such as cerebral palsy or spinal cord dysfunction, still have adequate neuromuscular control after proper training.

3.9. Epidemiology of Paralympic Powerlifting

Six studies [51–56] explored the epidemiological aspects of PP.

Lopes Silva et al. [51] retrospectively assessed 3107 athletes (1985 males and 1122 females) who took part in the last eight World Championships and six Paralympic Games in terms of sex/gender, chronological age, weight category, and competition achievements. The authors found that male athletes were older (33.2 ± 8.6 vs. 32.2 ± 7.5 years, $p = 0.001$, ES = 1.21, large) and stronger. Regarding the age of male athletes, there was a main effect of events ($p = 0.018$, ES = 0.001, small), even though no differences between those competing at Paralympic Games and World Championships ($p = 0.098$) could be found. Moreover, there was a main effect of competition achievement ($p = 0.001$, ES 0.009, small), with medalists being younger compared to non-medalists. Further, there was a main effect of the weight category ($p = 0.001$, ES = 0.014, small). Considering the age of female athletes, there was only a main effect for competition achievement ($p = 0.001$, ES 0.017, small), with medalists being younger when compared to non-medalists ($p = 0.001$), and a main effect for weight category ($p = 0.001$, ES = 0.031, moderate). Male athletes were able to lift heavier loads than females (168.0 ± 35.9 vs. 96.8 ± 24.4 kg, $p < 0.001$, ES = 2.20, large). A similar trend was reported for the relative load (2.06 ± 0.90 kg/body mass (BM) vs. 1.49 ± 0.61 kg/BM, $p < 0.001$, ES 0.71, small). The main effects of competition ($p = 0.001$, ES = 0.017, small), with higher values in the Paralympic Games compared to the World Championships, and of weight category ($p = 0.001$, ES = 0.215, moderate), were computed. Finally, an event and weight category interaction ($p = 0.045$, ES = 0.00, small) was found; for relative load, there was an event and ranking interaction ($p = 0.046$, ES = 0.002, small). Concerning the absolute load of female athletes, there was a main effect of events ($p = 0.001$, ES = 0.024, small), with higher values in Paralympic Games compared to World Championships. Furthermore, there was a main effect from the weight category ($p = 0.001$, ES = 0.344, large), also in terms of the relative load ($p = 0.001$, ES 0.124, large). Finally, in males, chronological age and body mass significantly correlated with the absolute and relative load, whilst in females, age was associated with the relative load as well as body mass with the absolute and relative load. In conclusion, the performances of both groups were better at the Paralympics than at the world championships. The medalists were younger. The lighter weight categories included participants of a younger age and with a greater relative load than the heavier competitors.

Willick et al. [52] analyzed the injury incidence rate and the injury incidence proportion in PP athletes during the London 2012 Paralympic Games (7 days). Out of 163 athletes participating in the competition, 38 injuries were reported by 38 different athletes. The injury incidence rate and the injury incidence proportion were 33.3 and 23.3, respectively. Lighter weight classes had fewer injuries than heavier weight classes. No significant differences between male and female athletes or age-specific effects could be found. In terms of the onset of injury, chronic-overuse injuries were the most frequent, followed by acute-on-chronic and acute traumatic injuries. Concerning the anatomical location of injuries, the shoulder/clavicle was the most injured area, followed by the chest and elbow.

Jarraya et al. [53] computed the injury frequency in PP athletes undergoing imaging (X-rays, ultrasound, and magnetic resonance imaging (MRI)) during the Rio 2016 Summer Paralympic Games. Of the 182 athletes participating in the competition, 20 underwent imaging. Of the 33 examinations performed, 18 injuries were reported affecting the upper extremities. The injuries mainly involved the tendons followed by the muscles and bone bruises.

Hamid et al. [54] determined the sociodemographic, clinical, and anthropometric physical parameters of Malaysian PP athletes during a Powerlifting Workshop and National Championship. Fifty-two athletes representing 13 different Malaysian states were recruited. Most of the participants were men (82.7%), and the mean age was about twenty years (24.50 $\pm$ 8.25 years). A spinal cord injury and lower limb amputation were the most frequent pathologies, with a percentage of 34.6% and 26.9%, respectively. About half of the powerlifters (42.3%) competed in international competitions, more than half (76.9%) had at least 1 year or more of experience, a minority (5.8%) also practiced other sports (athletics, basketball, and wheelchair tennis), and nearly all (97%) have completed basic education. The workouts generally had a frequency of two to four sessions per week with a duration of 90 min per session. Regarding the anthropometric characteristics, the authors found that women had a lower lean body mass (54.90, interquartile range (IQR) 14.32 kg, vs. 43.50, IQR 9.78 kg, $p = 0.031$) and higher percentages (19.80 $\pm$ 10.56% vs. 35.61 $\pm$ 6.08%, $p \leq 0.001$) and a greater amount of body fat (14.10 $\pm$ 11.55 kg vs. 26.50 $\pm$ 10.80 kg, $p = 0.003$) than men. Furthermore, males had significantly longer arm and forearm lengths compared with females (30.10, IQR 3.00 cm vs. 23.00, IQR2.13 cm; $p = 0.020$). In the analyses based on weight categories, body mass index (BMI) was significantly highest ($p < 0.001$) among the heavyweight class (42.08 $\pm$ 11.39 kg/m^2) followed by the middleweight (31.33 $\pm$ 5.46 kg/m^2) and lightweight (25.55 $\pm$ 7.05 kg/m^2) classses. The lean body mass among the lightweight, middleweight, and heavyweight classes was 45.90 $\pm$ 9.13 kg, 63.41 $\pm$ 8.29 kg, and 71.70 $\pm$ 10.16 kg, respectively, with significant differences between the middleweight and heavyweight ($p < 0.001$) and between the lightweight and middleweight (p-value < 0.001) classes. Significant differences could also be found in the body fat between the lightweight and heavyweight (30.71 $\pm$ 12.31 kg vs. 9.88 $\pm$ 6.04 kg, $p < 0.001$) classes and between the lightweight and middleweight (9.88 $\pm$ 6.04 vs. 17.41 $\pm$ 8.40, $p < 0.001$) classes. Similarly, in hip circumference, significant differences were found between the lightweight and middleweight (81.98 $\pm$ 20.51 cm vs. 108.72 $\pm$ 7.62 cm, $p < 0.001$) classes and between the middleweight and heavyweight (108.72 $\pm$ 7.62 vs. 118.38 $\pm$ 8.03, $p < 0.001$) classes. Both dominant and non-dominant arm girths during relaxation and tension were significantly greater in the heavier weight classes (p-value < 0.001). Finally, variables were found that have a significant correlation with the powerlifters' best lift. Specifically, strongly correlated variables were arm girth (r ranging from 0.549 to 0.694, p-value < 0.0001) and experience (r = 0.724, p-value < 0.0001). Weight and BMI, on the other hand, showed moderate correlations (r = 0.418, $p = 0.009$ and r = 0.462, $p = 0.008$), while lean body mass and age only showed weak correlations (r = 0.389, $p = 0.019$ and r = 0.352, $p = 0.030$).

van den Hoek et al. [55] compared world BP records of different weight classes in terms of absolute and relative strength (strength-to-weight ratio [$kg{\cdot}kg_{bw}{}^{-1}$]) between powerlifters with disabilities and powerlifters without disabilities. Surprisingly, the authors found similar results between the two athlete populations and, in some cases, higher world records for powerlifters with disabilities than their counterparts. Specifically, powerlifting world record holders without disabilities showed an absolute strength greater than those with a disability in 5 of 8 weight classes for women (47 kg, 52 kg, 57 kg, 76 kg, and 84 kg) and 6 of 8 weight classes for men (59 kg, 66 kg, 74 kg, 83 kg, 93 kg and +120 kg).

Regarding the relative strength, the values ranged, respectively, from 1.83 to 3.88 kg·kg_{bw}^{-1} for powerlifters with disabilities and from 1.49 to 3.35 kg·kg_{bw}^{-1} for powerlifters without disabilities (p = 0.118). For women, on the other hand, relative strength values ranged from 1.19–2.72 kg·kg_{bw}^{-1} for powerlifters with disabilities and from 1.14–2.22 kg·kg_{bw}^{-1} for powerlifters without disabilities, respectively (p = 0.432). Finally, among powerlifters with disabilities, the greatest relative strength was observed in the 49 kg weight class for males (3.88 kg·kg_{bw}^{-1}) and in the 50 kg weight class for women (2.72 kg·kg_{bw}^{-1}). Among powerlifters without disabilities, on the other hand, the greatest relative strength was observed in the under-66-kg weight class for males (3.35 kg·kg_{bw}^{-1}) and in the under-63-kg weight class for females (2.29 kg·kg_{bw}^{-1}).

Severin et al. [56] conducted a retrospective study with a dual aim: (1) to determine the average age of and weight lifted by 2079 athletes who participated in the Paralympic Games and World Championships, stratified by gender and body weight category and (2) to establish the age-related trajectory of the performance and derive estimates of the age at peak performance. Regarding the first aim, the authors found that the mean age for men and women in the heaviest body weight categories was 36 and 43 years, respectively. In addition, the average age of athletes in the heavier bodyweight categories was higher than that of athletes in the lighter bodyweight categories (p < 0.001). Particularly in men, age increases between 49 and 65 kg (3.9 ± 0.1 years, p = 0.002), 65 and 80 kg (2.5 ± 0.8 years, p = 0.03), and for the body weight categories 80 kg and >107 kg (3.3 ± 1.1 years, p = 0.07). For women, on the other hand, there were age increases ranging from 41 to 50 kg (4.4 ± 1.0 years, p < 0.001), 50 and 67 kg (5.6 ± 1.0 years, p < 0.001), 67 and 86 kg (3.6 ± 1.0, p = 0.02), and for body weight categories 86 and >86 kg (4.6 ± 1.1 years, p < 0.001). For the second aim, it was found that peak performance in men occurs at a younger age than in women (36.3 ± 0.5 years vs. 40.5 ± 0.7 years, p < 0.001). Furthermore, higher-level powerlifters achieved their peak performance earlier than their lower-level peers (37.1 ± 0.7 years vs. 39.7 ± 0.5 years, p = 0.003). Finally, the age at which athletes were most likely to reach their full potential (between 31 and 35 years of age) was lower than that measured (36 years for males and 41 years for females) using individual age-related trajectories.

3.10. New Analytical/Statistical Approaches for Kinematics Assessments, Internal Load Monitoring, and Predictions of Mechanical Outputs in Strength Exercises and in Paralympic Powerlifting

Six studies [57–62] developed new analytical/statistical approaches for kinematics assessments and predictions of mechanical outputs in strength exercises. The Functional ANOVA (FANOVA) model is a generalized regression model, with logistic, probit, and Poisson regression as special cases. FANOVA enables the modeling of multivariate predictor functions as specified sums of constant terms, main effects, and interaction terms. Ramos Dalla Bernardina et al. [57] recruited eight male and two female PP athletes aged 35.00 ± 7.01 years undergoing a set of five repetitions at intensities of 50% and 90% of 1RM. Mean velocity in the concentric and eccentric phases was assessed using ANOVA and FANOVA approaches to quantify asymmetries at different submaximal intensities In both analyses, a higher average velocity was found at an intensity of 50% compared to 90% of 1RM, specifically for the range of movement from 70% to 100% (p = 0.005). Whilst the two methodologies yielded similar results for the eccentric phase (no interaction between limb and intensity, and no main effect of limb, p = 0.801), the FANOVA approach enabled the authors to find an asymmetrical pattern in the concentric phase, in favor of the preferred limb, at the maximum intensity of the exercise. ANOVA failed to capture a significant interaction between limb and intensity (p = 0.999), as well as the main effect of asymmetry (p = 0.526), while the main effect of intensity could be found (p = 0.001), identifying higher mean velocities at an intensity of 50% compared to that of 90% of 1RM. When compared with ANOVA, FANOVA analyzes the entire profile of the velocity curve in the concentric and eccentric phases, allowing for a better understanding of the biomechanical characteristics of the movement with respect to the classical approach.

Bellitto et al. [58] conducted a case series analysis of one able-bodied athlete (male, 22 years) andthree PP athletes (one female and two female individuals, aged 20–40 years), undergoing three repetitions at intensities of 90% of 1RM with 3 min of rest. By means of kinematics, the authors evaluated the movements in the sagittal, frontal, and transverse planes. sEMG showed that PP athletes had high symmetry and low variability in the three movements of the bench. The able-bodied athlete had a lower level of repeatability and symmetry. Techniques of execution and muscle patterns were different for each athlete. The instrumental evaluation used allowed for the identification of similar kinematic performance patterns and specific muscle strategies for each athlete.

Loturco et al. [59] analyzed the relationship between load and barbell velocity (average velocity, average propulsive velocity, and peak velocity) to accurately predict distinct loading intensities (%1RM) during maximum contraction in a sample of eight males (aged 28.3 ± 3.6 years), five females (aged 25.4 ± 5.2 years), and four dwarfs (aged 29.4 ± 3.6 years). Associations between bar velocities and %1RM were strong for all the loading intensities (R^2 values ranging from 0.80–0.91), but the precision of the predictive modeling equations was lower (~5%) and higher (~20%) at lighter and heavier loading intensities (≤70% 1RM, and ≥70%1RM), respectively. Finally, very strong athletes perform BP 1RM assessments at lower velocities than reported in the scholarly literature.

Aidar et al. [60] assessed different methodologies (two-, and four-point methods with distal loads, and six-point methods with proximal loads) to evaluate BP maximum repetitions and their impacts on the measurement of the minimum velocity limit, load at zero velocity, and force velocity (FV) in a sample of 15 elite male PP athletes (aged 27.7 ± 5.7 years). The authors found that all methods exhibited a good ability to predict BP 1RM in PP.

Aidar et al. [61] compared dynamic (mean propulsive velocity, maximum velocity, power, and prediction of one maximum repeat) and static (maximum isometric strength, time to maximum isometric strength, rate of force development, impulse, variability, and fatigue index) indicators at different intensities in 11 national level PP athletes (aged 26.13 ± 7.22 years) vs. 12 regional level PP athletes (aged 29.25 ± 4.50 years). The authors found higher velocity values in PP at the regional level compared with the national level. Notably, there were differences for the mean propulsive velocity at 45% ($p = 0.041$), 55% ($p = 0.047$), and 75% ($p = 0.020$) of 1RM and for the maximum velocity at 50% ($p = 0.041$), 55% ($p = 0.0049$), 75% ($p = 0.013$), and 95% ($p = 0.040$) of 1RM. However, the national level has developed higher power rates than the regional level at 40% ($p = 0.004$), 45% ($p = 0.004$), 50% ($p = 0.023$), and 60% ($p = 0.032$) of 1RM and the maximum of the predicted repetition. Regarding static indicators, the national level developed a higher maximum isometric force ($p = 0.001$), impulse ($p = 0.001$) and variability ($p = 0.049$), whilst there were no differences in the time to maximum isometric strength ($p = 0.262$), rate of force development ($p = 0.276$), and fatigue index ($p = 0.180$). In conclusion, national-level athletes rely more on strength than velocity.

While the "Rating of Perceived Exertion" (RPE) scale can be used for internal load monitoring in athletes undergoing aerobic training, and it has been demonstrated to not be a useful and clinically meaningful tool to capture the strength training load intensity, a possible alternative in PP is given by a scale based on the repetitions in reserve (RIR), which examines how many repetitions the athlete estimates they can perform after the end of the set. Based on this perception, the athlete stipulates a score from 1–10 (1 corresponds to little-to-no effort and 10 to maximum effort). Specifically, the RIR-based scale values are 10, 9.5, 9, 8.5, 8, 7.5, 7, 5–6, 3–4, and 1–2 and are associated with 0, 0.5, 1, 1, 5, 2, 2.5, 3, 5, 6, and 7 repetitions (repetition estimate), respectively. Neto et al. [62] validated the RIR-based scale in a sample of 20 PP. In this study, participants were asked to perform a minimum of one repetition and up to a maximum of 4 for each different intensity (100%, 90%, 85%, 80%, and 75% of 1RM), and after each test, the RIR-based scale was evaluated. Subsequently, the number of repetitions performed was added to the estimate of repetitions provided by the RIR-based scale (estimate of total repetitions). Finally, the estimated total repetitions were compared with a maximal strength test (1RM) and a maximum repetitions test at different intensities (90, 85, 80, and 75% of 1RM). There were no significant differences between the repetitions of the maximum strength test and the estimated total repetition. Similarly, no significant differences were found between the estimated total repetition and the repetitions of the maximum strength test for 100%, 90%, 85%, and 80% of 1RM. However, repetitions performed at 75% of 1RM were significantly higher than the total estimated repetitions (median = 9.0 vs. 7.0 repetitions, Δ = 13.8%, SE = 0.4). To demonstrate the reliability of the scale, the correlation of the estimated total repetitions with the repetitions of the maximum strength tests for all load intensities was very high (intraclass correlation coefficient (ICC) = 0.91, p-value < 0.01). Using the Bland and Altman method, the difference between means was 0.9 repetitions, and the interval around differences was 6.4 repetitions. In terms of construct validity, the RIR-based scale exhibited a high correlation value with 1RM intensities (rho = 0.86, p-value < 0.05).

3.11. Bibliometrics-Based Analysis of Paralympic Powerlifting Scientific Output

Our bibliometrics analysis enabled us to identify 164 researchers (nodes), 103 (62.8%) of whom were interconnected (Figure 1). The resulting graph (Figure 2) consisted of 1229 links (edges), with a total link strength of 2065, and 19 clusters. The most prolific author (topologically speaking, the hub node) was Aidar, F. J., with 22 items/documents (representing 59.5% of the scientific output overviewed in the present scoping review). The list of the ten most productive scholars can be found in Table 1.

As can be seen from Figure 3, the distribution of documents is highly asymmetrical (median = 1, coefficient of skewness = 3.76, $p < 0.0001$, coefficient of kurtosis = 15.92, $p < 0.0001$). A total of 68.3% of scholars have authored one document, whilst one single author is responsible for about 60% of the PP-related scientific production. The main topological features of the scholarly community of authors on PP are shown in Table 2.

Table 1. The ten most productive authors on Paralympic powerlifting.

Author	Country	Number of Items (%)	Number of Links	Total Link Strength	Author Cluster
Aidar, F.J.	Brazil	22 (59.5%)	94	264	7
Cabral, B.G.	Brazil	15 (40.5%)	76	209	2
de Almeida-Neto, P.F.	Brazil	15 (40.5%)	74	207	2
de Matos, D.G.	Brazil/Canada	14 (37.8%)	63	188	1
Marçal, A.C.	Brazil	13 (35.1%)	62	182	1
Reis, V.M.	Portugal	11 (29.7%)	56	150	1
Clemente, F.M.	Portugal	11 (29.7%)	54	148	6
de Souza, R.F.	Brazil	11 (29.7%)	54	145	1
Garrido, N.D.	Portugal	10 (27.0%)	52	145	3
dos Santos, J.L.	Brazil	7 (18.9%)	46	98	3

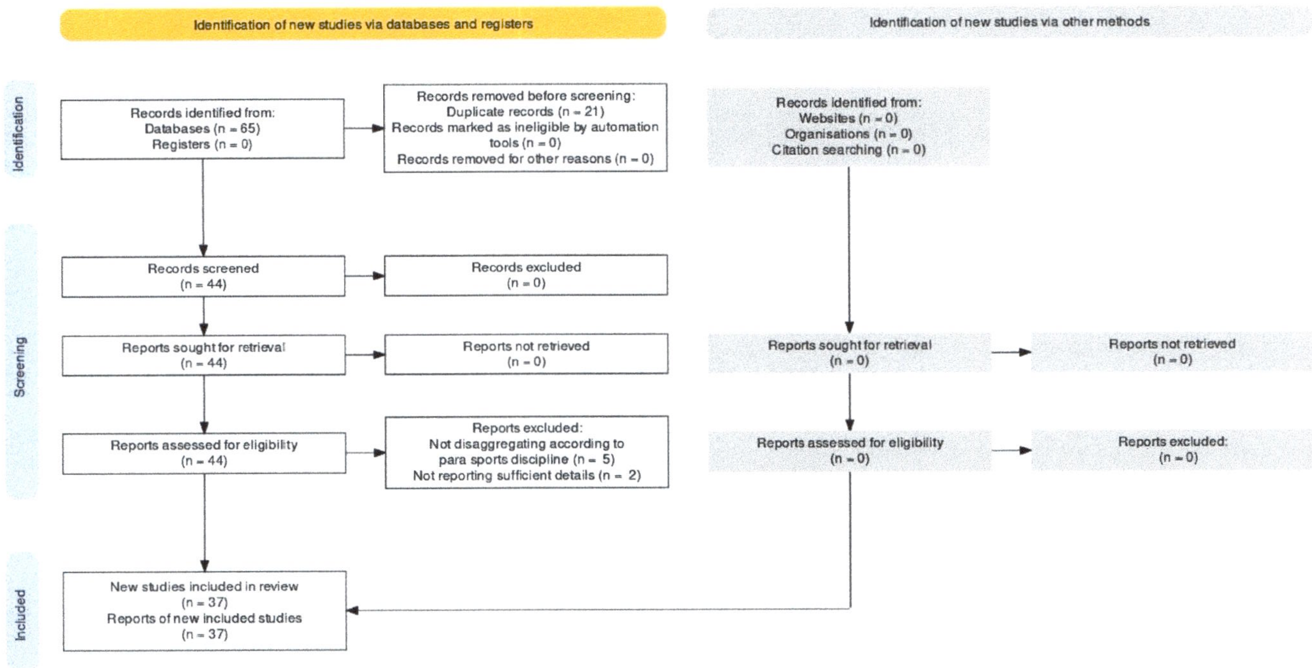

Figure 1. Flowchart adopted in the present scoping review.

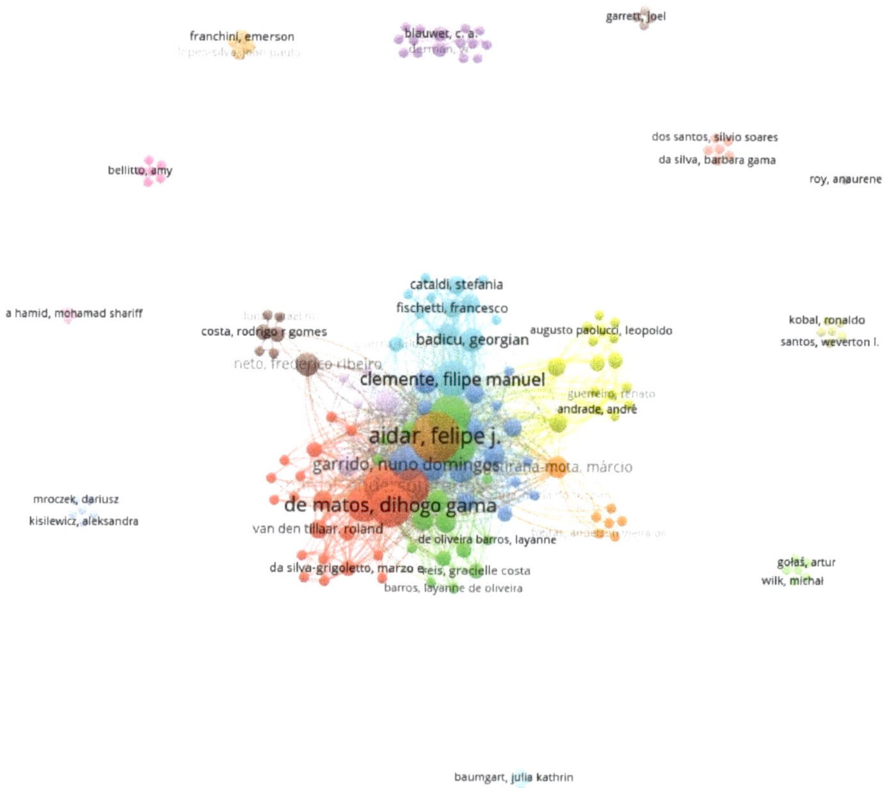

Figure 2. Bibliographic network showing connections between authors active in the field of Paralympic powerlifting.

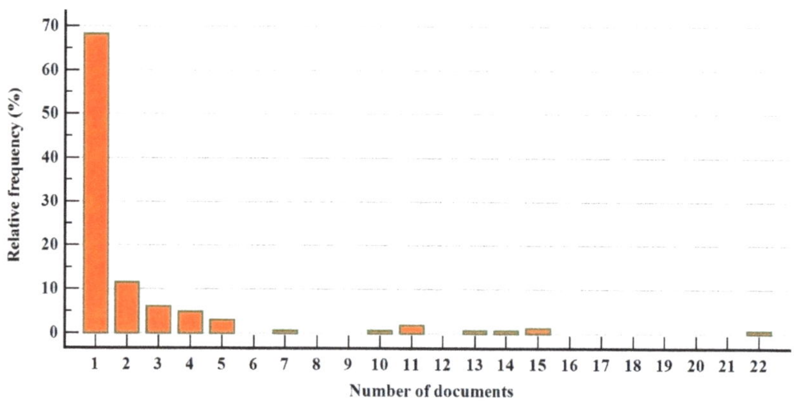

Figure 3. Distribution of Paralympic powerlifting-related documents broken down to authors.

Table 2. The main topological features of the scholarly community of authors on Paralympic powerlifting.

Topological Feature	Value
Average number of neighbors	20.78
Network diameter	4
Network radius	2
Characteristic path length	1.91
Clustering coefficient	0.84
Network density	0.20
Network heterogeneity	0.79
Network centralization	0.73
Connected components	11

Similar highly asymmetrical distributions can be found for other topological parameters, for instance, for neighborhood connectivity (Figure 4) and topological coefficients (Figure 5).

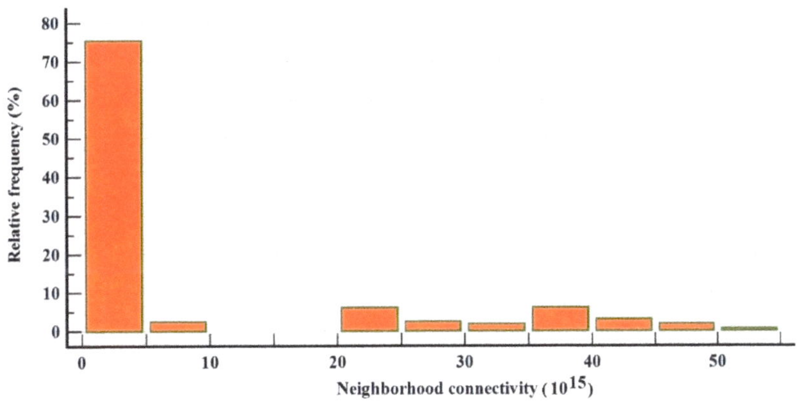

Figure 4. Distribution of neighborhood connectivity of the author network in the field of Paralympic powerlifting.

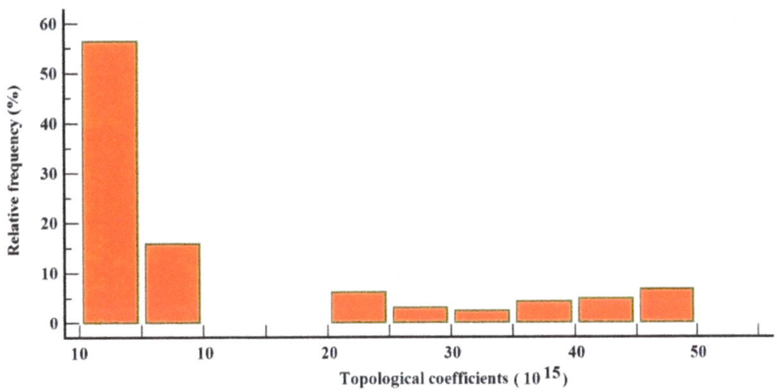

Figure 5. Distribution of topological coefficients of the author network in the field of Paralympic powerlifting.

Finally, in terms of publication years, 13 articles (35.1%) were published in 2022.

4. Discussion

Despite having already become a paralympic sports discipline in 1984 [63], only in the last few years has PP been attracting a lot of interest from the community of researchers, with the first scholarly contribution dating back to 2012 and with more than one-third of the scientific output being published this year (2022). As such, the scholarly discipline is quite recent and young. Moreover, the community dealing with this topic is poorly interconnected, with most authors contributing to just one article, and with one single author being a hub node of the author network. Distributions of the number of articles and authors/co-authors were found to be highly asymmetrical, indicating that this research is still in its infancy and has great room as well as great potential to grow. Reflecting this, many research topics are also overlooked and underdeveloped, with the currently available evidence being based on a few studies.

4.1. *Physiological and Psychological Responses to Warm-up, Training, Exercise, and Recovery in Paralympic Powerlifting*

Warm-ups have been acknowledged as instrumental in enhancing athletes' performance-related outcomes in different sports disciplines and in a wide range of exercises and physical activities, by increasing body temperature and thus decreasing stiffness, improving nerve conduction velocity, and optimizing metabolic efficiency [64]. However, disabled people may have impaired thermoregulatory responses to exercise and could benefit less from warm-ups. In PP, the warm-up, regardless of its design and format (in terms of type, intensity, and volume), has been shown by two studies [26,27] to improve performance (type, intensity, volume), even though the body of evidence is limited (being based on two studies only), and more research should be conducted to explore the effects of other designs of warm-up strategies.

Concerning training, the use of elastic bands (vs. the fixed-resistance methodology) in PP seems to promote overload, increase fatigue, and decrease strength, whilst it appears to be an effective and common practice in powerlifting [65]. However, this conclusion is drawn from one study only [28], warranting further research in the field. As well, the determinants of training in terms of the optimal preparation interval should be further investigated: the only study available [29] failed to detect any age-, sex-, and gender-specific differences.

In addition, disabled people have impaired cardiovascular, respiratory, neuromuscular, and thermoregulatory responses to exercise. However, regular training can compensate for these impairments and derangements [30,31], helping this specific population overcome their underlying limitations [47–50], reaching levels of relative and absolute strength sometimes greater than able-bodied athletes [55]. PP athletes experience unique stressors [32], even though, through anticipatory and proactive coping functions, self-consciousness, and strong positive beliefs, PP athletes can become confident, successful, and inspirational figures for other people with disabilities [33].

These results are in line with studies evaluating physiological responses in para-athletics athletes [66,67], providing further evidence that high-level and long-term training can overcome the difficulties associated with the disability [68].

Evidence drawn from the studies overviewed in the present review confirms that PP is a safe sports discipline that can be practiced by people with disabilities [51–56]. However, the data revealed a high rate of chronic overuse injuries of the upper limbs among PP athletes, with the highest injury incidence rate among all other sports, second only to 5-a-side football [69]. These injuries, if not treated promptly, could have functional consequences in everyday activities.

Concerning recovery strategies, pharmacological interventions (such as ibuprofen) were found to impact the immune and muscular systems, proving to be an important recovery strategy to reduce fatigue and improve performance, albeit without any effect on oxidative and anti-inflammatory stress markers, as shown in the two studies by Aidar et al. [42,43], whilst the results were mixed in the study by Fraga et al. [44], in which ibuprofen seemed to delay the anti-inflammatory response post-exercise. Another study [45] investigated the impact of creatine supplementation on recovery, which was found to impact one parameter only, showing a decrease in fatigue index values. Finally, another study [46] explored different post-workout recovery strategies (namely, passive recovery, dry needling, and cold-water immersion), finding that recovery strategies differentially contributed in terms of outcomes measured and timing of the return to baseline values of altered homeostasis induced by the training session.

4.2. Methodological and Statistical Advancements

Methodological and statistical advancements [57–62] have enabled a better assessment of performance outcomes, for which classical approaches relying on the null-hypothesis significant statistic may be misleading. A few studies have utilized the magnitude-based inference (MBI) model, which seems to be a promising and better statistical proposition compared with conventional inferential statistics to quantitatively analyze and interpret sports performance outcomes. FANOVA, as well, has been very recently introduced in the field of biomechanics and neuromechanics and has enabled the uncovering of specific patterns that classical methodologies failed to discover. Biomechanical studies conducted in PP failed to detect significant differences or found only slight differences in terms of the performance of PP under different BP conditions (such as with the legs tied and untied [34,35], using different grip widths [36,37], with the arched and flat techniques [38], at different distances from the bar to the chest [40], and in different sub-phases of the BP movement [41]). The use of novel, cutting-edge techniques could potentially result in the discovery of subtle differences. Moreover, studies on paralympic athletes could further benefit from big data analytics (BDA) and artificial intelligence (AI)-based techniques.

The 1RM test is the gold standard for defining and controlling athlete strength and can be used to track strength progress and calculate percentage loads. However, it is not a practical test, requires special attention, presents a high risk of injury, and could compromise the prescribed training session of the day. The study that examined the relationships between different loading intensities and movement velocities was able to accurately predict the maximum of one repetition. Furthermore, another practicable alternative for regular load monitoring was the RIR-based scale [62].

4.3. Gaps in Knowledge and Future Directions

Moreover, we identified some gaps in the knowledge concerning PP: namely, (1) psychological, (2) nutritional aspects, and (3) doping. The latter topic is particularly paramount, in that doping substances and methods/practices, including the intentional activation of autonomic dysreflexia, also called "boosting" [70], are well known to be widespread among PP athletes and other para-athletes [22,71]. Furthermore, there is a significant lack of studies that have stratified data and outcomes based on the type, cause, and severity of the disability and how these clinical features affect sports and physical performance. For example, it is known that super-compensation processes and fatigue responses are different among Paralympic athletes, and tailor-made programming is required for correct and safe psychophysical preparation [72,73].

While kinematics assessments have been widely investigated, the methodology of training and periodization theory related to peak performance represent research areas relatively under-explored and overlooked in the extant scholarly literature. For example, most studies attribute changes in performance only to the effectiveness of short-term programs rather than long-term training programs. In addition, there are no follow-up studies. However, it is possible that a training methodology carried out over longer periods of time leads to longer-lasting physiological adaptations and that acquired gains in strength, velocity, and endurance may fade away with training cessation [74].

Besides, despite the increasing presence of female athletes in the discipline of PP, very few studies have recruited women. In these studies, it emerges that the woman para-athletes are less strong and powerful, but little information is present on the differences in response to exercise, on the recovery times, and on the correct parameters of the load to be used compared to equally trained men.

Finally, there is a tremendous paucity of information about how the still ongoing "Coronavirus Disease 2019" (COVID-19) pandemic has impacted PP. Information and recommendations and the highlighting of potential strategies and approaches would be crucial as it is possible to predict that new emerging/re-emerging infectious outbreaks can be anticipated to occur in the next future.

Although there are studies that provide recommendations for endurance and team-sport para-athletes to maintain general and sport-specific conditioning [75–77], these methods of home-based training may not be valid for strength para-athletes due to the need to use specific pieces of bulky, heavy, and expensive equipment [78].

Author Contributions: Conceptualization, L.P. and N.L.B.; methodology, N.L.B.; software, N.L.B.; validation, L.P. and N.L.B.; formal analysis, N.L.B.; investigation, L.P. and N.L.B.; resources, L.P. and N.L.B.; data curation, N.L.B.; writing—original draft preparation, L.P. and N.L.B.; writing—review and editing, L.P., K.T., C.T., L.M. (Laura Mori), L.M. (Lucio Marinelli), A.C., E.F., V.F., P.O., J.D.K., A.A. and N.L.B.; visualization, N.L.B.; supervision, L.P. and N.L.B.; project administration, L.P. and N.L.B.; funding acquisition, J.D.K. and N.L.B. All authors have read and agreed to the published version of the manuscript.

Funding: This research was funded by Canada's International Development Research Centre (IDRC) and the Swedish International Development Cooperation Agency (SIDA) (Grant No. 109559-001). N.L.B. and J.D.K. acknowledge support from IDRC (Grant No. 109981). J.D.K. acknowledges support from New Frontier in Research Fund-Exploratory (Grant No. NFRFE-2021-00879) and NSERC Discovery Grant (Grant No. RGPIN-2022-04559).

Institutional Review Board Statement: Not applicable.

Informed Consent Statement: Not applicable.

Data Availability Statement: Not applicable.

Conflicts of Interest: The authors declare no conflict of interest.

References

1. Ferland, P.M.; Comtois, A.S. Classic Powerlifting Performance: A Systematic Review. *J. Strength Cond. Res.* **2019**, *33* (Suppl. 1), S194–S201. [CrossRef] [PubMed]
2. Bengtsson, V.; Berglund, L.; Aasa, U. Narrative review of injuries in powerlifting with special reference to their association to the squat, bench press and deadlift. *BMJ Open Sport Exerc. Med.* **2018**, *4*, e000382. [CrossRef] [PubMed]
3. Travis, S.K.; Mujika, I.; Gentles, J.A.; Stone, M.H.; Bazyler, C.D. Tapering and Peaking Maximal Strength for Powerlifting Performance: A Review. *Sports* **2020**, *8*, 125. [CrossRef] [PubMed]
4. International Paralympic Committee. *World Para Powerlifting Technical Rules and Regulations*; International Paralympic Committee: Bonn, Germany, 2020.
5. Mann, D.L.; Tweedy, S.M.; Jackson, R.C.; Vanlandewijck, Y.C. Classifying the evidence for evidence-based classification in Paralympic sport. *J. Sport. Sci.* **2021**, *39* (Suppl. 1), 1–6. [CrossRef] [PubMed]
6. Grant, M.J.; Booth, A. A typology of reviews: An analysis of 14 review types and associated methodologies. *Health Info. Libr. J.* **2009**, 91–108. [CrossRef]
7. Shi, P.; Bairner, A. Sustainable Development of Olympic Sport Participation Legacy: A Scoping Review Based on the PAGER Framework. *Sustainability* **2022**, *14*, 8056. [CrossRef]
8. Munn, Z.; Pollock, D.; Price, C.; Aromataris, E.; Stern, C.; Stone, J.; Barker, T.H.; Godfrey, C.M.; Clyne, B.; Booth, A.; et al. Investigating different typologies for the synthesis of evidence: A scoping review protocol. *JBI Evid. Synth.* 2022; *Epub ahead of print*. [CrossRef] [PubMed]
9. Khalil, H.; Tricco, A.C. Differentiating between mapping reviews and scoping reviews in the evidence synthesis ecosystem. *J. Clin. Epidemiol.* **2022**, *149*, 175–182. [CrossRef] [PubMed]
10. Arksey, H.; O'Malley, L. Scoping studies: Towards a methodological framework. *Int. J. Soc. Res. Methodol.* **2005**, *8*, 19–32. [CrossRef]
11. Westphaln, K.K.; Regoeczi, W.; Masotya, M.; Vazquez-Westphaln, B.; Lounsbury, K.; McDavid, L.; Lee, H.; Johnson, J.; Ronis, S.D. From Arksey and O'Malley and Beyond: Customizations to enhance a team-based, mixed approach to scoping review methodology. *MethodsX* **2021**, *8*, 101375. [CrossRef]

12. Bradbury-Jones, C.; Aveyard, H.; Herber, O.R.; Isham, L.; Taylor, J.; O'Malley, L. Scoping reviews: The PAGER framework for improving the quality of reporting. *Int. J. Soc. Res. Methodol.* **2021**, *25*, 457–470. [CrossRef]
13. Mbogning Fonkou, M.D.; Bragazzi, N.L.; Tsinda, E.K.; Bouba, Y.; Mmbando, G.S.; Kong, J.D. COVID-19 Pandemic Related Research in Africa: Bibliometric Analysis of Scholarly Output, Collaborations and Scientific Leadership. *Int. J. Env. Res. Public Health* **2021**, *18*, 7273. [CrossRef] [PubMed]
14. van Eck, N.J.; Waltman, L. Software survey: VOSviewer, a computer program for bibliometric mapping. *Scientometrics* **2010**, *84*, 523–538. [CrossRef] [PubMed]
15. Bastian, M.; Heymann, S.; Jacomy, M. Gephi: An Open Source Software for Exploring and Manipulating Networks. In Proceedings of the International AAAI Conference on Web and Social Media, Atlanta, GA, USA, 6–9 June 2022; Volume 3, pp. 361–362. Available online: https://ojs.aaai.org/index.php/ICWSM/article/view/13937 (accessed on 18 November 2022).
16. Shannon, P.; Markiel, A.; Ozier, O.; Baliga, N.S.; Wang, J.T.; Ramage, D.; Amin, N.; Schwikowski, B.; Ideker, T. Cytoscape: A software environment for integrated models of biomolecular interaction networks. *Genome Res.* **2003**, *13*, 2498–2504. [CrossRef] [PubMed]
17. Krnc, M.; Škrekovski, R. Group Degree Centrality and Centralization in Networks. *Mathematics* **2020**, *8*, 1810. [CrossRef]
18. Jacob, R.; Harikrishnan, K.P.; Misra, R.; Ambika, G. Measure for degree heterogeneity in complex networks and its application to recurrence network analysis. *R. Soc. Open Sci.* **2017**, *4*, 160757. [CrossRef] [PubMed]
19. Blauwet, C.A.; Chakraverty, J.; Derman, W.; Idrisova, G.; Martin, P.; Miller, S.C.; Morrissey, D.; Webborn, N. Shoulder Pain, Function, and Ultrasound-Determined Structure in Elite Wheelchair-Using Para Athletes: An Observational Study. *Med. Sci. Sport. Exerc.* **2022**, *54*, 896–904. [CrossRef] [PubMed]
20. Von Held, R.; Castilho, T.; Antunes, L.; Tavares, J.; Pivetta Petinati, M.F.; Winckler, C.; Neto, Z.; Scariot, R.; Küchler, E.C.; Brancher, J.A.; et al. Interleukin 1 alpha genetic polymorphisms as potential biomarkers for oral health-related quality of life in Para athletes. *Spec. Care Dent.* **2021**, *41*, 679–687. [CrossRef]
21. Durán Agüero, S.; Arroyo Jofre, P.; Varas Standen, C.; Herrera-Valenzuela, T.; Moya Cantillana, C.; Pereira Robledo, R.; Valdés-Badilla, P. Calidad Del Sueño, Somnolencia E Insomnio En Deportistas Paralímpicos De Elite Chilenos [Sleep Quality, Excessive Daytime Sleepiness And Insomnia In Chilean Paralympic Athletes]. *Nutr. Hosp.* **2015**, *32*, 2832–2837. [CrossRef]
22. Van de Vliet, P. Antidoping in paralympic sport. *Clin. J. Sport Med.* **2012**, *22*, 21–25. [CrossRef]
23. Echague, C.G.; Csokmay, J.M. Exercise-Induced Abdominal Wall Muscle Injury Resulting in Rhabdomyolysis and Mimicking an Acute Abdomen. *Obstet. Gynecol.* **2018**, *131*, 591–593. [CrossRef] [PubMed]
24. Silva, A.; Pinto Pinheiro, L.S.; Silva, S.; Andrade, H.; Pereira, A.G.; Rodrigues da Silva, F.; Guerreiro, R.; Barreto, B.; Resende, R.; Túlio de Mello, M. Sleep in Paralympic athletes and its relationship with injuries and illnesses. *Phys. Ther. Sport* **2022**, *56*, 24–31. [CrossRef] [PubMed]
25. Brancher, J.A.; Morodome, F.; Madalena, I.R.; Reis, C.; Von Held, R.; Antunes, L.; Winckler, C.; Salgueirosa, F.; Neto, Z.; Storrer, C.; et al. Salivary pH and oral health of Brazilian para-athletes: Saliva and oral health of para-athletes. *Spec. Care Dent.* **2021**, *41*, 505–511. [CrossRef] [PubMed]
26. Resende, M.A.; Vasconcelos Resende, R.B.; Reis, G.C.; Barros, L.O.; Bezerra, M.; Matos, D.G.; Marçal, A.C.; Almeida-Neto, P.F.; Cabral, B.; Neiva, H.P.; et al. The Influence of Warm-Up on Body Temperature and Strength Performance in Brazilian National-Level Paralympic Powerlifting Athletes. *Medicina* **2020**, *56*, 538. [CrossRef]
27. de Aquino Resende, M.; Aidar, F.J.; Vasconcelos Resende, R.B.; Reis, G.C.; de Oliveira Barros, L.; de Matos, D.G.; Marçal, A.C.; de Almeida-Neto, P.F.; Díaz-de-Durana, A.L.; Merino-Fernández, M.; et al. Are Strength Indicators and Skin Temperature Affected by the Type of Warm-Up in Paralympic Powerlifting Athletes? *Healthcare* **2021**, *9*, 923. [CrossRef]
28. Aidar, F.J.; Clemente, F.M.; de Lima, L.F.; de Matos, D.G.; Ferreira, A.; Marçal, A.C.; Moreira, O.C.; Bulhões-Correia, A.; de Almeida-Neto, P.F.; Díaz-de-Durana, A.L.; et al. Evaluation of Training with Elastic Bands on Strength and Fatigue Indicators in Paralympic Powerlifting. *Sports* **2021**, *9*, 142. [CrossRef]
29. Lopes-Silva, J.P.; Richardson, D.; Fukuda, D.H.; Franchini, E. Is there an optimal interval for medal winning performance in World Para Powerlifting competition? *Am. J. Phys. Med. Rehabil.* 2021; *Online ahead of print.* [CrossRef]
30. Paz, Â.A.; Aidar, F.J.; de Matos, D.G.; de Souza, R.F.; da Silva-Grigoletto, M.E.; van den Tillaar, R.; Ramirez-Campillo, R.; Nakamura, F.Y.; Costa, M.; Nunes-Silva, A.; et al. Comparison of Post-Exercise Hypotension Responses in Paralympic Powerlifting Athletes after Completing Two Bench Press Training Intensities. *Medicina* **2020**, *56*, 156. [CrossRef]
31. Aidar, F.J.; Paz, Â.A.; Gama, D.M.; de Souza, R.F.; Vieira Souza, L.M.; Santos, J.; Almeida-Neto, P.F.; Marçal, A.C.; Neves, E.B.; Moreira, O.C.; et al. Evaluation of the Post-Training Hypotensor Effect in Paralympic and Conventional Powerlifting. *J. Funct. Morphol. Kinesiol.* **2021**, *6*, 92. [CrossRef]
32. Silva, D.; Santos, M.; Aidar, F.; Cabral, B.; Stieler, E.; Resende, R.; Andrade, A.; Almeida-Neto, P.; Bulhões-Correia, A.; Guerreiro, R.; et al. Effect of strength training on psychophysiological aspects in Paralympic powerlifting athletes: A pilot study. *Hum. Mov.* **2022**, *23*, 150–159. [CrossRef]
33. Roy, A. Socio-cultural power dynamics and coping functions: A narrative case report of a female paralympian. *Asian, J. Sport. Med.* **2012**, *3*, 131–138. [CrossRef] [PubMed]
34. Guerra, I.; Aidar, F.J.; Greco, G.; de Almeida-Neto, P.F.; De Candia, M.; de Araújo Tinoco Cabral, B.G.; Poli, L.; Filho, M.M.; Carvutto, R.; Silva, A.F.; et al. Are sEMG, Velocity and Power Influenced by Athletes' Fixation in Paralympic Powerlifting? *Int. J. Environ. Res. Public Health* **2022**, *19*, 4127. [CrossRef] [PubMed]

35. Mota, M.G.; Aidar, F.J.; Rocha, J.C.S.D.; Santos, W.D.S.; Leite Junior, J.A.D.S.; Jesus, J.B.D.; Freitas, A.V.D.; Solidade, V.T.D. Avaliação de duas formas de execução, amarrado ou não no powerlifting paralímpico: Um estudo piloto. *Motricidade* **2020**, *16*, 56–63. [CrossRef]
36. Dos Santos, M.; Aidar, F.J.; Alejo, A.A.; de Matos, D.G.; de Souza, R.F.; de Almeida-Neto, P.F.; de Araújo Tinoco Cabral, B.G.; Nikolaidis, P.T.; Knechtle, B.; Clemente, F.M.; et al. Analysis of Grip Amplitude on Velocity in Paralympic Powerlifting. *J. Funct. Morphol. Kinesiol.* **2021**, *6*, 86. [CrossRef]
37. Dos Santos, M.; Aidar, F.J.; de Souza, R.F.; Dos Santos, J.L.; da Silva de Mello, A.; Neiva, H.P.; Marinho, D.A.; Marques, M.C. Does the Grip Width Affect the Bench Press Performance of Paralympic Powerlifters? *Int. J. Sport. Physiol. Perform.* **2020**, *15*, 1252–1259. [CrossRef]
38. Ribeiro Neto, F.; Dorneles, J.R.; Luna, R.M.; Spina, M.A.; Gonçalves, C.W.; Gomes Costa, R.R. Performance Differences Between the Arched and Flat Bench Press in Beginner and Experienced Paralympic Powerlifters. *J. Strength Cond. Res.* **2022**, *36*, 1936–1943. [CrossRef]
39. Mendonça, T.P.; Aidar, F.J.; Matos, D.G.; Souza, R.F.; Marçal, A.C.; Almeida-Neto, P.F.; Cabral, B.G.; Garrido, N.D.; Neiva, H.P.; Marinho, D.A.; et al. Force production and muscle activation during partial vs. full range of motion in Paralympic Powerlifting. *PLoS ONE* **2021**, *16*, e0257810. [CrossRef]
40. Aidar, F.J.; Clemente, F.M.; Matos, D.G.; Marçal, A.C.; de Souza, R.F.; Moreira, O.C.; Almeida-Neto, P.F.; Vilaça-Alves, J.; Garrido, N.D.; Dos Santos, J.L.; et al. Evaluation of Strength and Muscle Activation Indicators in Sticking Point Region of National-Level Paralympic Powerlifting Athletes. *J. Funct. Morphol. Kinesiol.* **2021**, *6*, 43. [CrossRef]
41. da Silva, B.G.; Miziara, I.M.; Furtado, D.A.; dos Santos, S.S.; Fidale, T.M.; Pereira, A.A. Electromyographical activity of the pectoralis, triceps, and deltoideus during the sub-phases of bench press in paralympic powerlifters. *Sport. Eng.* **2022**, *25*, 13. [CrossRef]
42. Aidar, F.J.; Fraga, G.S.; Getirana-Mota, M.; Marçal, A.C.; Santos, J.L.; de Souza, R.F.; Ferreira, A.; Neves, E.B.; Zanona, A.F.; Bulhões-Correia, A.; et al. Effects of Ibuprofen Use on Lymphocyte Count and Oxidative Stress in Elite Paralympic Powerlifting. *Biology* **2021**, *10*, 986. [CrossRef]
43. Aidar, F.J.; Fraga, G.S.; Getirana-Mota, M.; Marçal, A.C.; Santos, J.L.; de Souza, R.F.; Vieira-Souza, L.M.; Ferreira, A.; de Matos, D.G.; de Almeida-Neto, P.F.; et al. Evaluation of Ibuprofen Use on the Immune System Indicators and Force in Disabled Paralympic Powerlifters of Different Sport Levels. *Healthcare* **2022**, *10*, 1331. [CrossRef] [PubMed]
44. Fraga, G.S.; Aidar, F.J.; Matos, D.G.; Marçal, A.C.; Santos, J.L.; Souza, R.F.; Carneiro, A.L.; Vasconcelos, A.B.; Da Silva-Grigoletto, M.E.; van den Tillaar, R.; et al. Effects of Ibuprofen Intake in Muscle Damage, Body Temperature and Muscle Power in Paralympic Powerlifting Athletes. *Int. J. Environ. Res. Public Health* **2020**, *17*, 5157. [CrossRef]
45. Soares Freitas Sampaio, C.R.; Aidar, F.J.; Ferreira, A.; Santos, J.; Marçal, A.C.; Matos, D.G.; Souza, R.F.; Moreira, O.C.; Guerra, I.; Fernandes Filho, J.; et al. Can Creatine Supplementation Interfere with Muscle Strength and Fatigue in Brazilian National Level Paralympic Powerlifting? *Nutrients* **2020**, *12*, 2492. [CrossRef] [PubMed]
46. Santos, W.; Aidar, F.J.; Matos, D.G.; Van den Tillaar, R.; Marçal, A.C.; Lobo, L.F.; Marcucci-Barbosa, L.S.; Machado, S.; Almeida-Neto, P.F.; Garrido, N.D.; et al. Physiological and Biochemical Evaluation of Different Types of Recovery in National Level Paralympic Powerlifting. *Int. J. Environ. Res. Public Health* **2021**, *18*, 5155. [CrossRef] [PubMed]
47. Gołaś, A.; Zwierzchowska, A.; Maszczyk, A.; Wilk, M.; Stastny, P.; Zając, A. Neuromuscular Control During the Bench Press Movement in an Elite Disabled and Able-Bodied Athlete. *J. Hum. kinetics* **2017**, *60*, 209–215. [CrossRef] [PubMed]
48. Szafraniec, R.; Kisilewicz, A.; Kumorek, M.; Kristiansen, M.; Madeleine, P.; Mroczek, D. Effects of High-Velocity Strength Training on Movement Velocity and Strength Endurance in Experienced Powerlifters with Cerebral Palsy. *J. Hum. Kinet.* **2020**, *73*, 235–243. [CrossRef] [PubMed]
49. Teles, L.; Aidar, F.J.; Matos, D.G.; Marçal, A.C.; Almeida-Neto, P.F.; Neves, E.B.; Moreira, O.C.; Ribeiro Neto, F.; Garrido, N.D.; Vilaça-Alves, J.; et al. Static and Dynamic Strength Indicators in Paralympic Power-Lifters with and without Spinal Cord Injury. *Int. J. Environ. Res. Public Health* **2021**, *18*, 5907. [CrossRef]
50. Aidar, F.J.; Cataldi, S.; Badicu, G.; Silva, A.F.; Clemente, F.M.; Latino, F.; Greco, G.; Fischetti, F. Paralympic Powerlifting as a Sustainable Way to Improve Strength in Athletes with Spinal Cord Injury and Other Disabilities. *Sustainability* **2022**, *14*, 2017. [CrossRef]
51. Lopes-Silva, J.P.; Richardson, D.; Franchini, E. Chronological Age and Performance in Paralympic Powerlifters: Differences Between Sexes, Competition, and Weight Categories. *J. Sci. Sport Exerc.* **2022**, 1–9. [CrossRef]
52. Willick, S.E.; Cushman, D.M.; Blauwet, C.A.; Emery, C.; Webborn, N.; Derman, W.; Schwellnus, M.; Stomphorst, J.; Van de Vliet, P. The epidemiology of injuries in powerlifting at the London 2012 Paralympic Games: An analysis of 1411 athlete-days. *Scand. J. Med. Sci. Sport.* **2016**, *26*, 1233–1238. [CrossRef]
53. Jarraya, M.; Blauwet, C.A.; Crema, M.D.; Heiss, R.; Roemer, F.W.; Hayashi, D.; Derman, W.E.; Guermazi, A. Sports injuries at the Rio de Janeiro 2016 Summer Paralympic Games: Use of diagnostic imaging services. *Eur. Radiol.* **2021**, *31*, 6768–6779. [CrossRef] [PubMed]
54. AHamid, M.S.; Ghazali, S.S.; Karim, S.A. Anthropometric Characteristics of Malaysian Competitive Powerlifters with Physical Disabilities. *J. Health Transl. Med.* **2019**, *22*, 49–55. [CrossRef]
55. van den Hoek, D.; Garrett, J.; Howells, R.; Latella, C. Paralympians Are Stronger Than You Know: A Comparison of Para and Nondisabled Powerlifting Bench Press World Records. *J. Strength Cond. Res.* 2022; *Advance online publication.* [CrossRef]

56. Severin, A.C.; Baumgart, J.K.; Haugen, T.; Hogarth, L. Peak age and performance trajectories in Para powerlifters. *Am. J. Phys. Med. Rehabil.* 2022; *Advance online publication*. [CrossRef]
57. Ramos Dalla Bernardina, G.; Danillo Matos Dos Santos, M.; Alves Resende, R.; Túlio de Mello, M.; Rodrigues Albuquerque, M.; Augusto Paolucci, L.; Carpes, F.P.; Silva, A.; Gustavo Pereira de Andrade, A. Asymmetric velocity profiles in Paralympic powerlifters performing at different exercise intensities are detected by functional data analysis. *J. Biomech.* **2021**, *123*, 110523. [CrossRef] [PubMed]
58. Bellitto, A.; Marchesi, G.; Comini, M.; Massone, A.; Casadio, M.; De Luca, A. Electromyographic and Kinematic Evaluation of Bench Press Exercise: A Case Report Study on Athletes with Different Impairments and Expertise. *Sport Sci. Health* **2022**, 1–10. [CrossRef]
59. Loturco, I.; Pereira, L.A.; Winckler, C.; Santos, W.L.; Kobal, R.; McGuigan, M. Load-Velocity Relationship in National Paralympic Powerlifters: A Case Study. *Int. J. Sport. Physiol. Perform.* **2019**, *14*, 531–535. [CrossRef]
60. Aidar, F.J.; Brito, C.J.; de Matos, D.G.; de Oliveira, L.; de Souza, R.F.; de Almeida-Neto, P.F.; de Araújo Tinoco Cabral, B.G.; Neiva, H.P.; Neto, F.R.; Reis, V.M.; et al. Force-velocity relationship in Paralympic powerlifting: Two or multiple-point methods to determine a maximum repetition. *BMC Sport. Sci. Med. Rehabil.* **2022**, *14*, 159. [CrossRef]
61. Aidar, F.J.; Cataldi, S.; Badicu, G.; Silva, A.F.; Clemente, F.M.; Bonavolontà, V.; Greco, G.; Getirana-Mota, M.; Fischetti, F. Does the Level of Training Interfere with the Sustainability of Static and Dynamic Strength in Paralympic Powerlifting Athletes? *Sustainability* **2022**, *14*, 5049. [CrossRef]
62. Neto, F.R.; Dorneles, J.R.; Aidar, F.J.; Gonçalves, C.W.; Veloso, J.; Costa, R. Validation of the Repetitions in Reserve Rating Scale in Paralympic Powerlifting Athletes. *Int. J. Sport. Med.* **2022**, *43*, 366–372. [CrossRef]
63. World Para Powerlifting. History of para powerlifting. Available online: https://www.paralympic.org/powerlifting/about (accessed on 18 November 2022).
64. Ribeiro, B.; Pereira, A.; Neves, P.P.; Sousa, A.C.; Ferraz, R.; Marques, M.C.; Marinho, D.A.; Neiva, H.P. The Role of Specific Warm-up during Bench Press and Squat Exercises: A Novel Approach. *Int. J. Environ. Res. Public Health* **2020**, *17*, 6882. [CrossRef] [PubMed]
65. Shaw, M.P.; Andersen, V.; Sæterbakken, A.H.; Paulsen, G.; Samnøy, L.E.; Solstad, T. Contemporary Training Practices of Norwegian Powerlifters. *J. Strength Cond. Res.* **2022**, *36*, 2544–2551. [CrossRef] [PubMed]
66. Runciman, P.; Derman, W.; Ferreira, S.; Albertus-Kajee, Y.; Tucker, R. A descriptive comparison of sprint cycling performance and neuromuscular characteristics in able-bodied athletes and paralympic athletes with cerebral palsy. *Am. J. Phys. Med. Rehabil.* **2015**, *94*, 28–37. [CrossRef] [PubMed]
67. Runciman, P.; Tucker, R.; Ferreira, S.; Albertus-Kajee, Y.; Derman, W.A. Effects of induced volitional fatigue on sprint and jump performance in paralympic athletes with cerebral palsy. *Am. J. Phys. Med. Rehabil.* **2016**, *95*, 277–290. [CrossRef]
68. Puce, L.; Pallecchi, I.; Chamari, K.; Marinelli, L.; Innocenti, T.; Pedrini, R.; Mori, L.; Trompetto, C. Systematic Review of Fatigue in Individuals With Cerebral Palsy. *Front. Hum. Neurosci.* **2021**, *15*, 598800. [CrossRef]
69. Willick, S.E.; Webborn, N.; Emery, C.; Blauwet, C.A.; Pit-Grosheide, P.; Stomphorst, J.; Van de Vliet, P.; Patino Marques, N.A.; Martinez-Ferrer, J.O.; Jordaan, E.; et al. The epidemiology of injuries at the London 2012 Paralympic Games. *Br. J. Sport. Med.* **2013**, *47*, 426–432. [CrossRef]
70. Mazzeo, F.; Santamaria, S.; Iavarone, A. "Boosting" in Paralympic athletes with spinal cord injury: Doping without drugs. *Funct. Neurol.* **2015**, *30*, 91–98. [CrossRef]
71. Walter, M.; Krassioukov, A.V. Autonomic Nervous System in Paralympic Athletes with Spinal Cord Injury. *Phys. Med. Rehabil. Clin. North Am.* **2018**, *29*, 245–266. [CrossRef]
72. Puce, L.; Marinelli, L.; Pierantozzi, E.; Mori, L.; Pallecchi, I.; Bonifazi, M.; Bove, M.; Franchini, E.; Trompetto, C. Training methods and analysis of races of a top level Paralympic swimming athlete. *J. Exerc. Rehabil.* **2018**, *14*, 612–620. [CrossRef]
73. Puce, L.; Bragazzi, N.L.; Currà, A.; Marinelli, L.; Mori, L.; Cotellessa, F.; Chamari, K.; Ponzano, M.; Samanipour, M.H.; Nikolaidis, P.T.; et al. Not all Forms of Muscle Hypertonia Worsen With Fatigue: A Pilot Study in Para Swimmers. *Front. Physiol.* **2022**, *13*, 902663. [CrossRef]
74. Hill, K.G.; Woodward, D.; Woelfel, T.; Hawkins, J.D.; Green, S. Planning for Long-Term Follow-Up: Strategies Learned from Longitudinal Studies. *Prev. Sci. Off. J. Soc. Prev. Res.* **2016**, *17*, 806–818. [CrossRef] [PubMed]
75. Shaw, K.A.; Bertrand, L.; Deprez, D.; Ko, J.; Zello, G.A.; Chilibeck, P.D. The impact of the COVID-19 pandemic on diet, fitness, and sedentary behaviour of elite para-athletes. *Disabil. Health J.* **2021**, *14*, 101091. [CrossRef] [PubMed]
76. Cavaggioni, L.; Rossi, A.; Tosin, M.; Scurati, R.; Michielon, G.; Alberti, G.; Merati, G.; Formenti, D.; Trecroci, A. Changes in Upper-Body Muscular Strength and Power in Paralympic Swimmers: Effects of Training Confinement during the COVID-19 Pandemic. *Int. J. Environ. Res. Public Health* **2022**, *19*, 5382. [CrossRef] [PubMed]
77. Peña-González, I.; Sarabia, J.M.; Manresa-Rocamora, A.; Moya-Ramón, M. International football players with cerebral palsy maintained their physical fitness after a self-training program during the COVID-19 lockdown. *PeerJ* **2022**, *10*, e13059. [CrossRef]
78. Latella, C.; Haff, G.G. Global Challenges of Being a Strength Athlete during a Pandemic: Impacts and Sports-Specific Training Considerations and Recommendations. *Sports* **2020**, *8*, 100. [CrossRef]

healthcare

MDPI

Article

Training in Hypoxia at Alternating High Altitudes Is a Factor Favoring the Increase in Sports Performance

Ovidiu Dragos [1], Dan Iulian Alexe [2,*], Emil Vasile Ursu [1], Cristina Ioana Alexe [3], Nicoale Lucian Voinea [3,*], Petronela Lacramioara Haisan [1], Adelina Elena Panaet [4,*], Andreea Mihaela Albina [5] and Dan Monea [6]

[1] Department of Physical Education, University of Alba Iulia, 510009 Alba Iulia, Romania
[2] Department of Physical and Occupational Therapy, Faculty of Movement, Sports and Health, Sciences, "Vasile Alecsandri" University of Bacau, 600115 Bacau, Romania
[3] Department of Physical Education and Sports Performance, Faculty of Movement, Sports and Health, Sciences, "Vasile Alecsandri" University of Bacau, 600115 Bacau, Romania
[4] Doctoral School, National University of Physical Education and Sport Bucharest, 060057 Bucharest, Romania
[5] Sport Science and Physical Educational Doctoral School, Social and Humanities Sciences University of Craiova, 200585 Craiova, Romania
[6] Faculty of Physical Education and Sport, "BabeșBolyai" University, 400084 Cluj-Napoca, Romania
* Correspondence: alexedaniulian@ub.ro (D.I.A.); lucian.voinea@ub.ro (N.L.V.); panaet.adelina@ub.ro (A.E.P.)

Abstract: Training above 1800 m causes increases in hemoglobin, erythropoietin and VO2max values in the bodies of athletes. The purpose of this study is to prove that living at an altitude of 1850 m and training at 2200 m (LHTH+) is more effective than living and training at 2000 m (LHTH). Ten endurance athletes (age 21.2 ± 1.5 years, body mass 55.8 ± 4.3 kg, height 169 ± 6 cm, performance 3000 m 8:35 ± 0:30 min) performed three training sessions of 30 days, in three different situations: [1] living and training at 2000 m altitude (LHTH), [2] living at 1850 m and training at 2200 m (LHTH+), and [3] living and training at 300 m (LLTL). The differences in erythropoietin (EPO), hemoglobin (Hb) concentration, and VO2max values were compared before and at the end of each training session. Data analysis indicated that LHTH training caused an increase in EPO values (by 1.0 ± 0.8 mU/mL, $p = 0.002 < 0.05$.); Hb (by 1.1 ± 0.3 g/dL, $p < 0.001$); VO2max (by 0.9 ± 0.23 mL/kg/min, $p < 0.001$). LHTH+ training caused an increase in EPO values (by 1.9 ± 0.5 mU/ML, $p < 0.001$); Hb (by 1.4 ± 0.5 g/dL, $p < 0.001$); VO2max (by 1.7 ± 0.3 mL/kg/min, $p < 0.001$). At the LLTL training, EPO values do not have a significant increase ($p = 0.678 > 0.050$; 1 ± 0.1 mU/mL, 0.1 ± 0.9%.), Hb (0.1 ± 0.0 g/dL, 0.3 ± 0.3%), VO2max (0.1 ± 0.1, 0.2 ± 0.2%, $p = 0.013 < 0.05$). Living and training at altitudes of 2000 m (LHTH) and living at 1850 m training at 2200 m (LHTH+) resulted in significant improvements in EPO, Hb, and VO2max that exceeded the changes in these parameters, following traditional training at 300 m (LLTL). LHTH+ training has significantly greater changes than LHTH training, favorable to increasing sports performance. The results of this study can serve as guidelines for athletic trainers in their future work, in the complete structure of multi-year planning and programming, and thus improve the process of development and performance training.

Keywords: altitude; hemoglobin; erythropoietin; hypoxia; maximum volume of oxygen

check for updates

Citation: Dragos, O.; Alexe, D.I.; Ursu, E.V.; Alexe, C.I.; Voinea, N.L.; Haisan, P.L.; Panaet, A.E.; Albina, A.M.; Monea, D. Training in Hypoxia at Alternating High Altitudes Is a Factor Favoring the Increase in Sports Performance. *Healthcare* **2022**, *10*, 2296. https://doi.org/10.3390/healthcare10112296

Academic Editor: Felipe Aidar

Received: 6 October 2022
Accepted: 14 November 2022
Published: 16 November 2022

1. Introduction

For maximum training efficiency, the best solutions are sought to produce physiological changes favorable to performance. One method studied in performance sports is altitude training [1]. A series of studies show that the amount of oxygen in the breathed air decreases along with the increase in altitude, and the human body adapts to the conditions of reduced oxygenation [2,3]. These changes take place at the hematological level and result in easier transport of oxygen [4,5]. The hematological change which leads to easier transport of oxygen is the increase in hemoglobin mass [1,4,5]. All hematological and non-hematological changes result in increasing sports performance [6–8]. Numerous studies show the beneficial effect of altitude training on sports performance [9–11]. Wilber, R.L.A. demonstrated that living high (2500 m) and training low (1250 m) for 28 days increases the hemoglobin mass by 5% and VO2max by 4% [12]. Rodriguez, F.A. et al. showed that classical training of 45 swimmers at an altitude of 2320 m led to an increase in hemoglobin mass by 7.2 ± 3% after a 4-week training course at altitude [13]. Specialists' opinions are divided, with some studies stating that exposure to altitude does not bring major changes [14]. Gore, C.J. et al. highlighted the fact that athletes exposed to 4 weeks of intermittent exposure to hypobaric hypoxia (3 hours/day, 5 days/week at 4000–5500 m) had increased their erythrocyte volume index by 2.3% and hemoglobin mass by 1%, and the EPO concentration doubled in the first 6 hours. With all these changes, the conclusion was that intermittent exposure to hyperbaric hypoxia did not accelerate erythropoiesis despite the increase in serum EPO [14]. Some studies show physiological changes similar to those produced by altitude training [15–17]. Man, M.C. et al. present an alternative, although less explored, that has the potential to positively influence performance while avoiding some of the negative physiological consequences of hypoxia being sand training. Increases in VO2max and VMA after sand training were high (1.3 ± 0.1%; $p < 0.001$ and 1.2 ± 0.1%; $p < 0.001$), and the hemoglobin values also increased (3.3 ± 1.1%; $p = 0.035$) [15].

It is scientifically proven that physiological changes favorable to performance are triggered in the athletes' bodies after 21 days [2,4,12]. As a result, it is very difficult to complete a training session in a hyperbaric chamber [18], and for this reason, specialists are looking for the best conditions for living and training at an altitude that produce favorable effects for increasing sports performance [11].

Therefore, were compared the differences in hemoglobin (Hb), erythropoietin (EPO) concentrations, and running capacity (VO2max) in highly trained runners after 30-day training cycles at 2000 m (LHTH), high-altitude living (1850 m), training at 2200 m (LHTH+) and traditional low-altitude training at 300 m (LLTL). It was hypothesized that training at LHTL and LHTH+ would significantly increase blood parameters and physical performance compared to training at LLTL and greater improvement will be seen after LHTH+ training over time.

2. Materials and Methods

2.1. Participants and Study Design

Participants were 10 male athletes (age 21.2 ± 1.5; 1 athlete 19 years and 7 months; 9 athletes 22 years ± 7 months, body mass 55.8 ± 4.3 kg, height 169 ± 6 cm) who specialized in half-distance and long-distance races, with 3000 m 8:35.00 ± 0:30. The athletes went through the same training program for 30 days, in three separate training cycles. The difference between the training cycles was six months. The main inclusion criteria were competition in a national level event and that the participants were free from musculoskeletal injuries for at least 6 months before each training cycle of the study.

In total, 15 athletes were selected for the study, but in the end, only 10 could participate, by observing the training and health protocol in all three training sessions. The athletes went through the same training program for 30 days across three training cycles, separated by one year.

2.2. Sample Dimension

The G*Power software V 3.0.10 (Dusseldorf, Germany) was used to determine the sample size (the minimum number of subjects).

Analysis Of Variance (ANOVA) with repeated measurements was chosen to determine the sample size (see the image above), with the following input parameters:

1. Effect size f (ES = 0.58);
2. Error probability $\alpha = 0.05$;
3. Power (1-β err prob) = 0.8;
4. No. conditions = 3 (no. groups in the image);
5. No. of repetitions = 2 (before and after);
6. Correlation for repeated measurements = 0.5;
7. Non-sphericity correction = 1.

The result indicates a minimum sample size of 9 subjects to ensure a test power of 82.46%.

Standard meals were offered to the athletes at each training camp. In addition, all the athletes adhered to the same regimen of vitamin and mineral supplements. Anthropometric measurements, blood draws, and running performance tests were taken the day before and on the first day after each 30-day training program to determine changes in hemoglobin concentration and running performance. Blood samples were collected after 12-h fasting at the same time of day (±1 h), at each moment. Samples were stored < 48 h at 2–8 °C before analyses.

2.3. Training Schedule

The athletes completed three training courses, as follows:

In the first stage, the athletes performed a training cycle for 30 days at Piatra Arsă, (G1) at an altitude of 2000 m (LHTH). In the second stage, the same group of athletes performed another training that took place in Font Romeu, where they lived at the National Altitude Training Centre (1850 m) and trained at an altitude of 2200 m (LHTH+). Finally, the third training cycle took place at an altitude of 300 m (LLTL).

An example of a training program is detailed in Table 1. The training program was repeated in all three training cycles.

Each training stage had 50 training sessions. A total of 520 ± 20 km was covered.

2.4. Maximum Speed and Aerobic Capacity

The five-minute test required the athletes to run at full capacity for five minutes. VMA = distance achieved (in km) × 12. The five-minute test was used to determine the VMA and the formula VMA × 3.5 was used to predict the VO2max because all subjects were over 18 years of age [19]. A previous study confirms that it is a reliable and practical indirect method of estimating individual aerobic fitness in a trained population [20].

Chamoux et al. 1996 [20–22] state that VMA determined on the field depends on the duration of the effort and therefore on the used protocol. Examining the relationship between running speed and the running time log set from the world race record pace shows a significant point at 4.97 min, suggested as the reference time for the VMA. By convention, VMA could be measured on the field by a 5-minute test, regardless of sport.

2.5. Hemoglobin Concentration

Hb was determined from venous blood collected before and after each 30-day training session using a Diagon D-Cell 60 automated hematologyanalyzer (Diagon Ltd., Budapest, Hungary).

2.6. Erythropoietin Concentration

Serum EPO concentration was determined by the commercially available Human EPO Quantikine™ IVD ELISA kit (R&D Systems, Minneapolis, MN, USA).

Table 1. Example of a training program.

Day	Piatra Arsă-2000 m Altitude	Total Km-Running
1	S.T.$_1$ 4 km walking	4
2	S.T.$_2$ 6 km walking	6
3	S.T.$_3$ 6 km e.r.50% VMA/S.T.$_4$ 6 km e.r., segment strength-50% VMA	12
4	S.T.$_5$ 6 km e.r.50% VMA/S.T.$_6$ 8 km e.r., segment strength-60% VMA	14
5	S.T.$_7$ 8 km e.r.50% VMA/S.T.$_8$ 8 km e.r., segment strength-60% VMA	16
6	S.T.$_9$ 12 km r. uniform tempo, 60% VMA, segment. Strength	12
7	S.T.$_{10}$ 11 km e.r.50% VMA/S.T.$_{11}$ 6 km e.r. and 3 complete strength series-65% VMA	17
8	S.T.$_{12}$ 12 km r. uniform tempo, 65% VMA, segment. Strength/S.T.$_{13}$ 8 km r. uniform tempo, 10 × 100 m a.l.-65% VMA	20
9	S.T.$_{14}$ 14 km r. various land, segment strength and r.l.-70% VMA	14
10	S.T.$_{15}$ 14 km r. various land-75% VMA/S.T.$_{16}$ 8 km e.r., 3 series of ex. for strength	22
11	S.T.$_{17}$ 12 km r. uniform tempo, 70% VMA/S.T.$_{18}$ 10 km r. uniform tempo, 10 × 100 m r.l.-70% VMA	22
12	S.T.$_{19}$ 14 km r. uniform tempo, 75% VMA	14
13	S.T.$_{20}$ 12 km r. progressive various land 75–83% VMA/S.T.$_{21}$ 10 km r. uniform tempo, 70% VMA and 3 series of ex. for strength	22
14	S.T.$_{22}$ 6 km r. uniform tempo, 65% VMA, 30 × 100 m r. accelerated (100% VMA) with connection 100 m e.r. 4 km/S.T.$_{23}$ 10 km r. uniform tempo, stretching	24
15	S.T.$_{24}$ 8 km e.r., stretching 75% VMA/S.T.$_{25}$ 40 min r. (2min r. tempo sustained + 1 min conn. + 1 min r. tempo sustained + 1 min. connection) × 8 series (90% VMA)	24
16	S.T.$_{26}$ 14 km r. various land (75–80% VMA)	14
17	S.T.$_{27}$ 10 km r. various land and 10 × 100 m r.l. with 100 m e.r. 80% VMA/S.T.$_{28}$ 8 km r. uniform tempo, (75% VMA)	22
18	S.T.$_{29}$ 12 km r. tempo progressive-88–93% VMA/S.T.$_{30}$ 10 km e.r. (75% VMA)	22
19	S.T.$_{31}$ 14 km r. various land 80% VMA/S.T.$_{32}$ 10 km r. uniform tempo, (75% VMA)	24
20	S.T.$_{33}$ 12 km r. various tempo 92–94%VMA, 1 km e.r.	13
21	S.T.$_{34}$ 10 km e.r., 75% VMA/S.T.$_{35}$ 12 km e.r. segment strength (60% VMA)	22
22	S.T.$_{36}$ 16 km r. various land (65% VMA)	16
23	S.T.$_{37}$ 6 km e.r., 15 × 100 m with 100 m (95% VMA), 3 km e.r./S.T.$_{38}$ 10 km r. uniform tempo, 70% VMA	22
24	S.T.$_{39}$ 8 km e.r. 75%VMA/S.T.$_{40}$ 3 km e.r, 20 × 300 m with connection 100 m e.r. (30 s) 100%	20
25	S.T.$_{41}$ 2 h′ walk-forest	0
26	S.T.$_{42}$ 12 km r. 80% VMA/S.T.$_{43}$ 10 km r. uniform tempo, 75% VMA	22
27	S.T.$_{44}$ 12 km r. progressive various land 75–83% VMA/S.T.$_{45}$ 10 km r. uniform tempo, 70% VMA and 3 series of ex. for strength	22
28	S.T.$_{46}$ 6 km r. uniform tempo, 65% VMA, 30 × 100 m r. accelerated (100% VMA) with connection 100 m e.r. 4 km/S.T.$_{47}$ 10 km r. uniform tempo, stretching	24
29	S.T.$_{48}$ 8 km e.r., stretching 75% VMA/S.T.$_{49}$ 40 min r. (2min r. tempo sustained + 1 min conn. + 1 min r. tempo sustained + 1 min. connection) × 8 series (90% VMA)	24
30	S.T.$_{50}$ 16 km r. various land (65% VMA)	16

Abbreviations: r.—running; e.r.—easy running; r.l.—running launched; S.T. $_1$—session of training no. 1; VMA—maximum aerobic velocity.

2.7. Statistical Analyses

Statistical analyses were performed using SPSS software (v.26, IBM, Armonk, NY, USA). ANOVA for repeated measurements was used to determine whether characteristics (for example, body weight, Hb, EPO, VO2max) remained similar before each 30-day training session. Changes in these characteristics within each training session were detected using one-way ANOVA. ANOVA repeated measurements were further used to determine differences in relative change (the percentage difference from pre-training) in characteristics across training camps. A Bonferroni correction was used for multiple comparisons on pairs, and the Greenhouse–Geisser correction was used when sphericity was violated. Normality was assessed using the Shapiro–Wilk test. Statistical significance was set a priori at $p < 0.05$.

2.8. Sample Size

Statistical analysis was performed using SPSS v.26 software. The one-way ANOVA test with repeated measurements was used to analyze the evolution of the values of the characteristics EPO, Hb, and VO2max, whose values were measured at the beginning and end of each 30-day training period. The athletes trained in training stages of 30 days at different altitudes: at 2000 m (LHTH)-G1, living at 1850 m and training at 2200 m (LHTH+)-G2, and 300 m (LLTL)-G3.

One-way ANOVA with repeated measurements was also used to determine the evolution of each characteristic mentioned above, as well as the differences between the average values of each characteristic, at the end of each training period, in which the athletes trained at altitudes LHTH, LHTH+, namely LLTL.

The Bonferroni correction was used to compare multiple pairs of values. Mauchly's test was also used for sphericity, and the Greenhouse–Geisser test was used for correction when it was violated.

The data normality was checked using the Shapiro–Wilk test.

3. Results

3.1. Maximum Volume of Oxygen (VO2max-mL/kg/min)

LHTH resulted in a significant increase in the maximum volume of oxygen. It increased by 0.9 ± 0.23 mL/kg/min to 56.1 ± 2.2 mL/kg/min at the initial assessment and to 57.0 ± 2.2 g mL/kg/min at the final assessment, the percentage progress being 1.6 ± 0.5 mL/kg/min The increase is statistically significant, $p < 0.001$.

The maximal oxygen volume increased during LHTH+ by 1.7 ± 0.3 mL/kg/min, from 56.7 ± 2.0 mL/kg/min to 58.4 ± 2.1 mL/kg/min at the end of the training period. The percentage of increase is 2.9 ± 0.5%. The value $p < 0.001$ shows a statistically significant increase in the mean.

At LLTL, the average maximum volume of oxygen increased by 0.1 ± 0.1 mL/kg/min, from 56.9 ± 1.9 mL/kg/min to 57.0 ± 1.8 mL/kg/min after the end of the training period. In percentages, the increase is 0.2 ± 0.2%. The difference between the two means is statistically significant, $p = 0.013 < 0.05$.

The average values of the maximum oxygen volume recorded at the end of each training period at the three altitudes were compared with the one-way ANOVA test for repeated measurements. It turned out that there is at least one pair of average values with significant differences, $p = 0.004$.

There are statistically significant differences noticeable between the average values of the maximum oxygen volume between all pairs of values: LHTH vs. LHTH+, the difference of 1310 mL/kg/min, $p = 0.047 < 0.05$ and LHTH+ vs. LLTL, the difference of 1380 mL/kg/min, $p = 0.001 < 0.05$. Bonferroni adjustment was used for multiple comparisons.

It was determined that the *highest average increase in maximum oxygen volume at the end of the training period occurred in the cohort living at 1850 m and training at 2200 m*. The graph in Figure 1 shows the average relative (percentage) increases in the maximum oxygen volume for the preparation periods at the three altitudes.

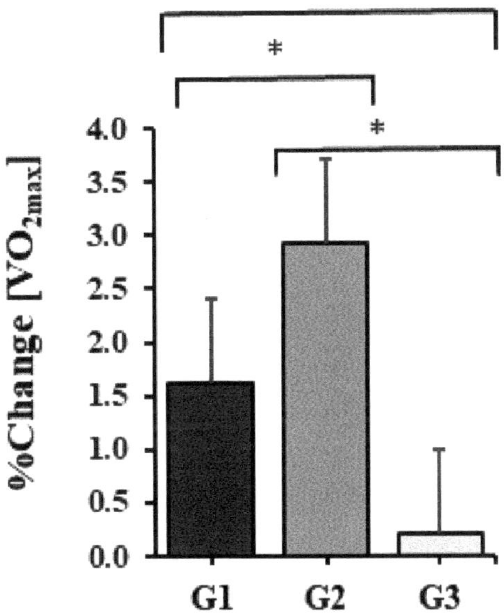

Figure 1. Relative before–after changes in VO2max concentration after 30 days of training at 2000 m altitude (G1), living at 1850 m and training at 2200 m (G2), namely 300 m (G3). Values displayed represent mean ± sd. Significant differences ($p < 0.05$) between training courses are marked with *.

3.2. Hemoglobin Concentration (Hb-g/dL)

Hb measured before the start of each training camp were similar ($p = 0.145$).

Each training session resulted in increases in hemoglobin values as follows.

LHTH increased by 1.1 ± 0.3 g/dL from 13.6 ± 0.4 mL/kg/min at the assessment before the training stage to 14.7 ± 0.5 g/dL at the assessment after the training stage, the percentage progress being 8.0 ± 1.8%. The increase is statistically significant, $p < 0.001$.

The average hemoglobin concentration LHTH+ increased by 1.4 ± 0.5 g/dL, from 13.6 ± 0.5 to 15.0 ± 0.7 g/dL at the end of the 30 days of training. The percentage increase is 10.9 ± 2.1%. The value $p < 0.001$ shows a statistically significant increase.

LLTH shows an increase in the average hemoglobin concentration of 0.1 ± 0.0 g/dL, from 13.7 ± 0.5 to 13.8 ± 0.5 in percentage, the increase being 0.3 ± 0.3%. The difference between the two means is statistically significant, $p = 0.015 < 0.05$.

The mean hemoglobin values recorded at the end of each training period at the three altitudes were compared with the one-way ANOVA test for repeated measurements. It turned out that there is at least one pair of mean values with significant differences, $p \leq 0.001$.

Statistically significant differences were noticed between the average hemoglobin concentrations among all pairs of values: LHTH vs. LHTH+, a difference of 0.35 g/dL, $p = 0.045 < 0.05$, LHTH, vs. LLTL, a difference of 0.87 g/dL, $p = 0.002 < 0.05$, LHTH+, vs. LLTL, a difference of 1.22 g/dL, $p < 0.001 < 0.05$. Bonferroni adjustment was used for multiple comparisons.

It was also noted that the greatest increase in Hb concentration was achieved at the end of the training period at LHTH+. The graph in Figure 2 highlights the average relative (percentage) increases in hemoglobin concentration for the training periods at the three altitudes.

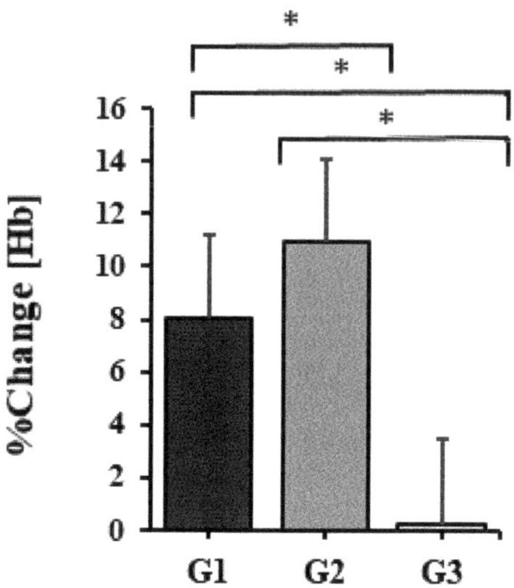

Figure 2. Relative before-after changes in Hb concentration after 30 days of training at 2000 m altitude (G1), living at 1850 m and training at 2200 m (G2), namely 300 m (G3). Values displayed represent mean ± sd. Significant differences ($p < 0.05$) between training courses are marked with *.

3.3. Erythropoietin Concentration

Differences in the erythropoietin (EPO) concentration before and after each training cycle were compared.

LHTH resulted in a significant increase in the average concentration of erythropoietin. This increased by 1.0 ± 0.8 mU/mL from 6.2 ± 1.9 at the initial assessment to 7.2 ± 2.5 at the final assessment, the percentage progress being 15.8 ± 8.4%. The increase is statistically significant, $p = 0.002 < 0.05$.

Following LHTH+, the mean erythropoietin concentration increased by 1.9 ± 0.5 mU/mL from 6.4 ± 1.8 to 8.3 ± 2.2 after 30 days of training. The percentage increase is 30.0 ± 5.6%. The value $p < 0.001$ shows a statistically significant increase.

LLTL does not bring a significant increase in the average concentration of erythropoietin, $p = 0.678 > 0.05$. In this situation, the average increase tends to be zero (0.1 ± 0.1 mU/mL), the average value measured before the beginning of the period is 8.9 ± 1.7 and the one at the end of the period is 9.0 ± 1.7. The percentage progress is 0.1 ± 0.9%.

Comparing the erythropoietin values recorded at the end of each training period, at the three altitudes, with the one-way ANOVA test for repeated measurements, it turned out that there is at least one pair of mean values with significant differences, $p < 0.001$.

There is only one statistically significant difference noticeable between mean erythropoietin concentrations in LHTH vs. LHTH+, $p < 0.001$, with Bonferroni adjustment for multiple comparisons.

It was also observed that *the highest increase in erythropoietin concentration was achieved at the end of the training period living at 1850 m and training at 2200 m.* This can also be seen from the graph in Figure 3, which shows the average percentage (relative) increases in erythropoietin concentration for the training periods at the three altitudes.

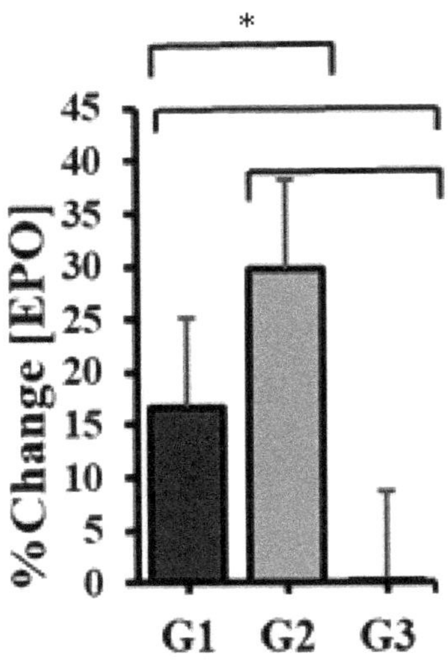

Figure 3. Relative before–after changes in EPO concentration, after 30 days of training at 2000 m altitude (G1), living at 1850 m and training at 2200 m (G2), namely 300 m (G3). Values displayed are mean ± sd. Significant differences ($p < 0.05$) between training courses are marked with *.

4. Discussion

This study aimed to assess changes in EPO, Hb concentrations, and running performance (VO2max) after 30 days, at a high altitude (2000 m), living at 1850 m and training at 2200 m, and the traditional training cycle at a 300 m altitude. Our main findings are that both high-altitude training and living at 1850 m and training at 2200 m resulted in significant improvements in EPO, Hb, and VO2max that exceeded changes in these parameters following traditional sea-level training. While training at high altitude caused greater relative increases in EPO and VO2max, living at 1850 m and training at 2200 m also resulted in greater increases in Hb, EPO, as well as sports performance (VO2max). The main findings of this study confirmed our initial hypothesis and suggest that the physiological changes triggered by 30 days of either high-altitude training or living at 1850 m and training at 2200 m are greater than those achieved by traditional training methods at the sea level.

The effect of training at high altitudes has been extensively researched [23–29]. Few studies have focused on high-altitude alternation [30]. Sharma, A.P. conducted research on running speed during training sessions wherein athletes lived at 2100 m and trained at 1400–2700 m, exercising over a range of intensities relevant to middle-distance running performance.

Movement speed in elite middle athletes is negatively affected at 2100 m natural altitude, with levels of impairment dependent on training intensity. Maintaining walking speed at certain intensities during altitude training may lead to greater perceived exertion [31].

The ten performance athletes in our study had a one-year training program individualized according to VMA values. Respecting the altitude adaptation period, at the end of the 30-day training period, the VO2max values increased by 1.6 ± 0.5% for LHTH and 2.9 ± 0.5% for LHTH+, which shows that the training burden incurred by a lack of oxygen leads to significant increases in sports performance.

Sports training at altitude can generally show an increase in aerobic capacity by 14% [32–34]. The acclimatization response to altitude depends on the individual physiological parameters, as is the case for the correlation between red blood cell mass that increases while the partial pressure of oxygen (PaO_2) decreases [35]. This is why the "threshold altitude" for many people is 2200 to 2500 m [36]. For this reason, in this study was chosen the alternation of altitude; thus, living at 1850 m altitude, the altitude at which the hypoxia phenomenon appears [23], and training at 2200 m altitude, where the need for oxygen is bigger [36], were chosen for study. Acclimatization to environmental hypoxia generates cardiorespiratory adaptations reflected in the transport and use of oxygen [37], increases the concentration of hemoglobin in the blood, results in a high buffering capacity against the homeostasis of acid and basic elements of the body, has benefits for the structural and biochemical properties of skeletal muscle [37], and increases pulmonary ventilation.

In our study, hemoglobin and erythropoietin concentrations at the end of the LHTH preparation period increased by 8.0 ± 1.8% and 15.8 ± 8.4% for LHTH+, the increases being higher: LHTH hemoglobin increases by 10.9 ± 2.1% and erythropoietin by 30.0 ± 5.6%, which supports the previous statements. On the other hand, maximal aerobic power is reduced as the variable changes; hematology compensates for this loss [38]. As mentioned above, altitude training may not be beneficial for everyone, as it initially depends on the handling and exposure time, which must be controlled according to the age, physical condition level, iron status, and energy requirements of each individual [33,39].

Stefan de Smet et al. [29] proved that gradual exposure to hypoxia in a normobaric chamber from 2000 m to 3250 m increased the total Hb mass by ~2.6% on average. Moreover, this increase was strongly correlated with the mean increase in sEPO, over the 5-week study intervention ($r = 0.78$, $p < 0.05$). In fact, the correlations between EPO and Hb mass gradually increased from the beginning (week 1, $r = 0.54$) to the end (week 5, $r = 0.81$) of the intervention period. This supports the rationality that maintaining high EPO levels during prolonged "living high" is crucial for increasing Hb mass at altitude. The current hypoxic protocol consistently increased sEPO concentrations from week 1 to week 5 in all subjects. This is likely due at least in part to the gradual increase in hypoxia from 16.4 to 14.0% FiO_2 (~2000 to 3250 m), which resulted in even lower arterial oxygen saturations at week 5 than at week 1.

According to a recent meta-analysis, "living high" is expected to increase Hb mass by ~1.08% for every 100 h of exposure to altitude above 2100 m [40]. This algorithm predicts a ~4% increase in Hb mass over 350–400 h at >2100 m. Consequently, a hypoxic dose expressed as "hour-kilometers" predicts a ~3.4% increase in Hb mass—linear model [41]. However, another study reported a 6.7% increase in Hb mass for only ~230 h of intermittent normobaric hypoxia, but at a constant altitude of 3000 m [42]. This could indicate that intermittent hypoxia may become more effective for increasing Hb mass at higher degrees of hypoxia.

All these studies support the fact that living and training at altitude causes hematological changes that lead to increased sports performance.

Our study showed that there are different hematological changes influenced by the altitude at which the athlete lives and trains, changes that must be taken into account when planning training courses at altitude.

Our study is not without limitations. Although the study was conducted on elite runners, the sample size was small. Furthermore, it was measured the Hb concentration rather than Hb mass. Additionally, differences in weather and higher ambient temperatures at LHTH+ could have led to changes in Hb mass (with heat training).Another limitation would be the assumption that the physiological changes in the two parameters EPO and HB acquired in the first stage LHTH positively influence the changes produced in the second stage LHTH+, even if there is a period of six months between the two races, in which the athletes have trained at an altitude of 300 m. This remains to be studied in future research.

5. Conclusions

The results of this study can serve as guidelines for athletic trainers in their future work, in the complete structure of multi-year planning and programming, and thus improve the process of development and performance training.

Both alternatives of training at altitude are beneficial for increasing sports performance. Coaches and technical teams of athletes can introduce them to training plans according to geographical and financial possibilities.

The alternative of living at 1850 m and training at 2200 m is more expensive from a financial point of view as it involves daily ascent and descent to and from altitude; however, it produces greater changes and is therefore more beneficial for increasing sports performance.

In conclusion, this study shows that living at an altitude of 1850 m and training at 2200 m is more effective for performance athletes, due to several factors that remain to be studied, than living and training at an altitude of 2000 m.

Author Contributions: Conceptualization O.D., D.I.A.; methodology, E.V.U., P.L.H.; software, N.L.V.; validation, C.I.A. and D.I.A.; formal analysis O.D., P.L.H.; investigation, O.D. and A.E.P.; resources, A.M.A.; data curation N.L.V.; writing—original draft preparation D.I.A., O.D. and D.M.; writing—review and editing, D.I.A., C.I.A. and N.L.V.; visualization, E.V.U.; supervision, D.M.; project administration C.I.A.; funding acquisition, P.L.H. and E.V.U. All authors have read and agreed to the published version of the manuscript.

Funding: This research received no external funding.

Institutional Review Board Statement: The study was conducted in compliance with the Declaration of Helsinki, and approved by the Ethics Committee of "Vasile Alecsandri" University of Bacau. Romania (decision no.27/3 October 2022, registered under no. 19264/2/ 3 October 2022).

Informed Consent Statement: Informed consent was obtained from all subjects involved in the study.

Data Availability Statement: Not applicable.

Conflicts of Interest: The authors declare no conflict of interest.

References

1. Man, C.M.; Ganera, C. A study on the influence of training at altitude (2000m) on the maximum aerobic velocity in athletics (mountain race). *Ovidius Univ. Ann. Ser. Phys. Educ. Sport/Sci. Mov. Health* **2015**, *15*, 135–146.
2. Green, H.J. Altitude Acclimatization, Training and Performance. *J. Sci. Med. Sport* **2000**, *3*, 299–312. [CrossRef]
3. Barnes, K.R.; Kilding, A.E. Strategies to Improve Running Economy. *Sport. Med.* **2014**, *45*, 37–56. [CrossRef] [PubMed]
4. Man, C.M.; Ganera, C. A study on the influence of training at altitude (2000 m) on the blood hemoglobin and erythrolein values in athletics (aerobic resistance). *Ovidius Univ. Ann. Ser. Phys. Educ. Sport/Sci. Mov. Health* **2015**, *15*, 409–419.
5. Flaherty, G.; O'Connor, R.; Johnston, N. Altitude Training for elite endurance athletes: A review for the travel medicine practitioner. *Travel Med. Infect. Dis.* **2016**, *14*, 200–211. [CrossRef] [PubMed]
6. Álvarez-Herms, J.; Julià-Sánchez, S.; Hamlin, M.J.; Corbi, F.; Pagès, T.; Viscor, G. Popularity of hypoxic training methods for endurance-based professional and amateur athletes. *Physiol. Behav.* **2015**, *143*, 35–38. [CrossRef]
7. Strzała, M.; Ostrowski, A.; Szyguła, Z. Altitude training and its influence on physical endurance in swimmers. *J. Hum. Kinet.* **2011**, *28*, 91–105. [CrossRef]
8. Man, C.M. *Pregătirea la Altitudine, Factor Favorizant Creșterii Performanței în Alergare Montană*; Risoprint: Cluj-Napoca, Romania, 2022; pp. 53–70.
9. Man, M.C.; Ganera, C. Study on changing arterial oxygen saturation level of athletes while performing a 21 days training course at an altitude of 2000 metres. *Ovidius Univ. Ann. Ser. Phys. Educ. Sport Sci. Mov. Health* **2016**, *16*, 198–208.
10. Viscor, G.; Torrella, J.R.; Corral, L.; Ricart, A.; Javierre, C.; Pages, T.; Ventura, J.L. Physiological and biological responses to short-term intermittent hypobaric hypoxia exposure: From sports and mountain medicine to new biomedical applications. *Front. Physiol.* **2018**, *9*, 814. [CrossRef]
11. Levine, B.D.; Stray-Gundersen, J. Dose-response of altitude training: How much altitude is enough? *Adv. Exp. Med. Biol.* **2006**, *588*, 233–247.
12. Wilber, R.L. Application of altitude/hypoxic training by elite athletes. *Med. Sci. Sport. Exerc.* **2007**, *39*, 1610–1624. [CrossRef] [PubMed]
13. Rodríguez, F.A.; Iglesias, X.; Feriche, B.; Calderón-Soto, C.; Chaverri, D.; Wachsmuth, N.B.; Schmidt, W.; Levine, B.D. Altitude training in elite swimmers for sea level performance (Altitude Project). *Med. Sci. Sport. Exerc.* **2015**, *47*, 1965–1978. [CrossRef] [PubMed]
14. Gore, C.J.; Rodríguez, F.A.; Truijens, M.J.; Townsend, N.E.; Stray-Gundersen, J.; Levine, B.D. Increased serum erythropoietin but not red cell production after 4 wk of intermittent Hypobaric Hypoxia (4000–5500 m). *J. App. Physiol.* **2006**, *101*, 1386–1393. [CrossRef]

15. Man, M.C.; Ganera, C.; Bărbuleț, G.D.; Krzysztofik, M.; Panaet, A.E.; Cucui, A.I.; Tohănean, D.I.; Alexe, D.I. The modifications of hemoglobin, erythropoietin values and running performance while training at mountain vs hilltop vs seaside. *Int. J. Environ. Res. Public Health* **2021**, *18*, 9486. [CrossRef] [PubMed]
16. Pereira, L.A.; Freitas, T.T.; Marín-Cascales, E.; Bishop, C.; McGuigan, M.R.; Loturco, I. Effects of training on sand or hard surfaces on sprint and jump performance of team-sport Players: A systematic review with meta-analysis. *Strength Cond. J.* **2021**, *43*, 56–66. [CrossRef]
17. Impellizzeri, F.M.; Rampinini, E.; Castagna, C.; Martino, F.; Fiorini, S.; Wisloff, U. Effect of plyometric training on sand versus grass on muscle soreness and jumping and sprinting ability in soccer players. *Br. J. Sport. Med.* **2007**, *42*, 42–46. [CrossRef]
18. Alexe, D.I.; Alexe, C.I.; Man, M.C.; Iconomescu, T.M.; Ilie, M. *Simulare de Condiții, Captarea Mișcării și Analiza Datelor în Cercetareasportului*; Risoprint: Cluj-Napoca, Romania, 2020; pp. 91–97.
19. Léger, L.; Mercier, D. Gross energy cost of horizontal treadmill and track running. *Sport. Med.* **1984**, *1*, 270–277. [CrossRef]
20. Melin, B.; Jimenez, C.; Charpenet, A.; Pouzeratte, N.; Bittel, J. Validation de deux tests de détermination de la vitesse maximale aérobie (VMA) sur le terrain Validation of two maximal aerobic speed (MAS) field tests. *Sci. Sport.* **1996**, *11*, 46–52. [CrossRef]
21. Chamoux, A.; Berthon, P.; Laubignat, J.F. Determination of maximum aerobic velocity by a five-minute test with reference to running world records. A theoretical approach. *Arch. Physiol. Biochem.* **1996**, *104*, 207–211. [CrossRef]
22. Berthon, P.; Fellmann, N.; Bedu, M.; Beaune, B.; Dabonneville, M.; Coudert, J.; Chamoux, A. A 5-min running field test as a measurement of maximal aerobic velocity. *Eur. J. Appl. Physiol. Occup. Physiol.* **1997**, *75*, 233–238. [CrossRef]
23. Nadarajan, V.S.; Ooi, C.H.; Sthaneshwar, P.; Thompson, M.W. The utility of immature reticulocyte fraction as an indicator of erythropoietic response to altitude training in elite cyclists. *Int. J. Lab. Hematol.* **2010**, *32*, 82–87. [CrossRef] [PubMed]
24. Chen, C.Y.; Hou, C.W.; Bernard, J.R.; Chen, C.C.; Hung, T.C.; Cheng, L.L.; Liao, Y.H.; Kuo, C.H. Rhodiola crenulata- and Cordyceps sinensis-based supplement boosts aerobic exercise performance after short-term high altitude training. *High Alt. Med. Biol.* **2014**, *15*, 371–379. [CrossRef] [PubMed]
25. Garvican, L.; Martin, D.; Quod, M.; Stephens, B.; Sassi, A.; Gore, C. Time course of the hemoglobin mass response to natural altitude training in elite endurance cyclists. scand. *J. Med. Sci. Sport.* **2010**, *22*, 95–103.
26. Heinicke, K.; Heinicke, I.; Schmidt, W.; Wolfarth, B. A Three-Week traditional altitude training increases hemoglobin mass and red cell volume in elite biathlon athletes. *Int. J. Sport. Med.* **2005**, *26*, 350–355. [CrossRef] [PubMed]
27. Panaet, A.E.; Alexe, C.I.; Marchis, C.; Man, C.M.; Grigore, V. Essay regarding the Need for a standard framework of assessment and measurement of flat feet in children. *Bull. Transilvania Univ. Brasov. Ser. IX Sci. Hum. Kinet.* **2021**, *14*, 235–246. [CrossRef]
28. Friedmann, B.; Jost, J.; Rating, T.; Weller, E.; Werle, E.; Eckardt, K.U.; Bartsch, P.; Mairbaurl, H. Effects of iron supplementation on total body hemoglobin during endurance training at moderate altitude. *Int. J. Sport. Med.* **1999**, *20*, 78–85. [CrossRef]
29. Man, M.C.; Ganera, C. A study on athletes' heart rate changing while performing a 21 days training course at an altitude of 2000 m. *Ovidius Univ. Ann. Ser. Phys. Educ. Sport/Sci. Mov. Health* **2016**, *16*, 537–548.
30. Millet, G.P.; Trigueira, R.; Meyer, F.; Lemire, M. Is altitude training bad for the running mechanics of middle-distance runners? *Int. J. Sport. Physiol. Perform.* **2021**, *16*, 1359–1362. [CrossRef]
31. Sharma, A.P.; Saunders, P.U.; Garvican-Lewis, L.A.; Clark, B.; Stanley, J.; Robertson, E.Y.; Thompson, K.G. The effect of training at 2100m altitude on running speed and session rating of perceived exertion at different intensities in elite middle-distance runners. *Int. J. Sport. Physiol. Perform.* **2017**, *12*, 2147–2152. [CrossRef]
32. Millet, G.P.; Debevec, T.; Brocherie, F.; Malatesta, D.; Girard, O. Therapeutic use of exercising in hypoxia: Promises and Limitations. *Front. Physiol.* **2016**, *7*, 224. [CrossRef]
33. Holloszy, J.O.; Coyle, E.F. Adaptations of skeletal muscle to endurance exercise and their metabolic consequences. *J. Appl. Physiol. Respir. Environ. Exerc. Physiol.* **1984**, *56*, 831–838. [CrossRef] [PubMed]
34. Klausen, K.; Robinson, S.; Michael, E.D.; Myhre, L.G. Effect of high altitude on maximal working capacity. *J. Appl. Physiol.* **1966**, *21*, 1191–1194. [CrossRef]
35. Weil, J.V.; Jamieson, G.; Brown, D.W.; Grover, R.F. The red cell mass-Arterial oxygen relationship in normal man. Application to patients with chronic obstructive airway disease. *J. Clin. Invest.* **1968**, *47*, 1627–1639. [CrossRef] [PubMed]
36. Levine, B.D.; Stray-Gundersen, J. A practical approach to altitude training: Where to live and train for optimal performance enhancement. *Int. J. Sport. Med.* **1992**, *13*, 209–212. [CrossRef] [PubMed]
37. Bailey, D.M.; Davies, B. Physiological implications of altitude training for endurance performance at sea level: A review. *Br. J. Sport. Med.* **1997**, *31*, 183–190. [CrossRef] [PubMed]
38. Jackson, C.G.; Sharkey, B.J. Altitude, training and human performance. *Sport. Med.* **1988**, *6*, 279–284. [CrossRef] [PubMed]
39. Hickson, R.C.; Bomze, H.A.; Holloszy, J.O. Linear increase in aerobic power induced by a strenuous program of endurance exercise. *J. Appl. Physiol. Respir. Environ. Exerc. Physiol.* **1977**, *42*, 372–376. [CrossRef]
40. De Smet, S.; van Herpt, P.; D'Hulst, G.; Van Thienen, R.; Van Leemputte, M.; Hespel, P. Physiological adaptations to hypoxic vs. Normoxic training during intermittent living high. *Front. Physiol.* **2017**, *8*, 347. [CrossRef]
41. Gore, C.J.; Sharpe, K.; Garvican-Lewis, L.A.; Saunders, P.U.; Humberstone, C.E.; Robertson, E.Y.; Wachsmuth, N.B.; Clark, S.A.; McLean, B.D.; Friedmann-Bette, B.; et al. Altitude training and hemoglobin mass from the optimised carbon monoxide rebreathing method determined by a meta-analysis. *Br. J. Sport. Med.* **2013**, *47*, 31–39. [CrossRef]
42. Garvican-Lewis, L.A.; Sharpe, K.; Gore, C.J. Time for a new metric for hypoxic dose? *J. Appl. Physiol.* **2016**, *121*, 352–355. [CrossRef]

healthcare

MDPI

Article

The Role of Volunteers in a Swimming Organization for Persons with Disabilities

Alena Vernerova [1,*], Ivana Marova [2] and Frantisek Chmelik [1]

1 Faculty of Physical Culture, Palacký University Olomouc, 779 00 Olomouc, Czech Republic
2 Faculty of Education, Masaryk University, 601 77 Brno, Czech Republic
* Correspondence: alena.ruzickova01@upol.cz; Tel.: +420-723849333

Abstract: Participation in leisure time physical activity (LTPA) has considerable health-related, psychological, and social benefits. However, the involvement of individuals with disabilities is considerably less than that of their peers without disabilities. A higher rate of participation of individuals with disabilities in LTPA may be achieved by the active involvement of volunteers. This study aimed to describe the importance of volunteer involvement in a swimming organization focused on individuals with disabilities, as perceived by all participants, including swimmers with disabilities, their parents, volunteers, and coaches. The organization uses volunteers as swimming instructors who work individually with swimmers with disabilities. The data were obtained through 11 semi-structured interviews with swimmers with disabilities and their parents, volunteers, and coaches. The interviews were transcribed verbatim and analyzed using a five-step inductive thematic analysis. As a result of the cooperation with the volunteer swimming instructors, swimmers with disabilities felt an improved range of movement, greater independence, and higher self-esteem than before they started using the services of the swimming organization. Consequently, even individuals with severe disabilities can participate in LTPA. Membership to the organization also provided space for the establishment of new social relations, and the instructors described them accepting persons with disabilities as their equals. More importantly, the involvement of volunteers enables organizations to provide respite care for parents.

Keywords: leisure time physical activity; volunteering; swimming; social inclusion; disability; adapted physical activity; respite care

check for updates

Citation: Vernerova, A.; Marova, I.; Chmelik, F. The Role of Volunteers in a Swimming Organization for Persons with Disabilities. *Healthcare* **2022**, *10*, 2149. https://doi.org/10.3390/healthcare10112149

Academic Editor: Felipe Aidar

Received: 24 August 2022
Accepted: 24 October 2022
Published: 28 October 2022

1. Introduction

The full and effective participation of an individual in society includes involvement in leisure time physical activity (LTPA). In addition to the proven health-related benefits, there are significant psychosocial implications.

LTPA has the potential to increase self-esteem and independence in daily life activities for persons with disabilities, leading to an improved quality of life [1]. It also creates a natural space for the socialization of individuals [2] and families with children with disabilities, especially those with severe forms of disability [3]. Physical activity can also lead to improvements in mental health and well-being at any age [4,5]. On the other hand, a lack of movement is a risk factor for declining skills with increasing age [6].

The participation of children with disabilities in leisure time activities may also be beneficial for their parents and other caregivers. Being a caregiver is very mentally demanding and is associated with a high degree of fatigue. Respite care provides caregivers with a short relief period and has the potential to improve their mental health and decrease the extent of long-term fatigue [7]. However, the offer is very limited, and caregivers tend to have concerns about the quality of the service or, by using the service, may have a feeling of failure in their role as a carer [8]. Respite care can also include camps or other types of organized LTPA, which have an added value not only for parents but also for their children with disabilities [9].

A suitable type of physical activity for persons with disabilities, often recommended by physicians, is swimming [10]. In addition to many other health benefits, movement in water allows people with disabilities to be free of the need to use compensatory devices and, to a large extent, the need for assistance [11].

Despite the considerable benefits that have been identified, persons with disabilities participate in LTPA significantly less often than their peers without disabilities [12,13]. This may be influenced by several external barriers such as structural barriers [14–17], insufficient financing, and low awareness of the possibility of participation [18–21], as well as internal factors, including, for example, a lack of motivation [22,23], personality factors of the individuals [24–26], and the presence of pain [27].

Volunteers represent an important element in increasing the involvement of people with disabilities in LTPA. The involvement of volunteers in LTPA has the potential to increase community-like feelings. Conversely, the absence of volunteers is considered a barrier to the participation in LTPA of persons with disabilities [28]. The quality of volunteer participation involves their feeling of meaningfulness of the perceived benefits [29]. These benefits include the opportunity to improve their organizational and communication skills, acquire new contacts, and learn to work in a team [30]. Student volunteering is perceived as having an added value by society. Thus, it increases the social status of volunteers, thereby increasing their chances of finding jobs and securing admission in universities owing to it being perceived as an asset [31].

Although the involvement of volunteers can be beneficial for all participants, few studies have considered it a factor in facilitating the involvement of persons with disabilities in LTPA. The present study aimed to describe the importance of volunteer involvement in a swimming organization focused on individuals with disabilities as perceived by all participants, including swimmers with disabilities, their parents, volunteers, and coaches.

2. Materials and Methods

2.1. Research Sample

2.1.1. Settings

This study involved a swimming sports club that focused on individuals with disabilities. This particular sports club was chosen because of organizational factors and the size of the club, which made it able to address enough participants. The swimming club was a nonprofit organization founded in 1995. It focused on leisure time activities, sports, rehabilitation, and swimming lessons for persons with disabilities. In addition to the swimming lessons, the club participates in para-swimming competitions and organizes summer swimming camps. The target group includes persons with disabilities from all age groups. Swimmers were divided according to their skills into groups of competitive, recreational, and rehabilitation swimmers. Recreational and rehabilitation swimmers were individually led by volunteer instructors who were in the pool with them during the swimming lesson. Volunteers and coaches in the organization not only participated as swimming instructors but also provided persons with disabilities assistance or other additional support, especially during swimming camps. The club had few paid staff; therefore, its operation was largely based on volunteers.

2.1.2. Recruitment

The study was conducted in accordance with the Declaration of Helsinki and approved by the Ethics Committee of the Faculty of Physical Culture, Palacký University, Olomouc. Informed consent was obtained from all the participants involved in the study.

For the purposes of the qualitative research, participants from each of the following groups were selected: (a) swimmers, (b) parents, (c) volunteers or coaches (referred to as instructors), and (d) one female participant who was both a swimmer and an instructor. Eleven interviews were conducted (three swimmers, three parents, four instructors, and one swimmer or instructor were interviewed). The interviewees were not parents of the interviewed swimmers. The description of the participants is presented in Table 1. To preserve anonymity, the names of the participants were replaced with pseudonyms.

Table 1. Descriptions of the participants.

		Swimmers (n = 4) *	Instructors (n = 5) *	Parents (n = 3)
Age (years), (M ± SD)		21 ± 2.6	24.8 ± 6.2	58.7 ± 5.9
Sex (*n*)	Male	1	2	2
	Female	3	3	1
Occupation (*n*)	Student	4	3	-
	Employed	-	2	2
	Unemployed	-	-	-
	Retired	-	-	1
Diagnosis (*n*)	Cerebral palsy	3	1	-
	Muscular dystrophy	1	-	-
Type of mobility device used (*n*)	None	2	5	3
	Manual wheelchair	1	-	-
	Power wheelchair	1	-	-
Participation (years), (M ± SD)		12.5 ± 8.2	5.8 ± 5.1	13.7 ± 4.6

* One participant provided two interviews, one in the role of a swimmer and another as an instructor; thus, her data was included in both groups. M, mean; SD, standard deviation.

The sample was established through deliberate sampling. The swimmers were contacted via their coaches. The inclusion criterion was an age of 15 years or older, and the exclusion criterion was an intellectual disability to provide relevant information. The first three swimmers who responded to the call were included in the study. The study sample also comprised parents who accompanied their children to the training sessions. Interviews with these parents were conducted during their children's swimming sessions and included parents of individuals with severe disability who needed all-day care. We assumed that the impact of the presence of volunteers in the organization on these parents would be more significant than in the case of parents of swimmers with mild or moderate disabilities. The instructors were chosen according to their length of experience and included new instructors with <5 years of experience in the organization, as well as experienced instructors with a history of >5 years, to ensure that various views and experiences were collected.

2.2. Procedures and Techniques

2.2.1. Data Collection

Data collection was performed through semi-structured interviews conducted by the first author. The interviews with swimmers and instructors had similarly structured questions and lasted for approximately 30 min. The interviews with parents lasted for approximately 20 min. The interviews were recorded, transcribed verbatim, and anonymized. The semi-structured interviews with all respondents were thematically divided into three parts. The first part was related to the characteristics of the individual, his or her interests, and previous experiences with LTPA. The second part focused specifically on the course of the training sessions, their interactions with their instructor, and the motivation for swimming, whereas the third part focused on the relationships with the organization and other events held by the organization, especially summer camps. The last part also included questions on the subjectively perceived positives and negatives of involvement in leisure organizations. The questions differed slightly for each group to make them relevant according to the role of the respondents within the organization. All responses were based on a retrospective view of the time spent in the organization and their recent feelings.

2.2.2. Data Analysis

The data were analyzed by the first author using a five-step inductive thematic analysis approach [32]. A thematic analysis method provides flexibility and enables the researcher to obtain an in-depth view when analyzing and reporting the themes within the data. In contrast to grounded theory or interpretive phenomenological analysis, this approach does not demand deep theoretical and technological expertise; therefore, it is more suitable for researchers early in their qualitative research careers, a description applicable to the first author [32]. In the first step, the interviews were transcribed verbatim by the first author and read repetitively to immerse herself in the data, search for patterns, and make coding notes. The transcribed interviews were encoded as a second step. Third, the codes were analyzed into subthemes and themes and combined into relevant overarching themes. Fourth, the key themes and subthemes were reviewed to ensure their relevance and entered into the data set [33]. Fifth, the themes were delivered to each group of participants separately (swimmers, instructors, and parents), after which the first author searched for relevant intersections between the groups. As a final part of the data analysis, the themes were reviewed by all the authors to ensure their relevance to the aim of the study.

For clarity, the authors evaluated the frequency of occurrence of the subthemes in each participant's group (Table 2). "X" illustrates a high frequency of occurrence, which was set as >15 mentions among swimmers and instructors and >10 among parents, "x" illustrates a medium frequency of occurrence, which was set as 10–14 mentions among swimmers and instructors and 5–9 among parents, and "o" illustrates a low frequency of occurrence, which was set as 1–9 mentions among swimmers and instructors and 1–4 among parents.

Table 2. Key themes and subthemes mentioned by the participants.

Overarching Themes	Key Themes	Subthemes	Participants		
			Swimmers	Instructors	Parents
Personal enrichment	Health and well-being	Movement development	X [a]	x	x
		Freedom of movement	x [b]	o [c]	o
		Enjoyment	X	X	X
	Self-esteem	Empowerment	x	X	x
		Surpassing oneself	o	x	o
		Meaningful time spending	x	X	o
		Swimming progress	o	x	x
	New possibilities	New experience	o	o	x
		Future work direction	o	o	
		Independence	o	o	x
Social interactions	Community	New friendships	X	X	X
		Feeling of belonging	X	X	X
		Safe space	X	x	x
	Social inclusion	Acceptance of disability	o	X	
		Mutual trust	x	x	o
Family support	Respite care	Change of scenery	o	o	o
		Time to rest	o	o	o

[a] X indicates a high frequency of mentions of a particular subtheme of each participant's group. [b] x indicates a medium frequency of mentions of a particular subtheme of each participant's group. [c] o indicates a low frequency of mentions of a particular subtheme of each participant's group.

3. Results

Three overarching themes were constructed based on the key themes and subthemes that emerged from the data analysis: (1) "Personal enrichment" described the individual benefits for all the participants, (2) "Social interactions" illustrated the social impact of the involvement in the organization, and (3) "Family support" represented the benefits for all families with children with disabilities. All themes were based on the cooperation of swimmers with the volunteers in the organization. Table 2 presents each subtheme reflecting the frequency of mentions of the specific groups of participants in the interviews (see Data Analysis). There are three tables that present the significant expressions for each subtheme according to the groups of participants that supported the research outcomes. Tables 3–5 present quotes from the swimmers, instructors, and parents, respectively.

Table 3. Swimmers' quotes according to the mentioned subthemes.

Key Themes	Sub-Themes	Quotes
Health and well-being	Movement development	"It has had a great impact on my daily life. When I move my body, I am aware of which muscle I am using at the moment. It also shows in my dancing skills. Even my coaches tell me I have a bigger range of movement. It has helped me to be more aware of my body and its possibilities."—Elena
	Freedom of movement	"I enjoy the movement in the water itself, we do what we want. What we can do best. I am not sure how to express it, but it gives us a feeling of freedom."—Gustav
	Enjoyment	"I enjoy the movement in the water itself, we do what we want. What we can do best. I am not sure how to express it, but it gives us a feeling of freedom."—Gustav
Self-esteem	Empowerment	"Once there was an event at the end of the season and there was no one who would go with me. So I was supposed to go all by myself by bus and I never go alone by bus because I am too scared. We agreed that someone would pick me up at the bus station but they forgot about me. After all, I got there by myself and felt so proud, because I surpassed myself and stepped up from my comfort zone." —Elena
	Meaningful time spending	"It is my free time and thanks to swimming, I feel more self-confident because I know I am spending my free time in a meaningful way.—Elena
	Swimming progress	"The first time they threw me into the water, I could barely hold myself on the pool edge when I wanted to talk. So I am able to see the progress."—Fiona
New possibilities	New experience	"Sometimes it leads to some completely different opportunities. For example, they were filming some documentary, TV show, or something like that. And they wanted to film something about our organization, about the cooperation of swimmers with instructors. They wanted someone who is physically impaired and talkative, so they chose me (laugh)."—Fiona
	Future work direction	"I found out I do not like when people try to motivate me, and that I would rather motivate others. So I became an instructor."—Denisa, swimmer/instructor
	Independence	"I found out I do not like when people try to motivate me, and that I would rather motivate others. So I became an instructor."—Denisa, swimmer/instructor
Community	New friendships	"I like the competitions a lot. We are meeting there with our friends from different sport clubs. One could say it is more of a social event than a sports event."—Gustav
	Feeling of belonging	"It seems to me that everybody is talking to everybody, and the swimmers and instructors are at the same level. That is what I like the most. Sometimes when I see different camps, the program is so childish, like we were babies! So, I like this approach way better."—Fiona
	Safe space	"I like, that every time we come to the training session you cannot see any person who works with us or whom you meet there that would not like to be there."—Gustav
Social inclusion	Mutual trust	"When I am at the training session, I know that someone would jump for me into the water if anything happens. At the very moment, when someone appears in front of me and we are swimming together, I feel more secure. I can relax and enjoy it more."—Elena
Respite care	Change of scenery	"I say it is a bit of an anti-educational camp (laughing). Because we get away from our parents and personal assistants and simply spend time with friends."—Fiona
	Time to rest	"Because when we are there for the whole week [camp] we simply live there and we get used to going to the restaurants and bakeries, everywhere we want to. I always feel like I am on vacation."—Fiona

Table 4. Instructors' quotes according to the mentioned subthemes.

Key Themes	Sub-Themes	Quotes
Health and well-being	Movement development	" . . . so when you are focusing on the right technique when you stretch them in the water when you are forcing the swimmers to prolong the movements, you can help them even from the physiological viewpoint. You can help them to both stretch the muscles and relax the joints."—Denisa
	Enjoyment	"I just want the swimmer to enjoy the lesson and I also want to enjoy it myself. For me, it is a relaxation. I jump into the water to chill. It also gives me different thoughts."—Claudie
Self-esteem	Empowerment	"So I tell him: 'Just try to do it two times by yourself, if anything goes wrong, I am here to catch you.' That's how I lead them to be more independent."—Boris
	Surpassing oneself	"Of course, I was scared during the first years of my volunteering. Well, I guess I am still a bit scared. Especially, because I am a technician I don´t know the diagnoses, and I didn´t know what to expect from the swimmers. After some time I discovered that they are actually grateful that I can properly stretch their muscles."—Claudie
	Meaningful time spending	"I feel like I am doing something meaningful with a part of my free time."—Boris
	Swimming progress	"Of course, I feel happy when I see that the swimmers are improving. That is probably the thing that fulfills me the most."—Anna
New possibilities	New experience	"Once I was with her [swimmer] in the Netherlands because she had a boyfriend there at the time. And he wanted her to visit him and her mum felt awkward about the idea of going with her. So I gladly accompanied her."—Claudie
	Future work direction	I started to volunteer in this organization. It opened my eyes and I realized this could be the right path for me. I still think this could be my future work direction."—Anna
	Independence	"It is important not to do things instead of them and to trust them, that they can do it by themselves. It is also important to overcome the inner need of helping them and just verbally motivate them to try to do it by themselves."—Tomas
Community	New friendships	"I feel more like a friend than an instructor to the swimmers. After one and a half year of volunteering in the organization I found many friends among the swimmers. With some of them, we also meet outside the swimming sessions and camps and it just makes me happy that they are more than just the swimmers for me."—Anna
	Feeling of belonging	"The members of the organization are more open than the mainstream society. They try to understand one another and be kind to each other. (. . .) They always try to find ways to make things possible than looking for problems. They try to overcome the obstacles together. It is easy to be accepted."—Tomas
	Safe space	"I have never met a bad person in the organization." —Anna
Social inclusion	Acceptance of disability	"When I see a person with a disability, I don't close my eyes anymore, I see it as something normal. I found out that they are normal people, and only some of them carry a chair with them. "– Claudia
	Mutual trust	"No foam board can replace a person. Foam boards can be very unstable. In our training, there are always hands of the instructor so the swimmers can lean on them. You cannot even imagine how huge the difference is. A person gives the swimmer real support."—Denisa
Respite care	Change of scenery	"Parents get time to rest and to go for a trip and the swimmers can have a beer or French fries without any remorse."—Claudie
	Time to rest	"The most important thing for both the parents and swimmers is that they are apart for half an hour."—Denisa

Table 5. Parent's quotes according to the mentioned subthemes.

Key Themes	Sub-Themes	Quotes
Health and well-being	Movement development	" . . . and we see that the range of movement in the shoulder joint is perfect now. His right arm movement was much worse. Or should I say it was much worse than the left arm. And thanks to swimming his movements of both arms are now almost identical."—Hynek
	Enjoyment	"He is at the age when he likes girls, naturally. So when he gets to train with a beautiful female instructor, oh how hard he tries!" (laugh)—Hynek
Self-esteem	Empowerment	"I just wanted him to learn how to swim. And I watched their approach towards the swimmers. The instructors are often very good swimmers so they give it their all. And it is visible in the results of the children from the organization. How far they have got! Because some of them were competing in European championships and that is incredible. Also, thanks to the volunteers."—Hynek
	Swimming progress	"I have never imagined that my son would be able to swim and now he can swim a 200 m backstroke, 200 m at once! That is amazing!"—Hynek
New possibilities	New experience	"That they are taken care of for the whole week in a different environment and she is always full of new experiences and then the whole year draws from it."—Iva
	Independence	"The swimming progress is great. At first, she was swimming only with assistance, and now we throw her into the water and she can swim by herself."—Iva
Community	New friendships	"She usually swims with the same instructor and she likes her and the instructor likes my daughter. So this beautiful friendship was created and I think she attends the training mostly because of the instructor."—Jan
	Feeling of belonging	"Once my nephew drove me and my daughter to the swimming camp and when he saw the warm-hearted welcome and the atmosphere he was amazed. Because he was a person who did not know anything about the organization. He saw it and he told me: ´wow, that is amazing!´"—Jan
	Safe space	"Well if I just mention the fact she always talks about the community where she feels very safe, and when there is a competition ahead, she is always very excited. She just loves the people there. She does not have many friends, which is sad. But she feels very safe among the swimmers and she just loves the whole community."—Iva
Social inclusion	Mutual trust	"I appreciate that they give all their energy to the swimmers and that the instructors make friendly connections with every single one of them and that they help the swimmers a lot."—Jan
Respite care	Change of scenery	"I think that, even though she is sometimes just floundering in the water, at least we leave the house once a week, and in a way, she looks forward to swimming, even though she is not achieving any real results."—Jan
	Time to rest	"I always find a sightseeing tour on the internet, and we set off with my wife for a week. And that makes us satisfied for the rest of the year."—Jan

3.1. Personal Enrichment

The overarching theme of personal enrichment comprised three key themes: health and well-being, self-esteem, and new possibilities.

Health and well-being: Swimmers often reported the rehabilitation aspect of swimming with an instructor. They experienced an improvement in their range of movement. Thanks to swimming, Elena reported experiencing not only a larger range of movement but also a greater awareness of her body (see Table 3).

Instructors mentioned that, thanks to the individual lessons, they could help swimmers stretch their stiff muscles during the training session and help them reach their body potential. They described how they liked to observe the improvement in the movement of the swimmers throughout the swimming lessons (see Table 4).

The same effect was observed by the parents in their children with disabilities; they reported mostly a greater range of motion, which they attributed to swimming, as mentioned by Hynek, a father of a 24-year-old man with a severe type of cerebral palsy (see Table 5).

Moreover, the swimmers described how water provided them with possibilities of movements that they were unable to perform outside water (for example, walking in water and a more effective relaxation of spasticity).

In addition to the physiological benefits, swimming also produces a psychological effect, as demonstrated by the reports from swimmers, such as Gustav, where most described the freedom they felt during swimming sessions (see Table 3). Parents appreciated that swimming offered their children a great opportunity to move, and in their opinion, it compensated for their children having to sit all day in a wheelchair.

Based on descriptions from the swimmers, the feeling of safety while swimming with an individual instructor was an important factor, which helped the swimmers to relax and fully enjoy the swimming sessions (see Table 3). The instructors often mentioned that they were not only focused on the swimming progress but mostly on the positive experiences of the swimmers and their own enjoyment in assisting the swimmers (see Table 4). They stressed the individual approaches and communication during this process. The presence of individual instructors was also an important factor for the parents, who reported that having an instructor of the opposite sex provided an additional unplanned motivation to the swimmers (see Table 5).

Self-esteem: Both the swimmers and instructors perceived a feeling of higher self-esteem due to their participation in the swimming organization. It was not linked only to the swimming lessons but also to the other events organized by the sports club. For example, Elena described how she succeeded in traveling all by herself to get to the club's event (Table 3). Thanks to the cooperation between the swimmers and instructors, both groups described how they had to overcome various challenges, which made them feel more confident in their abilities. In particular, the instructors described that they had to overcome their own fears during the training sessions, as stated by Claudia (see Table 4). Involvement in the organization brought a sense of meaningfulness to both instructors and swimmers. At the same time, they shared a feeling of fulfillment when swimmers made progress. According to both swimmers and instructors, this feeling of meaningfulness was important for strengthening their self-esteem (see Tables 3 and 4).

New possibilities arose among swimmers consequent to their becoming more independent, thanks to the trust, safe space, and support that they received from the instructors. Although swimmers with severe disabilities would not be able to participate without an instructor, some swimmers gradually became independent of their instructors and managed to swim on their own. This kind of progress was described by Iva, a parent of a 25-year-old blind woman with cerebral palsy (see Table 5). The feeling of independence described by the swimmers, was not only at the physical level but also at the psychological level when they could experience new life situations unaccompanied by parents, especially during the camps. Fiona especially enjoyed that they were not taken care of as children, which was quite common in other organizations based on her experience (see Table 3). The instructors mentioned having a different perspective on life owing to their involvement in the organization, and furthermore, this played a role in the instructors' choices for their future jobs. As Anna described, it helped her to consider her future path (see Table 4). Similarly, some swimmers became swimming coaches and, thus, served as models for other swimmers. A good example was Denisa, who used to be a swimmer at the international championship level but now participates in the organization as an instructor (see Table 4).

3.2. Social Interactions

The overarching theme of social interactions comprised two key themes: community and social inclusion.

Community: The organization had a friendly atmosphere and created a community where everyone felt welcomed. Therefore, it was easy to establish a relationship between the swimmers and instructors. Good relationships played a major role in keeping participants in the organization. Parents often mentioned how their children felt safe and welcomed in the community. Jan, the father of a 37-year-old woman who experienced traumatic brain damage, described how good friendships was one of the main reasons why his daughter attended the swimming sessions. Another parent, Iva, perceived that her daughter felt safe in the community (see Table 5). Swimmers had the opportunity to establish relationships with individuals with similar disabilities, as well as with people without disabilities. This was further confirmed by the fact that the swimmers and instructors often met outside training sessions and became friends, as Anna described (see Table 4). Participants from all groups (swimmers, instructors, and parents) often talked about the organization as if it were a family.

Social inclusion: Participants with disabilities described feeling equal to their instructors. In the words of Fiona, a swimmer, "swimmers and instructors are at the same level" (see Table 3). In addition, the instructors gained experience with people with disabilities. As a result, they accepted them as a normal part of society, and they overcame prejudices. This phenomenon was expressed by Claudia, an instructor, who said that it changed her view of people with disabilities (see Table 4).

3.3. Family Support

The last overarching theme was family support, and the main theme that emerged was respite care and its benefits for both parents and swimmers.

The swimmers benefited mainly from changing their environment and becoming independent of their parents, with whom they spend much more time than their peers without disabilities. In this way, they had the opportunity to get to know themselves in different social roles other than as a daughter or son. Fiona, a swimmer, described the swimming camp as an "antieducational camp", where she could be by herself without parents and personal assistants (see Table 3).

For parents, the swimming organization provided a substitute for respite care. During training sessions led by instructors, parents had time to rest from their caring responsibilities. An even stronger effect was described in talking about summer swimming camps where the volunteers worked as both instructors and personal assistants to the swimmers. These camps were beneficial for swimmers and their parents.

The parents appreciated that their children were taken care of by the instructors and that they could rest for a week. As Jan stated, he could go on a getaway trip with his wife to gain some energy for the year (see Table 5). The same benefits were perceived by the instructors, as Denisa realized even half an hour (the time of the swimming session) of the parents being apart from their children with disabilities proved to be very refreshing for both groups (see Table 4).

4. Discussion

All respondents agreed on the benefits stemming from the cooperation between the swimmers and instructors in the swimming organization. The participants described how they felt a greater range of movement and that they could perform movement patterns that they were unable to perform by themselves on the ground, thanks to cooperation with the instructors. The aquatic environment made the swimmers feel free and independent. Although the instructors attempted to lead swimmers toward the greatest possible degree of independence, simultaneously, they provided a safe environment that had the potential to increase the effect of this development. The development of independence and self-reliance in persons with disabilities can lead to an improved quality of life [1].

Another positive aspect was the sense of meaningfulness perceived by participants in the organization. The individuals included in the research described a feeling of freedom, meaningful fulfilment of free time, and consequently, increased self-esteem. Owing to sports, individuals with disabilities often feel pride, meaningfulness, and freedom [34]. In the present study, these feelings were described by both the swimmers and volunteers.

Previous studies have suggested a connection between volunteering and well-being, higher self-esteem, and a greater sense of belonging [35].

The positive climate in the organization was one of the main reasons why participants stayed. The swimmers and instructors often became friends, even outside the organization. Similar results were suggested by a study on participation in a wheelchair basketball organization, where participants felt welcomed and appreciated among their peers without disabilities [36]. This is a good step toward the inclusion of persons with disabilities in mainstream society. The direct experience of instructors with individuals with disabilities was subjectively correlated with better attitudes towards this group, which is consistent with the results from other studies [37–39]. The finding that the connection between individuals with and without disabilities supported a sense of belonging, respect, and acceptance, especially among persons without disabilities [28], was also supported by the results of the present study.

Leisure time organizations and sports clubs also play an important role in respite care. Families often feel a lack of opportunities for leisure, recreation, and social activities for their children with disabilities. At the same time, these activities give parents a necessary respite from all-day care [40]. Camps, which, in the present study, were summer swimming camps, were considered particularly beneficial by parents, as they could go on a holiday knowing that their child would be taken care of. The children are cared for by the instructors, without whom these camps would not take place. The findings of the present study cannot be generalized; however, other studies have confirmed that camp-like events had a positive impact on caregivers' mental health [9]. At the same time, it allowed individuals with disabilities to change their environment and provided an opportunity for recreation and personal growth [41]. The results of the present study were similar.

These results suggested several benefits of volunteer involvement in providing LTPA to individuals with disabilities. Despite the small sample size, this study clearly showed some positive patterns. It appeared that the involvement of volunteers contributed to improving the conditions for individuals with disabilities and their families. Therefore, greater attention should be paid to LTPA as a form of respite care, as this is an inspiring idea that has so far not been optimally used in the Czech Republic and in many other countries.

In contrast to previously published results [8], the parents in our study did not report any concerns about the quality of the services provided by the organization or that they felt unsuccessful in their role as carers when using the service. Future studies should therefore also address parents' possible negative perceptions about volunteers in leisure time organizations and sports clubs.

Limitations and Strengths

The first author had her own experience as an instructor in the organization. Despite her efforts to achieve the highest degree of objectivity, she realized that her experience could have been reflected in the interpretation of the results of the study. The study showed positive patterns; however due to the small sample size and specificity of the deliberately chosen swimming organization, the results cannot be generalized. It is unclear to what extent the results would be transferable to different sports organizations for people with disabilities. Therefore, future studies in different sports settings are encouraged to enable an investigation of other sports, with all the practical implications. Another limitation of this study was the short duration of the interviews conducted. A strength of the study was the comprehensive approach to the issue, which was analyzed from the perspectives of all the actors in the organization.

5. Conclusions

Owing to the cooperation between volunteers and coaches in the role of swimming instructors and swimmers with disabilities, the swimmers described a subjectively perceived improvement in their range of movement, increased independence, and development of self-esteem. Through their activities, the instructors helped individuals with disabilities participate in the organization. Moreover, involvement in the organization brought about new social relationships that continued to exist outside the organization. Thanks to these interactions, the instructors reported that it helped them accept people with disabilities as a normal part of society. The swimmers and volunteers described their involvement in the organization as a meaningful way of spending free time, which, according to them, led to a feeling of higher self-esteem. The parents appreciated all of the above benefits, especially that their child felt welcome and safe in the organization, and they valued that their children were taken care of during the swimming lessons and camps, which provided them time to rest from their carer responsibilities.

Author Contributions: Conceptualization, A.V., I.M. and F.C.; methodology, A.V. and I.M.; validation, A.V., I.M. and F.C.; formal analysis, A.V.; investigation, A.V.; data curation, A.V.; writing—original draft preparation, A.V.; writing—review and editing, A.V., I.M. and F.C.; visualization, A.V.; and supervision, I.M. and F.C. All authors have read and agreed to the published version of the manuscript.

Funding: This research received no external funding.

Institutional Review Board Statement: The study was conducted in accordance with the Declaration of Helsinki and approved by the Ethics Committee of the Faculty of Physical Culture, Palacký University Olomouc (protocol code 72/2016, date of approval 28 November 2016).

Informed Consent Statement: Informed consent was obtained from all the participants involved in the study.

Data Availability Statement: The data presented in this study are available upon request from the authors.

Conflicts of Interest: The authors declare no conflict of interest.

References

1. Sweet, S.N.; Martin Ginis, K.A.; Tomasone, J.R. Investigating Intermediary Variables in the Physical Activity and Quality of Life Relationship in Persons with Spinal Cord Injury. *Health Psychol.* **2013**, *32*, 877–885. [CrossRef] [PubMed]
2. Horvat, M.; Croce, R.V.; Pesce, C.; Fallaize, A. *Developmental and Adapted Physical Education*; Routledge: London, UK, 2019. [CrossRef]
3. Neyroud, M.C.; Newman, C.J. Parents' Perspectives on Adaptive Sports in Children with Profound Intellectual and Multiple Disabilities. *Children* **2021**, *8*, 815. [CrossRef] [PubMed]
4. Rodriguez-Ayllon, M.; Cadenas-Sánchez, C.; Estévez-López, F.; Muñoz, N.E.; Mora-Gonzalez, J.; Migueles, J.H.; Molina-García, P.; Henriksson, H.; Mena-Molina, A.; Martínez-Vizcaíno, V.; et al. Role of Physical Activity and Sedentary Behavior in the Mental Health of Preschoolers, Children and Adolescents: A Systematic Review and Meta-Analysis. *Sport. Med.* **2019**, *49*, 1383–1410. [CrossRef] [PubMed]
5. Kadariya, S.; Gautam, R.; Aro, A.R. Physical Activity, Mental Health, and Wellbeing among Older Adults in South and Southeast Asia: A Scoping Review. *BioMed Res. Int.* **2019**, *2019*, 6752182. [CrossRef]
6. Buchholz, A.C.; Martin Ginis, K.A.; Bray, S.R.; Craven, B.C.; Hicks, A.L.; Hayes, K.C.; Latimer, A.E.; McColl, M.A.; Potter, P.J.; Wolfe, D.L. Greater Daily Leisure Time Physical Activity Is Associated with Lower Chronic Disease Risk in Adults with Spinal Cord Injury. *Appl. Physiol. Nutr. Metab.* **2009**, *34*, 640–647. [CrossRef]
7. Remedios, C.; Willenberg, L.; Zordan, R.; Murphy, A.; Hessel, G.; Philip, J. A Pre-Test and Post-Test Study of the Physical and Psychological Effects of out-of-Home Respite Care on Caregivers of Children with Life-Threatening Conditions. *Palliat. Med.* **2015**, *29*, 223–230. [CrossRef]
8. Ashworth, M.; Baker, A.H. 'Time and Space': Carers' Views about Respite Care. *Health Soc. Care Community* **2000**, *8*, 50–56. [CrossRef]
9. Meltzer, L.J.; Johnson, S.B. Summer Camps for Chronically Ill Children: A Source of Respite Care for Mothers. *Child. Health Care* **2004**, *33*, 317–331. [CrossRef]
10. Matias, M.T.; Parent, M.M. Developing and Implementing a Community-Level Para-Swimming Program. *Int. J. Aquat. Res. Educ.* **2018**, *11*, 3. [CrossRef]
11. Kraus, J. *Dětská Mozková Obrna*; Grada: Prague, Czech Republic, 2004.
12. Jackson, J.; Williams, T.L.; McEachern, B.M.; Latimer-Cheung, A.E.; Tomasone, J.R. Fostering Quality Experiences: Qualitative Perspectives from Program Members and Providers in a Community-Based Exercise Program for Adults with Physical Disabilities. *Disabil. Health J.* **2019**, *12*, 296–301. [CrossRef]
13. Batshaw, M.L.; Roizen, N.J.; Lotrecchiano, G.R. *Children with Disabilities*, 7th ed.; Brookes Publishing: Baltimore, MD, USA, 2013.

14. Bloemen, M.A.; Takken, T.; De Groot, J.F.; Kruitwagen, C.L.J.J.; Rook, R.A.; Van den Berg-Emons, R.H.J.G.; Backx, F.J.G. Determinants of Physical Activity in Young Wheelchair-Users with Spina Bifida. *J. Rehabil. Med.* **2020**, *52*, jrm00115. [CrossRef]
15. Wright, A.; Roberts, R.; Bowman, G.; Crettenden, A. Barriers and Facilitators to Physical Activity Participation for Children with Physical Disability: Comparing and Contrasting the Views of Children, Young People, and Their Clinicians. *Disabil. Rehabil.* **2019**, *41*, 1499–1507. [CrossRef]
16. Menzies, A.; Mazan, C.; Borisoff, J.F.; Mattie, J.L.; Mortenson, W.B. Outdoor Recreation among Wheeled Mobility Users: Perceived Barriers and Facilitators. *Disabil. Rehabil. Assist. Technol.* **2021**, *16*, 384–390. [CrossRef]
17. Jaarsma, E.A.; Geertzen, J.H.B.; de Jong, R.; Dijkstra, P.U.; Dekker, R. Barriers and Facilitators of Sports in Dutch Paralympic Athletes: An Explorative Study. *Scand. J. Med. Sci. Sport.* **2014**, *24*, 830–836. [CrossRef]
18. MacEachern, S.; Forkert, N.D.; Lemay, J.F.; Dewey, D. Physical Activity Participation and Barriers for Children and Adolescents with Disabilities. *Int. J. Disabil. Dev. Educ.* **2021**, *69*, 204–216. [CrossRef]
19. Declerck, L.; Stoquart, G.; Lejeune, T.; Vanderthommen, M.; Kaux, J.F. Barriers to Development and Expansion of Adaptive Physical Activity and Sports for Individuals with a Physical Disability in Sports Clubs and Centres. *Sci. Sports* **2021**, *36*, 202–209. [CrossRef]
20. Shields, N.; Synnot, A. Perceived Barriers and Facilitators to Participation in Physical Activity for Children with Disability: A Qualitative Study. *BMC Pediatr.* **2016**, *16*, 9. [CrossRef]
21. Stephens, C.; Neil, R.; Smith, P. The Perceived Benefits and Barriers of Sport in Spinal Cord Injured Individuals: A Qualitative Study. *Disabil. Rehabil.* **2012**, *34*, 2061–2070. [CrossRef]
22. Cho, C.; Shin, W.; Kong, S. Participation in Regular Physical Activity According to the Type of Disability, Sex, Point of Disability Diagnosis, and Ability to Walk Independently in South Korea. *Healthcare* **2021**, *9*, 1079. [CrossRef]
23. Mckenzie, G.; Willis, C.; Shields, N. Barriers and Facilitators of Physical Activity Participation for Young People and Adults with Childhood-Onset Physical Disability: A Mixed Methods Systematic Review. *Dev. Med. Child Neurol.* **2021**, *63*, 914–924. [CrossRef]
24. Saebu, M.; Sørensen, M. Factors Associated with Physical Activity among Young Adults with a Disability. *Scand. J. Med. Sci. Sport.* **2011**, *21*, 730–738. [CrossRef] [PubMed]
25. Shikako-Thomas, K.; Shevell, M.; Schmitz, N.; Lach, L.; Law, M.; Poulin, C.; Majnemer, A. Determinants of Participation in Leisure Activities among Adolescents with Cerebral Palsy. *Res. Dev. Disabil.* **2013**, *34*, 2621–2634. [CrossRef] [PubMed]
26. Úbeda-Colomer, J.; Devís-Devís, J.; Sit, C.H.P. Barriers to Physical Activity in University Students with Disabilities: Differences by Sociodemographic Variables. *Disabil. Health J.* **2019**, *12*, 278–286. [CrossRef] [PubMed]
27. Mashola, M.K.; Korkie, E.; Mothabeng, D.J. Pain and Its Impact on Functioning and Disability in Manual Wheelchair Users with Spinal Cord Injury: A Protocol for a Mixed-Methods Study. *BMJ Open* **2021**, *11*, e044152. [CrossRef] [PubMed]
28. Labbé, D.; Miller, W.C.; Ng, R. Participating More, Participating Better: Health Benefits of Adaptive Leisure for People with Disabilities. *Disabil. Health J.* **2019**, *12*, 287–295. [CrossRef] [PubMed]
29. Man, K.E.; Williams, T.L.; Barnim, N.; Shirazipour, C.H.; Latimer-Cheung, A.E.; Tomasone, J.R. Exploring How the Process of Quality Participation Unfolds for Volunteers in Community-Based Exercise Programs for Persons with Disabilities. *Qual. Res. Sport. Exerc. Health* **2021**, *13*, 300–324. [CrossRef]
30. Opatřilová, D.; Vítková, M. *Speciálně Pedagogická Podpora dětí a Mládeže se Speciálními Vzdělávacími Potřebami Mimo Školu*; Masaryk University: Brno, Czech Republic, 2011.
31. Matulayová, T.; Jurníčková, P.; Doležel, J. *Motivace k Dobrovolnictví*; Palacký Univesity: Olomouc, Czech Republic, 2016.
32. Hsieh, H.F.; Shannon, S.E. Three Approaches to Qualitative Content Analysis. *Qual. Health Res.* **2005**, *15*, 1277–1288. [CrossRef]
33. Braun, V.; Clarke, V. Qualitative Research in Psychology Using Thematic Analysis in Psychology Using Thematic Analysis in Psychology. *Qual. Res. Psychol.* **2006**, *3*, 77–101. [CrossRef]
34. Aitchison, B.; Rushton, A.B.; Martin, P.; Barr, M.; Soundy, A.; Heneghan, N.R. The Experiences and Perceived Health Benefits of Individuals with a Disability Participating in Sport: A Systematic Review and Narrative Synthesis. *Disabil. Health J.* **2022**, *15*, 101164. [CrossRef]
35. Brown, K.M.; Hoye, R.; Nicholson, M. Self-Esteem, Self-Efficacy, and Social Connectedness as Mediators of the Relationship Between Volunteering and Well-Being. *J. Soc. Serv. Res.* **2012**, *38*, 468–483. [CrossRef]
36. Moss, P.; Lim, K.H.; Prunty, M.; Norris, M. Children and Young People's Perspectives and Experiences of a Community Wheelchair Basketball Club and Its Impact on Daily Life. *Br. J. Occup. Ther.* **2020**, *83*, 118–128. [CrossRef]
37. Kalargyrou, V.; Pettinico, W.; Chen, P.J. Attitudes toward People with Physical Disabilities: An Examination of Social Context, Discipline, Disability Type, and Demographics. *J. Vocat. Rehabil.* **2021**, *54*, 117–133. [CrossRef]
38. Fort, M.; Lundberg, N.; Zabriskie, R.; Eggett, D.; Prater, M.A.; Barney, K. Adolescent Summer Camp Volunteers' Attitudes Toward Peers with Disabilities. *Leis. Sci.* **2017**, *39*, 277–294. [CrossRef]
39. Iwakuma, M.; Miyamoto, K.; Murata, J. Changes in Perceptions of Japanese University Students toward Disability: A Mixed Methods Study. *Int. J. Disabil. Dev. Educ.* **2021**, *68*, 1–13. [CrossRef]
40. Palisano, R.J.; Almarsi, N.; Chiarello, L.A.; Orlin, M.N.; Bagley, A.; Maggs, J. Family Needs of Parents of Children and Youth with Cerebral Palsy. *Child Care Health Dev.* **2010**, *36*, 85–92. [CrossRef]
41. Engwall, K.; Hultman, L. Constructions of Childhood: The Assessment of Respite Care for Children with Disabilities in Sweden. *Eur. J. Soc. Work* **2021**, *24*, 617–628. [CrossRef]

healthcare MDPI

Article

Development and Validation of a Scale Measuring Intention toward Participating in Pro Bono of Pre-Service Physical Activity Instructors for the Activation of Physical Activity for the Disabled: Based on the Theory of Planned Behavior

Kyungjin Kim and Yonghwa Lee *

Department of Adapted Physical Activity, Korea Nazarene University, Cheonan-si 31172, Korea
* Correspondence: leedragonfire@kornu.ac.kr; Tel.: +82-10-5322-9583

Abstract: The purpose of this study was to develop and validate a scale for predicting the intention of pre-service physical activity instructors for persons with disabilities to participate in pro bono work, based on the Theory of Planned Behavior. This study analyzed 322 university students majoring in adapted physical activity in South Korea. To determine the purpose of the study, the EFA using SPSS 21.0 and CFA using AMOS 21.0 were used to confirm the validity of the measurement tool and the relationship between latent and observed variables. Further, the Cronbach's alpha was used to identify the internal reliability. As a result, first, the questionnaire used in this study was validated based on the theory. Second, the behavioral belief was influenced by teaching experience about physical activity for the disabled and knowledge about physical activity for the disabled. Third, the normative belief was influenced by the parents of people with disabilities, people with disabilities, family members, friends, and students in my department. Fourth, the control belief was influenced by the state of mind of physical activity instructors for people with disabilities, the ability to create an IEP, and the ability to do physical activity.

Keywords: pro bono; intention; pre-service physical activity instructor; people with disabilities; theory of planned behavior

check for updates

Citation: Kim, K.; Lee, Y. Development and Validation of a Scale Measuring Intention toward Participating in Pro Bono of Pre-Service Physical Activity Instructors for the Activation of Physical Activity for the Disabled: Based on the Theory of Planned Behavior. *Healthcare* **2022**, *10*, 2094. https://doi.org/10.3390/healthcare10102094

Academic Editor: Felipe Aidar

Received: 21 September 2022
Accepted: 18 October 2022
Published: 20 October 2022

1. Introduction

The population of persons with disabilities registered in 2021 was about 2,645,000, which has been maintained at about 5% of the total population of South Korea for 10 years, since 2010 [1]. An increase in the disabled population is the same as a decrease in the non-disabled population across the Organization for Economic Cooperation and Development (OECD) [2]. The number of disabled elderly people is increasing due to the increase in the elderly population, and the amount of people with birth defects is also increasing [3]. About 60% of disability occurs in old age [1]. As for the status of children with disabilities, the number of children with disabilities in the total child population in 2008 has been continuously increasing from 0.73% to 0.89% in 2018 [1]. Although the proportion of the population with disabilities is maintained or increased, the reality is that the level of health, which is significant for the daily life of the disabled, is not as good as that of the non-disabled. For example, 50.2% of the disabled reported the subjective health status of the disabled as bad [4]. In the case of chronic diseases, the prevalence of hypertension in the non-disabled adult group was 33.5% and the prevalence of diabetes mellitus was 13.0%. However, in the case of the disabled, hypertension was 46.9% and diabetes was 21.9%, which was higher than that of the non-disabled [5].

The importance of exercise is being emphasized to improve the health status of individuals with disabilities. Exercise maintains and improves physical strength and body functions through physical training, so it can be effective for health management as well as disease prevention [6]. When asked the purpose of physical activity for people with disabilities, 50.0% answered health promotion and management, and individuals with disabilities recognized that physical activity is important for the health of the disabled. However, in the case of the disabled, not only participation in sports but also the will to participate is shown to be low [7]. In the case of non-disabled people, it can be seen that 52.4% of them participate in physical activity more than twice a week, but for people with disabilities, that figure is 23.8%. Among those with no experience in physical activity, the amount of individuals with a view of "I have no intention of doing sports at all" or "I have no intention of doing it at all" is as high as 50.0% [7]. The reasons for not participating in physical activity for the disabled include cost, lack of sports facilities for the disabled, and the need for exercise equipment and auxiliary personnel (help for transportation, etc.). Although these problems are being improved, persons with disabilities point out the lack of life sports instructors for the disabled in regard to complementing the diversity of programs [6,7].

Currently, the Korean government is planning to approximately double the number of physical activity instructors for the disabled from 577 in 2018 to 1000 in 2022 [7]. This might be evidence that the current government is seriously aware of the lack of physical activity instructors for the disabled. However, it has been determined that more physical activity instructors for the disabled are needed to improve the quality of sports for the disabled and the continuously increasing proportion of disabled people in South Korea [8]. Therefore, pro bono work has been recently proposed as a method to solve such a problem. Pro bono, a shortened version of pro bono publico, is a Latin phrase that means "for the public good". Experts do not seek compensation based on their expertise, but provide material and mental help for the benefit of society, either directly or through charitable organizations [9]. The implementation of pro bono work can solve the shortage of physical activity instructors for the disabled and can help provide various programs.

The concept of pro bono work started with American lawyers providing legal services for the socially disadvantaged, and experts providing their knowledge and services free of charge [10]. Pro bono is an area of volunteer work, and provides services with respect to individual abilities, knowledge, experience and skills. Along with talent donation, it has recently established itself as a new trend in social contribution roles [10]. However, talent donation is short-term skilled volunteering that targets individuals as a form of volunteer activity or donation that provides one's professional abilities and skills to society, whereas pro bono, which also provides professional skills and is defined as a volunteer activity, offers services not only to individuals but also to organizations such as non-profit organizations and social enterprises [11]. In particular, pro bono work is not a short-term activity such as volunteering or talent donation, but a long-term social contribution activity. Pro bono is currently expanding not only to legal services but also to business, arts, marketing, education, and medical care across the world [12].

Most of the Korean and international studies related to pro bono work are the establishment of the concept of pro bono and the study of pro bono activation methods, and further research is currently being conducted [10–14]. Studies of pro bono related to law, education, design, and beauty are being conducted, but the reality is that there are no prior studies related to physical activity for the disabled [10,15,16]. In particular, studies on physical activity for the disabled through volunteer activities have been conducted, but there are no studies related to pro bono work, so research is needed to promote physical activity for the disabled through pro bono work [8,17–21].

In addition, theories based on various factors are being used in relation to physical activity for the disabled, including Theory of Planned Behavior, Theory of Reasoned Action, Health Belief Model, and Social Cognitive Theory. The Theory of Planned Behavior is one of the theories most widely used in relation to physical activity or sports for the disabled [22–25]. The Theory of Planned Behavior was developed based on the Theory of Reasoned Action of Fishbein and Ajzen [26], and it states that an individual's specific behavior is determined according to the intention to perform. The Theory of Planned

Behavior is a theory that supplements the problem that the individual's control over a specific behavioral intention is excluded from the Theory of Reasoned Action, and it expresses the factors of an individual's attitude, subjective norm, and control toward a specific behavioral intention [26,27]. Thus, the Theory of Planned Behavior can predict specific behavior according to behavioral intentions [27]. Hence, if the intention of physical activity experts for the disabled to participate in pro bono work can be analyzed for the revitalization of physical activity for the disabled, the behavior of pro bono participation can also be predicted through the Theory of Planned Behavior.

This study intends to provide basic data for the promotion of physical activity for the disabled by exploring and analyzing factors related to the intention toward participating in pro bono physical activity work for the disabled by pre-service physical activity instructors who are currently majoring in adapted physical activity at universities. Therefore, the purpose of this study is to develop and validate a scale for predicting the behavioral intention of physical activity instructors for people with disabilities to participate in pro bono work based on the Theory of Planned Behavior.

2. Materials and Methods

2.1. Participants

The selected participants of the study were 322 students who are currently majoring in adapted physical activity at universities in South Korea. The reason why university students were selected as the participants of this study is that they are preliminary physical activity instructors for the disabled. Furthermore, it is necessary to understand the intention of pre-service physical activity instructors for the disabled toward participating in pro bono work because future pro bono plans can be predicted. The demographic characteristics of participants in this study are outlined in Table 1.

Table 1. Demographic characteristics of participants.

Classification	Content	N	Percentage (%)
Gender	Male	209	64.9
	Female	113	35.1
Grade	Freshman	34	10.6
	Sophomore	107	33.2
	Junior	115	35.7
	Senior	66	20.5

2.2. Research Instrument

In order to develop a scale to explore and analyzing the intentions of pre-service physical activity instructors regarding pro bono participation, a survey which targeted university students from the department of adapted physical activity was conducted regarding the intention of participating in pro bono work for the promotion of physical activity for the disabled. A questionnaire was prepared based on Ajzen's "Constructing a theory of planned behavior questionnaire" [28]. In particular, in order to analyze the intention toward participating in pro bono work as accurately as possible, the question content and method were established based on the Theory of Planned Behavior and previous studies, and the final question was validated through consultation with experts. Based on the variables of the pre-service physical activity instructor's participation intention with respect to pro bono work derived through these questionnaires and expert opinions, a measure of the pre-service physical activity instructor's pro bono participation intention for promoting physical activity for the disabled was developed.

The Theory of Planned Behavior used in the questionnaire to develop the measure of intention for pre-service physical activity instructors to participate in pro bono work is a total of four variables: intention, behavioral belief, normative belief, and control belief. Among the variables of the questionnaire, the intention was a measure of "intention toward participating in Pro Bono", and the behavioral belief was a measure of "the degree of belief that certain outcomes may occur due to behavior in Pro Bono participation". The normative belief was a measure of "perceived groups and people with respect to Pro Bono behavior", and the control belief was a measure of "helping and hindering the practice of Pro Bono behaviors" [27,28]. In addition, this questionnaire used a 5-point Likert scale (e.g., 1 = strongly agree, 2 = agree, 3 = neither disagree or agree, 4 = disagree, and 5 = strongly disagree).

2.3. Research Process

In order to develop a questionnaire on the intention of pre-service physical activity instructors toward participating in pro bono work for the promotion of sports for the disabled, analysis of the literature and prior research were first investigated. Based on the collected data, modifications were made to fit Ajzen's sample questionnaire [28], and the pilot questionnaire was completed after review by 5 experts who study in the field of adapted physical activity and are faculty members at universities in South Korea. The completed questionnaire was distributed to 100 pre-service physical activity instructors, the collected data were used to evaluate the validity and reliability of the questionnaire, and the results were derived. Another expert meeting was held to discuss the derived results, and the questionnaire for this study was distributed to the study participants based on the completed questionnaire. This process was verified through the institutional review board (IRB) approval of Korea Nazarene University, and the questionnaire scale was developed for this study through the questionnaire validity and reliability test process based on the collected data.

2.4. Data Analysis

In this study, the exploratory factor analysis (EFA) was performed using SPSS 21.0 to confirm the validity of the measurement tool. The maximum likelihood method was used for factor extraction, and square rotation was used for factor rotation. To verify the relationship between latent and observed variables, confirmatory factor analysis (CFA) was performed using AMOS 21.0, and the significance level was set to $\alpha = 0.05$. The maximum likelihood method was used for the estimation method, and x2, Q, the root mean square residual (RMR), Tucker–Lewis index (TLI), comparative fit index (CFI), and normed fit index (NFI) were used for the selection of goodness-of-fit. In addition, conceptual reliability and mean variance extraction were analyzed in the process of confirming factor analysis to verify the reliability of internal consistency. Cronbach's alpha was used for the internal reliability analysis, and the significance level was set as $\alpha = 0.05$. Cronbach's alpha required 0.8 or higher for reliability.

3. Results

3.1. The Results of the EFA of the Pilot Questionnaire

The data of the pilot questionnaire for developing and validating a scale for predicting the pro bono participation intention of physical activity instructors for people with disabilities were randomly collected from 100 pre-service physical activity instructors in South Korea. The researchers conducted a series of EFA using SPSS 21.0 to identify the structure of the pilot questionnaire. The variables, measure of sampling adequacy, correlation matrix, and adequacy of factor analysis were calculated by the Kaiser-Meyer-Olkin (KMO) and Bartlett's Test of Sphericity [29]. In the EFA of the pilot questionnaire, the KMO for the measure of sampling adequacy was 0.935. A KMO value higher than 0.6 is considered good [30]. Bartlett's Test of Sphericity was significant (Bartlett's $\chi^2 = 6955.134$, df = 325, $p < 0.001$). In addition, the 68.625% of total variance was totally explained by 4 factors. The communality of retained questions ranged from 0.234 to 0.856 and the loadings of retained question ranged from −0.497 to 0.890. The variance of each factor was calculated as intention (16.534%), behavioral belief (18.636%), normative belief (18.667%), and control belief (14.788%). As a result, the questions of the communality or loading of less than 0.40

(e.g., Q1, Q25) and high multicollinearity were eliminated to improve the structure of the questionnaire. Therefore, the variables, measure of sampling adequacy, correlation matrix, and adequacy of factor analysis were appropriate to determine the purpose of this study. However, the final EFA, CFA, and internal reliability were conducted to enhance the factor structure (e.g., factor loading, internal consistency of factors) of the questionnaire. The results of the EFA of the pilot questionnaire are in Table 2.

Table 2. The results of the EFA of the pilot questionnaire.

No	Factors				Communality
	Intention	Behavioral Belief	Normative Belief	Control Belief	
Q1	0.199	0.034	0.890	0.131	0.324
Q2	0.103	0.079	0.873	0.176	0.790
Q3	0.180	0.069	0.853	0.163	0.789
Q4	0.148	0.118	0.831	0.167	0.809
Q5	0.208	0.171	0.807	0.236	0.856
Q6	0.219	0.263	0.638	0.302	0.839
Q7	0.269	0.849	0.127	0.194	0.505
Q8	0.252	0.829	0.128	0.234	0.820
Q9	0.166	0.811	0.099	0.330	0.806
Q10	0.256	0.799	0.076	0.331	0.790
Q11	0.312	0.775	0.157	0.258	0.849
Q12	0.286	0.617	0.146	0.143	0.824
Q13	0.805	0.287	0.296	0.191	0.755
Q14	0.803	0.283	0.147	0.203	0.812
Q15	0.775	0.121	0.373	0.232	0.792
Q16	0.770	0.273	0.308	0.159	0.852
Q17	0.761	0.283	0.360	0.221	0.781
Q18	−0.497	−0.271	0.057	−0.018	0.617
Q19	0.149	0.129	0.161	0.710	0.613
Q20	0.234	0.270	0.191	0.696	0.433
Q21	0.266	0.326	0.145	0.660	0.571
Q22	0.278	0.416	0.115	0.641	0.634
Q23	−0.041	0.057	0.234	0.602	0.676
Q24	0.178	0.133	0.208	0.582	0.650
Q25	0.342	0.400	0.216	0.537	0.234
Q26	−0.013	0.270	0.042	0.398	0.423
Total	4.299	4.845	4.853	3.845	
%Variance	16.534	18.636	18.667	14.788	
%Cumulative	16.534	35.170	53.837	68.625	

3.2. The Results of the EFA of the Final Questionnaire

The data in the final questionnaire were collected from 322 pre-service physical activity instructors in South Korea to develop and validate a scale for predicting the pro bono participation intention of physical activity instructors for people with disabilities. The final EFA was conducted to determine the structure of the final questionnaire. In the EFA of the final questionnaire, the KMO for the measure of sampling adequacy was 0.928. Bartlett's Test of Sphericity was significant (Bartlett's χ^2 = 5494.070, df = 153, $p < 0.001$). Further, the 80.312% of total variance was totally explained by 4 factors. The communality of retained questions ranged from 0.612 to 0.880 and the loadings of retained question ranged from 0.539 to 0.887 in all factors. The variance of each factor was calculated as intention (18.115%), behavioral belief (24.358%), normative belief (23.271%), and control belief (14.568%). Cronbach's alpha coefficients for intention, behavioral belief, normative belief, and control belief were 0.940, 0.948, 0.938, and 0.856. Therefore, the variables, measure of sampling adequacy, correlation matrix, and adequacy of factor analysis were improved and appropriate to identify the purpose of this study. The results of the EFA of the final questionnaire are in Table 3.

Table 3. The results of the EFA of the final questionnaire.

No	Factors				Communality
	Intention	Behavioral Belief	Normative Belief	Control Belief	
Q3	0.791	0.314	0.259	0.158	0.818
Q4	0.805	0.160	0.332	0.235	0.841
Q5	0.823	0.314	0.241	0.211	0.880
Q6	0.789	0.307	0.309	0.241	0.871
Q8	0.209	0.815	0.073	0.332	0.825
Q9	0.122	0.825	0.108	0.323	0.812
Q10	0.291	0.791	0.137	0.262	0.800
Q11	0.249	0.878	0.110	0.175	0.877
Q12	0.226	0.869	0.124	0.198	0.862
Q13	0.158	0.136	0.856	0.123	0.793
Q14	0.142	0.089	0.887	0.130	0.832
Q15	0.216	0.082	0.851	0.138	0.798
Q16	0.246	0.054	0.884	0.100	0.856
Q17	0.261	0.174	0.785	0.202	0.757
Q19	0.290	0.423	0.238	0.539	0.612
Q22	0.202	0.318	0.163	0.735	0.710
Q23	0.225	0.393	0.122	0.732	0.758
Q24	0.167	0.252	0.222	0.782	0.754
Total	3.261	4.384	4.189	2.622	
%Variance	18.115	24.358	23.271	14.568	
%Cumulative	18.115	42.473	65.744	80.312	
Cronbach α	0.940	0.948	0.938	0.856	

3.3. The Results of the CFA

A series of CFA were conducted to identify a relationship between the theory of planned behavior and variables in this study to support the structure of the questionnaire based on the relevant theory. In addition, the CFA was used to identify the adequacy of the model fit to the data. In the first CFA, the indexes of RMR, TLI, CFI, and NFI were calculated as RMR (0.051), TLI (0.912), CFI (0.923), and NFI (0.897). According to the researchers (30–32), the value of 0.05 or lower for RMR and the value of 0.09 or higher for TLI, CFI, and NFI were stated as a good model fit. However, the indexes of RMR and NFI did not meet this standard. As a result, six questions (Q2, Q7, Q18, Q20, Q21, Q26) were eliminated due to the low values of these questions in the squared multiple correlation (SMC), high multicollinearity, and modification index. In the final CFA, the indexes of RMR, TLI, CFI, and NFI were improved as follows: RMR (0.038), TLI (0.929), CFI (0.940), and NFI (0.919). The results of model fit of the series of CFA are in Table 4. The diagram of results of the measurement model is in Figure 1. Furthermore, all questions for each factor were measured to be significant (e.g., $p < 0.001$) based on the results of CFA. The results of CFA are in Table 5. Therefore, these index values can be predictable for the adequacy of validity of scale in the questionnaire and model fit.

Table 4. The results of model fit index of a series of CFA.

Classification	Goodness of Fit		
	Results of the First CFA		Results of the Final CFA
RMR	0.051	→	0.038
TLI	0.912	→	0.929
CFI	0.923	→	0.940
NFI	0.897	→	0.919

Table 5. The results of CFA.

Classification	Estimate	S.E.	C.R.
Intention → Q3	0.951	0.040	23.714 ***
Intention → Q4	0.952	0.039	24.484 ***
Intention → Q5	0.994	0.035	28.034 ***
Intention → Q6	1.000		
Behavioral Belief → Q8	0.939	0.038	24.796 ***
Behavioral Belief → Q9	0.908	0.038	23.654 ***
Behavioral Belief → Q10	0.963	0.040	23.921 ***
Behavioral Belief → Q11	1.000		
Behavioral Belief → Q12	0.942	0.034	27.702 ***
Normative Belief → Q13	0.914	0.042	21.823 ***
Normative Belief → Q14	0.928	0.040	23.348 ***
Normative Belief → Q15	0.933	0.039	23.829 ***
Normative Belief → Q16	1.000		
Normative Belief → Q17	0.847	0.039	21.782 ***
Control Belief → Q19	0.989	0.074	13.410 ***
Control Belief → Q22	0.993	0.073	13.511 ***
Control Belief → Q23	1.083	0.074	14.624 ***
Control Belief → Q24	1.000		

Note. S.E. = standard error, C.R. = construct reliability, *** $p < 0.001$.

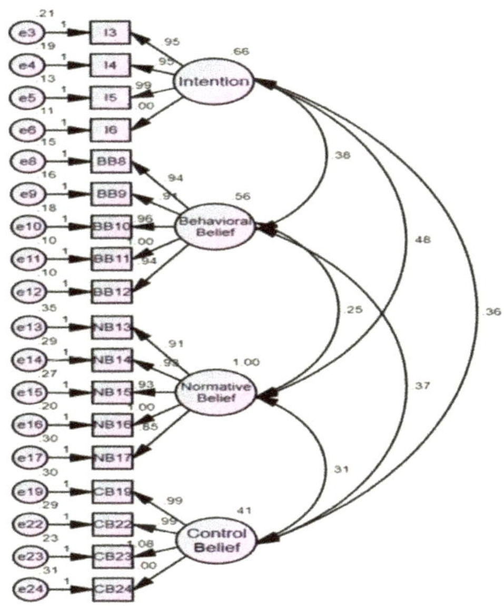

Figure 1. The diagram of results of the measurement model.

3.4. The Questions for Each Factor in the Final Questionnaire

The final questionnaire was developed and validated after the series of EFA and CFA to predict the behavioral intention of physical activity instructors for people with disabilities to participate in pro bono work based on the Theory of Planned Behavior. The questions for each factor in the final questionnaire are in Table 6.

Table 6. The questions for each factor in the final questionnaire.

Factor	No	Question
Intention	Q3	I strongly agree to participate in Pro Bono for the physical activity of people with disabilities.
	Q4	I will definitely participate in Pro Bono for the physical activity of people with disabilities.
	Q5	I will gladly participate in Pro Bono for the physical activity of people with disabilities.
	Q6	I will actively participate in Pro Bono for the physical activity of people with disabilities.
Behavioral Belief	Q8	Participating in Pro Bono for the physical activity of people with disabilities will require the teaching experience about physical activity for the disabled.
	Q9	Participating in Pro Bono for the physical activity of people with disabilities will require the theoretical learning about physical activity for the disabled that I have learned so far.
	Q10	My time effort to participate in Pro Bono for the physical activity of people with disabilities will be worthwhile.
	Q11	Physical activity coaching experience for people with disabilities will be valuable to participate in Pro Bono for physical activity.
	Q12	The knowledge of physical activity for people with disabilities will be valuable to participate in Pro Bono for physical activity.
Normative Belief	Q13	Parents of people with disabilities will think that I should participate in Pro Bono for the physical activity of people with disabilities.
	Q14	People with disabilities will think that I should participate in Pro Bono for the physical activity of people with disabilities.
	Q15	My family members will think that I should participate in Pro Bono for the physical activity of people with disabilities.
	Q16	My friends would think that I should participate in Pro Bono for the physical activity of people with disabilities.
	Q17	Students in my department will think that I should participate in Pro Bono for the physical activity of people with disabilities.
Control Belief	Q19	Physical activity instructors for people with disabilities must be able to participate in Pro Bono, which provides physical activity services for people with disabilities.
	Q22	Participation in Pro Bono providing physical activity services for people with disabilities depends on the mind of physical activity instructors for people with disabilities.
	Q23	Physical activity instructors for people with disabilities must be able to create an IEP (Individualized Education Plan) to participate in Pro Bono, which provides physical activity services for people with disabilities.
	Q24	Physical activity instructors for people with disabilities must have the ability to do physical activity to participate in Pro Bono, which provides physical activity services for people with disabilities.

4. Discussion

The purpose of this study was to develop and validate the scale for predicting the pro bono participation intention of pre-service physical activity instructors for persons with disabilities based on the Theory of Planned Behavior. Results were obtained relating to questionnaire scale development and validation for pre-service physical activity instructors for persons with disabilities participating in pro bono work. First, the questionnaire about "Intention Toward Participating in Pro Bono of Pre-service Physical Activity Instructors for the Activation of Physical Activity for the Disabled" was validated based on the Theory of Planned Behavior. In addition, there were four results based on the questionnaire; first, most participants in this study agreed to participate in pro bono work for the physical activity of people with disabilities, and the negative questions about Pro Bono participation have been eliminated due to disagreement of participants. This may be because the all participants in this study are majoring in an area closely related to physical activity for the disabled. Second, the teaching experience about physical activity for the disabled and the knowledge about physical activity for the disabled were required to participate in pro bono work for the physical activity of people with disabilities. Third, some people (e.g., parents of people with disabilities, people with disabilities, family members, friends, students in my department) may believe that pre-service physical activity instructors for the disabled should participate in pro bono work for the physical activity of people with disabilities. Fourth, some elements (e.g., the state of mind of physical activity instructors for people with disabilities, the ability to create an IEP, the ability to do physical activity) can be encouraged to control pro bono participation. The discussion based on the results is as follows:

First, it suggested that this questionnaire based on the Theory of Planned Behavior was appropriate to identify pre-service physical activity instructors' intention toward participating in pro bono work for people with disabilities. This questionnaire was categorized by Ajzen's "Constructing a theory of planned behavior questionnaire" [28–32]. Ajzen's guideline made it appropriate and valid to create the questionnaire. Furthermore, many studies related to physical activity instructors for persons with disabilities based on the Theory of Planned Behavior were conducted for development and validity of a scale measuring their behavioral intention. For instance, Jeong and Block [33] investigated general physical education teachers' intentions to teach students with disabilities. Lee, Yun, So [25], Rizzo, So, and Tripp [34], and Tripp and Rizzo [35] determined physical education teachers' intentions to teach people with disabilities. These researchers reported that the questionnaire used in their studies had an applicable and valid scale to determine the purpose of their studies. Eventually, it was possible to confirm their valid and reliable results, even though the purpose of the study was different, as stated by the previous studies related to this study.

Second, in regard to behavioral belief, teaching experience and knowledge about people with disabilities can help instructors participate in pro bono work for the physical activity of people with disabilities. It can be correlated to the results of a study [35] which found that physical education teachers who had teaching experience with students with disabilities had higher intentions to teach disabled students than those with no teaching experience in an inclusive physical education environment. In particular, many researchers reported that experiences with students with disabilities are significant for successful physical activity [36,37]. In addition, one study stated that pre-service physical education teachers with more education (e.g., undergraduate courses about children with disability) and information about students with disabilities had a positive attitude toward teaching students with disabilities [36]. Hence, it is deduced that experience with and knowledge of teaching the disabled are important factors in behavioral belief toward participating in pro bono work regarding physical activity of the disabled. Furthermore, it is determined that a study on whether these factors lead to actual behavior is needed.

Third, parents of people with disabilities, people with disabilities, family members, friends, and students in my department were the people who had a lot of influence on my participation in pro bono work for the physical activity of people with disabilities. The participants of this study were all university students studying as pre-service physical activity instructors. University students show high interest in human rights and social issues such as topics around persons with disabilities. [38]. In particular, one study [39] reported that many university students argue that equal opportunities should be provided to persons with disabilities, and this argument is evidence that students are sensitive to social pressures (i.e., demand of parents of people with disabilities or people with disabilities). In addition, some researchers [40] reported that parents and friends of university students play the most important roles in determining the behavior of university students who are in early adulthood, as they understand and help university students. Thus, these factors (i.e., parents of people with disabilities, people with disabilities, family members, friends, students in my department) must have had a lot of influence on the behavior of the pre-service physical activity instructors to participate in pro bono work, and it is necessary to find out what kind of influence they had.

Fourth, the state of mind of physical activity instructors for people with disabilities, the ability to create the IEP, and the ability to do physical activity can help to control the pro bono participation of physical activity instructors for people with disabilities. In the Theory of Planned Behavior, there is a correlation between each factor, and control belief and intention also have a correlation [26–28]. A willingness to do something can be interpreted as a person's state of mind and determination. Consequently, the control belief may be different depending on the person's mindset. The IEP is an educational program that comprises all areas of education, including educational goals, teaching, and evaluation for the education of students with disabilities based on the abilities of individual students with disabilities [41,42]. Furthermore, physical activity instructors can teach well if they know how to perform the physical activity they need to teach. These abilities (e.g., the ability to create the IEP and to perform physical activity) can increase the self-efficacy of instructors, and self-efficacy can improve self-confidence and control their behavior [43]. Then, it is necessary to find ways to improve these elements (e.g., the state of mind of physical activity instructors for people with disabilities, the ability to create an IEP, and the ability to do physical activity) to control successful behavior.

5. Research Limitations

There are some limitations. First, this study was conducted only by university students majoring in adapted physical activity, so it may be difficult to apply it in the actual field. Thus, future research should be conducted for physical activity instructors in the actual field. Second, this study was conducted only with participants in South Korea, so there may be cultural differences. Hence, it is necessary to expand the criteria for participants in future studies. Third, this study was conducted targeting pre-service physical activity instructors. It was not possible to know the actual participation in pro bono work. Consequently, in future studies, it is necessary to check whether the behavior was actually performed through a longitudinal study.

6. Conclusions

This study developed and validated a scale for predicting the pro bono participation intention of physical activity instructors for people with disabilities based on the Theory of Planned Behavior. The conclusions are as follows: first, the questionnaire developed in this study was validated based on the Theory of Planned Behavior. Second, the behavioral belief of participants was influenced by their teaching experience in physical activity for the disabled and knowledge about physical activity for the disabled. Third, the normative belief was influenced by the parents of people with disabilities, people with disabilities, family members, friends, and students in my department. Fourth, the control belief was influenced by the state of mind of physical activity instructors for people with disabilities, the ability to create an IEP, and the ability to do physical activity.

Author Contributions: Conceptualization, K.K. and Y.L.; Methodology, K.K.; Software, K.K.; Formal analysis, K.K.; Investigation, K.K. and Y.L.; Resources, K.K. and Y.L.; Data curation, K.K. and Y.L.; Writing—review and editing, K.K. All authors have read and agreed to the published version of the manuscript.

Funding: This work was supported by the Ministry of Education of the Republic of Korea and the National Research Foundation of Korea (NRF-2020S1A5B5A16082558).

Institutional Review Board Statement: The study approved by the Institutional Review Board of Korea Nazarene University (IRB approval no. IRB-Korea Nazarene University-2021-4).

Informed Consent Statement: Informed consent was obtained from all subjects involved in the study.

Data Availability Statement: The original contributions presented in the study are included in the article. Further inquiries can be directed to the corresponding author.

Conflicts of Interest: The authors declare no conflict of interest.

References

1. Korea Ministry of Health and Welfare. The Number of Registered Disabled People in South Korea. Available online: https://www.mohw.go.kr/react/jb/sjb030301ls.jsp?PAR_MENU_ID=03&MENU_ID=0321&SEARCHKEY=TITLE&SEARCHVALUE=%EC%9E%A5%EC%95%A0%EC%9D%B8 (accessed on 5 September 2022).
2. GBD 2017 Disease and Injury Incidence and Prevalence Collaborators. Global, regional, and national incidence, prevalence, and years lived with disability for 354 diseases and injuries for 195 countries and territories, 1990–2017: A systematic analysis for the Global Burden of Disease Study 2017. *Lancet* **2018**, *392*, 10–16.
3. World Health Organization. Congenital Anomalies. Available online: https://www.who.int/health-topics/congenital-anomalies#tab=tab_1 (accessed on 5 September 2022).
4. Korea Ministry of Health and Welfare. 2018 the Epidemiological Survey of Mental Disorders in Korea. Available online: http://www.bgnmh.go.kr/bgnmh/board/bgnmhHtmlView.jsp?menu_cd=BM_02_02_00_01&no=315 (accessed on 5 September 2022).
5. Choi, H.; Bai, P.; Lee, H. Association between away-from-home meals and hypertension in Korean adults: Analyzing data from the Korean National Health and Nutrition Examination Survey 2016–2017. *Korean J. Fam. Pract.* **2019**, *9*, 520–526. [CrossRef]
6. Koo, K.M.; Kim, K. Effects of physical activity on the stress and suicidal ideation in Korean adult women with depressive disorder. *Int. J. Environ. Res. Public Health* **2020**, *17*, 3502. [CrossRef] [PubMed]
7. Korea Ministry of Culture, Sports and Tourism. 2018 Survey on the Participation of Sports for the Disabled. Available online: https://www.mcst.go.kr/kor/s_policy/dept/deptView.jsp?pSeq=1730&pDataCD=0406000000&pType= (accessed on 5 September 2022).
8. Kang, B.; Baek, S. The effects of self-efficacy on professionalism and job satisfaction from instructors for disability sport. *Korean J. Adapt. Phys. Act.* **2014**, *22*, 47–59.
9. Junker, L.; Carlberg, E.B. Factors that affect exercise participation among people with physical disabilities. *Adv. Physiother.* **2011**, *13*, 18–25. [CrossRef]
10. Granfield, R.; Mather, L. *Private Lawyers and the Public Interest: The Evolving Role of Pro Bono in the Legal Profession*; Oxford University Press: Oxford, UK, 2009.
11. Choi, E.; Lee, J. The case study on the design Pro Bono: Focused on personal participation. *Arch. Des. Res.* **2012**, *10*, 72–73.
12. Shim, M.; Park, J. An exploratory study on Pro Bono sustainability. *Korean J. Contents.* **2016**, *16*, 211–223. [CrossRef]
13. Yun, J. A study on the Pro Bono activation plan for sustainable beauty. *J. Korean Converg. Soc.* **2018**, *9*, 403–415.
14. Lee, B. A study on the legislative cases of the state-based litigations -focused on the Pro Bono system. *Korean J. Law Res.* **2018**, *34*, 3–26. [CrossRef]
15. Bonilla Maldonado, D. The mandarins of the law Pro Bono legal work from a comparative perspective. *Indiana J. Glob. Leg. Stud.* **2020**, *27*, 131–188. [CrossRef]
16. Duncan, D. Easing conflict rules for brief Pro Bono legal advice: A small rule change regarding free legal advice could improve lawyer-community relations and improve access to legal services in Utah. *Utah Bar J.* **2019**, *32*, 24–26.
17. Kang, H.; Kim, W. The effects of disabled sports game volunteers' relationship commitment on disability acceptance attitude and perspective-taking ability. *Korean J. Sport Soc.* **2015**, *13*, 179–189.
18. Kim, Y.S. A study on the structural relationship among motives for volunteering for disabled sports, self-efficacy and career maturity. *Korean J. Adapt. Phys. Act.* **2019**, *27*, 113–126.
19. Park, H.; Kwon, W. The influence of university student volunteers' participation motivation to take adapted physical activity class on role conflict and pride. *Korean J. Adapt. Phys. Act.* **2014**, *22*, 33–45.
20. Sim, T.Y.; Park, J. The effect of participation in volunteer activities at sports events for the disabled on the perceptions, receptive attitudes, and physical activity values of university students regarding the disabled. *Korean J. Sport Soc.* **2019**, *17*, 1463–1474.

21. Cho, H.I.; Kim, J.T.; Shin, Y.A. The causal relationship among awareness of inclusive physical activity, physical activity value, and instruction attitude in undergraduates participating in adapted physical service activity. *Korean J. Adapt. Phys. Act.* **2013**, *21*, 69–80.
22. Kim, J.H.; Kim, K. Development and validation of a scale measuring intention of going to a disability mega sport event: Based on the Theory of Planned Behavior. *Korean J. Sport Leis. Stud.* **2018**, *73*, 391–405. [CrossRef]
23. Park, S.G.; Lee, H.S. Verification of predictive model of mutual cooperative behavior of disabilities without disability for students with disability in inclusive physical education setting using the Theory of Planned Behavior. *Korean J. Adapt. Phys. Act.* **2012**, *20*, 15–28.
24. Lee, H.S. Analysis of Model of Sport for All Participate Behavior with People with Physical Disabilities Applied to the TPB. *Korean J. Alliance Health Phys. Educ. Recreat. Danc.* **2012**, *51*, 431–440.
25. Lee, H.S.; Yun, S.M.; So, H.S. The Study of Physical Educators' Intention Toward Teaching Individuals with Disabilities: Validity and Relationship of Factors about PEITID-II-PS. *Korean J. Adapt. Phys. Act.* **2007**, *15*, 183–205.
26. Fishbein, M.; Ajzen, I. Misconceptions about the Fishbein model: Reflections on a study by Songer-Nocks. *J. Exp. Soc. Psychol.* **1975**, *12*, 579–584. [CrossRef]
27. Ajzen, I. The theory of planned behavior. *Organ. Behav. Hum. Decis. Process.* **1991**, *50*, 179–211. [CrossRef]
28. Ajzen, I. Constructing a Theory of Planned Behavior Questionnaire: Conceptual and Methodological Considerations. Available online: http://people.umass.edu/aizen/pdf/tpb.measurement.pdf (accessed on 5 September 2022).
29. Bartlett, M.S. Properties of sufficiency and statistical tests. *Math. Phys. Sci. Ser. A* **1937**, *160*, 268–282.
30. Hooper, D.; Coughlan, J.; Mullen, M.R. A study of a measure of sampling adequacy for factor-analytic correlation matrices. *Multivar. Behav. Res.* **2008**, *6*, 53–60.
31. Kline, R.B. *Principles and Practice of Structural Equation Modeling*, 3rd ed.; Guilford Press: New York, NY, USA, 2010.
32. Tucker, L.R.; Lewis, C. A reliability coefficient for maximum likelihood factor analysis. *Psychometrika* **1973**, *38*, 1–10. [CrossRef]
33. Jeong, M.; Block, M.E. Physical education teachers' beliefs and intentions toward teaching students with disabilities. *Res. Q. Exerc. Sport* **2011**, *82*, 239–246. [CrossRef] [PubMed]
34. Rizzo, T.L.; So, H.; Tripp, A. Validation of the physical educators' intentions toward teaching individuals with disabilities II preservice survey [Abstract]. *Res. Q. Exerc. Sport* **2007**, *78*, 102–103.
35. Tripp, A.; Rizzo, T. Disability labels affect physical educators. *Adapt. Phys. Act. Q.* **2006**, *23*, 310–326. [CrossRef]
36. Di Nardo, M.; Kudláček, M.; Tafuri, D.; Sklenaříková, J. Attitudes of preservice physical educators toward individuals with disabilities at University Parthenope of Napoli. *Acta Gymnica* **2014**, *44*, 211–221. [CrossRef]
37. Martin, K.; Kudláček, M. Attitudes of preservice teachers in an Australian University toward inclusion of students with physical disabilities in general physical education programs. *Eur. J. Adapt. Phys. Act.* **2010**, *3*, 30–48. [CrossRef]
38. Feeley, T.H. College students' knowledge, attitudes, and behaviors regarding organ donation: An integrated review of the literature. *J. Appl. Soc. Psychol.* **2007**, *37*, 243–271. [CrossRef]
39. Park, M.; Yoh, T.; Choi, Y.S.; Hums, M. Exploring attitudes toward the Paralympic games and its corporate sponsors. In Proceedings of the North American Society for the Sociology of Sport Conference (NASSS), Ottawa, ON, Canada, 4–7 November 2009.
40. Potwarka, L.R.; Nunkoo, R.; McCarville, R.E. Understanding television viewership of a mega event: The case of the 2010 Winter Olympics. *J. Hosp. Mark. Manag.* **2014**, *23*, 536–563. [CrossRef]
41. Block, M.E. *A Teachers' Guide to Including Children with Disabilities into General Physical Education*, 3rd ed.; Paul H. Brookes: Baltimore, MD, USA, 2007.
42. Winnick, J.P. *Adapted Physical Education and Sport*, 5th ed.; Human Kinetics: Champaign, IL, USA, 2010.
43. Hutzler, Y.; Zach, S.; Gafni, O. Physical education students' attitudes and self-efficacy towards the participation of children with special needs in regular classes. *Eur. J Spec. Needs Educ.* **2005**, *20*, 309–327. [CrossRef]

healthcare

MDPI

Article

A Study on the Establishment of Physical Activity Environment for People with Disabilities in South Korea

Ah-Ra Oh [1] and Kyungjin Kim [2,*]

1 Department of Exercise Rehabilitation & Welfare, Gachon University, 191 Hombakmoero, Yeonsu-gu, Incheon 21936, Korea
2 Department of Adapted Physical Activity, Korea Nazarene University, Cheonan-si 31172, Korea
* Correspondence: kkij1004@gmail.com; Tel.: +82-10-6613-6708

Abstract: The purpose of this study was to analyze the relative importance and priority of what factors should be reflected in the administration to efficiently consider the needs of people with disabilities for the physical activity (PA) environment in South Korea. To achieve the purpose of the study, 32 experts (e.g., faculty members, administrators) with more than 5 years of experience with PA for people with disabilities were asked to prioritize the factors that should be reflected in the PA environment. The questionnaire consisted of 4 factors in the upper-layer (H2), 8 factors in the middle-layer (H3), and 38 items in the low-layer (H4). The research instrument was composed of a pairwise comparison of decision elements to analyze the priority. For the analysis of the questionnaire data, the relative importance and priority were analyzed using Expert Choice 2000, a solution dedicated to priority analysis. The results are as follows. The relative importance of H2 was determined by programs, instructors, facilities, and information. In the relative importance among H3, the program type was determined as the highest factor in the program, and instructor expertise was determined as the highest factor in the instructor. The type of facility was determined as the highest factor in the facility, and the information provider was determined as the highest factor in the information. As a result of analyzing the priority of H4, it was found that the program within the sports facilities had the highest priority.

Keywords: physical activity environment; people with disabilities; South Korea; relative importance; priority

check for updates

Citation: Oh, A.-R.; Kim, K. A Study on the Establishment of Physical Activity Environment for People with Disabilities in South Korea. *Healthcare* **2022**, *10*, 1638. https://doi.org/10.3390/healthcare10091638

Academic Editor: Felipe Aidar

Received: 3 August 2022
Accepted: 23 August 2022
Published: 27 August 2022

1. Introduction

Physical activity (PA) can be defined as any body movement generated by skeletal muscle that necessitates power expenditure [1]. According to the latest PA guidelines of the World Health Organization (WHO), adults around the world, including individuals with disabilities, benefit from health advantages and reduce health risks when they do more then 150 minutes of aerobic exercise per week with moderate intensity or vigorous intensity [1]. However, most adults around the world do not meet the PA guidelines of WHO [2]. On average, people with disabilities participate less in PA and are more sedentary than people without disabilities [3]. For instance, only about 50% of individuals with disabilities are active, compared to about 75% of people without disabilities in the United States [2]. In addition, only one-third of people with disabilities participate in sports, while two-thirds of individuals without disabilities participate in sports in the United States [4]. Only 12% of adults with physical disabilities participated in PA with moderate intensity or vigorous intensity [5].

According to data from the 2020 National Survey on the Current Status of Participation of Lifetime Sports for Persons with Disabilities, conducted by the Korea Ministry of Culture, Sports, and Tourism [6], the participation rate of PA for people with disabilities in South Korea was 24.9%, which is more than three times higher than 17.9% 10 years ago. Even though the participation rate of PA in 2021 has been lowered to 20.2% due to the Coronavirus Disease-19 (COVID-19) pandemic, this rate is expected to increase in the future [6]. The reason why PA is encouraged around the world is that engaging in PA immediately produces positive results for adults with disabilities [7]. It has been found that being provided opportunities to engage in PA can improve the quality of life for individuals with disabilities both physically and psychologically [8]. Moreover, PA participation among people with disabilities can prevent diseases and help to save the national health insurance finance [9].

Although the participation in PA of individuals with disabilities has many advantages, it is very low compared to the 60.8% participation rate of people without disabilities in South Korea [6]. Many people with disabilities participate in PA near or at home rather than at public PA-related facilities or social sports clubs for persons with disabilities [10]. However, as for the place of PA for people with disabilities in South Korea, the highest percentage was in a park or hiking trail near their home (61.5%), followed by their home (31.8%) [6]. Many people with disabilities participate in PA near or at home rather than at public PA-related facilities or social sports clubs for persons with disabilities, but there is little service support for individuals. The reason for this issue is that the analysis of the PA environment was insufficient and the needs of people with disabilities were not reflected [11].

In South Korea, studies are continuing to identify the needs of people with disabilities to facilitate their participation in PA or to investigate factors that make it difficult for them to actively participate in PA [11–15]. Summarizing the results of these studies, it is argued that, for the people with disabilities to participate more actively than previously in PA, their inner will to participate is significant, but rather than that, they demanded that the environment for participation in PA should be improved. Among the demands of persons with disabilities, the problems related to the expansion of public PA-related facilities and movement were found to be the biggest [6]. However, it cannot be concluded that there is not enough public PA-related facilities for people with disabilities to exercise at home and around the house. Participation in PA at home or around the house may be due to the characteristics of the type of disability, or it may be because the average age of the persons with disabilities has increased, or it may be because they simply enjoy taking a walk around the house. Thus, it is necessary to understand the cause from various angles and viewpoints from the perspective of individuals with disabilities, beyond the simple structure of expanding the public PA-related facilities for people with disabilities. In addition, creating an environment required by persons with disabilities will increase the satisfaction of people with disabilities and will continue to participate in PA.

Since the 1990s, the Australian Government has launched several policies to increase the participation of people with disabilities in recreation and sports [16]. Based on numerous research results, the Australian Government has made efforts to improve the environment and accessibility of open spaces, sports facilities, leisure, and swimming pools [17]. In the studies of the United States and the Netherlands, lack of motivation and experience of participating in PA or sports were individual barriers to participation in PA, such as environmental barriers, transportation and access to public PA-related facilities and cost were problems [18–21]. In addition, Moran, Taliaferro, and Pate [22] stated barriers to participation in PA for people with disabilities include lack of training knowledge and lack of programs for persons with disabilities. These studies include a long research period and the PA environment of persons with disabilities. Though, studies in South Korea that actively reflect the needs of people with disabilities and PA services have not yet been provided. Therefore, the purpose of this study was to determine the relative importance and priority for establishing the PA environment based on the opinions on the PA of persons with disabilities presented in a pilot study [23] and to introduce methods for successful access to the PA of people with disabilities in South Korea.

2. Materials and Methods

2.1. Participants

The purpose of this study was to identify the priority for establishment of the PA environment for persons with disabilities by reflecting the needs of people with disabilities. The participants of this study selected 32 disabled PA experts who understood the purpose of the study and agreed to participate in this study. The participants consisted of 12 faculty members who majored in PA with more than 5 years of research experience and 20 administrators who had worked at the Korea Paralympic Committee for more than 5 years. The reasons why the participants of this study were selected as faculty members and administrators of the Korean Paralympic Committee were that they were key experts in planning and implementing the administration of PA for people with disabilities in South Korea. The purpose of the study was explained to the participants of this research, and the PA environment for people with disabilities that should be developed first to reflect the needs of individuals with disabilities was investigated. The demographic characteristics of experts participating in this study are in Table 1.

Table 1. Demographic characteristics of participants.

No.	Classification	Gender	Years of Experience	Age
1	Faculty	Female	11	34
2	Faculty	Male	10	41
3	Faculty	Male	14	54
4	Faculty	Male	5	32
5	Faculty	Male	5	39
6	Faculty	Female	5	33
7	Faculty	Male	17	51
8	Faculty	Male	8	48
9	Faculty	Male	8	39
10	Faculty	Male	5	40
11	Faculty	Male	6	32
12	Faculty	Male	5	46
13	Administrator	Male	13	48
14	Administrator	Male	21	40
15	Administrator	Female	11	45
16	Administrator	Male	14	39
17	Administrator	Male	21	48
18	Administrator	Male	10	42
19	Administrator	Male	6	42
20	Administrator	Male	11	40
21	Administrator	Male	14	42
22	Administrator	Male	12	41
23	Administrator	Female	5	29
24	Administrator	Female	5	25
25	Administrator	Male	7	35
26	Administrator	Female	8	36
27	Administrator	Female	13	42
28	Administrator	Male	10	41
29	Administrator	Female	5	29
30	Administrator	Male	5	30
31	Administrator	Male	24	49
32	Administrator	Female	9	36

2.2. Research Instrument

The study extracted the relative importance and priority using the priority analysis method (i.e., analytic hierarchy process (AHP)) to investigate which needs of the people with disabilities in the field of PA and experts' thoughts should be reflected in the administration for PA environment for persons with disabilities. The questionnaire was constructed in the form of a pairwise comparison questionnaire for priority analysis [24]. The AHP is an analysis method that is often used in the process of collecting the opinions of experts. It is one of the decision-making methodologies that utilize the knowledge, experience, and intuition of respondents through binary comparison between factors forming a hierarchical structure of decision-making [25]. In other words, it is used as a scientific method for the decision-making method to reach final decision-making by dividing the entire decision-making process into stages and then analyzing and interpreting them step-by-step [26,27].

The research instrument of this study was based on the results of a focus group interview (e.g., 35 persons with disabilities in South Korea) conducted by the pilot study [23] on the needs of people with disabilities for PA in South Korea. A total of 38 key factors were extracted, and a questionnaire was prepared. The hierarchical structure of the questionnaire was shown in Figure 1. A group of experts (e.g., 3 faculties specializing in PA and 3 PA administrators for people with disabilities) checked the facial validity and composition of the questions for the questionnaire. As a result, there was hierarchy (H)1 for the establishment of the PA environment for persons with disabilities. The questionnaire consisted of 4 factors (e.g., program, instructor, facility, information: H2) in the upper-layer and 8 sup-factors (e.g., type of program, content of program, expertise of instructor, competency of instructor, type of facility, operation of facility, provider of information and content of information: H3) in the middle-layer. In the case of pairwise comparison, the response score of participants was 'equivalent' from 1 and 'average' to 'very important' from 2 to 7, so the factors of both poles were compared and selected.

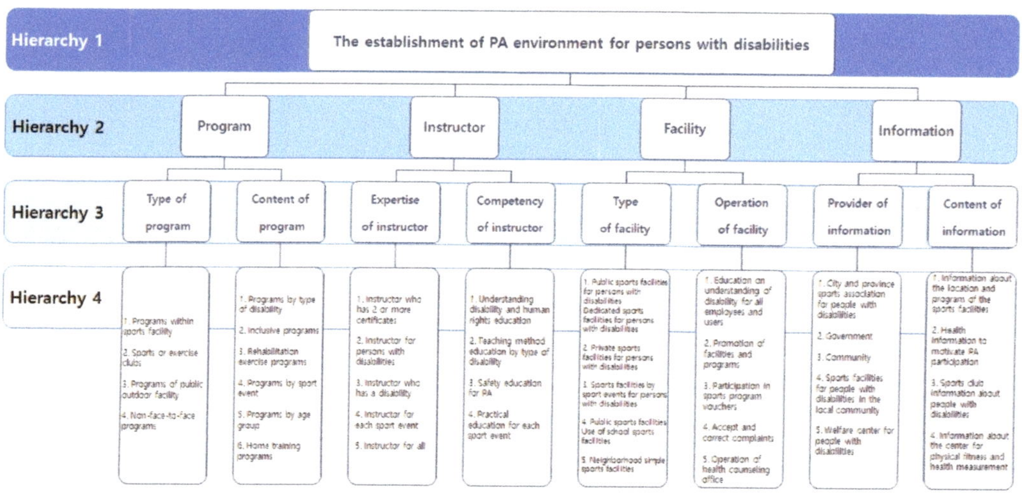

Figure 1. The hierarchical structure of the questionnaire.

2.3. Research Process

For the investigation of the study, the researchers first found two faculties based on PA for people with disabilities and two PA administrators in Korean Paralympic Committee. After that, the participants were secured by a snowball sampling method in which experts were introduced to other faculty members and PA administrators in Korean Paralympic Committee. A schedule was set with experts, and the purpose and contents of the study were explained to them. Since the pairwise comparison questionnaire is not a familiar questionnaire, the response method of the pairwise comparison was explained in detail. Participants in the study were asked to participate in the questionnaire, and the researchers collected it immediately after the questionnaire. In addition, the period of this study was 3 months from December 2021 to February 2022.

2.4. Data Analysis

The AHP was applied to analyze priorities for establishing the PA environment for people with disabilities. A hierarchical analysis is a method of calculating the relative importance between factors, and after identifying the hierarchical structure, priorities are selected through the analysis process [26,28]. The consistency index (CI) was verified to evaluate the logical contradiction of responses. The consistency is greater as the criterion of CI is closer to 0. In this study, consistency evaluation was conducted based on a value of 0.1 or less, which was generally accepted by previous studies [29,30]. As for the CI, when 0.1 or less appeared, it was confirmed that the consistency of the expert group for each question was high. The Expert Choice 2000 program was used to analyze priorities in this study.

3. Results

3.1. The Results of the Relative Importance of H2

In the relative importance of H2, the program showed the highest ranking as follows, followed by the instructor, facility, and information. The weight of the program was derived 38.9%, instructor (34.5%), facility (17.7%), and information (8.8%). The CI of the experts' responses was 0.07, indicating that the respondents' perceptions of the questions met consistency. The results of the relative importance of H2 for the establishment of the PA environment for people with disabilities are in Table 2.

Table 2. Results of the relative importance of H2 for the establishment of the PA environment for persons with disabilities.

Classification	Factor	CI	Order
The establishment of PA environment for persons with disabilities	Program	0.389	1
	Instructor	0.345	2
	Facility	0.177	3
	Information	0.088	4

Note: CI = 0.07.

3.1.1. The Results of the Relative Importance of the Program in H3

As for the relative importance of the program in H3, the type of program was the highest factor, followed by the content of the program. As for the degree of importance perception of priority, the weight for the type of program was analyzed as 79.6%, and the content of the program (20.4%). The CI of the experts' responses was 0.001, indicating that the respondents' perceptions of the questions met consistency. The results of the relative importance of the program among H3 are in Table 3.

Table 3. Results of the relative importance of the program in H3.

Classification	Factor	CI	Order
Program	Type of program	0.796	1
	Content of program	0.204	2

Note: CI = 0.001.

3.1.2. The Results of the Relative Importance of the Instructor in H3

As for the relative importance of the instructor in H3, the expertise of the instructor was the highest factor, followed by the competency of the instructor. As for the degree of importance perception of priority, the weight for the expertise of the instructor was analyzed as 73.1%, and the competency of the instructor (26.9%). The CI of the experts' responses was 0.001. The results of the relative importance of the instructor among H3 are in Table 4.

Table 4. Results of the relative importance of the instructor in H3.

Classification	Factor	CI	Order
Instructor	Expertise of instructor	0.731	1
	Competency of instructor	0.269	2

Note: CI = 0.001.

3.1.3. The Results of the Relative Importance of the Facility in H3

As for the relative importance of the facility in H3, the type of facility was the highest factor, followed by the operation of the facility. As for the degree of importance perception of priority, the weight for the type of facility was analyzed as 76.1%, and the operation of the facility (23.9%). The CI of the experts' responses was 0.001. The results of the relative importance of the facility among H3 are in Table 5.

Table 5. Results of the relative importance of the facility in H3.

Classification	Factor	CI	Order
Facility	Type of facility	0.761	1
	Operation of facility	0.239	2

Note: CI = 0.001.

3.1.4. The Results of the Relative Importance of the Information in H3

As for the relative importance of the information in H3, the provider of information was the highest factor, followed by the content of information. As for the degree of importance perception of priority, the weight for the provider of information was analyzed as 74.1%, and the content of information (25.9%). The CI of the experts' responses was 0.001. The results of the relative importance of the information among H3 are in Table 6.

Table 6. Results of the relative importance of the information in H3.

Classification	Factor	CI	Order
Information	Provider of information	0.741	1
	Content of information	0.259	2

Note: CI = 0.001.

3.2. The Results of the Relative Importance of H4 by H3

The results of the relative importance of low-layer (H4: e.g., programs within sports facility, sports or exercise clubs, programs of public outdoor facility, non-face-to-face programs, programs by type of disability, inclusive programs, rehabilitation exercise programs, programs by sport event, programs by age group, home training programs, instructor who has 2 or more certificates, instructor for persons with disabilities, instructor who has a disability, instructor for each sport event, instructor for all, understanding disability and human rights education, teaching method education by type of disability, safety education for PA, practical education for each sport event, public sports facilities for persons with disabilities, dedicated sports facilities for persons with disabilities, private sports facilities for persons with disabilities, sports facilities by sport events for persons with disabilities, public sports facilities, use of school sports facilities, neighborhood simple sports facilities, education on understanding of disability for all employees and users, promotion of facilities and programs, participation in sports program vouchers, accept and correct complaints, operation of health counseling office, city and province sports association for people with disabilities, government, community, sports facilities for people with disabilities in the local community, welfare center for people with disabilities, information about the location and program of the sports facilities, health information to motivate PA participation, sports club information about people with disabilities, information about the center for physical fitness and health measurement) by H3 were analyzed for the establishment of PA environment for persons with disabilities.

3.2.1. The Results of the Relative Importance of H4 by the Program in H3

As shown in Table 7, the results of the relative importance of H4 by the program in H3 included the composition of H4 by H3, weight, ranking, and CI. As a result of the analysis, first, as the relative importance of H4 in the type of program in H3, the weight for programs within sports facilities was 40.7%, sports or exercise clubs for individuals with disabilities (25.3%), programs of public outdoor facilities (24.7%), and non-face-to-face (e.g., YouTube, etc.) programs (9.3%). The CI of responses of the experts in this study was 0.01.

Table 7. Results of the relative importance of H4 by the program in H3.

Highest Factor	Sub-Factor	Sub-Item	Weight	Order	CI
Program	Type of program	Programs within sports facility	0.407	1	0.01
		Sports or exercise clubs	0.253	2	
		Programs of public outdoor facility	0.247	3	
		Non-face-to-face programs	0.093	4	
	Content of program	Programs by type of disability	0.302	1	0.01
		Inclusive programs	0.168	2	
		Rehabilitation exercise programs	0.164	3	
		Programs by sport event	0.162	4	
		Programs by age group	0.125	5	
		Home training programs	0.080	6	

Note: CI = 0.001.

As for the results of the relative importance of H4 by the content of the program in H3, the weight for programs by type of disability was 30.2%, inclusive (i.e., persons with and without disability) programs (16.8%), rehabilitation exercise programs (16.4%), program by sports events (16.2%), programs by age group (12.5%), and home training programs (8.0%). The CI of responses of the experts in this study was 0.01. The explanation of H4 by the program in H3 is in Table 8.

Table 8. Explanation of H4 by the program in H3.

Sub-Factor	Sub-Item	Explanation of Item
Type of program	Programs within sports facility	PA programs for people with disabilities in public and private sports facilities
	Sports or exercise clubs	PA programs in sports or exercise clubs for people with disabilities
	Programs of public outdoor facility	PA programs using public sports facilities in local parks
	Non-face-to-face programs	Non-face-to-face PA programs that can be performed at home
Content of program	Programs by type of disability	PA programs by type of disability
	Inclusive programs	PA programs for people with and without disabilities
	Rehabilitation exercise programs	Rehabilitation exercise programs that serve as a bridge to PA
	Programs by sport event	PA programs by each sport event
	Programs by age group	PA programs by age group
	Home training programs	PA programs that can be performed at home alone or with your family member

Note: CI = 0.001.

3.2.2. The Results of the Relative Importance of H4 by the Instructor in H3

As shown in Table 9, the results of the relative importance of H4 by the instructor in H3 included the composition of H4 by H3, weight, ranking, and CI. As a result of the analysis of instructor, first, as the relative importance of H4 in the expertise of instructor in H3, the weight for an instructor who has 2 or more certificates related to PA was 32.7%, instructor for persons with disabilities (29.2%), an instructor who has a disability (16.5%), instructor for each sport event (12.3%), and instructor for all (9.3%). The CI of responses of the experts in this study was 0.02.

Table 9. Results of the relative importance of H4 by the instructor in H3.

Highest Factor	Sub-Factor	Sub-Item	Weight	Order	CI
Instructor	Expertise of instructor	Instructor who has 2 or more certificates	0.327	1	0.02
		Instructor for persons with disabilities	0.292	2	
		Instructor who has a disability	0.165	3	
		Instructor for each sport event	0.123	4	
		Instructor for all	0.093	5	
	Competency of instructor	Understanding disability and human rights education	0.362	1	0.02
		Teaching method education by type of disability	0.334	2	
		Safety education for PA	0.154	3	
		Practical education for each sport event	0.151	4	

Note: CI = 0.001.

As for the results of the relative importance of H4 by the competency of instructor in H3, the weight for understanding disability and human rights education were 36.2%, teaching method education by type of disability (33.4%), safety education for PA (15.4%), and practical education for each sport event (15.1%). The CI of responses of the experts in this study was 0.02. The explanation of H4 by the instructor in H3 is in Table 10.

Table 10. Explanation of H4 by the instructor in H3.

Sub-Factor	Sub-Item	Explanation of Item
Expertise of instructor	Instructor who has 2 or more certificates	An instructor who has 2 or more certificates related to PA for all, people with disabilities, or athletes
	Instructor for persons with disabilities	An instructor who has a PA certificate for persons with disabilities
	Instructor who has a disability	An instructor who has a disability
	Instructor for each sport event	An instructor for each sport event
	Instructor for all	A PA instructor for all
Competency of instructor	Understanding disability and human rights education	Understanding the types of disability and reduce derogatory comments and discrimination through education on the human rights of persons with disabilities
	Teaching method education by type of disability	Teaching instructional methods suitable for the type of disability and teach communication methods (sign language, etc.)
	Safety education for PA	Improving the ability to cope with accidents that may occur during PA (ex. emergency rescue, etc.)
	Practical education for each sport event	Upgrading skills and knowledge about each sport event

Note: CI = 0.001.

3.2.3. The Results of the Relative Importance of H4 by the Facility in H3

As shown in Table 11, the results of the relative importance of H4 by the facility in H3 included the composition of H4 by H3, weight, ranking, and CI. As a result of the analysis, first, as the relative importance of H4 in the type of facility in H3, the weight for public sports facilities for persons with disabilities was 27.8%, dedicated sports facilities for persons with disabilities (22.3%), private sports facilities for persons with disabilities (14.8%), sports facilities by sports events for persons with disabilities (13.7%), public sports facilities (8.5%), use of school sports facilities (7.7%), and neighborhood simple sports facilities (5.3%). The CI of responses of the experts in this study was 0.01.

Table 11. Results of the relative importance of H4 by the facility in H3.

Highest Factor	Sub-Factor	Sub-Item	Weight	Order	CI
Facility	Type of facility	Public sports facilities for persons with disabilities	0.278	1	0.01
		Dedicated sports facilities for persons with disabilities	0.223	2	
		Private sports facilities for persons with disabilities	0.148	3	
		Sports facilities by sport events for persons with disabilities	0.137	4	
		Public sports facilities	0.085	5	
		Use of school sports facilities	0.077	6	
		Neighborhood simple sports facilities	0.053	7	
	Operation of facility	Education on understanding of disability for all employees and users	0.264	1	0.01
		Promotion of facilities and programs	0.261	2	
		Participation in sports program vouchers	0.199	3	
		Accept and correct complaints	0.154	4	
		Operation of health counseling office	0.123	5	

Note: CI = 0.001.

As for the results of the relative importance of H4 by the operation of facility in H3, the weight for education on understanding of disability for all employees and users was 26.4%, promotion of facilities and programs (26.1%), participation in sports program vouchers (19.9%), accept and correct complaints (15.4%), and operation of health counseling office (12.3%). The CI of responses of the experts in this study was 0.01. The explanation of H4 by the facility in H3 is in Table 12.

Table 12. Explanation of H4 by the facility in H3.

Sub-Factor	Sub-Item	Explanation of Item
Type of facility	Public sports facilities for persons with disabilities	A sports facility that people with disabilities prefer to use but can use together with people without disabilities
	Dedicated sports facilities for persons with disabilities	Sports facilities mainly used by people with disabilities
	Private sports facilities for persons with disabilities	A private sports facility that installs convenient facilities for people with disabilities and recruit members with disabilities
	Sports facilities by sport events for persons with disabilities	Sports facilities for people with disabilities specializing in sports
	Public sports facilities	Sports facilities created for residents
	Use of school sports facilities	School sports facilities opened as sports facilities for people with disabilities
	Neighborhood simple sports facilities	Sports equipment and facilities simply installed in community parks
Operation of facility	Education on understanding of disability for all employees and users	It is necessary to make it compulsory for employees and users to understand disability education so that users with disabilities can use it without discrimination
	Promotion of facilities and programs	Promotion of facility and program recruitment through text messages, SNS, website, etc. should be actively promoted
	Participation in sports program vouchers	It is necessary to prepare an environment in which sports program vouchers can be used.
	Accept and correct complaints	Efforts should be made to actively respond to and accept complaints when they are filed
	Operation of health counseling office	There is a need for a counseling office that can conduct and manage consultations on the health status of people with disabilities and how to maintain and improve their health in the future

Note: CI = 0.001.

3.2.4. The Results of the Relative Importance of the Information in H3

As shown in Table 13, the results of the relative importance of H4 by the information in H3 included the composition of H4 by H3, weight, ranking, and CI. As a result of the analysis of information, first, as the relative importance of H4 in the provider of information in H3, the weight for city and province sports association for people with disabilities was 26.1%, government (25.4%), community (19.7%), sports facilities for people with disabilities in the local community (15.4%), and welfare center for people with disabilities (13.4%). The CI of responses of the experts in this study was 0.01.

Table 13. Results of the relative importance of H4 by the information in H3.

Highest Factor	Sub-Factor	Sub-Item	Weight	Order	CI
Information	Provider of information	City and province sports association for people with disabilities	0.261	1	0.01
		Government	0.254	2	
		Community	0.197	3	
		Sports facilities for people with disabilities in the local community	0.154	4	
		Welfare center for people with disabilities	0.134	5	
	Content of information	Information about the location and program of the sports facilities	0.376	1	0.01
		Health information to motivate PA participation	0.232	2	
		Sports club information about people with disabilities	0.220	3	
		Information about the center for physical fitness and health measurement	0.171	4	

Note: CI = 0.001.

As for the results of the relative importance of H4 by the content of information in H3, the weight for information about the location and program of the sports facilities was 37.6%, health information to motivate PA participation (23.2%), sports club information about people with disabilities (22.0%), and information about the center for physical fitness and health measurement (17.1%). The CI of responses of the experts in this study was 0.01. The explanation of H4 by the information in H3 is in Table 14.

Table 14. Explanation of H4 by the information in H3.

Sub-Factor	Sub-Item	Explanation of Item
Provider of information	City and province sports association for people with disabilities	At the level of city and province sports associations for people with disabilities, health information should be provided to individuals with disabilities in the local community by text message or mail
	Government	The government should provide health information for people with disabilities through the mass media
	Community	Health information should be provided by text message or mail at the city hall or community center in the local community
	Sports facilities for people with disabilities in the local community	Health information should be provided to users with disabilities and their families in sports facilities
	Welfare centers for people with disabilities	Welfare centers should provide health information to users with disabilities and their families
Content of information	Information about the location and program of the sports facilities	Information on where and what programs are available for people with disabilities in the community
	Health information to motivate PA participation	Motivation of PA by providing information on PA and eating habits
	Sports club information about people with disabilities	Location and related information about sports clubs for people with disabilities and PA
	Information about the center for physical fitness and health measurement	Information on physical fitness certification center for people with disabilities

Note: CI = 0.001.

3.3. *The Results of the Priority of H4*

The results of the priority of H4 were analyzed for the establishment of the PA environment for individuals with disabilities. There was the priority of 1st to 40th of all H4. The priority of 1st to 40th of all H4 is in Table 15. The priority was as follows: programs within sports facilities (12.6%), instructor who has 2 or more certificates related to PA (8.2%), sports or exercise clubs for individuals with disabilities (7.9%), programs of public outdoor facilities (7.7%), instructor for persons with disabilities (7.4%), instructor who has a disability (4.2%), public sports facility for persons with disabilities (3.7%), education on understanding of disabilities and human rights (3.4%), instructor for each sport event (3.1%), teaching method education by type of disability (3.1%) and etc. The CI of responses of the experts in this study was 0.04.

Table 15. Results of the priority of H4.

Item	Weight	Order	Item	Weight	Order
Programs within sports facilities	0.126	1	Programs by sport event	0.013	21
Instructor who has 2 or more certificates related to PA	0.082	2	Inclusive programs	0.013	22
Sports or exercise clubs for individuals with disabilities	0.079	3	Rehabilitation exercise programs	0.013	23
Programs of public outdoor facilities	0.077	4	Community	0.013	24
Instructor for persons with disabilities	0.074	5	General public sports facilities	0.011	25
Instructor who has a disability	0.042	6	Promotion of facilities and programs	0.011	26
Public sports facility for persons with disabilities	0.037	7	Education on understanding of disability for all employees and users	0.011	27
Education on understanding of disabilities and human rights	0.034	8	Programs by age group	0.010	28
Instructor for each sport event	0.031	9	Use of school sports facilities	0.010	29
Teaching method education by type of disability	0.031	10	Sports facilities for people with disabilities in the local community	0.010	30
Public sports facility for persons with disabilities	0.030	11	Welfare centers for people with disabilities	0.009	31
Non-face-to-face programs	0.029	12	Information about the location and program of the sports facilities	0.009	32
Programs by type of disability	0.024	13	Participation in sports program vouchers	0.008	33
Instructor for all	0.024	14	Neighborhood simple sports facilities	0.007	34
Private sports facilities for persons with disabilities	0.020	15	Accept and correct complaints	0.007	35
Sports facilities by sport events for persons with disabilities	0.018	16	Home training programs	0.006	36
Government	0.017	17	Operation of health counseling office	0.005	37
City and province sports association for people with disabilities	0.017	18	Health information to motivate PA participation	0.005	38
Practical education for each sport event	0.014	19	Sports club information about people with disabilities	0.005	39
Safety education for PA	0.014	20	Information about the center for physical fitness and health measurement	0.004	40

Note: CI = 0.04.

4. Discussion

The aim of the study was to determine the relative importance and priority for the establishment of the PA environment for persons with disabilities by 32 experts with more than 5 years of experience with PA for people with disabilities. This study analyzed the relative importance and priority of establishing the PA environment based on the opinions on the PA of persons with disabilities offered in the pilot study. The relative importance and priority of establishing the PA environment for people with disabilities were analyzed by AHP. The discussion based on the results of the study was as follows; first, the results of the relative importance of H2 for the establishment of the PA environment for persons with disabilities was the rankings of program, instructor, facility, and information. The program was chosen as the highest factor in H2 to establish the PA environment for individuals with disabilities. However, there are no various PA programs for people with disabilities in South Korea. It may be helpful to motivate people with disabilities for participating in PA [23]. In both school and community settings, the PA programs for persons with disabilities are limited and require professional work [31]. For example, people with visual impairment cannot play regular baseball, but they can play it if they modify the game a little or modify the tool to put beads in the ball. Hence, modifying the program can be a successful key to participation in PA for people with disabilities [32]. After the program, it was found that the instructor was a key factor in establishing the PA environment. It was reported that learners' behavior or attitudes were affected by instructors' beliefs and values [33]. People with disabilities tend to rely on instructors due to various restrictions. This causes interference with the participation of persons with disabilities when the instructors negatively affect the participation of individuals with disabilities in PA [34]. The following factors included the facility and information. According to McGrath [8], it is important to provide playgrounds, leisure facilities, and swimming facilities to participate in sports and recreation for people with disabilities. In addition, the awareness of PA programs and sports facilities is essential for activating the PA of persons with disabilities [35]. The facilities should be built at the government level, and information can be obtained through individual efforts, so it is considered that the priority was lower than the factors of programs and instructors.

Second, the results of the relative importance of the program in H3 were the type of program and content of the program. The results of rankings of the relative importance of H4 by the type of program in H3 were programs within sports facilities, sports or exercise clubs, programs of public outdoor facilities, and non-face-to-face programs. The results of rankings of the relative importance of H4 by the content of the program in H3 were programs by type of disability, inclusive programs, rehabilitation exercise programs, programs by sports event, programs by age group, and home training programs. The highest item of H4 by the type of program in H3 was the programs within a sports facility. There are various PA programs (e.g., aqua aerobics, badminton, basketball, football, golf, table tennis, squash, swimming, volleyball, and weight training) for individuals without disabilities in more than 1070 facilities and swimming facilities in South Korea. However, the PA programs (e.g., badminton, boccia, goalball, swimming, table tennis, weight training) for people with disabilities are only played at about 70 sports facilities in South Korea [36]. These programs limit the participation in the PA for persons with disabilities and cannot satisfy their needs. Furthermore, the highest item of H4 by the content of the program in H2 was the programs by type of disability because it is necessary to modify the PA program according to the characteristics of the type of disability as in the baseball example of people with visual impairment. According to Disability Rights in the United Kingdom, inclusive PA programs should be provided for persons with and without disabilities to participate in PA [23]. Additionally, when providing PA programs reflecting the needs of people with disabilities, voluntary participation of individuals with disabilities is expected to increase and satisfaction might increase [37].

Third, the results of the relative importance of the instructor in H3 were the expertise of the instructor and competency of the instructor. The results of rankings of the relative importance of H4 by the expertise of instructor in H3 were instructor who has 2 or more certificates, instructor for persons with disabilities, instructor who has a disability, instructor for each sport event, instructor for all. The results of rankings of the relative importance of H4 by the competency of instructor in H3 were understanding disability and human rights education, teaching method education by type of disability, safety education for PA, practical education for each sport event. The highest item of H4 by the expertise of instructor and competency of instructor in H3 were the instructor who has 2 or more certificates related to PA and understanding disability and human rights education. The professionalism (i.e., formal training, knowledge, resources) of PA instructors who know the characteristics of people with disabilities and PA is very important due to the activation of PA for individuals with disabilities [38]. A study [39] found the teaching of an instructor with expertise has an important influence on the effectiveness of PA, and the results of only 6% of the experience of PA with a professional instructor indicate what the future direction is. In addition, the professionalism of the instructor can increase the satisfaction of the participants by providing high-quality classes to people with disabilities [38]. Finally, PA instructors should have expertise and knowledge about people with disabilities to effectively teach them.

Fourth, the results of the relative importance of the facility in H3 were the type of facility and operation of the facility. The results of rankings of the relative importance of H4 by the type of facility in H3 were public sports facilities for persons with disabilities, dedicated sports facilities for persons with disabilities, private sports facilities for persons with disabilities, sports facilities by sports events for persons with disabilities, public sports facilities, use of school sports facilities, and neighborhood simple sports facilities. The results of rankings of the relative importance of H4 by the operation of the facility in H3 were education on the understanding of disability for all employees and users, promotion of facilities and programs, participation in sports program vouchers, accept and correct complaints, and operation of a health counseling office. The highest item of H4 by the type of facility and operation of the facility in H3 was the public sports facilities for persons with disabilities and education on the understanding of disability for all employees and users. As mentioned earlier, sports facilities for persons with disabilities in South Korea are insufficient compared to sports facilities for people without disabilities [36]. Several studies [40,41] reported that environmental factors such as accessibility and convenience of sports facilities are very significant for PA and securing of sports facilities is essential in relation to PA of people with disabilities. Conclusively, the lack of sports facilities for people with disabilities indicates that they are not even provided with opportunities to participate in PA, and the lack of understanding about the disability of the employees can even destroy their reliance to participate in PA.

Fifth, the results of the relative importance of the information in H3 were the provider of information and content of information. The results of rankings of the relative importance of H4 by the provider of information in H3 were city and province sports association for people with disabilities, government, community, sports facilities for people with disabilities in the local community, and welfare center for people with disabilities. The results of rankings of the relative importance of H4 by the content of information in H3 were information about the location and program of the sports facilities, health information to motivate PA participation, sports club information about people with disabilities, and information about the center for physical fitness and health measurement. The highest relative importance of H4 by the provider of information and content of information in H3 was the city and province sports association for people with disabilities and information about the location and program of the sports facilities. The studies of Pia [42] and Lyusyena [43] stated that the right to know about persons with disabilities is very important, and the PA of individuals with disabilities has a positive effect on reducing medical expenses and improving the quality of life. An efficient method for transmitting information is needed so that the city and province sports associations for people with disabilities oversee administrative work on PA for individuals with disabilities in South Korea and can know best about the information about the location and program of the sports facilities. Thus, the role of the city and province sports associations for people with disabilities is critical for effective information delivery to persons with disabilities.

Sixth, the results of the priority of H4 (i.e., the priority of 1st to 40th) were the programs within sports facilities, instructor who has 2 or more certificates related to PA, sports or exercise clubs for individuals with disabilities, programs of public outdoor facilities, instructor for persons with disabilities, instructor who has a disability, public sports facility for persons with disabilities, education on understanding of disabilities and human rights, instructor for each sport event, teaching method education by type of disability and so on. The highest priority of H4 for the establishment of the PA environment for persons with disabilities was the programs within sports facilities because there was a lack of sports facilities for people with disabilities, but also programs for individuals with disabilities in South Korea [36]. According to Brenda and Deborah [40], sports facilities are essential for individuals with disabilities to participate in sports and recreation, and the various programs provided by the sports facilities provide positive effects on the participation of persons with disabilities in PA. In addition, the next priority of H4 was the instructor who has 2 or more certificates related to PA. As stated earlier, instructors have an influence on the PA of people with disabilities; for instance, an instructor with expertise can effectively teach people with disabilities and provide high-quality teaching [38]. On the other hand, a small number of people with disabilities are provided with PA by professional instructors in South Korea [39]. The results of the relative importance and priority presented above showed similar results. Consequently, if the relative importance and priority are taken into consideration and the PA environment for persons with disabilities is established, successful PA can be provided for individuals with disabilities.

Therefore, these findings demonstrated that the programs, instructors, facilities, and information are all necessary for the successful establishment of the PA environment for individuals with disabilities. However, it will be possible to save time and to establish an effective PA environment for persons with disabilities based on the results of the relative importance and priority presented in this study.

5. Research Limitations

There are several limitations. First, this study is difficult to generalize because it was limited to specific participants (e.g., faculty members researching PA for people with disabilities, administrators in the Korean Paralympic Committee) in South Korea. Therefore, future studies should be conducted using data from various participants (e.g., persons with disabilities, administrators in the city and province sports association for people with disabilities). Second, the participants of this study were only Korean people with disabilities. Therefore, the establishment of the PA environment for people with disabilities according to cultural differences was not considered. Therefore, future research should be conducted in consideration of the PA environment for individuals with disabilities recommended by the world association for adapted PA or WHO. Third, this study analyzed the priority that should be reflected in the administration for the establishment of the PA environment for persons with disabilities, but there are no specific administrative plans presented in this study. Therefore, there is a need for a study that specifically suggests administrative plans that reflect the needs of individuals with disabilities and the opinions of experts.

6. Conclusions

The purpose of this study was to analyze the priority of what factors should be reflected in the administration to efficiently consider the needs of persons with disabilities for the PA environment in South Korea. To achieve the purpose of the study, 32 PA experts were asked about the factors that should be reflected in the PA environment first through the questionnaire in the pairwise comparison format. The conclusions shown through the hierarchical analysis are as follows; first, the relative importance between H2 was determined by program, instructor, facility, and information. Second, in the relative importance among H3, the type of program was determined as the highest factor in the program, and the expertise of the instructor was determined as the highest factor in the instructor. The type of facility was determined as the highest factor in the facility, and the provider of information was determined as the highest factor in the information. Third, the results of analyzing the priority of H4, it was decided as the program within a sports facility had the highest priority.

Author Contributions: Conceptualization, A.-R.O. and K.K.; Methodology, A.-R.O.; Software, A.-R.O.; Formal analysis, A.-R.O.; Investigation, A.-R.O. and K.K.; Resources, A.-R.O. and K.K.; Data curation, A.-R.O. and K.K.; Writing-review and editing, K.K. All authors have read and agreed to the published version of the manuscript.

Funding: This work was supported by the Ministry of Education of the Republic of Korea and the National Research Foundation of Korea (NRF-2019S1A5A2A01041417).

Institutional Review Board Statement: The study approved by the Institutional Review Board of Gachon University (IRB approval no. 1044396-201911-HR-204-01).

Informed Consent Statement: Informed consent was obtained from all subjects involved in the study.

Data Availability Statement: The original contributions presented in the study are included in the article, further inquiries can be directed to the corresponding author.

Conflicts of Interest: The authors declare no conflict of interest.

References

1. Bull, F.C.; Al-Ansari, S.S.; Biddle, S.; Borodulin, K.; Buman, M.P.; Cardon, G.; Carty, C.; Chaput, J.P.; Chastin, S.; Chou, R.; et al. World Health Organization 2020 guidelines on physical activity and sedentary behaviour. *Br. J. Sports Med.* **2020**, *54*, 1451. [CrossRef] [PubMed]
2. Carroll, D.D.; Courtney-Long, E.A.; Stevens, A.C.; Sloan, M.L.; Lullo, C.; Visser, S.N.; Fox, M.H.; Armour, B.S.; Campbell, V.A.; Brown, D.R.; et al. Vital signs: Disability and physical activity-United States, 2009–2012. *Morb. Mortal. Wkly. Rep.* **2014**, *63*, 407–413. Available online: https://search-ebscohost-com.ezp.twu.edu/login.aspx?direct=true&db=cmedm&AN=24807240&site=ehost-live (accessed on 1 August 2022).
3. Barker, J.; Smith, B.K.; Doherty, A.; Foster, C.; Rahimi, K.; Ramakrishnan, R.; Woodward, M.; Dwyer, T. Physical activity of UK adults with chronic disease: Cross-sectional analysis of accelerometer-measured physical activity in 96 706 UK Biobank participants. *Int. J. Epidemiol.* **2019**, *48*, 1167–1174. [CrossRef]
4. US Department of Health and Human Services. *Healthy People 2010: Understanding and Improving Health*; Department of Health and Human Services: Washington, DC, USA, 2010. Available online: https://eric.ed.gov/?id=ED443794 (accessed on 1 August 2022).
5. Kosma, M.; Cardinal, B.J.; McCubbin, J.A. A pilot study of a web-based physical activity motivational program for adults with physical disabilities. *Disabil. Rehabil.* **2005**, *27*, 1435–1442. [CrossRef] [PubMed]
6. Korea Ministry of Culture, Sports, and Tourism. 2020 National Survey on the Current Status of Participation of Lifetime Sports for Persons with Disabilities. Available online: https://www.mcst.go.kr/kor/s_notice/press/pressView.jsp?pSeq=19356 (accessed on 1 August 2022).
7. Orr, K.; Evans, M.B.; Tamminen, K.A.; Arbour-Nicitopoulos, K.P. A scoping review of recreational sport programs for disabled emerging adults. *Res. Q. Exerc. Sport.* **2020**, *91*, 142–157. [CrossRef]
8. McGrath, R. A discourse analysis of Australian local government recreation and sport plans provision for people with disabilities. *Public Manag. Rev.* **2009**, *11*, 477–497. [CrossRef]
9. Junker, L.; Carlberg, E.B. Factors that affect exercise participation among people with physical disabilities. *Adv. Physiother.* **2011**, *13*, 18–25. [CrossRef]
10. Kim, Y.; Cho, J.; Fuller, D.K.; Kang, M. Correlates of physical activity among people with disabilities in South Korea: A multilevel modeling approach. *J. Phys. Act. Health* **2015**, *12*, 1031–1038. [CrossRef]
11. Han, J.D.; Koo, K.M.; Oh, A.R. Analysis on the demand for the people with disabilities for participation in lifetime sports. *Kor. J. Exerc. Rehabil.* **2010**, *6*, 101–110.
12. Koo, K.M.; Oh, A.R. Analysis on the factors of restraints against participation in the lifetime sport of visual and hearing impairment. *Kor. J. Phys. Educ.* **2012**, *51*, 423–430.
13. Koo, K.M.; Oh, A.R. Analysis on the constraint factors of physical disabilities in the lifetime sport. *Kor. J. Phys. Educ.* **2012**, *51*, 447–454.
14. Kim, K.S.; Oh, A.R.; Koo, K.M. The development of a model to sport for all on persons with disabilities. *Kor. J. Phys. Educ.* **2009**, *17*, 65–95.

15. Kim, H.M.; Lee, H.S.; Kim, S.H.; Park, J.W. Investigation of sports for all requirement types of people with intellectual disability: Focused on Q methodology. *Kor. J. Phys. Educ.* **2015**, *54*, 597–610.
16. Australian Sports Commission. *Active Australia: A National Participation Framework*; Australian Sports Commission: Canberra, Australia, 1997.
17. McGrath, R. What do they say they are doing? Thematic analysis of local government disability action plans. *Ann. Leis. Res.* **2008**, *11*, 168–186. Available online: https://search-ebscohost-com.ezp.twu.edu/login.aspx?direct=true&db=s3h&AN=35705285&site=ehost-live (accessed on 1 August 2022). [CrossRef]
18. Kars, C.; Hofman, M.; Geertzen, J.H.B.; Pepping, G.-J.; Dekker, R. Participation in sports by lower limb amputees in the province of Drenthe, the Netherlands. *Prosthet. Orthot. Int.* **2009**, *33*, 356–367. [CrossRef]
19. Scelza, W.M.; Kalpakjian, C.Z.; Zemper, E.D.; Tate, D.G. Perceived barriers to exercise in people with spinal cord injury. *Am. J. Phys. Med. Rehab.* **2005**, *84*, 576–583. [CrossRef]
20. Tasiemski, T.; Kennedy, P.; Gardner, B.P.; Blaikley, R.A. Athletic identity and sports participation in people with spinal cord injury. *Adapt. Phys. Activ. Q.* **2004**, *21*, 364–378. Available online: https://search-ebscohost-com.ezp.twu.edu/login.aspx?direct=true&db=psyh&AN=2004-19950-003&site=ehost-live (accessed on 1 August 2022). [CrossRef]
21. Van der Ploeg, H.P.; Streppel, K.R.M.; van der Beek, A.J.; Van der Woude, L.H.; Vollenbroek-Hutten, M.M.; Van Harten, W.H.; Van Mechelen, W. Successfully improving physical activity behavior after rehabilitation. *Am. J. Health Promot.* **2007**, *21*, 153–159. [CrossRef]
22. Moran, T.E.; Taliaferro, A.R.; Pate, J.R. Confronting physical activity programming barriers for people with disabilities: The empowerment model. *Quest* **2014**, *66*, 396–408. Available online: https://search-ebscohost-com.ezp.twu.edu/login.aspx?direct=true&db=s3h&AN=98903203&site=ehost-live (accessed on 1 August 2022). [CrossRef]
23. Oh, A.; So, W.Y. Assessing the needs of people with disabilities for physical activities and sports in South Korea. *Healthcare* **2022**, *10*, 265. [CrossRef]
24. Noble, E.E.; Sanchez, P.P. A note on the information content of a consistent pairwise comparison judgment matrix of an AHP decision maker. *Theory Decis.* **1993**, *34*, 99–108. [CrossRef]
25. Saaty, T.L.; Hu, G. Ranking by the eigenvector versus other methods in the analytic hierarchy process. *Appl. Math. Lett.* **1998**, *11*, 121–125. [CrossRef]
26. Saaty, T.L. An exposition of the AHP in reply to the paper remarks on the analytic hierarchy process. *Manag. Sci.* **1990**, *36*, 259–268. [CrossRef]
27. Schmoldt, D.L.; Kangas, J.; Mendoza, G.A.; Pesonen, M. *The Analytic Hierarchy Process in Natural Resource and Environmental Decision Making*; Springer Science & Business Media: Berlin/Heidelberg, Germany, 2013. Available online: https://search-ebscohost-com.ezp.twu.edu/login.aspx?direct=true&db=kdh&AN=BK0020194630&site=ehost-live (accessed on 1 August 2022).
28. Saaty, T.L. Decision making—The Analytic Hierarchy and Network Processes (AHP/ANP). *J. Syst. Sci. Syst. Eng.* **2004**, *13*, 1–35. [CrossRef]
29. Han, S. A practical approaches to decrease the consistency index in AHP. In Proceedings of the 2014 Joint 7th International Conference on Soft Computing and Intelligent Systems (SCIS) and 15th International Symposium on Advanced Intelligent Systems (ISIS), Kitakyushu, Japan, 3–6 December 2014; pp. 867–872.
30. Jiří, F.; Aleš, K. Judgment scales and consistency measure in AHP. *Procedia Econ. Fin.* **2014**, *12*, 164–173.
31. Kleinert, H.L.; Miracle, S.S.; Sheppard-Jones, K. Including students with moderate and severe disabilities in extracurricular and community recreation activities. *Teach. Excep. Child.* **2007**, *39*, 33–38. [CrossRef]
32. Johnson, C.C. The benefits of physical activity for youth with developmental disabilities: A systematic review. *Sci. Health Promot.* **2008**, *23*, 157–167. [CrossRef]
33. Ennis, C.D.; Ross, J.; Chen, A. The role of value orientations in curricular decision making: A rationale for teachers' goals and expectations. *Res. Q. Exerc. Sport.* **1992**, *63*, 38–47. [CrossRef]
34. Ennis, C.D.; Zhu, W. Value orientations: A description of teachers: Goals for student learning. *Res. Q. Exerc. Sport* **1991**, *62*, 33–40. [CrossRef]
35. Pitts, B.G.; Shapiro, D.R. People with disabilities and sport: An exploration of topic inclusion in sport management. *J. Hosp. Leis. Sports Tour. Educ.* **2017**, *21*, 33–45. [CrossRef]
36. Korea Paralympic Committee. Current Status of Sports Facilities Exclusively for the Disabled. Available online: https://sports.koreanpc.kr/front/sportsFacility/facility.do (accessed on 1 August 2022).
37. Kosciulek, J.F.; Merz, M. Structural analysis of the consumer-directed theory of empowerment. *Rehabil. Couns. Bull.* **2001**, *44*, 209–216. [CrossRef]
38. Moran, T.E.; Block, M.E. Barriers to participation of children with disabilities in youth sports. *Teach. Except. Child. Plus* **2010**, *6*, n3. Available online: https://search-ebscohost-com.ezp.twu.edu/login.aspx?direct=true&db=eric&AN=EJ879597&site=ehost-live (accessed on 1 August 2022).
39. Lee, Y.Y. Analysis of influencing factors on the effects of sports for all participation: Hierarchical regression analysis using the 2020 National Sports for All Participation Survey with Disabilities. *Kor. J. Adapt. Phys. Act.* **2021**, *29*, 125–139.
40. Hommond, A.M. The relationship between disability and inclusion policy and sports coaches' perceptions of practice. *Int. J. Sport Policy* **2022**, *14*, 471–487. [CrossRef]

41. Troped, P.J.; Saunders, R.P.; Pate, R.R.; Reininger, B. Addy CL. Correlates of recreational and transportation physical activity among adults in a New England community. *Prev. Med.* **2003**, *37*, 304–310. [CrossRef]
42. Pia, L.W. Sport, disability, and women: A study of organized Swedish disability sport in 1969-2012. *Sport Tour.* **2017**, *24*, 213–220.
43. Lyusyena, K. Sport for all and social inclusion of individuals with impairments: A case study from Brazil. *Societies* **2019**, *9*, 44.

healthcare

MDPI

Article

Improving Special Ability Performance of Badminton Players through a Visual Reaction Training System

Kuei-Pin Kuo [1], Chun-Chin Liao [2,*] and Chun-Chieh Kao [2,*]

1 Office of Physical Education, National Ping-Tung University of Science and Technology, 1 Shuefu Road, Neipu, Pingtung 91201, Taiwan; kweibin0422@gmail.com
2 Office of Physical Education, Ming Chuan University, 5 De Ming Road, Gui Shan District, Taoyuan City 333, Taiwan
* Correspondence: luck@mail.mcu.edu.tw (C.-C.L.); kao@mail.mcu.edu.tw (C.-C.K.); Tel.: +886-3-3507-001 (C.-C.K.)

Abstract: This study investigates the effects of a visual reaction training system (VRTS) in improving the footwork of badminton players. The participants comprised 20 high school male badminton players (mean age, 17.83 ± 1.57 years; mean height, 171.4 ± 11.52 cm; mean weight, 58.76 ± 9.32 kg) who first underwent a badminton footwork agility training program and subsequently, a fixed or random six-point footwork test and an agility *t*-test. A one-way repeated-measures analysis of variance with Bonferroni correction was performed to identify differences in terms of response time, movement time, and total shift time. The results measured at midtest and posttest after the training intervention revealed significant improvements in reaction ($p \leq 0.01$) and movement ($p \leq 0.05$) time for the fixed six-point footwork test ($p \leq 0.01$). The total time results for the fixed or random six-point footwork test and agility *t*-test at midtest and posttest after the training intervention revealed significant improvement ($p \leq 0.05$). Badminton footwork agility training conducted through the VRTS enhances the ability and agility of badminton players. Therefore, researchers and coaches should evaluate the footwork of badminton players by precisely measuring and quantify their ability.

Keywords: footwork; reaction time; agility; performance

Citation: Kuo, K.-P.; Liao, C.-C.; Kao, C.-C. Improving Special Ability Performance of Badminton Players through a Visual Reaction Training System. *Healthcare* **2022**, *10*, 1454. https://doi.org/10.3390/healthcare10081454

Academic Editor: Felipe Aidar

Received: 30 June 2022
Accepted: 31 July 2022
Published: 2 August 2022

1. Introduction

The initial speed of a shuttlecock following a badminton smash is faster relative to similar movements used in other sports. In international badminton tournaments, the fastest speeds ever recorded for singles and doubles matches are 417 and 426 km/h, indicating that badminton is a fast-paced sports in which players must react to each hit with rapid movements that require agility and strategy. Numerous studies have investigated the footwork and movements of badminton players, and their findings have been combined with sports science and technology in recent years and widely applied in badminton training. In one study, accelerators were used to obtain the step-related data of players during step training, and a quantitative analysis of average and maximum speeds was performed to effectively assess the speed and state of their movements to adequately improve their agility and overall athletic performance [1–4]. Badminton involves shots that require speed and explosive strength combined with agile footwork and movements that are applied tactically, and it has become a popular racket sport that is extensively developed worldwide [5].

Research has revealed a significant correlation between athletic performance and the agility of footwork movements [1–4,6]. Traditionally, agility was simply defined as the speed with directional changes [7]. Currently, agility is considered an open skill, and it was recently defined as a change in velocity or direction in response to a stimulus that cannot be preplanned [8]. Agility is defined as a rapid whole-body movement with a change of direction or speed in response to a stimulus. However, traditional agility tests do not address this definition and are preplanned with no stimulus. Compared to traditional agility testing, reactive agility testing is an effective and reliable agility testing method. Reactive agility tests can also be used as training exercises to improve skills by using sport-specific stimuli that preplanned agility exercises may not have. Players who can perform rapid movements are likely to dominate in badminton tournaments [9,10]. Therefore, the footwork of badminton players during rapid movements is a crucial basis for defining agility [11–13]. Although agility is a key ability required in sports, its definition has remained divergent until recently. Young et al. proposed that agility involves cognitive skills, physical qualities, and technical aspects. Cognitive skills comprise the time taken by an individual to make judgments and decisions as well as the reaction time of that individual [14]. Physical qualities refer to the linear sprint velocity of an individual (depending on the muscular, explosive, and reactive strength of their leg muscles) and their core muscular strength. Technical aspects comprise two indicators, namely, cognitive skills and physical qualities, which are applied strategically to perform sports techniques [15].

A badminton court comprises two halves that each measure 6.7 m in length and 6.1 m in width. The six primary directions of movement on the court are leftward and rightward in the forecourt, midcourt, and rear court. The strategies for reacting to an opponent and executing footwork vary depending on the movements made in these six directions, which include the cross-step in the forecourt and rear court and the lunge in the midcourt. Badminton players who are able to complete their footwork faster show greater average and maximum acceleration. Players deploy movement strategies with the center of the court as the starting and ending points for shifting and returning. Steps, lunges, and other types of footwork movements are performed to receive the shuttlecock and to return to a defensive position after each attack and defense as soon as possible to correctly per-form efficient (direction and distance) and high-quality (strength and intensity) shots. Immediately returning to the central position after performing a shot and following up with another shot is an efficient technique that increases a badminton player's probability of winning [1,2].

In recent years, numerous studies have analyzed the movements of badminton player by employing kinesiological research methods, and they revealed that footwork during badminton movements is a key indicator of a badminton player's athletic performance and a basis for evaluating their injury risk. Findings in the literature have also indicated that a higher percentage of the injuries sustained in badminton occur in the lower limbs than in other parts of the body [16,17]. Therefore, an appropriate examination of the quantitative data on agile reactions (of badminton players) can enable researchers to understand the variability of a player's overall trend, and overtraining and an unnecessary training load can be avoided by referring to these data and focusing on incidence statistics. Badminton movements are characterized by rapid changes in direction, which are required to achieve tournament-winning performance. A study investigated the plantar pressure variations in players with varying skill levels when they were performing lunges for net shots. Its results revealed that plantar pressure was distributed across the inner side of the feet among skilled players and across the outer side of the feet among average players; they also indicated that the difference in the distribution of pressure affected the motions of the players' lower limb joints [18].

Lower limb joint loading affects the athletic performance of badminton players. Studies have revealed that incorrect footwork movements have a negative effect on the state of lower limb joints and cause injuries [19–21]. For inappropriate footwork movements involving lunges, the body compensates by shifting the trunk inclination angle of the lower limb joints, which in turn affects the efficiency of shots and causes injuries [19,20,22]. In recent years, neuromuscular theories and research results have been widely applied in various types of sports training to enhance muscular strength while correctly and effectively reducing the correlation between injury risk and muscle-controlling nerves [23,24]. Therefore, the enhancement of footwork and movement is an essential training component for badminton players. The agility *t*-test proposed by the National Strength and Conditioning

Association of the United States is an effective method for measuring speed, explosive strength, and agility [25].

In recent years, the focus has shifted to training methods that are based on simulation of competition and the accurate monitoring of training outcomes through the processing of training results using quantitative methods (e.g., data collection). At present, few sport-specific scientific electronic devices with both training and testing features have been developed. Scientific quantitative training methods allow for the specific and effective modification and improvement of training programs for players with respect to their movement characteristics, advantages, and disadvantages. Numerous studies have used biomechanical methods to explore footwork movements. Although three-dimensional biomechanical motion capture systems enable researchers to effectively measure parameters of kinematics, dynamics, and athletic performance in the context of human activities, data collection is subject to environmental constraints that prevent the use of large research samples. The present study aimed to conduct intervention training and examine its outcomes with a self-developed visual reaction training system (VRTS) to test the system's effectiveness in routine badminton training. The training system was designed to provide coaches and players with various types of quantitative data on badminton agility and specific skills, allowing them to clearly modify their subsequent training programs based on the collected data and results and to improve the tournament performance of players.

2. Methods

2.1. Participants

This study assessed the agility and specific abilities of high school badminton players after they underwent 12 weeks of specific physical training that was based on the VRTS. Twenty male high school badminton players who received regular training were recruited as the participants of the present study; the 20 participants were all members of local high school badminton teams (mean age = 17.83 ± 1.57 years; mean height = 171.4 ± 11.52 cm; mean weight = 58.76 ± 9.32 kg; the right hand is the dominant hand for all participants). To prevent research participant effects from affecting the research results of the present study during the intervention phase, participants were only included if they (1) underwent at least 6 h of specialized badminton training spread across at least three sessions per week, (2) did not participate in any neuromuscular stimulation program during the first 6 months of training, (3) had no history of neuromuscular injury in the bones of their lower extremity within 1 year, and (4) understood the experimental procedure and provided informed consent (i.e., the participants' and their guardians' consent). Students were directly excluded if they had a relationship with the researcher. The present study was approved by the institutional review board of Antai Tian-Sheng Memorial Hospital, Antai Medical Care Cooperation (IRB approval number: 19-034-B, Pingtung, Taiwan).

2.2. Research Tools

VRTS

In accordance with the methodology of another study [3], the VRTS used in the present study mainly comprised a programmable logic controller and a human–machine interface. The RS232 communication protocol was used for data transmission, image conversion was conducted through the HMI, and a sequential function chart was used to write the internal syntax. The hardware devices comprised an infrared sensor module, light-emitting diode (LED) lights equipped with multicore control cables, and wireless I/O modules with a maximum transmission range of 100 m. Radio signals were transmitted through globally shared frequency bands between 2400 and 2480 MHz to send various types of data (e.g., trend analysis charts and time parameters) as feedback for coaches and players. The devices were tested using interclass correlation coefficients (ICCs) and demonstrated to exhibit high reliability and validity (ICC = 0.95) [3].

3. Research Procedures

Prior to the commencement of the study intervention, the purpose, methods, and procedures of the present study were explained to the participants. They then underwent a trial VRTS-based training session that enabled them to adapt to the study environment and familiarize themselves with the training equipment and methods, and the instruments were carefully inspected to ensure that they could record data. Before the formal training intervention, participants practiced familiarization with VTRS, and a rest period of at least 48 h was implemented between the end of the exercise and the start of the formal experiment to prevent participant fatigue and potential build-up. Additionally, the study was conducted for a total of 15 weeks, with participants completing the training period pretest (week 1), Phase 1 (weeks 2–7), and Phase 2 (weeks 9–14), and posttest (week 15). The pretest, midtest, and posttest were evaluated twice, and the best score was used as the experimental data (Figure 1).

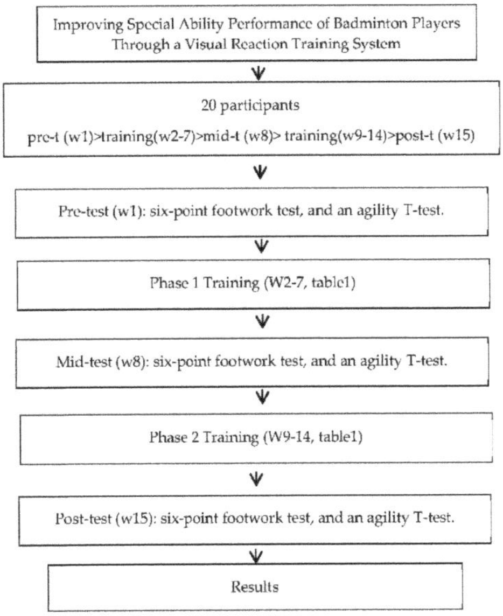

Figure 1. Research procedures.

For the pretest, midtest, and posttest of the present study, the 20 participants underwent a fixed-light-mode six-point footwork test, a random-light-mode six-point footwork test, and an agility *t*-test. The test procedures were as follows. A visual stimulus light signal panel that indicates movement direction was placed in front of the court near the center of the net. Optical sensors were installed on the left and right sides of the front court and rear court (4 m from the central position) and on the left and right sides of the midcourt (2.6 m from the central position). Each participant moved quickly from the central position (30 cm $\times$ 30 cm) according to the direction indicated by the indicator light. Figure 2 illustrates the six-point footwork test venue layout. However, the lights indicated movement directions through two modes. In the fixed mode, the indicator lights lighted up in a specific order (i.e., Corners 1, 2, 3, 4, 5, and 6), and the participants performed the footwork movement test in accordance with the light indications. In the random mode, the LED lights lighted up in a random order to simulate a game situation.

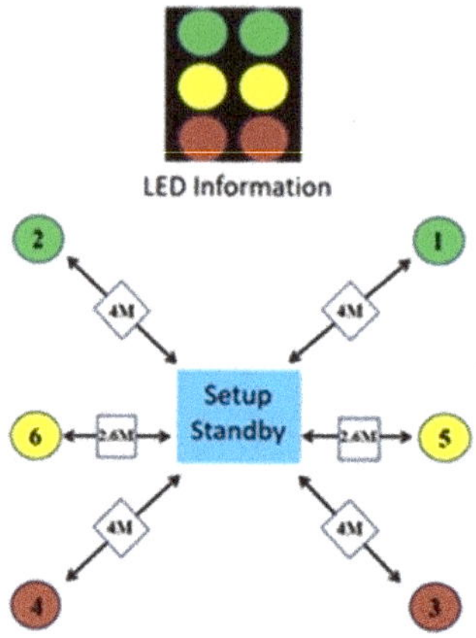

Figure 2. Six-point footwork test venue layout.

A participant performed the agility *t*-test by running straight from the starting position to Point A (4.7 m), moving laterally from Point A to Point B (2.6 m), moving laterally from Point B (pass Point A) to Point C (the distance between Points A and C = 2.6 m), moving laterally from Point C to Point A, and then running back to the starting position. The entire sequence from the starting position was as follows: starting position → A → B → A → C → A → starting position. The total distance covered was 19.8 m. Figure 3 illustrates the agility *t*-test venue layout.

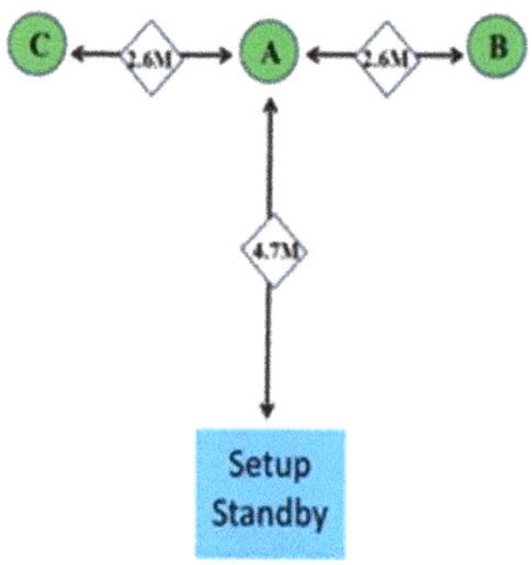

Figure 3. Agility *t*-test venue layout.

Prior to the pretest, midtest, and posttest as well as each training session, each player was asked to perform static stretching of a specific intensity followed by a dynamic warm up to ensure that they effectively warmed up their neuromuscular system and to minimize the risk of neuromuscular injury. The present study developed a training schedule by revising the training schedule used by Kuo et al. [3]. The content of the agility training for the footwork movements is presented in Table 1.

Table 1. Training content.

Week 1	**Pretest**	**T-Footwork Movement: 2n × 2N Six-Point Footwork 2C × 2n × 1N & 2R × 2n × 1N**
Week/Item and assignment	Fixed direction	Random direction
Weeks 2 and 3	2C × 2n × 2N Rest interval between sets = 30 s	2C × 3n × 1N Rest interval between sets = 30 s
Weeks 4 and 5	2C × 2n × 2N Rest interval between sets = 30 s	2C × 3n × 2N Rest interval between sets = 30 s
Weeks 6 and 7	2C × 2n × 2N Rest interval between sets = 20 s	2C × 3n × 2N Rest interval between sets = 20 s
Week 8	Midtest	T-footwork movement: 2n × 2N Six-point footwork: 2C × 2n × 1N & 2R × 2n × 1N
Weeks 9 and 10	2C × 3n × 2N Rest interval between sets = 20 s	2C × 3n × 2N Rest interval between sets = 20 s
Weeks 11 and 12	2C × 3n × 2N Rest interval between sets = 20 s	3C × 2n × 2N Rest interval between sets = 20 s
Weeks 13 and 14	2C × 3n × 2N Rest interval between sets = 20 s	1C × 5n × 2N Rest interval between sets = 10 s
Week 15	Posttest	T-footwork movement: 2n × 2N Six-point footwork: 2C × 2n × 1N & 2R × 2n × 1N

C = completion of fixed-mode six-point positions; R = completion of random-mode six-point positions; n = repetitions per set; N = number of sets.

4. Statistical Analysis

In the present study, a VRTS-based training intervention was conducted to enhance the agility of male high school badminton players. The system tested the players' agility and analyzed variabilities in their reaction time, action time, and the time taken to perform movements; the outcomes of the intervention were also examined. Data from the pretest, midtest, and posttest were collected using a computer, and a difference analysis was conducted using the SPSS 20.0 statistical software package (Version 20.0; SPSS, Chicago, IL, USA). The reaction and action time data collected during the fixed- and random-light-mode six-point footwork tests and the agility *t*-test were evaluated through a one-way repeated-measures analysis of variance (ANOVA). Training outcomes were assessed by performing a Bonferroni post hoc test, and the significance level α for the present study was 0.05.

5. Results

5.1. Differences in Fixed-Light-Mode Six-Point Footwork Test Results

Significant differences in the reaction times recorded during the fixed-light-mode six-point footwork test were observed for all six positions at 12 weeks after the start of the VRTS-based training (Corner 1, F = 93.298, $p \leq 0.01$; Corner 2, F = 62.714, $p \leq 0.01$; Corner 3, F = 38.633, $p \leq 0.01$; Corner 4, F = 123.514, $p \leq 0.01$; Corner 5, F = 317.821, $p \leq 0.01$; Corner 6, F = 33.673, $p \leq 0.01$). Additionally, the post hoc test results pertaining to the reaction times for the six positions indicated a significantly superior performance for the midtest and posttest compared to the pretest. Table 2 presents the reaction time results for the fixed-light six-point footwork test with respect to these positions.

Table 2. Reaction times for footwork movements in six-point positions in fixed and random modes.

	Pretest	Midtest	Posttest	F	Power
Fixed-mode six-point reaction time_Corner 1	0.715 ± 0.118	0.191 ± 0.072	0.209 ± 0.081	93.298 **	1.000
Fixed-mode six-point reaction time_Corner 2	0.739 ± 0.332	0.201 ± 0.065	0.139 ± 0.067	62.714 **	1.000
Fixed-mode six-point reaction time_Corner 3	0.679 ± 0.385	0.112 ± 0.074	0.151 ± 0.102	38.633 **	1.000
Fixed-mode six-point reaction time_Corner 4	0.758 ± 0.221	0.167 ± 0.238	0.131 ± 0.066	123.514 **	1.000
Fixed-mode six-point reaction time_Corner 5	0.684 ± 0.115	0.146 ± 0.083	0.119 ± 0.060	317.821 **	1.000
Fixed-mode six-point reaction time_Corner 6	0.686 ± 0.201	0.174 ± 0.087	0.148 ± 0.215	33.673 **	1.000
Random-mode six-point reaction time_Corner 1	0.778 ± 0.174	0.617 ± 0.452	0.636 ± 0.098	3.729 *	0.593
Random-mode six-point reaction time_Corner 2	0.952 ± 0.166	0.729 ± 0.352	0.659 ± 0.318	4.296 *	0.694
Random-mode six-point reaction time_Corner 3	0.901 ± 0.211	0.716 ± 0.179	0.563 ± 0.149	8.997 *	0.962
Random-mode six-point reaction time_Corner 4	0.981 ± 0.167	0.686 ± 0.277	0.665 ± 0.273	9.386 *	0.961
Random-mode six-point reaction time_Corner 5	0.830 ± 0.124	0.755 ± 0.178	0.659 ± 0.175	4.771 *	0.724
Random-mode six-point reaction time_Corner 6	0.858 ± 0.224	0.863 ± 0.253	0.769 ± 0.162	2.291	0.319

*: $p < 0.05$; **: $p < 0.01$.

Significant differences in the total movement times recorded during the fixed-light-mode six-point footwork test were observed for all six positions (Corner 1, F = 38.117, $p \leq 0.01$; Corner 2, F = 56.915, $p \leq 0.01$; Corner 3, F = 8.620, $p = 0.035$; Corner 4, F = 26.625, $p \leq 0.01$; Corner 5, F = 11.181, $p = 0.05$; Corner 6, F = 14.628, $p = 0.01$). The post hoc test results pertaining to the total action times at Corners 1, 2, 4, and 6 indicated a significantly superior performance for the midtest and posttest compared to the pretest; by contrast, a superior performance was achieved at Corner 3 for the midtest compared to the pretest and at Corner 5 for the posttest compared to the pretest. Table 3 presents the total action time results obtained through the fixed-light six-point footwork test.

Table 3. Time taken for footwork movements in six-point positions in fixed and random modes.

	Pretest	Midtest	Posttest	F	Power
Time for fixed-mode six-point footwork_Corner 1	3.485 ± 0.582	2.296 ± 0.335	2.279 ± 0.271	38.117 **	1.000
Time for fixed-mode six-point footwork_Corner 2	3.318 ± 0.132	2.654 ± 0.354	2.401 ± 0.108	56.915 **	1.000
Time for fixed-mode six-point footwork_Corner 3	3.701 ± 0.718	2.699 ± 0.261	3.127 ± 0.586	8.620 **	0.798
Time for fixed-mode six-point footwork_Corner 4	3.317 ± 0.294	2.892 ± 0.419	2.662 ± 0.245	26.625 **	1.000
Time for fixed-mode six-point footwork_Corner 5	2.568 ± 0.553	1.916 ± 0.248	1.799 ± 0.239	11.181 *	0.889
Time for fixed-mode six-point footwork_Corner 6	2.397 ± 0.571	1.701 ± 0.295	1.875 ± 0.166	14.628 **	0.993
Time for random-mode six-point footwork_Corner 1	3.778 ± 0.832	2.921 ± 0.619	2.801 ± 0.408	7.828 *	0.919
Time for random-mode six-point footwork_Corner 2	3.117 ± 0.199	2.729 ± 0.357	2.457 ± 0.112	21.033 **	1.000
Time for random-mode six-point footwork_Corner 3	3.369 ± 0.352	3.201 ± 0.292	3.152 ± 0.284	4.389 *	0.708
Time for random-mode six-point footwork_Corner 4	3.355 ± 0.296	2.822 ± 0.486	2.708 ± 0.321	13.995 **	0.996
Time for random-mode six-point footwork_Corner 5	2.509 ± 0.338	2.110 ± 0.371	1.993 ± 0.237	13.427 **	0.993
Time for random-mode six-point footwork_Corner 6	2.415 ± 0.372	1.836 ± 0.235	1.659 ± 0.226	20.016 **	1.000

*: $p < 0.05$; **: $p < 0.01$.

5.2. Differences in Random-Light-Mode Six-Point Footwork Test Results

Significant differences in the reaction times recorded during the random-light-mode six-point footwork test were observed for the following positions: Corner 1, F = 3.729, $p = 0.047$; Corner 2, F = 4.296, $p = 0.043$; Corner 3, F = 8.997, $p = 0.001$; Corner 4, F = 9.386, $p = 0.001$; Corner 5, F = 4.771, $p = 0.021$. Additionally, the post hoc test results indicated that the random-light-mode reaction times recorded at Corners 2, 3, and 5 were significantly superior for the posttest compared to the pretest. For Corner 4, a significantly superior performance was obtained for the midtest and posttest compared to the pretest. Table 2 presents the results of the random-light-mode six-point footwork test.

Significant differences in the total action times recorded during the random-light-mode six-point footwork tests were observed for all six positions (Corner 1, F = 7.828, $p = 0.003$;

Corner 2, F = 21.033, $p \leq 0.01$; Corner 3, F = 4.389, $p = 0.036$; Corner 4, F = 13.995, $p \leq 0.01$; Corner 5, F = 13.427, $p \leq 0.01$; Corner 6, F = 20.016, $p \leq 0.01$). The post hoc test results for action time indicated a significantly superior performance at Corners 2, 4, 5, and 6 for the midtest and posttest compared to the pretest. The post hoc test also revealed a superior performance at Corner 1 for the posttest compared to the pretest. Table 3 presents the total action time results for the random-light-mode six-point footwork test.

5.3. Differences in Agility t-Test Results

The results of the one-way repeated measures ANOVA revealed significant differences in the total movement times obtained through the fixed-light-mode test (F = 29.469, $p \leq 0.01$), random-light-mode test (F = 22.381, $p \leq 0.01$), and agility *t*-test (F = 48.229, $p \leq 0.01$). The Bonferroni post hoc test indicated a significantly superior performance for total movement time during the midtest and posttest compared to during the pretest. Table 4 presents the results of the agility tests.

Table 4. Movement time obtained through agility test.

	Pretest	Midtest	Posttest	F	Power
Total movement time for fixed-mode six-point footwork	19.010 ± 2.1721	14.208 ± 1.328	13.989 ± 1.436	29.469 **	0.999
Total movement time for random-mode six-point footwork	18.162 ± 1.917	16.663 ± 1.277	14.927 ± 1.259	22.381 **	1.000
Total movement time for T agility running	17.558 ± 1.443	14.594 ± 1.315	14.356 ± 1.108	48.229 **	1.000

**: $p < 0.01$.

6. Discussion

The self-developed VRTS tested in the present study was used to develop training schedules. The system provided data feedback that contributed to improving training outcomes. An electronic device was developed to facilitate the training of an essential badminton-specific skill (i.e., footwork during quick attacking and defensive movements) to improve the agility of players.

The participants underwent a 12-week agility training intervention that was based on the VRTS and comprised two types of badminton-specific footwork movements (i.e., six-point footwork and T-footwork). The results reveal significant differences in the reaction and action times recorded for the fixed-light-mode six-point footwork test. For the random-light-mode six-point footwork test, only the reaction times recorded at Corner 6 were not significantly different because the Corner 6 direction was to the left of the players, and in badminton footwork, only one step was required to complete the action at Corner 6. Therefore, the time taken was short, and the variability in action time was small. By contrast, the variability in reaction and action times was greater at other positions, and the results revealed significant differences when changes occurred in these positions. Furthermore, the results indicated that the VRTS-based training, which focused on the agility of players during movements, enabled them to improve their time performance from the pretest to the midtest. Additionally, their performance in the posttest was superior to their performance in the pretest and midtest, indicating that the VRTS-based training of footwork during movements allows high school players to effectively improve their reaction and action time performance.

The training of badminton-specific footwork is a major component of agility training. Additional information was obtained through scientific quantitative results regarding the training, and it served as further feedback for coaches and players. In contrast to inaccurate measurement methods (e.g., using stopwatches), the VRTS was designed based on exercise science, and it is light, portable, and straightforward to set up. When used with a computer and a sensor, the VRTS can precisely record various types of information regarding the agility of players; in addition, laboratory space constraints and other limitations are addressed through the system's accurate quantitative measurements such that the agile reactions of players can be monitored during training. The experimental results indicated that the system can effectively contribute to monitoring, recording, and analytical tasks during training and collect relevant quantitative data. The quantitative data that the system delivers to coaches and players can further facilitate the planning of subsequent training.

Studies have compared badminton players with varying skill levels by conducting badminton-specific speed and sprint tests. Their results indicated that badminton-specific speed tests are superior to general sprint tests for assessing agility performance because of their closer correlation with athletic performance in the context of badminton; precise training allows for effective player selection and training course design [26]. The findings of the present study indicated that both the reaction times and the action times of the participants adequately improved following VRTS-based training. The action time results of the participants revealed superior posttest results for the backhand side relative to the forehand side. For random-light reaction time, the results revealed a shorter reaction time for the forehand side than for the backhand side. The players moved by shifting their center of gravity after receiving stimulating information; this principle conforms with the theory of perception and decision-making in agility [2,18,19], indicating a crucial association between agility and specific athletic performance. Similarly, the results of the present study revealed significant improvements in the reaction time performance of its participants.

Studies have also indicated that the state of a player's central nervous system can be improved by enhancing their agility during routine training to facilitate their processing and decision-making regarding stimulating information, and their reaction speed also increased [27]. During the VRTS-based training of agility for footwork movements, indicator lights produced rapid and changing stimulating information that served as cues for the participants; this method effectively trained the players to reduce their reaction time, thereby improving their agility.

Ooi et al. tested the agility of elite and sub-elite Malaysian badminton players and reported the absence of significant differences between the two groups [28]. The training results obtained through tests conducted in other studies were similar because these tests focused only on fixed and specific directions. Through the implementation of a tournament simulation mode, the VRTS-based training provides increased variety. The random-light tournament mode stimulated the participants to react agilely, and significant differences were observed between pretest results and midtest and posttest results, indicating that the system substantially contributed to the training of the participants and improved their performance.

Studies have used the six-point position model to test the agility of players in various areas. The results indicated that, although agility is an ability required in various sports events, the six-point position agility test is more suitable for assessing the agility of badminton players than for assessing the agility of players of other sports; this is because badminton players perform agile movements within a smaller space relative to players of other sports. Moreover, sports science researchers should focus on simultaneous training and testing of badminton-specific abilities to enable badminton players to apply their skills and improve their athletic performance during tournaments more efficiently [29]. Based on the findings, the six-point footwork test is recommended for assessing the movements of badminton players during training sessions and tournaments. Based on six-point footwork tests that are conducted in fixed and random light modes, the VRTS measures a player's reaction time and action time. It provides effective feedback that further enhances the training and strategy of players with respect to their footwork movements, thereby enhancing their agility while reinforcing their shifting and running within a badminton court.

The results of a Taiwan-based retrospective study on badminton footwork suggested that the routine training of badminton players should involve visual stimulation training followed by motor control training. This training method can improve the perceptual and decision-making abilities of badminton players [30]. Accordingly, the present study obtained test data through simulated tournament scenarios and examined the changes in direction on the left and right sides of the forecourt, midcourt, and rear court. The ability to change direction was tested, participants were randomly provided with stimulating information, and their ability to move in various directions was measured. The training module used in the present study corresponds to theories regarding the definition of agility, and it covers information reception, reactions and actions, the ability to change direction, and other mechanisms. Another study recruited 43 badminton players (29 men and 14 women) and conducted an agility test that was similar to the one conducted in the present study. Its results indicated that specific tests are necessary for badminton players. Meanwhile, a wide range of data can be obtained through specific quantitative data-based tests, and athletic performance can be further improved with the aid of technology [31].

After a badminton player executes a shot, they must return to the center of the court and react to their opponent's returning shot by performing rapid six-point footwork or T-footwork movements to move to the forecourt, the rear court, or the sides of the court. Therefore, by determining the correct direction and rapidly moving to the correct position through the execution of appropriate footwork movements, players can correctly and effectively apply their skills and return shots [4]. In the present study, significant differences in agility *t*-test results were observed, indicating that the VRTS-based training can adequately improve the ability of badminton players to move rapidly in straight and lateral directions, enabling them to perform highly efficient shots.

7. Conclusions

The present study used a VRTS to train 20 male high school badminton players and demonstrated that the system substantially improved their reaction and action time performance, thereby enhancing their abilities and agility. The VRTS can provide quantitative data on badminton-specific training. A wide range of information is made available to coaches and players for testing, enabling them to facilitate specific training precisely and effectively and, thus, improve training outcomes and athletic performance.

During the training conducted for the present experiment, the test data pertaining to specific abilities and agility were collected only from male high school badminton players who received regular training; no VRTS-based test was conducted to collect data from female players. Future studies should recruit female players and players of varying technical levels, incorporate hitting actions, or simulate various tournament scenarios and include other evaluation indicators (e.g., electromyography, and photography-based motion analysis.). As an electronic training system, the VRTS is arranged according to different training methods and intensities, and research has proved that it can effectively improve an athlete's agility and mobility, and effectively improve training and performance in the context of badminton (or other sports). Therefore, the VTRS is a scientific instrument with both training function and detection and evaluation ability.

Author Contributions: Conceptualization, K.-P.K. and C.-C.L.; methodology, K.-P.K. and C.-C.K.; formal analysis, K.-P.K., C.-C.K. and C.-C.L.; data curation, K.-P.K. and C.-C.L.; writing (original draft preparation), C.-C.L.; writing—review and editing: K.-P.K., C.-C.L. and C.-C.K. All authors have read and agreed to the published version of the manuscript.

Funding: This work was supported by of the Ministry of Science and Technology, R.O.C. (MOST 109-2637-H-020-002).

Institutional Review Board Statement: The study was conducted according to the guidelines of the Declaration of Helsinki and approved by the Institutional Ethics Committee of the Antai Medical Care Cooperation Antai-Tian-Sheng Memorial Hospital Institutional Review Board (approval number: 21-005-B).

Informed Consent Statement: Informed consent was obtained from all subjects involved in the study.

Data Availability Statement: Not applicable.

Acknowledgments: Thanks to the junior high school badminton players who assisted in the successful completion of this study.

Conflicts of Interest: The authors declare no conflict of interest.

References

1. Chiu, Y.L.; Tsai, C.L.; Sung, W.H.; Tsai, Y.J. Feasibility of smartphone-based badminton footwork performance assessment system. *Sensors* **2020**, *20*, 6035. [CrossRef] [PubMed]
2. Latorre, E.C.; Zuniga, M.D.; Arriaza, E.; Moya, F.; Nikulin, C. Automatic Registration of Footsteps in Contact Regions for Reactive Agility Training in Sports. *Sensors* **2020**, *20*, 1709. [CrossRef] [PubMed]
3. Kuo, K.P.; Tsai, H.H.; Lin, C.Y.; Wu, W.T. Verification and evaluation of a visual reaction system for badminton training. *Sensors* **2020**, *20*, 6808. [CrossRef] [PubMed]
4. Hung, M.H.; Chang, C.Y.; Lin, K.C. Application of sports technology on badminton footwork analysis. *Qtly. Chin. Phys. Educ.* **2019**, *33*, 165–172. [CrossRef]
5. Chang, F.C.; Lian, W.Y.; Wang, C.M.; Chi, S.C. A study of developing a specific fitness battery test for badminton single players. *Sports Coach. Sci.* **2017**, *47*, 89–99. [CrossRef]
6. Chang, C.Y.; Chang, C.H.; Chen, K.C.; Ho, C.S.; Chen, Y.R. The Effect of Footwork and Response Capability in Elementary School Badminton Players by Six Weeks Agility Training. *Sports Coach. Sci.* **2016**, *44*, 57–66. [CrossRef]
7. Draper, J.A. The 505 test: A test for agility in horizontal plane. *Aust. J. Sci. Med. Sport* **1985**, *17*, 15–18.
8. Sheppard, J.M.; Young, W.B.; Doyle, T.L.A.; Sheppard, T.A.; Newton, R.U. An evaluation of a new test of reactive agility and its relationship to sprint speed and change of direction speed. *J. Sci. Med. Sport* **2006**, *9*, 342–349. [CrossRef]
9. Inglis, P.; Stephen, P.B. Reactive agility tests: Review and practical applications. *J. Aust. Strength Cond.* **2016**, *24*, 62–69.
10. Fiorilli, G.; Iuliano, E.; Mitrotasios, M.; Pistone, E.M.; Aquino, G.; Calcagno, G.; di Cagno, A. Are change of direction speed and reactive agility useful for determining the optimal field position for young soccer players. *J. Sports Sci. Med.* **2017**, *16*, 247.
11. Singh, J.; Raza, S.; Mohammad, A. Physical characteristics and level of performance in badminton: A relationship study. *J. Educ. Pract.* **2011**, *2*, 6–10. [CrossRef]
12. González-Fernández, F.T.; Sarmento, H.; Castillo-Rodríguez, A.; Silva, R.; Clemente, F.M. Effects of a 10-Week Combined Coordination and Agility Training Program on Young Male Soccer Players. *Int. J. Environ. Res. Public Health* **2021**, *18*, 10125. [CrossRef] [PubMed]
13. Andrašić, S.; Gušić, M.; Stanković, M.; Mačak, D.; Bradić, A.; Sporiš, G.; Trajković, N. Speed, Change of Direction Speed and Reactive Agility in Adolescent Soccer Players: Age Related Differences. *Int. J. Environ. Res. Public Health* **2021**, *18*, 5883. [CrossRef] [PubMed]
14. Young, W.B.; Dawson, B.; Henry, G.J. Agility and change-of-direction speed are independent skills: Implications for training for agility in invasion sports. *Int. J. Sports Sci. Coach.* **2015**, *10*, 159–169. [CrossRef]
15. Kuntze, G.; Mansfield, N.; Sellers, W. A biomechanical analysis of common lunge tasks in badminton. *J. Sports Sci.* **2010**, *28*, 183–191. [CrossRef]
16. Fu, L.; Ren, F.; Baker, J.S. Comparison of joint loading in badminton lunging between professional and amateur badminton players. *Appl. Bion. Biomech.* **2017**, *2017*, 1–8. [CrossRef]
17. Reeves, J.; Hume, P.A.; Gianotti, S.; Wilson, B.; Ikeda, E. A retrospective review from 2006 to 2011 of lower extremity injuries in badminton in New Zealand. *Sports* **2015**, *3*, 77–86. [CrossRef]
18. Mei, Q.; Gu, Y.; Fu, F.; Fernandez, J. A biomechanical investigation of right-forward lunging step among badminton players. *J. Sports Sci.* **2017**, *35*, 457–462. [CrossRef]
19. Liu, X.; Imai, K.; Zhou, X.; Watanabe, E. Influence of Ankle Injury on Subsequent Ankle, Knee, and Shoulder Injuries in Competitive Badminton Players Younger Than 13 Years. *Orthop. J. Sports Med.* **2022**, *10*, 23259671221097438. [CrossRef] [PubMed]
20. Herbaut, A.; Delannoy, J.; Foissac, M. Injuries in French and Chinese regular badminton players. *Sci. Sports* **2018**, *33*, 145–151. [CrossRef]
21. Phomsoupha, M.; Laffaye, G. The science of badminton: Game characteristics, anthropometry, physiology, visual fitness and biomechanics. *Sports Med.* **2015**, *45*, 473–495. [CrossRef] [PubMed]
22. Lin, C.F.; Hua, S.H.; Huang, M.T.; Lee, H.H.; Liao, J.C. Biomechanical analysis of knee and trunk in badminton players with and without knee pain during backhand diagonal lunges. *J. Sports Sci.* **2015**, *33*, 1429–1439. [CrossRef]
23. Kimura, Y.; Ishibashi, Y.; Tsuda, E.; Yamamoto, Y.; Hayashi, Y.; Sato, S. Increased knee valgus alignment and moment during single-leg landing after overhead stroke as a potential risk factor of anterior cruciate ligament injury in badminton. *Br. J. Sports Med.* **2012**, *46*, 207–213. [CrossRef]
24. Noyes, F.R.; Barber-Westin, S.D. Neuromuscular retraining in female adolescent athletes: Effect on athletic performance indices and noncontact anterior cruciate ligament injury rates. *Sports* **2015**, *3*, 56–76. [CrossRef]
25. Semenick, D. Testing protocols and procedures. In *Essentials of Strength Training and Conditioning*, 1st ed.; Baechle, T., Ed.; Human Kinetics: Champaign, IL, USA, 1994; pp. 258–273.
26. Madsen, C.M.; Karlsen, A.; Nybo, L. Novel speed test for evaluation of badminton-specific movements. *J. Strength Condit. Res.* **2015**, *29*, 1203–1210. [CrossRef] [PubMed]
27. Schmidt, R.A.; Lee, T.D. *Motor Control and Learning: A Behavioral Emphasis*, 5th ed.; Human Kinetics: Champaign, IL, USA, 2011.
28. Ooi, C.H.; Tan, A.; Ahmad, A.; Kwong, K.W.; Sompong, R.; Mohd Ghazali, K.A.; Liew, S.L.; Chai, W.J.; Thompson, M.W. Physiological characteristics of elite and sub-elite badminton players. *J. Sports Sci.* **2009**, *27*, 1591–1599. [CrossRef]
29. Loureiro, L.D.F.B.; Dias, M.O.C.; Cremasco, F.C.; da Silva, M.G.; de Freitas, P.B. Assessment of specificity of the badcamp agility test for badminton players. *J. Hum. Kinet.* **2017**, *57*, 191–198. [CrossRef]
30. Hong, Y.; Wang, S.J.; Lam, W.K.; Cheung, J.T.M. Kinetics of badminton lunges in four directions. *J. Appl. Biomech.* **2014**, *30*, 113–118. [CrossRef] [PubMed]
31. Loureiro, L.D.F.B.; de Freitas, P.B. Development of an agility test for badminton players and assessment of its validity and test–retest reliability. *Int. J. Sports Physiol. Perform.* **2016**, *11*, 305–310. [CrossRef]

healthcare

MDPI

Article

Gold Medals, Silver Medals, Bronze Medals, and Total Medals: An Analysis of Summer Paralympic Games from 1992 to 2016

Miguel Jacinto [1,2], Diogo Monteiro [2,3,4], Rui Matos [2,3] and Raul Antunes [2,3,5,*]

1 Faculty of Sport Sciences and Physical Education, University of Coimbra, 3004-531 Coimbra, Portugal; miguel.s.jacinto@ipleiria.pt
2 Life Quality Research Centre (CIEQV), 2411-901 Leiria, Portugal; diogo.monteiro@ipleiria.pt (D.M.); rui.matos@ipleiria.pt (R.M.)
3 ESECS—Polytechnic of Leiria, 2411-901 Leiria, Portugal
4 Research Center in Sport Sciences, Health Sciences and Human Development (CIDESD), 5001-801 Vila Real, Portugal
5 Center for Innovative Care and Health Technology (ciTechCare), Polytechnic of Leiria, 2411-901 Leiria, Portugal
* Correspondence: raul.antunes@ipleiria.pt; Tel.: +351-244-829-400

Abstract: The Paralympic Games (PG) are considered one of the biggest events in the world, with increasing coverage by media and participation. The present study aimed to investigate the variation in the number of gold, silver, bronze, and totals medals in the Summer PG from 1992 to 2016. Data related to the results were extracted from the International Paralympic Committee to an SPSS database. Descriptive statistics and Friedman's two-way analysis of variance by ranks were used to check the differences across medals in seven editions of the Summer PG, with the correspondent effect sizes. There was a peak in the maximum number of any type of medal between the 1996 and 2000 Summer PG and a decrease until 2008. After that, the number of any kind of medals has been increasing again. There were also significant differences with intermediate to large effect sizes when comparing more distant PG with more recent events. Several external factors can influence performance indicators (e.g., the number of medals) in a negative or positive way. An increase in the number of participants and a greater and better investment by the countries may explain part of our results. The preparation of an athlete must be based on a multidisciplinary team, and future organizing countries must take into account reports of previous events.

Keywords: athletes; disability; Paralympic Games; performance indicators; sports

check for updates

Citation: Jacinto, M.; Monteiro, D.; Matos, R.; Antunes, R. Gold Medals, Silver Medals, Bronze Medals, and Total Medals: An Analysis of Summer Paralympic Games from 1992 to 2016. *Healthcare* **2022**, *10*, 1289. https://doi.org/10.3390/healthcare10071289

Academic Editors: Felipe Aidar and José Carmelo Adsuar Sala

Received: 8 June 2022
Accepted: 11 July 2022
Published: 12 July 2022

1. Introduction

The Paralympic Games (PG), considering both the Summer and Winter PG, are a movement that was initiated during the Second World War in rehabilitation centres [1]. In these centres, where soldiers returned with various types of injuries, doctors used sport as a means of rehabilitating the body and mind and of contributing to reintegration into society [2–4]. In the space around the rehabilitation centres where small competitions were practiced, they quickly evolved into regional, national, and international events with the format that is now known worldwide as the PG [5,6]. The first PG took place in Rome in 1960 and involved 400 athletes from 23 different countries who competed in 57 medal events across eight sports [7].

On 22 September 1989, the International Paralympic Committee (IPC) was founded, being responsible for directing the Paralympic Movement, with the mission of guaranteeing and supervising its organization [8]. According to the IPC, the main objectives of the PG are: (i) to allow Paralympic athletes to achieve their best performance at the highest level of competition through adequate and adapted conditions and services in a solid environment; (ii) to provide visibility, differentiation, and opportunities that promote and demonstrate the spirit and values of the Paralympic Movement (courage, de-termination, inspiration, and equality); and (iii) to promote social development and leave a positive framework that benefits communities in the host country and around the world [8].

The PG take place every four years, immediately after the respective Olympic Games, in the same city that hosts them [8] and represent an opportunity to convey messages of peace, justice, integration, resilience, values, culture, resistance to the adverse effects of events, inclusion, change in attitudes, stereotyped behaviours, an environment free of urban and architectural barriers, and the greatest achievement for an athlete [4,9], with the number of participants increasing from event to event [10].

The 1992 Barcelona PG represented a turning point, as they presented a new classification concept [11], taking into account their health and functioning (according to the International Classification of Functioning, Disability, and Health) and sport participation, in contrast to a purely medical model [12,13]. This model is based on three steps: (i) determining if an athlete has an eligible impairment; (ii) determining if the athlete meets the minimum impairment criteria for a sport; and (iii) deciding an athlete's sports class [14]. This allows the athlete to participate on equal terms with other athletes [11]. These athletes go through an evidence-based classification process and are grouped into classes, depending on the degree of limitation and the modality practiced [11,14,15]. Nowadays, according to the IPC [14], the PG involve athletes with a series of deficiencies, namely, impaired muscle power, impaired passive range of movement, limb deficiency, leg length difference, short stature, hypertonia, ataxia, athetosis, vision impairment, and intellectual impairment.

There are currently 22 Paralympic sports held in the Summer PG [16]. Due to the different modalities, there are sports with only one class and others with up to 50 [14], with a high number of events. Subsequently, the first, second, and third place in each class are awarded gold, silver, and bronze medals, respectively.

During the first editions of the Summer PG (between 1960 and 1984), we saw an increase in the number of medals (from 113 to 975), mainly caused by the increase in classes and sporting events. Subsequently, there was a decrease in the number of medals between the 1984 and 1992 Summer PG (from 975 to 489) that was caused by a reduction in the number of sporting events. After this phase of decline, the number of medal events and sporting events remained stable. This number of medals remained stable, despite a slight increase in classes, due to the fact that some sports combined classes in the same event, while others excluded classes from certain events [17].

Previous studies mention that there is a clear advantage at the country level ($p < 0.05$) when it plays at home in the PG [18]. However, the causes are not clear, and further investigation is recommended. More recently, when investigating the Summer PG using a standardized measure of success, some authors confirmed that home advantage is predominant for countries ($p < 0.01$) and in some specific sports ($p < 0.05$) [19].

Knowing that the Paralympic Movement has grown and the number of athletes has increased and that the number of medals is related to the number of sporting events (stable since 1992) and to the number of classes (a slight increase), as far as we know, no study has analysed how the performance has evolved over the events. Therefore, the present study intends to investigate the variation in gold, silver, bronze, and total medals by event in the summer games from 1992 to 2016.

2. Materials and Methods

The results of each edition of the Summer PG between 1992 and 2016 were obtained by experienced researchers (M.J., R.A., and D.M.) through the results history file of the IPC [20] and downloaded to the software SPSS. For our analysis, we considered only the countries that were awarded gold in each of the seven selected editions ($n = 28$).

Statistical Analysis

Descriptive statistics, including the median, mean, standard deviation, and interquartile range, were calculated for all variables. The Shapiro–Wilk ($n < 50$) test was used to verify data normality. In addition, a Friedman's two-way analysis of variance by ranks was used (since the normality was not verified) to check the differences across gold, silver, and bronze medals in seven editions of the Summer PG (i.e., 1992 to 2016), with the correspondent effect sizes for nonparametric tests (Eta squared, η^2) [21]. The interpretation of the effect size using η^2 was based on the following criteria: <0.01, no effect; 0.01–0.04, small effect: 0.06–0.11, intermediate effect: and 0.14–0.20, large effect [22]. The significance level to reject the null hypothesis was set at 5% [23]. The analyses were conducted using IBM SPSS, version 27.0.

3. Results

Table 1 presents the descriptive statistics of the Summer PG (1992–1996), with means, standard deviations, medians, interquartile ranges, and total medals values.

Table 1. Descriptive statistics of Summer PG (1992–2016).

Variables	Mean	SD	Median	IQ	S_W	Total Medals
Gold 1992	15.68	3.48	9.0	18		439
Gold 1996	15.79	2.63	9.5	16		442
Gold 2000	15.96	2.97	8.5	22		447
Gold 2004	13.04	2.53	8.0	15	$p \leq 0.05$	365
Gold 2008	12.96	3.42	5.0	12		365
Gold 2012	13.04	3.49	8.0	9		365
Gold 2016	14.00	4.29	8.0	11		392
Silver 1992	15.11	2.98	9.5	19		423
Silver 1996	15.29	2.85	9.5	16		428
Silver 2000	14.75	2.61	8.0	22		413
Silver 2004	13.61	2.32	9.5	21	$p \leq 0.05$	381
Silver 2008	11.89	2.85	5.0	16		333
Silver 2012	13.04	2.85	7.5	13		365
Silver 2016	14.04	3.35	7.0	17		393
Bronze 1992	15.39	3.00	10.5	19		431
Bronze 1996	15.75	3.05	10.5	18		441
Bronze 2000	15.46	2.56	10.0	17		433
Bronze 2004	13.29	2.29	7.0	22	$p \leq 0.05$	372
Bronze 2008	11.79	2.28	6.0	17		330
Bronze 2012	13.04	2.79	7.5	14		365
Bronze 2016	12.93	2.50	7.5	13		362
Total Medals 1992	46.14	9.26	32.5	58		1292
Total Medals 1996	46.82	8.30	30.0	46		1311
Total Medals 2000	46.18	7.81	27.5	65		1293
Total Medals 2004	39.93	6.75	22.5	59	$p \leq 0.05$	1118
Total Medals 2008	36.64	8.35	16.0	42		1026
Total Medals 2012	38.46	8.99	20.5	31		1077
Total Medals 2016	38.14	9.79	19.5	29		1068

Legend: SD—standard deviation; IQ—interquartile range; S_W—Shapiro-Wilk.

We can verify that the peak of each of the analysed variables occurred in 1996, except for the gold medals, which had their peak in the year 2000 (Table 1 and Figures 1–4). After that, there was a decrease until the PG of 2008, as the number of gold and silver medals has been increasing since then, although far from the values previously achieved (Table 1 and Figures 1–4).

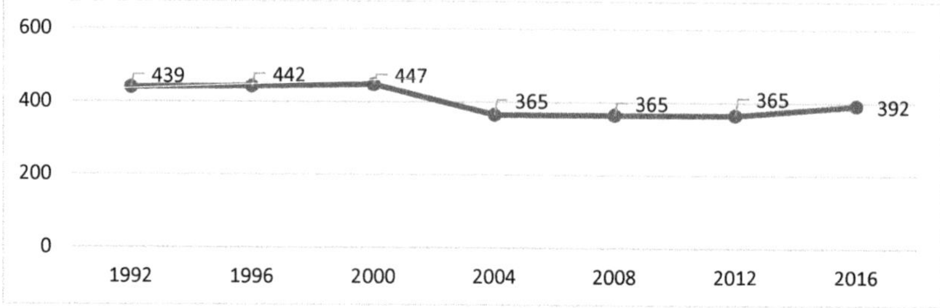

Figure 1. Gold medals evolution all over the editions.

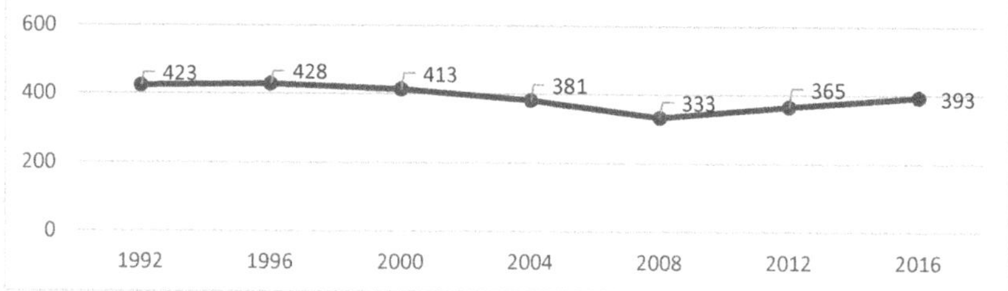

Figure 2. Silver medals evolution over all the editions.

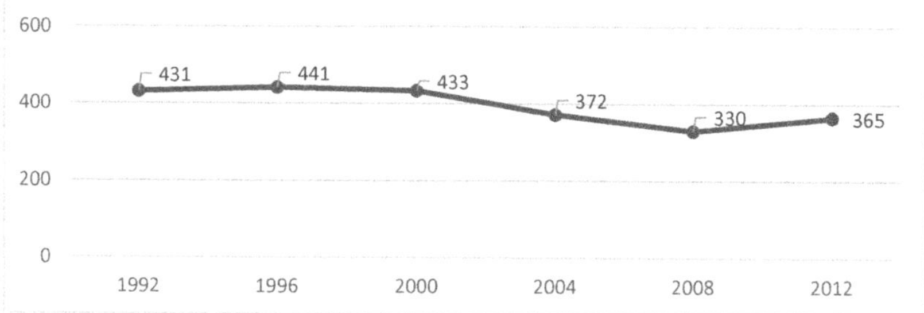

Figure 3. Bronze medals evolution over all the editions.

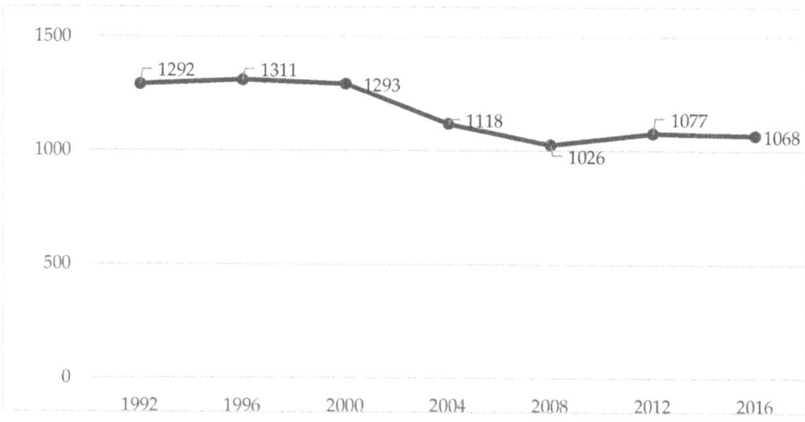

Figure 4. Total medals evolution over all the editions.

The figures show some stabilization in the number of medals across the seven analysed editions.

Table 2 presents the differences across gold, silver, and bronze medals in seven editions of Summer PG (i.e., 1992 to 2016) with the corresponding effect sizes for nonparametric tests.

Table 2. Variation in medals for the Summer PG (1992–2016).

Medals	F_r Value	Z	p	η^2
Gold				
1992–1996		−0.91	0.12	-
1992–2000		−0.29	0.62	-
1992–2004		0.34	0.54	-
1992–2008		1.01	0.07	-
1992–2012		0.70	0.23	-
1992–2016		0.09	0.12	-
1996–2000		0.63	0.28	-
1996–2004		1.25	0.03	0.06
1996–2008		1.93	≤0.01	0.13
1996–2012		1.60	0.01	0.09
1996–2016	$F_r = 17.98$; $p \leq 0.01$	1.80	≤0.01	0.12
2000–2004		0.63	0.28	-
2000–2008		1.30	0.02	0.06
2000–2012		0.98	0.09	-
2000–2016		1.18	0.04	0.05
2004–2008		0.68	0.24	-
2004–2012		0.36	0.54	-
2004–2016		0.55	0.34	-
2008–2012		−0.32	0.58	-
2008–2016		−0.13	0.83	-
2012–2016		0.20	0.73	-
Silver				
1992–1996		0.46	0.42	-
1992–2000		−0.09	0.88	-
1992–2004		0.02	0.98	-
1992–2008		1.36	0.02	0.07
1992–2012		0.52	0.37	-
1992–2016		0.66	0.25	-
1996–2000		0.38	0.52	-
1996–2004		0.48	0.40	-
1996–2008		1.82	≤0.01	0.12
1996–2012	$F_r = 13.66$; $p = 0.03$	0.98	0.09	-
1996–2016		1.13	0.05	0.05
2000–2004		0.11	0.85	-
2000–2008		1.45	0.01	0.08
2000–2012		0.61	0.29	-
2000–2016		0.75	0.19	-
2004–2008		1.34	0.02	0.06
2004–2012		0.50	0.39	-
2004–2016		0.14	0.81	-
2008–2012		−0.84	0.15	-
2008–2016		−0.70	0.23	-
2012–2016		0.14	0.81	-

Table 2. *Cont.*

Medals	F_r Value	Z	p	η^2
Bronze				
1992–1996		−0.16	0.78	-
1992–2000		−0.75	0.19	-
1992–2004		0.23	0.69	-
1992–2008		1.23	0.03	0.05
1992–2012		0.52	0.37	-
1992–2016		0.55	0.34	-
1996–2000		−0.59	0.31	-
1996–2004		0.39	0.50	-
1996–2008		1.40	0.02	0.07
1996–2012		0.68	0.24	-
1996–2016	$F_r = 14.53; p = 0.02$	0.71	0.21	-
2000–2004		0.98	0.09	-
2000–2008		1.98	≤0.01	0.14
2000–2012		1.27	0.03	0.06
2000–2016		1.30	0.02	0.06
2004–2008		1.10	0.08	-
2004–2012		0.29	0.62	-
2004–2016		0.32	0.58	-
2008–2012		−0.71	0.22	-
2008–2016		−0.68	0.24	-
2012–2016		0.04	0.95	-
Total Medals				
1992–1996		−0.27	0.64	-
1992–2000		−0.66	0.25	-
1992–2004		0.36	0.54	-
1992–2008		1.41	0.02	0.07
1992–2012		0.77	0.18	-
1992–2016		0.77	0.18	-
1996–2000		−0.39	0.50	-
1996–2004		0.63	0.28	-
1996–2008		1.68	≤0.01	0.1
1996–2012		1.03	0.08	-
1996–2016	$F_r = 19.23; p \leq 0.01$	1.04	0.07	-
2000–2004		1.01	0.08	-
2000–2008		2.07	≤0.01	0.15
2000–2012		1.43	0.01	0.07
2000–2016		1.50	0.01	0.08
2004–2008		1.05	0.06	-
2004–2012		0.39	0.47	-
2004–2016		0.41	0.48	-
2008–2012		−0.64	0.27	-
2008–2016		−0.64	0.26	-
2012–2016		0.01	0.55	-

Legend: F_r—Friedman test; Z—Z-Score; *p*—*p*-value; η^2—Eta squared.

For gold medals, there were differences with intermediate effect sizes, essentially for the 1996 Summer PG compared to the 2004 to 2016 Summer PG. Likewise, there were differences with intermediates effect sizes when comparing the 2000 Summer PG with 2008 and 2016. Knowing that gold medals have a greater "weight", 1996 was the edition with a greater preponderance compared to the last four editions.

Regarding silver medals, there were differences with intermediate effect sizes when comparing the results of the 1992–2008, 1996–2008, 1996–2016, 2000–2008, and 2004–2008 Summer PG.

Considering bronze medals, there were differences with intermediate effect sizes when comparing the 1992–2008, 1996–2008, and 2000 Summer PG and the last three events.

Likewise, when analysing the total number of medals, differences with intermediate to large effect sizes were verified for the same events as the bronze medals.

4. Discussion

The present study aims to investigate the variation in gold, silver, bronze, and total medals in the Summer PG from 1992 to 2016 in a selected sample (countries that were awarded gold in each of the seven selected editions).

Through the performed analyses, there was a peak in the number of any type of medal between the 1996 and 2000 Summer PG and a decrease until the year 2008. Apparently, this number of any type of medal has been increasing again. Likewise, the differences were significant when comparing more distant PG with more recent ones.

Given that the number of events, countries, and participants has increased, a greater distribution of medals may justify the results obtained in this study. However, the literature had already shown that the various indicators (e.g., medals) were stable [16], which is something we confirmed in Figures 1–4. If we analyse the editions separately, we see that there was a slight decrease in the number of medals from 2004, which can be interpreted in light of several factors that will be discussed below. Several reports, which are mostly unofficial, reveal the existence of various problems with doping and fraud in sport (classification) at the PG [24]. Since 2004, these issues have been overseen by the IPC [25] with greater rigor and control [26,27]. This fact may have a decreasing effect on the analysed variables (medals won).

Another factor to consider is the prevalence of various injuries and illnesses between the 2000 and 2008 PG [28,29]. The sample of countries selected for the analysis in our study may have been affected by these issues in the period in which there was a decrease in medals.

People with disabilities were rarely seen in the media and in public spaces before the PG. The Paralympic Movement acted as a showcase for its participants, giving visibility and helping to challenge stereotypes and stigmas as well as opening new doors [30]. However, the media can promote both positive and negative/stigmatizing images about people with disabilities [31–34], and they should be aware of their importance for the Paralympic Movement. Some athletes might not be prepared for such exposure, and their performance may be affected.

This increase in media exposure, greater interest and expectations for sports results (pressure), a high-intensity training environment, and below-average performances lead athletes to exhaustion, physical and psychological injuries, and lower incomes [35–37]. As the intensity of training and the number of sporting events increase (qualifications for the PG), life beyond sport is impaired, and this can be another destabilizing factor for sporting performance [38–40].

In the same sense, the effects of continuous support for athletes, together with the expectations of institutions/organizations/countries, parents, media scrutiny, and the thought that employment will depend on sports results, can lead to coach exhaustion, which impairs the quality of training and, subsequently, the athletes' performance [41–44].

Likewise, several factors may be contributing to the decrease in the number of barriers to the practice of physical activity [45] and the increase in the number of people enrolled in this practice [46], which positively impacts the number of people participating in the PG and performance indicators. Although the interest in the psychological skills of athletes started in the 1980s [47], the development of psychological skills training programs in Paralympic sports is recent [48–50]. It is a systematic and consistent practice of mental or psychological skills aimed at improving performance and increasing pleasure and physical activity self-satisfaction and includes training in arousal regulation, imagery, self-talk, goal setting, and concentration [50]. A multidisciplinary team is important before the competition, during the competition, and after the competition, controlling all the issues that can negatively influence an athlete and providing the ideal conditions for the Paralympic athlete to be able to be at the fullest of their performance indicators in the events of the PG. As an example, Israel only started providing psychological support to its athletes in 2000 [51].

Currently, we observe an increase in the social and scientific interest in the athlete's personality, preparation, and sports results [5,52,53], and the training of psychological skills must be integrated with physical training, enhancing both variables [50,54]. This fact may be one of the reasons why the values of the number of medals won are increasing again.

Another issue that may justify the fact that the value seems to be increasing again is the existence of previously published literature that assesses the risk and identifies critical success factors (public health, surveillance, assessment and control, safety, environmental health, outbreaks of infectious diseases, weather conditions, travel information—public transport, economic assessment, and allergies, among others) that will help to formulate recommendations and organizational plans that manage the identified risks [55–59]. This aspect is essential, not only for the organizing country but also for the entourage that will participate in the PG, since the knowledge of the conditions they will encounter is complete and allows them to prepare accordingly [58–60]. A simple example is the fact that weather conditions, namely, temperature and humidity, can influence the performance of athletes [61–63]. A prior knowledge of these issues allows adjusting and adapting the structure of the training plan to the conditions that the athlete will find in the competition and the reorganization of future events.

An individual's eating strategies can significantly influence their physical performance [64]. A nutritional plan for athletes should be differentiated according to their disability, sport, frequency and intensity of exercise, and occupation [65–68]. Correct nutrition guarantees energy needs and recovery during and after exercise [37], while insufficient nutrition can increase the risk of injury and illness and decrease performance [69]. Despite being scarce, studies on the nutritional knowledge of athletes with disabilities and its relationship with sport have increased [37,70–72], as this is also a key element for performance indicators.

There are still some studies that address that the game/modality itself has evolved in technical, tactical, and physical terms over the years, a fact that has been proven in the PG [73–75], which is currently considered a high-performance sport. The use of technology in Paralympic sport created tools capable of eliminating disadvantages or measuring them and compensating for performance [76] as well as the development of more, better adapted, and more accurate tools to assess physical [77] and physiological [78] responses and may justify an increase in the number of medals.

Reducing the number of medals may not mean a decrease in performance. The study by Hassani et al. [79] did not find differences in the performance of amputees from 2004 to 2012. Since Paralympic sport has increased interest, increased participation (more athletes and new participating countries) and a greater commitment by countries make the distribution of medals among the countries greater [80]. In this way, the usual winners, namely, the countries analysed in this study, are faced with greater and better competitiveness, and the reduction in the number of medals is not necessarily negative when analysing the PG events.

This document is aligned with the studies on different performance indicators in the PG, where the variation in medals over the last seven editions of the event was studied. Our results point to variations in the number of medals by the sample we selected for analysis. There are several factors (independent variables) that can justify it. However, after the starting point of our study, this conclusion will have to be reached by future studies that study the countries' individual paths. Likewise, more qualitative studies, focusing on athletes, are needed to understand all the issues around preparation, competition, and the experience after participation in the PG.

In addition, future studies should analyse the moderating effect of the organizing country or continent on the number of participants compared to the number of medals.

5. Conclusions

Considering the seven editions of the Summer PG from 1992 to 2016, the present study intends to investigate the variation in gold, silver, bronze, and total medals. There was a variation, with the 1996 and 2000 editions having the highest number of medals won by the sample of this study. A decrease followed. However, it is possible to verify an increase in the last editions.

Faced with high-performance events, the number of participants increasing in the PG, and a greater commitment by countries, we will witness greater competitiveness among athletes, which could lead to a greater distribution of medals, depending on countries, reducing the number of those who can always earn one or more.

Pre- and post-PG reports are also essential to create knowledge that can help in the development of strategies to be adopted during preparations and in future events and to minimize external factors that can negatively affect athletes' performance.

Author Contributions: Conceptualization, M.J., R.A., R.M. and D.M.; methodology, M.J., R.A., R.M. and D.M.; software, M.J. and D.M.; validation, M.J., R.A., R.M. and D.M.; formal analysis, M.J. and D.M.; investigation, M.J.; resources, M.J., R.A. and R.M.; data curation, M.J., R.A., R.M. and D.M.; writing—original draft preparation, M.J. and D.M.; writing—review and editing, M.J., R.A., R.M. and D.M.; visualization, R.A., R.M. and D.M.; supervision, R.A., R.M. and D.M.; project administration, M.J., R.A., R.M. and D.M.; funding acquisition, M.J., R.A., R.M. and D.M. All authors have read and agreed to the published version of the manuscript.

Funding: This research was funded by the Portuguese Foundation for Science and Technology, I.P., Grant/Award Number UIDB/04748/2020.

Institutional Review Board Statement: Not applicable.

Informed Consent Statement: Not applicable.

Data Availability Statement: https://www.paralympic.org/results/historical (accessed on 1 June 2022).

Conflicts of Interest: The authors declare no conflict of interest.

References

1. Silver, J.R. Ludwig Guttmann (1899–1980), Stoke Mandeville Hospital and the Paralympic Games. *J. Med. Biogr.* **2012**, *20*, 101–105. [CrossRef]
2. Goodman, S.; Wales, H.T.P. *Spirit of Stoke Mandeville: The Story of Sir Ludwig Guttmann*; Collins: London, UK, 1986; p. 191.
3. Guttmann, L. *Textbook of Sport for the Disabled*; HM+M: Aylesbury, UK, 1976.
4. Gold, J.R.; Gold, M.M. Access for all: The rise of the Paralympic Games. *J. R. Soc. Promot. Health* **2007**, *127*, 133–141. [CrossRef] [PubMed]
5. DePauw, K.P.; Gavron, S.J. *Disability Sport*, 2nd ed.; Human Kinetics: Champaign, IL, USA, 2005; p. 408.
6. International Paralympic Committee. Paralympic Games—All Editions. Available online: https://www.paralympic.org/paralympic-games (accessed on 1 June 2022).
7. International Paralympic Committee. Rome 1960 Paralympic Games. Available online: https://www.paralympic.org/rome-1960 (accessed on 28 June 2022).
8. International Paralympic Committee. About the International Paralympic Committee. Available online: https://www.paralympic.org/ipc/history (accessed on 1 June 2022).
9. Pelliccia, A.; Adami, P.E. Tokyo 2020 summer Olympic and Paralympic Games: The games of innovation and resilience. *J. Sports Med. Phys. Fit.* **2021**, *61*, 1037–1038. [CrossRef] [PubMed]
10. Dehghansai, N.; Lemez, S.; Wattie, N.; Baker, J. A Systematic Review of Influences on Development of Athletes with Disabilities. *Adapt. Phys. Activ. Q.* **2017**, *34*, 72–90. [CrossRef]
11. Tweedy, S.M.; Vanlandewijck, Y.C. International Paralympic Committee position stand–background and scientific principles of classification in Paralympic sport. *Br. J. Sports Med.* **2011**, *45*, 259–269. [CrossRef] [PubMed]
12. Sherrill, C. Disability Sport and Classification Theory: A New Era. *Adapt. Phys. Act. Q.* **1999**, *16*, 206–215. [CrossRef]
13. Legg, D.; Steadward, R. The Paralympic Games and 60 years of change (1948–2008): Unification and restructuring from a disability and medical model to sport-based competition. *Sport Soc.* **2011**, *14*, 1099–1115. [CrossRef]
14. International Paralympic Committee. Classification. Available online: https://www.paralympic.org/classification (accessed on 1 June 2022).
15. Tweedy, S.; Williams, G.; Bourke, J. Selecting and modifying methods of manual muscle testing for classification in Paralympic sport. *Eur. J. Adapt. Phys. Act.* **2010**, *3*, 7–16. [CrossRef]

16. International Paralympic Committee. Paralympic Sports. Available online: https://www.paralympic.org/sports (accessed on 1 June 2022).
17. Baumgart, J.K.; Blaauw, E.R.; Mulder, R.; Severin, A.C. Frontiers in Sports and Active Living. Changes in the Number of Medal Events, Sport Events, and Classes during the Paralympic Games: A Historical Overview. 2022. Available online: https://www.frontiersin.org/article/10.3389/fspor.2021.762206 (accessed on 5 June 2022).
18. Wilson, D.; Ramchandani, G. Home advantage in the Winter Paralympic Games 1976–2014. *Sport Sci. Health* **2017**, *13*, 355–363. [CrossRef]
19. Wilson, D.; Ramchandani, G. An investigation of home advantage in the Summer Paralympic Games. *Sport Sci. Health* **2017**, *13*, 625–633. [CrossRef]
20. Paralympic Games Results. Available online: https://www.paralympic.org/results/historical (accessed on 5 June 2022).
21. Fritz, C.O.; Morris, P.E.; Richler, J.J. Effect size estimates: Current use, calculations, and interpretation. *J. Exp. Psychol. Gen.* **2012**, *141*, 2–18. [CrossRef] [PubMed]
22. Cohen, J. *Statistical Power Analysis for the Behavioral Sciences*, 2nd ed.; Routledge: New York, NY, USA, 1988; p. 567.
23. Ho, R. *Handbook of Univariate and Multivariate Data Analysis with IBM SPSS*; CRC Press: Boca Raton, FL, USA, 2013; p. 572.
24. Collier, R. Most Paralympians inspire, but others cheat. *CMAJ* **2008**, *179*, 524. [CrossRef] [PubMed]
25. International Paralympic Committee. Anti-Doping. Available online: https://www.paralympic.org/antidoping (accessed on 1 June 2022).
26. Sobolevsky, T.; Krotov, G.; Dikunets, M.; Nikitina, M.; Mochalova, E.; Rodchenkov, G. Anti-doping analyses at the Sochi Olympic and Paralympic Games 2014. *Drug Test. Anal.* **2014**, *6*, 1087–1101. [CrossRef] [PubMed]
27. Pereira, H.M.G.; Sardela, V.F.; Padilha, M.C.; Mirotti, L.; Casilli, A.; de Oliveira, F.A.; Cavalcanti, G.d.A.; Rodrigues, L.M.L.; de Araujo, A.L.D.; Levy, R.S.; et al. Doping control analysis at the Rio 2016 Olympic and Paralympic Games. *Drug Test. Anal.* **2017**, *9*, 1658–1672. [CrossRef]
28. Sobiecka, J. Injuries and ailments of the Polish participants of the 2000 Paralympic Games in Sydney. *Biol. Sport* **2005**, *22*, 353–362.
29. Liang, X.Y.; Lan, L.; Chen, W.N.; Zhang, A.P.; Dai, J.P. Disease distribution and medical resources during the Beijing 2008 Olympic and Paralympic Games. *Chin. Med. J.* **2011**, *124*, 1031–1036.
30. de Souza, D.L.; Brittain, I. The Rio 2016 Paralympic Games: The Visibility of People with Disabilities in Brazil as a Possible Legacy. *Commun. Sport* **2022**, *10*, 334–353. [CrossRef]
31. de Leseleuc, E.; Pappous, A.; Marcellini, A. La cobertura mediática de las mujeres deportistas con discapacidad. Análisis de la prensa diaria de cuatro países europeos durante los Juegos Paralímpicos de Sidney 2000. *Apunt. Educ. Física Deportes* **2009**, *1*, 97.
32. Poffo, B.N.; Velasco, A.P.; Kugler, A.G.; Furtado, S.; dos Santos, S.M.; Fermino, A.L.; de Souza, D.L. Media and Paralympic Games in Brazil: Investigating stigmas in Folha de S. Paulo's coverage. *Movimento* **2017**, *23*, 1353–1366. [CrossRef]
33. Silva, C.F.; Howe, P.D. The (In)validity of Supercrip Representation of Paralympian Athletes. *J. Sport Soc. Issues* **2012**, *36*, 174–194. [CrossRef]
34. A Mídia Diante da Deficiência: Além dos Estereótipos. Comunicar. Available online: https://recyt.fecyt.es/index.php/comunicar/article/view/25250 (accessed on 7 June 2022).
35. Foskett, R.L.; Longstaff, F. The mental health of elite athletes in the United Kingdom. *J. Sci. Med. Sport* **2018**, *21*, 765–770. [CrossRef] [PubMed]
36. Schaal, K.; Tafflet, M.; Nassif, H.; Thibault, V.; Pichard, C.; Alcotte, M.; Guillet, T.; Helou, N.E.; Berthelot, G.; Simon, S.; et al. Psychological balance in high level athletes: Gender-based differences and sport-specific patterns. *PLoS ONE* **2011**, *6*, e19007. [CrossRef] [PubMed]
37. Nor, N.M.; Manaf, H.; Azhari, N.A.M. A Conceptual Model for Developing a Valid and Reliable Questionnaire on Nutritional Knowledge and Supplement Habits Among Disabled Athletes in Malaysia. *Curr. Res. Nutr. Food Sci. J.* **2017**, *5*, 223–229. [CrossRef]
38. Kristiansen, E.; Hanstad, D.V.; Roberts, G.C. Coping with the media at the Vancouver Winter Olympics: 'We all make a living out of this'. *J. Appl. Sport Psychol.* **2011**, *23*, 443–458. [CrossRef]
39. Pensgaard, A.M. Consulting under pressure: How to help an athlete deal with unexpected distracters during Olympic Games 2006. *Int. J. Sport Exerc. Psychol.* **2008**, *6*, 301–307. [CrossRef]
40. Pensgaard, A.M.; Ursin, H. Stress, control, and coping in elite athletes. *Scand. J. Med. Sci. Sports* **1998**, *8*, 183–189. [CrossRef]
41. Bentzen, M.; Lemyre, P.N.; Kenttä, G. Development of Exhaustion for High-Performance Coaches in Association with Workload and Motivation: A Person-Centered Approach. *Psychol. Sport Exerc.* **2015**, *25*, 22. [CrossRef]
42. Hawkins, P. The coaching profession: Some of the key challenges. *Coach. Int. J. Theory Res. Pract.* **2008**, *1*, 28–38. [CrossRef]
43. Olusoga, P.; Butt, J.; Hays, K.; Maynard, I. Stress in Elite Sports Coaching: Identifying Stressors. *J. Appl. Sport Psychol.* **2009**, *21*, 442–459. [CrossRef]
44. Dehghansai, N.; Pinder, R.A.; Baker, J.; Renshaw, I. Challenges and stresses experienced by athletes and coaches leading up to the Paralympic Games. *PLoS ONE* **2021**, *16*, e0251171. [CrossRef]
45. Jacinto, M.; Vitorino, A.S.; Palmeira, D.; Antunes, R.; Matos, R.; Ferreira, J.P.; Bento, T. Perceived Barriers of Physical ActivityParticipation in Individuals with Intellectual Disability—A Systematic Review. *Healthcare* **2021**, *9*, 1521. [CrossRef] [PubMed]
46. Bloemen, M.; Van Wely, L.; Mollema, J.; Dallmeijer, A.; de Groot, J. Evidence for increasing physical activity in children with physical disabilities: A systematic review. *Dev. Med. Child Neurol.* **2017**, *59*, 1004–1010. [CrossRef] [PubMed]

47. Goldberg, G.; Shephard, R.J. Personality profiles of disabled individuals in relation to physical activity patterns. *J. Sports Med. Phys. Fitness.* **1982**, *22*, 477–484. [PubMed]
48. De la Vega, R. Mental training of a boccia athlete participating in the London 2012 Paralympic Games. In *Global Practices and Training in Applied Sport, Exercise, and Performance Psychology: A Case Study Approach*; Cremades, J.G., Tashman, L.S., Eds.; Routledge/Taylor & Francis Group: New York, NY, USA, 2016; pp. 105–112.
49. Hanrahan, S.J.; Andersen, M.B. *Routledge Handbook of Applied Sport Psychology: A Comprehensive Guide for Students and Practitioners*; Routledge: London, UK, 2010; p. 584.
50. Weinberg, R.S.; Gould, D. *Fundamentals of Sport and Exercise Psychology*, 6th ed.; Human Kinetics: Champaign, IL, USA, 2015.
51. Blumenstein, B.; Orbach, I. Psychological Preparation for Paralympic Athletes: A Preliminary Study. *Adapt. Phys. Activ. Q.* **2015**, *32*, 241–255. [CrossRef] [PubMed]
52. Bawden, M. Providing sport psychology support for athletes with disabilities. In *The Sport Psychologist's Handbook: A Guide for Sport-Specific Performance Enhancement*; Wiley: Hoboken, NJ, USA, 2008; pp. 665–683.
53. Gilbert, K.; Schantz, O.J.; Schantz, O. *The Paralympic Games: Empowerment or Side Show?* Meyer & Meyer Verlag: Aachen, Germany, 2008; p. 256.
54. Martin, J. Mental preparation for the 2014 Winter Paralympic Games. *Clin. J. Sport Med.* **2012**, *22*, 70–73. [CrossRef]
55. Enock, K.E.; Jacobs, J. The Olympic and Paralympic Games 2012: Literature review of the logistical planning and operational challenges for public health. *Public Health* **2008**, *122*, 1229–1238. [CrossRef]
56. Heggie, T.W. Traveling to Canada for the Vancouver 2010 Winter Olympic and Paralympic Games. *Travel Med. Infect. Dis.* **2009**, *7*, 207–211. [CrossRef]
57. Nakamura, S.; Wada, K.; Yanagisawa, N.; Smith, D.R. Health risks and precautions for visitors to the Tokyo 2020 Olympic and Paralympic Games. *Travel Med. Infect. Dis.* **2018**, *22*, 3–7. [CrossRef]
58. Shaw, M.T.M.; Leggat, P.A.; Borwein, S. Travelling to China for the Beijing 2008 Olympic and Paralympic Games. *Travel Med. Infect. Dis.* **2007**, *5*, 365–373. [CrossRef]
59. Fagher, K.; Baumgart, J.K.; Solli, G.S.; Holmberg, H.C.; Lexell, J.; Sandbakk, Ø. Preparing for snow-sport events at the Paralympic Games in Beijing in 2022: Recommendations and remaining questions. *BMJ Open Sport Exerc. Med.* **2022**, *8*, e001294. [CrossRef]
60. Groschl, S. Planning and organizing the Olympic and Paralympic Games: The case of Rio 2016. *Sport Bus. Manag. Int. J.* **2021**, *11*, 365–383. [CrossRef]
61. Goosey-Tolfrey, V.; Swainson, M.; Boyd, C.; Atkinson, G.; Tolfrey, K. The effectiveness of hand cooling at reducing exercise-induced hyperthermia and improving distance-race performance in wheelchair and able-bodied athletes. *J. Appl. Physiol.* **2008**, *105*, 37–43. [CrossRef] [PubMed]
62. Maltais, D.; Wilk, B.; Unnithan, V.; Bar-Or, O. Responses of children with cerebral palsy to treadmill walking exercise in the heat. *Med. Sci. Sports Exerc.* **2004**, *36*, 1674–1681. [CrossRef]
63. Bhambhani, Y. Physiology of wheelchair racing in athletes with spinal cord injury. *Sports Med.* **2002**, *32*, 23–51. [CrossRef] [PubMed]
64. Flueck, J.L. Nutritional Considerations for Para-Cycling Athletes: A Narrative Review. *Sports* **2021**, *9*, 154. [CrossRef] [PubMed]
65. Jeoung, B.; Kim, J. Analysis and Evaluation of Nutritional Intake and Nutrition Quotient of Korean Athletes with Disabilities in the Tokyo Paralympic Games. *Nutrients* **2021**, *13*, 3631. [CrossRef] [PubMed]
66. Blauwet, C.A.; Brook, E.M.; Tenforde, A.S.; Broad, E.; Hu, C.H.; Abdu-Glass, E.; Matzkin, E.G. Low Energy Availability, Menstrual Dysfunction, and Low Bone Mineral Density in Individuals with a Disability: Implications for the Para Athlete Population. *Sports Med.* **2017**, *47*, 1697–1708. [CrossRef]
67. Sanz, S.; Moya, M.; Costa, G.; Rice, I.; Urbán, T.; López-Grueso, R. Nutritional strategies in an elite wheelchair marathoner at 3900 m altitude: A case report. *J. Int. Soc. Sports Nutr.* **2019**, *16*, 1–10.
68. Egger, T.; Flueck, J.L. Energy Availability in Male and Female Elite Wheelchair Athletes Over Seven Consecutive Training Days. *Nutrients* **2020**, *12*, 3262. [CrossRef]
69. Burke, L.M.; Hawley, J.A.; Wong, S.H.S.; Jeukendrup, A.E. Carbohydrates for training and competition. *J. Sports Sci.* **2011**, *29*, S17–S27. [CrossRef]
70. Rastmanesh, R.; Taleban, F.A.; Kimiagar, M.; Mehrabi, Y.; Salehi, M. Nutritional Knowledge and Attitudes in Athletes with Physical Disabilities. *J. Athl. Train.* **2007**, *42*, 99–105. [PubMed]
71. Graham-Paulson, T.S.; Perret, C.; Smith, B.; Crosland, J.; Goosey-Tolfrey, V.L. Nutritional Supplement Habits of Athletes with an Impairment and Their Sources of Information. *Int. J. Sport Nutr. Exerc. Metab.* **2015**, *25*, 387–395. [CrossRef] [PubMed]
72. Deguchi, M.; Yokoyama, H.; Hongu, N.; Watanabe, H.; Ogita, A.; Imai, D.; Suzuki, Y.; Okazaki, K. Eating Perception, Nutrition Knowledge and Body Image among Para-Athletes: Practical Challenges in Nutritional Support. *Nutrients* **2021**, *13*, 3120. [CrossRef]
73. Sánchez-Pay, A.; Sanz-Rivas, D. Competitive Evolution of Professional Wheelchair Tennis from the Paralympic Games in Athens 2004 to Rio 2016: An Observational Study. *Int. J. Environ. Res. Public Health* **2021**, *18*, 3157. [CrossRef]
74. Vorobev, S.A.; Baryaev, A.A. Peculiarities of athletic training at final stage of annual training cycle for 2021 paralympic games. *Teor. I Prakt. Fiz. Kult.* **2020**, *2020*, 48–50.
75. Jakub, K.; Ryszard, K.; Ryszard, P. A comparative analysis of sports levels in the selected swimming competitions of the paralympic games in the years 1992–2008. *J. Orthop. Trauma Surg. Relat. Res.* **2011**, *6*.

76. Dyer, B.; Woolley, H. Desenvolvimento de uma prótese transtibial específica para ciclismo de alta performance para os Jogos Paralímpicos de Londres 2012. *Prosthet. Orthot. Int.* **2017**, *41*, 498–502. [CrossRef]
77. Willems, A.; Paulson, T.A.W.; Keil, M.; Brooke-Wavell, K.; Goosey-Tolfrey, V.L. Dual-Energy X-Ray Absorptiometry, Skinfold Thickness, and Waist Circumference for Assessing Body Composition in Ambulant and Non-Ambulant Wheelchair Games Players. Frontiers in Physiology. 2015. Available online: https://www.frontiersin.org/article/10.3389/fphys.2015.00356 (accessed on 31 May 2022).
78. Weissland, T.; Faupin, A.; Borel, B.; Leprêtre, P.M. Comparison between 30–15 Intermittent Fitness Test and Multistage Field Test on Physiological Responses in Wheelchair Basketball Players. Frontiers in Physiology. 2015. Available online: https://www.frontiersin.org/article/10.3389/fphys.2015.00380 (accessed on 31 May 2022).
79. Hassani, H.; Ghodsi, M.; Shadi, M.; Noroozi, S.; Dyer, B. An Overview of the Running Performance of Athletes with Lower-Limb Amputation at the Paralympic Games 2004–2012. *Sports* **2015**, *3*, 103–115. [CrossRef]
80. International Paralympic Committee. Tokyo 2020 Sees More Countries than Ever Winning Medals at a Paralympics. Available online: https://www.paralympic.org/news/tokyo-2020-sees-more-countries-ever-winning-medals-paralympics (accessed on 1 June 2022).

healthcare

MDPI

Article

Tokyo 2020: A Sociodemographic and Psychosocial Characterization of the Portuguese Paralympic Team

Tânia Mira [1], Diogo Monteiro [2,3,4], Aldo M. Costa [1,3,5], Pedro Morouço [2,6], Rui Matos [2,4] and Raúl Antunes [2,4,6,*]

1 Department of Sport Sciences, University of Beira Interior, 6201-001 Covilhã, Portugal; taniaslmira@gmail.com (T.M.); amcosta@ubi.pt (A.M.C.)
2 ESECS, Polytechnic of Leiria, 2411-901 Leiria, Portugal; diogo.monteiro@ipleiria.pt (D.M.); pedro.morouco@ipleiria.pt (P.M.); rui.matos@ipleiria.pt (R.M.)
3 Research Center in Sport Sciences, Health Sciences and Human Development (CIDESD), 5001-801 Vila Real, Portugal
4 CIEQV—Life Quality Research Centre, Polytechnic of Leiria, 2411-901 Leiria, Portugal
5 Health Science Research Center (CICS-UBI), 6201-001 Covilhã, Portugal
6 Center for Innovative Care and Health Technology (ciTechCare), Polytechnic of Leiria, 2411-901 Leiria, Portugal
* Correspondence: raul.antunes@ipleiria.pt

Abstract: The importance of practicing sports and its impact on the quality of life of people with disabilities is fundamental. Characterizing subjective well-being, resilience, and social influence in the practice of adapted sports, namely in those who participate in elite sport in Portugal, is truly important to support a set of initiatives to promote higher levels of practice. Thus, this study describes the Portuguese delegation at the Tokyo 2020 Paralympic Games through sociodemographic and psychosocial (positive and negative affect, life satisfaction, resilience, and social support) variables. The study involved 31 of the 33 athletes of the Portuguese Paralympic team aged between 15 and 58 years (34.45 ± 11.7 years), with 21 men and 10 women. Individual-level sociodemographic data gave us a clear insight into the reality of adapted sport in Portugal. The high values of life satisfaction, high positive affect and low negative affect, as well as high levels of resilience and social support seem to be important variables for these athletes. The data from the present study highlighted the importance of understanding the characteristics of Paralympic athletes, in order to better understand the reality of Paralympic sport in Portugal.

Keywords: Paralympic Games; Tokyo 2020; sociodemographic; well-being; resilience; social support

check for updates

Citation: Mira, T.; Monteiro, D.; Costa, A.M.; Morouço, P.; Matos, R.; Antunes, R. Tokyo 2020: A Sociodemographic and Psychosocial Characterization of the Portuguese Paralympic Team. *Healthcare* **2022**, *10*, 1185. https://doi.org/10.3390/healthcare10071185

Academic Editor: Felipe Aidar

Received: 24 May 2022
Accepted: 22 June 2022
Published: 24 June 2022

1. Introduction

One of the problems for people with disabilities is that from childhood they are not encouraged to have active lives, ending up living sedentary lives with significant health problems and barriers to physical activity [1]. Therefore, the physical inactivity of this population could increase the risk of developing secondary conditions, such as loneliness, fatigue, obesity [2]. A healthy lifestyle is as essential for promoting health and well-being and disease prevention for people without disabilities as for people with disabilities. Therefore, several authors [3,4] showed the importance of sports practice in people with disabilities.

In this regard, well-being has been one of the most studied variables. It gives people a better feeling of self-confidence, enthusiasm, leadership skills, and sociability. Happy people tend to be healthier, more efficient, successful, and they tend to volunteer in society [5,6].

Subjective well-being emerges as a subjective approach to quality of life [7,8]. People evaluate their life based on important domains (e.g., work, marriage, and health) or the affections and emotions they feel (e.g., joy, anxiety, and depression) [7,9–12]. Subjective well-being of the hedonic premise has a complex and multifaceted nature, and is divided into three components: satisfaction with life (cognitive), positive affect, and negative affect [10,13,14]. Cognitive assessments are characterized by life satisfaction and a sense of personal achievement, and affective appraisals assume the presence of positive affect (i.e., positive emotions and moods) and the absence of negative affect (i.e., negative emotions and moods) [6,7,15–17]. Positive affect is characterized by hedonic contentment experienced at a given moment, based on the description of an emotional state rather than on a cognitive judgment. In contrast, negative affect is characterized by a transitory state that includes negative experiences. In its turn, life satisfaction is a cognitive assessment that the person makes of certain areas of their life, depending on the comparison of real-life circumstances with what they define as a model [8,13].

Studies [18–21] revealed the positive associations between the practice of physical activity and increased well-being [12,22–25]. Some authors [26–28] showed the positive relationship between sports practice and subjective well-being in the disabled population. Well-being has been studied because of its role in actively coping with adversity [29]. Personal growth often involves experiences with obstacles, failure, and disappointment. Incidents such as these are necessary to find internal strengths and reintroduce resources while at the same time allowing one to become aware of one's own limitations and vulnerabilities. This theme leads us to the study of resilience. In line with that, Fletcher and Sarkar [30] define resilience as "*The role of mental and behavioral processes in promoting personal assets and protecting the individual from the potential negative effect of stress*" (p. 675). Reacting positively to adversity depends on the hardships they have been subjected to and their respective adaptation [31]. Resilience is characterized as a dynamic process influenced by the environment and how the person relates to it, which allows for identifying the best attitude in each context [32].

With the increasing development and importance of the concept of resilience, many recent investigations have emerged within the scope of regular and adapted sports [30,33–41]. Participation in sports by people with disabilities has implications for resilience, access to social support, opportunities, and meaningful social experiences for people who faced traumatic injuries [42]. Athletes with disabilities show significant levels of resilience [42–44].

Due to inherent characteristics and problems, people with disabilities seem to be a vulnerable risk group for mental disorders such as depression, anxiety, stress, frustration, lack of motivation, and social impairment [45,46]. Many of the sports initiated during rehabilitation can be continued for pleasure throughout the life of the person with a disability. Pleasure is the primary motivational factor in the willingness to continue in sport [47]. People with physical disabilities who have participated in adapted sports have higher life satisfaction compared to people with physical disabilities who do not participate in any adapted sport [48–50]. People with disabilities who try to have an active lifestyle accept their disability better than inactive people; sport presents itself as a tool that promotes health, quality of life, social integration, self-confidence [48,49,51], satisfaction, quality of life, and self-esteem [48,49,51,52]. Sport decreases the suicidal tendencies of people with disabilities and promotes a more independent and motivated attitude [48,49].

Despite all the benefits mentioned, access to sports for people with disabilities is difficult due to the various barriers, which include a lack of understanding and awareness about inclusion, few opportunities and limited programs, inaccessibility of facilities, transportation difficulties, and lack of information and resources [51]. The support given to people with disabilities influences the promotion and maintenance of physical exercise in sports facilities [52]. Social support shows the person that they are loved, cared for, esteemed, and an integral part of a network of mutual obligations [53]. The origin of social support can be considered informal from family, friends, neighbors or social groups that accompany them daily, or formal when it comes from social institutions such as hospitals, doctors, social workers, and other specialists [54].

In studies that have been carried out on this topic, especially among young people, social support has been considered to be a positive influence in the sporting context [54]. Sheridan et al. [55] conducted a systematic review of social support in youth sports. They concluded that coaches, parents, and peers impact the development of youth sports through their positive influence on several factors. They also found that social support, over time, changed negatively, which can harm the athlete in both elite sport and physical activity [55]. This makes us aware of this need, properly in adjusting the athlete's support pattern throughout the career.

More recently, Ascione et al. [56] referred to sport as a fundamental context in supporting the person with disabilities, contributing to enhancing and helping psychological issues that allow the development of their abilities. Through the practice of sports, the person with a disability and the others around them experience and assess their limits, using them positively as resources and qualities, accepting the difficulties.

In this regard, Martin [57] said that there are more studies with elite athletes, namely in adapted sports, since there is a significant difference between the number of studies published in regular sport than adapted sport. In addition, the variables under analysis in the present study (e.g., social support, well-being, and resilience) are important variables, particularly for this type of population, due to encouraging the participation and involvement of athletes using the strategies presented by Hellison [58]. This highlights the following: provide options for the activity to be performed (including the possibility of temporarily stopping the task/activity); allow the choice of the pace of participation, intensity and number of attempts; individualize and optimize the coach–athlete relationship through feedback, challenges and proposed activities. Moreover, Martin and Wheeler [59] stated that sport is an appropriate environment for these subjects to develop their own mechanisms in terms of resilience, since sometimes they are not accepted in other domains, and through sport they have the possibility to promote and develop their own skills, abilities, and personal resources, and consequently improve their coping strategies.

Thus, the present study aimed to characterize the Portuguese delegation at the Tokyo 2020 Paralympic Games through sociodemographic (age, gender, profession, education, and sports practice) and psychosocial variables (positive and negative affect, life satisfaction, resilience, and social support).

2. Materials and Methods

2.1. Study Design and Procedures

With the approval of the study by the ethics committee of the University of Beira Interior (CE-UBI-Pj-2018-076), there was initial contact with the Paralympic Committee of Portugal, to whom the study purpose was explained. Authorization was requested to carry it out with the Paralympic athletes who participated in the Tokyo 2020 Paralympic Games. Data were collected from questionnaires just after participation in the Tokyo 2020 Paralympic Games, between October and November 2021. The procedure explains the study's objectives, and guarantees the principle of confidentiality. Informed consent was given by the participants, prior to data collection. Therefore, each athlete was provided with a link to access a Google Form, in which authorization was requested to carry out the study. The use of an online questionnaire was intended to facilitate the participation of all Portuguese Paralympic athletes, including athletes with visual impairments and athletes with intellectual disabilities, who in turn had the collaboration of coaches for this purpose. Regarding the completion of the questionnaires by the participants with intellectual disabilities ($n = 4$), the clubs were contacted in order to provide support in reading and understanding them, namely through specialists with training for the application of the questionnaires.

2.2. Participants

A total of 31 out of 33 athletes of the Portuguese Paralympic team aged between 15 and 58 years, with a mean age of 34.45 ± 11.7 years, with 21 men (36.29 ± 11.49 years) and

10 women (30.60 ± 11.84 years). Respondents were fully informed about the aim of the study. They were also told that they could stop at any time. Participants did not receive compensation for their participation.

2.3. Variables/Instruments

The sociodemographic questions were developed specifically for this study, having been reviewed by four experts. The other four questionnaires are validated instruments for the Portuguese population, evaluating four domains: sociodemographic data, life satisfaction, positive and negative affections, resilience, and social influence. To access information regarding the number of clubs in which there are sports modalities adapted for practice in Portugal, we accessed the website of the Portuguese Paralympic Committee, which contains a platform (Sport Inclusion Map) that allows us to find this information by searching by sport or geographical area [60].

To assess the Social Support perceived by athletes with disabilities, a scale based on the recommendations of Jago et al. [61], adapted with the objective assessment of children's perceptions of friends and parental influences on physical activity, was divided into four dimensions: coach, parents, friends, and best friend. When asked about the support that the athlete has from their coach/parents/friends/best friend regarding exercise and sport ("encourages", "practices", "accompanies", and "talks"), athletes responded on a Likert-type scale, with five levels, ranging from 1 ("rarely") to 5 ("often").

Subjective well-being was assessed through Satisfaction with Life Scale [62]. For the present study, the Portuguese version was used [63]. This scale presents five items (1. "In most ways my life is close to my ideal", 2. " The conditions of my life are excellent", 3. "I am satisfied with my life", 4. " So far I have gotten the important things I want in life" and 5. "If I could live my life over again I would change almost nothing"), which are answered on a seven-point Likert scale, with 7 levels, ranging from 1 ("Strongly disagree") to 7 ("Strongly agree").

Positive and negative affect were evaluated through PANAS—The Positive and Negative Affect Schedule [64]. The Portuguese version of PANAS (PANAS-VRP) [65] was used in the present study. The PANAS-VRP presents 10 items (five items for positive affect: "inspired", "alert", "excited", "enthusiastic" and "determined" and five items for negative affect: "fear", "worried", "nervous", "scared" and "perturbed") that are answered on a five-point Likert scale which varies between 1 ("Not at all or very slightly") and 5 ("Extremely").

To assess resilience, the Brief Resilience Scale (BRS) [66], in the Portuguese version [67], was used. This scale is composed of six items that are answered on a five-point Likert scale, as follows: ("1. I tend to recover quickly after difficult situations", "2. I find it difficult to cope with stressful situations", "3. I do not take much time to recover from a stressful situation", "4. I find it difficult to recover quickly when something bad happens", "5. I usually cope with difficult times without much worry" and "6. I tend to take a long time to overcome problems in my life"), with five levels, ranging from 1 ("I totally disagree") to 5 ("I totally agree").

2.4. Data Analysis

Considering the aim of the present study, a descriptive analysis was employed via SPPS v.27 (IBM, Armonk, NY, USA). Based on the central limit theorem, a sample greater than or equal to 30 approximates a normal distribution and therefore is often considered enough for the central limit theorem to hold [68]. In this regard, a descriptive analysis of location and central tendency measures (mean) and dispersion measures (standard deviation) were performed.

In addition, in order to measure the associations across studied variables, a Pearson bivariate correlation was performed. Cohen's (1988) criterion was considered to interpret the magnitude of the correlation coefficients ($r < 0.3$ = low, $r > 0.3$ and <0.5 = medium, and $r > 0.5$ = high) [69] and the significance level to reject the null hypothesis was set at 5% [70].

3. Results

The sample's sociodemographic characteristics that focus on the characterization of age, gender, disability, academic qualification, professional situation, type of sport, years of practice, weekly practice frequency, and training hours per week are presented in Table 1.

Table 1. Summary of the descriptive statistics for the sample's sociodemographic characteristics ($n = 31$).

Variables	*n* (%)	Mean ± SD
	31	
Age (Years)		34.45 ± 11.7
Gender		
Male	21 (67.7%)	
Female	10 (32.3%)	
Disability		
Motor	24 (77.4%)	
Visual	3 (9.7%)	
Intellectual	4 (12.9%)	
Academic qualification		
1st Cycle of Basic Education	1 (3.2%)	
2nd Cycle of Basic Education	1 (3.2%)	
3rd Cycle of Basic Education	5 (16.1%)	
Upper Secondary Education	17 (54.8%)	
Bachelor's degree	4 (12.9%)	
Undergraduate degree	1 (3.2%)	
Master's degree	2 (6.5%)	
Ph.D. degree	0 (0%)	
Professional situation		
Student	9 (29%)	
Public service	5 (16.1%)	
Outsourced account	4 (12.9%)	
Personal account	3 (9.7%)	
Unemployed	1 (3.2%)	
Retired	3 (9.7%)	
Other	6 (19.4%)	
Type of Sport		
Para Athletics	9 (29%)	
Para Badminton	1 (3.2%)	
Boccia	9 (29%)	
Para Canoe	2 (6.5%)	
Para Cycling	2 (6.5%)	
Equestrian	1 (3.2%)	
Judo	1 (3.2%)	
Para Swimming	6 (19.4%)	
Years of practice		
4 to 7 years	4 (12.9%)	
8 to 11 years	11 (35.5%)	
12 or more	16 (51.6%)	
Weekly training frequency		
3 per week	4 (12.9%)	
4 per week	3 (9.7%)	
5 per week	3 (9.7%)	
More than 5 per week	21 (67.7%)	
Training hours per week		
2 to 6 h	6 (19.4%)	
7 to 10 h	3 (9.7%)	
11 to 14 h	8 (25.8%)	
15 to 18 h	7 (22.6%)	
19 to 22 h	4 (12.4%)	
More than 22 h	3 (9.7%)	

Note: SD, standard deviation.

As can be seen in Table 1, the results are based on 31 athletes from eight Paralympic sports. Most athletes had motor disabilities.

The most common academic qualification is secondary education, followed by the third cycle of basic education. The first cycle is usually from between 6 and 9 years old, the second cycle is usually from between 10 and 12 years old and the third cycle is usually from between 13 and 15 years old.

Regarding the professional situation, the distribution is more varied. Most are employed or students and a small percentage are unemployed.

In relation to years of practice, it can be noted that about half of the sample has been practicing for more than 12 years. In relation to the number of training sessions per week the majority, they train more than five times per week and the number of hours of training per week is quite variable.

Figure 1 shows the distribution of athletes according to their residence districts. Thus, the majority of athletes reside in the districts of Lisbon and Porto.

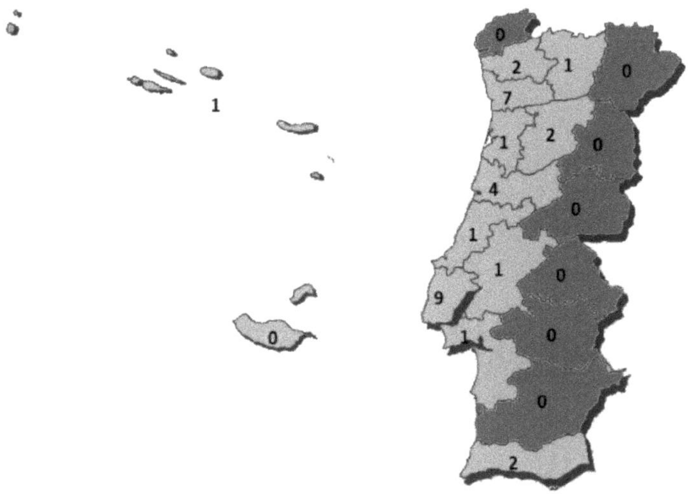

Figure 1. Distribution of athletes according to their districts in Portugal (light gray districts with athletes in the Tokyo 2020 Paralympic Games, dark gray districts without Paralympic athletes).

On the Portuguese Paralympic Committee website platform, we found 204 clubs with sports adapted to practice in Portugal [60]. With this data, Lisbon and Porto are the districts with the most clubs (Figure 2). Still regarding the geographical distribution, it is worth noting the asymmetry between the coast and interior of Portugal, where most clubs are located in the coastal area of the country.

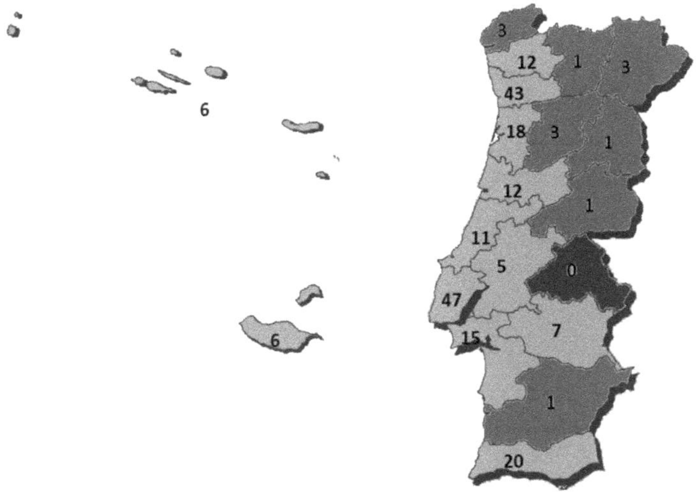

Figure 2. Distribution of adapted sports clubs by districts of Portugal.

The variables of satisfaction with life, positive affect, negative affect, resilience, and social influence were analyzed and are presented in Table 2. Our results show that athletes perceive a positive affect superior to negative affect. Regarding social support, the perception of support by the coach is the one with the highest value.

Table 2. Summary of the descriptive statistics for the sample variables (n = 31).

Variables	Mean		
	Mean ± SD	(95% CI)	Median (IQR)
Life Satisfaction	5.24 ± 0.97	4.88–5.59	5.00 (1.00)
Positive affect	3.96 ± 0.64	3.73–4.20	4.00 (0.60)
Negative affect	1.72 ± 0.64	1.48–1.95	1.60 (1.00)
Resilience	3.73 ± 0.77	3.45–4.01	3.80 (1.00)
Social Support			
Coach	3.48 ± 0.58	3.26–3.69	3.50 (0.75)
Parents	2.55 ± 0.89	2.22–2.88	2.50 (1.25)
Friends	3.00 ± 0.76	2.72–3.28	3.00 (1.00)
Best Friend	2.83 ± 0.94	2.49–3.18	3.00 (1.75)

Notes: SD, standard deviation; 95% CI, confidence interval 95%; IQR, interquartile range.

Results for the association between different variables are summarized in Table 3.

Table 3. Bivariate correlations between variables.

	1	2	3	4	5	6	7	8
1. Life Satisfaction	1	-	-	-	-	-	-	-
2. Positive affect	0.47 **	1	-	-	-	-	-	-
3. Negative affect	−0.18	−0.05	1	-	-	-	-	-
4. Resilience	0.28	0.08	−0.53 **	1	-	-	-	-
5. Social Support—Coach	0.08	0.37	0.06	0.01	1	-	-	-
6. Social Support—Parents	0.13	0.51 **	−0.19	0.18	0.34	1	-	-
7. Social Support—Friends	0.26	0.43 *	0.12	0.22	0.34	0.27	1	-
8. Social Support—Best Friend	0.06	0.26	−0.15	0.12	0.30	0.23	0.62 **	1

**. $p < 0.001$; *. $p < 0.05$.

The bivariate correlation was observed between life satisfaction and positive affect (medium), between positive affect with social support by the parents (high) and between positive affect with social support by the friends (medium). Resilience displayed a negative and significant association with the negative affect (high).

4. Discussion

The purpose of the present study was to describe the Portuguese delegation at the Tokyo 2020 Paralympic Games through sociodemographic (age, gender, disability, academic qualification, professional situation, type of sport, years of practice, weekly frequency, and training hours per week) and psychosocial variables (positive and negative affect, life satisfaction, resilience, and social support).

Thirty-three Portuguese athletes competing in eight sports participated in the 2020 Paralympics Games [71]. We found that 32.3% are female athletes and 67.7% are male athletes regarding sociodemographic data. This difference must, however, be analyzed considering that the number of women who practice sport or exercise regularly is lower than that of men [72]. On the other hand, there are no significant differences between the number of men and women with disabilities in the world [73].

While the 2020 Olympics were near gender parity for the first time, there are still deeply rooted gender stereotypes in Paralympic sport. Indeed, there has been a gradual increase in female participation in the Olympic Games, from 11% in Rome 1960 to around 45% in London 2012. However, in the Paralympic Games, it has increased much more slowly from a higher base of 21% in the Heidelberg 1972 Paralympics to 35% compared in London 2012 [74]. As early as 1995, Olenik et al. [75] noted that women with disabilities who aspire to reach the highest levels of sports performance face double discrimination—disability and gender discrimination.

When we analyze the weekly training hours of these athletes, the answers are pretty variable. Interestingly, the three athletes who train the most hours per week (more than 22 h) are in the same sport: swimming. Similarly, athletes who train the fewest hours per week (between 2 and 6 h) are boccia players. In a study conducted by Fagher et al. [76] with the Swedish Paralympic team, the average hours trained is 9 h per week.

As a suggestion for a future study, it would be interesting to analyze data on the number of weekly training hours of the other Paralympic teams for comparison.

Our results showed another important fact: only one athlete presents himself in the condition of unemployed. Few studies have been conducted on the elite athlete with a disability to the best of our knowledge. It is interesting how Bundon et al. [77] address this topic, noting that the research that has been done to understand how and why elite athletes with disabilities end their sporting careers. The research was conducted in the 1990s and is already outdated since the context has changed. There was concern about losing their income from the sport and there was little certainty about professional integration post-career in sport, mainly due to lack of work experience. These authors also found that the progression of certain types of disability may force some to leave the sport earlier than anticipated [77]. They discuss how previous generations of Paralympians struggled to find time to train while working or studying, paying the costs of their participation in sport. Currently, they have access to funding but face the difficulty of professional integration post-sports career [77–79]. The report of the Disability and Human Rights Observatory [80] showed a trend of growth of workers with disabilities in the public and private sectors.

We also noticed that seven districts do not present any athletes and, as we can see in the image in darker gray, they are primarily inland districts (Viana do Castelo, Bragança, Guarda, Castelo Branco, Portalegre, Évora and Beja). This may reflect the scarce supply and accessibility of adapted sports in the interior area at a national level. With the presented data, we can see that the districts that have more clubs with adapted sports disciplines are the districts with more athletes in the Paralympic Games: Porto and Lisbon. The islands are represented by the Azores with one athlete, and Madeira had no athletes participating in the Tokyo 2020 Games. Darcy [74] noted that resource-rich nations dominate medal-winning nations; he concluded that a more concerted effort must be made to help resource-poor governments strategically improve their participation rates in adapted sport. We can perceive our country's needs at the level of the most resource-poor districts, be they structural or human. This is a robust practical implication of this work: knowing and identifying where the athletes are coming from and comparing this with the number of clubs is another contribution to the implementation of policies to promote adapted sports practice in our country. A competitive environment requires the elaboration of strategic actions that allow the achievement of pre-established objectives. It would be interesting to understand this reality by applying the model of Bosscher et al. [81] who designed the SPLISS (Sports Policies Leading to Sports Success) model, which compares and measures the effectiveness of national sports policies by training. They defined the critical factors that must be carried out for a country to increase the chances of international sports success. As we have seen, the most common academic qualification is secondary education, followed by the third cycle of primary education. Although the study conducted by the Directorate-General for Education and Science Statistics (DGEEC) [80] showed that in Portugal, the number of students with disabilities attending higher education increased by 57% compared with 2017/18, in our sample, the number of athletes with a university education is still far from the desired values. These results help us reflect on the need to encourage academic careers, making it possible to reconcile them with the dual career of sports training. The dual career aims to give the high-performance athlete the possibility to combine, in a fair way, a sporting career with an academic career [82].

Saphiro and Pitts [83], in their research, concluded that sports management scholars and practitioners do not identify sport, leisure, recreation and physical activity for the disabled as part of the business of the sport industry. Less than one-tenth of all published articles address sport for disability. There is a lack of information across the curriculum areas of sports management and in sport for people with disabilities. These authors suggest scholarship and advancement of studies in disability sport in sport business management.

It is important to increase the opportunities for disabled people through education, training, employment, transport, sports, and recreational activities. Therefore, investing in education centers in order to promote the practice of sports and its prolonged practice in these people are key issues not only in sports policy, but must be the position of sports in social policy in general [84].

The overall sample verified that athletes have high values of satisfaction with life, high positive affect, and low negative affect. These results seem to align with previous studies, which concluded that Paralympic athletes have interactions with others, disabled and non-disabled athletes, that give them opportunities to establish new relationships and friendships, increasing life satisfaction [85].

These results for subjective well-being are interesting; studies point to the fact that affect and life satisfaction allow for a significant increase in health, longevity, work, earnings, social relationships, and benefits to society [6]. Côté-Leclerc et al. [86], in their study, found that the positive effect of adapted sport on the quality of their lives acts mainly through personal factors (behavior and health), social participation (interpersonal relationships) and the environment (societal perception and support of the environment). Well-being gives people higher self-confidence, enthusiasm, leadership skills and sociability. Happy people tend to be healthier, more efficient, successful and they tend to volunteer more in society, businesses, and other organizations, individual and governmental, enabling them to increase performance [6,7]. Similar results were found by Hammond's study [87] which analyzed these variables in Paralympic athletes and concluded that they represent a very high functioning group within the population, with high levels of subjective wellbeing. In other study, Silva et al. [88] showed that the subjective well-being are positively affected by sport participation of athletes with disabilities.

We also found a high value for resilience. This data reinforces the literature that states athletes with disabilities show significant levels of resilience [42–44,86]. Hariharan et al. [89] found that resilient people with disabilities had higher emotional intelligence and more positive perceptions of their environment. These positive perceptions of emotional resources allow people with disabilities to overcome barriers and difficulties. In their experiences, athletes face countless hours of training, often repetitive and with implications for stress levels, time to recover from injuries that prevent them from performing, and competitive anxiety with the agony of failure. For these reasons, athletes need physical stamina, talent, and mental toughness [21,90,91]. Thus, they must possess a greater ability to cope with challenges and adversity.

In what concerns social support for physical activity or sport's practice, we verified that the coach has the highest value of the most influence on the athlete, followed by friends, best friends and, lastly, parents. In recent years, studies on social support have increased considerably; from family, friends, and coaches [92,93] to a variety of support staff in a multidisciplinary team [94,95], social support is essential for well-being, allows better integration in society and better achievement of goals. Banack et al. [96], reinforce the importance of the relationship of the Paralympic athlete with the coach in the support of autonomy. Many of the athletes, depending on the disability, need the coach as an assistant in basic activities in training and in competition. Although in our study parental support appears last in degree of importance, Shapiro and Malone [97] refer to family support as extremely important, especially in younger athletes. This result may have to do with the fact that the athletes are older than 16. Social support relationships are all important for access to sport by people with disabilities however, the higher the competitive level, the greater the social support relationships [98].

Our results showed that there is an association between life satisfaction and positive affect, which is in line with the conceptual framework of subjective well-being [7,11,13,62] and with some studies conducted recently [99,100]. The association between the positive effect and the social support of parents and friends reinforces the importance that this support seems to have in the emotional states of the athletes, confirming some of the evidence in the literature [97,98].

Regarding resilience and its negative association with negative affect seems to indicate a possible buffer effect of resilience for negative emotional experiences [101–103]. Although these associations are interesting, they need to be clarified in future studies.

Despite the importance of the present study, some limitations must be acknowledged and should be addressed in future studies. This study was conducted in Portugal, thus results cannot be generalized to other countries and contexts. It will also be very interesting to relate, in future studies, the psychological variables (e.g., well-being, resilience, social support) with demographic variables and with the variables of sports practice (e.g., years of practice). However, this work may have an important contribution to understanding the reality of Paralympic sport in Portugal.

5. Conclusions

The sociodemographic (age, gender, profession, education, sports practice) and psychosocial (positive and negative affect, life satisfaction, resilience, and social support) variables could characterize the Tokyo 2020 Paralympic team. The disparity between the team's total number of men and women is still a reality. Training hours per week are pretty heterogeneous among athletes. The offer and accessibility to adapted sports at the national level are considerably lower in the inner part of the country.

In the sample, we found that Portuguese Paralympic athletes have high values of life satisfaction, high positive affect, low negative affect, and good levels of resilience. Additionally, our results showed that the coach has the most decisive influence on the athlete, followed by friends, best friends, and parents. The coach is indeed the most critical figure in this social influence.

These findings are important and could be considered for further analysis and evaluation of the reality of adapted sport in Portugal, supporting the idea that more public development policies are needed for people with disabilities to access adapted physical activity and sport.

Author Contributions: Conceptualization, T.M., D.M. and R.A.; methodology, T.M., D.M. and R.A.; validation, T.M., D.M., A.M.C., P.M. and R.A.; formal analysis, T.M., D.M. and R.A; investigation, T.M., D.M. and R.A.; data curation, R.M. and R.A.; writing—original draft preparation, T.M., D.M. and R.A.; writing—review and editing, T.M., D.M., A.M.C., P.M., R.M. and R.A.; visualization, D.M., A.M.C., P.M. and R.A.; supervision, D.M. and R.A.; funding acquisition, P.M. and R.A. All authors have read and agreed to the published version of the manuscript.

Funding: This research was supported by National Funding through the Portuguese Foundation for Science and Technology, I. P., under the project number UIDB/04045/2020 and the project number UIDB UIDB/04748/2020.

Institutional Review Board Statement: This study was approved by the Ethics Committee of the University of Beira Interior (CE-UBI-Pj-2018-076).

Informed Consent Statement: Informed consent was taken from all participants in the study.

Data Availability Statement: Additional data are available upon request to the author for correspondence.

Acknowledgments: We thank the Portuguese Paralympic Committee and the athletes who allowed and contributed to this study.

Conflicts of Interest: The authors declare that they have no conflict of interest.

References

1. Saphiro, D.; Martin, J. Multidimensional Physical Self-Concept of Athletes with Physical Disabilities. *Adapt. Phys. Act. Q.* **2010**, *27*, 294–307.
2. Laskowski, E. The role of exercise in the treatment of obesity. *PMR* **2012**, *4*, 840–844. [CrossRef] [PubMed]
3. Slater, D.; Meade, M.A. Participation in recreation and sports for persons with spinal cord injury: Review and recommendations. *NeuroRehabilitation* **2004**, *19*, 121–129. [CrossRef] [PubMed]
4. Medola, F.; Busto, R.; Marçal, A.; Júnior, A.; Dourado, A. Sports on quality of life of individuals with spinal cord injury: A case series. *Rev. Bras. Med. Esporte* **2011**, *17*, 254–256. [CrossRef]
5. Diener, E.; Kesebir, P.; Lucas, R. Benefits of accounts of well-being—For societies and for psychological science. *Appl. Psychol. Int. Rev.* **2000**, *57*, 37–53. [CrossRef]
6. Ryan, R.M.; Deci, E.L. On happiness and human potentials: A review of research on hedonic and eudaimonic well-being. *Annu. Rev. Psychol.* **2001**, *52*, 141–166. [CrossRef]
7. Diener, E. Subjective well-being—The science of happiness and a proposal for a national index. *Am. Psychol.* **2000**, *55*, 34–43. [CrossRef]
8. Albuquerque, A.; Tróccoli, B. Desenvolvimento de uma escala de bem-estar subjetivo. *Psicol. Teor. Pesqui.* **2004**, *20*, 153–164. [CrossRef]
9. Diener, E. Assenssing subjective well-being—Progress and opportunities. *Soc. Indic. Res.* **1994**, *31*, 103–157. [CrossRef]
10. Diener, E.; Suh, E.M.; Lucas, R.E.; Smith, H.L. Subjective well-being: Three decades of progress. *Psychol. Bull.* **1999**, *125*, 276–302. [CrossRef]
11. Diener, E.; Ryan, K. Subjective well-being: A general overview. *S. Afr. J. Psychol.* **2009**, *39*, 391–406. [CrossRef]
12. Moraes, M.; Corte-Real, N.; Dias, C.; Fonseca, A.M. Um olhar sobre a prática desportiva, bem-estar subjetivo e integração social de imigrantes … em Portugal e no mundo. *Psicol. Soc.* **2012**, *24*, 208–216. [CrossRef]
13. Diener, E.; Oishi, S.; Lucas, R.E. Personality, culture, and subjective well-being: Emotional and cognitive evaluations of life. *Annu. Rev. Psychol.* **2003**, *54*, 403–425. [CrossRef]
14. Ryff, C.; Keyes, C. The Structure of Psychological Well-Being Revisited. *J. Personal. Soc. Psychol.* **1995**, *69*, 719–727. [CrossRef]
15. Dias, C.; Corte-Real, N.; Corredeira, R.; Barreiros, A.; Bastos, T.; Fonseca, A. A prática desportiva dos estudantes universitários e suas relações com as autopercepções físicas, bem-estar subjectivo e felicidade. *Estud. Psicol.* **2008**, *13*, 223–232. [CrossRef]
16. Giacomoni, C. Bem-estar subjetivo: Em busca da qualidade de vida. *Temas Psicol. SBP* **2004**, *12*, 43–50.
17. Waterman, A.S. Two conceptions of happiness: Contrasts of personal expressiveness (eudaimonia) and hedonic enjoyment. *J. Personal. Soc. Psychol.* **1993**, *64*, 678–691. [CrossRef]
18. Caddick, N.; Smith, B. The impact of sport and physical activity on the well-being of combat veterans: A systematic review. *Psychol. Sport Exerc.* **2014**, *15*, 9–18. [CrossRef]
19. Hogan, C.L.; Catalino, L.I.; Mata, J.; Fredrickson, B.L. Beyond emotional benefits: Physical activity and sedentary behaviour affect psychosocial resources through emotions. *Psychol. Health* **2015**, *30*, 354–369. [CrossRef]
20. Mack, D.E.; Wilson, P.M.; Gunnell, K.E.; Gilchrist, J.D.; Kowalski, K.C.; Crocker, P.R.E. Health-Enhancing Physical Activity: Associations with Markers of Well-Being. *Appl. Psychol. Health Well Being* **2012**, *4*, 127–150. [CrossRef]
21. Smith, A.L.; Ntoumanis, N.; Duda, J.L.; Vansteenkiste, M. Goal Striving, Coping, and Well-Being: A Prospective Investigation of the Self-Concordance Model in Sport. *J. Sport Exerc. Psychol.* **2011**, *33*, 124–145. [CrossRef] [PubMed]

22. Downward, P.; Rasciute, S. Does sport make you happy? Na analysis of the well-being derived from sports participation. *Int. Rev. Appl. Econ.* **2011**, *25*, 331–348. [CrossRef]
23. Ku, P.; Kenneth, F.; Chang, C.; Sun, W.; Chen, L. Cross-Sectional and Longitudinal Associations of Categories of Physical Activities with Dimensions of Subjective Well-being in Taiwanese Older Adults. *Soc. Indic. Res.* **2014**, *117*, 705–718. [CrossRef]
24. Ku, P.; McKenna, J.; Fox, K.R. Dimensions of Subjective Well-being and Effects of Physical Activity in Chinese Older Adults. *J. Aging Phys. Act.* **2007**, *15*, 382–397. [CrossRef]
25. Olsson, L.; Hurtig-Wennlof, A.; Nilsson, T. Subjective well-being in Swedish active seniors and its relationship with physical activity and commonly available biomarkers. *Clin. Interv. Aging* **2014**, *14*, 1233–1239.
26. Albrecht, G.; Devlieger, P. The disability paradox: High quality of life against all odds. *Soc. Sci. Med.* **1999**, *48*, 977–988. [CrossRef]
27. Chow, S.; Lo, S.K.; Cummins, R. Self-perceived quality of life of children and adolescents with physical disabilities in Hong Kong. *Qual. Life Res.* **2005**, *14*, 415–423. [CrossRef]
28. Emerson, E.; Honey, A.; Madden, R.; Llewellyn, G. The Well-Being of Australian Adolescents and Young Adults with Self-Reported Long-Term Health Conditions, Impairments or Disabilities: 2001 and 2006. *Aust. J. Soc. Issues* **2009**, *44*, 39–53.
29. Ryff, C.D. Self-realisation and meaning making in the face of adversity: A eudaimonic approach to human resilience. *J. Psychol. Afr.* **2014**, *24*, 1–12. [CrossRef]
30. Fletcher, D.; Sarkar, M. A grounded theory of psychological resilience in Olympic Champions. *Psychol. Sport Exerc.* **2012**, *13*, 669–678. [CrossRef]
31. Morgan, P.B.C.; Fletcher, D.; Sarkar, M. Defining and characterizing team resilience in elite sport. *Psychol. Sport Exerc.* **2013**, *14*, 549–559. [CrossRef]
32. Angst, R. Psicologia e resiliência: Uma revisão da literatura. *Psicol. Argum.* **2009**, *27*, 253–260. [CrossRef]
33. Bejan, R.; Tonita, F. The role of the resilience in coping with stress in sports. *Soc. Behav. Sci.* **2013**, *117*, 402–407. [CrossRef]
34. Besharat, M.A. Relationship of Alexithymia with Coping Styles and Interpersonal Problems. *Procedia-Soc. Behav. Sci.* **2010**, *5*, 614–618. [CrossRef]
35. Cevada, T.; Cerqueira, L.S.; de Moraes, H.S.; dos Santos, T.M.; Pompeu, F.; Deslandes, A.C. Relationship between sport, resilience, quality of life, and anxiety. *Rev. Psiquiatr. Clin.* **2012**, *39*, 85–89. [CrossRef]
36. Fontes, R.D.D.; Brandao, M.R.F. Resilience in sport: An ecological perspective on human development. *Mot. Rev. Educ. Fis.* **2013**, *19*, 151–159. [CrossRef]
37. Fletcher, D.; Sarkar, M. Psychological Resilience A Review and Critique of Definitions, Concepts, and Theory. *Eur. Psychol.* **2013**, *18*, 12–23. [CrossRef]
38. Lu, F.J.H.; Lee, W.P.; Chang, Y.K.; Chou, C.C.; Hsu, Y.W.; Lin, J.H.; Gill, D.L. Interaction of athletes' resilience and coaches' social support on the stress-burnout relationship: A conjunctive moderation perspective. *Psychol. Sport Exerc.* **2016**, *22*, 202–209. [CrossRef]
39. Neves, A.; Hirata, K.; Tavares, M. Imagem corporal, trauma e resiliência: Reflexões sobre o papel do professor de Educação Física. *Rev. Quadrimestral Assoc. Bras. Psicol. Esc. Educ.* **2015**, *19*, 97–104. [CrossRef]
40. Nicholls, A.; Morley, D.; Perry, J. The Model of Motivational Dynamics in Sport: Resistance to Peer Influence, Behavioral Engagement and Disaffection, Dispositional Coping, and Resilience. *Front. Psychol.* **2016**, *6*, 2010. [CrossRef]
41. Sarkar, M.; Fletcher, D. Psychological resilience in sport performers: A review of stressors and protective factors. *J. Sports Sci.* **2014**, *32*, 1419–1434. [CrossRef] [PubMed]
42. Machida, M.; Irwin, B.; Feltz, D. Resilience in Competitive Athletes With Spinal Cord Injury: The Role of Sport Participation. *Qual. Health Res.* **2013**, *23*, 1054–1065. [CrossRef] [PubMed]
43. Cardoso, F.L.; Sacomori, C. Resilience of athletes with physical disabilities: A cross-sectional study. *Rev. Psicol. Deporte* **2013**, *23*, 15–22.
44. Sirorska, I.; Gerc, K. Athletes with disability in the light of positive psychology. *Balt. J. Health Phys. Act.* **2018**, *10*, 64–76. [CrossRef]
45. Ferreira, J.; Fox, K. Physical self-perceptions and self-esteem in male basketball players with and without disability: A preliminar analysis using the physical self-perception profile. *Eur. J. Adapt. Phys. Act.* **2008**, *1*, 35–49. [CrossRef]
46. Sahlin, B.; Lexell, J. Impact of Organized Sports on Activity, Participation, and Quality of Life in People with Neurologic Disabilities. *PMR* **2015**, *7*, 1081–1088. [CrossRef]
47. Martin, J.J. Transitions out of competitive sport for athletes with disabilities. *Ther. Recreat. J.* **1996**, *30*, 128–136.
48. Frank, C.; Land, W.M.; Schack, T. Mental representation and learning: The influence of practice on the development of mental representation structure in complex action. *Psychol. Sport Exerc.* **2013**, *14*, 353–361. [CrossRef]
49. Blauwet, C.; Willick, S.E. The Paralympic Movement: Using Sports to Promote Health, Disability Rights, and Social Integration for Athletes with Disabilities. *PMR J. Inj. Funct. Rehabil.* **2012**, *4*, 851–856. [CrossRef]
50. Yazicioglu, K.; Yavuz, F.; Goktepe, A.; Tan, A. Influence of adapted sports on quality of life and life satisfaction in sport participants and non-sport participants with physical disabilities. *Disabil. Health J.* **2012**, *5*, 249–253. [CrossRef]
51. Misener, L.; Darcy, S. Managing disability sport: From athletes with disabilities to inclusive organisational perspectives. *Sport Manag. Rev.* **2014**, *17*, 1–7. [CrossRef]
52. Javorina, D.; Shirazipour, A.; Allan, V.; Latimeur-Cheung, A. The impact of social relationships on initiation in adapted physical activity for individuals with acquired disabilities. *Psychol. Sport Exerc.* **2020**, *50*, 101752. [CrossRef]
53. Cobb, S. Social support as a moderator of life stress. *Psychosom. Med.* **1976**, *38*, 300–314. [CrossRef] [PubMed]

54. Dunst, C.; Trivette, C. Assessment of social support in early intervention programs. In *Handbook of Early Childhood Intervention*; Meisels, S., Shonkoff, J., Eds.; Cambridge University Press: New York, NY, USA, 1990; pp. 326–349.
55. Sheridan, D.; Coffee, P.; Lavallee, D. A systematic review of social support in youth sport. *Int. Rev. Sport Exerc. Psychol.* **2014**, *7*, 198–228. [CrossRef]
56. Ascione, A.; Belfiore, P.; Di Palma, D. Sports program to promote the well-being of people with disabilities. *Acta Med. Mediterr.* **2018**, *34*, 1261–1263.
57. Martin, J. *Handbook of Disability Sport and Exercise Psychology*; Oxford University Press: New York, NY, USA, 2018.
58. Hellison, D. *Teaching Responsability through Physical Activity*; Human Kinetics: Champaign, IL, USA, 1995.
59. Martin, J.; Wheeler, G. Psychology. In *Handbook of Sports Medicine and Science—The Paralympic Athlete*; Vanlandewijck, Y., Thompson, W., Eds.; John Wiley & Sons. Ltd.: Oxford, UK, 2011; pp. 116–135.
60. Comité Olímpico de Portugal. Available online: https://paralimpicos.pt/mapa-inclusao-desportiva (accessed on 27 February 2022).
61. Jago, R.; Fox, K.; Page, A.; Brockman, R.; Thompson, J. Development of scales to assess children's perceptions of friend and parental influences on physical activity. *Int. J. Behav. Nutr. Phys. Act.* **2009**, *6*, 67. [CrossRef]
62. Diener, E.; Emmons, R.A.; Larsen, R.J.; Griffin, S. The Satisfaction with Life Scale. *J. Personal. Assess.* **1985**, *49*, 71–75. [CrossRef]
63. Neto, F. The satisfaction with life scale: Psychometrics properties in an adolescent sample. *J. Youth Adolesc.* **1993**, *22*, 125–134. [CrossRef]
64. Watson, D.; Clark, L.A.; Tellegen, A. Development and validation of brief measures of positive and negative affect: The PANAS scales. *J. Personal. Soc. Psychol.* **1988**, *54*, 1063–1070. [CrossRef]
65. Galinha, I.; Pereira, C.; Esteves, F. Versão reduzida da escala portuguesa de afeto positivo e negative—PANAS-VRP: Análise fatorial confirmatória e invariância temporal. *Rev. Psicol.* **2014**, *28*, 53–65. [CrossRef]
66. Smith, B.W.; Dalen, J.; Wiggins, K.; Tooley, E.; Christopher, P.; Bernard, J. The brief resilience scale: Assessing the ability to bounce back. *Int. J. Behav. Med.* **2008**, *15*, 194–200. [CrossRef] [PubMed]
67. Silva-Sauer, L.; Torre-Luque, A.; Smith, B.W.; Lins, M.C.; Andrade, S.; Fernández-Calvo, B. Brief resilience scale (brs) portuguese version: Validity and metrics for the older adult population. *Aging Ment. Health* **2020**, *25*, 1554–1563. [CrossRef] [PubMed]
68. Hair, J.F.; Black, W.C.; Babin, B.J.; Anderson, R.E. Multivariate Data Analysis. 2019. Available online: www.cengage.com/highered (accessed on 27 March 2022).
69. Cohen, J. *Statistical Power Analysis for the Behavioral Sciences*; Lawrence Erlbaum Associates: Hillsdale, NJ, USA, 1988.
70. Ho, R. *Handbook of Univariate and Multivariate Data Analysis with IBM SPSS*, 2nd ed.; CRC Press: New York, NY, USA, 2014.
71. Comité Paralímpico de Portugal. Available online: https://comiteolimpicoportugal.pt/wp-content/uploads/Toquio-2020-Guia-Desportivo.pdf (accessed on 15 March 2022).
72. World Health Organization & World Bank. *World Report on Disability 2011*; World Health Organization: Geneva, Switzerland, 2011.
73. European Opinion Research Group. *Special Eurobarometer 472*; European Commision: Brusels, Belgium, 2018.
74. Darcy, S. "Behemoths and the Also-Rans": The International Paralympic Movement as a Pyramid Built on Quicksand. In *The Palgrave Handbook of Paralympic Studies*; Brittain, I., Beacom, A., Eds.; Palgrave Handbooks: London, UK, 2018.
75. Olenik, L.; Matthews, J.; Steadward, R. Women, Disability and Sport: Unheard Voices. *Canadian Woman Studies* **1995**, *15*, 4.
76. Fagher, K.; Dahstrom, O.; Jacobsson, J.; Timpka, T.; Lexell, J. Injuries and illnesses in Swedish Paralympic athletes—A 52-week prospective study of incidence and risk factors. *Scand. J. Med. Sci. Sports* **2020**, *30*, 1457–1470. [CrossRef]
77. Bundon, A.; Ashfield, A.; Smith, B.; Goosey-Tolfrey, V. Struggling to stay and struggling to leave: The experiences of elite para-athletes at the end of their sport careers. *Psychol. Sport Exerc.* **2018**, *37*, 296–305. [CrossRef]
78. Wheeler, G.D.; Malone, L.A.; VanVlack, S.; Nelson, E.R.; Steadward, R.D. Retirement from disability sport: A pilot study. *Adapt. Phys. Act. Q.* **1996**, *13*, 382–399. [CrossRef]
79. Wheeler, G.D.; Steadward, R.D.; Legg, D.; Hutzler, Y.; Campbell, E.; Johnson, A. Personal investment in disability sport careers: An international study. *Adapt. Phys. Act. Q.* **1999**, *16*, 219–237. [CrossRef]
80. Observatório da Deficiência e direitos Humanos. *Pessoas com Deficiência em Portugal*; Instituto Superior de Ciências Sociais e Políticas, Universidade de Lisboa: Lisboa, Portugal, 2021.
81. De Bosscher, V.; De Knop, P.; Van Bottenburg, M.; Shibli, S. A Conceptual Framework for Analysing Sports Policy Factors Leading to International Sporting Success. *Eur. Sport Manag. Q.* **2006**, *6*, 185–215. [CrossRef]
82. Picamilho, S.; Saragoça, J.; Teixeira, M. Dual careers in high sporting performance in europe: A systematic literature review. *Motricidade* **2021**, *17*, 290–305.
83. Saphiro, D.; Pitts, B. What Little Do We Know: Content Analysis of Disability Sport in Sport Management Literature. *J. Sport Manag.* **2014**, *28*, 657–671.
84. Walker, C.M.; Hayton, J.W. Navigating austerity: Balancing 'desirability with viability'in a third sector disability sports organisation. *Eur. Sport Manag. Q.* **2017**, *17*, 98–116. [CrossRef]
85. Ondrušova, Z.; Pitekova, R.; Bardiovsky, M.; Galikova, Z. Sport and doing sport s by the disabled posttraumatic return to life. *Clin. Soc. Work* **2013**, *4*, 65–70.

86. Côté-Leclerc, F.; Duchesne, G.; Bolduc, P.; Gélinas-Lafrenière, A.; Santerre, C.; Desrosiers, J.; Levasseur, M. How does playing adapted sports affect quality of life of people with mobility limitations? Results from a mixed-method sequential explanatory study. *Health Qual. Life Outcomes* **2017**, *15*, 22. [CrossRef] [PubMed]
87. Hammond, T. *The Subjective Well-Being of Paralympic Athletes*; Deakin University: Geelong, Austrália, 2014.
88. Silva, A.; Monteiro, D.; Sobreiro, P. Effects of sports participation and the perceived value of elite sport on subjective well-being. *Sport Soc.* **2021**, *23*, 1202–1216. [CrossRef]
89. Hariharan, M.; Karimi, M.; Kishore, M.T. Resilience in persons with disabilities: Role of perceived environment and emotional intelligence. *J. Indian Acad. Appl. Psychol.* **2014**, *40*, 97–102.
90. Jones, G.; Hanton, S.; Connaughton, D. What Is This Thing Called Mental Toughness? An Investigation of Elite Sport Performers. *J. Appl. Sport Psychol.* **2002**, *14*, 205–218. [CrossRef]
91. Vallerand, R.J.; Losier, G.F. An integrative analysis of intrinsic and extrinsic motivation in sport. *J. Appl. Sport Psychol.* **1999**, *11*, 142–169. [CrossRef]
92. Rosenfeld, L.; Richman, J.; Hardy, C. Examining social support networks among athletes: Description and relationship to stress. *Sport Psychol.* **1989**, *3*, 23–33. [CrossRef]
93. Barefield, S.; McCallister, S. Social support in the athletic training room: Athletes' expectations of staff and student athletic trainers. *J. Athl. Train.* **1997**, *32*, 333.
94. Gould, D.; Guinan, D.; Greenleaf, C. Factors affecting Olympic performance: Perceptions of athletes and coaches from more and less successful teams. *Sport Psychol.* **1999**, *13*, 371–394. [CrossRef]
95. Burns, L.; Weissensteiner, J.; Cohen, M. Lifestyles and mindsets of Olympic, Paralympic and world champions: Is an integrated approach the key to elite performance? *Br. J. Sports Med.* **2019**, *53*, 818–824. [CrossRef] [PubMed]
96. Banack, H.; Sabiston, C.; Bloom, G. Coach Autonomy Support, Basic Need Satisfaction, and Intrinsic Motivation of Paralympic Athletes. *Res. Q. Exerc. Sport* **2011**, *82*, 722–730. [CrossRef] [PubMed]
97. Shapiro, D.; Malone, L. Quality of life and psychological affect related to sport participation in children and youth athletes with physical disabilities: A parent and athlete perspective. *Disabil Health J.* **2016**, *9*, 385–391. [CrossRef]
98. VaezMousavia, M.; Mousavib, A.; Mohammadic, F. Psychological Characteristics of Iranian Para-athletes. *Int. J. Mot. Control Learn.* **2021**, *3*, 46–56.
99. Busseri, M.A. Examining the structure of subjective well-being through meta-analysis of the associations among positive affect, negative affect, and life satisfaction. *Personal. Individ. Differ.* **2018**, *122*, 68–71. [CrossRef]
100. Jovanović, V.; Joshanloo, M. The Contribution of Positive and Negative Affect to Life Satisfaction across Age. *Appl. Res. Qual. Life* **2021**, *17*, 511–524. [CrossRef]
101. Ryff, C.D.; Singer, B. Flourishing under fire: Resilience as a prototype of challenged thriving. In *Flourishing: Positive Psychology and the Life Well-Lived*; Keyes, C.L.M., Haidt, J., Eds.; American Psychological Association: Washington DC, USA, 2003; pp. 15–36.
102. Ong, A.D.; Bergeman, C.S.; Bisconti, T.L.; Wallace, K.A. Psychological resilience, positive emotions, and successful adaptation to stress in later life. *J. Personal. Soc. Psychol.* **2006**, *91*, 730–749. [CrossRef] [PubMed]
103. Cohn, M.A.; Fredrickson, B.L.; Brown, S.L.; Mikels, J.A.; Conway, A.M. Happiness unpacked: Positive emotions increase life satisfaction by building resilience. *Emotion* **2009**, *9*, 361–368. [CrossRef]

healthcare

MDPI

Article

Assessing the Needs of People with Disabilities for Physical Activities and Sports in South Korea

Ahra Oh [1] and Wi-Young So [2,*]

1 Department of Exercise Rehabilitation & Welfare, Gachon University, 191 Hombakmoero, Yeonsu-gu, Incheon 21936, Korea; dhdkfk@gachon.ac.kr

2 Sport Medicine Major, College of Humanities and Arts, Korea National University of Transportation, Chungju-si 27469, Korea

* Correspondence: wowso@ut.ac.kr; Tel.: +82-43-841-5993; Fax: +82-43-841-5990

Abstract: This study's objective was to understand the physical activities and sports-related needs of people with disabilities in South Korea and how those needs should be reflected in policy and practice to improve these people's quality of life. Accordingly, focus group interviews were conducted with 35 people with disabilities who had participated in physical activities. Interviews were conducted one-on-one or in small groups of three or four. The interview questions related to their participation experiences in physical activities and sports, their difficulties with such participation, and their thoughts on what was needed to improve their participation. For data analysis, the interviews were transcribed and the content analyzed, with content triangulation performed for validity. From this, a total of 307 meaningful references were derived, comprising four categories, eight theme clusters, and 40 themes. The current physical activities and sports programs for people with disabilities in South Korea are led by the government to provide an environment for them to participate; however, to improve the quality of life for these people, these must be transformed into consumer-centric programs. To provide an opportunity for people with disabilities to choose the exercise program of their choice, it is necessary to research in advance what kind of exercise program these people want, centering on the local community. To strengthen the professionalism of disabled sports instructors, it is necessary to provide a stable environment for them in sports facilities and continue training them to build capacity. In terms of facilities, the expansion of sports facilities that can be used by people with disabilities is an urgent priority, and the opinions of users with disabilities must be actively collected and addressed in the operation of these facilities. Additionally, at the national level, information should be continuously provided through mass media and the Internet so that people with disabilities can know the importance of physical activity and sports and manage their own health. To that end, it would be helpful to conduct an in-depth analysis of countries with effective participation policies for people with disabilities and consider how these could be adapted to the situation in Korea.

Keywords: people with disabilities; physical activities; South Korea; social determinants of health; focus group interviews

check for updates

Citation: Oh, A.; So, W.-Y. Assessing the Needs of People with Disabilities for Physical Activities and Sports in South Korea. *Healthcare* **2022**, *10*, 265. https://doi.org/10.3390/healthcare10020265

Academic Editor: Felipe Aidar

Received: 26 December 2021
Accepted: 26 January 2022
Published: 29 January 2022

1. Introduction

Since the 1988 Seoul Paralympic Games, there has been a growth in South Korea (henceforth "Korea") of sports and physical activities for people with disabilities, with the full support of the Korean government [1]. Since then, the government launched has its first and now its third "Plan for the Promotion of Sports for People with Disabilities" covering 2008 to 2022, and continues to develop these plans [2].

In 2019, the Ministry of Culture, Sports and Tourism, which is in charge of sports administration in Korea, received a budget increase of 145% "to stimulate physical activities and sports" in the country [3]. In addition, this government agency is responsible for promoting projects such as the building of 150 sports facilities for people with disabilities by 2025, arranging for 1200 adapted instructors for the disabled by 2022, and introducing free sports lessons for the disabled [4]. The enlarged budget called for the expansion of these established sports programs and the recruitment of adapted sports instructors (instructors for the disabled people with disabilities) for existing sports facilities [5].

In a study by Sá, Maria Manuel, and four others, the reason that people with disabilities in Portugal did not participate in physical activity and sports was primarily because of a lack of suitable sports facilities. Such people also experience various problems, such as in relation to their financial situation [6]. In the United States, depending on the region, people with disabilities continue to experience various barriers to accessing sports facilities, and according to a survey of 50 sports facilities for people with disabilities in Oregon, major barriers included the entrance, customer service, and shower facilities [7]. Studies that investigated accessibility to most sports facilities for people with disabilities reflected the opinions of people with disabilities in the study [8–10].

Unfortunately, according to 2018 survey data on where people with disabilities participate in physical activities and sports, most (61.5%) respondents indicated that they exercised in a park or used a hiking trail near their homes, with 31.8% exercising at home [4]. In other words, although the government is investing heavily in sports centers for people with disabilities, 87.1% of the people with disabilities surveyed indicated that they were not using these facilities, but instead pursuing such activities either at home or in nearby parks.

When the Korean government established a quantitative target for the stimulation of physical activities and sports, local governments made efforts to achieve this target [11]. As a result, the plan has not effectively supported physical activities and sports for people with disabilities based on their needs [12].

For the Korean government's administration of sports and physical activities for people with disabilities to become effective, it needs to be centered on the concerns of the disabled. This means that the government needs to focus on how to "empower" people with disabilities and create an environment where they can make decisions about their own lives [13]. This is in accordance with the right to self-determination, which is frequently emphasized in the field of sports and physical activity for people with disabilities [14]. In so doing, the Korean government's supplier-centric administrative system for sports for people with disabilities can be transformed into a consumer-centric system.

Early consumer-centric studies that focused on performance [15–19] reported that a consumer-centric service delivery system not only affects the quality of life of people with disabilities positively but also helps to improve their social participation and empowerment [20–27]. To that end, the needs of people with disabilities should be assessed. Subsequently, based on this assessment, an environment can be provided in which they can easily participate in the sports they choose, increase their physical activity, and enhance their quality of life. Many studies have confirmed that the psychological and physiological health and quality of life of people with disabilities improve through participation in sports and physical activity [28–32].

Disability Rights United Kingdom, the United Kingdom's leading charitable organization for persons with disabilities, is funded by Sports England and runs a program called Get Yourself Active. This program enhances the general understanding of the benefits of physical activity for disabled persons and provides the environment and opportunities for people with disabilities to participate voluntarily [33]. Similarly, the Netherlands and Canada have improved the quality of life for people with disabilities by providing national support that independently promotes sports, recreation, and physical activity for these individuals [34].

The Korean government has conducted the "Physical Activities and Sports for People with Disabilities Survey" every year since 2006. However, there are only two multiple-choice questions that ask about their needs in the context of facilities for physical activities and sports [3]. Thus, there are no customer data on whether such facilities are required, as the questions do not touch on the diverse and in-depth needs of people with disabilities in terms of the programs and exclude any reference to aspects such the facilities, leaders, or facility management. Thus, to provide effective consumer-centric services, an in-depth analysis of the needs of people with disabilities in Korea in terms of physical activities and sports is necessary. To that end, we use a focus group interview (FGI) approach to gather data to analyze the needs of people with disabilities in Korea in depth.

For qualitative studies, the FGI method, which utilizes an interview guide of open-ended questions, supports a detailed examination of participant experiences, perceptions, opinions, emotions, and knowledge [35]. In addition, by sharing opinions on a topic freely, the participants and interviewers can interact, understanding not only each individual's thoughts, but also gaining ideas from the group as a whole [36]. Accordingly, many scholars in social science, health science, and evaluation research use FGIs to obtain detailed information that cannot be readily obtained through quantitative surveys [37–40]. In this study, by using FGIs, we are able to assess the needs of Korean consumers with disabilities in terms of their requirements for participation in physical activities and sports, and identify the underlying environmental issues driving these needs. Ultimately, our objective is to understand the physical activities and sports-related needs of people with disabilities in Korea and how those needs should be reflected in policy and practice to improve their quality of life.

2. Materials and Methods

2.1. Participants

The purpose of the FGIs was to collect qualitative data from people who had experienced "a specific situation" consistent with our objective [41]. The groups comprised 35 people with disabilities who had participated in physical activities and sports in Korea. When recruiting focus groups in social science research, a mixed group is more effective than a homogeneous group to obtain various viewpoints and experiences [42]. In similar studies, participants in FGIs represented various ages, environments, and disabilities and included subjects with various experiences in physical education to cover both negative and positive experiences, as well as physical activity and quality of life [43–45].

In our study, to obtain abundant data in the recruitment process, we considered two factors when screening for people with disabilities who had experience participating in physical education. The first factor was the size of the participant's city. For the study, we tried to consider needs based on the size of the city by recruiting from both small and large cities in Korea. The second factor was employment status. We deemed that needs would differ based on employment status, since there could be a difference in leisure time between those who were and were not employed.

Regarding the type of disability, in the FGIs, we included a family member who could communicate the opinions of participants with intellectual disabilities, as well as those with physical and visual impairments. The characteristics of the participants are shown in Table 1.

2.2. Procedure

To design the focus group guide, we first conducted a literature review on the status of physical activities and sports for people with disabilities in Korea and other countries. The questions for the FGIs were based on what we discovered in this process. Next, we collected data through one-on-one and small-group interviews. These data were coded, and subsequently, through further analysis of the coded data, we derived the participants' physical activities and sports environment-related needs that could improve their quality of life.

2.3. Data Collection

In the first stage of data collection, the current situation was analyzed by collecting domestic and overseas research on physical activities and sports for people with disabilities. The literature review included data between 2018 and 2020 from the "Physical Activities and

Sports for People with Disabilities Survey" [3,46,47]—conducted annually in Korea—and data from the United Kingdom's "Get Yourself Active" [48] and Germany's "Survey Among People with Disabilities in Leipzig on Participation in Sport" [49]. A summary of the review is presented in Table 2.

Table 1. Participant characteristics.

Name	Gender	Age	Type	City Size	Job	Name	Gender	Age	Types	City Size	Job
P1	Male	62	CP	Small	No	P18	Male	23	ID	Small	No
P2	Male	45	SCI	Small	Yes	P19	Female	27	ID	Small	No
P3	Female	22	SCI	Small	Yes	P20	Female	63	CP	Small	No
P4	Male	50	MD	Small	No	P21	Male	43	SCI	Small	Yes
P5	Male	26	ID	Large	Yes	P22	Female	48	VD	Large	Yes
P6	Male	24	CP	Large	Yes	P23	Male	47	VD	Large	Yes
P7	Female	60	SCI	Small	No	P24	Male	61	CD	Large	No
P8	Male	36	SCI	Large	Yes	P25	Male	24	CP	Small	Yes
P9	Female	29	CP	Large	Yes	P26	Female	50	VD	Large	No
P10	Male	48	CD	Large	Yes	P27	Female	43	VD	Large	Yes
P11	Male	25	CP	Small	No	P28	Male	59	CD	Large	No
P12	Male	34	CP	Large	No	P29	Male	60	CD	Large	No
P13	Male	35	VD	Large	Yes	P30	Male	66	VD	Large	Yes
P14	Male	30	VD	Large	Yes	P31	Female	31	SCI	Small	Yes
P15	Female	53	SCI	Small	No	P32	Female	54	VD	Small	Yes
P16	Male	56	SCI	Small	No	P33	Male	61	VD	Large	No
P17	Female	48	CD	Large	No	P34	Male	37	SCI	Small	Yes
						P35	Male	21	SCI	Small	Yes

ID: intellectual disability, VD: vision disability, SCI: spinal cord injury, CP: cerebral palsy, CD: cerebrovascular disease, MD: muscular dystrophy.

In the second stage, the FGI questions were based on the content of the literature review. The questions were completed and reviewed by two associates with PhDs in sports for disabled persons. In the third stage, 35 people with disabilities who had experience in physical activity and sports were recruited.

We recruited these individuals by reaching out to welfare centers and gyms that could identify people with disabilities who would be willing to participate. Subsequently, via e-mail or telephone, we explained the purpose of the study, the interview method, and the time required. Twelve people agreed to participate via email, and twenty-three people agreed to participate via phone. The interview content was also explained, giving the individuals time to contemplate the topic. In the fourth stage, interviews were conducted with small groups of three or four people.

The interview questions were framed according to the method suggested by Krueger and Casey [35], comprising an opening question, an introductory question, a transition question, a key question, and an ending question. The questions are presented in Appendix A.

At the time of the interviews, general information about the interview was provided, consent was obtained for voluntary participation, and a consent form was completed. The content of the consent form included information about the recording of the interview, the destruction of recorded material after the study was completed, the protection of personal information and confidentiality, the participant's freedom to stop participating in the study, and the fee for participation in the study. Field notes were made during the interviews, and the one-on-one interviews took, on average, 40 min; the small-group interviews lasted, on average, one hour and 30 min. All interviews were conducted in Korean and subsequently translated into English for the study.

Table 2. Review summary.

Item	Survey on the Participation in Sports for People with Disabilities in Korea		Survey on the Participation in Sports for People with Disabilities in the United Kingdom and Germany
Reference	2018–2020 Physical Activities and Sports for People with Disabilities Survey		United Kingdom: http://www.activityalliance.org.uk/ (accessed on 21 June 2021). Germany: http://www.dguv-forum.de/files/594/09-36-126_DGUV_Forum_9-2009.pdf (accessed on 21 June 2021)
Review Summary	Participation	. Sports facilities you want to use near your home: "Parks" in 2018, "Public sports facilities for disabled people" in 2019 and 2020. (However, "Parks" were excluded from the selection in 2019 and 2020.) . Current sports facilities: From 2018 to 2020, the first priority was the park and the second was the home. . Participation type: "Walking and jogging" ranked first in both 2018 and 2020. . Needs for participating in physical education: "Support for participation fee" was required in 2018–2020.	. Club-centric: The United Kingdom operates 2711 sports clubs for people with disabilities, centered on 27 sports organizations. In Germany, 1 in 10 people with disabilities join a sports club. . Inclusive facilities and programs: In the United Kingdom, under the "Inclusive Design" policy, Inclusive Fitness Initiative (IFI) sports facilities and sports facilities for people with disabilities coexist together. There are about 400 such facilities across the United Kingdom. . In Germany, when building sports facilities, the regulation of "indoor gym without obstacles" is applied (wheelchair sports, sports for the visually impaired, rehabilitation sports, swimming pools, etc.). . Legal basis: In the United Kingdom, whether the "Inclusive Design" was reflected was determined by how faithfully the Disability Discrimination Act (DDA) obligations were fulfilled. In Germany, according to the German Industrial Standards Association (18040-1), public sports facilities and leisure facilities must be built so that they are not inconvenient.
	Non-participation	. Reason for non-participation: Poor health ranked first. . Events you want to participate in in the future: Walking ranked first.	

2.4. Data Analysis and Research Rigor

We analyzed our data according to the FGI content analysis method suggested by Krueger and Casey [35]. First, to exclude any research bias, a research assistant unaffiliated with the study transcribed the FGI content in the form of verbatim records. Second, the transcribed content was compared with the audio files again, and based on the field notes written during the interview process, we added the results of our observations into the transcripts. Third, to analyze the content of the raw data, data were transcribed into Microsoft® Office Word 2019 (Microsoft Corporation, Redmond, WA, USA) and read repeatedly. Subsequently, to extract the themes, meaningful words were entered into Microsoft® Office Excel 2019 (Microsoft Corporation, Redmond, WA, USA). We classified and then reclassified common characteristics of the themes. By repeating the classification process, we were able to identify and analyze common attributes in the responses in terms of frequency, specificity, emotion, and richness. Finally, we determined the categories by extracting themes and theme clusters through this process [48].

We verified the rigor of the study according to the quality assurance criteria of Sandelowski [50]. First, to check reliability, immediately after each interview, the interview was summarized and explained to confirm that the participant and interviewer were in agreement on what had been posited and discussed. Second, we checked the accuracy of the recordings by collating the transcript and audio files several times. All the interviews were transcribed verbatim to ensure data reliability. In particular, the participants with experience participating in physical activity and sports were asked open-ended questions regarding their experiences to enable us to collect sufficient data to reflect their perspectives accurately. After the interviews, the participants' actions and reactions were recorded in interview logs. These were transcribed within one week of the interviews to ensure that there were no omissions or distortions of the data. In addition, by applying the pause in judgment approach, we were able to avoid any preconceived notions or prejudice in the interview and analysis processes. To ensure suitability, data collection and analysis continued until theoretical saturation was reached. This meant that we were able to capture all the requirements of people with disabilities in terms of physical activities and the sports environment. The validity of the method suggested by Guba and Lincoln [51] was determined as follows: the results were reviewed by a qualitative analysis expert and two sports doctors for people with disabilities; additionally, one professor in sports for people with disabilities reviewed the content that reflected their feedback. The final results were shared with the 35 participants in writing or by e-mail so that they could review these and provide feedback as to any content that needed to be corrected or deleted. As a result, we were able to confirm the accuracy of our final research results.

3. Results

A total of 307 meaningful references were derived from the FGIs. Conversations judged to be outside the purpose of the study were deleted, and only meaningful words that fit the purpose were extracted. As captured in the data, the requirements for improving physical activities and sports participation among people with disabilities were classified into programs, facilities, instructors, and health-related information. The themes and theme clusters are listed in Table 3.

3.1. *Program Needs*

The study participants asked for greater support for the facilities where the programs were held, as well as for greater diversification in the programs available in the sports centers.

3.1.1. Equal Support

Participants requested programs that allowed them to exercise in an environment similar to one for people without disabilities.

> *"People without disabilities have many private sports facilities close to home and can exercise alone in parks, but very few private sports facilities offer exercise programs for people with disabilities. However, it is too expensive to use. Even the exercise equipment placed in the park has nothing that wheelchair-bound people can [use]."*
>
> Participant 2
>
> *"A lot of people are exercising while watching YouTube at home these days, but when I look at them, most people with disabilities can't do them. However, there is no movement channel for people with disabilities, and I thought that the government should operate a movement channel for people with disabilities."*
>
> Non-participant 8

3.1.2. Availability of Various Programs in Sports Centers

The participants were dissatisfied with the fact that only programs at sports centers for people with disabilities were open to them, because these were too limited.

> *"My son is gaining weight and he needs to exercise, but it is difficult to exercise because he hates moving. I like the ball, so I want to teach basketball or soccer, but the sports center doesn't have a ball sports program for the intellectually disabled, so I can't exercise."*
>
> Non-participant 1
>
> *"I have severe disabilities, so I always go to exercise with my parents. When I exercise, my parents just wait."*
>
> Participant 11

Table 3. Results of environmental needs of physical activities and sports of people with disabilities.

Category	Theme Cluster	Theme
Programs	Equivalent support of the program	Physical activities and sports program for people with disabilities in public and private sports facilities
		Non-face-to-face exercise programs that can be done at home
		An exercise program conducted by a sports club for people with disabilities
		Exercise programs using exercise equipment installed in local parks
	Opening of various programs within the sports center	Physical activities and sports programs according to type of disability
		Physical activities and a sports program for each sport
		Physical activities and a sports program for people with and without disabilities
		Rehabilitation sports programs
		Exercise programs that you can do with your family
		Exercise programs by age group
Facilities	Strengthening the professionalism of instructors	A qualified instructor for physical activities and sports for people with disabilities
		An instructor with professional qualifications in sports
		Sports instructors with disabilities
		Qualified as a disabled sports instructor and as an instructor for those without disabilities
		Instructors with past exercise specialist qualifications
	Improvement of the leadership skills of instructors	Understanding the types of disabilities; education on human rights for persons with disabilities
		Continuous upgrading of skills and knowledge about the sport
		Emergency response ability
		Education in communication methods with people with disabilities (sign language, etc.)
Instructor	Needs to expand facilities available to people with disabilities	Expansion of sports facilities exclusively for people with disabilities
		Expansion of universal sports facilities
		Expansion of sports facilities created for local residents
		Expansion of sports facilities for people with disabilities specializing in sports
		School sports facilities for people with disabilities
		Installation and expansion of convenience facilities for people with disabilities in private sports facilities
		Installation and expansion of sports equipment and facilities in community parks
	Improvement of facility operation aspects	Active acceptance of complaints
		Active promotion of facility and program recruitment
		An environment where there are free tickets to sports classes
		Mandatory education on understanding disabilities for employees and users
		Counseling room for health checkups, maintenance, and promotion
Health information provision	The needs of the entity providing health information	Provision of health information for people with disabilities through mass media at the government level
		Provision of health information by text message or mail at the city hall or community center level of the local community
		Provision of health information by text message or mail to people with disabilities in the local community at the level of the Sports Association for People with Disabilities in the local community
		Provision of health information to disabled users and their families at the welfare center level
		Provision of health information to disabled users and their families at the level of sports facilities
	Content of health information	Information that can motivate exercise by providing information on "disability and exercise," "necessity of exercise," "healthy eating habits,", etc.
		Information on where and what programs are available for people with disabilities in the community
		Locations and related information on sports clubs for people with disabilities
		Related information on physical fitness centers for people with disabilities, etc.

3.2. *Leader Needs*

Participants asked for the professional improvement of sports instructors responsible for physical activities for people with disabilities and the enhancement of instructors' leadership abilities.

3.2.1. Strengthening Instructor Professionalism

Public sports centers or sports centers for people with disabilities are required to appoint leaders with the correct qualifications, namely, qualified instructors for general physical activities and sports for people with disabilities, as well as for adapted elite sports, universal sports, and rehabilitation sports.

> *"Even at the sports center for people with disabilities, there are leaders who do not have qualifications as a sports coach for people with disabilities. A leader who is not qualified to teach disabled sports is teaching my daughter, and I thought this was wrong. My daughter has a very poor understanding, so I have to teach it little by little, but if I don't do it after a demonstration, I just neglect it for the duration of the activity."*
>
> Non-participant 2

> *"I learned swimming from someone who was a disabled sports player in the past, and he definitely teaches me well. I knew exactly how much my disability was, so he taught me in a way that was easy to understand. Apparently, leaders of people without disabilities, even if they are qualified, do not have direct experience with disabilities, so I think there is a limit."*
>
> Participant 3

3.2.2. Improving Instructor Leadership Skills

The participants said that many leaders did not have the basic abilities to teach physical activities and sports to people with disabilities, emphasizing that improvement in this area was urgently needed. Such improvement included understanding disabled persons, human rights education about people with disabilities, continuous training in sports emergencies and response ability, and improvement in instruction methods.

> *"I felt like my coach was ignoring me while I was working out. You cannot do this movement because you are severely disabled. Advanced tactics cannot be used. It hurt my heart when I talked about things like that."*
>
> Participant 6

> *"I went to learn to swim. I'm blind, and coach did a demonstration by saying, "Look at me and follow me ... " (laughs). "Coach! I'm blind!" I was very confused. When we exercise, we need a lot of tactile guidance, but it was very difficult to understand the movement because he kept explaining it in words."*
>
> Participant 13

3.3. *Sports Facility Needs*

The participants indicated that existing sports facilities should be expanded and their operations improved.

3.3.1. Expansion of Facilities for People with Disabilities

Respondents indicated that very few sports facilities were convenient for people with disabilities people to use. The discussion focused on the need for a specific sports facility for people with disabilities, a universal sports facility, a public sports facility, a sports facility for each sport (pool, lawn ball court, etc.), and a school sports facility. Additionally, some requested the installation and expansion of sports equipment for disabled people in the local park.

> *"There are very few gyms or swimming pools that are wheelchair accessible to people with disabilities. The weight training equipment is placed so closely that it is difficult for a wheelchair to pass through, and the equipment itself is hardly usable by a wheelchair user. The swimming pool is also very difficult to get into in a wheelchair, and there are very few places where the shower or changing rooms are accessible for people with disabilities."*
>
> Participant 10

> *"Even if a non-disabled sports facility is equipped with facilities for people with disabilities, people with disabilities and people without disabilities can exercise together, but it is a*

pity that there are so few convenient facilities. So, it is difficult to move while exercising at a sports facility for people with disabilities, far from our home. Too much time is wasted."

Participant 4

3.3.2. Improvements at Sports Facilities

Some respondents indicated that the needs of people with disabilities could be accommodated quickly, and the environment readily improved in sports facilities. First, they mentioned the simple need for better publicity regarding the available exercise programs. Second, the general feeling was that they should be able to use the facilities for free. Third, other exercisers, together with the facility staff, should be educated on the different types of disabilities. Finally, several referred to the need for a room for health counseling.

"When I go to the gym to play badminton, the time for people with disabilities to play is set from 3 to 6 pm. It's only available on weekends for working people. There are many people who play badminton even on weekdays, so I spend more time waiting than playing. So, even if I ask for an increase in time allotment, I don't think they will increase it, and they say no. In my opinion, I wish there was no separate time for people with disabilities and those without disabilities. There are six courts, so it's frustrating because even if they suggest that it would be better to leave only one or two of them empty for people with disabilities, they won't accept it. They don't even tell you clearly why you shouldn't do that, so I stopped working out because I felt bad."

Non-participant 7

"I didn't even know there was a gym for people with disabilities around my house. I wish they could tell you where the sports center for people with disabilities near my house is and what kind of exercise programs there are by phone or text message. Blind people like us can exercise only when they receive information via text message or phone calls."

Non-participant 15

3.4. Health Information

Participants responded that they had difficulty receiving information about their health. People with disabilities in Korea receive little information on how to maintain and improve their health. Such information is difficult to find unless it is personally sought out. In addition, as the average age of people with disabilities increases, the number of disabled people who are unable to obtain information on their own through their mobile phones or via the Internet is increasing.

"Health information for people without disabilities is easy to find on TV or in the mass media, but we cannot find health information about people with disabilities unless we search for it ourselves. I am old and I can't even use a computer. So, if someone doesn't tell you, you don't even know where and what the facilities are. I would like the community to provide information about sports facilities and programs near the house by text message or mail."

Non-participant 13

"I also want to go to a club and exercise with people with disabilities similar to mine. I want to know if there is a disabled sports club in my neighborhood. If there is, I would like to know what kind of sports clubs there are, and if there are clubs with people similar to my age. They said they didn't know … if I asked the welfare center … If you don't have a club, you can't help it, but it may be that you have a club and you are not able to join it. It would be nice if there was a place that would provide such health information."

Non-participant 11

The respondents were looking for health information that included content on the importance of exercise programs, as well as information that could motivate them to participate in exercise programs. In addition, they asked for information on the locations of sports facilities, physical fitness measurements, physical activities, and sports programs. They looked to the government as well as the private sector to provide better health information for people with disabilities.

4. Discussion

Using FGIs, we were able to analyze in depth the requirements of people with disabilities for their participation in physical activities and sports. As a result, the demands for physical activities and sports of people with disabilities were largely divided into four categories: programs, instructor, facilities, and health information provision. We will focus on these four categories.

Among the first requirements mentioned was equal support for such programs for people with disabilities as well as their establishment within sports centers. There are 1078 gyms and swimming pools in public sports facilities for people without disabilities in Korea. These facilities include programs for weight training, badminton, basketball, volleyball, kendo, table tennis, futsal, golf, children's physical education, squash, swimming, and aqua aerobics—a very diverse list [52]. Meanwhile, there are just 68 public sports facilities exclusively for people with disabilities, and the programs at these facilities are limited to weight training, swimming, table tennis, badminton, and goalball [53]. These programs do not address the needs of people with disabilities. An environment should be provided that would allow for the self-determination needed to satisfy the three basic psychological needs of autonomy, competence, and enhancement of one's internal motivation and positive experiences [54,55]. In contrast, Disability Rights United Kingdom provides universal physical activities and sports programs that include both people with and without disabilities, offering many opportunities for people with disabilities to participate in physical activities and sports [48]. Previous studies have shown that when people with disabilities are able to voluntarily participate in these programs, their satisfaction and quality of life increase [24,56]. The Korean and sports organizations for people with disabilities should also reflect these individuals' needs in order to provide an environment in which people with disabilities can manage their own physical activities and sports.

The second requirement concerned instructors. Respondents mentioned the need for enhancing instructor professionalism and improving leadership abilities. In 2015, Korea established the National Qualification System for Adapted Sports Instructors. However, it is still difficult to employ sports instructors at sports facilities for people with disabilities, as well as at those for people without disabilities [57]. Moreover, in Korea, there is no legal restriction on hiring unqualified sports instructors at sports facilities for people with disabilities [58]. Therefore, instructors without leadership certificates may be teaching people with disabilities. Even instructors licensed to provide sports guidance to people with disabilities are not clear about their roles in such sports facilities and have difficulties due to unstable environments [59]. Similar problems are occurring in other countries as well. The budget for coaches is low, and the job pay is also low [60–62]. Therefore, a law should be enacted to only allow the employment of licensed instructors at gyms for people with disabilities, and an environment in which such instructors can work stably should be provided.

There is also the need to improve the working environment for instructors so that they can teach and be leaders [63]. In Japan, for people with disabilities, sports instructors (beginner, intermediate, and advanced), sports coaches, sports trainers, and sports doctors are subdivided, and their roles are clearly defined [64]. In Ireland, its National Disability Authority has a coaching program that supports FGIs among people with disabilities, providing information for physical education teachers, coaches, trainers, managers, and educators. Through such information, adequate sports programs can be developed and provided [43]. In addition, a program to develop the leadership capabilities of instructors should also be provided. Many scholars state that instructors should practice self-reflection on guidance. For this, an opportunity should be provided for instructors to learn how to reflect on their coaching through workshops [65–67]. Additionally, coaching networks for leaders should be created and nurtured. It is desirable to provide information on coaching networks to leaders in national sports organizations for people with disabilities [68]. Korea also needs to improve the roles and development of instructors to be able to provide programs at a level that can satisfy people with disabilities.

The third requirement concerned the expansion of sports facilities that could support people with disabilities, along with their improvement. These results also tend to be consistent with previous studies [6–10]. In Korea, facilities where persons with disabilities can exercise are exclusive facilities for people with disabilities or simple sports facilities in local community parks [57]. These facilities are few and far between compared with sports facilities for people without disabilities. This means, for those who want to participate, they have no choice but to travel long distances to utilize such facilities [69]. Research on the causes that prevent persons with disabilities from participating in sports in Korea, as well as potential solutions, is ongoing [70,71]. Previous studies have found that the biggest hindrance to exercise participation among people with disabilities is distance from the exercise facility. In Australia, the perceived barriers to participation in physical activity among children with disabilities also included the lack of transportation and inadequate facilities [72]. Due to such problems, the Netherlands provides travel expenses for people with disabilities to commute to exercise facilities [34]. As a small country, Korea faces difficulties in expanding its facilities. In line with Dutch policy, if people with disabilities could be provided with travel expenses to commute to sports facilities, their participation in physical activities and sports could increase.

Problems related to the operation of sports facilities are often due to a lack of understanding of people with disabilities by the sports facilities' staff as well as by other exercisers. Human rights issues such as this are continuously emerging in the field of sports for people with disabilities in Korea. Barriers to sports facilities and communication with persons with disabilities not only restrict access but also threaten the quality of participation and render participation unsustainable. Even if individuals participate in physical activity or sports, they have negative stereotypes about the facility operators, which can lead to cessation of participation [73,74]. To promote continued participation in physical activity and sports, it is necessary to focus on whether people with disabilities experience the basic right to use sports facilities [75].

Min and Cho [76] stated that a lack of understanding of people with disabilities' human rights by the staff at sports facilities for people with disabilities in Korea lowered the satisfaction of people with disabilities who used these facilities. To address these problems, many sports experts for people with disabilities in Korea are working hard to finance the Sports Basic Act, which would give "everyone the right to participate in sports and physical activities and sports without discrimination" [77]. The European Sports Charter states that everyone has the right to participate in sports and that sports must be based on ethics and human dignity [78]. In Australia, the opportunity to participate in physical activity and leisure is recognized as a "right" by law and is considered an essential element contributing to quality of life [79]. As one means of improving facility operations, Korea also needs to enact a Sports Basic Act to legally regulate discrimination against people with disabilities and support their participation at such facilities.

The fourth requirement concerned health information. From one participant who referenced health information, various health information provisions were identified. The health information requested included information that could motivate individuals to participate in sports, as well as more information on the location of sports facilities for people with disabilities. From our interviews, we learned that most people with disabilities do not receive information related to physical activities and sports program availability. Moreover, although they search for health-related information, the information is very limited.

People with disabilities face different barriers to participation in sports and physical activity than people without disabilities [80]. Information about sports and physical activities needs to be better promoted and provided at both national and local levels [28]. In 2014, the English Federation of Disability Sport published a report called "Talk to Me" to encourage people with disabilities to participate in sports. The report set out 10 principles for reaching people with disabilities and offering them sports programs. The first principle was to employ various means of publicity such as social media, local broadcasting, posters, and word of mouth to promote these programs [81]. Ireland has established departments within government ministries and legal institutions to reach out to citizens and ensure equal opportunity for participation in physical activity, as people with disabilities do not have sufficient access to such information. Such actions have created partnerships that raise awareness of the problem, mobilize support, and disseminate information assistance. At the same time, appropriate programs for people with disabilities can be organized and coordinated, primarily within communities and mainstream organizations [43].

In addition, it is very important for health care workers in the community to provide health information and to encourage participation in sports. People with disabilities have a greater reliance on health care workers than the general public [82]. Therefore, health care workers in the community should recommend health information and exercise participation to people with disabilities [83]. In previous research, to create an opportunity to encourage health information and exercise participation, it was necessary to use social capital especially for people with disabilities [84–86]. In particular, for people with disabilities, social capital is shared among members through trust, such as social acceptance, life skills, and friendship [85]. In particular, suggestions through social capital for people with disabilities who are participating in sports can promote interaction and participation in exercise [87]. Recently, social capital has been utilized through social networks [83].

In Korea, the government needs to take the initiative to support various means of publicity for such programs, encouraging local communities to pursue these as well so that people with disabilities can obtain health information more readily. If Korea can effectively address the physical activity and sports-related needs of people with disabilities, their quality of life will definitely improve.

5. Conclusions

In this study, we used FGIs to determine the needs of people with disabilities in Korea to encourage their participation in physical activities and sports. We found that in terms of programs, more improvement is needed in terms of instructors, facilities, and the provision of health information. Thus far, the approach to physical activities and sports in Korea for people with disabilities has been supplier-centric rather than consumer-centric. Thus, insufficient efforts have been made to listen to the needs of people with disabilities and reflect these in current plans. To improve the quality of life for people with disabilities in Korea, their needs should be reflected in terms of support for their physical activities and engagement in sports.

To provide an opportunity for people with disabilities to choose the exercise program of their choice, it is necessary to research in advance what kind of exercise program people with disabilities want, centering on the local community. To strengthen the professionalism of leaders, it is necessary to provide a stable environment for them in sports facilities and continue training them for capacity building. In terms of facilities, the expansion of sports facilities that can be used by people with disabilities is an urgent priority, and the opinions of users with disabilities must be actively collected and addressed in the operation of these facilities. Additionally, at the national level, information should be continuously provided through mass media and the Internet so that people with disabilities can know the importance of physical activity and sports and manage their own health. To that end, it would be helpful to conduct an in-depth analysis of countries with effective participation policies for people with disabilities and consider how these could be adapted to the situation in Korea.

Some limitations of our study warrant comment and suggest directions for future research. As we analyzed the needs of people with disabilities in small groups using the FGI method, it is difficult to generalize these findings. Thus, based on our results, a larger, quantitative consumer-oriented survey among people with disabilities that could assess their needs in the context of physical activities and sports should be conducted to confirm our results. Additionally, although we identify areas for improvement, further studies should confirm which areas should be improved first.

Author Contributions: Design, A.O. and W.-Y.S.; study conduction, A.O. and W.-Y.S.; data collection, A.O. and W.-Y.S.; data analysis, A.O. and W.-Y.S.; data interpretation, A.O. and W.-Y.S.; writing—original draft preparation, A.O. and W.-Y.S.; writing—review and editing, A.O. and W.-Y.S. All authors have read and agreed to the published version of the manuscript.

Funding: This work was supported by the Ministry of Education of the Republic of Korea and the National Research Foundation of Korea (NRF-2019S1A5A2A01041417).

Institutional Review Board Statement: The study was conducted according to the guidelines of the Declaration of Helsinki, and approved by the Institutional Review Board of Gachon University (IRB approval no. 1044396-201911-HR-204-01).

Informed Consent Statement: Informed consent was obtained from all subjects involved in the study. Written informed consent has been obtained from the participants to publish this paper.

Data Availability Statement: The data presented in this study are available on request from the author.

Conflicts of Interest: The authors declare no conflict of interest.

Appendix A

Table A1. Semi-structured focus group interview questions.

Question Classification		Question Content	
Opening question Brief introduction		Tell us your name? When did you become disabled?	
Introductory question Experience participating in physical activities and sports		Do you have experience participating in physical activities and sports?	
		Participant	How did you get involved?
		Non-Participant	Why did not you participate in physical activities and sports?
Transition question Difficulty participating in physical activities and sports		Participant	What difficulties did you have in participating in physical activities and sports?
		Non-Participant	Have you ever tried to participate in physical activities and sports?
			What difficulties did you face when trying to participate in physical activities and sports?
Key question Needs for physical activities and sports	Programs	Participant	What needs are there for the physical activities and sports program? Please explain in detail.
		Non-Participant	If I participate in physical activities and sports, are there any needs for the program? Please explain in detail.
	Facilities	Participant	What needs do you have for physical activities and sports facilities? Please explain in detail.
		Non-Participant	If I participate in physical activities and sports, are there any needs for the facility? Please explain in detail.
	Instructor	Participant	What needs are there for instructors in physical activities and sports? Please explain in detail.
		Non-Participant	Are there any needs for an instructor if you participate in physical activities and sports? Please explain in detail.
	Health information provision	Participant Non-Participant	What needs do you have for providing health information? Please explain in detail.
Ending question Interview impression		Have you ever talked with people around you about the environment of physical activities and sports?	
		Have you tried to change the environment of physical activities and sports yourself?	
		Have you ever felt that your quality of life has increased or decreased through physical activities and sports?	
		How do you feel about the interview?	

References

1. Ministry of Culture Sports and Tourism. Available online: https://www.mcst.go.kr/kor/s_notice/press/pressView.jsp?pSeq=16857&pMenuCD=0302000000&pCurrentPage=26&pTypeDept=23&pSearchType=01&pSearchWord= (accessed on 4 September 2021).
2. Lee, D.C.; Kim, K.J. A Study on the Improvement Plans of Sport Voucher Service for Individuals with Disabilities. *J. Adapt. Phys. Act. Exerc.* **2021**, *29*, 117–128.
3. Ministry of Culture Sports and Tourism. 2018 Disability Physical Activities and Sports Survey Result Report. Sejong City: Ministry of Culture, Sports and Tourism. March 2019. Available online: https://www.mcst.go.kr/kor/s_policy/dept/deptView.jsp?pDataCD=0417000000&pSeq=1467 (accessed on 31 March 2021).
4. Jung, Y.K.; Moon, K.M.; Lee, H.S. Analysis of Research Trends on Disabled Sports in Korea. *J. Adapt. Phys. Act. Exerc.* **2019**, *27*, 15–28.
5. Cho, K.H. A Parasports Activation Plan for Sports Welfare. *J. Korea Entertain. Ind. Assoc.* **2021**, *15*, 189–204. [CrossRef]
6. Manuel, S.M.; Rui, A.; Machado, M.C.; Osvaldo, M.; João, T. Accessibility of Sports Facilities for Persons with Reduced Mobility and Assessment of Their Motivation for Practice. *Work* **2012**, *41*, 2017–2023. [CrossRef]
7. Cardinal, B.J.; Spaziani, M.D. ADA compliance and the accessibility of physical activity facilities in western Oregon. *Am. J. Health Promot.* **2003**, *17*, 197–201. [CrossRef] [PubMed]
8. Clark, M.; Cary, S.; Diemert, G.; Ceballos, R.; Atteberry, I.; Vue, F.; Trieu, S. Involving communities in community assessment. *Public Health Nurs.* **2003**, *20*, 456–463. [CrossRef]
9. Lindsey, E.; McGuinness, L. Significant elements of community involvement in participatory action research: Evidence from a community project. *J Adv. Nurs.* **1998**, *36*, 652–658. [CrossRef]
10. Riley, B.B.; Rimmer, J.H.; Wang, E.; Schiller, W.J. A Conceptual Framework for Improving the Accessibility of Fitness and Recreation Facilities for People with Disabilities. *J. Phys. Act. Health* **2008**, *5*, 158–168. [CrossRef]
11. Kim, K.I.; Park, B.D.; Lee, C.W. Problems and Tasks for Policy in Component of Lifetime Sports of People with Disability. *J. Korean Soc. Sport Policy* **2014**, *30*, 103–118.
12. Oh, Y.P. A Study on Development Plan of Systemic Korea Sports Association for the Disabled. *Korean J. Sport Sci.* **2014**, *25*, 527–539.
13. Robbins, S.P.; Chatterjee, P.; Canda, E.P.; Richardson, F.; Franklin, C.; Robbins, S.P.; Canda, E.R. *Contemporary Human Behaviour Theory-A Critical Perspective for Social Work*, 3rd ed.; Pearson PLC: London, UK, 2012; pp. 323–344, ISBN 3-978-02-0503-312-6.
14. Brittain, I.; Biscaia, R.; Gérard, S. Ableism as a regulator of social practice and disabled peoples' self-determination to participate in sport and physical activity. *Leis. Stud.* **2020**, *39*, 209–224. [CrossRef]
15. Doty, P.; Kasper, J.; Litvak, S. Consumer-Directed Models of Personal Care: Lessons from Medicaid. *Milbank Q.* **1996**, *74*, 377–409. [CrossRef] [PubMed]
16. Prince, J.M.; Manley, S.; Whiteneck, G.G. Self-managed versus agency-provided personal assistance care for individuals with high tetraplegia. *Arch. Phys. Med. Rehabil.* **1995**, *76*, 19–23. [CrossRef]
17. Richmond, G.W.; Beatty, P.W.; Tepper, S.; DeJong, G. The effect of consumer-directed personal assistance services on productivity outcomes of people with physical disabilities. *J. Rehabil. Outcomes Meas.* **1997**, *1*, 48–51.
18. Beatty, P.W.; Richmond, G.W.; Tepper, S.; DeJong, G. Personal assistance for people with physical disabilities: Consumer-direction and satisfaction with services. *Arch. Phys. Med. Rehabil.* **1998**, *79*, 674–677. [CrossRef]
19. Kim, K.M.; Fox, M.H.; White, G.W. Comparing out comes of persons choosing consumer-directed or agency-directed personal assistance services. *J. Rehabil.* **2006**, *72*, 32–43.
20. Kosciulek, J.F. The consumer-directed theory of empowerment. *Rehabil. Couns. Bull.* **1999**, *42*, 196–213.
21. Kosciulek, J.F. Implications of consumer direction for disability policy development and rehabilitation service delivery. *J. Disabil. Polic Stud.* **2000**, *11*, 82–89. [CrossRef]
22. Kosciulek, J.F. Research application of the longitudinal study of the vocational rehabilitation service program. *Rehabil. Couns. Bull.* **2004**, *47*, 173–180. [CrossRef]
23. Kosciulek, J.F. Structural Equation Model of the Consumer-Directed Theory of Empowerment in Vocational Rehabilitation Context. *Rehabil. Couns. Bull.* **2005**, *49*, 40–49. [CrossRef]
24. Kosciulek, J.F.; Merz, M. Structural analysis of the consumer-directed theory of empowerment. *Rehabil. Couns. Bull.* **2001**, *44*, 209–216. [CrossRef]
25. Tilly, J.; Wiener, J.M.; Cuellar, A.E. Consumer-directed home and community-based services programs in five countries: Policy issues for older people and government. *Generations* **2000**, *24*, 74–83.
26. Crozier, M.; Muenchberger, H.; Colley, J.; Ehrlich, C. The disability self-direction movement: Considering the benefits and challenges for an Australian response. *Aust. J. Soc.* **2016**, *48*, 427–455. [CrossRef]
27. Cherry, E.; Stancliffe, R.J.; Emerson, E.; Renata, T. Policy Implications, Eligibility, and Demographic Characteristics of People with Intellectual Disability Who Access Self-Directed Funding in the United States. *Intellect. Dev. Disabil.* **2021**, *59*, 123–140. [CrossRef] [PubMed]
28. Casey, A.F.; Wang, X.; Boucher, J. Test of Self-Determination Theory in Swimmers with and without Down Syndrome. *Inclusion* **2014**, *2*, 54–64. [CrossRef]

29. Yazicioglu, K.; Yavuz, F.; Goktepe, A.S.; Tan, A.K. Influence of adapted sports on quality of life and life satisfaction in sport participants and non-sport participants with physical disabilities. *Disabil. Health J.* **2012**, *5*, 249–253. [CrossRef] [PubMed]
30. Sahlin, K.B.; Lexell, J. Impact of Organized Sports on Activity, Participation, and Quality of Life in People with Neurologic Disabilities. *J. Inj. Funct. Rehabil.* **2015**, *7*, 1081–1088. [CrossRef] [PubMed]
31. Côté-Leclerc, F.; Boileau Duchesne, G.; Bolduc, P.; Gélinas-Lafrenière, A.; Santerre, C.; Desrosiers, J.; Levasseur, M. How does playing adapted sports affect quality of life of people with mobility limitations? Results from a mixed-method sequential explanatory study. *Health Qual. Life Outcomes* **2017**, *15*, 1–22. [CrossRef]
32. Erdoğdu, M.; Yüksel, M.F.; Işık, B.; Boyalı, E.; Erdağı, K.; Sevindi, T. The effects of acute moderate intensity training on hematological parameters in elite para-badminton athletes. *J. Men's Health* **2022**. [CrossRef]
33. Disability Rights, UK. Increasing Participation in Physical Activity and Sport. Available online: https://www.disabilityrightsuk.org/policy-campaigns/briefings-reports-responses (accessed on 1 June 2021).
34. Hoekstra, F.; Roberts, L.; van Lindert, C.; Martin Ginis, K.A.; van der Woude, L.H.V.; McColl, M.A. National approaches to promote sports and physical activity in adults with disabilities: Examples from the Netherlands and Canada. *Disabil. Rehabil.* **2019**, *41*, 1217–1226. [CrossRef]
35. Krueger, R.A.; Casey, M.A. *Focus Groups: A Practical Guide for Applied Research*, 5th ed.; Sage Publications: Thousand Oaks, CA, USA, 2014; pp. 64–67, 138–159, ISBN 978-1-4833-6524-4.
36. Rosenthal, M. Qualitative research methods: Why, when, and how to conduct interviews and focus groups in pharmacy research. *Curr. Pharm. Teach. Learn.* **2016**, *8*, 509–516. [CrossRef]
37. Ansay, S.J.; Perkins, D.F.; Nelson, C.J. Interpreting outcomes: Using focus groups in evaluation research. *Fam. Relat. Interdiscip. J. Appl. Fam. Stud.* **2004**, *53*, 310–316. [CrossRef]
38. Hennink, M.M. *International Focus Group Research: A Handbook for the Health and Social Sciences*; Cambridge University Press: Atlanta, GA, USA, 2007; p. 280, ISBN 978-051-161-194-58.
39. Alasuutari, P.; Bickman, L.; Brannen, J. *The SAGE Handbook of Social Research Methods*; Sage: Thousand Oaks, CA, USA, 2008; ISBN 978-1-4129-1992-0.
40. David, W.S.; Prem, N.S. *Focus Groups: Theory and Practice*, 3rd ed.; Sage: Thousand Oaks, CA, USA, 2014; p. 40, ISBN 978-1452270982.
41. Merton, R.K.; Kendall, P.L. The focused interview. *Am. J. Sociol.* **1946**, *51*, 541–557. [CrossRef]
42. Nijstad, B.A.; Paulus, P.B. Group Creativity: Common Themes and Future Directions. In *Group Creativity: Innovation Through Collaboration New York*; Paulus, P.B., Ed.; Oxford University Press: Oxford, UK, 2003; pp. 326–339, ISBN 978-019-514-730-8.
43. National Disability Authority. Physical Activity, Health and Quality of Life among People with Disabilities an Analysis of the SLÁN Data. Available online: https://nda.ie/publications/health/health-publications/physical-activity-health-and-quality-of-life-among-people-with-disabilities-an-analysis-of-the-sl%C3%A1n-data-.html (accessed on 1 June 2021).
44. Line, M.; Borgunn, Y. Disability leisure: In what kind of activities, and when and how do youths with intellectual disabilities participate? *Scand. J. Disabil. Res.* **2017**, *19*, 245–255. [CrossRef]
45. Shields, N.; Synnot, A. Perceived barriers and facilitators to participation in physical activity for children with disability: A qualitative study. *BMC Pediatr.* **2016**, *16*, 9. [CrossRef]
46. Ministry of Culture, Sports and Tourism, 2020 Disability Physical Activities and Sports Survey Result Report. Available online: https://www.mcst.go.kr/kor/s_policy/dept/deptView.jsp?pDataCD=0406000000&pSeq=1730 (accessed on 31 March 2021).
47. Ministry of Culture, Sports and Tourism, 2019 Disability Physical Activities and Sports Survey Result Report. Available online: https://www.mcst.go.kr/kor/s_policy/dept/deptView.jsp?pDataCD=0417000000&pSeq=1294 (accessed on 31 March 2021).
48. Get Yourself Active. Increasing Participation in Physical Activity and Sport Evaluation of Get Yourself Active. Available online: http://www.getyourselfactive.org/wp-content/uploads/2019/06/GYA-final-report_FINAL_29.03.19.pdf (accessed on 1 June 2021).
49. Landessportbund Berlin. Survey among People with Disabilities in Leipzig on Participation in Sport. Available online: https://www.behindertensport-sachsen.de/index.php?id=113 (accessed on 31 June 2021).
50. Sandelowski, M. The problem of rigor in qualitative research. *Adv. Nurs. Sci.* **1986**, *8*, 27–37. [CrossRef]
51. Lincoln, Y.S.; Guba, E.G. *Naturalistic Inquiry*; Sage: Thousand Oaks, CA, USA, 1985; p. 290, ISBN 978-0803924314.
52. Statistics Korea Government Official Work Conference. Available online: http://www.index.go.kr/potal/main/EachDtlPageDetail.do?idx_cd=2751#quick_02; (accessed on 1 June 2021).
53. Korea Paralympic Committee. Current Status of Sports Facilities Exclusively for the Disabled. Available online: https://sports.koreanpc.kr/front/sportsFacility/facility.do (accessed on 1 June 2021).
54. Gunnell, K.E.; Crocker, P.R.; Wilson, P.M.; Mack, D.E.; Zumbo, B.D. Psychological need satisfaction and thwarting: A test of basic psychological needs theory in physical activity contexts. *Psychol. Sport Exerc.* **2013**, *14*, 599–607. [CrossRef]
55. Ryan, R.M.; Deci, E.L. *Self-Determination Theory: Basic Psychological Needs in Motivation, Development, and Wellness*; Guilford Publishing: New York, NY, USA, 2017.
56. Kosciulek, J.F. Consumer direction in disability policy formation and rehabilitation service delivery. *J. Rehabil.* **1999**, *65*, 4–9.
57. Ko, K.M. Field experience and Conflict of Sports for All Instructors for People with Disabilities. *J. Sport Leis.* **2018**, *72*, 399–412. [CrossRef]

58. Kang, Y.S.; Song, K.Y. Exploring the Expertise and the Process of Expertise Development of the Disability Sports Instructors. *Korean J. Phys. Educ.* **2018**, *57*, 357–373. [CrossRef]
59. Kim, K.I.; Park, B.D.; Kim, S.Y.; Oh, Y.P. An Analysis on the Duties for Adapted Physical Sports Instructor Using DACUM Technique. *J. Korean Soc. Sport Policy* **2015**, *33*, 17–31.
60. Burkett, B. Coaching athletes with a disability. In *Routledge Handbook of Sports Coaching*; Potrac, P., Gilbert, W., Denison, J., Eds.; Routledge: London, UK, 2013; pp. 196–209.
61. Cregan, K.; Bloom, G.A.; Reid, G. Career evolution and knowledge of elite coaches of swimmers with a physical disability. *Res. Q. Exerc. Sport* **2007**, *78*, 339–350. [CrossRef] [PubMed]
62. McMaster, S.; Culver, D.; Werthner, P. Coaches of athletes with a disability: A look at their learning experiences. *Qual. Res. Sport Exerc. Health* **2012**, *4*, 226–243. [CrossRef]
63. Lee, N.H.; Roh, H.K. Ideal and Reality of Disability Sports Instructors: Focusing on the Changes after Getting the Government Authorized Licence of Disability Sports Instructor. *J. Adapt. Phys. Act. Exerc.* **2018**, *26*, 1–16.
64. Japanese Para-Sports Association. Instructor Training Overview. Available online: https://www.jsad.or.jp/leader/leader_aim_method.html (accessed on 1 June 2021).
65. Cassidy, T.; Potrac, P.; McKenzie, A. Evaluating and reflecting upon a coach education initiative: The CoDe of rugby. *Sport Psychol.* **2006**, *20*, 145–161. [CrossRef]
66. Culver, D.; Trudel, P. Cultivating coaches' communities of practice: Developing the potential for learning through interactions. In *The Sport Coach as Educator: Re-Conceptualising Sports Coaching*; Jones, R.L., Ed.; Routledge: London, UK, 2006; pp. 97–112.
67. Gallimore, R.; Gilbert, W.; Nater, S. Reflective practice and ongoing learning: A coach's 10-year journey. *Reflective Pract. Int. Multidiscip. Perspect.* **2014**, *15*, 268–288. [CrossRef]
68. Taylor, S.L.; Werthner, P.; Culver, D. A Case Study of a Parasport Coach and a Life of Learning. *Int. Sport Coach. J.* **2014**, *1*, 127–138. [CrossRef]
69. Kim, M.H.; Kim, K.I. Strategies to Increase Participation in Sports and Physical activity among Persons with Disabilities: A Review of National Surveys. *J. Adapt. Phys. Act. Exerc.* **2019**, *27*, 61–72.
70. Oh, A.; Koo, K.M. Analysis on the Constraint Factors of Physical Disabilities in the Lifetime Sport. *Korean J. Phys. Educ.* **2012**, *51*, 447–454.
71. Lee, H.S.; Park, J.W.; Kim, S.H.; Kim, H.M. Investigation of sports for all requirement types of People with intellectual Disability: Focused on Q methodology. *Korean J. Phys. Educ.* **2015**, *54*, 597–609.
72. Shields, N.; Synnot, A.J.; Barr, M. Perceived barriers and facilitators to physical activity for children with disability: A systematic review. *Br. J. Sports Med.* **2012**, *46*, 989–997. [CrossRef] [PubMed]
73. Shirazipour, C.H.; Evans, M.B.; Caddick, N.; Smith, B.; Aiken, A.B.; Martin Ginis, K.A.; Latimer-Cheung, A.E. Quality participation experiences in the physical activity domain: Perspectives of veterans with a physical disability. *Psychol. Sport Exerc.* **2017**, *29*, 40–50. [CrossRef]
74. Evans, M.B.; Shirazipour, C.H.; Allan, V.; Zanhour, M.; Sweet, S.N.; Ginis, K.A.M.; Latimer-Cheung, A.E. Integrating insights from the parasport community to understand optimal Experiences: The Quality Parasport Participation Framework. *Psychol. Sport Exerc.* **2018**, *37*, 79–90. [CrossRef]
75. Allan, V.; Smith, B.; Côté, J.; Ginis, K.A.M.; Latimer-Cheung, A.E. Narratives of participation among individuals with physical disabilities: A life-course analysis of athletes' experiences and development in parasport. *Psychol. Sport Exerc.* **2018**, *37*, 170–178. [CrossRef]
76. Min, S.H.; Cho, J.H. Development of Physical Activity Model for Persons with Disabilities from Human Rights Paradigm Perspective. *J. Adapt. Phys. Act. Exerc.* **2017**, *25*, 17–41.
77. Min, S.H.; Cho, J.H. Analyses of Implications on the Sport Innovation Recommendations and Application toward the Adapted Sport Sector. *Korean J. Phys. Educ.* **2020**, *59*, 339–353. [CrossRef]
78. Council of Europe. The European Sports Charter. Available online: https://www.coe.int/en/web/sport/european-sports-charter (accessed on 1 June 2021).
79. Lord, E.; Patterson, I. The Benefits of Physically Active Leisure for People with Disabilities: An Australian perspective. *Ann. Leis. Res.* **2008**, *11*, 123–144. [CrossRef]
80. Martin Ginis, K.A.; Ma, J.K.; Latimer-Cheung, A.E.; Rimmer, J.H. A systematic review of review articles addressing factors related to physical activity participation among children and adults with physical disabilities. *Health Psychol. Rev.* **2016**, *10*, 478–494. [CrossRef]
81. Activity Alliance Is the Operating Name for the English Federation of Disability Sport. Talk to Me. October 2014. Available online: https://www.activityalliance.org.uk/how-we-help/research/1878-talk-to-me-october-2014 (accessed on 1 June 2021).
82. van der Ploeg, H.P.; van der Beek, A.J.; van der Woude, L.H.; van Mechelen, W. Physical activity for people with a disability: A conceptual model. *Sports Med.* **2004**, *34*, 639–649. [CrossRef] [PubMed]
83. Wilhite, B.; Shank, J. In praise of sport: Promoting sport participation as a mechanism of health among persons with a disability. *Disabil. Health J.* **2009**, *2*, 116–127. [CrossRef]
84. Devine, M.A.; Parr, M.G. "Come on in, but not too far": Social capital in an inclusive leisure setting. *Leis. Sci.* **2008**, *30*, 391–408. [CrossRef]

85. Portes, A. Social capital: Its origins and application in modern sociology. *Annu. Rev. Sociol.* **1998**, *24*, 1–24. [CrossRef]
86. Dattilo, J.; Caldwell, L.; Lee, Y.; Kleiber, D. Returning to the community with a spinal cord injury: Implications for therapeutic recreation specialists. *Ther. Recreat. J.* **1998**, *32*, 13–27.
87. Field, J. *Social Capital*; Routledge: Oxford, UK, 2003.

healthcare MDPI

Article

The Effect of an Alternative Swimming Learning Program on Skills, Technique, Performance, and Salivary Cortisol Concentration at Primary School Ages Novice Swimmers

Konstantinos Papadimitriou * and Dimitrios Loupos

Faculty of Physical Education and Sport Science of Thessaloniki, Aristotle University of Thessaloniki, 57001 Thermi, Greece; loupo@phed.auth.gr
* Correspondence: kostakispapadim@gmail.com; Tel.: +30-6980265800

Abstract: The playful training method shows positive effects on sports learning, thus the aim of the present study was to compare the effect of two different swimming learning programs. In an 8-week intervention with a training frequency of three times per week, 23 healthy primary school-aged novice swimmers (13 boys, 10 girls) aged 9.0 ± 0.9 participated. They were split into control (CG) and alternative (AG) groups and evaluated on skills (Start, Sink), backstroke (BK) and breaststroke (BR) technique, performance (Skills time, Kicks Time), and salivary cortisol concentration. According to the results, "Start" had a greater percentage of success in AG, at the first (CG = 9.1% vs. AG = 58.3%, $p = 0.027$) and third (CG = 63.6% vs. AG = 100%, $p = 0.037$) measurement. Additionally, greater scores were found in technique for AG in both BK ($p = 0.009$, $\eta^2 = 0.283$) and BR ($p = 0.020$, $\eta^2 = 0.231$). Salivary cortisol concentration was decreased for both groups ($p < 0.001$) and greater in CG at the second measurement ($p < 0.001$). The alternative swimming learning program was found to be more efficient or equally effective, compared with the standardized method in-water skills, swimming technique and performance, and in salivary cortisol concentration.

Keywords: backstroke; breaststroke; start; sink; cortisol

check for updates

Citation: Papadimitriou, K.; Loupos, D. The Effect of an Alternative Swimming Learning Program on Skills, Technique, Performance, and Salivary Cortisol Concentration at Primary School Ages Novice Swimmers. *Healthcare* **2021**, *9*, 1234. https://doi.org/10.3390/healthcare9091234

Academic Editor: Felipe Aidar

Received: 3 August 2021
Accepted: 16 September 2021
Published: 19 September 2021

1. Introduction

The playful training method for learning a sport or a technique has been used by coaches on children at various sports and levels. The aim of playful training is to entertain the children and to make them feel spontaneous, with and without rules, and demand to succeed via their participation in the training [1]. The benefits of the method are the faster technique assimilation and pleasure that children show with their participation in a program that contains organized games for the learning of specific skills [2]. The background of this learning approach originates from the theory of constructivism, which makes learning ability more effective when the trainee participates in the understanding and enjoyment of a movement than when he remains a passive receiver. Additionally, it is highlighted that with the playful approach, exhausting, boring, and high repeatability exercises, which are contained in a classic training method and are often used by coaches, are avoided [3].

In tennis, a six-week intervention study was conducted on 62 children aged 11 years old, targeted to learn the sport through a playful learning program (Play and Stay) [1]. The sample was divided into an interventional and a control group. The interventional group used the learning skills via a normal game, whereas the control group used several exercises that coaches use for the same skills' methodological teaching. The skills were assessed, namely service, forehand, and backhand, before the intervention, at the sixth week, and one week later from the intervention's end. Study results showed that the 36 children who participated in the intervention group had a greater improvement in the skills that were taught compared with the 26 children who followed the classic learning [1].

Another sport in which the effect of playful training method was assessed was table tennis. In the study 56 students participated and they were divided into control and playful training groups. The target was to learn the technical elements of table tennis such as service, attack, and ball guidance. According to the results, after 48 min of training twice a week during the academic year, there was a greater improvement in attack and service in the playful training group [4].

Common results about the effectiveness of playful teaching in sports show several reviews and meta-analyses. Additionally, the authors have reported a disagreement about the using adult-oriented training on children, due to the monotony which that kind of training presents, and as a result, the children abandon their activity [5,6]. In another meta-analysis, a total of 15 studies has shown that a program which contains playful exercises positively affects the participation of children in training. Specifically, these exercises motivate them to participate in a sport which is more enjoyable. Moreover, the playful exercises contribute to the development of motor learning, game and execution skills, and decision-making in the training.

Back to the interventional studies, Blatsis [2] examined the effect of the International Amateur Athletic Federation (IAAF) Kids program on 226 children aged 11–12 years old, 102 of whom were trained in a playful manner, while the rest were trained with a classic learning method on different track and field skills. The study was conducted over a period of 12 weeks. The results revealed that the playful method was more effective than the classic one in parameters such as Yo-Yo test, long jump, and agility.

The playful teaching approach was utilized by Miller [7] too, who assessed the effect of that kind of teaching, compared with a classical method in common skills such as throwing, handling, and perceptual ability. Intervention's duration was seven weeks with the participation of 107 students aged about 10 years old. According to the results, it was observed that playful training was more effective on performance improvement, in pleasure questionnaire scores, and perceptual ability, in contrast with the control group.

Similarly, in 40 children aged 12–13 years old it was found that the playful approach promotes the learning effectiveness of traditional Malaysian games. The duration of the intervention was eight weeks, with three training sessions of one hour per week. The content of traditional games included skills such as running, jumping, space perception, and children's socialization, since such games do not contain any participation numerical limitation. Program effects were evaluated through speed, agility, and balance tests. The results showed that the children who used the playful approach were improved significantly in the factors that were evaluated [8].

In swimming, the only alternative learning approach, apart from the use of high repetition standardized exercises, was used for the development of the sense and perception of the forces exerted from the water on the children's body during their movement. Thus, in swimming, the use of an alternative training approach targeting on fun and learning, such as "Play and Stay" or "IAAF Kids" programs, must be further studied [9]. According to the literature, the authors show that the target of playful method is to increase: (a) children's will to participate, (b) fun, and (c) mood via their participation in a sport [1,2].

Cortisol concentration is a useful indicator for the examination of children's mood [10]. In a study with 117 children, aged 3 to 6 years old, the cortisol concentration was examined in the morning and afternoon. The children were divided into three groups depending on the level of care (low, medium, or high) which was provided by each daycare center, where they were attending at least three times per week. A reduced cortisol concentration was found in the daycare centers with high-quality services. In contrast, in the children who participated in daycare centers with lower care services, a higher cortisol concentration was observed [10].

In swimming, the cortisol concentration tended to decline after an acute period in low-intensity exercise as opposed to high-intensity exercise [11]. Similarly, after acute high-intensity exercise in children aged from 9 to 10 years old, increased cortisol concentration was found [12].

Thus, because of the lack of literature about the effect of playful training in swimming, and the use of an approach that targets mimetic ability, game, and the sensation of the body in the water, the aim of the present study was to compare the effect of a classic versus an alternative swimming learning program on skills (Start, Sink), on backstroke (BK) and breaststroke (BR) technique, on swimming performance (Skills time, Kicks Time), and in salivary cortisol concentration on primary school ages novice swimmers.

2. Materials and Methods

2.1. Participants

Power analysis indicated that a sample size of 10 participants per group would be needed to detect significant differences [13]. Participants were recruited via an annual summer swimming program. Inclusion criteria were (a) healthy participants, (b) aged between 8–10 years old, (c) novices at swimming, (d) biological maturation (≤ 2) (Tanner's scale) [14], and participation in the sport at least after their fifth year of age [15]. Exclusion criteria were (a) non the inclusion, (b) pharmaceutical treatment, (c) any disorder, or (d) participation in another sport during the intervantion.

A total of 40 swimmers participated in the intervention. Twenty-three of them completed all of the measurements and had more than 75% percent attendance, while none of them continued the follow-up measurements. The 23 novice swimmers (13 boys, 10 girls), (Median, SD) aged 9.0 ± 0.9, were recorded for their height, weight, training age, attendance, training volume, and Tanner's scale, which is a five-point scale which defines physical measurements of development based on external primary and secondary sex characteristics. Humans' biological maturation affects learning ability [15] (Table 1).

Table 1. Swimmers' anthropometrics and intervention details.

Groups	Age (y)	Height (m)	Weight (kg)	Tanner (*n*)	Training Age (y)	Attendances (*n*)	Training Volume (m)
CG	9.1 ± 0.8	1.4 ± 0.1	33.8 ± 8.1	1.5 ± 0.7	2.2 ± 1.1	16.3 ± 2.1	400 ± 100
AG	9.0 ± 0.9	1.4 ± 0.1	33.3 ± 5.7	1.5 ± 0.5	3.0 ± 1.9	16.1 ± 2.8	200 ± 100

CG = Control Group, **AG** = Alternative Group.

Then, the 23 swimmers were randomly split into two groups according to demographic characteristics (age, height, weight, Tanner's scale, training age, ($p > 0.05$)) (Table 1), the baseline values of the Kicks time (sec) test ($p > 0.05$), and their preference. These groups were the control (CG) and alternative (AG), in which 11 and 12 swimmers participated, respectively. Before the intervention all the swimmers and their parents were informed about the study's process and the safety of the measurements. Then, a consent form was signed by parents to ensure swimmers' participation. The study was planned and conducted according to the Code of Research Ethics of Aristotle University of Thessaloniki.

2.2. Intervention's Details

A parallel randomized design was used to compare the effects of two swimming learning programs (Standardized (CG) vs. Alternative (AG)) in-water skills, swimming technique and performance, and salivary cortisol concentration. The duration of the intervention was eight weeks [16], with three training sessions per week [17] and one day off between each session. The duration of each training session in both groups was 45′ and included 3–4 exercises. The repetitions of each exercise occurred according to the swimmers' ability to make it successful. The intervention was conducted in an open 17.5 m pool, 27 degrees Celsius, during the summer months (June to August) at Sohos, Thessaloniki, Greece. No follow-up period was occurred because it was the summer holiday period for all the participants.

Groups' training sessions comprised swimming exercises for the skills of start and sink and for the styles of backstroke and breaststroke. These skills were chosen because they are necessary for those ages. Additionally, the styles of backstroke and breaststroke were chosen because of the difference in the move's symmetry, the multiple muscle activation, and the novelty of their use compared with freestyle, which is usually used in studies.

The main difference between the groups (CG and AG) was the approach that the skills and styles were taught. The CG followed a usual training approach which contained standardized exercises that swimming instructors use in high repetitions. On the other hand, the AG used alternative exercises named Tec Pa, in which the children had to use their imagination, and during each exercise experience from daily situations was added with the use of different kinds of objects which helped the children to make a more precise move.

The study was organized with the contribution of five swimming coaches to ensure the blinded measurements and objectivity. Thus, one coach was used to plan the swimming sessions, one to train both groups according to the plans, two more to assess the swimmers in the three measurements during the intervention, and the last one to analyze the variables by which the swimmers were assessed.

2.3. *Alternative vs. Standardized Exercises*

Table 2 and Appendix A show some of the exercises that were used between the two groups. The target of both groups was to instruct the same skills and technique but with a different approach. Tec Pa's alternative exercises were targeting to increase the swimmers' imaginations and the ability to find solutions during an exercise.

Specifically, the swimmers sometimes had to play the role of a soldier, fire worker, diver, etc., using different objects which helped them to precisely perform the skills or the styles' moves. In contrast, the CG had to perform a number of exercises in which the swimmers should follow the coach's demands without the use of their imagination or of some objects that could help the learning process.

Table 2. Exercises between CG and AG.

CG	AG	Learning Target
		**Breaststroke kick** **CG**: Passive repetition **AG**: Dancing
		**Backstroke body position** **CG**: Star position **AG**: Tube for pillow

Table 2. *Cont.*

CG	AG	Learning Target
		**Start** **CG**: Entrance from the pool's wall **AG**: Soldier's entry
		**Sink** **CG**: Diving try in small pool **AG**: Ring door

2.4. *Measurements*

The measurements occurred before (June), in the middle (4 weeks) (July) and at the end (8 weeks) (August) of the intervention (Table 3). At the beginning of each month and in the same day, the children were evaluated for their technique (Backstroke (BK), Breaststroke (BR)), then for their swimming skills (Start, Sink 1 & 2) and performance. In the middle of the intervention (4th week), in the second training session of the week the salivary cortisol was collected before and after swimming training.

Table 3. Measurements' schedule.

0 Weeks	4 Weeks	8 Weeks
Technique Skills and Performance	Technique Skills and Performance Saliva cortisol concentration (Before and After training)	Technique Skills and Performance

2.5. *Technique's Evaluation*

Swimmers in both groups and in the three measurements were evaluated in BK and BR techniques by the same experienced swimming coach with the use of Tec Pa cards [18]. Tec Pa is an evaluation tool which assesses six key points of a swimming styles' technique. These key points are the position of the head, the position of the body, the elbows, the knees, the ankles, and the full body coordination. All swimmers in each group had to swim 15 m of each style (BK and BR) with the command to swim slowly and as carefully as possible. Their unique attempts in both styles were recorded on a camera which was placed on a high spot for better evaluation from the coach. Then, one coach assessed swimmers' technique by watching the videos and recording swimmers' scores via Tec Pa.

2.6. *Skills and Performance Measurement*

After the evaluation of the technique, the Skills and Performance evaluation followed. The skills included "Start", in which the swimmers had to enter the pool first with their hands and then with the other parts of the body. Then, they had to swim for 5 m as far as the pool's rope keeping their head outside the water. When the swimmers reached the pool's rope, they performed the first of the two dives, "Sink 1". The swimmers had to dive under the lane's rope without any of their body parts touching it. After the first dive they swam for another 5 m as far as the opposite side of the pool. The exact process was repeated while performing the second dive "Sink 2", and the skills measurement was finished.

Skills were recorded as successful, with one point, or unsuccessful, with zero points. Additionally, the time that the swimmers needed to complete these Skills (Skills' Time) was recorded. When the swimmers completed the skills, they took a kickboard and immediately continued with the kicks' performance (Kicks' Time), in which the swimmers covered the distance of 35 m as fast as possible. At the end of this process, the coach stopped the stop-watch (TYR Z - 100 LAP) and the swimmers had completed their try (Figure 1). To ensure the reliability of the measurements, during the evaluation of swimmers' performance, the try of each swimmer were recorded via a digital video camera (Sony DCR-HC52 MiniDV Handycam Camcorder with 40x Optical Zoom). Additionally, the coach had an assistant coach who was observing all the processes and was noting the result of each swimmer.

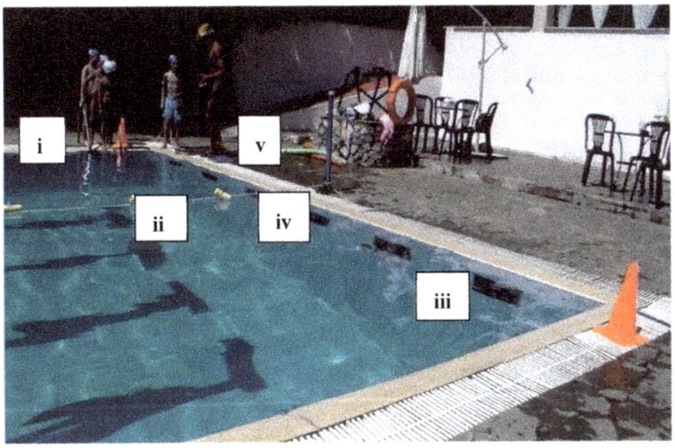

Figure 1. Skills and Performance test. **i** = Start: Entrance in the pool, **ii** = Sink 1: Dive under the pool's lane for first time, **iii** = Swim: Swim until the opposite side of the pool, **iv** = Sink 2: Dive under the pool's lane for second time, **v** = Kicks' Time: Took the kickboard for the 35 m of free kick.

The conceptualization of this skills and performance test was chosen to make the children feel that they were participating in a game instead of the usual test that several authors utilize to evaluate children's' performance. Both groups enjoyed that type of evaluation and this gave confidence to the children for further training participation.

2.7. Saliva Cortisol Concentration

The saliva cortisol concentration measurement occurred only at the fourth week of the intervention to examine the children's mood between the two swimming learning programs. A total of 0.5 ml of saliva was collected from all the swimmers before and immediately after the swimming training. Saliva was collected in tubes that were saved in a portable fridge, then the samples were analyzed in the laboratory with the ELISA method [19].

The measurement's validity was ensured by following the process of Hanrahan et al. [20]. Thus, the children were informed to avoid food, liquid consumption, brushing their teeth, and chewing gum 30 min before the measurement. At the end of training, five minutes before the sampling, swimmers washed their mouth with cold water.

2.8. Statistical Analysis

The variables' values were shown as median with standard deviation (±). Descriptive statistic and test of normality (Shapiro–Wilk) ($p > 0.05$) for all the variables were used for a sample of fewer than 50 participants. Categorical variables of "Start" and two "Dives" (Sink 1, Sink 2) between the two groups were analyzed using Fisher's Exact Test (χ^2) for 2 × 2 Table. Additionally, Chochran's Q Test was used to examine possible difference between three measurements.

Continue variables of performance and technique were analyzed with the parametric analysis of two–way ANOVA with repeated measures (group * measurements), checking for possible within or between subjects' effects. Additionally, the measurements were checked for Homogeneity and Sphericity ($p > 0.05$). When homogeneity did not meet, the ratio of G2/G1 was checked (G2/G1 > 1.5). Additionally, Mauchly's test and Greenhouse Geisser were used for the measurements' sphericity. Possible statistically significant difference between subjects' effects were analyzed via Syntax, making pairwise comparisons between groups with Bonferroni's post hoc test.

Additionally, two–way ANOVA was used to measure cortisol concentration (groups * measurements), checking Levene's test for homogeneity ($p > 0.05$) and possible interaction between groups with Wilk's lambda. In all continuous variables, the Effect Size (ES) with Partial Eta square (η^2) were calculated. The analysis was performed with the statistical software IBM SPSS Statistics for Windows, Version 27.0. Armonk, NY: IBM Corp. The level of significance was set at $a = 0.05$.

3. Results

3.1. Categorical Variables

Start, Sink 1, and Sink 2

According to Fisher's exact analysis, the categorical variable of "Start" had a statistically significant difference, with a greater percentage of successful tries, in AG, at the first (CG = 9.1% (1/11 participants) vs. AG = 58.3% (7/12 participants), $p = 0.027$) and third (CG = 63.6% (7/11 participants) vs. AG = 100% (12/12 participants) ($p = 0.037$)) measurement, respectively. Additionally, according to Cochran's analysis both of "Start" ($p = 0.001$), "Sink 1" ($p = 0.003$), and "Sink 2" ($p = 0.046$) variables, there was a statistically significant difference between the three measurements (Table 4).

Table 4. Percentage of successful tries within groups in the three measurements.

	Start (N%)				Sink 1 (N%)				Sink 2 (N%)			
M	CG	AG	Fisher's (p–Value)	Cochran's (p–Value)	CG	AG	Fisher's (p–Value)	Cochran's (p–Value)	CG	AG	Fisher's (p–Value)	Cochran's (p–Value)
M 1	9.1	58.3	0.027 *		36.4	50	0.680		45.5	66.7	0.414	
M 2	36.4	66.7	0.220	0.001 **	90.9	83.3	1	0.003 **	45.5	75	0.214	0.043 **
M 3	63.6	100	0.037 *		90.9	75.0	0.590		100	75	0.217	

M = Measurement, M 1 = Measurement 1, M 2 = Measurement 2, M 3 = Measurement 3, CG = Control Group, AG = Alternative Group, * = Statistically significant difference within groups (Fisher's, p–value), ** = Statistically significant difference between measurements (Cochran's, p–value).

3.2. Continuous Variables

According to the normality test (Shapiro–Wilk), normality was found in a sample with fewer of 50 participants ($p > 0.05$), thus followed parametric analysis in all continuous variables.

3.3. Skills Time, Kick Time, Sum Time

Box's test of equality of covariance metrices found statistically significant differences ($p = 0.000$), and thus analyzed the ratio of G2/G1. The ratio was less than 1.5, so there was not any violation of homogeneity. Mauchly's test for the sphericity analysis, in Skills, Kick, and Sum Time, was less than 0.75 ($p < 0.05$). Thus, to avoid any violation of sphericity, we checked Greenhouse Geisser. The degrees of Freedom were modified for Skills Time (F (1.165, 24.486) = 3.695, p = 0.061), Kicks Time (F (1.391, 29.218) = 3.862, p = 0.046), and Sum Time (F (1.266, 26.580) = 4.391, p = 0.038).

In between subject effects, statistically significant difference interactions were found in the Skills Time between groups in (F (1,21) = 9.720, p = 0.005, η^2 = 0.316). Thus, Syntax analysis and, specifically, Bonferroni pairwise comparisons were utilized to find the differences between groups. The difference observed at the first measurement (40.4 ± 16.5 vs. 26.0 ± 5.3 sec, (95% CI (3.925, 24.802)), p = 0.009). Moreover, a statistically significant difference was found overall between measurements ($p < 0.001$) (Table 5).

Table 5. Performance variables within groups in the three measurements.

	Skills Time (sec)			Kicks Time (sec)			Sum Time (sec)		
M	**CG**	**AG**	**Eta (η^2)**	**CG**	**AG**	**Eta (η^2)**	**CG**	**AG**	**Eta (η^2)**
M 1	40.4 ± 16.5 *	26.0 ± 5.3	0.316	112.9 ± 34.7 **	93.8 ± 24.7	0.035	153.8 ± 49.5 **	120.4 ± 27.0	0.101
M 2	30.4 ± 7.7 **	26.3 ± 5.7		77.8 ± 11.2 **	80.8 ± 21.4		108.0 ± 11.9 **	107.3 ± 26.3	
M 3	26.8 ± 5.2 **	23.2 ± 3.8		77.2 ± 12.8	72.7 ± 17.4		105.1 ± 13.3	95.8 ± 20.8	

M = Measurement, M 1 = Measurement 1, M 2 = Measurement 2, M 3 = Measurement 3, CG = Control Group, AG = Alternative Group, * = Statistically significant difference between groups, ** = Statistically significant difference between measurements.

3.4. Saliva Cortisol Concentration

Box's test of equality of covariance metrices had no statistically significant difference (p = 0.067); moreover, Levene's test observed the p–value to be greater than 0.05, suggesting that there was not any violation in homogeneity. Then, an interaction between groups was found in the Multivariate test (Wilk's lambda = 0.599, F (2.000, 20.000) = 6.696, p = 0.006). In pairwise comparison, a statistically significant difference in the second measurement was found between groups (CG vs. AG: 0.058 ± 0.12 vs. 0.122 ± 0.12 µg/dl, (95% CI (−0.99, −0.28), p = 0.001). Moreover, statistically significant decrement in saliva cortisol concentration was observed between the two measurements, ($p < 0.001$) (Figure 2).

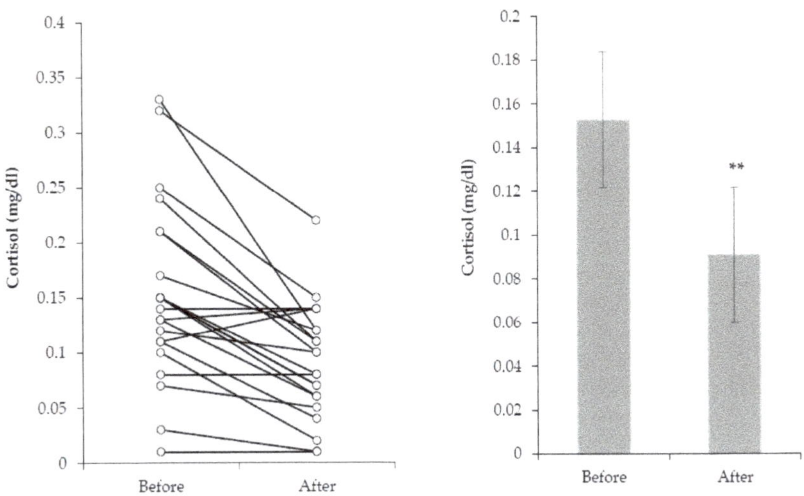

(**a**) (**b**)

Figure 2. Saliva cortisol concentration before and after training, (**a**): for each swimmer, (**b**): mean values between groups. ** = Statistically significant difference between measurements.

3.5. Tec Pa's Backstroke and Breststroke Scores

Box's test of equality of covariance metrices found statistically significant differences ($p = 0.044$), thus analyzed the Ratio of G2/G1. The ratio was less than 1.5 so there was not violation of homogeneity. Using Mauchly's test for Sphericity analysis, in BK and BR, ε was close to 1 ($p > 0.05$). Thus, checked Sphericity assumed for measurement (BK: F (2,42) = 51.388, $p = 0.000$ and BR: F (2,42) = 15.995, $p = 0.000$) and for measurement x group in which there was not any interaction (BK: F (2,42) = 2.491, $p = 0.095$ and BR: F (2,42) = 2.245, $p = 0.118$).

In between subject effects, statistically significant differences were found between groups in both of BK ($p = 0.009$, $\eta^2 = 0.283$) and BR ($p = 0.020$, $\eta^2 = 0.231$). Thus, Syntax analysis and specifically Bonferroni pairwise comparisons were utilized to find the differences between groups. In BK, we observed a statistically significant difference in the third measurement (CG vs. AG: 6.6 ± 1.6 vs. 9.8 ± 1.4, 95% CI (−4.475, −1.931), $p = 0.000$), whereas a difference was observed in BR in the second (CG vs. AG: 1.3 ± 1.6 vs. 3.1 ± 2.2, 95% CI (−3.495, −0.126), $p = 0.036$) and third (CG vs. AG: 1.9 ± 2.5 vs. 4.5 ± 3.1, 95% CI (−5.031, −0.151), $p = 0.038$) measurement. Moreover, statistically significant differences were found between measurements in each group ($p < 0.001$) (Figure 3).

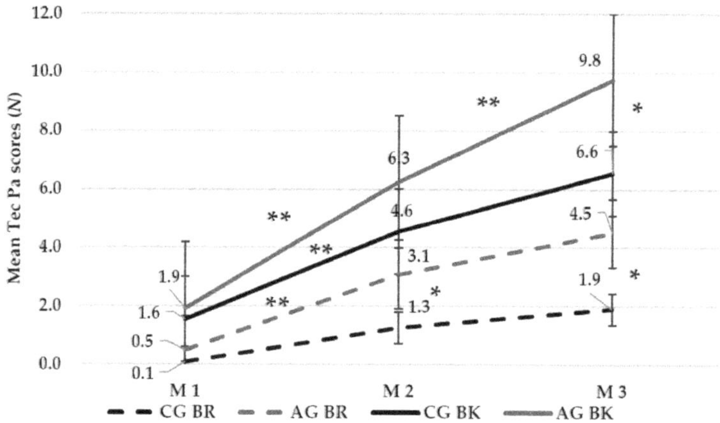

Figure 3. Swimmers' mean score in Backstroke and Breaststroke. M 1 = Measurement 1, M 2 = Measurement 2, M 3 = Measurement 3, CG = Control Group, AG = Alternative Group, BR = Breaststroke, BK = Backstroke, * = Statistically significant difference between groups, ** = Statistically significant difference between measurements in each group.

4. Discussion

The main objective of the study was to discover if an alternative swimming learning approach could give beneficial results on primary school-aged novice swimmers. Often, swimming coaches choose to teach young swimmers a variety of standardized swimming exercises which increase the boredom and restricts learning effectiveness. On the other hand, the main findings of the study indicate that a swimming learning approach which targets creative games and fun could make the swimming training more interesting and effective on skills and technique learning.

4.1. Movement Perception for Faster Skills' and Technique's Learning

The present study was conducted by the participation of young swimmers (7–9 years old). The aim of it was the children to learn the skills of start and dive, the techniques of BK and BR, and to improve their performance. The swimmers were chosen at these ages because according to the literature it is the most crucial age for faster learning [21].

Additionally, an additional feature of the sample's selection was that at those ages they usually start swimming, and the main content of the courses is the specific skills and styles.

The most common learning approach which is used is through standardized exercises that are constantly repeated and prevent children from developing their imagination and ideas. In recent years, there has been a tendency to use a more playful approach. Many studies examined the effectiveness of that kind of training in sports such as track and field, tennis, football, and general skills, through the use of movements that children use in their daily routine [1,2,4–8].

The present study was based on the findings of the above research, comparing a standardized learning training approach with an alternative that targets mimicry and moving patterns which are usually used in a daily situation. Study results confirm that an alternative learning approach gives better results [2]. No similar research was found in swimming to compare the data. Only Magias and Pill [9] used a more distinct approach which helped the swimmers to develop the perception of the forces exerted on the body from the water.

The target in AG was to limit the faults that are usually observed at a move during an exercise and to give the children a better perception of their body movements. In the existing literature, athletes' ability to perceive their movement was not mentioned. In the study, an important learning factor is movements perception. Generally, each child needs a different learning approach. However, common evidence on a learning process is the moves perception. Through the perception of an error, it is possible to learn the technique faster.

4.2. Technique, Skills and Performance

In our study, the alternative exercises provided the opportunity for faster and more effective skills and technique assimilation. The playful spirit and content of the lessons created a positive learning background for both BK and BR styles. Additionally, the liquid element and the forces produced in the water did not seem to affect the children's learning ability. Instead, they were found to have a better understanding of their body's moves. This finding is in accordance with Magias and Pill's [9] study results.

On performance variables (Skills' time, Kicks' time, and Sum time) in both groups were observed statistically significant improvements. Probably, the stimuli of the two training protocols have the same improvement in endurance. However, on AG compared to the CG less training volume (meters) was used because the emphasis was on the quality of movements' execution and not on the quantity.

Additionally, for AG, those workouts, which contained more training volume (m) than the others, were performed in different directions inside the pool, in contrast to the CG that followed the usual route from one side of the pool to the other within the pool's lane. The target was to differentiate the way that endurance is trained, taking the idea from the "IAAF Kids" [2] which used road exercises of various directions and obstacles.

In the studies of Papadimitriou and Savvoulidis [22,23], it was stated that endurance is a parameter that can be improved in childhood with a variety of training stimuli. In the present study, the training target was to learn the technique of BK and BR, but also, was to improve endurance. Since the endurance improved in both groups by performing technical exercises, it is understandable that with less fatigue in training the children can be improved in endurance.

4.3. Salivary Cortisol Concertation

Salivary cortisol concentration was used to examine children's exercise stress levels [24]. Researchers use this index to understand the stress levels in acute or long time periods [25]. According to the literature, salivary cortisol concertation in both infants [26] and children [27] gave reliable results and showed that children's mood depends on it and when they are engaged with one activity the cortisol's concentration values alter.

The present study was based on the research of Sims et al., [10] who examined the effect of service quality in three daycare centers in relation to salivary cortisol concentration, based on samples taken from children. The results of the research showed that the children with the highest quality of service at daycare centers had the lowest salivary cortisol values.

In the study, it was found that the salivary cortisol concentration had no statistically significant difference at the first measurement. Therefore, the 45′ between groups possibly do not affect the salivary cortisol concentration. According to the literature, cortisol reached a peak at around 08:30am, then cortisol levels slowly decrease until the completion of the 24 h cycle [28]. Moreover, the circadian rhythm of each person differs, because cortisol's Acrophase values vary from 07:59 to 09:05 am [28]. In contrast, statistically significant decrease was observed from the pre to post training measurements in both groups. The result is consistent with the literature about the effect of circadian rhythm, low intensity exercise, and the mood of participation on cortisol's concentration reduction [10,11,28,29].

Another statistically significant difference which was observed in the second measurement between the groups, indicated that in CG, the cortisol concentration reduced more than in AG. Additionally, another difference is the rate of cortisol's reduction during the respective hours that our measurements were performed. It was found that on children, the cortisol concentration from 09:30 to 10:15 am reduced by 10.5%, while the AG who trained at the same hours the reduction rate was 31.4%. Continuing from 10:15 to 11:00 am, the reduction rate on children is 14.7%, while the CG's reduction rate was 48.7% [30,31].

The difference between groups is probably due to the fact that at the time of the day the CG participated, the environmental conditions were more delightful because the sunshine was more intense and brighter than AG's hour. Therefore, there is a greater proportionate decrease in cortisol concentration at the same hours with an increased rate, possibly due to the circadian rhythm, low intensity exercise, and increased mood. However, further studies, at these ages are necessary.

4.4. Fear as Attenuate Factor on Skills and Technique's Learning

According to the results of the study, there was a greater improvement for AG at the skill of "Start" and at the BK and BR technique. In "Sink 1 and 2" similar improvement in both groups was observed. However, these two skills are very difficult for children to assimilate, especially when they are novices, due to the fear that exists when they immerse their head in the water.

Additionally, another measurement which was found statistically different between groups was in the first measurement of Skill's time. That difference was observed because of the fear that the children felt in the first measurement, mainly in the CG. Thus, they needed more time to think how to perform each skill.

Usually, fear resulted from a previous traumatic experience or an attempt to protect themselves from an injury [32]. It is observed that children, when entering the water, choose to enter on foot or hold their nose to dive. These reactions are observed due to the safety that children feel when they step on their feet and because of the protection of their nose and mouth from the water's possible entry. Therefore, in the study, fear was a reaction that was observed during the tests and training. After a short time period, the methodical teaching in both groups was contributed to overcoming the children's fear. However, AG overcame this fear faster than CG, because the training's content was focused on fun and recreational thinking.

According to the study results, the alternative swimming learning approach could be used in whole or as part of a training session. Children seem to prefer participating in a training session which gives the opportunity to think creatively and to learn, without recurring exhausting exercises. To make this happen, it is important the swimming coaches have the mood to create alternative solutions which will solve children's motor learning difficulties faster than the usual standardized exercises that mostly utilize.

5. Conclusions

The alternative swimming training program was found to be more efficient or equally effective, compared to the standardized method, for teaching the skills of "Start" and "Sink", at the improvement of BK and BR technique, at performance, and in the reduction of salivary cortisol concentration. Therefore, it is helpful for coaches to steer their swimming learning programs to the alternative form to achieve faster and more effective learning outcomes.

6. Study Limitations

In the present study, the swimmers' age that was used in the intervention did not meet in any other study. Thus, the evaluation of skills and performance variables in those ages is novel. Despite this, there are some limitations in the study that probably affect the results of the study (Table 6).

Table 6. Study's limitations.

Limitation	Problem	Future Solution
The weather conditions were unstable.	Limited the presence of children in the training.	To take part in an indoor pool.
Due to illness, the presence of some children was small.	Smaller samples were used for the statistical analysis.	Smaller intervention periods.
The start time of training differed between the two groups by 45 min.	The AG had earlier training than CG, thus there were complaints from the children of AG.	The training must be starting at the same time, probably on different days.

Author Contributions: Conceptualization, K.P. and D.L.; Methodology, K.P. and D.L.; Software, K.P.; Validation, D.L.; Formal Analysis, K.P.; Investigation, K.P. and D.L.; Resources, K.P.; Data Curation, K.P.; Writing—Original Draft Preparation, K.P. and D.L.; Writing—Review and Editing, K.P. and D.L.; Visualization, K.P.; Supervision, D.L.; Project Administration, K.P and D.L.; Funding Acquisition, no funds. All authors have read and agreed to the published version of the manuscript.

Funding: This research had no funds.

Institutional Review Board Statement: The study was conducted according to the to the Code of Research Ethics of Aristotle University of Thessaloniki with protocol code 199/2-2-2017, which was confirmed on 17th of February 2017.

Informed Consent Statement: Informed consent was obtained from all subjects' parents involved in the study by signatured the statement's participation in which was described the study's process and the safety of the measurements.

Data Availability Statement: Not applicable.

Acknowledgments: The authors would like to thank the swimming coach who participated in the swimmers' training and assessment. Additionally, the head of the Laboratory of Biological Evaluation of Human Performance Vasilios Mougios and his partners who contributed to cortisol's analyzation and the English professor for her valuable contribution in the manuscript's corrections.

Conflicts of Interest: The authors declare no conflict of interest.

Appendix A. Weekly Training Plan between Groups (CG vs. AG)

2nd Week						
Days	**Monday**		**Wednesday**		**Friday**	
Target	**CG**	**AG**	**CG**	**AG**	**CG**	**AG**
Entrance in the pool	Starts from the pool side	Press the cockroaches with your foot and get in the pool	Starts from the pool side	Get in the cycle from the pool's side	Starts from the pool side	Hands skateboard with pool noodle until all body enters the pool
Back stroke's body position and kicks	Kicks with the kick board in different positions	Clean the pool from the balls with kicks	Kicks with the kick board in different positions	Swimming holidays around the pool with a pool noodle on hands	Kicks with the kick board in different positions	Battles with tie ropes on hips
Breaststroke's stroke coordination	Making the move outside the pool, then in the water the same moves	Karate lesson outside the pool, then the same move with a pool noodle on the chest	Making the move outside the pool, then in the water the same moves	Karate lesson outside the pool, then ball hunting	Making the move outside the pool, then in the water the same moves	Karate lesson outside the pool, then the same move with a pool noodle on the chest
Sinking in the water	Grabbing the wall of the pool, sink the body in the water	Dive grabbing a rope which is tie in the pool's bottom	Grabbing the pool's wall, sink of the body in the water	Dives with a slide at the side of the pool	Grabbing the pool's wall, sink of the body in the water	Dive grabbing a rope which is tie in the pool's bottom

References

1. Koronaios, V. The Effect of "Play and Stay" Program in Volleyball Skills Learning and in Satisfaction Level in Primary School Students. Ph.D. Thesis, Aristotle University of Thessaloniki, Thessaloniki, Greece, 2012.
2. Blatsis, P.; Saraslanidis, P.; Barkoukis, V.; Manou, V.; Tzavidas, K.; Hatzivasiliou, H.; Palla, S. The Implementation of IAAF Kids Athletics in Elementary Schools: Can It Enhance the Student's Motivation to Participate in Physical Education and Improve their Physical Performance? *Inq. Sport Phys. Educ.* **2015**, *13*, 22–36.
3. Light, R.; Wallian, N. A Constructivist-Informed Approach to Teaching Swimming. *Quest* **2012**, *60*, 387–404. [CrossRef]
4. Zhang, P.; Ward, P.; Li, W.; Sutherland, S.; Goodway, J. Effects of Play Practice on Teaching Table Tennis Skills. *J. Teach. Phys. Educ.* **2012**, *31*, 71–85. [CrossRef]
5. Harveya, S.; Jarrettb, K. A review of the game-centered approaches to teaching and coaching literature since 2006. *Phys. Educ. Sport Pedagog.* **2013**, *19*, 278–300. [CrossRef]
6. Jarrett, K.; Harvey, S. Recent trends in research literature on game-based approaches to teaching and coaching games. In *Contemporary Developments in Games Teaching*, 1st ed.; Light, R., Quay, J., Harvey, S., Mooney, A., Eds.; Routledge: Abingdon, UK, 2014; p. 16.
7. Miller, A.; Christensen, E.; Eather, N.; Gray, S.; Sproule, J.; Keay, J.; Lubans, L. Can physical education and physical activity outcomes be developed simultaneously using a game-centered approach? *Eur. Phys. Educ. Rev.* **2016**, *22*, 113–133. [CrossRef]
8. Alli, G.C.; Mohamad, R.A.; Rabiu, M.M.; Norlaila, A.K.; Ahmad, B.H.; Musawi, M. The Effectiveness of traditional games intervention program in the improvement of form one school-age children's motor skills related performance components. *J. Phys. Educ. Sport* **2017**, *3*, 925–930.
9. Magias, T.; Pill, S. Teaching swimming for movement variability: An application of Teaching Games for Understanding-Game Sense. In Proceedings of the 28th ACHPER International Conference, Melbourne, Australia, 27–29 November 2013; p. 93.
10. Sims, M.; Guilfoyle, A.; Parry, T.S. Children's cortisol levels and quality of child care provision. *Child Care Health Dev.* **2006**, *32*, 453–466. [CrossRef]
11. Tharp, G.D.; Barnes, M.W. Reduction of saliva immunoglobulin levels by swim training. *Eur. J. Appl. Phys. Occup.* **1990**, *60*, 61–64. [CrossRef] [PubMed]
12. Budde, H.; Windisch, C.; Kudielka, B.M.; Voelcker-Rehage, C. Saliva cortisol in school children after acute physical exercise. *Neur. Lett.* **2010**, *483*, 16–19. [CrossRef] [PubMed]

13. Tsirigkakis, S.; Mastorakos, G.; Koutedakis, Y.; Mougios, V.; Nevill, A.M.; Pafili, Z.; Bogdanis, G.C. Effects of two workload-matched high-intensity interval training protocols on regional body composition and fat oxidation in obese men. *Nutrients* **2021**, *27*, 1096. [CrossRef] [PubMed]
14. Singer, R.N. Motor learning as a function of age and sex. In *Physical Activity, Human Growth and Development*; Lawrence, R., Ed.; Academic Press: Cambridge, MA, USA, 1973; p. 182.
15. Blanksby, B.A.; Parker, H.E.; Bradley, S.; Ong, V. Children's readiness for learning front crawl swimming. *Aust. J. Sci. Med. Sport* **1995**, *27*, 34–37.
16. Jerszyński, D.; Antosiak-Cyrak, K.; Habiera, M.; Wochna, K.; Rostkowska, E. Changes in Selected Parameters of Swimming Technique in the Back Crawl and the Front Crawl in Young Novice Swimmers. *J. Hum. Kinet.* **2013**, *37*, 161–171. [CrossRef]
17. Helena, A.; Rocha, D.A.; Marinho, S.S.; Ferreira, A.M.C. Management and teaching methodology of swimming lessons in the Portuguese primary schools. *Fund. Técn. Cient. Desp.* **2014**, *10*, 45–59.
18. Papadimitriou, K.; Papadimitriou, N.; Gourgoulis, V.; Barkoukis, V.; Loupos, D. Assessment of Young Swimmers' Technique with Tec Pa Tool. *Central Eur. J. Sport Sci. Med.* **2021**, *34*, 39–51.
19. Chennaoui, M.; Bougard, C.; Drogou, C.; Langrume, C.; Miller, C.; Gomez-Merino, D.; Vergnoux, F. Stress biomarkers, mood states, and sleep during a major competition: "Success" and "failure" athlete's profile of high-level swimmers. *Front. Physiol.* **2016**, *7*, 94. [CrossRef] [PubMed]
20. Hanrahan, M.A.K.; McCarthy, R.N.; Kleiber, R.N.C.; Lutgendorf, S.; Tsalikian, E. Strategies for salivary cortisol collection and analysis in research with children. *Appl. Nurs. Res.* **2006**, *19*, 95–101. [CrossRef] [PubMed]
21. Janacsek, K.; Fiser, J.; Nemeth, D. The best time to acquire new skills: Age-related differences in implicit sequence learning across the human lifespan. *Dev. Sci.* **2012**, *15*, 496–505. [CrossRef] [PubMed]
22. Papadimitriou, K.; Savvoulidis, S. Does High Intensity Interval Training (HIIT), have an effect on young swimmers' performance? *J. Swim. Res.* **2017**, *25*, 20–28.
23. Papadimitriou, K.; Savvoulidis, S. The Effects of Two Different HIIT Resting Protocols on Children's Swimming Efficiency and Performance. *Central Eur. J. Sport Sci. Med.* **2020**, *30*, 15–24. [CrossRef]
24. Cordero, A.M.J.; López, S.A.M.; Villar, M.N.; García, G.I.; López, R.M.A.; Piñero, O.A.; Castell, C.E. Salivary cortisol as an indicator of physological stress in children and adults· a systematic review. *Nutr. Hosp.* **2014**, *29*, 960–968.
25. Bouget, M.; Rouveix, M.; Michaux, O.; Pequignot, J.M.; Filaire, E. Relationships among training stress, mood and dehydroepiandrosterone sulphate/cortisol ratio in female cyclists. *J. Sports Sci.* **2006**, *24*, 1297–1302. [CrossRef]
26. Hertsgaard, L.; Gunnar, M.; Larson, M.; Brodersen, L.; Lehman, H. First time experiences in infancy: When they appear to be pleasant, do they activate the adrenocortical stress response? *Dev. Psych.* **1992**, *25*, 319–333. [CrossRef] [PubMed]
27. Williamson, D.; Dewey, A.; Steinbekg, D. Mood change through physical exercise in nine to ten-year-old children. *Percept. Mot. Ski.* **2001**, *93*, 311–316. [CrossRef]
28. Chan, S.; Debono, M. Replication of cortisol circadian rhythm: New advances in hydrocortisone replacement therapy. *Ther. Adv. Endocrinol. Metab.* **2010**, *1*, 129–138. [CrossRef] [PubMed]
29. Jin, P. Changes in heart rate, noradrenaline, cortisol and mood during Tai Chi. *J. Psychosom. Res.* **1989**, *33*, 197–206. [CrossRef]
30. Hindmarsh, P.C.; Geertsma, K. *Congenital Adrenal Hyperplasia. A Comprehensive Guide*; Academic Press: London, UK, 2017; p. 10.
31. Bartels, M.; de Geus, E.J.C.; Kirschbaum, C.; Sluyter, F.; Boomsma, D.I. Heritability of daytime cortisol levels in children. *Behav. Gen.* **2003**, *33*, 421–433. [CrossRef]
32. Daou, M.; Hutchison, Z.; Bacelar, M.; Rhoads, J.A.; Lohse, K.R.; Miller, M.W. Does learning a skill with the expectation of teaching it impairs the skill's execution under psychological pressure. *J. Exp. Psychol. Appl.* **2019**, *25*, 219–229. [CrossRef] [PubMed]

healthcare MDPI

Article

Are Strength Indicators and Skin Temperature Affected by the Type of Warm-Up in Paralympic Powerlifting Athletes?

Marcelo de Aquino Resende [1], Felipe J. Aidar [2,3,4,5], Roberta Barreto Vasconcelos Resende [1], Gracielle Costa Reis [1], Layanne de Oliveira Barros [2], Dihogo Gama de Matos [2,6], Anderson Carlos Marçal [2,3], Paulo Francisco de Almeida-Neto [7], Alfonso López Díaz-de-Durana [8], María Merino-Fernández [9], José Vilaça-Alves [10], Breno Guilherme de Araújo Tinoco Cabral [7], Eduardo Borba Neves [11], Victor Machado Reis [10], Filipe Manuel Clemente [12,13] and Nuno Domingos Garrido [10,*]

1 Department of Physical Education, Tiradentes University (UNIT), Aracaju 49010-390, Brazil; marcelo.aquino@souunit.com.br (M.d.A.R.); roberta.resende@souunit.com.br (R.B.V.R.); gracielle.reis@souunit.com.br (G.C.R.)
2 Group of Studies and Research of Performance, Sport, Health and Paralympic Sports (GEPEPS), Federal University of Sergipe (UFS), Sao Cristovao 49100-000, Brazil; fjaidar@gmail.com (F.J.A.); layanneoliveira@cepiexpansao.com.br (L.d.O.B.); dematosd@myumanitoba.ca (D.G.d.M.); acmarcal@yahoo.com.br (A.C.M.)
3 Program of Physical Education, Federal University of Sergipe (UFS), Sao Cristovao 49100-000, Brazil
4 Program of Physiological Science, Federal University of Sergipe (UFS), Sao Cristovao 49100-000, Brazil
5 Department of Physical Education, Federal University of Sergipe (UFS), Sao Cristovao 49100-000, Brazil
6 Cardiovascular & Physiology of Exercise Laboratory, University of Manitoba, Winnipeg, MB R3T 2N2, Canada
7 Department of Physical Education, Federal University of Rio Grande do Norte (UFRN), Natal 59078-970, Brazil; paulo220911@hotmail.com (P.F.d.A.-N.); brenotcabral@gmail.com (B.G.d.A.T.C.)
8 Sports Department, Physical Activity and Sports Faculty-INEF, Universidad Politécnica de Madrid, 28040 Madrid, Spain; alfonso.lopez@upm.es
9 Faculty of Health Sciences, Universidad Francisco de Vitoria (UFV), 28223 Madrid, Spain; m.merino.prof@ufv.es
10 Research Center in Sports Sciences, Health Sciences and Human Development (CIDESD), Trás os Montes and Alto Douro University, 5001-801 Vila Real, Portugal; josevilaca@utad.pt (J.V.-A.); vmreis@utad.pt (V.M.R.)
11 Universidade Tecnológica Federal do Paraná (UTFPR), Curitiba 80230-901, Brazil; eduardoneves@utfpr.edu.br
12 Escola Superior Desporto e Lazer, Instituto Politécnico de Viana do Castelo, Rua Escola Industrial e Comercial de Nun'Álvares, 4900-347 Viana do Castelo, Portugal; filipe.clemente5@gmail.com
13 Instituto de Telecomunicações, Delegação da Coilhã, 1049-001 Lisboa, Portugal
* Correspondence: ndgarrido@gmail.com

Citation: de Aquino Resende, M.; Aidar, F.J.; Vasconcelos Resende, R.B.; Reis, G.C.; de Oliveira Barros, L.; de Matos, D.G.; Marçal, A.C.; de Almeida-Neto, P.F.; Díaz-de-Durana, A.L.; Merino-Fernández, M.; et al. Are Strength Indicators and Skin Temperature Affected by the Type of Warm-Up in Paralympic Powerlifting Athletes? *Healthcare* **2021**, *9*, 923. https://doi.org/10.3390/healthcare9080923

Academic Editor: João Paulo Brito

Received: 24 April 2021
Accepted: 29 June 2021
Published: 22 July 2021

Abstract: (1) Background: the present study aimed to evaluate the effect of different types of warm-ups on the strength and skin temperature of Paralympic powerlifting athletes. (2) Methods: the participants were 15 male Paralympic powerlifting athletes. The effects of three different types of warm-up (without warm-up (WW), traditional warm-up (TW), or stretching warm-up (SW)) were analyzed on static and dynamic strength tests as well as in the skin temperature, which was monitored by thermal imaging. (3) Results: no differences in the dynamic and static indicators of the force were shown in relation to the different types of warm-ups. No significant differences were found in relation to peak torque ($p = 0.055$, F = 4.560, $\eta 2p = 0.246$ medium effect), and one-repetition maximum ($p = 0.139$, F = 3.191, $\eta 2p = 0.186$, medium effect) between the different types of warm-ups. In the thermographic analysis, there was a significant difference only in the pectoral muscle clavicular portion between the TW (33.04 ± 0.71 °C) and the WW (32.51 ± 0.74 °C) ($p = 0.038$). The TW method also presented slightly higher values than the SW and WW in the pectoral muscles sternal portion and the deltoid anterior portion, but with p-value > 0.05. (4) Conclusions: the types of warm-ups studied do not seem to interfere with the performance of Paralympic Powerlifting athletes. However, the thermal images showed that traditional warm-up best meets the objectives expected for this preparation phase.

Keywords: warm-up; muscle force; performance; resistance training; thermal imaging; physiology

1. Introduction

The warm-up was identified as essential to maximize the athlete's performance in different sports and physical activities [1]. When addressing performance in adapted sports and Paralympic powerlifting, the warm-up has also been presented as a determinant for performance [1]. Warm-ups aim to improve nerve conduction, combined with an increase in temperature [2–4]. Specific warm-ups have been shown to improve strength [5–7], however, variations in the type of warm-up can be harmful [8].

The warm-up performed before training and competitions seems to increase body temperature, providing a decrease in stiffness, an increase in the rate of nerve conduction and an increase in metabolic efficiency [2,3], an improvement in muscle strength and power production [9], and an improvement in mechanical efficiency and contraction speed [10,11]. In this sense, it seems that during short-term static stretching, neuro-muscular activation and muscle-tendon stiffness seem to be unaffected. Among other factors, this may be due to an elevated muscle temperature, which tends to lead to an increase in the speed of conduction of muscle fibers and a better binding of contractile proteins (actin, myosin) [12,13], and stretching can provide this improvement.

On the other hand, with specific warm-ups with higher loads, the capacity to produce force tends to increase [14], that is, the force tends to improve [7]. A specific warm-up tends to increase strength, improving efficiency, training intensity, with improvements in strength and velocity [14–16]. However, variations in the type of warm-up can be harmful [8]. Currently, there is no consensus between the effect of different types of warm-ups [17–19], and the indications of the types of warm-ups are still very controversial [7]. Thus, the study raised the following hypotheses regarding strength and temperature: (i) traditional warm-up tends to be better; (ii) warm-up as stretching tends to be better; and (iii) there are no differences between the types of warm-up.

Therefore, the present study aimed to evaluate the effect of different types of warm-ups on the strength and skin temperature of Paralympic powerlifting athletes. It was hypothesized that the warm-up methods are not capable of altering the performance of Paralympic powerlifting athletes.

2. Materials and Methods

2.1. Sample

Fifteen male Paralympic powerlifters volunteered for this study. Every participant was a competitor involved in national competitions and was eligible for this sport under the International Paralympic Committee (IPC). All participants met the functional classification criteria of the IPC [20], with disabilities in the lower limbs, with the unique classification being legible and ineligible. Participants were required to have participated in a minimum of one competition at the national level over the past 12-month period and the average prior experience in the sport was 2.43 ± 1.03 years. The physical impairments of the participants were varied as follows: four had spinal cord injuries at or below the eighth thoracic vertebra, four had amputations, two had polio, one had cerebral palsy, and one had arthrogryposis. The participants mean age and body mass was 28.47 ± 5.79 years and 81.75 ± 17.33 kg, respectively. Body mass was assessed with specifically adapted equipment as described by Resende et al. [19].

The athletes participated voluntarily and signed an informed consent form in accordance with Resolution 466/2012 of the National Commission for Research Ethics (CONEP) of the National Health Council and the ethical principles of the latest version of the Declaration of Helsinki 2013 (and the World Medical Association). This study was approved by the Research Ethics Committee of the Federal University of Sergipe, CAAE: 2.637.882 (date of approval: 7 May 2018).

2.2. Experimental Design

The study comprised 3 weeks which included 9 sessions separated by a minimum of 48-h. The first three sessions (Week 1) were dedicated to baseline measurements of thermal images on Session 1, and to familiarization with the dynamic strength tests on Session 2 (1-RM and mean propulsive velocity) and the isometric strength tests on Session 3 (impulse, variability, peak torque). In Week 2 (Sessions 4 to 6), the participants performed in random order the three experimental conditions herein (3 types of warm-ups) followed 10-min later by the dynamic strength tests [21]. Skin temperature was measured immediately post-warm-up. In Week 3 (Sessions 7 to 9), the participants performed in random order the three experimental conditions herein (3 types of warm-ups) followed 10-min later by the isometric strength tests.

All testing was performed in an acclimated room, at the same time of day for and under the same environmental conditions (23 °C to 25 °C of temperature and relative humidity of ~60%). The athletes were asked to maintain the same routine during the evaluation days, avoiding strenuous exercise and refraining from consuming caffeine for 48-h before the test. This can be explained once caffeine tends to interfere in power, velocity, in static and fatigue states, which could interfere in the study's results [22–25].

The three types of exercise condition in terms of warm-up were: (i) exercise without any previous warm-up; (ii) exercise after traditional warm-up (which included dynamic resistance exercises); and (iii) exercise after a stretching warm-up (including 3 exercises as shown in Figure 1). A full explanation of the three types of war-up is described elsewhere [19,26].

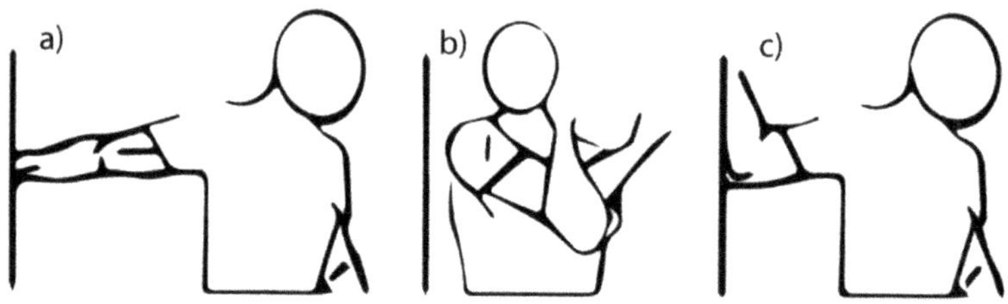

Figure 1. Stretches used as a warm-up method (**a**) shoulder, (**b**) triceps, and (**c**) pectoralis major.

2.2.1. Stretching Warm-Up

The participants performed only three static stretching exercises for deltoids, chest, and triceps, as is shown in Figure 1 [26]. Stretching was performed gradually and slowly until the discomfort threshold at the subjective limit point and thus remained in the position for 30 s. The exercises were repeated 3 times with an interval of 10 s [26].

2.2.2. Traditional Warm-Up

The participants performed the previous warm-up for the upper limbs, using three exercises (abduction of the shoulders with dumbbells, military press with dumbbells, and medial and lateral rotation of the arm to warm up the rotator cuff with dumbbells) with a set of 20 repetitions in approximately 10 min. Subsequently, a specific warm-up was performed on the bench press using only the barbell (20 kg) without extra weight, with 10 slow repetitions (3.0 × 1.0 s, eccentric × concentric) and 10 fast repetitions (1.0 × 1.0 s, eccentric × concentric). Next, the participants performed five repetitions at 30% of 1RM, followed by three repetitions at 50% of 1RM, a repetition at 70% of 1RM, a repetition at 80% of 1RM, and a repetition at 90% of 1RM. Between the series, the participants rested for 5 min [19,26].

2.3. Procedures

2.3.1. Skin Temperature Measurement

Thermal image acquisition was performed in a room prepared without natural light, with no airflow directed to the collection site. Ambient temperature conditions were maintained at around 24 °C ± 1 °C, and relative humidity around 50% using an air conditioner and monitored by a hygrometer (HIGHMED, model HM-01, USA) [2].

Participants were instructed not to perform vigorous physical activity in the previous 24 h, not to consume alcohol or caffeine, and not to use any type of cream or lotion on the skin in the 6 h immediately prior to the evaluation. To obtain the thermograms, the athlete remained seated and did not make sudden movements, did not cross the arms, and did not scratch for a period of at least 10 min for acclimatization [2,27].

Images were captured by an infrared camera model FLIR T640sc (Flir, Stockholm, Sweden) measuring range −40 °C to 2000 °C, accuracy 2%, sensitivity < 0.035, an infrared spectral band of 7.5–14 μm, refresh rate of 30 Hz, resolution of 640 × 480 pixels. The software used for thermal image analysis was FLIR TOOLS (Flir, Stockholm, Sweden). The region of interest evaluated was the anterior and posterior faces of the trunk and arms [2,28]. Figure 2 presents an illustration of the thermal images acquired.

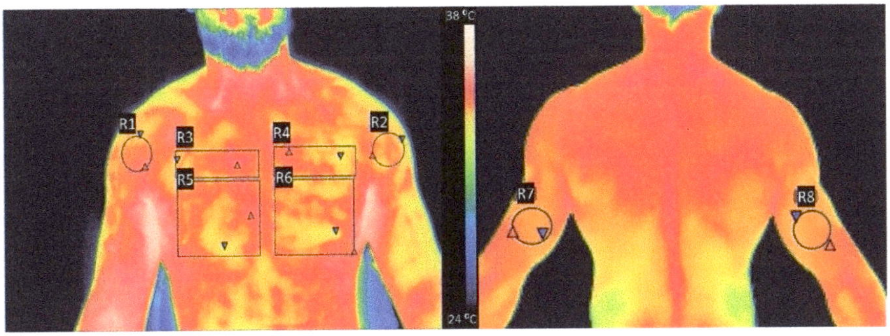

Figure 2. Illustration of the regions of interest (ROI) in the thermal images acquired.

2.3.2. Dynamic Strength Measurements (1-RM and Mean Propulsive Velocity—MVP)

In every testing herein, a 2.1 m long official adapted bench (Eleiko Sport AB, Halmstad, Sweden), approved by the International Paralympic Committee [20], was used. The barbell was a 2.2 m long, 20 kg weight official bar (Eleiko Sport AB, Halmstad, Sweden). The 1-RM assessment in bench press exercise was performed following the protocol proposed by Fleck and Kraemer [29]. A 3.0 to 5.0 min rest was provided between attempts. A valid and reliable [30] linear position transducer (Chronojump, BoscoSystem, Barcelona, Spain) was attached to the bar to measure the velocity of movement. The maximum speed averages were collected with the 1-RM load [31].

2.3.3. Isometric Force Measurements (Impulse, Variability, and Peak Torque)

The isometric evaluation was performed by having the participants press the bar at a distance of 15 cm from the chest. Impulse, variability, g and peak torque (PT) were measured with the help of a force sensor (Chronojump, BoscoSystem, Barcelona, Spain) and a goniometer FL6010 (Sanny, São José dos Campos, Brazil). Details of this testing can be found elsewhere [19].

2.4. Statistical Analysis

After confirmation of normality and homogeneity assumptions, one-way ANOVA with Bonferroni's post hoc was performed to compare the measurements post- the three types of warm-up. A repeated-measures analysis of variance was used to evaluate the performance between the warm-up conditions, followed by Bonferroni post hoc comparison tests. To check the effect size, partial Eta squared ($\eta 2p$) was used, adopting values of low effect ($\leq$0.05), medium effect (0.05 to 0.25), high effect (0.25 to 0.50), and very high effect (>0.50) for ANOVA [32]. A d value <0.2 was considered a trivial effect, 0.2 to 0.6 a small effect, 0.6 to 1.2 a moderate effect, 1.2 to 2.0 a large effect, 2.0 to 4.0 a very large effect, and $\geq$4.0 an extremely large effect [33]. Cohen "d" was calculated as the difference between the mean divided by the pooled SD to estimate the effect size for between-lift comparison [32].

All statistical analyses were performed using the computerized package Statistical Package for the Social Science (SPSS), version 22.0 (IBM Corp, Armonk, NY, USA). The level of significance was set at $p < 0.05$. Data are presented as means (X) ± standard deviation (SD) and 95% confidence interval (95% CI).

3. Results

The participants' 1-RM in bench press was 119.07 ± 43.15, which corresponded to a mean of 1.50 ± 0.38 times their body mass. Values above 1.4 (1RM/body weight) in the bench press, are considered to classify elite athletes [34].

The results found in the dynamic indicators of force, MPV, and power, and static indicators of force, impulse, and variability in relation to the different types of warm-up are shown in Table 1.

Table 1. Dynamic and static force indicators (mean ± standard deviation, 95% CI) in relation to different types of warm-up.

Warm-Up	MPV (m/s) X ± DP (IC 95%)	Power (W) X ± DP (IC 95%)	Impulse (N.s) X ± DP (IC 95%)	Variability (N) X ± DP (IC 95%)
Without Warm-up (A)	0.12 ± 0.06 (0.09–0.16)	137.69 ± 90.80 (87.41–187.97)	4022.23 ± 1341.43 (3279.36–4765.09)	46.74 ± 30.06 (30.10–63.38)
Traditional (B)	0.11 ± 0.05 (0.09–0.14)	128.86 ± 69.70 (90.26–167.46)	3964.91 ± 1240.10 (3278.17–4651.66)	40.57 ± 17.72 (30.76–50.38)
Stretching (C)	0.10 ± 0.04 (0.07–0.12)	105.77 ± 50.77 (77.65–133.88)	3740.41 ± 1114.96 (3122.96–4357.85)	41.26 ± 23.42 (28.29–54.22)
A vs. B	$p = 0.62$ d = 0.18	$p = 0.77$ d = 0.11	$p = 0.90$ d = 0.04	$p = 0.50$ d = 0.25
A vs. C	$p = 0.29$ d = 0.39	$p = 0.25$ d = 0.43	$p = 0.54$ d = 0.23	$p = 0.58$ d = 0.20
B vs. C	$p = 0.55$ d = 0.22	$p = 0.31$ d = 0.38	$p = 0.61$ d = 0.19	$p = 0.93$ d = 0.03
p	0.272	0.383	0.293	0.999
η2p	0.122 ##	0.116 ##	0.121 ##	0.030 #

$p < 0.05$ (ANOVA two-way, and Bonferroni post hoc, ES η2p). A vs. B; A vs. C and B vs. C (test t and ES Cohen "d"). ES: effect size, # low effect, ## medium effect. MPV: mean propulsive velocity.

Table 2 shows no differences in the dynamic and static indicators of the force in relation to the different types of warm-up. The results found for peak torque (Nm) and 1 maximum repetition (kg) are shown in Figure 3.

Table 2. Skin temperature over active muscles in different types of warm-up (mean ± SD and CI 95%).

Muscles	WW (°C)	TW (°C)	SW (°C)	WW vs. TW	WW vs. SW	TW vs. SW	p-Value	η2p
Pectoral Sternal	31.77 ± 1.18 (31.11–32.42)	32.23 ± 0.80 (31.79–32.68)	32.06 ± 1.09 (31.45–32.67)	$p = 0.238$ d = 0.456	$p = 0.505$ d = 0.255	$p = 0.642$ d = 0.178	0.261	0.091 a
Pectoral Clavicular	32.51 ± 0.74 * (32.10–32.92)	33.04 ± 0.71 * (32.65–33.43)	33.02 ± 0.55 (32.72–33.32)	$p = 0.064$ d = 0.731	$p = 0.049$ * d = 0.782	$p = 0.934$ d = 0.031	0.038 *	0.276 b
Anterior Deltoid	32.31 ± 0.69 (31.93–32.69)	32.52 ± 0.78 (32.09–32.95)	32.64 ± 0.60 (32.31–32.97)	$p = 0.457$ d = 0.285	$p = 0.230$ d = 0.465	$p = 0.061$ d = 0.741	0.145	0.099 a
Triceps	31.47 ± 0.93 (30.96–31.99)	31.99 ± 0.54 (31.70–32.29)	32.01 ± 0.80 (31.57–32.46)	$p = 0.082$ d = 0.684	$p = 0.112$ d = 0.623	$p = 0.939$ d = 0.029	0.108	0.193 a

* $p < 0.05$ (ANOVA). (WW in comparison with TW). η2p = partial eta square. "a": medium effect and "b": high effect. d: Cohen' d. WW: without warm-up, TW: traditional warm-up and SW: stretching warm-up.

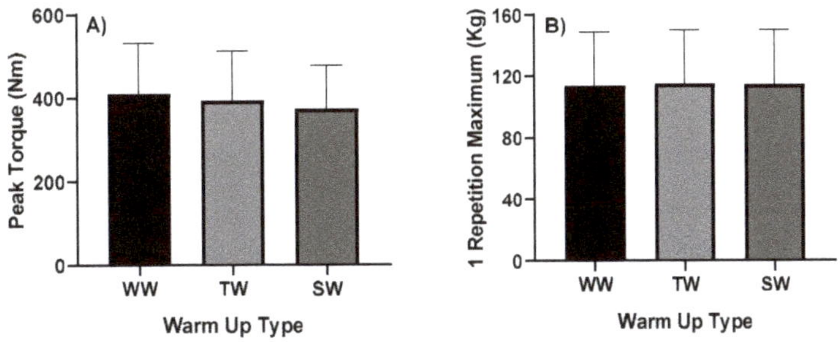

Figure 3. Evaluation of (**A**) peak torque (N.m) and (**B**) 1 repetition maximum (Kg), with different types of warm-up. WW: without warm-up, TW: traditional warm-up, and SW: stretching warm-up.

No significant differences were found in relation to the (A) peak torque (p = 0.055, F = 4.560, η2p = 0.246 medium effect), and (B) 1 repetition maximum (p = 0.139, F = 3.191, η2p = 0.186, medium effect) between the different types of warm-up.

4. Discussion

The objective of our study was to evaluate the different types of warm-up: without warm-up, traditional warm-up, and warm-up with stretching, on thermographic and strength indicators. The results of the mean propulsive velocity (MPV) did not show differences between the types of warm-up, however, the condition without warm-up (WW) was the one that presented the highest average propulsive speed (1.12 $\pm$ 0.06 m/s), followed by traditional warm-up (TW) (0.11 $\pm$ 0.05 m/s), and warm-up with stretching (SW) (0.10 $\pm$ 0.04 m/s).

A study that evaluated the influence of specific warm-up on strength performance found that participants were able to achieve a higher propulsive speed in the second and third sets in the squat, and with a tendency to decrease propulsive speed in the bench press. The time for propulsive speed was shorter after a warm-up with progressive intensity, demonstrating that speed can be affected by warm-up, tending to decrease with more activities [7]. In the horizontal bench press, the MPV does not tend to be greater at the beginning of the training, which is explained by the lower muscle mass involved, when compared to other exercises, in addition to being a relatively simple movement [35]. Thus, it seems that a more relaxed muscle tends to establish a higher speed than after a more traditional warm-up. The reduction in movement speed during strength work tends to indicate fatigue [14,36]. On the other hand, stretching exercises for sports training [37] and for maximum tests or for competition are highly questionable and would normally be related to loss of performance [38]. Still, the elapsed time of the warm-up with the use of stretching must observe an interval greater than three minutes before the warm-up continues [26].

Concerning power, despite not showing differences between the three types of warm-ups, the condition without warm-up showed a higher power (137.69 $\pm$ 90.80 W), followed by traditional warm-up (128.86 $\pm$ 69.70 W), and warm-up with stretching (105.77 $\pm$ 50.77 W). If we consider that power is the product of strength times speed, speed in resistance training can be considered very important when assessing muscle strength [39,40]. Whether traditional or even with pre-activation, the warm-up aims to increase the muscle temperature, the activation of the motor unit, and the myofiber water content [41,42]. Moderate to heavy exercises with loads varying between 20–90% of a maximum repetition tend to improve sprint and jump, especially in participants trained and familiar with the exercise load [43,44]. However, our findings indicate that WW and TW tend to be better than SW. On the other hand, contrary to this, dynamic and static stretching tend to be favorable as a warm-up strategy [12,26]. In active individuals, dynamic stretching increased the height of the vertical jump. On the other hand, agility tends to be positively impacted by stretching. Dynamic stretching can improve an athlete's power [45].

The same kinetics occurred in relation to the static components of the force, where there were no differences in impulse, and the WW method obtained the highest value (4022.23 ± 1341.43 N.s), followed by TW (3964.91 ± 1240.10 N.s) and of the SW (3740.41 ± 1114.96 N.s). In the same direction, the participants tested after 6.0 min of swimming warm-up or warm-up on land, with three repetitions (pull-over at 85% of the maximum of one repetition). Speed, force, acceleration, impulse, rate of force development (RFD) were evaluated. Warm-up on land with higher loads increased RFD (34.52 ± 16.55 vs. 31.29 ± 13.70 N/s; Δ = 9.35%), and stroke rate (64.70 ± 9.84 vs. 61.56 ± 7.07 Hz; Δ = 5.10%) compared to traditional water warm-up but decreased speed, strength, acceleration, impulse and power [46]. That is, traditional warm-up can decrease the impulse, and a lighter warm-up tends not to decrease the impulse. Likewise, exercises with high load resistance have been used to facilitate the improvement of neuromuscular performance. Traditional warm-up has its use restricted, despite its specificity and practicality for sports performance. Thus, when verifying the effect of repeated exercises on performance, where 43 participants were evaluated performance was quantified through vertical jump, relative thrust, and normalized peak strength at baseline. No improvements were found for the relative impulse in repeated trials, the sixth trial was significantly less than the baseline (2.35 ± 0.38 vs. 2.26 ± 0.35 N·s·kg; $p \leq 0.001$). This indicates that the repetition of traditional warm-ups can lead to fatigue, which tends to interfere with performance [47].

In variability, although there are no differences between the types of warm-up, the least variability was TW (40.57 ± 17.72 N), followed by SW (41.26 ± 23.42 N) and WW (46.74 ± 30.06 N). This may indicate that traditional warm-up tends to promote a more stable situation on a muscular level than other warm-up types, noting that there were no significant differences between the warm-up methods.

There were also no differences in peak torque, however, the WW method showed higher values (409.58 ± 120.99 Nm), followed by TW (393.74 ± 118.48 Nm) and SW (373.14 ± 103.51 Nm). One study evaluated standard warm-up or drop jump (plyometric protocol) or a slow walk (control protocol). Post-activation potentiation was assessed by changes in isometric muscle contractions. The plyometric protocol increased the peak contraction torque (PTT), the rate of torque development (RTD) and the impulse significantly (by 23, 39 and 46%, respectively). Peak contraction torque, RTD, and impulse, decreased significantly after standard warm-up. Thus, standard warming did not enhance but may have reduced the muscle's ability to generate strength [48]. The data in this study contradict our findings.

In the 1RM test, the three methods also showed no differences, however, the TW method (114.80 ± 34.98 kg) showed higher values, followed by the SW (114.53 ± 35.20 kg) and the WW (113.80 ± 34.80 kg). A specific warm-up can increase the production of strength after maximum or almost maximum muscle stimulation [14]. The effects of warming on athletic success have gained great attention in recent studies. Authors [19] evaluated different types of warm-up, with the participation of 15 elite Brazilian male athletes from Paralympic powerlifting (age, 24.140 ± 6.21 years; body weight, 81.67 ± 17.36 kg). A significant difference was observed for the maximum isometric strength, in the without warm-up (WW) in relation to traditional warm-up (TW) and stretching warm-up (SW) ($p = 0.005$, $\eta 2p = 0.454$, high effect). On the other side, no significant differences were observed in the RFD, fatigue index (FI), and time in the different types of warm-up ($p > 0.05$). No significant differences were observed in relation to the maximum repetition ($p = 0.121$, $\eta 2p = 0.275$, medium effect) or the maximum speed ($p = 0.712$, $\eta 2p = 0.033$, low effect) between the different types of warm-up. The different warm-up methods do not seem to provide significant differences in strength indicators in this population, and this could be explained by the displacement they use to the upper limbs, the target of the study [19].

In the thermographic analysis, there was a significant difference only in the pectoral muscle clavicular portion between the TW (33.04 ± 0.71 °C) and the WW (32.51 ± 0.74 °C) ($p = 0.038$). The TW method also presented slightly higher values than the SW and WW in the pectoral muscles sternal portion and in the deltoid anterior portion, but with a

p-value > 0.05. These results are in agreement with authors who studied thermal response to resistance training [49]; since traditional warm-up involves specific resistance exercises for the primary muscles that are recruited in the main work.

The physiological reason for the increase in skin temperatures observed in the pectoral muscle clavicular portion (TW protocol) might be the increase in the recruitment of motor units, which occurs during the traditional warm-up, needed to prepare the muscles for the considerable effort needed to overcome the weight of the barbell and give it acceleration [50].

Authors [49] reported an increase in skin temperature over the muscles that were the main responsible for the movement requested after the exercise. Neves et al. [28] reported that the warming of ROI in arm exercise seems to be related to exercise volume. In this sense, since the traditional warm-up protocol included a large volume of exercises, it promoted an increase in blood flow to the pectoral muscle clavicular portion and, consequently, a greater heat dissipation by the skin over this muscle.

From the hypotheses raised, our findings, and the confrontation with the literature, we ended up supporting the idea that, for Paralympic athletes, the type of warm-up tends not to impact performance in terms of temperature and strength indicators.

The study used the functional classification adopted by the International Paralympic Committee. Thus, it can be mentioned as limitations of this study, the control of variables such as balance, food, and life habits.

5. Conclusions

It can be concluded that the type of warm-up does not seem to interfere with the performance of Paralympic powerlifting athletes. However, although there are no significant differences between the warm-up methods, the thermal images showed that traditional warm-up best meets the objectives expected for this preparation phase. In a competition, it could be enough to provide better performance and classification.

The results found may have been influenced by the condition of being in a wheelchair and requiring the use of the upper limbs and trunk muscles for displacement, thus promoting the maintenance of these muscle groups in a state of activity similar to what is observed after the warm-up protocols.

Another important point is that in high-level competitions and especially in the Paralympic Games, many weight categories were classified by results with differences of less than 5.0%. In this sense, in competitions, when determining the type and warm-up, the traditional would be the best indicated in high-level competitions and, in training, any type of warm-up could be used.

Author Contributions: Conceptualization, M.d.A.R., F.J.A. and R.B.V.R., methodology, F.J.A., G.C.R. and L.d.O.B.; software, D.G.d.M. and A.C.M.; validation, P.F.d.A.-N., A.L.D.-d.-D. and M.M.-F., formal analysis, B.G.d.A.T.C., investigation, J.V.-A., E.B.N. and V.M.R., resources, N.D.G.; data curation, F.M.C. and B.G.d.A.T.C., writing—original draft preparation, M.d.A.R., F.J.A., R.B.V.R. and G.C.R., writing—review and editing, B.G.d.A.T.C., E.B.N., V.M.R., F.M.C. and N.D.G.; visualization, A.L.D.-d.-D., M.M.-F. and J.V.-A.; supervision, L.d.O.B. and D.G.d.M., project administration, A.C.M. and P.F.d.A.-N. All authors have read and agreed to the published version of the manuscript.

Funding: This research received no external funding.

Institutional Review Board Statement: The study was conducted according to the guidelines of the Declaration of Helsinki, and approved by the Research Ethics Committee of the Federal University of Sergipe, CAAE: 2.637.882 (date of approval: 7 May 2018).

Informed Consent Statement: Informed consent was obtained from all participants involved in the study.

Data Availability Statement: The data that support this study can be obtained from the address https://www.asuswebstorage.com, accessed on 1 July 2021.

Conflicts of Interest: The authors declare no conflict of interest.

References

1. McGowan, C.J.; Pyne, D.B.; Thompson, K.G.; Rattray, B. Warm-Up Strategies for Sport and Exercise: Mechanisms and Applications. *Sports Med.* **2015**, *45*, 1523–1546. [CrossRef]
2. Almeida Barros, N.; Aidar, F.J.; DEMatos, D.G.; DESouza, R.F.; Neves, E.B.; de Araujo Tinoco Cabral, B.G.; Carmargo, E.A.; Reis, V.M. Evaluation of Muscle Damage, Body Temperature, Peak Torque, and Fatigue Index in Three Different Methods of Strength Gain. *Int. J. Exerc. Sci.* **2020**, *13*, 1352–1365.
3. Bishop, D. Warm-up I: Potential mechanisms and the effects of passive warm-up on exercise performance. *Sports Med.* **2003**, *33*, 439–454. [CrossRef]
4. Bishop, D. Warm-up II: Performance changes following active warm-up and how to structure the warm-up. *Sports Med.* **2003**, *33*, 483–498. [CrossRef] [PubMed]
5. Gil, M.H.; Neiva, H.P.; Garrido, N.D.; Aidar, F.J.; Cirilo-Sousa, M.S.; Marques, M.C.; Marinho, D.A. The Effect of Ballistic Exercise as Pre-Activation for 100 m Sprints. *Int. J. Environ. Res. Public Health* **2019**, *16*, 1850. [CrossRef] [PubMed]
6. Gil, M.H.; Neiva, H.P.; Sousa, A.C.; Marques, M.C.; Marinho, D.A. Current approaches on warming up for sports performance: A critical review. *Strength Cond. J.* **2019**, *41*, 70–79. [CrossRef]
7. Ribeiro, B.; Pereira, A.; Neves, P.P.; Sousa, A.C.; Ferraz, R.; Marques, M.C.; Marinho, D.A.; Neiva, H.P. The Role of Specific Warm-up during Bench Press and Squat Exercises: A Novel Approach. *Int. J. Environ. Res. Public Health* **2020**, *17*, 6882. [CrossRef] [PubMed]
8. Neiva, H.P.; Marques, M.C.; Barbosa, T.M.; Izquierdo, M.; Viana, J.L.; Teixeira, A.; Marinho, D.A. Warm-up volume affects the 100 m swimming performance: A randomized crossover study. *J. Strength Cond. Res.* **2015**, *29*, 3026–3036. [CrossRef]
9. Faulkner, S.H.; Ferguson, R.A.; Gerrett, N.; Hupperets, M.; Hodder, S.G.; Havenith, G. Reducing muscle temperature drop after warm-up improves sprint cycling performance. *Med. Sci. Sports Exerc.* **2013**, *45*, 359–365. [CrossRef] [PubMed]
10. Racinais, S.; Oksa, J. Temperature and neuromuscular function. *Scand. J. Med. Sci. Sports* **2010**, *20* (Suppl. 3), 1–18. [CrossRef] [PubMed]
11. Mohr, M.; Krustrup, P.; Nybo, L.; Nielsen, J.J.; Bangsbo, J. Muscle temperature and sprint performance during soccer matches–beneficial effect of re-warm-up at halftime. *Scand. J. Med. Sci. Sports* **2004**, *14*, 156–162. [CrossRef]
12. Chaabene, H.; Behm, D.G.; Negra, Y.; Granacher, U. Acute Effects of Static Stretching on Muscle Strength and Power: An Attempt to Clarify Previous Caveats. *Front. Physiol.* **2019**, *10*, 1468. [CrossRef]
13. Gray, S.R.; De Vito, G.; Nimmo, M.A.; Farina, D.; Ferguson, R.A. Skeletal muscle ATP turnover and muscle fiber conduction velocity are elevated at higher muscle temperatures during maximal power output development in humans. *Am. J. Physiol. Regul. Integr. Comp. Physiol.* **2006**, *290*, R376–R382. [CrossRef] [PubMed]
14. Junior, D.; Junor, A.; Serpa, É.; Gomes, W.; Soares, E.; Lopes, C.; Teixeira, L.; Marchetti, P. Different warm-ups on the maximum repetition performance in resistance training. *Rev. Bras. Med. Esporte* **2014**, *20*, 461–464.
15. Silva, L.M.; Neiva, H.P.; Marques, M.C.; Izquierdo, M.; Marinho, D.A. Effects of warm-up, post-warm-up, and re-warm-up strategies on explosive efforts in team sports: A systematic review. *Sports Med.* **2018**, *48*, 2285–2299. [CrossRef] [PubMed]
16. Marinho, D.A.; Gil, M.H.; Cardoso Marques, M.; Barbosa, T.M.; Neiva, H.P. Complementing Warm-up with Stretching Routines: Effects in Sprint Performance. *Sports Med. Int. Open* **2017**, *1*, E101–E106. [CrossRef] [PubMed]
17. Pareja-Blanco, F.; Rodríguez-Rosell, D.; Sánchez-Medina, L.; Sanchis-Moysi, J.; Dorado, C.; Mora-Custodio, R.; Yáñez-García, J.M.; Morales-Alamo, D.; Pérez-Suárez, I.; Calbet, J.; et al. Effects of velocity loss during resistance training on athletic performance, strength gains and muscle adaptations. *Scand. J. Med. Sci. Sports* **2017**, *27*, 724–735. [CrossRef] [PubMed]
18. Brandenburg, J. The acute effects of prior dynamic resistance exercise using different loads on subsequent upper-body explosive performance in resistance-trained men. *J. Strength Cond. Res.* **2005**, *19*, 427–432.
19. Resende, M.A.; Vasconcelos Resende, R.B.; Reis, G.C.; Barros, L.O.; Silva Bezerra, M.R.; Matos, D.G.; Marçal, A.C.; Almeida-Neto, P.F.; Cabral, B.G.A.T.; Neiva, H.P.; et al. The Influence of Warm-Up on Body Temperature and Strength Performance in Brazilian National-Level Paralympic Powerlifting Athletes. *Medicina* **2020**, *56*, 538. [CrossRef]
20. International Paralympic Comitê (IPC). Sports. Available online: https://www.paralympic.org/powerlifting (accessed on 10 January 2020).
21. Adelsberger, R.; Tröster, G. Effects of stretching and warm-up routines on stability and balance during weight-lifting: A pilot investigation. *BMC Res.* **2014**, *7*, 938. [CrossRef]
22. Filip-Stachnik, A.; Krzysztofik, M.; Kaszuba, M.; Leznicka, K.; Kostrzewa, M.; Del Coso, J.; Wilk, M. Effects of Acute Caffeine Intake on Power Output and Movement Velocity During a Multiple-Set Bench Press Exercise Among Mild Caffeine Users. *J. Hum. Kinet.* **2021**, *78*, 219–228. [CrossRef]
23. Burke, L.M. Caffeine and sports performance. *Appl. Physiol. Nutr. Metab.* **2008**, *33*, 1319–1334. [CrossRef] [PubMed]
24. Raya-González, J.; Rendo-Urteaga, T.; Domínguez, R.; Castillo, D.; Rodríguez-Fernández, A.; Grgic, J. Acute Effects of Caffeine Supplementation on Movement Velocity in Resistance Exercise: A Systematic Review and Meta-analysis. *Sports Med.* **2020**, *50*, 717–729. [CrossRef]
25. Wilk, M.; Filip, A.; Krzysztofik, M.; Gepfert, M.; Zajac, A.; Del Coso, J. Acute Caffeine Intake Enhances Mean Power Output and Bar Velocity during the Bench Press Throw in Athletes Habituated to Caffeine. *Nutrients* **2020**, *12*, 406. [CrossRef] [PubMed]
26. De Souza, R.F.; de Matos, D.G.; Nogueira, A.C.; Ferreira, A.R.P.; de Freitas Zanona, A.; Aidar, F.J. Analysis of muscle recovery time after acute stretching at peak torque of the hamstring muscles. *Med. Dello Sport* **2019**, *72*, 171–180.

27. Marins, J.; Fernández-Cuevas, I.; Arnaiz-Lastras, J.; Sillero-Quintana, M. Applications of Infrared Thermography in Sports. A Review. *Rev. Inter. Med. Cienc. Activ. Física Depor.* **2015**, *15*, 805–824.
28. Neves, E.B.; Salamunes, A.C.C.; de Oliveira, R.M.; Stadnik, A.M.W. Effect of body fat and gender on body temperature distribution. *J. Therm. Biol.* **2017**, *70*, 1–8. [CrossRef]
29. Fleck, S.J.; Kraemer, W.J. *Designing Resistance Training Programs*, 4th ed.; Human Kinetics: Champaign, IL, USA, 2004.
30. Pérez-Castilla, A.; Piepoli, A.; Delgado-García, G.; Garrido-Blanca, G.; García-Ramos, A. Reliability andconcurrent validity of seven commercially available devices for the assessment of movement velocity atdifferent intensities during the bench press. *J. Strength Cond. Res.* **2019**, *33*, 1258–1265. [CrossRef]
31. García-Ramos, A.; Ha, G.G.; Padial, P.; Feriche, B. Reliability of power and velocity variables collectedduring the traditional and ballistic bench press exercise. *Sports Biomech.* **2018**, *17*, 117–130. [CrossRef]
32. Cohen, J. Statistics a power primer. *Psychol. Bull.* **1992**, *112*, 155–159. [CrossRef]
33. Hopkins, W.G.; Marshall, S.W.; Batterham, A.M.; Hanin, J. Progressive statistics for studies in sports medicine and exercise science. *Med. Sci. Sports Exerc.* **2009**, *41*, 3–13. [CrossRef] [PubMed]
34. Ball, R.; Weidman, D. Analysis of USA powerlifting federation data from January 1, 2012–June 11, 2016. *J. Strength Cond. Res.* **2018**, *32*, 1843–1851. [CrossRef] [PubMed]
35. Evans, A.K.; Durham, M.P.; Hodgkins, T.D.; Sinclair, D.R.; Adams, K.J. Acute effect of bench press on power output during a subsequent ballistic bench throw. *Med. Sci Sports* **2001**, *33*, 325. [CrossRef]
36. Sanchez-Medina, L.; González-Badillo, J.J. Perda de velocidade como um indicador de fadiga neuromuscular durante o treinamento de resistência. *Med. Sci. Sport Exerc.* **2011**, *43*, 1725–1734.
37. Behm, D.G.; Blazevich, A.J.; Kay, A.D.; McHugh, M. Acute Effects of Muscle Stretching on Physical Performance, ROM and Injury Incidence in Healthy Active Individuals: A Systematic Review. *Appl. Physiol. Nutr. Metab.* **2015**, *41*, 1–11. [CrossRef] [PubMed]
38. Kallerud, H.; Gleeson, N. Effects of stretching on performances involving stretch-shortening cycles. *Sports Med.* **2013**, *43*, 733–750. [CrossRef]
39. González-Badillo, J.J.; Marques, M.C.; Sánchez-Medina, L. The importance of movement velocity as a measure to control resistance training intensity. *J. Hum. Kinet.* **2011**, *29*, 15–19. [CrossRef]
40. González-Badillo, J.J.; Sánchez-Medina, L. Movement velocity as a measure of loading intensity in resistance training. *Int. J. Sports Med.* **2010**, *31*, 347–352. [CrossRef]
41. Blazevich, A.J.; Babault, N. Pós-ativação potenciação cersus pós-ativação aprimoramento de desempenho em humanos: Perspectiva histórica, mecanismos subjacentes e questões atuais. *Frente. Physiol.* **2019**, *10*, 1359. [CrossRef]
42. Tomlinson, K.A.; Hansen, K.; Helzer, D.; Lewis, Z.H.; Leyva, W.D.; McCauley, M.; Pritchard, W.; Silvestri, E.; Quila, M.; Yi, M.; et al. The Effects of Loaded Plyometric Exercise during Warm-Up on Subsequent Sprint Performance in Collegiate Track Athletes: A Randomized Trial. *Sports* **2020**, *8*, 101. [CrossRef]
43. Jo, E.; Judelson, D.A.; Brown, L.E.; Coburn, J.W.; Dabbs, N.C. Influence of recovery duration after a potentiating stimulus on muscular power in recreationally trained individuals. *J. Strength Cond. Res.* **2010**, *24*, 343–347. [CrossRef]
44. Duncan, M.J.; Thurgood, G.; Oxford, S.W. Effect of heavy back squats on repeated sprint performance in trained men. *J. Sports Med. Phys. Fit.* **2014**, *54*, 238–243.
45. Anderson, B.L.; Harter, R.A.; Farnsworth, J.L. The Acute Effects of Foam Rolling and Dynamic Stretching on Athletic Performance: A Critically Appraised Topic. *J. Sport Rehabil.* **2020**, *13*, 1–6. [CrossRef] [PubMed]
46. Cuenca-Fernández, F.; Batalha, N.M.; Ruiz-Navarro, J.J.; Morales-Ortiz, E.; López-Contreras, G.; Arellano, R. Post high intensity pull-over semi-tethered swimming potentiation in national competitive swimmers. *J. Sports Med. Phys. Fitness* **2020**. [CrossRef]
47. Horan, S.A.; Watson, S.L.; Lambert, C.; Weeks, B.K. Lunging. Exercise Potentiates a Transient Improvement in Neuromuscular Performance in Young Adults. *J. Strength Cond. Res.* **2015**, *29*, 2532–2537. [CrossRef]
48. Johnson, M.; Baudin, P.; Ley, A.L.; Collins, D.F. A Warm-Up Routine That Incorporates a Plyometric Protocol Potentiates the Force-Generating Capacity of the Quadriceps Muscles. *J. Strength Cond. Res.* **2019**, *33*, 380–389. [CrossRef]
49. Uchôa, P.; Matos, F.; Neves, E.B.; Saavedra, F.; Rosa, C.; Reis, V.M.; Vilaça-Alves, J. Evaluation of two different resistance training volumes on the skin surface temperature of the elbow flexors assessed by thermography. *Infrared Phys. Technol.* **2018**, *93*, 178–183. [CrossRef]
50. Kuniszyk-Jóźkowiak, W.; Jaszczuk, J.; Czaplicki, A.; Szyszka, P. Variability of shoulder girdle temperature in the initial phase of the snatch in weightlifting. *Acta Bioeng. Biomech.* **2019**, *21*, 143–148. [CrossRef]

healthcare

MDPI

Article

Cut-Off Points of Visceral Adipose Tissue Associated with Metabolic Syndrome in Military Men

Samir Ezequiel da Rosa [1,*], Amina Chain Costa [2], Marcos S. R. Fortes [1], Runer Augusto Marson [1], Eduardo Borba Neves [1], Laercio Camilo Rodrigues [3], Paula Fernandez Ferreira [1] and Jose Fernandes Filho [3]

[1] Brazilian Army Physical Fitness Research Institute (IPCFEx), Rio de Janeiro 22291-090, Brazil; profdr1.divpesq@ipcfex.eb.mil.br (M.S.R.F.); profdr2.divpesq@ipcfex.eb.mil.br (R.A.M.); eduardoneves@utfpr.edu.br (E.B.N.); paula.fernandez@eb.mil.br (P.F.F.)

[2] Federal Fluminense University (UFF), Niterói 24210-240, Brazil; aminacosta@id.uff.br

[3] Federal University of Rio de Janeiro (UFRJ), Rio de Janeiro 21941-901, Brazil; laercio.rodrigues@eb.mil.br (L.C.R.); jff@eefd.ufrj.br (J.F.F.)

[*] Correspondence: samirdarosa@hotmail.com

Abstract: Visceral adipose tissue (VAT) has high metabolic activity and secretes a larger number of adipokines that are related to the inflammatory process. Quantifying VAT could estimate the risk of developing Metabolic Syndrome (MetS). This study was designed to determine the VAT cut-off points assessed by DXA associated with MetS in military men. In total, 270 (37.5 ± 6.9 years) military men from the Brazilian Army (BA) participated in the study. Anthropometric measurements, assessment of body composition by dual X-ray absorptiometry (DXA), hemodynamics and biochemical tests were performed. The Student's *t* test, independent samples, Person's correlation, ROC curve, Youden Index and positive (PPV) and negative predictive value (NPV) were used. The MetS prevalence was 27.4%, which means that 74 (38.0 ± 7.3 years) military men had at least three risk factors of MetS present. The cutoff point of VAT with the highest balance between sensitivity (77.0%) and specificity (69.9%) was 1025.0 cm^3 (1086.0 g). An area on the ROC curve was 0.801 ($p < 0.000$), which was very good precision. VAT ≥ 1025.0 cm^3 (1086.0 g) is associated with the risk factors of MetS and is, therefore, a predictor of the disease with good indicators of sensitivity and specificity and a robust indicator of MetS.

Keywords: visceral adipose tissue; military; metabolic syndrome; cut-off points; DXA

Citation: da Rosa, S.E.; Costa, A.C.; Fortes, M.S.R.; Marson, R.A.; Neves, E.B.; Rodrigues, L.C.; Ferreira, P.F.; Filho, J.F. Cut-Off Points of Visceral Adipose Tissue Associated with Metabolic Syndrome in Military Men. *Healthcare* **2021**, *9*, 886. https://doi.org/10.3390/healthcare9070886

Academic Editors: Felipe Aidar and Chrysi Koliaki

Received: 28 April 2021
Accepted: 18 June 2021
Published: 14 July 2021

1. Introduction

Obesity is characterized by excessive accumulation of adipose tissue with damage to health and it is considered a worldwide epidemic conditioned mainly by the food and physical activity profile [1]. It is also the main risk factor for Chronic Non-communicable Diseases (NCDs) such as diabetes, stroke, hypertension, cardiovascular diseases and Metabolic Syndrome (MetS) [1]. The global prevalence of MetS in the population varies according to the diagnostic criterion used and geographic and sociodemographic factors [2,3]. The latest consensus, Joint Interim Statement (JIS), pointed out that about 20% to 25% of the world's adult civilian population has three of the five risk factors for the disease [4]. A recent study, using JIS criteria and involving 2719 (27.7 ± 8.59 years) male military selected to participate in the United Nations peacekeeping mission in HAITI, showed that 12.2% of the soldiers had risk factors for MetS [5].

Scientific evidence shows that MetS is associated with obesity, mainly with the accumulation of visceral adipose tissue (VAT), and consequently with cardiovascular risk [3,6]. Even if the subcutaneous adipose tissue (SAT) represents about 80% of the total body fat, it is VAT that has greater metabolic activity secreting a large number of adipokines, such as Leptin, which are related to inflammatory processes [7]. Furthermore, VAT is also considered as an independent risk factor for pathophysiological changes in MetS [3]. Thus, quantifying the VAT may be key to assess the risk of developing NCDs, including metabolic complications [3,7,8].

Some anthropometric measurements can estimate the amount of VAT, including waist circumference (WC) and associate it with risk factors, but these present limitations [9]. However, imaging techniques such as computed tomography (CT) and magnetic imaging resonance (MIR) can be accurately measured VAT and associated with some risk factors [10]. However, they expose the patient to high radiation [10]. The view of this dual X-ray absorptiometry (DXA) is a reference method for assessing body composition with the advantages of high precision, low radiation and short scanning time [11,12].

Despite the fact that some studies have investigated the association between excess VAT and the association with cardio-metabolic risk, few have proposed VAT cutoff points using DXA [11–19]. Only two studies, using GE's DXA, were found to associate VAT with cardio-metabolic risk factors [18,19]. However, no study involving VAT cut-off points associated with MetS in militaries has been found. A cutoff point can facilitate the diagnosis of people with the risk factors for metabolic syndrome, preventing them from being subjected to biochemical tests, blood pressure assessment and anthropometric measurements.

In this context, the objective of the present study was to determine the VAT cutoff points assessed by "DXA" associated with MetS in military men.

2. Materials and Methods

2.1. Study Design and Population

This is a cross-sectional study carried out in a convenience sample of 270 male military men, aged 22 to 60 (37.5 $\pm$ 6.9) years. They were selected from the group of volunteer military personnel who participated in the MetS Monitoring Program conducted by the Brazilian Army Physical Fitness Research Institute (IPCFEx) between 2017 and 2019. In this program, all military men received a complete health assessment by specialized professionals from IPCFEx. Active-duty male military personnel who were students at the Army Command and General Staff School (ECEME), the Officer Improvement School (EsAO) and the Sergeants School of Logistics (EsLog) were included. In addition, militaries selected to integrate individual peacekeeping missions of the United Nations and militaries from BA Organizations in the city of Rio de Janeiro were included. Military retired personnel and those who underwent any type of recent abdominal surgery were excluded. Female military personnel were also excluded due to the small number evaluated (only 27 women had participated until the end). This is illustrated in Figure 1.

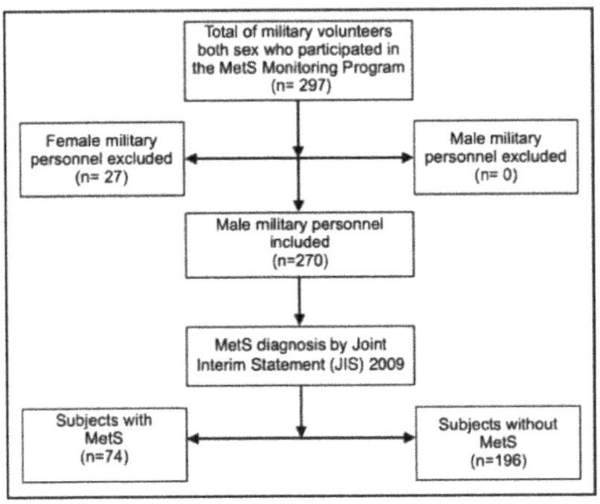

Figure 1. Schematic description of the study, with subject who participated of the Metabolic Syndrome (MetS) Monitoring Program conducted by the Brazilian Army Physical Fitness Research Institute (IPCFEx).

All the participants signed the informed consent form when they became aware of the procedures and risks to which they would be submitted. This research was registered in the National Research Ethics System, submitted and approved by the Ethics Council of the Naval Marcílio Dias Hospital, n° 1.551.242, CAAE n° 47835615.5.0000.5256 on 11 July 2019.

2.2. Data Collect

This took place in the IPCFEx laboratories in four stages during the same day in the morning, with the participant fasting for 12 h overnight. Blood samples were included for biochemical analysis in the IPCFEX Clinical Analysis Laboratory. Blood pressure assessment, anthropometric and body composition evaluation by DXA were realized in the IPCFEX Body Composition Laboratory.

2.3. Blood Collection and Biochemical Analyzes

Initially, blood samples (8 mL) were collected, in vacutainer tubes without anticoagulant, by a trained professional from 7 to 9 a.m. The blood samples were analyzed immediately after collection. Serum aliquots were separated after centrifugation (3000 rpm for 15 min) in the device model Centurion vector inverter system with 32 tubes (Centurion Scientific, Stoughton, Chichester, UK). The concentrations of triglycerides (TG), glucose (GL) and high-density lipoprotein (HDL-c) were determined using a biochemistry analyzer, model bt 3000 plus (Wiener Lab, Rosário, BA, Argentina). The serum levels were analyzed using the endpoint enzymatic colorimetric methodology, with GOD-PAP (glucose oxidase + peroxidase) by spectrophotometry, in the case of GL, GPO/PAP (glycerol phosphate oxidase + peroxidase), in the case of TG and colorimetric without precipitation CHO/PAD/TOOS (N-ethyl-N-3-disodium toluidine), in the case of HDL-c. The collections followed all the recommendations of the Brazilian Society of Clinical Pathology/Laboratory Medicine and according to Resolution n° 306/2004 from National Health Surveillance Agency for the management and disposal of samples [20,21].

2.4. Blood Pressure Assessment

Afterwards, Systolic Blood Pressure (SBP) and Diastolic Blood Pressure (DBP) were measured according to the Brazilian Guideline of Arterial Hypertension for the Use of Ambulatory Blood Pressure Monitoring of the Brazilian Society of Cardiology [22].

2.5. Anthropometric Evaluation

Then, military men underwent an anthropometric assessment, conducted by two physical education professionals from the IPCFEx, following the protocol standardized by Fernandes Filho [23]. The technical errors of measurement inter and intra-evaluators were considered acceptable, being 1.35% and 0.97%, respectively [24]. Total body mass (BM) was determined with those evaluated in the orthostatic position (OP), barefoot, using only a bathing suit a digital scale, model P150M (Lider, Araçatura, São Paulo, Brazil), with a maximum load of 200 kg. Height was measured with a metal stadiometer (Sanny, São Bernarndo do Campo, São Paulo, Brazil), with an accuracy of 2 mm. The subjects were standing, in OP, keeping contact with the device by the heel. To measure the WC, an anthropometric measuring tape, model SN 4010 (Sanny, São Bernarndo do Campo, São Paulo, Brazil), was used, with those evaluated in an OP and the abdomen relaxed. WC was measured at the point with the lowest circumference line of the last rib with the tape placed in a horizontal plane and with the individual in respiratory apnea, to minimize possible instability in the spine.

2.6. DXA Body Composition

The body composition assessment was performed using DXA, iLunar model, from GE Healthcare (GE Healhcare, Madison, WI, USA), with the enCore 2015 software (version 14.10.022). Before each acquisition DXA scanner was calibrated according to the manufacturer's instructions [12,14,16]. Furthermore, the calibration column phantom was applied weekly. From the scan of the whole body, the data of total fat mass (FM), total lean mass (LM), percentage of total body fat (%BF-DXA) and the fat mass index (FMI), FM (kg)/Height^2 (m^2), were obtained. VAT was measured and a region-of-interest is automatically defined whose caudal limit is placed at the top of the iliac crest and its height is set to 20% of the distance from the top of the iliac crest to the base of the skull to define its cephalad limit [12,14,16]. VAT mass (g) was automatically transposed into volume (cm^3) using a constant correction factor (0.94 g/mL). The measurements in the calibration block (daily) presented acceptable coefficients of variation 1.0% [12,14,16].

2.7. MetS Diagnosis

The diagnosis of MetS followed the parameters of the JIS with a combination of three or more cutoff points: central obesity (WC men $\geq$ 90 cm), HDL-c (men $\leq$ 40 mg/dL and/or use of medication for control), TG (men $\geq$ 150 mg/dL and/or use of medication for control), GL (men $\geq$ 100 mg/dL and or use of medication for control) and high levels of SBP $\geq$ 130 mmHg and/or DBP $\geq$ 85 mmHg and/or use of medication for control [4].

2.8. Statistical Analysis

Descriptive statistics were performed to characterize the sample universe surveyed using the measures of location (mean) and dispersion (SD). The Kolmogorov–Smirnov test was used to test the normality of the data distribution. In this sense, a parametric analysis was used. The Student's t-test, from independent samples, compared the anthropometric, hemodynamic, biochemical and body composition variables of the DXA among the military personnel without MetS risk factors (WMetSRF) and with the referred risk factors (MetSRF). The variation coefficient percentage (%CV) was calculated using the formula: %CV = (standard deviation (SD)/mean) $\times$ 100. To measure the reliability of measurements it was calculated the intra-class correlation coefficient (ICC) and Cronbach's alpha coefficients (α). The effect size was calculated by Cohen's d [25]. The Pearson correlation test was used to verify the association with the VAT obtained by DXA (VAT-DXA). The Receiver Operator Characteristic (ROC) curve was constructed to establish the VAT cutoff points. The Youden Index was used to determine the performance of the test and to determine more precisely which cutoff point of VAT with more balance [26]. The positive predictive values (PPV) and negative predictive values (NPV) were defined, respectively, as the probability that the military present the risk factors for MetS based the VAT equal to or above the cutoff point and does not present the risk factors by the VAT below the cutoff point [27]. The level of significance adopted was 95% ($p < 0.05$) and statistical analyses were performed by SPSS version 17 (Armonk, Nova York, NY, USA).

3. Results

After applying the criteria for the diagnosis of MetS, 74 militaries were diagnosed with the disease, a prevalence of 27.4%. Table 1 presents the general descriptive data of the 270 male military personnel evaluated and the comparison between the MetSRF and WMetSRF groups. Military personnel diagnosed with MetS had significantly higher anthropometric, hemodynamic, body composition and biochemical measurements than the group without the diagnosis ($p < 0.05$). Height alone was not significantly different between groups. Furthermore, the size of the effect in most of parameters was "large" (d = 0.80–1.29) [25]. Only four parameters showed "medium" effect size (d = 0.50–0.79) [25].

Table 2 shows the associations among anthropometric, hemodynamic, biochemical, body composition and VAT-DXA (cm^3) variables by groups. In the group without risk factors for the disease, strong and significant associations were observed between VAT and BM, FM, BMI, FMI, %BF-DXA and WC. This group also presents significant associations between VAT and age, LM, TG and glucose. VAT was negatively associated with HDL-c concentrations. In the MetSRF group VAT had strong association with FMI, FM, %BF-DXA and WC and moderate association with BM and BMI. In addition, it presented a weak association with age and glucose. In both groups, no associations were found between VAT, height, SBP and DBP.

Table 1. Descriptive data of the military evaluated and comparison between groups (n = 270).

Parameters (n)	WMetSFR (196) Mean ± SD	MetSFR (74) Mean ± SD	p Value *	Effect Size (d)	95%CI	ICC	CV	α
Age	36.0 ± 6.3	38.0 ± 7.3	0.026	0.30	0.04–0.57	0.421	1.71	0.448
Height (cm)	177.5 ± 6.0	177.5 ± 6.2	0.829	0.02	0.23–0.29	−0.061	1.61	−0.060
BM (kg)	80.9 ± 12.3	94.5 ± 12.3	0.000	0.98	0.70–1.26	0.084	2.18	0.108
BMI	25.7 ± 3.6	29.8 ± 6.2	0.000	1.03	0.76–1.32	0.150	6.61	0.197
LM (kg)	58.8 ± 5.9	62.5 ± 6.5	0.000	0.60	0.33–0.88	−0.038	0.36	−0.041
FM (kg)	20.8 ± 8.4	28.9 ± 8.7	0.000	0.95	0.67–1.23	0.024	10.28	0.030
FMI (kg/m^2)	6.6 ± 2.6	9.2 ± 2.7	0.000	0.97	0.69–1.25	0.044	13.30	0.057
%BF-DXA	24.5 ± 6.7	30.1 ± 5.7	0.000	0.87	0.59–1.15	0.029	8.41	0.037
VAT (cm^3)	806.4 ± 597.6	1550.6 ± 716.8	0.000	1.18	0.89–1.46	−0.189	27.87	−0.296
VAT (g)	761.2 ± 563.9	1462.8 ± 676.2	0.000	1.18	0.89–1.46	−0.189	27.85	−0.296
WC (cm)	87.1 ± 8.6	96.3 ± 7.6	0.000	1.14	0.85–1.42	−0.087	1.98	0.121
Triglycerides (mmol/L)	83.4 ± 38.0	117.8 ± 55.7	0.000	0.78	0.51–1.06	0.011	1.71	0.014
Glucose (mmol/L)	94.5 ± 8.6	100.7 ± 10.0	0.000	0.58	0.41–0.96	−0.361	0.82	−0.367
HDL-c (mmol/L)	54.4 ± 16.0	46.9 ± 10.8	0.000	0.52	0.24–0.79	0.087	8.08	0.101
SBP (mmHg)	117.1 ± 9.7	130.0 ± 12.8	0.000	1.21	0.92–1.49	−0.319	1.56	−0.628
DBP (mmHg)	80.0 ± 6.2	90.0 ± 11.3	0.000	1.28	0.98–1.56	−0.007	4.80	−0.010

WMetSRF: military group without metabolic syndrome, MetSRF: military group with metabolic syndrome, SD: standard deviation, %CV: Coefficient of variation, ICC: intra-class correlation coefficient, α: Cronbach's alpha coefficients, BMI: body mass index, WC: waist circumference, BM: total body mass, FM: total fat mass, LM: total lean mass, FMI: fat mass index, %BF-DXA: percentage body fat, VAT: visceral adipose tissue, HDL-c: high-density lipoprotein, SBP: systolic blood pressure, DBP: diastolic blood pressure. DXA: dual X-ray absorciometry. * p value obtained by Student's t-test. (d) Cohen's d Effect Size.

Table 2. Correlation between VAT-DXA and independent variables of militaries without MetS and with MetS.

Variables	VAT-DXA			
	WMetSRF		MetSRF	
Independent Variables	r *	p *	r *	p *
Age	0.280	0.000	0.363	0.000
Height (cm)	0.071	0.323	0.124	0.291
BM (kg)	0.775	0.000	0.548	0.000
BMI	0.800	0.000	0.644	0.000
FMI (kg/m^2)	0.872	0.000	0.747	0.000
LM (kg)	0.331	0.000	0.056	0.637
FM (kg)	0.880	0.000	0.722	0.000
%BF-DXA	0.825	0.000	0.722	0.000
WC (cm)	0.885	0.000	0.836	0.000
Triglycerides (mmol/L)	0.260	0.000	0.164	0.163
Glucose (mmol/L)	0.216	0.002	0.343	0.003
HDL-c (mmol/L)	−0.175	0.014	−0.138	0.241
SBP (mmHg)	0.033	0.643	0.019	0.874
DBP (mmHg)	0.119	0.098	0.127	0.282

WMetSRF: military group without metabolic syndrome, MetSRF: military group with metabolic syndrome, BM: total body mass, FM: total fat mass, LM: total lean mass, FMI: fat mass index, %BF-DXA: percentage body fat DXA, VAT: visceral adipose tissue, WC: waist circumference, HDL-c: high-density lipoprotein, SBP: systolic blood pressure, DBP: diastolic blood pressure, * p value obtained by Person correlation.

VAT cutoff points with degrees of sensitivity and specificity and predictive values are shown in Table 3. A VAT cutoff point that showed best balance in the specificity and sensitivity test was 1025 cm^3, which corresponded to 1086 g, with a sensitivity of 77.0%, specificity of 69.9%, PPV of 49.1% and NPV of 89.0%.

Table 3. VAT cutoff points with other relationships of sensitivity, specificity and predictive values.

VAT Cutoff (cm^3)	Sensitivity (%)	Specificity (%)	Youden Index **	PPV (%)	NPV (%)
48.0	100.0	0.0	0.00	27.4	0.0
568.5	95.9	44.9	0.41	39.7	3.3
811.5	85.1	57.7	0.43	43.3	91.1
1025.0 *	**77.0**	**69.9**	**0.47**	**49.1**	**89.0**
1417.0	56.8	83.2	0.40	56.0	83.6
2062.5	23.0	95.9	0.35	69.2	77.0
4201.0	0.0	100.0	0.00	27.2	100.0

VAT: visceral adipose tissue, * more balanced VAT cutoff found, ** index evaluation of the overall discriminative power of a diagnostic procedure, PPV: positive predictive value, NPV: negative predictive value.

This statement can be seen in the analysis of the ROC curve (Figure 2), which revealed, with the help of the Youden Index, PPV and NPV, that the VAT cutoff point with the greatest balance between sensitivity had an area on the ROC curve was 0.801 ($p < 0.001$) [26,27].

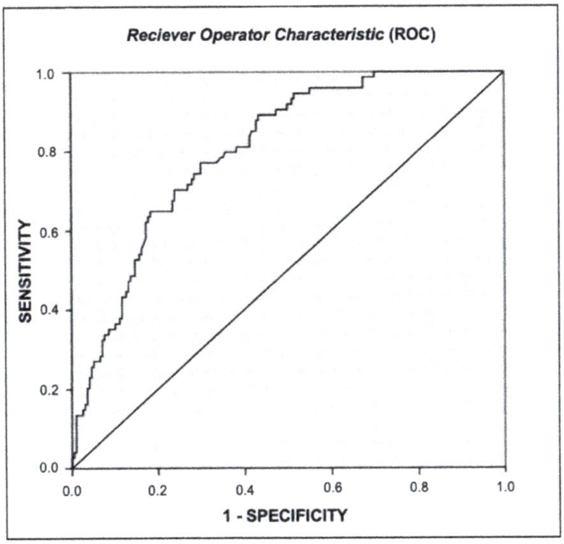

Figure 2. ROC curve for cut-off point of visceral adipose tissue associated with Metabolic Syndrome.

4. Discussion

The present study determined the VAT cutoff points assessed by DXA associated with MetS in BA military men. At the end, it was observed that the VAT $\geq$ 1025 cm^3, which is equivalent to 1086 g, showed a better ability to predict the disease in these individuals.

The prevalence of MetS has grown exponentially in the world and in Brazil, even in military personnel that have good physical conditioning [5,28–30]. Recently, Rostami and collaborators (2019) postulated, after a systematic review with meta-analysis, that the average prevalence of MetS in military personnel from the Armed Forces of the four continents is 8.0% [30]. They also suggested that the prevalence in this group is lower when compared to the civilian population, because they are encouraged to have a healthier lifestyle and to perform physical training with regular frequency [30].

In Brazil, a survey involving military and MetS analyzed 1383 military personnel from the Brazilian Navy, in active service, and concluded that the prevalence of MetS was 17.6%, being the HDL-c the most prevalent risk factor in the population, which was present in 43% of the individuals, followed by high blood pressure (26.3%), hypertriglyceridemia (19.3%) and fasting glucose (6.6%) [29]. Likewise, Fortes et al. postulated that the prevalence of

MetS in 2719 (27.7 years) Brazilian military personnel selected to participate in the UN peacekeeping mission in HAITI, from 2014 to 2017, was 12.2%, using the JIS criteria [4]. They also stated that both WC and BMI can be considered as good predictors of changes in the physiological markers of MS, especially in the military [4]. This prevalence was lower in relation to that found in the article under discussion (27.4%) whose average age was 38.0 years, therefore higher than in the surveys mentioned above. Perhaps here is the answer to this difference, as the prevalence of MetS increases with age, regardless of the diagnostic criteria used [2–4,30].

It is well described in the literature that biochemical, anthropometric and blood pressure markers are altered in the presence of MetS [5,29–31]. Rosa and collaborators found significantly lower mean values of WC, HDL-c, SBP and DBP in Brazilian military personnel without MetS risk factors, indicating a lower risk of DCNs [28].

Gámez et al. conducted a prospective cross-sectional survey with 51 Cuban military personnel MetSRF and 43 WMetSRF and found that %BF, HLD-c, glucose, TG, SBP, DBP and WC variables showed greater differences between group means. Similar to the findings described above, the study under discussion suggests that military personnel diagnosed with MetS risk factors have significantly worse health indicators when compared to individuals without risk [31]. The data obtained in this study confirm those described in a recent systematic review, suggesting that people diagnosed with MetS have a worsening in quality of life when compared to those who presented the disease [32].

In recent years, DXA has been a reliable alternative to CT and MRI to estimate total and regional fat [12,17,18]. In the present research, the VAT found in the individuals with MetS was significantly higher compared to the group WMetSRF; in fact, it was almost double. Current findings describe the occurrence of an association between VAT, measured by DXA, with cardiac and metabolic risk factors including high levels of glucose, hypertension, increased WC, BMI and high %BF, but none of the studies evaluated this outcome in the military population [6,7,12–19].

On the other hand, Sasai et al. prove that the VAT of adults, with BMI ranges from 19 to 54 kg/m^2, was inversely associated with HDL-c and positively with TG, WC, %BF and BMI, corroborating the finding in the present study [8]. Nicklas and collaborators suggested that the VAT-DXA of American women, aged 45 to 73 years, is positively correlated with WC and that, in turn, is related to all risk factors for MetS, except total and low cholesterol density lipoproteins (LDL) [17]. Another research study showed that the VAT-DXA (cm^3) of 229 women, diagnosed with obesity, was associated with the variables of WC, SBP, DBP, HDL-c, TG and glucose [18]. In the military, although research involving VAT and risk factors for MetS was not found, Rosa and collaborators carried out a study with 262 male soldiers, aged between 19 and 49 years, selected for the peace mission of the UN in Haiti, using GE's DXA, iLunar model, and observed an inverse association between HDL-c and EC, showing indirect instruments that are independent predictors of NCDs [33].

Although research points to the occurrence of associations between VAT and BP, in the present article, there were not associations between VAT and BP in both groups [34]. Differently from what literature describes, in the group with MetS it was not possible to observe a negative association between VAT and HDL-c concentration. This association was only observed in the group without disease. It is possible that the change in HDL-c does not accompany the change in VAT, justifying the absence of association in this group.

Considering the scientific literature studied, VAT cutoff points were not found; these were measured by DXA, in cm^3, and associated with MetS in the active military population. The first cutoff point associated with metabolic and coronary risk was established by Nicklas and collaborators had used GE's DXA, model DPX-L Lunar, which presents VAT in area (cm^2) [18]. The results of this study showed that women, with a mean of 59.0 ± 6.0 years, had a higher risk of having metabolic and coronary problems if they had a VAT $\geq$ 163 cm^2.

Ten years later, Kelly and collaborators established VAT cutoff points, using the DXA, Hologic Discovery, also reading in area (cm^2) and suggested that women with

VAT $\geq 100\ cm^2$ would have an increased metabolic risk for coronary heart disease, while those with VAT $\geq 160\ cm^2$ had an even higher metabolic risk [35].

Only two studies determined VAT cutoff points, in volume (cm^3) associated with MetS risk factors using the GE's DXA [18,19].

In the first, the researchers obtained cutoff points for women of European and African American descent (BMI 30.0 kg/m^2), using the ROC curve (area under curve, AUC, 0.749) with a balance between sensitivity and specificity (50%) [18]. This research postulated cardio-metabolic risk associations for European women with a VAT $\geq 1713\ cm^3$ and for African American women a VAT $\geq 1320\ cm^3$ [18]. In another finding, involving 421 young Europeans of both sexes, aged 20 to 30 years, it was observed that, in men, VAT $\geq 761\ cm^3$ was associated with risk factors for cardio-metabolic and VAT $\geq 239\ cm^3$ for women [19]. The area under the ROC curve was 0.914 for men and 0.839 for women [19].

As you can see, the different cutoff points attributed so far vary from one another and are different from the one found in this article. Part of this difference is attributed to the way of quantifying the VAT, being in area or volume and to the different characteristics of the studied populations [17–19,31]. When interpreting the area under the ROC curve found in the current article, whose value was 0.801 ($p < 0.001$), it is observed that it has very good diagnostic accuracy [26,27]. The Youden Index, measuring the performance of the test, calculated by deducting 1 from the sum of sensitivity and specificity of the test, helped in the discovery of the cutoff point with more balanced sensitivity (77.0%) and specificity (69.9%) (Table 2) [15,26,27].

In this study the VAT value $\geq 1025\ cm^3$ (1086 g) showed a better balance relationship with PPV and NPV. This means that if the military has visceral adiposity $\geq 1025\ cm^3$ he has a 49.1% chance of having MetS, and if he has a VAT < 1025 cm^3 he has 89.0% chance of not having MetS.

Unlike sensitivity and specificity, predictive values (PV) are dependent on the prevalence of the disease in the population examined. Therefore, the PV should not be transferred to another population with a different prevalence of the disease. Prevalence affects PPV and NPV differently. The PPV is increasing, while the NPV decreases with the increase in the prevalence of the disease in the population. These values of PPV and NPV are in a medium zone where they have the highest efficiency and the best cost–benefit ratio [27]. A possible explanation for this is in the sample size, as the 57 individuals who presented risk factors for MetS also had a VAT $\geq 1025\ cm^3$. However, no studies were found in the literature that involved the positive and negative prediction of MetS and the amount of visceral adiposity.

It is relevant to understand that the simple comparison of VAT values over time does not give information on the risk category to which the subject is exposed. With a cut-off point as a reference, the subjects can have a way to estimate their situation regarding the risk of being in the condition of MetS with only one exam (DXA). This cut-off point will also serve as a strategy to complete clinical information in the diagnosis of diseases, especially in subjects who are facing some metabolic disorders related to excess fat.

It is important to recognize some limitations in the present study: VAT-DXA cutoff points associated with risk factors for MetS were investigated exclusively in men; the generalization of the results was restricted to the military men aged between 22 and 60. Even so, this article presents a strong point because it is the first study that determined VAT cutoff points (cm^3), assessed by DXA, GE iLunar, associated with MetS in military personnel from BA. It is important to highlight that no other similar study was found in the scientific literature, even in other populations.

5. Conclusions

The results of the present study suggest that VAT $\geq 1025.0\ cm^3$ (1086.0 g), determined by DXA, GE iLunar, is associated with risk factors for the disease and can, therefore, predict it with good indicators of sensitivity and specificity.

These findings may be can be extrapolated to the Brazilian male population, as the BA is an institution formed by a heterogeneous sample of Brazilian society. Brazilians from different regions of the country join the Brazilian army in different ways. Whether by mandatory military conscription, or by public contests held annually. For this reason, such findings can be used, in daily clinical practice, by all male Brazilians within the studied age range.

They can also serve as a support for future investigations and treatments of MetS, improving the health and quality of life of the military, thus increasing its operability.

Author Contributions: S.E.d.R. conceived the study and care about conceptualization, data curation, formal analysis, methodology, software, resources, interpretation of data and writing draft. A.C.C., M.S.R.F., R.A.M., E.B.N., L.C.R. and J.F.F. took care about data curation, formal analysis, methodology, software, resources, interpretation of data and writing review and editing. P.F.F. had analyzed and interpreted all biochemical dates and also took care about data curation and methodology. All authors have read and agreed to the published version of the manuscript.

Funding: This research received no external funding.

Institutional Review Board Statement: Not applicable.

Informed Consent Statement: Informed consent was obtained from all subjects involved in the study.

Data Availability Statement: All data generated in this study are contained within this publication.

Acknowledgments: This project was supported by Brazilian Army Research Institute Physical Fitness (IPCFEx) which constantly develops studies about the Brazilian Army health and operability.

Conflicts of Interest: The authors declare no conflict of interest.

References

1. Blüher, M. Obesity: Global Epidemiology and Pathogenesis. *Nat. Rev. Endocrinol.* **2019**, *15*, 288–298. [CrossRef]
2. Saklayen, M.G. The Global Epidemic of the Metabolic Syndrome. *Curr. Hypertens. Rep.* **2018**, *20*, 12. [CrossRef]
3. McCracken, E.; Monaghan, M.; Sreenivasan, S. Pathophysiology of the Metabolic Syndrome. *Clin. Dermatol.* **2018**, *36*, 14–20. [CrossRef]
4. Alberti, K.G.M.M.; Eckel, R.H.; Grundy, S.M.; Zimmet, P.Z.; Cleeman, J.I.; Donato, K.A.; Fruchart, J.-C.; James, W.P.T.; Loria, C.M.; Smith, S.C. Harmonizing the Metabolic Syndrome. *Circulation* **2009**, *120*, 1640–1645. [CrossRef]
5. de Sá Rego Fortes, M.; da Rosa, S.E.; Coutinho, W.; Neves, E.B. Epidemiological Study of Metabolic Syndrome in Brazilian Soldiers. *Arch. Endocrinol. Metab.* **2019**, *63*, 345–350. [CrossRef]
6. Jemtel, T.H.L.; Samson, R.; Milligan, G.; Jaiswal, A.; Oparil, S. Visceral Adipose Tissue Accumulation and Residual Cardiovascular Risk. *Curr. Hypertens. Rep.* **2018**, *20*, 77. [CrossRef] [PubMed]
7. Sam, S. Differential Effect of Subcutaneous Abdominal and Visceral Adipose Tissue on Cardiometabolic Risk. *Horm. Mol. Biol. Clin. Investig.* **2018**, *33*, 438–448. [CrossRef] [PubMed]
8. Sasai, H.; Brychta, R.J.; Wood, R.P.; Rothney, M.P.; Zhao, X.; Skarulis, M.C.; Chen, K.Y. Does Visceral Fat Estimated by Dual-Energy X-ray Absorptiometry Independently Predict Cardiometabolic Risks in Adults? *J. Diabetes Sci. Technol.* **2015**, *9*, 917–924. [CrossRef] [PubMed]
9. Madden, A.M.; Smith, S. Body Composition and Morphological Assessment of Nutritional Status in Adults: A Review of Anthropometric Variables. *J. Hum. Nutr. Diet.* **2016**, *29*, 7–25. [CrossRef] [PubMed]
10. Fang, H.; Berg, E.; Cheng, X.; Shen, W. How to Best Assess Abdominal Obesity. *Curr. Opin. Clin. Nutr. Metab. Care* **2018**, *21*, 360. [CrossRef] [PubMed]
11. Kelly, T.L.; Wilson, K.E.; Heymsfield, S.B. Dual Energy X-ray Absorptiometry Body Composition Reference Values from NHANES. *PLoS ONE* **2009**, *4*, e7038. [CrossRef]
12. Ofenheimer, A.; Breyer-Kohansal, R.; Hartl, S.; Burghuber, O.C.; Krach, F.; Schrott, A.; Wouters, E.F.M.; Franssen, F.M.E.; Breyer, M.-K. Reference Values of Body Composition Parameters and Visceral Adipose Tissue (VAT) by DXA in Adults Aged 18–81 Years—Results from the LEAD Cohort. *Eur. J. Clin. Nutr.* **2020**, *74*, 1181–1191. [CrossRef]
13. Lang, P.-O.; Trivalle, C.; Vogel, T.; Proust, J.; Papazyan, J.-P.; Dramé, M. Determination of Cutoff Values for DEXA-Based Body Composition Measurements for Determining Metabolic and Cardiovascular Health. *BioResearch Open Access* **2015**, *4*, 16–25. [CrossRef]
14. Kaul, S.; Rothney, M.P.; Peters, D.M.; Wacker, W.K.; Davis, C.E.; Shapiro, M.D.; Ergun, D.L. Dual-Energy X-ray Absorptiometry for Quantification of Visceral Fat. *Obesity* **2012**, *20*, 1313–1318. [CrossRef] [PubMed]

15. Rothney, M.P.; Catapano, A.L.; Xia, J.; Wacker, W.K.; Tidone, C.; Grigore, L.; Xia, Y.; Ergun, D.L. Abdominal Visceral Fat Measurement Using Dual-Energy X-ray: Association with Cardiometabolic Risk Factors. *Obesity* **2013**, *21*, 1798–1802. [CrossRef] [PubMed]
16. Ergun, D.L.; Rothney, M.P.; Oates, M.K.; Xia, Y.; Wacker, W.K.; Binkley, N.C. Visceral Adipose Tissue Quantification Using Lunar Prodigy. *J. Clin. Densitom.* **2013**, *16*, 75–78. [CrossRef] [PubMed]
17. Nicklas, B.J.; Penninx, B.W.J.H.; Ryan, A.S.; Berman, D.M.; Lynch, N.A.; Dennis, K.E. Visceral Adipose Tissue Cutoffs Associated With Metabolic Risk Factors for Coronary Heart Disease in Women. *Diabetes Care* **2003**, *26*, 1413–1420. [CrossRef] [PubMed]
18. Bi, X.; Seabolt, L.; Shibao, C.; Buchowski, M.; Kang, H.; Keil, C.D.; Tyree, R.; Silver, H.J. DXA-Measured Visceral Adipose Tissue Predicts Impaired Glucose Tolerance and Metabolic Syndrome in Obese Caucasian and African-American Women. *Eur. J. Clin. Nutr.* **2015**, *69*, 329–336. [CrossRef]
19. Miazgowski, T.; Kucharski, R.; Sołtysiak, M.; Taszarek, A.; Miazgowski, B.; Widecka, K. Visceral Fat Reference Values Derived from Healthy European Men and Women Aged 20–30 Years Using GE Healthcare Dual-Energy X-ray Absorptiometry. *PLoS ONE* **2017**, *12*, e0180614. [CrossRef]
20. Andriolo, A.; Faulhaber, A.C.L.; Junior, A.P.; Martins, A.R.; de Oliveira Machado, A.M.; Ballarati, C.A.F.; Soares, C.A.S.; dos Ssantos Ferreira, C.E.; Granato, C.F.H.; de Oliveira Galoro, C.A.; et al. *Recomendações Da Sociedade Brasileira de Patologia Clínica/Medicina Laboratorial (SBPC/ML): Colet e Preparo Da Amostra Biológica*, 1st ed.; Manole Ltda: Rio de Janeiro, Brazil, 2014; Volume 1.
21. de Vigilância Sanitária, A.N. Resolução RDC nº 306, de 07 de Dezembro de Dispõe Sobre o Regulamento Técnico para o Gerenciamento de Resíduos de Serviços de Saúde 2004. Available online: https://www.saude.mg.gov.br/images/documentos/res_306.pdf (accessed on 8 July 2021).
22. Malachias, M.; Souza, W.; Plavnik, F.; Rodrigues, C.; Brandão, A.; Neves, M.; Bortolotto, L.; Franco, R.; Figueiredo, C.; Jardim, P.; et al. Capítulo 3—Avaliação Clínica e Complementar. *Arq. Bras. Cardiol.* **2016**, *107*, 1–83. [CrossRef]
23. Filho, J.F. *A Prática Da Avaliação Física: Testes, Medidas, Avaliação Física Em Escolares, Atletas e Academias de Ginástica*, 3rd ed.; SHAPE: Rio de Janeiro, Brazil, 2003; Volume 1.
24. dos Santos Ribeiro, G.; Fragoso, E.B.; Nunes, R.D.; Lopes, A.L. Erro Técnico de Medida Em Antropometria: Análise de Precisão e Exatidão Em Diferentes Plicômetros. *Rev. Educ. Física J. Phys. Educ.* **2019**, *88*. [CrossRef]
25. Sawilowsky, S.S. New Effect Size Rules of Thumb. *J. Mod. Appl. Stat. Methods* **2009**, *8*, 597–599. [CrossRef]
26. Li, C.; Chen, J.; Qin, G. Partial Youden Index and Its Inferences. *J. Biopharm. Stat.* **2019**, *29*, 385–399. [CrossRef] [PubMed]
27. Obuchowski, N.A.; Bullen, J.A. Receiver Operating Characteristic (ROC) Curves: Review of Methods with Applications in Diagnostic Medicine. *Phys. Med. Biol.* **2018**, *63*, 07TR01. [CrossRef]
28. da Rosa, S.E.; Lippert, M.A.; Marson, R.A.; de Sá Rego Fortes, M.; Rodrigues, L.C.; Filho, J.F. Physical Performance, Body Composition And Metabolic Syndrome In Military Personnel From The Brazilian Army. *Rev. Bras. Med. Esporte* **2018**, *24*, 422–425. [CrossRef]
29. da Costa, F.F.; Montenegro, V.B.; Lopes, T.J.A.; Costa, E.C. Combinação de Fatores de Risco Relacionados à Síndrome Metabólica Em Militares Da Marinha Do Brasil. *Arq. Bras. Cardiol.* **2011**, *97*, 485–492. [CrossRef] [PubMed]
30. Rostami, H.; Tavakoli, H.R.; Rahimi, M.H.; Mohammadi, M. Metabolic Syndrome Prevalence among Armed Forces Personnel (Military Personnel and Police Officers): A Systematic Review and Meta-Analysis. *Mil. Med.* **2019**, *184*, e417–e425. [CrossRef]
31. Gámez, A.A.; Sotolongo, O.G.; Cuza, E.R.; Helps, A.B.; Vaillant, R.A. El Síndrome Metabólico Como Factor de Riesgo Para La Disfunción Endotelial. *Rev. Cuba. Med. Mil.* **2007**, *36*. Available online: http://scielo.sld.cu/scielo.php?script=sci_arttext&pid=S0138-65572007000100002 (accessed on 8 July 2021).
32. Saboya, P.P.; Bodanese, L.C.; Zimmermann, P.R.; da Silva Gustavo, A.; Assumpção, C.M.; Londero, F. Metabolic Syndrome and Quality of Life: A Systematic Review. *Rev. Lat. Am. Enfermagem* **2016**, *24*. [CrossRef]
33. da Rosa, S.E.; Filho, J.F.; de Sá Rego Fortes, M.; Chain, A.C.; Martinez, E.C. Serum Biochemical Markers and Anthropometric Measurements in the Brazilian Army Militaries Selected for the United Nations' Peacekeeping Mission in Haiti. *Glob. J. Res. Anal.* **2015**, *4*, 38–40.
34. Bosch, T.A.; Dengel, D.R.; Kelly, A.S.; Sinaiko, A.R.; Moran, A.; Steinberger, J. Visceral Adipose Tissue Measured by DXA Correlates with Measurement by CT and Is Associated with Cardiometabolic Risk Factors in Children. *Pediatr. Obes.* **2015**, *10*, 172–179. [CrossRef] [PubMed]
35. Kelly, T.L. Practical and technical advantages of DXA visceral fat assessment compared with computed tomography. *Age* **2010**, *36*, 50.

MDPI
St. Alban-Anlage 66
4052 Basel
Switzerland
www.mdpi.com

Healthcare Editorial Office
E-mail: healthcare@mdpi.com
www.mdpi.com/journal/healthcare

www.ingramcontent.com/pod-product-compliance
Lightning Source LLC
Chambersburg PA
CBHW061808210926
51850CB00006B/641
9783036590530